American Sociology and Holocaust Studies

The Alleged Silence and the Creation of
the Sociological Delay

Perspectives in Jewish Intellectual Life

Series Editor: Giuseppe Veltri (University of Hamburg)

American Sociology and Holocaust Studies

The Alleged Silence and the Creation of the Sociological Delay

ADELE VALERIA MESSINA

Boston
2017

Library of Congress Cataloging-in-Publication Data

Names: Messina, Adele Valeria, 1982- author.

Title: American sociology and Holocaust studies: the alleged silence and the creation of the sociological delay / Adele Valeria Messina.

Description: [Boston]: Academic Studies Press, [2016]

Series: Perspectives in Jewish intellectual life | Includes bibliographical references and index.

Identifiers: LCCN 2016037750 | ISBN 9781618115478 (hardcover)

Subjects: LCSH: Holocaust, Jewish (1939–1945)—Historiography. | Sociologists—Attitudes. | National socialism and sociology. | Genocide—Sociological aspects. | Holocaust, Jewish (1939–1945)—Influence.

Classification: LCC D804.348.M49 2016 | DDC 940.53/18072073—dc23 LC record available at https://lccn.loc.gov/2016037750

ISBN 978-1-64469-662-0
ISBN 978-1-61811-548-5 (electronic)

Copyright © 2017 Academic Studies Press
All rights reserved

Book design by Kryon Publishing
www.kryonpublishing.com

Published by Academic Studies Press in 2017
28 Montfern Avenue
Brighton, MA 02135, USA
press@academicstudiespress.com
www.academicstudiespress.com

... Every man in regard of his intellect is connected with Divine Word [logos], being an impression of, or a fragment or ray of that blessed nature ...

–Philo, *On the Creation*

And yet He is there, in silence, in filigree.

–Elie Wiesel, in a 1978 interview with John S. Friedman

To my father,
When your voice pauses my heart,
I remember all the times that you asked me:
"Would you like to read, for me, a tale?"

Contents

Acknowledgments xi
Preface   xiii
Introduction xv
    The Famous October 2001 Conference:
    The Sociological Turning Point xviii
    Methodology.. xxiv
        English-Language Sources............................ xxviii
        Chronology xxx
The Outline of the Book xxxi

1. Sociological Thinking about the Holocaust in the
   Postwar Years, 1945–1960s 1
   1.1. A Preliminary 1
   1.2. A Totalitarian Order...................................... 9
   1.3. Reflections on Anti-Semitism: Frankfurt School Reactions to
       Nazi Atrocities.. 14
   1.4. An Open Case: Talcott Parsons and National Socialism, from
       Active Political Engagement to the Years of Silence 26
       1.4.1. Parsons's Seven Published Papers 29
       1.4.2. The Seven Unpublished Writings 31
       1.4.3. Years of Silence (1946–1948)......................... 37
       1.4.4. The Parsons Controversy over His "Role in
            Bringing Nazi Sympathizers to the U.S.". 44
   1.5. The German Army in Shils and Janowitz 57
   1.6. The NSDAP and the Consensus: Between
       Heberle and Lipset 66
       1.6.1. The Modern Society behind the Political Man......... 70
       1.6.2. Lipset's Election Analysis 75
   1.7. "Good People and Dirty Work": Hughes.................... 80

1.7.1. Beyond the Banality of Evil..........................82
1.7.2. The Theory of Flow and Empirical Evidence at the
       Basis of Hughes's Thinking 90
1.7.3. Halfway between Modern Industry and
       National Socialist Society 93
1.7.4. "Good People" according to Critical Essays and Reviews ...95
1.7.5. "The Gleichshaltung".................................102
1.7.6. A Self-Coördination Case...........................107
1.7.7. Hughes's Delay Roots in the American Sociological
       Tradition 112
1.8. Summary 121

2. The Destruction of the Jews in a Sociological Perspective
   during the 1970s 122
   2.1. Preface 122
   2.2. Auschwitz in the Light of Anna Pawełczyńska:
        From Violence to Values................................ 125
        2.2.1. Inside the Time and Space of Auschwitz 131
        2.2.2. The Hodological Space in the Structure of Terror 135
        2.2.3. Resistance as Defense of the Dimension of Life by
               Group Dynamics................................. 140
               2.2.3.1. Resistance as Communication 144
               2.2.3.2. The Market as Defense Mechanism
                        Par Excellence 147
               2.2.3.3. Resistance as Movement and Organization 150
        2.2.4. The Institutions of the Criminal State 154
        2.2.5. Auschwitz as Modern State 159
   2.3. Jews in Poland... 161
        2.3.1. Twenty-one Years after Celia Heller 169
               2.3.1.1. Polish Nationalism during the
                        Soviet Occupation..........................172
               2.3.1.2. Polish Collaboration during the German
                        Occupation................................ 177
   2.4. Injustice in the Eyes of German Workers.................. 182
        2.4.1. An Obedient Proletariat 186

        2.4.2. "Was du für Volk und Heimat tust, ist
                immer recht getan!" 191
        2.4.3. The Early Nazists for Abel, Merkl, and Moore 194
        2.4.4. Surrender to Authority in Concentration Camps 197
   2.5. How Many Victims of the Holocaust? 200
        2.5.1. Within a Statistical Framework 205
        2.5.2. Space and Time as Coordinates..................... 209
        2.5.3. Moral Solidarity................................... 213
        2.5.4. Jewish Victims 221
        2.5.5. International Debate after Publication 222
        2.5.6. An Intellectual Diatribe: Horowitz and Fein.......... 227
        2.5.7. Ben-Baruch's Position 231
        2.5.8. Accounting for Genocide and the Sociological
                Tradition... 232
   2.6. Summary.. 234

3. Toward a Sociology of Genocide, 1980–1989 235
   3.1. Genocide as a Government Solution
        during the 1980s 235
   3.2. The Significance of Genocide 239
   3.3. When States Sponsor Genocide 241
        3.3.1. Between Nation-State and International Law: The Role of
                International Organizations........................... 243
   3.4. A General Theory on State-Sponsored Genocide:
        Baum and Horowitz..................................... 248
        3.4.1. The Holocaust as Crime of State in Sofsky............ 251
        3.4.2. The Organization of Work 255
   3.5. The Sociological Frame of Katz 256
        3.5.1. Individuals and the Factory System.................. 258
   3.6. Tec and Sociological Categories of Genocide 261
        3.6.1. The Meaning of Resistance......................... 264
   3.7. "The Holocaust as the test of modernity".................. 268
        3.7.1. Between England and Poland....................... 269
        3.7.2. From *Memories of Class* to *Modernity
                and the Holocaust* *271*

  3.7.3. Suffering in Society 275
  3.7.4. The Holocaust as a Product of Modernity 281
  3.7.5. His Sociological Lesson 288
  3.7.6. A Samizdat Phenomenon 290
  3.7.7. Some Literary Critics 294
  3.7.8. An Open Problem on the Modernity Thesis 304
 3.8. Summary. 309

4. **The Problem of the Holocaust after 1989** 310
 4.1. After the Fall of the Berlin Wall 310
 4.2. From Collective National Memory to Cosmopolitan Memory. . . 313
  4.2.1. Levy and Sznaider in the Wake of Ulrich Beck 320
 4.3. Between Memory and Political Acting: The Holocaust
   in Global Society 327
 4.4. Alexander and Durkheim: "What Holds
   Society Together?". 335
  4.4.1. Τραγῳδία as Interpretation of the Human Condition. . 337
  4.4.2. Trauma Theory: From Cultural Trauma to
    Universal Value. 341
 4.5. Genre Studies and the Jewish Question 348
 4.6. The Post-Holocaust Sociology of the
   Social Movements 355
  4.6.1. The Warsaw Ghetto Uprising as Social Movement. 356
  4.6.2. The Conditions of Collective Action 363
  4.6.3. Leadership Question: Three Cases in Comparison 366
  4.6.4. The Geography of Resistance in Warsaw,
    Vilna, and Łódź. 374
 4.7. Anti-Semitism in Brustein 377
 4.8. Summary. 379

Conclusions: The Alleged Delay. 381
Watershed Events 385
Bibliography 392
Index 447

Acknowledgments

My grateful thanks go to a number of people who have been generous with their time and pleasant in disposition while helping me with this book.

My special gratitude goes to Antonella Salomoni for her support throughout this project and without whose professional assistance it would not have been conceivable. The University of Calabria, Italy, deserves particular mention: the publication of this volume has been possible thanks to a financial contribution by the Department of Political and Social Sciences of Unical (field research *La storiografia della shoah: Concetti, correnti, problemi* headed by Salomoni).

I also acknowledge with pleasure my gratitude to Rick Helmes-Hayes, Martin Oppenheimer, and Jack N. Porter, and to Christopher Simpson and Viviana Salomon for their e-mail conversations with me during my doctorate work, and for their suggestions and willingness to help.

I am indebted to Hanna K. Ulatowska, who hung around with me in Warsaw in December 2011. I am grateful for her translation from Polish to English in my interviews with Holocaust survivors Anna Pawełczyńska and Zofia Posmysz-Piasecka.

My personal recognition is owed to Rosalba Silvaggio, who was gracious and patient in reading some portions of the book while still in draft, and to Kirsten Lawson for having seen some parts of the initial version of the manuscript. I am also happily indebted to my friend Valentina Decembrini. In achieving success of the final version, the most appreciation goes to Scott Barker for having read and copyedited, with perseverance, wit, and keen intelligence, the entire volume.

I must also thank the editors, Gregg Stern and Faith W. Stein and particularly the production editor, Kira Nemirovsky, for overseeing the entire publication process.

The book has benefited from Andrew I. Port's preface: I am especially grateful to him for his critical reading of the volume and for his expert knowledge. I would just like to say: thank you.

My greatest thanks are reserved for Giuseppe Veltri for his never-ending moral, intellectual, and insightful support, and for having read and discussed many parts and points of the manuscript with me. I acknowledge my special indebtedness to him for his generosity with his time in helping me advance my ideas and especially for having conceived the title. His positive criticism generates a sense of gratitude beyond my capacity to express in words—without him this book never would have been possible.

Obviously, the final responsibility rests with me—all errors are my own.

Preface

At a time when references to the Holocaust saturate American popular culture and the media, and at a time when the so-called Final Solution has come to epitomize absolute evil in the United States – a country that opened a museum in the heart of its capital dedicated to an event that took place, on foreign soil, more than two decades before finally opening one dedicated to the history of African Americans – it is difficult to imagine a time when the Holocaust was not considered *the* moral and historical touchstone, *tout court*. In fact, as historian Peter Novick and others have shown, the history of the Holocaust – or rather its reception – has a history itself: it did not always receive the same level of public or scholarly attention that it does today. And the same holds true for Germany. Raul Hilberg, the late doyen of Holocaust studies in the United States, once observed that the genocide of the European Jews attracted some attention in the Federal Republic in the 1960s as a result of the Eichmann and Auschwitz trials, but was not a focal point of the "sixty-eighters," i.e., the youthful participants in the protest movement that rocked Germany in the latter part of the decade by asking their parents' generation what they had done during the Third Reich. It was not until a decade later, in fact, with the broadcast of the American miniseries *Holocaust* in West Germany in 1979, that the Final Solution finally entered popular consciousness there; it has since become a perennial source of public discussion.

That the reception of the Holocaust has a history that changed over time has generally become an accepted idea – one that has also come to be accepted with regard to the field of American sociology, as Adele Valeria Messina reminds us in this fine study, the first one-volume synthesis in English of the history of the sociology of the Holocaust in the United

States. But, as the author shows, there was no "delay" in approaching the Holocaust: rather, it was a topic that attracted attention in American sociological circles immediately after 1945 – and even during the war itself. Drawing on an abundance of evidence, Messina not only debunks that misperception, but also persuasively describes the reasons how and why the idea of a "missing tradition" in American sociology came about.

As a historian of modern Germany, there is another aspect of this review of American sociological studies of the Holocaust from the end of the Second World War through the present that I find especially attractive: by alerting us to a number of important studies that have unjustly been long neglected, it points to ways in which historians can better integrate the sociological tradition of Holocaust studies into their own field. And, as the author herself concludes, her monograph strongly suggests the need to revisit the sociological traditions of other countries as well, where the study of the Holocaust may very well have an equally rich heritage. By alerting us to this possibility, Messina has performed a valuable service to her own field, as well as to cognate ones such as my own.

Andrew I. Port
Professor of History, Wayne State University
Editor, *Central European History*

Introduction

Just as with many good things that happen by chance, this book has also come to be by happenstance: it is a bit associated with a fortunate event. When I started to approach the Holocaust topic, by reading *Modernity and the Holocaust* (1989) by Zygmunt Bauman, I sincerely knew almost nothing of what it really meant. In my mind, I thought I knew enough about the Holocaust: around 6 millions of Jews were killed. That's all I needed to know. But in working with a feeling that I had upon trying to look at it more closely, I started to examine any writing related to the topic I could find. One day my eyes accidentally fell on an article by Burton P. Halpert: "Early American Sociology and the Holocaust: The Failure of a Discipline" (2007). I had never read such a thing: it was absolutely new for me. So I proceeded with the abstract, and then my eyes ran over this passage:

> American sociology, established as an academic discipline in 1905, passed through two early developmental stages, Christian reformism and sociological positivism, together forming the basis for what was taught and researched in the academy. Topics not fitting this religious and positivistic paradigm were dismissed by the leaders of the discipline. Included among the neglected topics was the Holocaust, the paradigmatic genocide of the twentieth century. Permeated with religious ideology and anti-Semitism, American sociology as practiced in the leading universities in the United States institutionalized a professional milieu that precluded recognition of the Holocaust, even after World War II.[1]

---

1 Burton P. Halpert, "Early American Sociology and the Holocaust: The Failure of a Discipline," *Humanity & Society* 31 (2007): 6.

I really understood that something was amiss in my mind and that the Holocaust was a more deeply felt question. Contemporaneously I was becoming fascinated with Italian book *Auschwitz e gli intellettuali* by Enzo Traverso.[2] These two works, like two heavy stones, were making room in my consciousness and thought, and "like a beacon in the night" they were starting to illuminate my research. Actually, I was finding myself facing a new perspective of study. This was my starting point: I wanted to have more knowledge of the scholars of sociology and about the failure of sociology concerning the Holocaust.

Halpert's statement—that "American Sociology permeated with religious ideology and anti-Semitism institutionalized a professional milieu that precluded recognition of the Holocaust"—became a nagging, burdensome question for me: I continuously asked myself how Christian reformism and sociological positivism could be related to the Holocaust. Once more conscious of this, I commenced to peruse whatever Holocaust sources (symposium publications, papers, articles, books, essays, letters to the editor, reviews, and so on) and more and more to look at any writing about sociology and the destruction of the Jews. So, step by step, I was focusing on the approach sociology adopted in studying the Holocaust.

Since Halpert's article seemed to confirm the thesis according to which the post-Holocaust sociology started with *Modernity and the Holocaust* by Bauman, I wanted to verify that. Thus this book resulted from two questions: Does post-Holocaust sociology only start with *Modernity and the Holocaust* by Bauman in 1989 and after the fall of Berlin Wall? This is a concern of my study. The second question has to do with the role Bauman's book played in both American sociology and the wider Holocaust discussion, namely, should it be considered an exception in the field, as most scholars appear to think it is. In searching for an answer to these questions, I started to examine the sociology of the Holocaust and its related themes, and I ran into a set of unforeseen and astonishing outcomes beyond the Holocaust and concerned with academic realm.

I hope to make the reader aware of the "Jewish problem" of sociology and provide what this academic discipline urgently needs: a one-volume history

---

2   Enzo Traverso, *Auschwitz e gli intellettuali: La shoah nella cultura del dopoguerra* (Bologna: il Mulino, 2004 [1997]).

of the sociology of the Holocaust, that is, a single volume suited for a broad audience.[3] Moreover, although I run the clear risk of some omissions, I hope that my approach will be sufficient to point out the fundamental issues.

Since my original doubt occupied me with reviewing the history of sociology, this book is going to offer the first résumé in English of up-to-date research on the sociology surrounding the destruction of the Jews during World War II: a genocide that did not have its beginning in "mobile killing operations" and "killing center operations," as Raul Hilberg states. The destruction of the Jews, between 1933 and 1945, was prepared by certain steps: a definition by decree, concentration phases, and deportations.[4]

Even if this book affords a guide to the current state of knowledge, it does not aim to present itself as the last word on the subject. Filled with new elements and aspects that challenge contemporary and common scholarly theses, the volume tries to examine, as well as it can, the sociological literature that studied the Holocaust from the end of the conflict to the present day. Further, I will investigate the event of the Holocaust by retracing some stages of the sociological scholarship. Thus I am going to analyze sociology as academic *corpus* and as a discipline, namely, the sociological devices and concepts adopted by sociologists over the years in comprehending the Holocaust and the focus of sociological thoughts confronted by the event. Additionally, in rethinking the sociology of the Holocaust, the book will move across the history of the same sociology. However, the focus on almost every page is on the "alleged delay of sociology" in the comprehension of the Jewish genocide.

Before 1989, the year *Modernity and the Holocaust* by Bauman was published, scholars used to speak of a sociological problem, in the sense that the sociologists "have been reluctant to study the Holocaust"[5] or "have so far failed to explore in full the consequence of the Holocaust."[6]

---

3 Ronald J. Berger, review of *Sociology Confronts the Holocaust: Memories and Identities in Jewish Diasporas*, ed. Judith M. Gerson and Diane L. Wolf, *Shofar: An Interdisciplinary Journal of Jewish Studies* 27, no. 1 (2008): 151, accessed October 2, 2009, doi:10.1353/sho.0.0275.
4 Raul Hilberg, *The Destruction of the European Jews* (Chicago: Quadrangle, 1961), 43–53, 106–635; David Cesarani, *Final Solution: The Fate of the Jews 1933–1949* (London: Macmillan, 2016).
5 Fred E. Katz, "A Sociological Perspective to the Holocaust," *Modern Judaism* 2, no. 3 (1982): 273.
6 Zygmunt Bauman, "Sociology after the Holocaust," *British Journal of Sociology* 39, no. 4 (1988): 469.

Briefly put, few sociological works dealt with the Holocaust, with the exception of, for example, *Accounting for Genocide* by Helen Fein in 1979.[7] "The upshot of sociologists' silence," in Fred Katz's words, "is that distinctive sociological contributions to knowledge of the Holocaust remain relatively untapped."[8] Hence, the exigency and urgency for a book on the sociology of the Holocaust that collects and analyzes sociological works (authors and their theories) that have dealt with the phenomenon, especially because things seem not to have changed much since Barry Dank stated in 1979 that "there is in essence no American sociological literature on the Holocaust."[9] Therefore, this book attempts to solve the problem. I will start with an important conference, offering as balanced an outline of as many facets of its points as possible.

THE FAMOUS OCTOBER 2001 CONFERENCE: THE SOCIOLOGICAL TURNING POINT

An international conference on "Sociological Perspectives on the Holocaust and Post-Holocaust Jewish Life" took place at Rutgers University in New Jersey, October 25 to 27, 2001. In the working conference, sociologists and specialists well acquainted with Holocaust discourse and its familiar topics (from Jewish identity and migration to collective memory, by way of ethnicity and so on) participated.

What mattered, in the eyes of these academics, in those three days of the conference, was principally the analysis and the viewpoint of the situation, that is, sociology's status in respect to the Holocaust. A big role in the satisfactory outcome of the symposium was played, particularly, by Judith M. Gerson—associate professor of Sociology and Women's and Gender Studies at Rutgers University, where she is also an affiliate faculty

---

7 Helen Fein, *Accounting for Genocide: National Response and Jewish Victimization during the Holocaust* (New York: Free Press, 1979).
8 Katz, "A Sociological Perspective to the Holocaust," 273.
9 Barry M. Dank, review of *On the Edge of Destruction: Jews of Poland between the Two World Wars*, by Celia S. Heller, *Contemporary Sociology* 8, no. 1 (1979): 129. For example, Bauman speaks of a symposium on "Western Society after the Holocaust" summoned in 1978 by the Institute for the Study of Contemporary Social Problems, but it was only one episode. See Jack N. Porter, "The Holocaust as a Sociological Construct," *Contemporary Jewry* 14, no. 1 (1993): 185.

member of the Department of Jewish Studies and a recipient of a residential research fellowship at the Center for Advanced Holocaust Studies at the United States Holocaust Memorial Museum—and by Diane L. Wolf, professor of sociology and a member of the Jewish Studies Program at the University of California, Davis.

Hosted by the Institute for Women's Leadership of the Rutgers University, "Sociological Perspectives" aimed at favoring a scholarly dialogue and interchange between intellectuals and researchers working in Holocaust Studies and related fields for enhancing Holocaust research in sociology and called for a comparative analysis, as evident from invited papers and contributions.

Thanks to the support of several organizations (such as the American Sociological Association, the National Science Foundation's Fund for the Advancement of the Discipline, the Lucius N. Littauer Foundation, and the Research Council of Rutgers University) and the concrete and solid work by many scholars, the conference took place and, first and foremost, it was possible to address relevant questions surrounding why Holocaust Studies programs were considered marginal to most academic disciplines and why sociologists had not taken up this issue years before.

During the conference, scholars mostly agreed that there had been a delay of sociology in studying the genocide of the Jews—a recurring expression was "silence" (of sociology) in relation to the Holocaust—and that there was a "dearth of a sociological understanding of the Shoah."[10]

In almost a general scholarly consensus, it seemed that only *Modernity and the Holocaust* by Bauman had broken the silence of sociological studies on the Holocaust. And this was in 1989, after the fall of Berlin Wall,

---

10   Among numerous presentations, I mention the following: "Remembrance without Recognition: Jewish Life in Germany Today" by Y. Michal Bodemann; Post-Holocaust Identity Narratives: A Sociological Approach to Collective Consciousness, Memory and History" by Debra Renee Kaufman; "Availability, Proximity, and Identity in the Warsaw Ghetto Uprising: Adding a Sociological Lens to Studies of Jewish Resistance" by Rachel L. Einwohner; "'On Halloween We Dressed Up Like KGB Agents': Identity Strategies of Second-Generation Soviet Jews" by Kathie Friedman-Kasaba; "The Holocaust and Jewish Identity and Identification in the United States" by Chaim I. Waxman; and "The Holocaust and the Formation of Cosmopolitan Memory" by Daniel Levy. See Judith M. Gerson and Diane L. Wolf, eds., *Sociology Confronts the Holocaust: Memories and Identities in Jewish Diasporas* (Durham, NC: Duke University Press, 2007), 3, 11.

when the book was published. Indeed, the fall of the Berlin Wall constitutes a decisive moment in the history of Europe because next the collapse of communism, the resulting opening of the archives of the East, and the outbreak of civil war in ex-Yugoslavia (1991–95) all led several social scientists to reapproach, in their academic discussions and with new perspectives, the causes of the genocide of the Jews. It is not an accident that, in 1999, a workshop on "The Holocaust and Contemporary Genocide" took place at the University of Minnesota: almost as if in response to the genocide against Kosovar Albanians in 1998–99. The civil war in the ex-Yugoslavia awakened the "historical sociology of genocide."[11] This will be more evident in Chapter 3.

Now, Bauman's wake-up call for sociology's involvement with the Holocaust essentially meant two things: first, that before *Modernity and the Holocaust* only a few sociological works dealing with the topic existed, and, second, that these few sociological studies did not contain appropriate sociological tools or a formulation of a theoretical system that analytically treated the extermination of the Jews. After the publication of Bauman's study, Gerald E. Markle in 1995 and Debra Kaufman in 1996, for instance, tackled the problem.[12]

"A 'glaring paucity' of sociological scholarship exists on the Holocaust" (as stated in the opening pages of *Modernity and the Holocaust* [xiii]) became a kind of call to action for some sociologists:[13] thus in the 1990s, Jack N. Porter dealt with the presumed delay of the sociological discipline. According to Martin Oppenheimer's speculations, there are specific reasons for the lack of sociological studies on the Holocaust. Briefly,

> 1. that sociologists avoid "deviant cases"—because these incline them to description more than to analysis; 2. that grand narratives lead their authors astray methodologically, and evoke harsher-than-usual reactions from competing paradigms (as some of the historians have

---

[11] Michael Freeman, "Genocide, Civilization and Modernity," *British Journal of Sociology* 46, no. 2 (1995): 207.
[12] See Jack N. Porter, "Toward a Sociology of the Holocaust," *Contemporary Jewry*, 17 (1996): 145–48.
[13] Cf. Gerson and Wolf, *Sociology Confronts the Holocaust*, 11.

learned); 3. that "big" subjects like these are a poor fit for journal publication; 4. that American sociologists do not command the relevant languages; 5. that there is an uneasy fear of being academically ghettoized; 6. or worse, that there is fear of being labeled opportunist, for climbing onto the bandwagon of the Holocaust Industry ("shoah-business").[14]

The October 2001 conference rightly represents a turning point in sociological studies related to the Holocaust: it brought to fruition a productive and fertile scholarly movement; since that time the number of academic courses and scholarships, in several universities, have grown at great speed: indirectly, most of them are a consequence and product of that conference. Examples of course offerings included Sociology and the Holocaust (fall 2005 at New York University), Sociology of the Holocaust (spring 2007 at the University of Nebraska), Holocaust and Genocide Studies (in 2009 at Keene State College), and Sociology of the Holocaust at the University of Warwick in the same year.

The papers given in 2001 to the scholars of that conference were original contributions and resulted in a book: *Sociology Confronts the Holocaust* (2007). However, the contributions to the book are not simply from the 2001 conference proceedings: rather, that conference had invited, or compelled, a review of the sociological literature, categories, and methods and forced scholars to think of the Holocaust in terms of sociological devices.[15] The book edited by Gerson and Wolf is rooted in this context.

"Whether sociology itself has a 'Jewish problem,' or its scholars lack the language skills, historical background, or mere interest to study it,

---

14 Elihu Katz, review of *Sociology Confronts the Holocaust: Memories and Identities in Jewish Diasporas*, ed. Judith M. Gerson and Diane L. Wolf, *Social Forces* 87, no. 4 (2009): 2222, accessed October 2, 2009, doi:10.1353/sof.0.0198.
15 See the list of scholars "who have read at least one paper in 2007," http://www.jstor.org/stable/10.1086/590978?seq=1#page_scan_tab_contents (accessed September 28, 2015). The conference was in 2001, and the book came from that conference in 2007. The 2001 conference has compelled many sociologists to deal with or face the Holocaust: for instance, just the simple assessment of the papers, by referees, becomes an occasion to speak of the sociology of the Holocaust. In reviewing the papers there is already a kind of dissemination of the sociology of the Holocaust.

Sociology Confronts the Holocaust attempts to 'bring the study of the Holocaust and its aftermath up to speed in sociology,'"—so Lynn Rapaport began her review of the volume edited by Gerson and Wolf, one year after its release.[16] For the editors, and not only them, it was necessary to heal and to recover the lost time, just as had Bauman and Fein, who were greatly appreciated by the academic community for their "heroic efforts to approach the horror of the Holocaust sociologically."[17]

As stated by Martin Oppenheimer, in their twenty-three-page contribution, Gerson and Wolf outline "some of the strands of research that do exist." Oppenheimer's "critique" of Gerson and Wolf's edition weaves a series of relevant issues.[18]

If the October 2001 conference represents a turning point and if that conference came out of the aim to reconsider the status of sociology, the 2007 book, as a result of that symposium, may be properly conceived as the volume opening and inaugurating the sociological scholarship confronting the genocide of the Jews.

So, what more can be added to Gerson and Wolf's work? Is it possible to say something not yet said? The present book accepts the invitation by the two editors, in 2007, and by Berenbaum[19] in 2010, to "bring together what until now have been distant fields of knowledge."[20] At this point, the reader might ask: Which questions does this volume intend to answer?

Actually, I will ask myself a series of questions, of which the first is this: Does a book on English-speaking sociologists tackling the Holocaust exist? Or better: Do we know of a volume that collects and criticizes and at the same time, as a compendium, gathers the history of post-Holocaust sociology from 1945 to 2016? In other words, is there a book on "sociology

---

16 Lynn Rapaport, review of *Sociology Confronts the Holocaust: Memories and Identities in Jewish Diasporas*, ed. Judith M. Gerson and Diane L. Wolf, *American Journal of Sociology*, 113, no. 6 (2008): 1794. See Gerson and Wolf, *Sociology Confronts the Holocaust*.
17 Katz, review of *Sociology Confronts the Holocaust*, 1.
18 Martin Oppenheimer, "The Sociology of Knowledge and the Holocaust: A Critique," in Gerson and Wolf, *Sociology Confronts the Holocaust*, 331–36. See Gerson and Wolf, *Sociology Confronts the Holocaust*, 11–33.
19 Michael Berenbaum, review of *Sociology Confronts the Holocaust: Memories and Identities in Jewish Diasporas*, ed. Judith M. Gerson and Diane L. Wolf, *Journal of Contemporary History* 45, no. 2 (2010): 505–7, doi:10.1177/00220094100450020110.
20 Gerson and Wolf, *Sociology Confronts the Holocaust*, 9.

and the Holocaust" criticizing the discipline from within (i.e., sociologists who studied the event; concepts, categories, and methods applied to analyze it; theoretical system elaborated and so on)? It seems not. Thus, this book seeks to fill a gap or to provide a kind of missing link in the history of sociology. But, I hope it will also deepen and enhance Holocaust Studies (because herein the destruction of the Jews is illustrated differently, namely, with sociological tools not used previously). Finally, it links disciplines, such as history and sociology, that often diverge.

Other questions still arise in my mind—a kind of doubt, such as, has sociology really had a "Jewish problem"?[21] Has it "been slow to 'confront' the topic,"[22] as affirmed by most scholars? I naïvely ask myself: Is all this really true? And more profoundly: Was there really a delay? Have the scholars arguing that there was a delay read the entire sociological literature since 1945 connected with the Holocaust? This book intends to be a kind of response to Gerson and Wolf's volume and to the common assumption that there was a delay in post-Holocaust sociology. Therefore, at this point the matter is simple: if sociologists did not analyze the entire post-Holocaust sociological literature, the problem does not exist (in the sense that they only need to read the literature). On the contrary, if they have read everything, there may be a problem, because there may not have been a delay. In this case, I asked myself why these authors did not realize or recognize, reviewing the sociological literature, that there was not a delay. And yet: Did they not ask what caused the alleged delay? That is, why have scholars been led to speak of "delay," and even to arguing this thesis? Did they not attempt to theorize systematically the origins of this alleged delay in any publications? To these and other questions, this book tries to give the answer that the delay could be half true.

I will attempt to explain why authors who did indeed study the Holocaust were not considered by other scholars, in their own time and later; why observers, over the years, have come to speak of an absence of sociology in the study of the Holocaust; and why this sociological tradition is omitted, ignored to the point of creating, for most scholars, "a missing

---

21 Berger, review of *Sociology Confronts the Holocaust*, 151.
22 Rapaport, review of *Sociology Confronts the Holocaust*, 1794.

tradition." Thus, I endeavor to show in what way we can speak of a *missing sociological tradition*.

METHODOLOGY

The methodological ways with which I approached these matters were conceived as a tool that aims principally to answer my questions, and the method I adopted shows the liaison between the world of scientific research and the construction and dissemination of sociological knowledge in a dynamic context profoundly modified by new online multimedia devices.

In the beginning of my research, there was a timely and simple interrogative: Were there any sociological writings related to the Holocaust before the publication of *Modernity and the Holocaust* by Bauman in 1989? In order to clear up my doubts, I decided to peruse everything. To verify if, before Bauman's book, there really was no sociological work dealing with the destruction of the Jews and related topics, I poured over—as much as I could—the entire sociological literature since 1945.

I did not just look for great theories or eminent names of good reputation, that is, those known to most or all of the academic community. Rather, I looked at any book, essay, article, doctoral dissertation, book review, paper, letter to the editor, conference announcement, and fellow list surrounding and related to the Holocaust. For example, I also investigated the list of the names of the *American Journal of Sociology* (*AJS*) board and read annotations to the names of the directors of the journal. At this point, the reader might ask why I did this. I'd answer by saying that the reading of academic positions together with scholarly publications allows me to enter into the academic realm and to *inter*-read the scientific context that accounts for the conditions for the dissemination of research topics: this will be a key point in understanding the alleged delay of sociology.

Therefore, some readers may still ask how the research has been carried out. I literally browsed and considered all the online academic sociological journals: I used EBSCO*host* databases, particularly since 1945, in order to, I repeat, see which authors have written on the genocide of the Jews of Europe and its related themes.

This means that I utilized key concepts typical of the sociological discipline and those concerned with the Holocaust (such as "movement," "bureaucracy," "totalitarianism," "political violence"). With different combinations accommodated by Boolean operators, I researched abstracts, titles, articles, reviews of articles, and so on, or I looked for the related names of the authors in editorial contributions, letters to the director, and conference proceedings.

I've stated that I started with 1945 and the end of World War II, but actually I went back to 1933 (the year of Hitler's assumption of power) and even to the 1920s to acquaint myself with the academic realm of sociological research and its research funding.

I chose to adopt the method of online academic reviews for two reasons: first, because it is highly innovative and accurate—in the field of history, this method has recently brought significant relevant results, as demonstrated by the researches of Gisella Fidelio, Christian Fleck, Maurizio Ridolfi, and Carlo Spagnolo.[23] Through the online scientific reviews it is possible to contribute to writing history or, in other words, it is possible to do history through the reviews. Second, the method of online academic reviews provided me innovative interfaces with an optimization of the value of my work along with the breadth and depth of contents. In other words, to resolve my doubts and satisfy my curiosity, I had to sift post-Holocaust sociology: only such a research method could allow for "premium online information resources," primary sources, and open access to full-text searches, in short, a scientific, well-equipped knowledge.[24]

There was a conference that showed how this method is a fertile and useful tool of investigation that took place in Viterbo, Italy, May 25–26, 2006, promoted by the faculty of the Department of Political Science at the University of Tuscia and under the aegis of the Italian Society for the Study of Contemporary History (Sissco), with the organization of the Centre of Studies for the History of Mediterranean Europe.[25] I imagined that sociologists could take advantage of this new historical approach. Hence my choice to adopt it for the present work: I pored over writings, articles, and dissertations in sociology. However, I have to inform the

---

23 See also http://www.technologysource.org/article/free_online_scholarship_movement/ (accessed October 28, 2015).
24 See https://www.ebscohost.com/ (accessed February 13, 2016).
25 See http://www.sissco.it/articoli/la-storia-contemporanea-attraverso-le-riviste-549/ (accessed June 28, 2016).

reader of an important aspect: in going through the literature, I have tried to always keep in mind some guidelines that oriented my research: when a sociological work was written; who is the author of the piece; to which school of thought the author belongs; what is the content of the study; which sociological tools have been adopted (such as totalitarianism, movement, etc.); was is published after World War II? (in which year? and under which masthead?); and, finally, who was the author and when did he or she emigrate after Hitler's rise—keeping in mind the impact of the scholarly production of refugee sociologists on American culture.

It was in this manner that I acquainted myself with works by sociologists (by referring to their school, too, when possible) on the destruction of the Jews of Europe. I analyzed in which years the studies were published, and in which academic reviews, by measuring their productivity and the degree of appreciation for their works.[26] These measurements, productivity (how many written works the scholar has produced), and visibility (how many times the name of the authors appear in articles and reviews on EBSCO), and also the degree of appreciation of these works (calculated based on the number of citations that the academic environment has reserved for them) allowed me to verify the alleged delay and why there was said to be a delay.

I considered two broad periods: one from 1945 and following, and one that covers the years prior to World War II, examining all the publications that, at least once, have in the title of the article or book review terms related to the Jewish question. This method, halfway between hemerographia and metasociology, allows the measurement of some important indexes for this study, such as "the speed of publication" of research and "the

---

26 Cf. Maurizio Ridolfi, ed., *La storia contemporanea attraverso le riviste* (Soveria Mannelli: Rubbettino, 2008), 7–11; Christian Fleck, "Per un profilo prosopografico dei sociologi di lingua tedesca in esilio," in "L'Europa in esilio: La migrazione degli intellettuali verso le Americhe tra le due guerre," ed. Renato Camurri, *Memoria e Ricerca: Rivista di storia contemporanea* 16, no. 31 (2009): 81–101. On the use of databases, electronic journals, A-Link, and other university services in support of research and teaching, see http://www.aib.it/aib/com/bc04/programma.htm3 (accessed March 29, 2009). The interface of EBSCO research allows interaction with other electronic resources present in the collection. There are more than 100 databases both of property and of user license and more than 8,000 reviews in full-text, OPAC catalogs, index, and abstracts for approximately 12,000 publications and coverage in PDF for 6,000+ titles and peer-reviewed journals. See Gisella Fidelio, "La ricerca bibliografica on-line" (2010), http://www.sssub.unibo.it/pagine_principali/fidelio.pdf (last access March 29, 2009).

scientific impact" of it on the academic public. For example, I visited the digital library JSTOR, which operates as an "open service," and that permitted me to access to the contents of the archives and of particular publications for my research. A wide range of international journals was selected, classified by the publishing group and thematic content (to measure productivity and the rate of diffusion of the works relating to the matter). Additionally, through EBSCO, I could work with different databases, which, by surveying numerous international journals, facilitates access to older international publications and gives acquaintance with the quantitative diffusion of publications and intellectual quality of the author's sociological production by electronic catalog. I can say that I have conducted a kind of little scientometrical analysis.[27] As the reader will see in Chapter 1, on the database JSTORE (acronym of *JournalStorage*, listing 85 journals) a research for "total author" allowed me to measure the visibility of Hughes and Parsons.

In retracing the entire sociological literature from 1945 on, I touched upon previously ignored or marginal subjects of investigation: from perusing online academic reviews, unknown papers emerged and cleared up my doubts related to the question of the alleged delay of sociology. I will attempt to demonstrate all that.

I will describe, decade by decade, and in detail, which works concerning the Holocaust were conducted after World War II. Hence the more primarily descriptive nature of the book rather than that critical. I will also try to explain for what reasons these studies were not considered by their own contemporary academy or by later scholars.

This book aims at unearthing these works and describing their themes of focus. I will not criticize them, but I will limit myself to presenting and introducing them, organically, to an academic audience, because my aim in this book is primarily to demonstrate that it might be an error to speak of sociological silence in post-Holocaust sociology. I have to say, additionally, that this perusal permitted me to revise several important views of sociology: for example, when and how this discipline was born in American academies. It allowed me to approach the topic using *AJS* and the *American Sociological Review* (*ASR*), the most important

---

27 See Fleck, "Per un profilo prosopografico dei sociologi di lingua tedesca in esilio," 96, table 4.

sociological academic journals, which founded sociology itself, since they disseminate research activities. Meanwhile, I will identify the fathers of sociology and the of the American Social Gospel. And still further, I'll see how sociology developed, especially after 1945—since it was my key focus or my chronological device—in Europe, the country/place of the destruction of the Jews (for example, in Poland by addressing the Pawełczyńska and Bauman cases) and in the United States (the destination of emigration and the country hosting German refugee sociologists).

Precious for my research were e-mail dialogues that I had with Jack N. Porter, Martin Oppenheimer, Rick Helmes-Hayes, Christopher Simpson, and Viviana Salomon during my doctorate research, particularly in 2011, and three Holocaust-survivor interviews conducted with Anna Pawełczyńska, Hanna K. Ulatowska, and Zofia Posmysz-Piasecka in Warsaw in December 2011.

English-Language Sources

I privileged this research-online-perusing with sources in English: I considered above all English papers and writings: the most availability is in English and much came out on the discipline of American sociology. This perusing through the online reviews permitted me to sift and scrutinize the sociological discipline in detail. That several of these writings were unnoticed, for different reasons, is what I will attempt to explain.

In particular, I deal with the sociology of English speakers for specific functional reasons. First of all because American sociology claims to be universal and provide a more complete overview. Second because of the visibility and radius of influence it had and still has. I am aiming at creating a valid, general, and "immune" discourse, which means that I intentionally decided not to initiate a work starting from a particular perspective that might be called "German." I preferred to avoid, for example, all what in Italian might defined as "*tedesco-foro* discourse" (an Italian coinage from Greek φόρος, "bringing, bearing," and Old High German *theod*, "German people").[28] Therefore, hereafter, when I speak of sociology I refer above all to an "Anglophone sociology," so to speak.

---

28 I would like to thank Giuseppe Veltri for the expression "*tedesco-foro* discourse" and for his suggestions.

Moreover, German sociology makes an inner and indirect discourse. Anyway, it does not mean that I will not address German scholars in this volume, but simply I do not start from a German viewpoint. The importance of German sociology (of the Holocaust), as I will try to demonstrate, deserves a separate book, which I intend to tackle in a specific way in the near future. Here I will limit myself, for instance, to citing *Value-Free Sociology* by Sven Papcke, a relevant work in German sociology that the scholar conducted with Martin Oppenheimer.[29]

Another reason I thought of has to do with the United States as a country (and not only because, at the end of World War II, it needed to express itself in the language of the victor). The United States became the container-country hosting refugee scholars from Europe: sociologists spoke the language of the country in which they were welcomed. In Germany, sociology was interrupted in 1933 because the best scientific minds were exiled and sociology as theoretical appointment was widely discredited. Nationalistic German sociology was born, but I will speak of this in another place. However, in postwar Germany, sociology proceeded only with difficulties.

Finally, there is a pragmatic reason: it is impossible to sip and taste the sociology of any country, after World War II, in any language. It is an encyclopedic work, for now, a scholarly prodigy. This reduction, on the basis of the language, is guided by a goal: that this new history of sociology, now, deserves to be made available and exposed to academic public. In my opinion, it is more worthwhile to show the results of my historical interpretation of the status of the sociology, that is, it is not appropriate to speak of an absolute silence of sociology in dealing with the Holocaust or to state that the sociological discipline was on delay in addressing the destruction of the Jews.

Rather, I will attempt to demonstrate that the indifference or disinterest argued openly since 1989 by the academic field of sociology was—as the reader will see later—implicitly or explicitly "prepared": in the academic realm, there were conditions to expel this topic from the research agenda.

---

29 I personally thank Martin Oppenheimer for having recommended to me this study: Sven Papcke and Martin Oppenheimer, "Value-Free Sociology: Design for Disaster German Social Science from Reich to Federal Republic," *Humanity & Society* 8, no. 3 (1984): 272–82. Martin Oppenheimer, e-mail message to author, May 31, 2011.

Chronology

The chronological approach I have adopted for this volume is an attempt to better address the facts and to allow the reader to comprehend more thoroughly what exactly happened when. This will help the reader with a preparatory account leading to the alleged delay of sociology. It will be useful to focus attention on sociological traditions (such as the Chicago School of Everett C. Hughes) and on how sociology evolved, specialized, and differentiated. This is the reason I will touch on the initial interest for sociology in "evolutionary theory" and the "economic determinism" popular in Europe until the 1980s, American functionalism (debated in the 1940s–60s), and the rising partitioning of sociology: as the reader will note, it helps to comprehend the context in which the alleged delay was rooted.[30] I will also touch on the period at the end of the Vietnam War, when the legacy of American ameliorism of the early twentieth century—of which the traces were still strong in 1950s and 60s—and the easy consensus in quantitative sociology had come to an end, while theoretical and permanent divides arose in the discipline. (There was a decline in general theory-building, and a lot of theory-building grew within specialties, even if communication among these specialties was lacking, which process gave rise to "national methodological preferences," a continuous development locally and temporarily in sociology.)[31]

This book intends to be just the start of a long research work that could be an innovative study in analyzing the sociology of any country after the end of World War II: step-by-step, year after year, department by department. It wouldn't be difficult to imagine that sociologists would take an interest in this new approach: one that would review French sociology, for example, and thus examine which institutions supported which research after World War II in France, and which authors wrote on the Holocaust. The Polish Academy of Sciences could use this approach, or German and Israeli sociology after the Congo crisis in 1960s. Or even the sociology in Japan that replaced the earlier philosophical approach

---

30 Robert E. L. Faris and William Form, "Sociology," *Encyclopædia Britannica Online*, 1–4, accessed September 1, 2015, http://www.britannica.com/topic/sociology.
31 Ibid., 8.

Introduction | xxxi

with an empirical research method, or industrial sociology at the end of the global conflict. So to speak, it could be of use to any sociological study or department across the world.

This book does not pretend to be exhaustive. It is far from finished; rather it hopes to inaugurate and "hug the road" to this kind of strand on post-Holocaust sociology.

Coming back to the timeline, the method of reconstruction of events by date allows, one to consider the contextual framework with an interpretative and explanatory clarity. In fact, there is a multiple usefulness in adopting chronological order: by perusing the online academic sociological reviews year by year it is possible to glance at and examine who promoted which research project and in which scientific reviews. It may monitor how since the 1960s sociology was differentiated and how the editions and publications on the Holocaust increased after 1975, when sociology started, as academic discipline, a period of segmentation. It can look at when a sociological faculty or the American Sociological Society was established, and which arguments were more studied (in which country and in which years). As I will attempt to demonstrate, a review of these aspects is linked with the aims of this book: the origins of the alleged delay. Sociology as discipline is based on, depends on, and is built by the scientific reviews and the dissemination of works and by the establishment of a faculty at a particular institution. It would be very interesting—but this isn't the right place for it—to account for the institution of the Centre for Advanced Study (CAS) in Sofia, Bulgaria, since its establishment in 2000: how it was developed says a lot about the period of the Cold War and the anti-Semitism still present today in Europe.

THE OUTLINE OF THE BOOK

This book results from my doctoral research on sociology with respect to the destruction of the Jews from 1933 to the present day. It comprises four chapters: Chapter 1, "Sociological Thinking about the Holocaust in the Postwar Years, 1945–1960s," focuses the reader's attention on a very crucial time: the end of the war and the beginning of the Cold War. The chapter will explain how scholars acquainted with sociological tools attempted to comprehend just what happened, namely, the destruction of a nation, the Jews. Chapter 2, "The Destruction of the Jews in a Sociological Perspective during the 1970s," deals with sociological works written during the 1970s, the historical environment in which they were conceived, and the authors who were devoted to this theme. A particular focus is on the sociological tools they adopted. Chapter 3, "Toward a Sociology of Genocide, 1980–1989," addresses post-Holocaust sociology and its noteworthy, ever-increasing production in the 1980s. The Chapter 4, "The Problem of the Holocaust after 1989," is rightly dedicated to analyzing post-Holocaust sociology after the fall of communism and upon the opening of the secret archives in the territories of the former Soviet Union.

Chapter 1. I outline sociological studies related to the Holocaust and conducted during and soon after World War II, but, unfortunately, they were few. An exception is the open case of Talcott Parsons. I will sketch his interest in the Jewish question from his sociological writings related to the destruction of the Jews to the silent years after 1948. I will explain the academic and cultural circumstances in which sociological researches related to the Holocaust formed and the difficulties of different types that faced scholars approaching the Jewish question from the end of the war until the 1960s, when a turning point took place in the discipline of sociology and more sociology scholars started to address specific aspects of the destruction of the Jews. I will try to illustrate the reasons why during the 1960s scholars were becoming more sensitive to the Holocaust, which had been invisible to most intellectuals, and why authors had delayed the publication of their works until such a late date. A series of political and cultural events (for example, the Six-Day War) will be recalled along with some traditions of thought that affected sociology in approaching the theme. This chapter aims at illustrating where the alleged delay of sociology took root and how academic sociology legitimized the delay.

These are works whose sociological outlines and concepts—such as anti-Semitism, mass ideology, and the banality of evil—even if they seem to return in other writings of the Holocaust, present a crucial difference between them, a difference apparent on every page. These are the studies of the Frankfurt School, Parsons's writings, the researches by

Edward A. Shils and Morris Janovitz related to the *Wehrmacht* in World War II and the study on the NSDAP by Seymour Lipset. Also, the conceptual link of totalitarian power seems to bind these writings together. Special attention is given to the eight-page essay "Good People and Dirty Work" by Everett C. Hughes on the banality of evil. With this essay, the sociological tradition of Chicago School enters into post-Holocaust sociology. Written in 1948, the study was published in 1962, the year in which Hannah Arendt prepared her report on the Adolf Eichmann trial as a correspondent for *The New Yorker*, which appeared in the magazine in February and March 1963. I will explain how the Jews became a social problem by consensus and the difficulties faced by sociologists in addressing the Jewish question and publishing Jewish works in the postwar years, when intellectuals were strongly influenced by the power balance of the Cold War.

Chapter 2. I describe how important the rethinking of post-Holocaust sociology was in the 1970s: especially in the years that the Yom Kippur War influenced events and thinking. I will try to explain how the legacy of the Six-Day War endured and how echoes were still heard of "The Commanding Voice of Auschwitz" by Emil L. Fackenheim:

> When at Jerusalem in 1967 the threat of total annihilation gave way to sudden salvation it was because of Auschwitz, not in spite of it, that there was an abiding astonishment. Nothing of the past was explained or adjusted, no fears for the future were stilled. Yet the very clash between Auschwitz and Jerusalem produced a moment of truth—a wonder at a singled out, millennial existence which, after Auschwitz, is still possible and actual.[32]

I hope to illustrate how in little less than a decade the situation changed: the focus on the Jewish question gradually grew as if there was a kind of awakening in sociology. I will present the works characterizing this period, their

---

32 Emil L. Fackenheim, *God's Presence in History: Jewish Affirmations and Philosophical Reflections* (New York: New York University Press, London: University of London Press, 1970), 95–96.

common thread, the analytical categories adopted by scholars, and the impact on scholarship. Notable will be the sociological analysis of the concentration and death camp Auschwitz-Birkenau elaborated by Anna Pawełczyńska: a noteworthy work for her original concept of hodological space of Auschwitz and for her new conception of resistance, conceived by her in a period in which "resistance" in Holocaust Studies was a theme not yet much explored or addressed, especially in the literature related to the camps.

In this chapter, I also outline the original thesis, for social sciences, of Celia Heller: in 1977 she unearthed that at the base of genocide of the Jews in Poland there was Polish nationalism and anti-Semitism, an important thesis that in 2001 would strongly emerge in *Neighbors* by the historian Jan T. Gross.[33] Moreover, the reader's attention will be focused on what Barrington Moore means by "surrender to moral authority" in dealing with the Jewish question.

Finally, the second chapter will examine *Accounting for Genocide*, the most comprehensive sociological work, even to this day, conceived with statistical data. Published by Helen Fein in 1979 and based on crucial sociological categories (national anti-Semitism, Nazi control), it deserves to be considered post-Holocaust sociology. However, this volume did not receive the same plaudits in the academic realm that *Modernity and* obtained in 1989. I will attempt to explain why.

Chapter 3. This chapter addresses the sociological orientation adopted by scholars in the nine years before the fall of Berlin Wall in 1989. I will outline the sociological shift that characterized sociology in addressing the extermination of the Jews in the early 1980s. These years essentially featured a noteworthy and ever-increasing production that has to be linked with increased and overall attention for what was happening contemporarily in several countries on the African continent. The event termed "genocide" becomes an analytic tool: I describe how, starting from and around the concept or the definition of genocide, a series of sociological writings aiming at investigating the extermination of the Jews developed. I hope to show how in these years post-Holocaust sociology developed by starting

---

33 See Jan T. Gross, *Neighbors: The Destruction of the Jews Community in Jedwabne* (Princeton, NJ: Princeton University Press, 2001).

from the juridical definitions of "genocide" and "state." I will explain how authors used the juridical notion of genocide in a sociological way to explain the Holocaust. I will also attempt to demonstrate that these scholars were active politicians or had a big role in political life of their countries. Thus, it is possible to say that Holocaust Studies in these nine years, from 1980 to 1989, can be labeled more properly as "genocide sociological studies." It will be my intention to put in evidence how some scholars, such Leo Kuper and Irving L. Horowitz, acquainted themselves with juridical sciences and recognized the centrality of the political dimension following a multidisciplinary conference on the Holocaust and genocide in 1982, and thus helped to define the concept of "state-sponsored genocide." These scholars contributed to delineating a sociology of genocide or, in other words, to defining a sociology of the genocidal state. It follows that these studies will affect the political scene, in the sense that several government policies will be taken into account with respect to their agenda. These works find manifestation in Wolfgang Sofsky's later work.

I also aim to trace the sociological frame outlined by Katz, who individuates the "routinization" and the "bureaucratization" phases in the extermination of the Jews and the role of *Einsatzgruppen* and the reproposition of banality of evil.

Additionally, the focus will be on the sociological categories adopted by Nechama Tec, who presented her post-Holocaust sociology in 1982 with her own personal history, *Dry Tears*, and up through *Defiance* in 1993. I illustrate how in her long sociological path she considers basics elements of Holocaust Studies (such as Polish nationalism, anti-Semitism, resistance, rescuers, survivors, bystanders) and uses tools typical of sociology (statistical data, survivors interviews), showing the need of a dialogue between sociology and history.

Finally, I will discuss *Modernity and the Holocaust* by Bauman. I retrace his formation, the English exile period, starting in 1968, and how it was decisive in his recognition of the negative consequences of anti-Semitism in Poland and the recognition of human suffering. This latter becomes, for the author, an indispensable sociological notion for analyzing several problems of society. The concept of human suffering was studied and classified into four types according to four specific historical periods. For

Bauman, at the base of his works there is human suffering. However, I will attempt to explain why Bauman, who was a victim of Polish anti-Semitism, chose to explain the destruction of the Jews not by referring to this but through the category of modernity. This is my open question.

Chapter 4. This chapter is longer than the others because almost twenty-five years of post-Holocaust sociology are scrutinized—from 1990 to the present day. I focus first and foremost on the news and novelties sociology dealt with and on the issues the discipline had to confront. I especially outline how the era of globalization and the sociological categories related to it changed the sociological approach towards the Holocaust, prompting Holocaust Studies and sociology itself into a sort of renewal. It will be clearer in the works of Daniel Levy, Natan Sznaider, and Jeffrey Alexander. At the same time, it will be demonstrated that since 1990 the topic of the Holocaust has been approached in different ways, with the result of crossing the theme with other, unexpected, categories (such as those of gender, collective memory, and collective action) and with different issues (such as migration in Israel and the experience of the second-generation survivors). I attempt to illustrate how these mixings create some confusion in distinguishing the writings proper to the Holocaust from those related to affiliated themes and how the introducing of the category of gender in these studies brought some innovation to the research.

I also trace the passage from collective national memory to cosmopolitan memory in Holocaust sociology during the age of globalization. The conception of the Holocaust in modern society will be confronted with the conception of the Holocaust in the new global society, where it becomes a "moral touchstone"—a global icon of evil—in a period in which everything changes.

Finally, I outline how Rachel L. Einwohner updates sociological studies of the Holocaust thanks to a new conception of the Jewish resistance as social movement. I will focus attention on her three comparative cases studies. What has been hitherto lacking is the effort to draw out these sociological researches into a synthetic and comprehensive description. It is this mission the present book aims so far as possible to fulfill. I hope that through the use of sociology and history I will help render the

Holocaust more comprehensible and explain the "sociological delay." We can say that this delay had real and concrete roots.

I will attempt to demonstrate how the alleged delay of sociology was rooted in the cultural realm of sociology, or found its *raison d'être* in its own historical development as a discipline, namely, when it set itself apart from moral philosophy and evolved into a specialized academic discipline. We can see this in sociology in the United States, where the legacy of biologism and industrial scientific progress of the early 1920s was continuing to endure in the postwar years.

In covering aspects ranging from the Social Gospel to the Cold War by the way of World War II, I will attempt to demonstrate the following: (1) it is not appropriate to speak of a "delay of sociology" (and if it is, it has to be called a "desired" delay); (2) it is not appropriate to say that since 1989 the Holocaust has a been a subject of sustained research in sociology; (3) it is not appropriate to state that there were not scholarly works written related to the Holocaust in the postwar years.

In other words, I hope to help to show that a reassessment of post-Holocaust sociology is useful, necessary, and fertile; to start to demolish the common misconception that sociology has delayed the study of the destruction of the Jews; and, finally, to readdress some of major lines of interpretation of important scholars and to encourage more systematic research in the future.

Finally, this book illustrates another aspect: how the sociology of the Holocaust can be integrated into the discussion of historians. That sociology and history were academic disciplines not in close dialogue with each other on this topic over these years is evidenced by that fact that Holocaust sociology seems not to be affected by the four main strands of historiography of the Holocaust: functionalism-structuralism, intentionalism, Freiburg School, and recent theories of Otto Dov Kulka and Ian Kershaw. Most sociological works seem to handle the Holocaust separately. Obviously, there are some exceptions: for instance, Fein was affected by Hilberg's groundbreaking work, *The Destruction of the European Jews*, and by the intentionalist Lucy S. Dawidowicz, in 1975, with her *The War against The Jews, 1933–1945*. But these are special cases. Actually, by analyzing any of these sociological works, it is possible for the reader, working backwards, to find traces and references of intentionalism or intentionalist theories; however, it is work that the reader can only do a posteriori. At any rate, this approach is possible starting from the 1960s, when the first publication of Hilberg's work inaugurated the history of the Holocaust and when history as a discipline started to approach the theme. This happened because history at first analyzed the event starting from perpetrator documents—Nazi papers in German archives, writings of the Third Reich, or collections of sources scattered in many different languages across Europe—and the main aim was that of preparing the Nuremberg case and other cases against Nazi criminal wars. The attention was not focused on the victims, but on the perpetrators. This approach led, erroneously, to the idea that only history as academic discipline—by its appropriate devices and methods—was able to study and examine the Holocaust. It was shaping the event in scholars' minds. And for many years studies on the Holocaust saw the prevalence of historical disciplines, even monopolization by historians.[34] But, as I'll attempt to demonstrate in this book, several sociologists approached the theme apart from historians. Even if I have tried to outline to the best of my possibilities the historical and sociological approach, I believe that more than one reader will disagree with my assessments or interpretation. I apologize if sometimes, in analyzing the works of individual authors, one has the impression of getting lost in sociological devices and explanations. However, this method seems to be the most appropriate. In order to test my thesis, it will be necessary to enter specifically and singularly into these writings. I aim at opening the scholarly mind to debate, and not only to satisfy an intellectual curiosity but also with the goal of continuing the research on what happened. And I hope I hit the target.

---

34   See notes 3 and 5, below (chapter 1).

CHAPTER 1
Sociological Thinking about the Holocaust in the Postwar Years, 1945–1960s

I heard the Brown Shirts in the streets of Nuremberg in 1930 singing, "The German youth is never so happy as when Jewish blood spurts from his knife"; I wrote "Good People and Dirty Work" and used it as a special lecture at McGill University where in the 1930s I taught a course on Social Movements that came to be known as "Hughes on the Nazis."

—Everett C. Hughes

1.1. A PRELIMINARY

After the end of World War II, when worldwide society came to terms with modern civilization, which involved the extermination of inferior races, change seemed to happen fast. Nevertheless, a small number of scholars or politicians considered the extermination of the Jews as the event that, for a variety of factors, transformed the contemporary world: it took more than thirty years for the world to become aware of what had happened. Social sciences are well suited to describing makeovers of a society. In outlining these various sciences all definitions are ideal types, and it seems quite impossible to find a completely exhaustive description. These sciences investigate the fundamentals, representative manifestations of social life, aspects, processes, and structures of social organization. Social sciences are all those disciplines with objectives, different areas of research, peculiar and specific analysis tools, often complementary, which, although having a similar methodological and epistemological horizon as background, do not end in a unitary and equal theory.[1]

---

1 Cf. Adam Kuper and Jessica Kuper, eds., *The Social Science Encyclopedia* (London: Routledge, 1985), 784; Raymond Boudon and François Bourricaud, "Storia e Sociologia," in *Dizionario critico di sociologia*, ed. Lorenzo Infantino (Rome: Armando, 1991), 488–95.

At the end of World War II, although it was difficult to account for, as precisely as possible, the complex chain of events that had recently taken place, nevertheless, it was necessary to analyze what had occurred. How had modern society come to the extermination of the Jews? A set of historical-political situations and strange cultural contingencies led some intellectuals to reflect on the experience, touched as they were by the totalitarian Nazi regime, and they were forced to flee Germany and go into exile, were direct witnesses of the Nazi massacres, or were Holocaust survivors.[2] To examine how these social scientists approached the Jewish question and, particularly, the Holocaust after the war, means to analyze the procedures and devices through which modern liberal society becomes the mirror of a state that has removed moral responsibility from the individual, which places among its projects genocide. Following the insight of Maurice Duverger, who considers the social sciences as the study of social phenomena in the broadest sense, it may be good to review the ways in which these disciplines and scholars have reacted to the extermination of the Jews of Europe. On the basis of (especially) German sources, these researchers, convinced that the story of the destruction of European Jewry goes through the writings of the Nazi state, focused on the responsibility of the perpetrators of the genocide and the way in which the National Socialist state came to the annihilation of the Jews of Europe.[3] This historical study prospective concerned with perpetrators and the German state was reflected in the post-Holocaust sociology of the 1950s and 60s, which is evident in "The Gleichshaltung" by Hughes (1955) or in Lipset's work of 1960.[4] Historical attention to the victims, starting symbolically with *While Six Million Died*, in 1967, is rather visible in sociological works of the

---

2 See Traverso, *Auschwitz e gli intellettuali*.
3 See Gerald Reitlinger, *The Final Solution: The Attempt to Exterminate the Jews of Europe, 1939–1945* (London: Vallentine Mitchell, 1953); Joseph Tenenbaum, *Race and Reich: The Story of an Epoch* (New York: Twayne, 1956); Hilberg, *The Destruction of the European Jews*; Maurice Duverger, *I Metodi delle Scienze Sociali* (Milan: Etas Kompass, 1967); Karl A. Schleunes, *The Twisted Road to Auschwitz: Nazi Policy toward German Jews, 1933–1939* (Urbana–Champaign: University of Illinois Press, 1970); Uwe Dietrich Adam, *Judenpolitik im Dritten Reich* (Düsseldorf: Droste, 1972); Léon Poliakov, *Histoire de l'antisémitisme*, Vol. 4: *L'Europe suicidaire (1870–1933)* (Paris: Calmann-Lévy, 1977).
4 Everett C. Hughes, "The Gleichshaltung of the German Statistical Yearbook," *The American Statistician* 9, no. 5 (1955): 8–11, accessed March 2, 2016, http://www.jstor.org/

1970s:[5] especially in Fein—as one will see—who dedicates a part of her *Accounting for Genocide* to the victims. The founding researches of Léon Poliakov, Gerald Reitlinger, and Raul Hilberg, in 1950s to the 1970s, were followed by a phase in which historians were more oriented towards specific issues and ran the risk of losing sight of the overall context of the events. Only in the last two decades has there been a revival of research on global dimensions.[6]

Here I will not analytically address post-Holocaust historiography: this is not my aim; instead I am going to attempt to explore if and how post-Holocaust sociological studies were confronted (or not confronted) in the postwar period with historical works, since documents in archives and collections of sources, scattered across Europe, were mostly monopolized by historians. I will briefly focus attention on the historiographical debate, within which it is possible to distinguish four research strands, as Yehuda Bauer notes in his *Rethinking the Holocaust*.

First, the functionalist theory, according to which the Nazi policy of annihilation was a mechanism by discontinuous and irregular rhythms dictated by a system that moved independently of the people and their ideas. The functionalists, called also structuralists, focus on the social and economic structures of German society, the mechanism of the regime

---

stable/2685502; Seymour M. Lipset, *Political Man: The Social Bases of Politics* (Garden City, NY: Doubleday, 1960).

5 Cf. Philip Friedman, *Their Brothers' Keepers: The Christian Heroes and Heroines Who Helped the Oppressed Escape the Nazi Terror* (New York: Crown, 1957); Arthur D. Morse, *While Six Million Died: A Chronicle of American Apathy* (New York: Random House, 1967); David S. Wyman, *Paper Walls: America and the Refugee Crisis, 1938–1941* (Amherst: University of Massachusetts Press, 1968); Jacob Presser, *The Destruction of the Dutch Jews* (New York: Dutton, 1969); Isaiah Trunk, *Judenrat: The Jewish Councils in Eastern Europe under Nazi Occupation* (New York: Macmillan, 1972); Ari J. Sherman, *Island Refugee: Britain and Refugees from the Third Reich, 1933–1939* (London: Elek, 1973); Bernard Wasserstein, *Britain and the Jews of Europe, 1939–1945* (Oxford: Clarendon, 1979); Michael R. Marrus and Robert O. Paxton, *Vichy France and the Jews* (New York: Basic Books, 1981); Israel Gutman, *The Jews of Warsaw, 1939–1943: Ghetto, Underground, Revolt* (Bloomington: Indiana University Press, 1982); Dina Porat, *The Blue and the Yellow Star of David: The Zionist Leadership in Palestine and the Holocaust, 1939–1945* (Cambridge, MA: Harvard University Press, 1990).

6 See Saul Friedländer, *The Origins of Nazi Genocide: From Euthanasia to the Final Solution* (Chapel Hill: North Carolina University Press, 1995); Yehuda Bauer, *Rethinking the Holocaust* (New Haven, CT: Yale University Press, 2001).

machine, on bureaucracy, whose actions are dependent on the objectives to be achieved. In this respect, Dan Diner speaks of "a methodological retreat into the description of structures."[7] Economic, political, and social crises are put at the center of reflection. These crises, starting from the last decades of the nineteenth century, transformed Germany into an authoritarian regime with a dictator acting as an arbiter between the power centers in a struggle between them. Genocide is conceived of as an unexpected result. If, on the one hand, functionalism denounces the rivalry between different authorities, then, on the other, it emphasizes how personal power is established in a cultural context imbued with racism and anti-Semitism. According to some of its greatest exponents, such as Hans Mommsen, Götz H. Aly, and Karl A. Schleunes, a decisive role in the extermination was carried out by the bureaucratic apparatus, while political structures and, consequently, the ideology and decisions of central government played a most marginal part.[8]

Instead, the intentionalist school considers the Nazi anti-Jewish policy in a linear manner: by stressing the ideology of the Aryan race and the role of the dictatorship. For Eberhard Jäckel, Helmut Krausnick, Gerald Fleming, and Lucy Dawidowicz, decisional and intentional factors of the central government (personified by Hitler) were essential in the extermination of the Jews and Jewry.[9] Intentionalist scholars especially argue the centrality of Hitler in the anti-Jewish policy of extermination and his almost divine role compared with that of the other Nazi leaders. The tension between both historiographical schools is clear, and they seem to have been superseded by the Freiburg School, for which ideology and local collaboration were the main analytical and explanatory keys of

---

7 See Dan Diner, *Beyond the Conceivable: Studies on Germany, Nazism, and the Holocaust* (Berkeley: California University Press, 2000), 165.

8 See Hans Mommsen, *Auschwitz, 17. Juli 1942: Der Weg zur europäischen "Endlösung der Judenfrage"* (Munich: Deutscher Taschenbuch Verlag, 2002); Götz H. Aly, *Hitler's Beneficiaries: Plunder, Racial War, and the Nazi Welfare State* (New York: Henry Holt, 2005).

9 Cf. Helmut Krausnick, "Judenverfolgung," in *Anatomie des SS-Staates*, band 2, ed. Hans Buchheim et al. (Olten; Freiburg: Walter, 1965), 338–55; Eberhard Jäckel, *Hitler's Weltanschauung: A Blueprint for Power* (Middletown, CT: Wesleyan University Press, 1972); Lucy S. Dawidowicz, *The War against the Jews, 1933–1945* (New York: Holt, Rinehart and Winston, 1975); Gerald Fleming, *Hitler und die Endlösung* (Wiesbaden: Limes, 1982).

the genocide. Ulrich Herbert, the greatest supporter of this viewpoint currently, has studied, along with Christian Gerlach, Dieter Pohl, and Michael Zimmermann, the mass killings perpetrated on local initiative between the end of 1941 and the beginning of 1942 in Belarus, Lithuania, in eastern Galicia, and in the general government.[10] For these authors, behind the extermination campaigns carried out for economic reasons (to get rid of superfluous mouths to feed) or political-demographic motivations (to search for new settlements for German and Polish nationals), there was an ideological substratum, powered by an anti-Semitic intelligentsia, who considered the projects of the Nazi elite as normal. The transfer of entire populations, in the specific case of the Jews, constituted for the central and peripheral authorities, always coordinated with each other in the times and methods, a major goal in order to obtain a living space in which to extend their own national hegemony. In this regard, as Bauer remembers, Herbert refers to the continuous communication between Berlin and the periphery.[11]

Finally, it is relevant to mention the studies of Otto Dov Kulka and Ian Kershaw[12] to explain which role, especially for Kershaw and the sociologist Peter Merkl, anti-Semitism played in extermination: their research shows how a high percentage of members of the *Nationalsozialistische Deutsche Arbeiterpartei* (NSDAP), and a large segment of the German population, was not radically anti-Semitic. Rather there were moderate feelings of discomfort towards the Jews.[13] In its propaganda, the NSDAP never really

---

10 See Dieter Pohl, *Nationalsozialistische Judenverfolgung in Ostgalizien, 1941–1944: Organisation und Durchführung eines staatlichen Massenverbrechens* (Munich: Oldenbourg, 1996); Michael Zimmermann, *Rassenutopie und Genozid: Die nationalsozialistische "Lösung der Zigeunerfrage"* (Hamburg: Christians, 1996); Christian Gerlach, *Krieg, Ernährung, Völkermord: Forschungen zur deutschen Vernichtungspolitik im Zweiten Weltkrieg* (Hamburg: Hamburger Edition, 1998); Ulrich Herbert, hrsg., *Nationalsozialistische Vernichtungspolitik, 1939–1945: Neue Forschungen und Kontroversen* (Frankfurt: Fischer, 1998).
11 Cf. Bauer, *Rethinking the Holocaust*.
12 Ian Kershaw, *Der Hitler-Mythos: Volksmeinung und Propaganda im Dritten Reich* (Stuttgart: Deutsche Verlags-Anstalt, 1980); Otto Dov Kulka and Eberhard Jäckel, eds., *The Jews in the Secret Nazi Reports on Popular Opinion in Germany, 1933–1945* (New Haven, CT: Yale University Press, 2010).
13 Cf. Peter H. Merkl, *Political Violence under the Swastika: 581 Early Nazis* (Princeton, NJ: Princeton University Press, 1975).

pushed the theme of anti-Semitism: its program points were mass unemployment, social and economic crisis, and the defeat of Germany during the Great War. But all of these points were in conformity with a moderate anti-Semitic spirit present in public opinion, and that had as its outcome the removal of the Jews from their economic and political positions. Hitler mostly affected false intellectuals or intellectuals of lower rank, namely, teachers, students, lawyers, but also Protestant pastors, engineers, soldiers, and aristocrats, who, after 1918, found themselves sharing the same social and political disappointments. Moved by resentment and eager to occupy the positions of the Jews, they saw the NSDAP as a remedy for social diseases. What attracted them was the thought that Aryan people could ensure safety and be at the center of a global empire.[14]

To complete this broad overview, it is proper to remember that several sociological writings, in 1960s, were affected by the theological and philosophical reflections of Emil L. Fackenheim and Richard L. Rubinstein.[15] The elevation of the genocide of the Jews to the rank of metaphysical category makes the Holocaust an event that, surpassing human understanding, cannot be compared with other historical events.[16] Additionally, the conceptual category of genocide (typical of the discipline of anthropology) plays a sizable role: the literature emerging has allowed the comparison of the Holocaust and other genocidal types in history, making it an easier event to understand. As Bauer recalls in *Rethinking the Holocaust*, the difference should not be seen in terms of suffering, as suffering cannot be measured (namely, there are no differences in terms of numbers, either in

---

14 Cf. Bauer, *Rethinking the Holocaust*.
15 Cf. James E. Dittes, review of *Christian Beliefs and Anti-Semitism*, by Charles Y. Glock and Rodney Stark, *Review of Religious Research* 8, no. 3 (1967): 183–87; Richard L. Rubenstein, *The Cunning of History: The Holocaust and the American Future* (New York: Harper Colophon: 1978); Rubenstein, "Was Dietrich Bonhoeffer a 'Righteous Gentile'?" International Journal on World Peace 17, no. 2 (2000): 33–46; Emil L. Fackenheim, "Jewish Faith and the Holocaust: A Fragment," *Commentary*, August 1, (1968): 30–36; Fackenheim, *Quest for Past and Future* (Boston: Beacon, 1968); Ian Kershaw, *The Nazi Dictatorship: Problems and Perspectives of Interpretation* (London: Edward Arnold, 1985); Hans Jonas, *Der Gottesbegriff nach Auschwitz: Eine jüdische Stimme* (Frankfurt: Suhrkamp, 1987); Sebastian Rejak, "Judaism Facing the Shoah: American Debates an Interpretations," *Dialogue & Universalism* 13, no. 3/4, (2003): 81–102.
16 See Enzo Traverso, *The Origins of Nazi Violence* (New York: The New Press, 2003), 1–12.

absolute or in percentage), but rather one should understand the causes, factors, and procedures separately.[17] For an improved comprehension of the Holocaust, as total and unique genocide, the science *of* and *on* crime has contributed since the 1990s.[18]

It is important enough to remember in which works, for Porter, emerged the relevance of sociology or of sociological tools in understanding the Holocaust: especially from Rubenstein's and Hilberg's studies,[19] in which a historian and a theologian find fruitful concepts, such as modernity, bureaucracy, and authority, in Max Weber's sociology.[20] At this point, one may ask if sociology really ignored notions such as the totalitarian regime, extermination camps, authority, responsibility, resistance, and so on, and reread the Holocaust themes in postwar sociology, which means "sieving sociological studies."[21] A review of the thesis supporting the delay of sociology in the studying of the Holocaust appears to be indispensable, given that, since the rise of Hitler to power, several intellectuals started to

---

17   Cf. Christian P. Scherrer, "Towards a Theory of Modern Genocide: Comparative Genocide Research: Definitions, Criteria, Typologies, Cases, Key Elements, Patterns and Voids," *Journal of Genocide Research* 1, no. 1 (1999): 13–23, doi:10.1080/14623529908413932; Stephen C. Feinstein, "Art of the Holocaust and Genocide: Some Points of Convergence," *Journal of Genocide Research* 1, no. 2 (1999): 233–55, doi:10.1080/14623529908413953; Gunnar Heinsohn, "What Makes the Holocaust a Uniquely Unique Genocide?" *Journal of Genocide Research* 2, no. 3 (2000): 411–30; Zygmunt Bauman, "Categorical Murder, or: How to Remember the Holocaust," in *Re-presenting the Shoah for the Twenty-first Century*, ed. Ronit Lentin (New York: Berghahn, 2004), 25–40.

18   See Irving L. Horowitz, *Taking Lives: Genocide and State Power* (New Brunswick, NJ: Transaction, 1982); Ryan D. King and William I. Brustein, "A Political Threat Model of Intergroup Violence: Jews in Pre–World War II Germany," *Criminology* 44, no. 4 (2006): 867–91, doi:10.1111/j.1745-9125.2006.00066.x; Andrew Woolford, "Making Genocide Unthinkable: Three Guidelines for a Critical Criminology of Genocide," *Critical Criminology*, 14 (2006): 87–106, doi:10.1007/s10612-005-3197-7.

19   Cf. Rapaport, review of *Sociology Confronts the Holocaust*, 1794–96; Rubenstein, *The Cunning of History*; Benno W. Varon, *Professions of a Lucky Jew* (New York: Cornwall, 1992); Porter, "The Holocaust as a Sociological Construct," 184.

20   See Max Weber, *Economy and Society: An Outline of Interpretive Sociology* (Berkeley: University of California Press, 1978).

21   The expression recalls the metaphor "sieve the history" by Walter Benjamin, used by Traverso, *Auschwitz e gli intellettuali*, 9, 40n1. See Piotr Sztompka, "The Renaissance of Historical Orientation in Sociology," *International Sociology* 1, no. 3 (1986): 321–37, doi:10.1177/026858098600100308; Barbara Engelking, "Reflections on the Subject of Polish-Jewish Relations during World War II," *Polish Sociological Review* 137 (2002): 103–7.

reflect on the crisis of the liberal state in Europe. In accordance with Hilberg and Cesarani, the Holocaust actually started in the 1930s with anti-Jewish measures. The intellectuals in question were mainly European scholars who, forced to leave Germany in 1933, took refuge in the United States. Their works, of great interest for analyzing the structure of the National Socialist Party, trace the deterioration of liberal values pursuant to the advent of National Socialism. Among the works dealing with the promulgation of the Nuremberg racial laws, defining fascism, are the researches of the Institute for Social Research in Frankfurt. For instance, linking fascism and anti-Semitism is Max Horkheimer, while Otto Kirchheimer is distinguished for the fact that, in analyzing Nazi criminal law, he suggests two phases in legal theory after 1933: one authoritarian and one racist.[22]

As concerns concepts like responsibility, democracy, or the banality of evil, it is useful to evoke Morris Janowitz's investigations into the Secret Service: from his hundreds of interviews, it emerged that German respondents, "aware of the existence" of the concentration camps, "denied knowing" what was happening or deviating from their responsibility—Janowitz reported this in 1946![23]

---

22 After the Nazi power conquest in Germany in 1933, the Institute was closed for "tendencies hostile to the State." The members of the Frankfurt School—the most famous were Max Horkheimer, director from 1931, Theodor L. W. Adorno, Herbert Marcuse, Erich Fromm, Friedrich Pollock, Leo Lowenthal, and Walter Benjamin—all emigrated to the United States, with the exception of the last, who did not leave Europe, but committed suicide in 1940 while attempting to cross the border between occupied France and Spain; see Max Horkheimer, Erich Fromm, and Herbert Marcuse, *Studien über Autorität und Familie: Forschungsberichte aus dem Institut für Sozialforschung* (Paris: Felix Alcan, 1936); Max Horkheimer, "Die Juden und Europa," *Zeitschrift für Sozialforschung* 8, no. 1/2 (1939):115–37; Otto Kirchheimer, "Criminal Law in National Socialist Germany," *Studies in Philosophy and Social Sciences* 8, no. 3 (1939), 444–63; W. Rex Crawford, ed., *The Cultural Migration: The European Scholar in America* (Philadelphia: University of Pennsylvania Press, 1953); Martin Jay, *The Dialectical Imagination: A History of the Frankfurt School and the Institute of Social Research, 1923–1950* (London: Heinemann, 1973); H. Stuart Hughes, *The Sea Change: The Migration of Social Thought, 1930–1965* (New York: Harper & Row, 1975); Lewis A. Coser, *Refugee Scholars in America: Their Impact and Their Experience* (New Haven, CT: Yale University Press, 1984); Max Horkheimer and Th. L. W. Adorno, eds., *Lezioni di sociologia* (Turin: Einaudi, 2001 [1956]).

23 See Rudolph Heberle, *From Democracy to Nazism: A Regional Case Study on Political Parties in Germany* (Baton Rouge: Louisiana State University Press, 1945); Morris Janowitz, "German Reactions to Nazi Atrocities," *American Journal of Sociology* 52, no. 2 (1946):

1.2. A TOTALITARIAN ORDER

Studying how sociology approached the Holocaust at the end of the World War II means to fathom the reaction of intellectuals faced with the genocide of the Jews at a fairly crucial time, not too distant from the events from which echoed the dimensions of the Cold War that was to govern international relations.[24]

When World War II ended, very few people cared about the genocide of the Jews: about a destruction process initiated with administrative devices, with a definition by decree in April 1933. (As Hilberg states, the destruction process starts with the "definition," which is then implemented by a series of decrees). The Holocaust did not occupy an essential position; on the contrary, it was secondary in the culture and reality of the postwar period, marked by socioeconomic transformations, new definitions of boundaries, and regime changes. The legacy of an enduring anti-Semitism weighed heavily on this indifference or silence. This is rather evident in the field of sociological studies. Retrieving the first attempts to study the Holocaust involves searching for exceptions, *extra-ordine* works: above the ordinary, beyond the obvious inconvenience of facing similar issues. It is not uncommon to encounter sociologists who faced difficulty in the study of the problem and were forced to delay the publication of their research.[25]

By the end of the war and throughout the 1950s, one can distinguish a period characterized by only a few works, almost all of which dealt with the themes of German fascism or militarism or political and ideological components of the German state. A turning point came during the 1960s when research on specific aspects of the extermination of the Jews increased. In this period, especially in the 1960s, more social scientists started to become sensitive to this event, which was invisible to the majority of intellectuals or, better, more scholars approached the theme

---

141–46, doi: 10.1086/219961; Jessie Bernard, *American Community Behavior* (New York: Dryden, 1949); Gerson and Wolf, *Sociology Confronts the Holocaust*, 14.

24 Cf. Nigel West, *Venona: The Greatest Secret of the Cold War* (London: HarperCollins, 1999); Traverso, *Auschwitz e gli intellettuali*, 9; Salvatore Zappalà, *La tutela internazionale dei diritti umani: Tra sovranità degli Stati e governo mondiale* (Bologna: il Mulino, 2011), 40.

25 See Traverso, *Auschwitz e gli intellettuali*, 9–48.

with fewer difficulties. To pave the way to this was the Russell–Einstein Manifesto, introduced in London on July 9, 1955, by some leading scientists: among them, Einstein and Russell, who, in the center of the Cold War, begged the world to avoid more destruction. This meant that several sociologists identified the problem, analyzed it with sociological tools, and spread publicly results from their research. It happened because a set of events (of cultural order and within the academy) and other factors, such as public international policies, were changing. In other words, a succession of circumstances allowed it to occur.

At the center of these sociological works, one can find the categories of anti-Semitism, mass ideology, social movement, and the banality of evil. The greatest innovation that scholarship reached was exactly the combination of these concepts with the reality of the concentration camp system: it signified that their researches investigated how ordinary or good people contributed to the reality of the totalitarian system.

Among the noteworthy contributions of this period are works by the Frankfurt School, Talcott Parsons, Edward A. Shils and Morris Janovitz, Seymour M. Lipset, and Everett C. Hughes. What these scholars demanded is roughly as follows: What reasons led good people to consent to the policy of National Socialist racial hygiene? New interpretations were kick-started by the Eichmann trial in Israel.[26] That is an important theme and it is crucial for seeing how quickly the effects triggered by the decision of the State of Israel to seize and prosecute in Jerusalem one of the most central administrators of the extermination morphed into a serious discussion about the Holocaust and human justice, both in historical and in sociological scholarship. This demonstrates well the fate of a difficult discussion in the academy.

Once again, it is important to consider the international political context, which had profoundly changed by the end of the war: there was communism on the one hand and capitalism on the other. Hence a series of political and economic policies on behalf of one or the other position, and the collaboration of the Western scientific community, especially by the

---

26   See Antonella Salomoni, "I libri sulla Shoah: Una guida storiografica suddivisa per periodi e per temi," *Storicamente* 5, no. 23 (2009): 2, accessed October 24, 2009, doi:10.1473/stor200.

United States, with intelligence services in the fight against communism, a collaboration that exclusively procured the publication of research with a focus on these issues. Government and private foundations funding universities had a big role in establishing what and who was to be researched within academic institutions, which often needed federal and private support to conduct their agenda and research programs. Particularly, governmental policies had specific aims: since 1945, Western policy prioritized the defeat of communism. Other topics did not receive sufficient financial resources to be addressed and be made public; some issues, such as the destruction of the Jews, in sociological research, were set aside. During this competitive coexistence, there were other interests in that period and "in the name of the Cold War," but the Holocaust as the object of research was not among the key interests of academics.[27] In all these studies a shared element, "the common thread running through them and unites them," revolved around the concept of "totalitarian power" on which the cited authors reflect through the categories of "totalitarian order" and "anti-Semitic discrimination."[28] According to the classical literature, the term "totalitarian state" appears for the first time explicitly in 1939 during a "Symposium on the Totalitarian State." On the occasion, a group of American scholars set in place a set of knowledge, economic, and political terms against the dangers of this type of regime. During the World War II years, however, the term "totalitarianism," rather than as a historical interpretive category, was stated as an instrument of moral condemnation against another regime. But it was in 1951 that the term received a peculiar

---

27 See Christopher Simpson, *Blowback: The First Full Account of America's Recruitment of Nazis, and Its Disastrous Effect on Our Domestic and Foreign Policy* (New York: Weidenfeld and Nicolson, 1988); Jon Wiener, "Talcott Parsons' Role Bringing Nazi Sympathizers to the U.S.," *The Nation*, March 6, 1989, 309; Sigmund Diamond, *Compromised Campus: The Collaboration of Universities with the Intelligence Community, 1945-1955* (Oxford: Oxford University Press, 1992); Martin Oppenheimer, "To the Editor," *Sociological Forum* 12, no. 2 (1997): 339–41.

28 Traverso, *Auschwitz e gli intellettuali*, 15. In general, a conceptual outline of the history of the category of "totalitarianism" includes a before, which appears in an elaboration of totalitarianism intertwined with the kind of fascism—of which the totalitarian phenomenon would be a variety—and an after, in which the two categories instead are to separate and occupy two different disciplines; see Mariuccia Salvati, "Antifascismo e totalitarismo nelle scienze sociali tra le due guerre," *Contemporanea* 4 (2002): 623–26. Let me thank Tiziana Noce for having suggested Salvati's work.

definition by political scientist and philosopher Hannah Arendt. With *Elemente und Ursprünge totaler Herrschaft*, where *Herr* means "lord" and *schaft* "power," she examines what "concern[s] a total lordship." The next year, in London, Israeli historian Jacob L. Talmon gave birth to *The Origins of Totalitarian Democracy*. Through *Totalitarian Dictatorship and Autocracy* in 1956, Carl J. Friedrich and Zbigniew Brzezinski instead represent the totalitarian phenomenon as a form of autocracy centered on modern technology and the legitimacy of the masses:[29]

> The history of the concepts—as J. Petersen recalled in his groundbreaking paper of 1975 referring back to *Begriffsgeschichte* initiated by Koselleck in Germany—is an invaluable tool for a historical approach, capable of returning to us the ways in which political passions were experienced, expressed and elaborated in certain historical periods. Totalitarianism as an ideal type is that of Friedrich and Brzezinski, totalitarianism as a historical concept has a story which is more complex and changeable.[30]

Among the texts symbolically opening reflections, at the end of the World War II, there were the analysis on anti-Semitism in the United States, *Escape from Freedom* by Erich Fromm (1941), and the inquiry on fascism written by Adorno starting from a 1942 paper dedicated to Aldous Huxley, author of *Brave New World* (1932). *Escape from Freedom,* perhaps the best

---

29 Cf. "Symposium on the Totalitarian State," *Proceedings of the American Philosophical Society* 82, no. 1 (1940), i–vi, 1–102; Salvati, *Antifascismo e totalitarismo nelle scienze sociali tra le due guerre*, 646–47. See Hannah Arendt, *The Origins of Totalitarianism* (New York: Harcourt, Brace & Co., 1951); the German edition, Arendt, *Elemente und Ursprünge totaler Herrschaft: Antisemitismus, Imperialismus, totale Herrschaft* (Frankfurt: Europäische Verlagsanst, 1955); Jacob L. Talmon, *The Origins of Totalitarian Democracy* (London: Seecker and Warburg, 1952); Carl J. Friedrich and Zbigniew Brzezinski, *Totalitarian Dictatorship and Autocracy* (Cambridge, MA: Harvard University Press, 1956); Valerio Marchetti, "Resistenza ebraica, antisemitismo, totalitarismo," in *Nazismo, fascismo, comunismo: Totalitarismi a confronto*, ed. Marcello Flores (Milan: Bruno Mondadori, 1998), 259–88.

30 Salvati, "Antifascismo e totalitarismo nelle scienze sociali tra le due guerre," 624, with reference to "La nascita del concetto di 'Stato totalitario' in Italia," in *Annali dell'Istituto storico italo-germanico in Trento*, ed. Jens Petersen (Bologna: il Mulino, 1975), 1:145 (my translation).

known research by Fromm, an exile in the United States since 1934, explores the "psychological aspects that have contributed to the crisis of democracy and the rise of fascism."[31] As Mariuccia Salvati points out, they are identified by the author "in the mechanisms of escape from freedom produced by insecurity in the modern individual, in search of 'new secondary bonds' (authoritarianism, for example) instead of lost primary bonds. These aspects, aggravated by economic crisis, would have been particularly felt by members of the lower middle class who welcomed Nazi ideology with ardent support."[32] Instead, as concerns Adorno's text, it consists of the reading of Huxley's novel in the light of National Socialism: the text, devoted to modern mass society, is a laboratory of American capitalism. Adorno, who for the first time confronts the Jewish question, expresses positive opinions towards *Brave New World*: in his eyes, it contains many interesting elements to analyze the totalitarian German regime.[33]

Whereas Huxley shows that industrial society ends with a perfectly rationalized class system, that is, with planned state capitalism and then with a society marked by total domination, in "Aldous Huxley und die Utopie," Adorno argues that the new world, characterized by modern technology submissive to the ideology of the new order, leads to a totalitarian society, which is rationalized and industrial.[34] His lesson seems to be clearer thanks to what Traverso says about it in *Auschwitz e gli intellettuali*. Briefly, according to Adorno, there is a tight weave between the new totalitarian order and modern techniques. The state of Hitler is not the natural result of German history or culture, but rather the realization of the most recent trends of Western civilization in which, once the contradictions of society are eliminated, a new world occurs, a paradise (παράδεισος) where modern technique produces a total and perfect order. The author refers to cancellation of individual subjects, and to the individual living in modern mass society where there are no particular differences among individuals and where there is no longer a proper

---

31 Salvati, "Antifascismo e totalitarismo nelle scienze sociali tra le due guerre," 629; see Erich Fromm, *Escape from Freedom* (New York: Farrar and Rinehart, 1941).
32 Salvati, "Antifascismo e totalitarismo nelle scienze sociali tra le due guerre," 629.
33 Cf. Traverso, *Auschwitz e gli intellettuali*, 117–18.
34 Ibid.

pace for an organic society, with conflicts among social parts. As stated by Traverso, Adorno's essay announces, at last, a "telluric catastrophe" from which there is no escape, if human consciousness does not intervene to stop these kinds of ideological tendencies. However, the catastrophe of telluric proportions mentioned by Adorno is to be fulfilled and would take the form of extermination camps.[35]

1.3. REFLECTIONS ON ANTI-SEMITISM: FRANKFURT SCHOOL REACTIONS TO NAZI ATROCITIES

From 1933, about 500,000 German-speaking people, mostly Jews, expelled from Nazified Germany, sought refuge in the United States. Among them, although it is problematic to determine the exact number of intellectuals who actually reached the United States in those years, the "intellectual and cultural avant-garde of the Twenties" were included.[36] On the basis of a full-bodied literature, as Claus-Dieter Krohn says, this migration constituted the most important movement "of talents and intelligences" that has ever occurred in history: this exodus of intellectuals, commonly referred to as "emigre German-speaking scientists and scholars" revolutionized American history, its academic culture, and its entire social life.[37] It is remarkable to retrace representations that, through the years, have been given to the phenomenon of exile. In the popular imagination, the figure of the exile sometimes coincides with that of successful people who, in spite of misfortunes, achieve a position of power in a welcoming society, but other times being in exile signifies being in a different world. This condition is depicted as an experience of detachment from the realm in which a person is born and raised and is represented as a situation of

---

35 Ibid.
36 See Claus-Dieter Krohn, "L'esilio degli intellettuali tedeschi negli Stati Uniti dopo il 1933," *Memoria e Ricerca: Rivista di storia contemporanea* 16, no. 31 (2009): 13; Renato Camurri, "Idee in movimento: L'esilio degli intellettuali italiani negli Stati Uniti (1930–1945)," *Memoria e Ricerca*, 43. Camurri notes that other than Great Britain and Palestine, these intellectuals mostly went to the United States and South America.
37 Cf. Peter Gay, "Weimar Culture: The Outsider as Insider," in *The Intellectual Migration: Europa and America, 1930–1960*, ed. Donald Fleming and Bernard Bailyn (Cambridge, MA: Harvard University Press, 1969), 12.

solitude. As Adorno writes, in one of the fragments of *Minima Moralia*, the exile "will always be a nomad, a wanderer," and his native tongue will always be "expropriated."[38]

The impact that this shift of knowledge had on American culture raised several problematic issues. First, the Frankfurt School, during the war years, was forced to revise its study purposes and to redefine the institutional structure or solve the conflicting positions between Robert MacIver and Robert Lynd within the Department of Sociology at Columbia University, that is, the internal opposition within the Institute between the more speculative vein of the department, headed by MacIver, and the empirical antagonists gathered around Lynd.[39] These factors internal to the Department of Sociology at Columbia University coincided with the new phase of the Frankfurt School's empirical research in accordance with the interest of federal and private funding of research. According to the letter written by Lowenthal, January 23, 1942, and addressed to Horkheimer, the fight would be resolved in favor of Lynd. The director of the Institute was in favor of the dissolution of ties between the Institute and Columbia University. This fact, namely, the preference for Lynd's empirical research, compared to MacIver's more speculative approach, accounts for the atmosphere of American sociology in the years in which quantitative research projects and those without a real political impact or far from concrete real problems were preferred and enjoyed more public space. It is the period, for sociology, that Robert E. L. Faris and William Form call one of "explosive growth"[40] in which the discipline developed significantly and was also preparatory to the its rising segmentation at the end of Vietnam War. The chasm between theory and empirical research in sociology endured

---

38   "Exile is strangely compelling to think about but terrible to experience. It is the unhealable rift forced between a human being and a native place, between the self and its true home: its essential sadness can never be surmounted. The achievements of exile are permanently undermined by the loss of something left behind forever"; see Edward W. Said, *Reflections on the Exile and Other Essays* (Cambridge, MA: Harvard University Press, 2000), 137. See Camurri, "Idee in movimento," 45 with reference to Adorno, *Minima Moralia*; Enzo Traverso, *Cosmopoli: Figure dell'esilio ebraico-tedesco* (Verona: Ombre Corte, 2004).
39   See Jay, *The Dialectical Imagination*, 219; Halpert, "Early American Sociology and the Holocaust," 6–23.
40   Faris and Form, "Sociology," 1.

in the academy and took the shape of a functionalist-conflict debate, that one finds, especially starting from 1948, in Talcott Parsons, the scholar who epitomized functionalism and gained a successful position among scholars.

Looking back at postwar sociological works, let me be precise that although researches such as *Dialectic of Enlightenment* (1947), *Anti-Semitism among American Labor: Report on a Research Project Conducted by the Institute of Social Research of Columbia University* (written in the years 1944–45, but unpublished), *Eclipse of Reason* (1947), and, finally, *Studies in Prejudice* (1949–1950) have different focuses, they do, however, all share an anti-Semitic view.[41] If in 1942 Neumann wrote that the German people were "the least anti-Semitic of all," by the mid-1940s onwards, during the exile period, anti-Semitism instead became a central issue, which the Frankfurt School would not be able to leave out of consideration.[42] Thus, in the previous decade, anti-Semitism was an outdated theme for the School. As recalled by Traverso, "Anti-Semitism certainly did not dominate the historical scene," but, above all, "the birth of modern anti-Semitism—the transformation of the age-old exclusion on religious grounds into racial hatred affirmed in the name of science—attracted minimal attention from contemporaries or indeed went completely unnoticed."[43] At the end of the 1940s, instead, despite the reflections that were facing modern mass society and concentrating on the concept of prejudice, the interest headed towards the anti-Semitic question in Germany, having the American context as an ideal and material laboratory.

Once arrived in the United States, in contact with the American racist and anti-Semitic energies, the Frankfurt School sociologists realized the

---

41 Cf. Max Horkheimer and Theodore L. W. Adorno, *Dialectic of Enlightenment*, ed. Gunzelin Schmid Noerr, trans. Edmund Jephcott (Stanford: Stanford University Press, 2002 [1947]). Max Horkheimer, *Eclipse of Reason* (New York: Oxford University Press, 1947); Max Horkheimer and Samuel H. Flowerman, eds., *Studies in Prejudice* (New York: Harper & Brothers, 1949–1950); Catherine Collomp, "La Scuola di Francoforte in esilio: Storia di un'inchiesta sull'antisemitismo nella classe operaia americana," in "L'Europa in esilio: La migrazione degli intellettuali verso le Americhe tra le due guerre," ed. Renato Camurri, *Memoria e Ricerca: Rivista di storia contemporanea* 16, no. 31 (2009): 121–40.
42 Cf. Franz Neumann, *Behemoth: The Structure and Practice of National Socialism, 1933–1944* (New York: Oxford University Press, 1942).
43 Traverso, *The Origins of Nazi Violence*, 6.

strength of anti-Semitic prejudice in German society. Since the threat was the prejudice in itself, what mattered to the Frankfurt School, and also concerned them, was the force of prejudice in modern society.

It is on its character that they dwelled, tracing the different expressions, the degree of intensity, and possible explanations. They were certain that prejudice could easily be manipulated in favor of a political plan of a fascist kind. In the late 1930s, and above all in the early 1940s, the theme of authoritarianism began to be read through the phenomenon of anti-Semitism. When possibilities of publishing in France began to decrease due to the German invasion, and they were forced to publish in English (meanwhile the name of their review changed from *Zeitschrift fur Sozialforschung* to *Studies in Philosophy and Social Science*, and methods and perspectives of research turned into other forms), exiles of the Frankfurt School finally captured the essence of Nazism and took notice of anti-Semitism. Under the Weimar Republic, there had been benefits from some situations: there was a set of practices, attitudes, or anti-Semitic speeches, but there were few obstacles to the exercise of professions or use of services for Jews, a situation that soon changed.

As historian Traverso notes, between 1943 and 1947 the sociological theory of the School was "new," rich in categories pertaining to the process of rationalization, of Enlightenment ancestry. It was "new" in the sense that, before this time, there was no in-depth theory of the anti-Semitic phenomenon; and it was still "new" from a conceptual point of view, because the dialectic of the Enlightenment of the Frankfurt School differed from the traditional view of anti-Semitism. This theory was developed during the exile, at the end of World War II, when the Nazi atrocities were well known: they were only new because of the timing—the School had not taken the time to reflect on anti-Semitism.[44]

The Enlightenment leads to modern progress, from an economic, political, social point of view, in the broadest sense, and leads to a process of rationalization in society. In the 1940s, the notion of the Enlightenment underwent a fundamental change, because it was no longer just the cultural correlate of the rising middle class, but it tended to include the

---

44 Cf. Traverso, *Auschwitz e gli intellettuali*, 119–21.

full range of Western thought. "Enlightenment here," writes Horkheimer to Lowenthal in 1942, "is identical with bourgeois thought, nay, thought in general, since there is no other thought properly speaking than in cities."[45] Horkheimer and Adorno's theory on anti-Semitism can be traced back to the years 1943–44. The text, ready in 1944, and published only in 1947, in Amsterdam, was to receive some attention in the late 1960s after its re-release in Germany. It is important to understand the reason why an important work such this, and above all elaborated by the Frankfurt School, remained unnoticed in the late 1940s, both at the time of drafting in 1944 and at releasing in 1947. It is relevant since this work was prepared in the midst of the war; the scholars of the former Frankfurt School were refugee scholars in exile in the United States; there was an inner, well-concealed prejudice against the Jews among the nation's elite colleges; and, finally, there was the problem of funding and publishing houses. At this point, it is crucial to examine which publishing houses and which foundations, at the end of the war, supported them and published their works. Actually, this aspect or the locution "at the end of the war" is meaningful and evokes another aspect always related to the difficulties in publishing writings dealing with the recent past, in this case, the Holocaust.

Thus, there was a delay in the publication of sociological works at the end of the war, when one had to come to terms with the destruction of the Jews. This notice is well evidenced by Gerson and Wolf. Let me recall it briefly. A political Jew, Paul M. Neurath, after his camp experience started in 1938 in Dachau and then in Buchenwald, until his escape in 1939, put immediately into writing everything that happened, everything he photographed with his eyes, ears, and mind: he recorded in his mind, with all his senses, anything that occurred during his internment in order to tell every fact to the world at the end of the war when he left the camp. He memorized every aspect, especially because he could not write in the camp. He became a perfect social observer who participates in the event itself:[46] unconsciously he became a social scientist, and after the war, at the

---

45 Cf. Jay, *The Dialectical Imagination*, 258.
46 Paul M. Neurath, *The Society of Terror: Inside the Dachau and Buchenwald Concentration Camps*, ed. Christian Fleck and Nico Stehr (Boulder, CO: Paradigm, 2005), 286n18, Neurath's letter to Robert MacIver, March 29, 1942.

university, he would become acquainted with the sociological devices to explicate his experiences. It can be said that he grew to be a social scientist during his internment.

Neurath's work came into being as a doctoral dissertation, defended successfully in 1943, but by the end of the World War II, in Neurath's words, "publishers didn't want to print any more about concentration camps without gas chambers."[47] His *Society of Terror* was published posthumously, in 2005, thanks to Christian Fleck and Nico Stehr, who edited the volume. Neurath's case demonstrates several problems sociologists encounter when dealing with the genocide of the Jews within the academy: in his case, Columbia University and the political context of the Cold War. His sociological work on concentration camps represents a novelty for the innovative sociological method he adopts (he interviews "10 former fellows prisoners"[48]) and for the recounting of "various everyday resistances," "ordinary men,"[49] and this during the years of the war. In other words, at the end of the war there were several sociologists who attempted to account for the Holocaust: Neurath was one of them, and his study serves to rethink the so-called sociological delay.

Coming back to the phrase "at the end of the war," this means that specific political responsibilities (at the end of the conflict) and a public admission that the abandonment of the Jews had been allowed and prepared over the years, step-by-step, by any country. Therefore, in the early 1960s, when Eichmann was on put trial in Jerusalem by Israel's intelligence agency, Mossad, and he was widely judged and condemned, circumstances finally brought notice of the Frankfurt School's work and other related works. The Six-Day War in 1967 also brought such issues to the fore, when the fear of another destruction of the Jews came into the

---

47 Ibid., 297.
48 Lynn Rapaport, review of *The Society of Terror: Inside the Dachau and Buchenwald Concentration Camps*, by Paul M. Neurath, *American Journal of Sociology* 112, no. 4 (2007): 1263–65, accessed March 4, 2016, doi:10.1086/513546.
49 To deal with Neurath's case goes beyond the scope of my book. To it I will devote a separate paper. For additional features, see Andrew Woolford, review of *The Society of Terror: Inside the Dachau and Buchenwald Concentration Camps*, by Paul M. Neurath, *Canadian Journal of Sociology Online*, September-October 2006, accessed March 4, 2016, http://www.cjsonline.ca/reviews/societyofterror.html.

consciousness. And, right from that date, many burning questions and reflections were raised by Fackenheim: issues that compelled the world, the political and scholarly world, to reflect upon what was happening to humans. Precisely these events predisposed the reissuing of *Dialektik der Aufklärung* in Germany by S. F. Verlag in 1969.

Dialektik der Aufklärung, a creative processing and synthesis of the interdisciplinary study of the School during the exile period, is characterized by the concepts of capitalism-alienation, mass psychology, and instrumental-final rationality. The first category, borrowed from Marx, interpreted in the light of Lukács, helps to explain the phenomenon of a society built "on the mercantile reification of social relations."[50] Thanks to a process of economic rationalization, brought forward by capitalism, modern industrial civilization is born and the Jews cooperate with it. Hitler's racist anti-Semitism reassumes old religious prejudice and pushes to go beyond the traditional Marxist view: precapitalist and archaic origins of anti-Semitic phenomenon must be analyzed differently by Marx. Starting from the 1940s, the Institute applies less and less Marxist ideology in its own studies. This has been linked with the neglect of Marxism by American sociology until 1960, when a neo-Marxist phase (an amalgam of theories by Marx and Weber) gained approval and corroboration among several sociologists until the breakup of communism and "the introduction of postindustrial doctrines".[51]

Totalitarian capitalism of the Third Reich destroyed liberal society and the achievements of emancipation, of which the Jews were protagonists and who were considered the "colonizers of progress."[52] Fake modern social order attracts a destroying will towards the Jews. In *Dialectic of Enlightenment*, Adorno and Horkheimer no longer regard the concept of class as a form of global oppression, but just that of anti-Semitism, a terrible force upon the Jews, the exact opposite of the concentration of power, the real focal point of injustice. In other words, the Jews were starting to become the new proletariat of the world.[53]

---

50 Cf. Traverso, *Auschwitz e gli intellettuali*, 119–21.
51 Faris and Form, "Sociology," 2.
52 Cf. Traverso, *Auschwitz e gli intellettuali*, 119–21, 133n48.
53 Cf. Collomp, "La Scuola di Francoforte in esilio," 127–28n21.

The School's theory on the anti-Semitism of the Enlightenment gets at the core of the genocide of the Jews. As evident from the title of Horkheimer's book, the good ideas of Enlightenment are going to be eclipsed. Often the reflection of the Frankfurt School on the Holocaust devolves to Adorno's lapidary aphorism with which the author concludes an essay in 1949—"to write poetry after Auschwitz is barbaric." To understand this statement, we must remember the context, which is crucial for avoiding ambiguity or misunderstanding.[54] To put it concisely, the phrase belongs to one of the earliest writings that Adorno completed after having just returned, in 1949, to Germany, a country ravaged by war and still in ruins. The University of Frankfurt facilitated the repatriation of the Institute for Social Research, as it believed that it would be able to use its contacts with the American academic world, albeit not according to its orientation. At that time, Adorno was aware of being an intellectual from the outside, a former emigrant now back in Adenauer's Germany, and he was conscious of people living in the 1960s in a country where Auschwitz and its horror had been removed: while former Nazis surrounded him, he conceived his famous aphorism:

The price paid by Adorno will be—as Günther Anders would have reproached him—that of a "double life," in which a radical thought always sublimated by a hermetic language was accompanied by the "rise of action," in other words by political passivity in the face of the reality.[55]

Unquestionably, the condition of exiles returning to their homeland had specific characteristics. In the 1940s and 50s, while the Frankfurt School was in a foreign land it gave the face of mass totalitarian society to anti-Semitism. In that context, the individual, when it seems he is enjoying maximum freedom or independence is instead deprived of his critical thinking and, rather than being a distinguished person among many individuals, he is compelled to share a common mentality, a mutual personality to not be an individual anymore.[56]

---

54 See Traverso, *Auschwitz e gli intellettuali*, 109, 130n1.
55 Ibid., 111, 131n13; the author refers to a letter from Anders to Adorno, August 27, 1963 (my translation).
56 See Herbert Marcuse, *One-Dimensional Man: Studies in the Ideology of Advanced Industrial Society* (Boston: Beacon, 1964).

The *Minima Moralia*, written between 1944 and 1947, and published later in 1951 by Adorno, proposes a reflection on the need to think of Auschwitz, and it was then completed with *Negative Dialectics* in 1966. As far as I can see, the two texts, based on *Studies on Prejudice*, provide closure to the lessons of the Institute for Social Research on the Jewish question in the late 1950s and up to about the mid-1960s. In this phase we can note the idea of a critical theory summed up in Adorno's words with the famous formula "ticket mentality," emphasizing how after Auschwitz the otherness strives to be tolerated or understood.[57] The studies of the immediate postwar period, especially those on prejudice, the *Minima Moralia* and *Negative Dialectics*, highlight how, in the context of authoritarian regimes, the individual is withdrawn into the masses and presents a mentality unwilling to accept any label against any form of difference. For the Frankfurt School, anti-Semitism was an expression of this Enlightenment mentality. Humanist and emancipatory aspirations, followed by the French Revolution, had promoted equality among human beings, but they could not find a rich soil in bourgeois society: equality is supported by the bourgeoisie, but in a unilateral way that does not allow for the recognition of differences and does not create respect for cultural, religious, ethnic, or gender dissimilarities. Anyone who does not come under conformist standards of the Puritan and bourgeois ethics, which was the dominant order, is cast aside. This form of "repressive" equality led to the assertion of the totalitarian principle of identity and then to the triumph of totalitarian racism, according to which the principle of equality gave way to the discrimination and persecution of those who were different. In fascist totalitarian regimes, social plurality is suppressed and, due to the mechanism of the authoritarian personality, the crushing of the "nonidentical" makes inroads. For this reason, in *Minima Moralia* Adorno pronounces against totalitarian *ratio* and recognizes the advent of a truly emancipated society only when any difference is accepted. However, in *Negative Dialectics* something changes: Adorno states that the concentration and extermination camp of Auschwitz has confirmed the philosopheme of pure identity as death and the end of any contradiction

---

57 Cf. Traverso, *Auschwitz e gli intellettuali*, 124–26.

through a mass of alienated civilians, unable to rise.⁵⁸ The involvement with Nazi criminals does not require a conscious participation.⁵⁹ As Traverso notes, the research was written in a "hot-formed" period, during the destruction of the Jews: that is why it is so significant.

Adorno and Horkheimer conceive Nazism as an incessant self-destruction of reason: they pose the representation of the extermination as an effect of Western civilization, according to their dialectic intuition. In the Western world, that of the UN Universal Declaration of Human Rights, a set of elements accumulated in previous decades are brought to light in a violent manner. Namely, the Industrial Revolution, the development of mass society, the rationalization of public administration within the state, the modernization of armies, the progress of sciences and applied technology, all these lead to new uses of rationality. Auschwitz compels us to review the power of Western rationalism and the Enlightenment.⁶⁰ The Frankfurt School, especially Adorno, felt the need to think about Auschwitz: from *Minima Moralia* to *Negative Dialectics* one may find a common thread that identifies the social premises at the base of Nazism.⁶¹ Especially because, at the end of the war, there was not a denazification process in power institutions. What lacked was a public admission of guilt: governments presented no admission of accountability for what happened. This meant that destruction against the minorities could happen again.

To examine those elements featuring the Nazi society, these scholars use the notions of anti-Semitism, prejudice, and authoritarianism: phenomena all present in Nazi and American society, which they adopt as a research laboratory (ideal and material), just at the end of the conflict, when the extermination was almost completed. Their minds were set on avoiding a totalitarian state making inroads in the United States: in other words, they wanted to stop a new possible extermination. Hence, their attention to American authoritarianism in American mass society.

---

58 Cf. Th. Adorno, *Negative Dialektik* (Frankfurt: Suhrkamp, 1966).
59 Cf. Traverso, *Auschwitz e gli intellettuali*, 126, 134n64.
60 Cf. Jeffrey Herf, *Reactionary Modernism: Technology, Culture, and Politics in Weimar and the Third Reich* (New York: Cambridge University Press, 1984).
61 See Enzo Traverso, *Il totalitarismo: Storia di un dibattito* (Milan: Bruno Mondadori, 2002).

This research started with a focus on American working people: they studied the anti-Semitism in American labor. Initially, the study (whose result was unexpected and alarming) was spread in a limited manner and only in typescript from the Institute. What aroused curiosity was that this research had not been considered by labor historians who had studied American laborers during and after World War II, nor was it considered by historians of Jewish culture in the United States. As Catherine Collomp does, it could be asked who commissioned the research and, first and foremost, why it has never been published.[62] The survey, born from a research project on anti-Semitism, saw the program published in the summer 1941, in *Studies in Philosophy and Social Science* (*SPSS*). It was commissioned by the Jewish Labor Committee (JLC) and subsidized initially by the American Jewish Committee (AJC).[63] This research has never been published, even though several attempts were made up to 1953. What warrants attention is the research itself, which paves the way for studies on prejudice. In the research, the concept of "scapegoat" is clearly elaborated, while the prejudice is presented as the element building the totalitarian society. For these scholars, what mattered was avoiding another Holocaust in an America full of prejudice against the Jews. Hence, the cyclic structure of their research accounting for it: from American to Nazi society and back again. The research-outcomes are shocking, especially because in the 1940s America was fighting against Germany and above all because Jews were integrated among American labor and within the larger society. Most of them were part of the Jewish Labor Movement, while the International Ladies Garment Workers' Union (ILGWU) and Amalgamated Clothing Workers of America (ACWA) were among the organizations promoting the Congress of Industrial Organizations (CIO), the federation that, starting in 1936, organized the factory workers, as Collomp remembers. At this point, they measure intensity and visibility of prejudice among people: what emerges is that the prejudice is manipulated in favor of a political fascist plan and orientation to absolve social and economic tensions. There were the Silver Shirts and German American

---

62 Collomp, "La Scuola di Francoforte in esilio," 122.
63 Ibid., 127–28.

Bund, both in favor of Nazi ideologies. In 1942, an official revelation of what was happening to the Jews in Europe, even if on a delayed basis, appeared, but anti-Semitism did not diminish. In public opinion there was the conviction that the number of victims was altered and did not correspond to the reality. The JLC, caring about the social-democratic rights of laborers and aware of tensions among laborers, wanted to avoid further tensions and conflicts among them, especially since the end the war saw a reduction in the production of arms and, therefore, a reduction in the labor force.

The JLC, established in 1934 to fight Nazism in defense of democracy and in support of labor and Jews in Europe and in America, was the first organization in the United States to publicize the destruction of the Jews in April 1945 through a photo exhibition, "Heros and Martyrs of Europe's Ghettos," in New York, partly dedicated to the Warsaw Uprising.[64] At the end of the war, another research project on the prejudice against Jews appeared, which brought to light social tensions (typical of labor factory) stemming from the prejudice itself. The work in question was that of Everett C. Hughes of the Chicago School.

As concerns *American Labor*, the research was conducted by Friedrich Pollock, with the help of Leo Lowenthal, Paul Massing, and A. R. L. Gurland, and it surveyed 566 laborers using a sample of five geographical areas—the East Coast; the New York, New Jersey, and Philadelphia areas; Pittsburgh, with the steelworks; Detroit, with war industries (automotive industry converted into weapons production); and the West Coast, especially Los Angeles and San Francisco. The research dealt specifically with industry laborers, particularly, those in arms and weapons manufacturing, where a great number of laborers were employed in a short period of time. The selected sample presented a high percentage of unionized laborers (23.8% AFL; 38.5% CIO) and a number of white-collar workers, small wholesalers, and professionals: 68 percent were manual laborers; 6 percent managers; 9 percent white-collar employees; 6.7 percent sellers and wholesalers; and 8 percent professionals. The development of the research was targeted: 270 volunteer laborers were instructed how to

---

64 Ibid., 124.

conduct interviews among other laborers who were not aware of being interviewed, avoiding, in this way, certain pressures or conditions. The seven questions of the interview verified where episodes of anti-Semitic propaganda occurred in the workplace or community. On the basis of the answers, the researchers could classify the grade of anti-Semitism into eight categories: from an extreme hostility (which precedes the physical extermination of the Jews) to a good attitude. The key-answer measuring the anti-Semitic grade resulted from the question number 5, which related to their personal thinking about Nazis actions against Jews in Germany.[65]

The researchers found that 30.7 percent of the population sample had strong prejudices, while 30.9 percent were not hostile to the Jews. Noteworthy was the third group, representing "uncertain" responders and therefore, for scholars, those easily manipulatable and indoctrinable, fit for anti-Semitic militancy. This method of hidden interviews allowed for simple and candid answers, from which several prejudices emerged. Among blue-collar workers, anti-Semitism was stronger, while a high level of education was found to lower anti-Semitic prejudice.

1.4. AN OPEN CASE: TALCOTT PARSONS AND NATIONAL SOCIALISM, FROM ACTIVE POLITICAL ENGAGEMENT TO THE YEARS OF SILENCE

By stating that sociology was not late in studying the destruction of the Jews,[66] I mean that there were sociologists who approached the phenomenon and studied the event with sociological tools—even during the postwar years, and among them Talcott Parsons. Moreover, in sustaining that these scholars were unnoticed and their researches were ignored by the academy, I mean that, despite their efforts in approaching the Jewish question, they were impeded in their attempt to disseminate their scientific results: these obstacles and impediments were at the core of the so-called absence of sociology in Holocaust Studies. A sociological

---

65 Cf. ibid., 131.
66 As Hilberg and Cesarani explain in their works, it is a process that comprehends anti-Jewish practices in 1930s, a definition by decree, concentration and mobile killing operations, deportations and killing center operations. See note 4, above (Introduction).

tradition emerged that dismissed the study of the Holocaust, namely, it created a missing sociological tradition, having in Parsons a significant symbol.[67] Starting from 1937, as Porter asserts in his 1994 "Sociological Forum," Parsons counteracted German propaganda and Nazism and saved various German immigrants and Austrian refugees.[68] He "was one of the first in the United States to publicly denounce the Nazi movement and call for active and unconditional opposition to it."[69] In these years, Parsons wrote much about the Jewish question. What is astonishing is that, after the war, his stand against Nazism was all but silenced: there then appeared a profound silence about Nazism in his work. Reflecting on this, I asked myself why. To comprehend better what happened, on the basis of his available writings, I divided his approach to the Jewish question into three phases. In the first, from 1937 to 1946, he wrote and disseminated several papers against the Nazi movement and its anti-Jewish practices (he was acting as a fire-flagman and, having glimpsed Nazi ideology menaces in Europe and in America, denounced them). The second phase runs from 1946 to 1948: in these two years, during which Parsons seems to be a silent Calliope,[70] he did not deal with the Jewish question, even to the point of abandoning any direct engagement in the fight against Nazis. In the third phase, (1948–79) hardly widely known, he was an intellectual "bridging former Nazis collaborators in the U.S.A."[71] His interest in the Jewish question in 1937–46 is very noteworthy because he handled Jewish matters and National Socialism during the years of Nazi dominance. These writings attest that sociology addressed these themes at the time of events.

I assert this after reading Uta Gerhardt's 1993 work about Parsons, which is available as a collection of fourteen writings in sociology on

---

67 I would like to thank Giuseppe Veltri for the notion on "missing sociological tradition" and for his comments on it.
68 See Jack N. Porter, "Toward a Sociology of National Socialism," review of *Talcott Parsons on National Socialism*, by Uta Gerhardt, *Sociological Forum* 9, no. 3 (1994): 506.
69 Mike F. Keen, review of *Talcott Parsons on National Socialism*, by Uta Gerhardt, *American Journal of Sociology* 99, no. 5 (1994): 1359.
70 The expression "silent Calliope" comes out from Traverso's expression "muse arruolate" ("enrolled/enlisted muses"), which he uses in his *Auschwitz e gli intellettuali* in explaining the attitude of some intellectuals during the Nazism; see Traverso, *Auschwitz e gli intellettuali*, 15–18.
71 Wiener, "Talcott Parsons' Role Bringing Nazi Sympathizers to the U.S.," 305–9.

National Socialism. Among these papers, Gerhardt unearthed his wartime writings—seven articles diffused in a limited edition and another seven articles never published before her edition. Nevertheless, those seven published articles did not receive much notice or consideration from scholars: they were not disseminated among academics. This is notable because these writings provide evidence of some sociologists who dealt with the Jewish question, especially during the Nazi era. Yet more worthy of reflection is that after 1946, Parsons never wrote anything on Nazism and that after 1948, when he arrived in Germany, he actually recruited former Nazis.

However, it is important to introduce his sociological writings related to the Jewish question to see how he sociologically understood the destruction of the Jews.

Parsons was born in Colorado Springs, Colorado, on December 13, 1902, and after biology and medical studies at Amherst College he was at the London School of Economics until he went to Germany, in 1925, thanks to a scholarship in sociology and economics at Heidelberg University, where he earned his doctorate with a thesis on the origins of capitalism in Weber and Sombart. Back in the United States, he taught at Harvard from 1927 to 1973. Now, when I state that he recognized the Nazi inferno, I refer to his sociological writings of 1937–46 concerning Nazism and its anti-Jewish actions. Gerhardt deserves credit for having unearthed these valuable works and then collecting them in one edition. She accidentally discovered this treasure during her personal research on the sociology of professions, a theme precious to Parsons: she uncovered his writings among Parson's medical discourses. This is worthy of note: narrative medicine was the core of Parsons's sociology. Medical discourse is the sociological key for reading his work because the devices typical of medical discourse led Parsons to tackle the social problem of totalitarianism in society and to offer a solution. He acts as the doctor who analyzes people affected by some evil and makes a diagnosis: against totalitarian pathology, he offers a recipe to the patient faced with the (social) evil and how to overcome it. How he approached the destruction of the Jews is clearer in these fourteen writings gathered by Gerhardt. To understand what I mean when I state that he was among the first sociologists dealing with the

Jewish genocide, it is proper to identify a common thread among them that underlines the sociological categories he adopted.

1.4.1. Parsons's Seven Published Papers

On April 25, 1942, when Parsons for the inauguration of the Eastern Sociological Society gave a speech titled "Some Sociological Aspects of the Fascist Movements." In the discourse, first published in 1942, in *Social Forces*, he uses typical elements of the sociology of Durkheim to expose the rise of the political fascist (mass) movement in modern society, both in Italy and in Germany. His "ongoing" analysis continues in "Max Weber and the Contemporary Political Crisis," the sixth article, according Gerhardt's order in the 1993 edition. Some of its parts appeared in the fourth volume of *Review of Politics*, in 1942, where, by using tools and concepts of Weberian sociology, Parsons elaborates a long examination of National Socialism and its consequences after the rise of the NSDAP. Also in 1942, he recognized, in "Propaganda and Social Control," that the NSDAP had risen to power thanks to propaganda, a "kind of attempt to influence attitudes, and hence directly or indirectly the actions of people, by linguistic stimuli, by the written or spoken word."[72] It seems that in wartime Parsons stood as a sentinel in the academic realm, especially in understanding that propaganda brought the Nazis to power and social control. He returned to Nazism in the following years. He participated in a conference in New York, in May–June 1944, during which a group of psychiatrics, anthropologists, sociologists, and other scholars attempted to comprehend the role played by institutions in the maintenance of social order. (Previously there was the Tehran Conference and its political discussions about combating National Socialist Germany. This meeting of the Allied powers constituted a kind of turning point, corroborated his antifascist cause, and validated his ideas about the importance of having democratic social institutions that would collaborate in the fight against authoritarianism and anti-Semitism.) At the New York conference,

---

72   Uta Gerhardt, *Talcott Parsons on National Socialism* (New York: Aldine de Gruyter, 1993), 243. See Talcott Parsons, "Propaganda and Social Control," *Psychiatry* 5 (1942): 551–72.

Parsons prepared a rapport, published for the first time in *Psychiatry* in 1945 with the title "The Problem of Controlled Institutional Change," where much of this material was reproduced, with the exception of the analytic introduction appearing as appendix 5 of the same piece.[73] As the war was coming to an end, he was dealing with the problem of the collapse of modern democracy and the rise of the mass socialist movement owing to the lack of valid institutions capable of resolving the social tensions of modern society and integrating its deviant components. In his introduction, he focuses on the role of "institutional patterns": the "'backbone' of the social system."[74] When, in 1944–45, Parsons asks himself what one needs do in the face of the collapse of democratic and liberal organisms, and investigates which social tensions led to the fall of the democratic regime in Germany after the Great War, he clearly shows his interest in and appreciation for the Jewish question and its related consequences. For Parsons, the cause of the democratic crisis, at the end of the Great War, was the difference in the way of thinking, attitudes, or culture existing within German society, where there were idealistic, romantic, and antisocial components together with parts methodical, gregarious, and submissive. For him, National Socialism harnessed emotional tensions of romanticism towards political objectives that were clearly nationalist, with expansionist ambitions and legitimated by use of violence.

Unlike the United States, Germany failed in a natural development of democratic institutions: this led to the rise of National Socialism, a charismatic movement with an ideological structure. He had already spoken of the conditions of democracy in 1942 when he analyzed the social structure of pre-Nazi German, a theme better developed (namely, that National Socialism was a movement resulting from modernization) in "Certain Primary Sources and Patterns of Aggression in the Social Structure of the Western World," elaborated for the occasion of the conference on "Science, Philosophy and Religion" in Chicago in September 1946 and published in *Psychiatry* in the following year.[75] At the basis of the text again was National Socialism as a movement that harnesses the

---

73 See Gerhardt, *Talcott Parsons on National Socialism*, 322.
74 Ibid., 292.
75 Ibid., 325–47.

tensions of the Western modernization process. He introduces a topic familiar to the Frankfurt School, namely, the authoritarian structure of the German family (the authority of *pater familias* and women's submissive attitude). Instead, in "Racial and Religious Differences as Factors in Group Tensions," published in 1945, he exposes, using the categories of Durkheim, how the end of solidarity among groups, integration, and the social tensions between religious groups or ethnic minorities degenerates into forms with no democratic structure or legitimate sources of power.[76]

1.4.2. The Seven Unpublished Writings

Parsons can be seen as a standard-bearer for the fight against Nazism with his seven unpublished writings. As a prominent booster of Harvard University, he became inextricably linked with the democracy program. In 1940 Parsons elaborated a very long text that precociously offered surprising intuition concerning the control exercised against dissidents during the war: "Memorandum: The Development of Groups and Organizations Amenable to Use against American Institutions and Foreign Policy and Possible Measures of Prevention," prepared for the Council for Democracy. Through some sociological categories, such as social stratification, social mobility, ethnos, and social movement, Parsons analyzed the situation both in Germany and in the United States, which, like Germany, presented a strong social and economic insecurity with a strong nationalist component. Given that in Germany these factors had contributed to the rise of Nazism, Parsons's problem dealt with the comprehension of how to avoid the rise of fascist movements in the United States. The central question of his article was simple: What political attitudes do people have to adopt to impede the rise of totalitarian movements? Hence, the *memorandum* to remember to maintain liberal institutions. According to him, both international politics and social measures play a big role. Especially, social system stability depends on the level of integration among individuals belonging to it. Already in 1940, Parsons had

---

76 Cf. William Buxton, review of *Talcott Parsons on National Socialism*, by Uta Gerhardt, *Canadian Journal of Sociology* 19, no. 3 (1994): 426–27.

enumerated the features of National Socialism: those concerning race, socialism, anti-intellectualism, militarism, and particularism, even if its fundamental components remained propaganda and ideology. It is proper to stress that Parsons studied the economic problems that affected American society in the early twentieth century: sounding the warning, he perceived that a totalitarian movement could arise in the United States, as it did in Germany. For this reason, for him, it was important to address the problem of anti-Semitism and its horrendous consequences. Nevertheless, "The Sociology of Modern Anti-Semitism" only appeared in an edited version not authorized by Parsons in *Jews in a Gentile World* (1942), edited by Isacque Graeber and Steuart H. Britt.[77] We can recall that in the 1930s, America was in the grip of the Great Depression, and both intolerance and anti-Semitism were ordinary. When Parsons received the draft for the release of the text, he disagreed with the revisions of the two editors and gave them an accurate version, but they did not take it into account. Despite that, Parsons did not prepare further *errata corrigenda* after publication of the Graeber and Britt edition.[78] I will limit myself here to underlining some differences between the two versions: they are evident in the last periods of the essay. In the original text one may read: "In other words, it is by means of serious study, by means of an objective analysis, and not through emotional thinking that a successful tackling of the problem may be attempted."[79] In the Graeber and Britt edition it reads: "In other words, a rational policy toward anti-Semitism cannot consist in suppressing and punishing its expressions, but only in some analogous way in an attempt to control its deeper causes. Mere indignant repression of an evil is the treatment of symptoms, not of disease."[80]

Parsons had raised a real problem for America. His position was such a multidimensional topic that everyone could read and deal with it. Gerhardt

---

77 Gerhardt, *Talcott Parsons on National Socialism*, 131; Isacque Graeber and Steuart Henderson Britt, eds., *Jews in a Gentile World: The Problem of Anti-Semitism* (New York: Macmillan, 1942); Porter, "Toward a Sociology of National Socialism," 507–8n4.
78 See Buxton, review of *Talcott Parsons on National Socialism*, 425; Porter, "Toward a Sociology of National Socialism," 507.
79 Gerhardt, *Talcott Parsons on National Socialism*, 150–51.
80 Graeber and Britt, *Jews in a Gentile World*, 122.

recovered the original title and versions of Parsons's manuscript.[81] In the text, the principal subject was an anti-Semitism that stemmed from disorganization and modern insecurity. But the context in which Parsons wrote was not easy for him:

> In 1979, Parsons, troubled by the original article, wrote a postscript to the article that addressed the problem of Germany's change since 1945 and noted that the horrendous scope of Nazi atrocities had become known only *after* his article had been published. According to footnote 106 in Gerhardt's book, the manuscript carried a handwritten note by Victor Lidz, Parsons's literary executor, that the essay should be "edited and prepared for publication by S. Z. Klausner after T. P.'s death." That essay, along with Samuel Klausner's commentary, did in fact appear in *Contemporary Jewry* (1980).[82]

As concerns "National Socialism and the German People," it is instead a transcription of a 1942 broadcast. Parsons, after he introduces National Socialism as a problem, explicates some of the possible causes of German fascism:[83] first and foremost, social insecurity resulting from the rapid industrialization; second, the role played by Junkers, in whom converged a militant tradition and authoritarianism, and, finally, the *Volksgeist*.[84] Parsons in the war years recognized, thanks to notions of social anomie, class, tradition, and social movement, that Nazism constituted a specific aspect of modernity. National Socialism was not an invention of a few men: it was rooted in the culture and tradition of Germany. "But what of the situation," he asks, "when the Nazi movement is broken?"[85]

Worthy of attention is "Nazis Destroy Learning, Challenging Religion," which appeared on November 23, 1938, in *Radcliffe News*.

---

81 This reconstruction work has been possible thanks to manuscripts and notes in archives at Harvard University (42.41, box 2: "Unpublished Manuscripts"). Cf. Gerhardt, *Talcott Parsons on National Socialism*, 131.
82 Porter, "Toward a Sociology of National Socialism," 508n4.
83 Cf. Gerhardt, *Talcott Parsons on National Socialism*, 219n (reference to radio broadcast, WRUL, May 21, 1942).
84 Cf. ibid., 222–24.
85 Ibid., 219.

Although it is the shortest among Parsons writings, it actually illustrates the risks of Nazism very well:

> In my opinion, National Socialism is far more than a "political" movement in any narrow sense. It reaches down to the deepest foundations of institutional structure generally. Seen in this perspective the treatment of the Jews, tragic as it is for the victims, is only a small part of the significance of the movement, perhaps even more of symptomatic importance than itself the major danger.[86]

Parsons recognized the Jews as victims of Nazism and perceived the threat and tragic consequences of this movement—it was "far more than a 'political' movement." It moved against science and knowledge, democratic institutions and religious universalism: it pierced the fundamental values of reason and ethics, putting in crisis the concept of authority and the universalism of values on which democratic institutions depend.

"New Dark Ages Seen If Nazis Should Win" appeared in a limited edition on September 28, 1940, in the *Boston Evening Transcript* as an analysis of National Socialism.[87] But the more innovative text seems to be "Academic Freedom" (1939), which Parsons wrote at the moment World War II broke out. It was an important piece, never published, in which he put into discussion the quality of academic research under Nazism: freedom of thinking and teaching were particularly in peril. To some extent, Parsons reexposed what his friend and colleague Hartshorne had denounced in the late 1930s:

> Corresponding to the freedom of inquiry in investigation is the freedom of teaching. If the academic man is to transmit to his students the genuine results of academic work, of liberal analysis and investigation in his subject, he must clearly be free, within the

---

86 Ibid., 82.
87 There was a limited edition of two articles: "Nazis Destroy Learning, Challenging Religion," *Radcliff News*, November 23, 1938; and "New Dark Ages Seen If Nazis Should Win," *Boston Evening Transcript*, September 28, 1940. Cf. Gerhardt, *Talcott Parsons on National Socialism*, 81–83, 153–57.

technical part of his field, to carry the argument wherever objective considerations may lead. Within the limits of what is truly technical in this sense clearly only academic experts in the field in question are qualified to decide what should and should not be taught. Once the legitimacy of academic treatment of the subject be granted all this follows.[88]

More urgent for Parsons was a sociological definition of the democratic state in the light of European events. This was evident in "Sociological Reflections on the United States in Relation to the European War"—which institutions to be defended, in America and Europe, was the Parsons's problem.[89]

I decided to focus attention on the 1937–46 writings because these address burning topics related to Jews and their destruction with the end of democracy and its negative consequences. They deserve to be reconsidered and brought back to scholarly attention. Parsons was a sociologist famed for other sociological theories. Thanks to his own sociology of Nazism, the discipline seems not to have been late in the study of the destruction of the Jews. Parsons recognized Nazism as a social evil from the outset: he analyzed it sociologically. Moreover, if he had spread his results, the path of the sociology of Nazism would have been different since other scholars would have benefited from his ideas.

His sociology dealing with Nazism concerned the genocide of the Jews: the Holocaust resulted from Nazism, which, for him, was a social movement in reaction to modernization. When he analytically explained, step-by-step, how German society prepared itself for Nazism's rise in reaction to modernity and other innovations, he clarified that the Jews were considered supporters of modernity since they practiced all the professions typical of modernity and, consequently, they were an ongoing social problem. In 1942, he illustrated that in pre-Nazi Germany many political factors, religious sentiments, and social and economic tensions led in the Weimar Republic to the rise of Nazi power and consequently to

---

88 Ibid., 96.
89 Ibid., 189–90.

the collapse of the republic and the establishment of the Third Reich. Seeing in this works Weberian sociology traces, it seems appropriate to look at the thesis of historian Jeffrey Herf of "reactionary modernism," in 1984. What is important is that Parsons aimed at recognizing the theoretical import of Nazism, its nightmarish results, and that it was a social deviance, hitherto unknown. He aimed that other scholars would be able to recognize it and thus oppose it.[90]

To some extent, Parsons seemed to be a social psychologist analyzing all German society with its structure of evil. After Horkheimer and Fromm, Parsons stands as the third sociologists who links National Socialism with anti-Semitism.[91] Let me underline a point here. When Parsons wrote these articles, there was not an academic audience able to welcome these contributions, even if he was president of ASA (1949) and head of the Department of Social Relations at Harvard (1946–56). I wondered why they were not disseminated; and I noted that Carnegie had established the Russian Research Center at Harvard, of which I'll have more to say later, and financed some research by Parsons in that period, and after the war, too; nevertheless, for research related to the burning questions of the time, support was not offered.[92] Parsons's wartime writings were not disseminated or, more precisely, some were not published, but even those that were published were not properly disseminated. This seemed to happen as a matter of course, since attention after World War II was reserved for themes (as we will see below) aimed at creating an America perfectly functional and, primarily, devoted to the fight against communism. In fear of the Red menace, the academy closed in on itself by pressuring scholars, directly or indirectly, to divert any investigation or research project concerned with the truth about the Holocaust or what had happened in Europe during the war. It was an attitude that arose in the face of accountability for what had occurred. Let me highlight here

---

90 Porter, "Toward a Sociology of National Socialism," 506, 509, 510.
91 See ibid.; Buxton, review of *Talcott Parsons on National Socialism*; Keen, review of *Talcott Parsons on National Socialism*, 1359–61.
92 Cf. Jennifer Platt, *A History of Sociological Research Methods in America, 1920–1960* (Cambridge: Cambridge University Press, 1996); Franz Neumann et al., *Il nemico tedesco: Scritti riservati sulla Germania nazista (1943–1945)*, ed. Roberto Laudani (Bologna: il Mulino, 2012).

that Parsons's writings were finally noticed through and after the 1993 Gerhardt edition. What is interesting is that, starting from this edition, a Parsons controversy commenced. Seeing the debate that took place in 1996 led me to review Parsons's approach to the Holocaust theme and to subdivide his sociology (concerning the Jewish question) into three periods, which I now delineate.

1.4.3. Years of Silence (1946–1948)

When I assert that the so-called delay of sociology has been constructed in the realms of sociology, step-by-step and over the years, my mind runs to those Parsons writings that, though dealing with anti-Semitism, racism, and totalitarianism, have not been published; or those published that have not been adequately disseminated among scholars. This is astonishing. I observed that in 1946–48 Parsons ceased to say anything about what happened in Europe, after his long period as a political activist engaged in denouncing Nazi perils. Why did Parsons stop addressing the Jewish question? I wondered if there was a personal episode, linked with this cessation, that could explain what happened or if something occurred in sociology to stop Parsons from treating these issues. Thus we need to ask: What were the main research themes in those years and who decided the research agenda?

After Gerhardt's edition, an all-time debate started, and it is still ongoing, with no resolution in sight: the problem concerns with the postwar years. Something of personal nature seemed affect him over the tragic death of his young colleague, Edward Y. Hartshorne, Jr., in 1946, when he was shot to death on a German motorway near Nuremberg, Germany, by bullets fired from a moving car; the assailants were never identified and no details were disclosed. Porter's take:

> A young colleague of Parsons, a sociologist by the name of Edward Yarnall Hartshorne, Jr. (1912–1946), was shot to death in a bizarre "drive-by" shooting on the German autobahn. Parsons never wrote about national socialism, not even about Germany, after 1948. I discuss this in my earlier review. There are many questions. Who

shot Hartshorne? What effect did his death have on Parsons? Was there a connection between Hartshorne's death and Parsons' search for "consultants" to the Russian Research Center?[93]

What is strange is that from that moment Parsons rarely returned to writing anything or to giving seminars on Germany and National Socialism.[94] Hartshorne was the sociologist who had studied Nazi control of German universities, and he was also a close friend of Parsons. With the publication of Hartshorne's *German Universities and National Socialism* in 1937, Parsons was profoundly affected by his friend's book.

Parsons's sociology, the most prominent in postwar American sociology (with its structural and functional emphasis), encountered much success in academic circles after the war, when other schools of thought, such as those of Simmel or Sorokin related to the moral reconstruction of society, were set aside in favor of a functionalist and systemic sociology in agreement with the dominant power centers or advocates of the status quo, into the late 1960s or at least until at the beginning of the 1970s. Sorokin, for example, dedicated himself in the postwar years to the study of social phenomena and the moral reconstruction of humanity. Thanks to funding from Eli Lilly, a U.S. philanthropist, in 1946 he began studying altruistic love in rebuilding human society by publishing in 1948 *The Reconstruction of Humanity*. The following year, he founded the Harvard Research Center in Creative Altruism. Such interventions raised disagreements and dissensions by a number of sociologists, including, especially, Parsons, for whom Sorokin, in 1956, wrote *Fads and Foibles in Modern Sociology*. Some years later, in 1959, he published *Public Power and Morality*, a kind of indictment against the governments and ruling classes of the world, with a copy to Dwight D. Eisenhower and Nikita Khrushchev.[95] These were the years of a thaw in the Cold War.

But, coming back to the reasons why Parsons's studies about totalitarianism were dismissed, I investigated how much the international

---

93 Jack N. Porter, "Talcott Parsons and National Socialism: The Case of the 'Ten Mysterious Missing Letters,'" *Sociological Forum* 11, no. 4 (1996): 609.
94 Cf. Porter, "Toward a Sociology of National Socialism," 506.
95 Cf. Pitirim A. Sorokin, *Fads and Foibles in Modern Sociology and Related Sciences* (Chicago: Henry Regnery, 1956); Pitirim A. Sorokin and Walter A. Lunden, *Power and Morality: Who Shall Guard the Guardians?* (Boston: Porter Sargent, 1959).

relations between the U.S. and Soviet blocs affected decisions after World War II, when any aspect of public life was reinterpreted in the light of the Cold War. In many ways competitive coexistence seems to explain the delay in studying the Holocaust. The sociological thought of Parsons's friend Hartshorne had often affected his research time and methods: he particularly had understood the dangers and threats that intellectuals were forced to suffer under National Socialism:[96]

> On the occasion of Parsons's farewell dinner at Harvard in May 1973, he paid tribute to their friendship by saying that Hartshorne was "one of our real stars." Hartshorne had successfully masterminded the reopening of German universities in the American occupation zone in 1945–1946, and had deeply influenced Parsons's thinking on German going back to the late 1930s.[97]

Richard J. Evans has recently brought attention to the mysterious disappearance of Hartshorne.[98] However, to date, very little is known about the case. Hartshorne in his *German Universities and National Socialism* had denounced the limits of university research under the Nazis. Born in New Hampshire in 1912, he was far outside the German and European mentality. In the 1930s he was an entry-level instructor in sociology at Harvard University. During his doctorate work at the University of Chicago's Department of Anthropology and Sociology, he was interested in German history and in what was happening in that context. His love for liberalism and for an academy free from governmental control in the United States, and Condorcet's ideas about equal rights and public education and thanks to a scholarship funded by the Social Science Research Council in 1935–36, led him to assess the autonomy of research within universities and academies in Germany. As a traveling sociologist in a strange country, he could look at the reality with extreme objectivity and avoid any suspicion

---

96 Cf. Porter, "Toward a Sociology of National Socialism," 509.
97 Ibid., 507.
98 Richard J. Evans, *The Third Reich at War* (New York: Penguin, 2009); Evans, review of *The Night of Broken Glass: Eyewitness Accounts of Kristallnacht* by Uta Gerhardt and Thomas Karlauf, *The Guardian*, April 11, 2012, accessed May 8, 2012, http://www.guardian.co.uk/books/2012/apr/11/night-broken-glass-kristallnacht-review.

from the Nazi powers. But why were Hartshorne's studies important? His formation at Harvard and the Chicago approach let Hartshorne analyze official sources, such as laws, decrees, statistical data, and accounted for the collapse of German universities under Nazism, where professors and students were selected in the name of racial ideology: after a long examination, he concluded that 1,145 professors and 539 assistants were eliminated from universities at the end of 1936, and the Berlin and Frankfurt universities both lost one-third of their faculties, and Heildelberg lost a quarter. New programs were planned in accordance with Nazi ideals, faculties were repopulated, and Party celebrations in honor of Hitler were established, while unjustified dismissals became a daily routine:[99]

> "It is the task of the German universities," declares an unpublished Ministerial decree of November 24, 1934, "to put scientific research into the closest possible relationship with the national political needs of our people." To this end the administration was reorganized, the faculty reconstituted and retrained, the student body newly disciplined, and to this end the academic curriculum was remodeled.[100]

Hartshorne, close to the Frankfurt School and the psychoanalytic approach, provided a rationale for a set of farewells to the main German Institutes not in accordance with Nazi policies, such as the Kaiser Wilhelm Institute case:[101]

> Admission to the university and even more, the selection of professors is based upon "non intellectual" criteria of physical, political, and "racial" fitness. Independent research is destroyed; under the slogan "All for the Fatherland," a monopoly of the party is established. On the other hand, the fight against Einstein is not sufficiently described. The name of Theodor Lessing is missing. It

---

99 See Edward Y. Hartshorne, Jr., *The German Universities and National Socialism* (London: Allen and Unwin, 1937), 36, 85.
100 Ibid., 106.
101 Ibid., 135.

is characteristic that a foreigner did not hear that this important German professor was murdered by the Nazis.[102]

What is interesting is that, together with the historian Sidney Fay and the psychologist Gordon Allport, Hartshorne gathered personal stories of refugees from Nazi Germany after *Kristallnacht*. From this came a competition, *Mein Leben in Deutschland vor und nach dem 30 Januar 1933*, with prize money of $1,000 for the best account.[103] By April 1, 1940, more than 250 manuscripts were received: 155 from the United States, 31 from Great Britain, 20 from Palestine, and 6 from Shanghai. The authors were mostly Jews who escaped from Germany after *pogroms*; particularly, academics, professors, doctors, and lawyers from Berlin and Vienna.[104]

In 1940s, when sociology underwent a period of consolidation, Hartshorne and Parsons, together with Abel, worked together on the Nazi question at the Harvard School of Overseas Administration.[105] Well, it is again the sociologist Gerhardt who unearthed Parsons's and Hartshorne's writings.[106] Hartshorne taught about his project on Nazism at Harvard in 1939: in his view, the Nazis were criminals able to tyrannize a silenced majority. He also conceived the title of the volume that gathered together the 263 essays: *Nazi Madness*. But the collection, which was supposed to appear in 1941, was never published because—according to some sources—Hartshorne was called upon at the Research and Analysis Branch (R&A) of Office of the Coordinator of Information (COI) when the United States entered the war (as were Neumann and Kirchheimer in the role of political analysts), and he did

---

102 Walter Hirsch, "The Autonomy of Science in Totalitarian Societies," *Social Forces* 40, no. 1 (1961): 19, doi:10.2307/2573466.
103 See Detlef Garz, Sandra Tiefel, and Fritz Schütze, "'An alle, die Deutschland vor und während Hitler gut kennen': Autobiographische Beiträge deutscher Emigranten zum wissenschaftlichen Preisausschreiben der Harvard University aus dem Jahr 1939," *Zeitschrift für Qualitative Forschung* 8, no. 2 (2007): 179–88; Friedrich Wissmann and Ursula Blömer, hrsg., "*Es ist Mode geworden, die Kinder in die Lesslerschule zu schicken": Dokumente zur Privaten Waldschule von Toni Lessler in Berlin Grunewald* (Oldenburg: BIS-Verlag, 2010).
104 Cf. Karl Löwith, *Mein Leben in Deutschland vor und nach 1933: Ein Bericht* (Stuttgart: J. B. Metzler, 1986).
105 Cf. Uta Gerhardt, *Talcott Parsons: An Intellectual Biography* (Cambridge: Cambridge University Press, 2002), 90–91, 108–9.
106 See Uta Gerhardt and Thomas Karlauf, eds., *The Night of Broken Glass: Eyewitness Accounts of Kristallnacht* (Malden, MA: Polity, 2012 [2009]).

not have time to review the material. Gerhardt and Thomas Karlauf selected and published twenty-one of these essays in 2009. According to other sources, the essays were never disseminated because Harvard University would not let Hartshorne do it, and he therefore abandoned Harvard for the R&A Branch of COI, where he did not face any restrictions or pressure concerning his publications. But his case is still open at this date and research is ongoing.[107]

Nazi Madness was intended to be a contribution in opposition to U.S. isolationism, and many times Hartshorne had invited the government to abandon this stance and to intervene against the Nazis.[108] Before Hartshorne's death, Parsons also stood against American isolationism and for a possible intervention in Europe. We can read his opinions in the letter addressed to Fraser Taylor on September 28, 1939. Hartshorne, as a convinced anti-Nazi, after the United States entered the war, followed U.S. troops in Europe, prepared reports, and was dedicated to the postwar denazification process in several German schools, until 1946, when he was shot.

What it is surprising is that for decades these accounts remained unnoticed in Harvard's archives and that they were brought to light only after 1989, just as happened for Parsons writings. Some of Hartshorne's essays, unearthed by Gerhardt in 1995, were gathered in *Nie mehr zuruck in dieses Land* and edited by Propylaen Verlag in 2009. Their importance lies in that they are part of a research sociological project on Nazism, and on some of the German people who rescued Jews (as in the case of Marie Kahle).[109]

To give a more complete overview of the work of Hartshorne, let me remember that in 1943 Hartshorne became a professor at the Psychological Warfare Branch of the Office of War Information (OWI)—an agency of

---

107 Cf. Evans, *The Third Reich at War*; Evans, review of *The Night of Broken Glass*. See James F. Tent, ed., *Academic Proconsul: Harvard Sociologist Edward Y. Hartshorne and the Reopening of German Universities, 1945–1946. His Personal Account* (Trier: Wissenschaftlicher Verlag Trier, 1998).

108 In Parson Papers, 42.8.2, box 3, quoted in Gerhardt, *Talcott Parsons on National Socialism*, 65n58; in "New Dark Age Seen If Nazis Should Win," which appeared in a limited manner, on September 28, 1940, in the *Boston Evening Transcript*; in "Memorandum" (in which he speaks of prevention); and in "The Problem of Controlled Institutional Change: An Essay in Applied Social Science," *Psychiatry* 8 (1945): 79–101.

109 Cf. Neil J. Smelser, "Psychological Trauma and Cultural Trauma," in *Cultural Trauma and Collective Identity*, ed. Jeffrey C. Alexander et al. (Berkeley: University of California Press, 2004), 31–59.

the U.S. government during World War II from June 1942 to September 1945—to consolidate information services, and, in particular, to track the presence of foreign spies in the United States. The Research and Analysis Branch collected and investigated tactical and political information. It was directed by William Langer of Harvard University and established by Col. William Donovan, and for which Hartshorne had been in service. It was a total war and "the *intelligence* also has to be total").[110] After the assassination attempt against Hitler on July 20, 1944, Hartshorne was transferred to London and then back to the United States. At the end of the war, he was the main person responsible for reopening German universities in the occupation zone. In 1945, he was at the Psychological Warfare Division, a U.S. division of Supreme Headquarters Allied Expeditionary Force (SHAEF) under General Eisenhower. And before the reopening of the German university system, in April 1945, he returned to Marburg, Germany, because he was on the trail, along with an investigative team, of the *SS-Obergruppenführer* Max Amann. He was committed to denazification and to reopening all seven universities in the U.S. occupation zone, and he oversaw the process in Bavaria, especially after the American newspapers, in the spring of 1946, reported on the failure of the program, as is evident in an interview conducted by Marcuse with Jürgen Habermas in 1978. In the piece, he said, "Those whom we had listed first as 'economic war criminals' were very quickly back in the decisive positions of responsibility in the German economy. It would be very easy to name names here."[111]

Always on the move, Hartshorne, while at the service of Office of War Information, did not remain for more than four days in the same place. But when he discovered that the U.S. government was allowing former Nazis to enter the United States illegally, as a radical anti-Nazi, he informed Moscow of the ratline designed to help war criminals.

---

110 Reference to the *Joint Psychological Warfare Committee, Functions of the OSS*, in *War Report of the OSS* (New York: Walker and Co., 1976), 2:348, quoted in Neumann et al., *Il nemico tedesco*, 11–12. See Allan M. Winkler, *The Politics of Propaganda: The Office of War Information, 1942-1945* (New Haven, CT: Yale University Press, 1978); Bradley F. Smith, *The Shadow Warriors: OSS and the Origins of the CIA* (New York: Basic Books, 1983).

111 Charles Reitz, "Marcuse in America—Exile as Educator: Deprovincializing One-Dimensional Culture in the U.S.A.," *Fast Capitalism* 5, no. 2 (2009), accessed June 30, 2016, https://www.uta.edu/huma/agger/fastcapitalism/5_2/Reitz5_2.html.

These actions in divulging the ratline were fatal for him.¹¹² To the Counter Intelligence Corps, the passing on of such information was quite uncomfortable.¹¹³ As Porter has said concerning Hartshorne's death, several hypotheses have been advanced: it remains a mystery whether Hartshorne was a CIA agent shot dead by the Soviet secret police or was murdered by Nazi sympathizers, or some other scenario, and very little is known about the causes of the end of his career at Harvard.¹¹⁴

1.4.4. The Parsons Controversy over His "Role in Bringing Nazi Sympathizers to the U.S."

Porter states: "In short, I found many issues unresolved in the Cold War years from 1946 to 1954 at Harvard University, especially the role of Talcott Parsons and Clyde Kluckhohn in allegedly bringing Nazi collaborators to the United States."¹¹⁵

The controversy is related to the so-called delay of post-Holocaust sociology since 1948; following the death of Hartshorne, Parsons completely modified his sociological method of research, passing from a valutative sociology dealing with burning topics to an a-valutative one that marked the entire path of the sociological tradition for almost two decades, well known as "systems theory."

---

112 The meaning of the term *ratline* is significant and is appropriate if one thinks of the sense of the corresponding Italian, *grisella*, a marine term: a cord stairway that leads to the peak of a ship, the last refuge when it sinks.

113 See Robin W. Winks, *Cloak and Gown: Scholars in the Secret War, 1939–1961* (New York: Morrow, 1987); Allen Weinstein and Alexander Vassiliev, *The Haunted Wood: Soviet Espionage in America—The Stalin Era* (New York: Random House, 1999); Philip Deery and Mario Del Pero, *Spiare e tradire: Dietro le quinte della guerra fredda* (Milan: Feltrinelli, 2011). See Evans, review of *The Night of Broken Glass*. Thanks to Laudani, today it is known that, for some time, Neumann was, during his service at the OSS, also an informer for the KGB under the code name of "Ruff," making available to Soviets top-secret material; everything was known to U.S. intelligence services through the Venona project. See Neumann et al., *Il nemico tedesco*, 20–21.

114 See Porter, *Toward a Sociology of National Socialism*, 506–7; Martin Oppenheimer, "Social Scientists and War Criminals," *New Politics* 6, no. 23 (1997), accessed May 31, 2011, http://nova.wpunj.edu/newpolitics/issue23/oppenh23.htm.

115 Porter, *Talcott Parsons and National Socialism*, 603. Cf. Wiener, "Talcott Parsons' Role Bringing Nazi Sympathizers to the U.S." 305–9.

The unresolved Hartshorne episode invites scholars to investigate the background of sociological research in the United States after World War II. This exploration is going to involve another aspect: his "ten mysterious letters," which emerged after Gerhardt's 1993 edition. Here we want to examine Parsons's role [in] bringing Nazi sympathizers to the United States. This aspect broadens the overview of the role sociology played after the war and during the Cold War. Concerning this period, only selected topics will be addressed. Arguments not concerned with the fight against communism are dismissed. Hence, in this context, my thesis that scholars were impeded in their study of some themes and prevented from disseminating freely their views and research results takes its root. Sociologists were not free to approach the Holocaust with its related themes, such as anti-Semitism. In this way, they had to delay disseminating their views on the Holocaust.[116] The Parsons debate is an issue deserving particular attention and reflection. Here, I will attempt to consider just those elements useful to my aims in this book.[117]

Everything starts with the release of the 1993 Gerhardt edition. After the commendations in *Sociological Forum* by Porter for the attention with which Parsons addressed sociologically National Socialism, the same Porter, in 1996, put in evidence other aspects of Parsons's case.[118] As Oppenheimer observes: "Porter was unaware of Wiener's *Nation* piece at the time and when he found out about it (from me), he was understandably upset. He (and I) tried to have a correction to his review published."[119]

This opened up a lively academic dispute on Parsons's papers that were edited by Gerhardt and on the sociology of Parsons concerning National Socialism, termed the "Parsons controversy." The discovery of his having provided safe haven for Nazi collaborators inflamed the debate surrounding the political significance of his sociological theories. The value-free sociology of Parsons dominated in the field until the end of 1960s and

---

116 See Edward A. Shils, "Limitations on the Freedom of Research and Teaching in the Social Sciences," *Annals of the American Academy of Political and Social Science* 200 (1938): 144–64, http://www.jstor.org/stable/1022348.
117 I am preparing a more proper essay about the Parsons controversy.
118 Porter, "Toward a Sociology of National Socialism"; Porter, "Talcott Parsons and National Socialism", 603–11.
119 Oppenheimer, "Social Scientists and War Criminals."

the early 1970s when a new generation of sociologists understood and declared that the neutral sociology of Parsons did, indeed, hide the political status quo and the ideology of the Cold War. The discovery at the end of 1980s of Parsons's engagement in bringing Nazi sympathizers to the United States legitimated the position of these sociologists. The rising intellectual turmoil, to some extent, recalled the Arendt controversy at the publication of her *Banality of Evil* in 1963.[120]

Opening the debate was a letter sent by Oppenheimer to Porter, dated February 8, 1995, in which he says that Gerhardt, in her edition, did not mention "controversial issues" concerning Parsons and omitted "the case of ten mysterious missing letters," from which could be seen Parsons's role in bringing Nazi sympathizers to the United States to hold academic appointments and the Harvard Russian Research Center (HRRC).[121]

Porter immediately tried to review his previous version, but the editor of *Sociological Forum* rejected the debate, suggesting as "inappropriate" letters exchanged between Porter and Oppenheimer and that the journal was not fit for addressing the question.[122] "The sociological establishment then circled the wagons to protect Parsons. The journal refused to publish any amendment to Porter's review, much less any letters about it, for about two years."[123] Only in December 1996, with the new editor, Richard Hall, was Porter able to report, in *Sociological Forum*, the attention on Parsons, answering publicly the brouhaha. In Porter's view there was no attempt to sully Parsons, rather he intended to bring to light "the bluteh (Yiddish for "mud") of Cold War politics" a politics that led him to abandon any kind of research with practical feedback in political and social life.[124]

I decided to briefly report this debate because it accounts for how the strategies of the Cold War affected research projects and community research. Also, the controversy raised other tensions: in the same number in which Porter was edited, "two lengthy defenses of Parsons"—in

---

120   Talcott Parsons, *Professioni e libertà*, ed. Marco Santoro (Rome: Armando, 2011).
121   Cf. Porter, "Talcott Parsons and National Socialism," 603, 611. Oppenheimer sent another letter to Porter, January 31, 1995, and one to Gerhardt, November 13, 1995. See Oppenheimer, "Social Scientists and War Criminals."
122   Cf. Porter, "Talcott Parsons and National Socialism," 603.
123   Oppenheimer, "Social Scientists and War Criminals."
124   Cf. Porter, "Talcott Parsons and National Socialism," 604, 609.

Oppenheimer's words—appeared: "Truth, Misinterpretation, or Left-wing McCarthyism?" by Dennis H. Wrong, and "Scholarship, Not Scandal" by Gerhardt.[125] Well, the Porter and Oppenheimer criticisms hung on the studies of Thomas Charles O'Connell, the outstanding researcher, with Christopher Simpson, who read the famed missing letters. His studies were gathered in his dissertation "Social Structure and Science: Soviet Studies" (1990). I personally tried to consult this thesis, and in 2001 I requested it from Ann Arbor, Michigan, according to standard e-mail procedure, but I never received an answer.[126] Parsons and his sociology of Nazism deserve a separate study. The controversy arose because his initial interest in the Jewish question changed at the death of Hartshorne and, definitively, during the Cold War. Two works explain the context, one by Christopher Simpson and one by Jon Wiener,[127] as mentioned by Oppenheimer:

> University of California (Irvine) historian Jon Wiener stumbled upon Charles O'Connell's doctoral dissertation, then still in draft form, and wrote an article for *The Nation* (March 6, 1989) describing in some detail Parsons' involvement with trying to smuggle "Nazi collaborators" into the U.S. as Soviet studies experts. Gerhardt, it turns out, was aware of Wiener's article when she wrote her book.[128]

The key words seem to be "Soviet" and "experts." Parsons recruited Nazi sympathizers since they were Soviet experts, and this Soviet expertise was particularly requested by the U.S. government to help fight the Red menace.

When Winston Churchill, in a speech on March 5, 1946, gave us the term "Iron Curtain," all research thereafter was directed to the contest

---

125 Dennis H. Wrong, "Truth, Misinterpretation, or Left-wing McCarthyism?" *Sociological Forum*, 11, no. 4 (1996): 613–21; Uta Gerhardt, "Scholarship, Not Scandal," *Sociological Forum* 11, no. 4 (1996): 623–30; Oppenheimer, *Social Scientists and War Criminals*.
126 On the O'Connell dissertation—Charles O'Connell, "Social Structure and Science: Soviet Studies" (PhD diss., UCLA, 1990)—it can be consulted at UCLA, Department of Sociology, or it can be requested from University of Microfilms International of Ann Arbor. See Oppenheimer, "To the Editor"; Porter, "Talcott Parsons and National Socialism," 609.
127 Cf. Simpson, *Blowback*; Wiener, "Talcott Parsons' Role Bringing Nazi Sympathizers to the U.S."
128 Oppenheimer, "Social Scientists and War Criminals."

against the Soviets and their sphere. The Nazi sympathizers in question, such as Nicholas Poppe, were aware of the murder of the Jews. This is important. The historian Wiener wrote: "Poppe defected to the Nazis in 1942, the day they arrived in the Caucasus town where he was teaching. Simpson reported that Poppe 'actively collaborated in the creation of the quisling government' in one of the ethnic minority areas, an administration that promptly expropriated Jewish property and murdered the region's Jews."[129] In 1948, Parsons received his assignment to recruit Poppe, known for his expertise on the Caucasus, Soviet ethnics, and Jewish communities in the Soviet Union. In the name of the Cold War and to obtain information or insights concerning the Soviet Union, anything useful for unearthing Soviet operations became precious, and thus questions about or investigations into what happened to the Jews (even in those areas) were overshadowed. As for intelligence sources, a plan labeled "secret" was prepared on Soviet social scientists in 1948 by Norman Davies:

> The Davies project fit in well with what the Carnegie people had in mind for the Harvard Russian Research Center. A reconnaissance of various potential sources of data (the refugees) needed to be undertaken. Shortly after the formalization of the HRRC, Director Kluckhohn dispatched Executive Committee member Talcott Parsons to carry out this mission. Parsons travelled in Germany, Austria, England and Sweden from June to August 1948, during which time he was in touch with diplomatic and military officials, intelligence personnel, scholars, and a few Soviet displaced persons in order to identify those who might be useful in various ways to the HRRC. He also wrote approximately ten letters to Kluckhohn describing his travels and his contacts. (Two scholars have seen these letters and quote from them in their work: O'Connell, and Sigmund Diamond, the Columbia sociologist and historian, whose *Compromised Campus*,

---

129 Wiener, "Talcott Parsons' Role Bringing Nazi Sympathizers to the U.S.," 306.

1992, devotes several chapters to the HRRC). Some interesting names appear in these letters. Nicholas Poppe is one of them.[130]

For the U.S. fear of a second Red threat was in play above all by the end of the 1940s until 1953, when the Thaw era commenced with Stalin's death, the know-how of these informers constituted a golden basis of information against the Red menace, and "Nicholas Poppe, a sophisticated intellectual well-versed in Soviet affairs was a star in this respect."[131] It is essential to say that he was not accepted immediately by the U.S. Department of State. Edward Mason, professor at Harvard, helped with his entrance into the United States, and he was contacted by Parsons. Mason, as a member of the executive committee of the Russian Center and a consultant for the Department of State, kept in touch with political executives of the Warfare division of the State Department, particularly with George F. Kennan, author of the policy of "containment." Thanks to the friendship between Mason and Kennan, Poppe arrived in Washington in 1949, under the false name of Joseph Alexandros.[132] At the end of the war, Poppe was a refugee in Britain, to the embarrassment of the military government, since he is wanted as a war criminal. But as can be seen by reading the Wiener and Oppenheimer pieces, the Army Counter Intelligence Corps was asked "if it is possible for U.S. intelligence authorities to take him off their hands and see that he is sent to the U.S. where he can be 'lost,'" as stated in a secret memorandum of May 1947 and rediscovered by Simpson.[133] After the end of the war, Parsons worked at the Harvard Russian Research Center: he

---

130 Oppenheimer, "Social Scientists and War Criminals," 5.
131 Ibid. On the Dudin Group, Nazi collaborators of the Vlasov army, and the Cold War, see correspondence between Martin Oppenheimer and Jack N. Porter (January 31–February 8, 1995), and letters of Martin Oppenheimer to Uta Gerhardt (November 13, 1995). Cf. Simpson, *Blowback*; Wiener, "Talcott Parsons' Role Bringing Nazi Sympathizers to the U.S."
132 Cf. Wiener, "Talcott Parsons' Role Bringing Nazi Sympathizers to the U.S.," 306-9; Oppenheimer, "Social Scientists and War Criminals." For the relationship concerning Parsons, Poppe, the Russian Research Center, the academic realm of Harvard, and the Carnegie Foundation, see "Social Network Diagram for Talcott Parsons," last accessed May 17, 2011, http://www.namebase.org/cgi-bin/nb06?_PARSONS_TALCOTT_.
133 See Wiener, "Talcott Parsons' Role Bringing Nazi Sympathizers to the U.S.," 306; Oppenheimer, "Social Scientists and War Criminals".

had the mission on behalf of army intelligence officers and State Department officials to flush out some former military Soviet supporters of Nazis:

> Talcott Parsons knew that the man he called "our friend Poppe" had collaborated with the Nazis. ... The work Parsons did on Poppe's behalf indicates his willingness to overcome moral objections to collaboration, as well as his self-proclaimed "value-neutrality" in scientific norms, in the name of cold war activism.[134]

I cannot discuss the entire case here, but I direct the reader to pieces by Oppenheimer, Porter, and Wiener, scholars well acquainted with the facts. I shall limit myself to looking at the sociology of Parsons during the Cold War years. By examining Wiener's and Oppenheimer's writings, I learned about O'Connell dissertation, "Social Structure and Science: Soviet Studies," and about Parsons's postwar activities. Let me stress that in the Harvard archives, O'Connell found the ten letters mentioned above. Parsons wrote them to a colleague, Clyde Kluckhohn, head of the Center. These letters show that the main man among Russian contacts was Nicholas Poppe, an expert on the languages of Soviet areas: he was a professor at the University of Leningrad from 1925 to 1941 and knew "the location and size of Jewish communities in the Soviet Union."[135]

Parsons, in the ten letters of the summer of 1948, says he did know Poppe and "dedicated himself to obtaining a U.S. entry visa and a Harvard appointment" for Poppe—a difficult task, since Poppe "was not only a Nazi collaborator but had been banned from entering the United States and had recently been the object of a U.S. manhunt in Germany for extradition to the Soviet Union."[136]

Parsons' German summer of 1948 tells us a great deal about the historical role of liberal scholars in the early Cold War as well as the academic liaison with covert CIA operations, contacts with fugitives

---

134 Wiener, "Talcott Parsons' Role Bringing Nazi Sympathizers to the U.S.," 308.
135 Ibid., 306. Poppe's case is reported in the *U.S. General Accounting Office Report* of 1985.
136 Ibid., 306. See Porter, "Talcott Parsons and National Socialism," 605–6.

hiding underground on forged documents, desperate to escape either Soviet or Nuremberg Tribunals.[137]

Everything seems to be linked with the establishment of Harvard Russian Research Center. What I intend to underline, remembering my focus (that the sociological delay, in the approaching the Jewish question, occurred in the name of the Cold War politics), is that these Nazi collaborators, wanted by the Soviets, entered United States thanks to Harvard, with academic appointments in exchange for collaboration: "In the war against the Communists, anything and everything went, even morality. It is in this convoluted atmosphere that the story begins."[138] In this context we see that a sociological thinking free from political duties in relation to communism never took root. In the name of fighting communism and of individualistic ethics, collaboration with former Nazis was able to provide useful information on the Soviet system.

These Soviet experts passed information about the Soviets on to the Harvard Russian Research Center in order to save their own lives. The letter, a "smoking gun," in Porter's words, is on page 223 of O'Connell's doctoral dissertation and is based on Parsons's letter to Kluckhohn of June 30, 1948, in which "Parsons tells Kluckhohn of meeting with a British intelligence man named Rhodes, who had Poppe's dossier, marked 'Top Secret' on his desk. Parsons tells Kluckhohn that if a way can be found to get Poppe into the U.S., the British will take care of letting him out of Germany."[139]

Parsons's letters to Kluckhohn led Porter to raise many interesting questions: "(One intriguing question I have: How did Parsons' letters to Clyde Kluckhohn come to be controlled by Merle Fainsod and his daughters?) Indeed, Parsons' letters to Kluckhohn reveal a mixture of certainty and ambiguity regarding the exploitation of former Nazi collaborators as

---

137 Porter, "Talcott Parsons and National Socialism," 607. "Parsons developed relationships with other former Nazi collaborators on his German trip in 1948" (Wiener, "Talcott Parsons' Role Bringing Nazi Sympathizers to the U.S.," 308). On his contacts with Leo Dudin of the Vlasov army, and Vladimir Pozdniajov, former lieutenant colonel of Red Army, and on army intelligence officers and Harvard, see ibid., 308–9.
138 Porter, "Talcott Parsons and National Socialism," 604.
139 Ibid., 606; Oppenheimer, "Social Scientists and War Criminals."

scholarly resources for Harvard."[140] Porter, in an e-mail to me on May 31, 2011, writes that "it is a fascinating mystery." What presses me to reflect upon this case, or on what happened to those letters, is the way he informed me: "The 'ten letters' exist but are sealed by the Fainsod family," and "the Parsons family (especially, son Prof. Charles Parsons who is a prof of philosophy at Harvard) and Harvard are both sensitive to this matter and how it can be misused by Leftists who may be anti-Parsons." In Porter's article, he says:

> I waited in order to get hold of "ten mysterious letters" that show Parsons' role in all this. They can be found in the Merle Fainsod Collection of the Harvard Archives, but it was taking a great deal of time to get permission from the archives and from Fainsod's two daughters. I could not wait any longer. I also waited to find the article by Jens Kaalhauge Nielsen in Robertson and Turner (1991), and I urge everyone to read it and to compare it to the Jon Wiener (1989) essay in *The Nation*.
>
> The entire issue revolves around certain individuals who may or may not have been Nazi collaborators. At a curious juncture in history, two things happened: one, many post–World War II refugees were trying to get into America, some of them Nazi collaborators; and two, Harvard University was trying to recruit refugee scholars for their new Russian Research Center. There was bound to be a collision.[141]

From O'Connell's information, it is evident that after 1951, "Harvard appears to sever its ties with them [Soviet displaced persons]."[142] Nevertheless, this debate, far from resolved, is now useful for understanding the status of sociologists in a "wider perspective," that is, when academic research is not free and unfettered, but rather conditioned by political intentions.

---

140 Porter, "Talcott Parsons and National Socialism," 606, reference is to O'Connell, "Social Structure and Science," 223.

141 Ibid., 604. See Wiener, "Talcott Parsons' Role Bringing Nazi Sympathizers to the U.S.," 308–9.

142 Porter, "Talcott Parsons and National Socialism," 606.

Briefly, the main American universities, as with the HRRC, could not deal with the Holocaust theme, which concerned a matter of accountability and a very recent event calling for political accountabilities or for a kind of public admission of guilty. Behind Parsons's a-valutative sociology (for which political issues are not addressed and considered of no importance and not fit for social sciences) lies the purpose of maintaining the status quo. A liberal Harvard in fighting communism accepted the collaboration with Nazi collaborators or Nazi sympathizers after the Holocaust.

I can now focus attention on criticisms directed at Parsons after the Gerhardt edition came out. To be more precise, I have preferred to divide them into two main currents: on the one hand, those pro-Parsons, namely, those, such as Gerhardt, Wrong, and Nielsen, who ignore his political activities during the Cold War years. On the other, scholars, such Simpson, Wiener, O'Connell, Oppenheimer, and Porter, who, on the contrary, put into light a hitherto less well-known aspect of his European missions at the end of the war. Among pro-Parsons scholars, for example, Jens K. Nielsen, in 1991, introduced the sociologist of Harvard as a clear and passionate opponent of fascism, Nazism, and McCarthyism, criticizing strongly the 1989 positions by Wiener. I suggest the reader examine his assumptions.[143] To acquaint us better with the facts, as suggested by Porter, the answer can be found only in the Fainsod Papers, never seen by Nielsen, but seen by O'Connell, who examined them for his doctoral dissertation.[144] What strikes my eye is that Parsons, during 1947–49, was head of the Department of Social Relations at Harvard, and in 1949 he was president of the American Sociological Society, later American Sociological Association (his colleague Kluckhohn was president of the American Anthropological Association in 1947). This means that Parsons had relevant positions at Harvard and that he had financing so he could have publicized and disseminated his writings about National Socialism if he had wanted to. I reflect on this because

---

143 Cf. Jens K. Nielsen, "The Political Orientation of Talcott Parsons: The Second World War and Its Aftermath," in *Talcott Parsons: Theorist of Modernity*, ed. Roland Robertson and Bryan S. Turner (London: Sage, 1991), 217–33; Porter, "Talcott Parsons and National Socialism," 605–7; O'Connell, "Social Structure and Science," 222–24.

144 Porter, "Talcott Parsons and National Socialism," 608, reference to O'Connell, "Social Structure and Science," 233–36.

scholars became aware of these pieces only thanks to Gerhardt in 1993. The Carnegie Corporation founded the HRRC, and Parsons, in 1949, needed $10,000 to reestablish the American Sociological Association, and $25,000 for his book *Toward a General Theory of Action* (1951). In 1961, he received $30,000 for his other personal research. Also, his department received the amounts of $150,000 and $125,000 from the Carnegie Corporation.[145] (This is found in the interview with Talcott Parsons, March 22, 1967, at the Carnegie Oral History Project, Columbia University Archives.)

I attempted to find some answers to unresolved questions, exploring, even if briefly, the realm of Harvard, in the pre–World War II years, in the voices of some scholars. What helped me was a Norwood essay written in 2004 dealing with the academic conditions facilitating some strands of research. In blocking the approach to the Holocaust, some attitudes and views assumed by academics and alumni of Harvard at the time, such as the "dismissal of Jews from the professions,"[146] played a relevant role. The anti-Semitic mentality and outrage in the prewar years discouraged scholars from treating Jewish themes and the Holocaust during and after the war. Illuminating is the following piece:

> President Conant remained publicly indifferent to the persecution of Jews in Europe and failed to speak out against it until after Kristallnacht, in November 1938. He was determined to build friendly ties with the Universities of Heidelberg and Goettingen, even though they had expelled their Jewish faculty members and thoroughly Nazified their curricula, constructing a "scholarly" foundation for vulgar antisemitism, which was taught as "racial science."... President Conant's behavior was certainly influenced by the anti-Jewish prejudice he harbored. His predecessor as Harvard's president, A. Lawrence Lowell, had voiced his antisemitism publicly, notably during the controversy in 1922 surrounding his proposal that Harvard introduce a formal quota to reduce Jewish enrollment.

---

145 Ibid., 607; Talcott Parsons and Edward A. Shils, *Toward a General Theory of Action* (Cambridge, MA: Harvard University Press, 1951).
146 See next note.

In justifying a quota, President Lowell, a vice president of the Immigration Restriction League, had declared that "a strong race feeling on the part of the Jews" was a significant cause of the "rapidly growing anti-Semitic feeling in this country."[147]

In the postwar period, in an atmosphere of great tension between the two main world powers, what happened to the Jews in Europe was "frozen": Harvard, as did other American universities, reduced the importance of the analysis of Nazism in favor of other questions privileged by the ruling class:

> Parsons' 1948 German trip raises some larger questions about the relationship between academic sociology and political life: Is there something about ahistorical social theory that leads its practitioners to "forget" the history of the Nazis' crimes? Is there something about "value-free" social science that leads its practitioners to ignore the value of bringing collaborators to justice? In the end, Parsons proves to be another case in a depressingly familiar story: that of leading liberal scholars in the United States making political commitments in the name of the cold war, blinding themselves to moral issues and making a mockery of their claims to objective scholarship.[148]

Several researches of this period were conducted by the Office of Strategic Services (OSS), which were aimed at defeating of communism.[149] Today the "Parsons controversy" is largely well known: it is important because it brings to light the status of post-Holocaust sociology, illuminating why this event was studied, but rather dismissed, but then, finally, research pathways were opened to investigate it adequately. It recalls international

---

147 Stephen H. Norwood, "Legitimating Nazism: Harvard University and the Hitler Regime, 1933–1937," *American Jewish History* 92, no. 2 (2004): 190.
148 Wiener, "Talcott Parsons' Role Bringing Nazi Sympathizers to the U.S.," 309. Cf. Abbott Gleason, *Totalitarianism: The Inner History of the Cold War* (Oxford: Oxford University Press, 1995); Salvati, *Antifascismo e totalitarismo nelle scienze sociali tra le due guerre*, 627.
149 Cf. Martin Oppenheimer, "Footnote to the Cold War: The Harvard Russian Research Center," *Monthly Review* 48 (1997): 7–17. Several scholars and intellectuals entered OSS and OWI to help identify vulnerabilities in the war against communism.

relations during the Cold War and the difficulties liberal Harvard faced when handling the Nazi question and anti-Semitic issues:

> The matter of Talcott Parsons's "missing years" is known, but not widely. It would seem that there are people who prefer to keep it that way. Still, what harm would it do to satisfy historical objectivity nearly years later? Is it that Parsons' many sociological disciples, people whose careers are based on "Parsonian sociology," are embarrassed by these disclosures and feel they must therefore either deny Parsons' role, or somehow justify it as a matter of saving face? Or are Parsons and the HRRC really not the issue? Does a description of power structure networks and their responsibility for formulating university research agendas, and the interlock between those networks and "top" universities and intelligence and other "defense" agencies, get too close to undermining the myth of scholarly objectivity and thereby the respectability of the university, a status that has been in careful repair since the end of the Vietnam War?[150]

Only free access to the ten missing letters could enlighten us on forgotten aspects.[151] The publication of these letters, to date inaccessible, would not only settle the inflamed debate but would also reveal further issues related to post-Holocaust sociology:

> However from my knowledge of the Holocaust, Poppe is definitively a Nazi war criminal.... Poppe worked for the notorious Wannsee Institute and gave of his talents and skill as an SS research social scientist to help round up Jews and other ethnic groups inside the Soviet Union. In short, he was a kind of "Nazi sociologist" (my phrase). He would have been convicted of war crimes and sentenced, if not to death, then to a long prison sentence if caught. He would

---

150 Oppenheimer, "Social Scientists and War Criminals."
151 See Tony Judt, *Postwar: A History of Europe since 1945* (New York: Penguin, 2005); Judt, *Reappraisals: Reflections on the Forgotten Twentieth Century* (New York: Penguin, 2008).

have been placed on a watch list like Kurt Waldheim and never allowed into this country. He slipped through, however, as did hundreds of other collaborators during the Cold War. Look at the case of Paul de Man and Mircea Eliade, two accomplished academics who were also later found to be Nazi collaborators.[152]

1.5. THE GERMAN ARMY IN SHILS AND JANOWITZ

At this point, it is important to stress that 1948 was a crucial year for post-Holocaust sociology. In that year, Edward A. Shils and Morris Janowitz, members of the Chicago School, conducted a survey on the social structure of the German army. It comes as no surprise that the work had its origin in Chicago. Far from being a military history, as the title "Cohesion and Disintegration in the Wehrmacht in World War II" might suggest, in the article various aspects of Nazi policy are exposed along with the social construction of prejudice. Let me retrace what these scholars of Chicago elaborate and in which sociological way they link the German army to Nazism and the Holocaust. When, in the text, we read that the "passionate aggressiveness" of the *Wehrmacht* was used to protect a Germany that considered itself surrounded by dark and threatening forces (with reference to Bolsheviks, Jews, and blacks), it is clear that it refers to the image of a country that is defenseless and in danger. Although most of the German soldiers had no interest in the Nazi political system, conditions to discredit the Jews arose.[153] At the end of the 1940s, the topic of the *Wehrmacht* occupied a secondary position in postwar culture and this marginalization, in some respects, continued in the later years, especially owing to the common opinion that the army belonged only slightly to National Socialism and was a military body in itself, distinct and intact. Shils and Janowitz instead study organic solidarity within

---

152   Porter, "Talcott Parsons and National Socialism," 608-609, reference to O'Connell, "Social Structure and Science," 217–18.
153   Cf. Edward A. Shils and Morris Janowitz, "Cohesion and Disintegration in the Wehrmacht in World War II," *Public Opinion Quarterly* 12 (1948): 303.

the German army to understand what prompted the army to continue fighting despite the defeat of Germany. The authors found the "hard core" explaining the ideological nature lying behind the *Wehrmacht* and, principally, the force of Nazi ideology.[154]

Here some sociological key factors are highlighted: precisely, how both researchers of Chicago identify interesting elements helping to understand the process of Nazification and subsequently the destruction of the Jews. For example, the following phrases help to acquaint us better with the connection between Nazi Party and the army:

> Even before the outbreak of the war, the Nazi party took an active hand in the internal high policy of the Wehrmacht and in the selection of the Chief of Staff and his entourage. From September 1939 to the signing of the capitulation in May 1945 this process of Nazification continued steadily until the Wehrmacht was finally rendered powerless to make its own decisions. Nazi party control over the Wehrmacht was designed to insure (1) that Nazi strategic intentions would be carried out, (2) that capitulation would be made impossible, and (3) that internal solidarity down to the lowest private would be maintained.[155]

When Shils and Janowitz, diverging from the common contemporary opinion, state that the *Wehrmacht* did not exhibit typical features of Wilhelmine military ethics, because it was to be a mass that did not embrace the values of the German *nation* as such, they stress a particular feature of the Nazi propaganda—some fanatics were seeking to obey an authority in the name of the Second Reich's honor code. The *Wehrmacht* soldiers were recruited on the basis of "ethical or political loyalties": to be part of this military organization was to be an aggregation of individuals who were not nationalized according to Wilhelmine military ethics. Rather, joining the army were adults with economic difficulties during the Weimar Republic who hoped to find, with the advent of National

---

154 Ibid., 304. See Murray I. Gurfein and Morris Janowitz, "Trends in Wehrmacht Morale," *The Public Opinion Quarterly* 10, no. 1 (1946): 78.
155 Shils and Janowitz, "Cohesion and Disintegration in the Wehrmacht in World War II," 306-7.

Socialism, a solution to their material problems, or young people, between twenty-four and twenty-eight years old and easily indoctrinable. Shils and Janowitz unearthed the role played by the ancient German military code in the formation of social cohesion of the *Wehrmacht* and how it favored the advent of Nazi power.[156] Written perhaps only to account for the trauma of the World War II, however, the article is much more. It combines elements drawn from many fields of the social sciences: from psycho-sociology to international relations, by way of comparative politics and urban studies. Acquainted with the concepts of "armed forces" and "civil–military relations" and with the international context of World War II, the authors show the importance of social control over civilian institutions. After denouncing what the *Wehrmacht* was, the text is a real invitation to civic consciousness. It may be considered a pioneering work both in post-Holocaust sociology, because the *Wehrmacht* is presented as a "primary social group," and in sociology in general, since the University of Chicago in the 1940s was specializing in quantitative research of social groups. In addition, it offers a great contribution to social sciences in the field of military studies: Shils and Janowitz propose an original explanation of the reasons that led the *Wehrmacht* to support Hitler and his policies during World War II:[157]

> For the authors, in attempting to determine why the German Army in World War II fought so stubbornly to the end, have made an intensive study of the social structure of this army, of the symbols to which it responded, of the Nazi attempts to bolster its morale, and the Allied attempts to break it down.[158]

---

156 Cf. ibid., 284, 292–97, 303–5; Aly, *Hitler's Beneficiaries*. See Eric Dunning and Stephen Mennell, "Elias on Germany, Nazism and the Holocaust: On the Balance between 'Civilizing' and 'Decivilizing' Trends in the Social Development of Western Europe," *British Journal of Sociology* 49, no. 3 (1998): 339–57.
157 Cf. Ernest M. Doblin and Claire Pohly, "The Social Composition of the Nazi Leadership," *American Journal of Sociology* 51, no. 1 (1945): 42–49, doi:10.1086/219712; Robert J. MacCoun, Elizabeth Kier, and Aaron Belkin, "Does Social Cohesion Determine Motivation in Combat? An Old Question with an Old Answer," *Armed Forces & Society* 32, no. 4 (2006): 646–654, doi:10.1177/0095327X05279181.
158 Shils and Janowitz, "Cohesion and Disintegration in the Wehrmacht in World War II," 280.

Starting from the initial theme of the *Wehrmacht*, Shils and Janowitz explain in an early and alternative way what Hitlerism was and how "the ignorance of the German troops about important military events" was "a part of Nazi policy."[159] Terror and elimination of the opposition and, especially, the meaning of *Gemeinschaft* were among the elements typical of National Socialist ideology and of the old Prussian military code. What is interesting is that the *Wehrmacht* operates with the sociological notions of authority and obedience to authority that Shils and Janowitz adopt in their examination.

Their sociological innovation was also that they advocated, among other scholars, for the prompt recognition or public admission of massacres committed in regions in the East: they examine the differences between fighting methods on the Eastern Front and that of Western occupation. Behind the term "brutality" lies the executions committed in the Soviet areas to the east. In fact, "The experience of the German soldiers in Russia in 1941 and 1942 increased this repugnance by direct perception of the primitive life of the Russian villager. But probably more important was the projection onto the Russians of the guilt feelings generated by the ruthless brutality of the Germans in Russia during the occupation period."[160] According to the authors, the *Wehrmacht* did not play a mere secondary role in the Third Reich policies of extermination:

> When the Nazi party salute was introduced in 1944, it was accepted as just one more army order, about equal in significance to an order requiring the carrying of gas masks. The introduction of the *National Socialistische Fuhrungsoffizierte* (Guidance, or Indoctrination Officer), usually known as the NSFO, was regarded apathetically or as a joke. The contempt for the NSFO was derived not from his Nazi connection but from his status as an "outsider" who was not a real soldier. The especially Nazified Waffen SS divisions were never the object of hostility on the part of the ordinary soldier, even when the responsibility for atrocities was attributed to them. On the contrary,

---
159 Ibid., 300.
160 Ibid., 301.

the Waffen SS was highly esteemed, not as a Nazi formation, but for its excellent fighting capacity. Wehrmacht soldiers always felt safer when there was a Waffen SS unit on their flank.[161]

What is relevant is the sociological way in which Shils and Janowitz present the structure of this military body: first, they define the institution of *Wehrmacht* as a primary social group, putting the social cohesion at the center of the analysis. Following a functionalist and microsociological approach, they study—with close attention to inside roles and attitude patterns—how the *Wehrmacht* functioned. As concerns the National Socialist society, they introduce it as a "secondary group," organized and regulated. Their institutional perspective allows for the consideration also of a set of interinstitutional relations. Namely, it helps to compare this body with Nazi German society and to understand the relationships between the several institutions in National Socialist society—how they functioned and what caused their disorganization. What is so remarkable is their multilevel analysis that reflects not only the sociology of William I. Thomas (visible in the similarity that they trace between primary groups and institutions in society) but also that of Durkheim, according to which any primary social group is held together by ties of solidarity, defined as moral bonds of solidarity.[162]

There are rules or principles to which members of the group obey and for which the group remains alive in a cohesive way. Therefore, the elements that hold this military group are strong social ties, guaranteeing in turn the "soldier's company."

Shils and Janowitz identify two broad categories within the infantry: on the one hand, the faithfuls, those who fight until the end of the conflict, and second, the deserters, the few who defect.

Since the authors were interested in understanding what underpinned social cohesion in the *Wehrmacht* of the faithful who fought until the end of the war, and what instead favored the disruption causing others to

---

161 Ibid., 303–4.
162 See William I. Thomas, *The Unadjusted Girl: With Cases and Standpoint for Behavior Analysis* (Boston: Little, Brown, 1923); Shils and Janowitz, "Cohesion and Disintegration in the Wehrmacht in World War II," 280.

defect, they resorted to the sociological concepts of social cohesion and social disintegration.¹⁶³ Indeed, behind the two types of attitudes (loyalty and desertion) was the willingness on the part of Shils and Janowitz to confront strategies adopted by the Third Reich.

Very interesting in their research is the method they used to conduct interviews among prisoners of war and their data analysis of combat observers. It was an entirely new method of investigation for scholarship on the Jewish question and reflected the typical approach of the Chicago School. It can be said that with Shils and Janowitz—and as it will late with Hughes—the Chicago School made room for the studying the Holocaust.

Coming back to the interviews, it turns out how the *Wehrmacht*, a modern military body, was a primary social group, like the family or a community of friends. By reading that the *Wehrmacht* was the only community, it is clear that for both authors the characteristic of uniqueness, representative of a primary social group, is the element that gives identity and stability to the group.¹⁶⁴ What makes it without parallel is the idea of *Gemeinschaft*: the soldiers of the *Wehrmacht* felt the duty to fight, live, and die for their land.¹⁶⁵ Here is what emerged from an interview:

> Thus wrote an idealistic German student in the first world war. A German sergeant, captured toward the end of the second world war, was asked by his interrogators about the political opinions of his men. In reply, he laughed and said, "When you ask such a question, I realize well that you have no idea of what makes a soldier fight. The soldiers lie in their holes and are happy if they live through the next day. If we think at all, it's about the end of the war and then home."¹⁶⁶

When Shils and Janowitz notice that "the primary group continues to be the major source of social and psychological sustenance through

---

163 Shils and Janowitz, "Cohesion and Disintegration in the Wehrmacht in World War II," 280.
164 Ibid., 283.
165 Ibid., 286: "These were, on the whole, young men between 24 and 28 years of age who had had a gratifying adolescence in the most rewarding period of National Socialism. They were imbued with the ideology of *Gemeinschaft* (community solidarity)."
166 Ibid., 284.

adulthood,"¹⁶⁷ it is evident that the *Wehrmacht*, like the family, had the function to raise the individual: it played a fundamental role in the process of formation of persons until maturity. This process of primary education, which forms individual identity, generates affection, loyalty, and in some respects even addiction of the individual to the group. Since persons take shape in the group, they identify themselves with the group. In other words, the primary group of the *Wehrmacht* is cohesive and has a unique feeling, an *idem sentire*, like a feeling in the gut. In other words, an ἀλλὰ φρονεῖν. It is continuously indoctrinated in the same values and beliefs as those of National Socialist ideology:

> This extraordinary tenacity of the German Army has frequently been attributed to the strong National Socialist political convictions of the German soldiers....
>
> The capacity of the primary group to resist disintegration was dependent on the acceptance of political, ideological, and cultural symbols (all secondary symbols) only to the extent that these secondary symbols became directly associated with primary gratifications.¹⁶⁸

As a child feels attitudes of total trust towards his own mother and family, in the same way those who served in the *Wehrmacht* exhibited attitudes of loyalty and trust, mutual respect, love between individuals, to the point of putting the interests of the group—the German *Gemeinschaft*—before those of the individual. Shils and Janowitz's study is based on the idea of a substitution of the *Wehrmacht*, which educates the soldiers, for the family, which educates children. The attentions they gave to the psychological aspect brought them close to the Frankfurt School approach. Moreover, when they speak of a forced socialization based on a social control exercised among members of the *Wehrmacht*, they evidence the role of ideology, indoctrination, and propaganda: "In order to strengthen the traditional Wehrmacht indoctrination efforts, the Nazi Party appointed in

---

167 Ibid.
168 Ibid., 281.

the winter of 1943 political indoctrination officers, called *National Socialistische Fuhrungsoffiziere* (NSFO), to all military formations."[169]

Shils and Janowitz can measure the social cohesion level within the group since this element is the basis of unconditional loyalty or of military defection. Among the factors that ensure maximum cohesion are language and belonging to the same ethnic group, the *Volksdeutsche*, that is, cultural variables encouraging social integration. When a large number of soldiers share them, the social cohesion is greater and the degree of disintegration or defection from the army decreases. On the contrary, ethnic language and age differences among soldiers limit the process of assimilation, to which must then be added factors of a personal nature, such as the instability of the individual, or deviant people. In fact, "In the Wehrmacht, desertions and surrenders were most frequent in groups of heterogeneous ethnic composition in which Austrians, Czechs, and Poles were randomly intermixed with each other."[170] On this kind of solidarity, the political indoctrination of National Socialists ran its course. The cohesive strength of the group creates an experience of community in order to minimize or completely eliminate disagreements in the group, creating a corps without differences, that is, an amorphous mass of great force, and where the ties of solidarity depend on the construction of the "other" as an enemy to eliminate:

> The factor of spatial proximity in the maintenance of group solidarity in military situations must not be underestimated. In February and March of 1945, isolated remnants of platoons and companies were surrendering in groups with increasing frequency. The tactical situation of defensive fighting under heavy American artillery bombardment and the deployment of rear outposts forced soldiers to take refuge in cellars, trenches, and other underground shelters in small groups of three and four. This prolonged isolation from the nucleus of the primary group for several days worked to

---

169 Ibid., 307.
170 Ibid., 285. In the campaigns of North Africa (1943) and France and Germany (1944–45) defections were attributable, according to interviewees' answers, to the coerced condition and the lack of the feeling of empathy among Germans in army units.

reinforce the fear of destruction of the self, and thus had a disintegrative influence on primary group relations.[171]

As scholars of the Chicago School, Shils and Janowitz knew well that physical distance creates social distance, and, therefore, moral detachment ultimately causes the disintegration of social relations. For them, fear, growing stronger in the last few months of the war, disintegrated the group: loyalty and trust in Hitler failed; faced with the evidence of the loss of the war, the first signs of crisis in the Hitler myth came into view:

> An intense and personal devotion to Adolph Hitler was maintained in the German Army throughout the war. There could be little doubt that a high degree of identification with the Fuhrer was an important factor in prolonging German resistance.... The trust in Hitler remained at a very high level even after the beginning of the serious reverses in France and Germany … Even when defeatism was rising to the point at which only one tenth of the prisoners taken as of March 1945 believed that the Germans had any chance of success, still a third retained confidence in Hitler.[172]

From interviews conducted with German prisoners, for older men, Hitler was the one who could ensure economic security after the difficult period of the Weimar years: he was seen as the only one capable of protecting against uncertainty, and this made the strength of his charisma understandable.[173] According to the concept of the authoritarian personality, we can see how the *Wehrmacht* took the place of the father figure in society for the younger Nazi fanatics. This community educated, disciplined, and trained the impulse of its devotees. At the same time, it constituted a factor of discontinuity with the familial authority, with the tradition in the German patriarchal family. There was a component, immediately suppressed, that would never identify with Hitler, nor consider him as a father, and nourish sentiments of hatred towards him. For Shils and

---

171 Ibid., 288–89.
172 Ibid., 304.
173 Cf. ibid.

Janowitz this aspect depended on the different symbolic meaning given to authority.[174]

1.6. THE NSDAP AND THE CONSENSUS: BETWEEN HEBERLE AND LIPSET

In scrutinizing the sociology of 1940s to 1960s—in the years during which several sociologists tried to intensify empirical research and quantitative analysis—we can notice that some relevant works approached the Jewish question with measurement, data, and detailed studies. These works resulted from interest in historical and political sociology that grew after the war. Due to the sociological categories and contents used, post-Holocaust sociology could have benefited from these studies, if they had spread or noticed.

To start, in thinking of national party consensus, the mind immediately runs to *Political Man* by Seymour M. Lipset and his study of the people who voted for Hitler, ensuring his electoral success in 1933. Actually, five years after Hitler's rise, in 1938, another sociologist, Theodore Abel, dealt with the growing popularity of the Nazi movement in *When Hitler Came to Power*.

Here, before analyzing Lipset's work or before trying to better understand his research, it is important to introduce one more sociologist, the émigré scholar Rudolf Heberle, who addressed some key questions for the causes of the success of the Hitler movement, before and after 1933, by explaining how the perception of the Nazi movement changed over time. In the wake of Hans Gerth's studies, Heberle was interested in understanding the reasons that led to the birth of the Nazi Party and accounting for how, within the NSDAP, support for the Führer was maintained.[175]

Heberle's *From Democracy to Nazism* appeared in 1945 when the war was coming to an end.[176] Following the ecological approach of the Chicago

---

174 Ibid., 305.
175 Cf. Theodore Abel, *Why Hitler Came into Power* (Cambridge, MA: Harvard University Press, 1938); reprinted as *The Nazi Movement: Why Hitler Came into Power* (New York: Atherton, 1966); Hans Gerth, "The Nazi Party: Its Leadership and Composition," *American Journal of Sociology* 45, no. 4 (1940): 517–41, http://www.jstor.org/stable/2770263.
176 Heberle, *From Democracy to Nazism*.

School, Heberle analyzes the NSDAP's growing consensus in the region of Schleswig-Holstein, a rural area of Germany. At the base of the Jutland Peninsula, between the Baltic Sea and the North Sea, Schleswig-Holstein is a very wide region, which includes the present-day Schleswig-Holstein and the Danish county of South Jutland. Since 1920, the former Duchy of Schleswig, *Sønderjylland* in Danish, was divided between Germany and Denmark: particularly, North Schleswig was yielded to Denmark after a referendum held at the end of the Great War, following the German defeat. The term *Holstein* comes from Old Norse and Saxon, *Holseta Land*, "land of the woods," while the term *Schleswig* corresponds with the name from the town of Schleswig, from *Schlei*, "inlet in the east," and from *vik*, "settlement" in the ancient Saxon. This "land of the woods," rich in plains and without mountains (the highest point is the Bungsberg, with a height of only 168 meters), with many lakes, especially in the eastern part of Holstein, called "Holstein Switzerland" (*Holsteinische Schweiz*), was studied by Heberle to examine the collapse of electoral support for the democratic parties. *From Democracy to Nazism* arises as an experimental study on political parties in Germany and the rise of National Socialism, starting with a regional case, where it was easier to record the changing of the electorate in favor of the Nazi totalitarian party.

As a student of Ferdinand Tönnies—Heberle was his son-in-law, too[177]—at the University of Kiel, Heberle inherited from the master the theoretical-sociological approach together with a predisposition for field research, the so-called socio-geography (*Soziografie*). These elements made him absolutely the first author able to apply social ecology—as an analysis system pertaining to sociology and geography—to the study of the NSDAP. With a multifaceted education (from 1926 to 1929 he was a researcher at the Rockefeller Foundation and maintained study relationships with *Deutsche Notgemeinschaft der Deutschen Wissenschaft*), he defended his research: a case study representing a bulwark no one could disregard, neither the method adopted nor the information contained therein. In a period very close to the conflict, Heberle excelled in analyzing social attitudes, the psychological conditions of the residents in Schleswig-Holstein, their electoral behavior, and the link between environmental factors and the

---

177 See Papcke and Oppenheimer, "Value-Free Sociology," 279.

structure of society. We read that Hitlerism influenced countryside dwellers especially:[178] electoral support came from the middle class, which included small holders and small entrepreneurs, social groups remaining on the margins and not part of the leading sectors in modern industrial economy.

The case of Schleswig-Holstein explains how NSDAP's support was given by parties that, prior to 1933, had nationalist positions: the subdivision of the land of the woods, that is, the partition of the borders of Schleswig-Holstein, was one of the major points of NSDAP's program. In addition, Lipset, a scholar of movements and political parties, was profoundly influenced by Heberle's study:

> The German-American sociologist Rudolf Heberle has demonstrated in a detailed study of voting patterns in Schleswig-Holstein that the conservatives lost the backing of the small property owners, both urban and rural, whose counterparts in nonborder areas were most commonly liberals, while they retained the backing of the upper-strata conservatives.[179]

Some years later, in 1960, in Lipset's *Political Man*, particularly in the section devoted to the conditions of the democratic regime, when he parsed the fascism of right, left, and center wings, he attempted above all to fathom the reasons or, rather, the conditions that encouraged and prepared the breeding ground for the authoritarian turn within a liberal political system. In this regard, Lipset writes that extremist movements have many points in common: "They appeal to the disgruntled and the psychologically homeless, to the personal failures, the socially isolated, the economically insecure, the uneducated, unsophisticated, and authoritarian persons at every level of the society."[180] As Heberle states, such movements were sustained and carried by "those who for some reason or other had failed to make a success in their business or occupation, and those who had lost their social status or were in danger of losing it.... The masses of the organized [Nazi] party members consisted therefore before

---

178 Heberle, *From Democracy to Nazism*, 32.
179 Lipset, *Political Man*, 142, with reference to Heberle, *From Democracy to Nazism*.
180 Ibid., 175.

1933 largely of people who were outsiders in their own class, black sheep in their family, thwarted in their ambitions."[181]

Forced to immigrate to the United States in 1938 with his family, Heberle succeeded in publishing his research only in 1945, followed by the 1970 and 1971 editions, in a period when the Khrushchev Thaw, from the early 1950s to the early 1960s, still echoed with its benefits. It is crucial to remember this political turning point that changed public consciousness, allowing more scholars to approach burning political issues, such as the consensus to NSDAP.

In the second edition of the book, Heberle points out the connection between his work and certain political trends or movements, called the extreme Right in the United States.[182] Nevertheless, his work remained largely unnoticed: it was mainly due to Lipset, who in *Political Man* quoted different parts of his study, if critics paid attention to *From Democracy to Nazism*. Among Heberle's and Lipset's studies, despite of some years between them, it seems there was a sociological continuum that marks the transition from democracy to Nazism. Thus, in 1960, Lipset deepened the discourse, initiated by Heberle, trying to figure out which political parties guaranteed the political victory of the National Socialist Party. Nevertheless, above all, they explored the community basis of party election by handling ideological arguments differently from the scholars prominent in structural theories. One has to remember that these pieces were written in a period in which the "functionalist-conflict debate" was strong.

Like Abel, Lipset immediately showed his interest in knowing who voted for Hitler: What slice of the German population was in favor of his policy and the destruction of the Jews? The point from which Lipset starts is the analysis of Hitler's electoral constituency in the years 1928–33. This choice has its own explanation: according to Lipset, popular legitimacy is a key element, which cannot be ignored in trying to understand the nature of the social strata that supported Hitler, ensuring a lasting consensus. He studied the social bases of electoral support for the NSDAP, allowing him to identify "who voted for Hitler" and to fathom the ways in which

---

181   Ibid. quoting Heberle, *From Democracy to Nazism*, 10.
182   Here I focus on the second edition of scholar's work; see Heberle, *From Democracy to Nazism: A Regional Case Study on Political Parties in Germany* (New York: H. Fertig, 1970), vii.

common citizens and ordinary people supported Nazi totalitarianism and its policy of racial hygiene. Hence it becomes essential to explore political orientations prior to 1933 to apprehend the reasons that prompted the electorate "to move" their vote in favor of the NSDAP. Therefore the author's choice of speaking, from the title, of "social bases" (of consensus).

Lipset's research followed the work of Abel (1938)—according to whom the support for the NSDAP did not come from the so-called middle class, but from the upper class—and of Heberle (1945). Lipset deserves credit for having incorporated the assumptions of both of his guides. What is interesting is that he took into account more case studies about the social causes of obedience to Hitler. His study completed aspects that Heberle only hinted at. To crown it all, Lipset was the best critic of Heberle: he was the one who appreciated the work to the point of resuming his thesis, supporting it, and making it more convincing. Lipset's rediscovery of these works deserves much appreciation: if Abel's and Heberle's researches were noticed among their contemporary scholars and within their academy, maybe these works could have established good scholarship on the social bases (of consensus) for a totalitarian power in a modern society. However, again, this scholar opportunity was missed.[183] Moreover, this inattention in subsequent years finds a possible answer within segmentation of the discipline that arose in the 1970s and that let sociologists abandon matters concerning voting and party studies (that instead became the research object of political scientists). In other words, Lipset's study seems not to belong to sociology but to the politological realm. This shift removed the attention of sociologists to Lipset's work, letting the field forget his analysis for the NSDAP and his interest in the Jewish question.

1.6.1. The Modern Society behind the Political Man

> Once a politically active middle class is in existence, the key distinction between "left" and "right" political tendencies no longer suffices as a means of differentiation between supporters and opponents of democracy. As Chapter V shows, the further distinction between

---

[183] Cf. Papcke and Oppenheimer, "Value-Free Sociology," 279.

left, right, and center, each with a characteristic ideology and social base, and each with a democratic and an extremist tendency, clarifies the problem of "authoritarianism," and its relationship to the stage of economic development.[184]

To make the issue clearer, it is crucial to analyze Lipset's research in detail. Briefly, his study begins with a question concerning the constituency of the German electorate. The survey, mainly based on the voting results and the election, was conducted in two precise historical periods: the pre-Nazi period (1928–32) and in 1933, when the NSDAP political victory occurred. He examines the voting behavior of Germans, but, unlike Heberle, he does not only consider the case of the rural state of Schleswig-Holstein (a region on the edge of the rest of the country, i.e., occupying a position that is geographically on the borders). This element of extremity, to which we will return, is one of many characteristics on which National Socialist policy relied by supporting the autonomy of regionalist positions against Berlin-centric positions of Prussia. This aspect explains that Lipset's most important priority concerns the changing of electoral support among Germans. If we come back now to the previous question, it can be said that he also examines Lower Saxony (a northwestern state of Germany and a noncentral region by its geographical position) and Bavaria.

In his research, halfway between an ecological approach and a statistical method (with the adoption of concepts such as ideology, social and political movement, social class, and authority), the most important tool is the category of mass: the most irrational social force of modernity. In measuring the NSDAP's consensus through correlation coefficients, with regard to the variables that contributed to the popular legitimacy and National Socialist influence during the Weimar Republic, he refers to the factors of religious nature (Protestants supported the National Socialist policy to a greater extent than did Catholics) and gender (among men the consensus was higher).

What is of account is the relevance Lipset attributes to masses. After completing a historical analysis of modern society and its evolution, Lipset deals with the important sociological notion (related to the Holocaust) of mass. He identifies two types of it. The first is of the "popular" kind and is

---

184   Lipset, *Political Man*, 95–96.

characterized by a political activism that goes against people's rights (the frame of reference is the United States in the late 1950s). The second type, based on what occurred in South Africa during Apartheid, takes the name of "working" (mass) for the fact that it goes against the freedom of the individual. In his ideal types of mass as indistinct collectivity, he also includes commercial and industrial employees, lower officials and workers. It has to be said that Lipset, choosing as analytical tool that of mass, reproposes, in 1960s, the lesson elaborated many times by the Frankfurt School and not widely shared, in a time that the first backlash against the functionalism of Parsons was starting to become more evident. Lipset's lesson reformulates the fact that inside of the mass forms the prejudice and is established and nourished—as in the case of South Africa by ethnic nationalism—a fertile ground in which the roots of forms of racist discrimination are shaped by maintaining the power of the current class. The attention to the South African case is useful for Lipset in explaining what happened in Nazi Germany: when he refers to Tingsten's search on South Africa, he puts in evidence the strength of racism and the role of the masses that in South Africa were related to processes of industrialization and capitalist trade.[185] His discourse becomes more interesting in his use of categories of movement and social class, when he defines what National Socialism was and what its policy of extermination was: specifically, National Socialism is presented as a revolutionary social movement as a working-class authoritarianism along with a right-wing fascism. Lipset (interested in the political behavior of the individual in modern mass society) is intent on asserting his own preference for a democratic society.[186]

In the shadow of totalitarianism, past and present, Lipset tries to discover the conditions necessary for maintaining a stable democratic government: he repeatedly returns to the social reasons that lead to the formation of extremist political movements threatening democratic institutions. His effort to retrieve data in support of his thesis, seeing that there is a connection between certain socioeconomic conditions and the occurrence or duration of democratic regimes, has to be inserted

---

185 See Lipset, *Political Man*, 130.
186 See Shmuel N. Eisenstadt, *Paradoxes of Democracy: Fragility, Continuity, and Change* (Washington, DC: Woodrow Wilson Center Press, 1999).

into the wider discourse of democracy in general.[187] Lipset immediately presents Nazism as a right-wing fascism, an extremist form of middle-class spirit. For the most part, this form is suggested by the lower layers (small holders, small traders, small artisans, and small farmers) of society, and it will stand out for its extremist positions: this class will vote for Hitler for social and economic reasons, related to the evolution of industrial and capitalist society.[188] In reading this piece, one remembers what the sociologist Martin Trow maintained, namely, that the middle class living in an industrial society of full maturity expresses feelings of frustration, to which National Socialism seemed to search for a cure: Hitlerism enjoyed a broad consensus because it offered neither moderate nor reformist solutions, but rather it ensured economic security and favorable situations by limiting the power of monopoly capital and the action of labor unions.[189] What matters is that Lipset's analysis focuses on the extreme power of fascism with its social roots, produced by a process of rapid industrialization or, on the contrary, by its slow development.

If in some ways Lipset reconstructs Heberle's thesis, in other ways he overturns Abel's ideas, according to which the Nazi variant is not an expression of the middle class, but rather of wealthy industrial capitalists.[190] Despite the divergence between Lipset in 1960 and Abel in 1938, the attention to the Nazi movement is almost new in the sociological scholarship approaching these similar themes. Again, let me stress that Abel, Heberle,

---

187 Lipset's sociological interest focuses on man living in the *polis*. Lipset devotes four broad sections to these politician's conditions. For example, in the first, "The Conditions of the Democratic Order," he tackles working-class authoritarianism and fascism of the Left, Right, and center. There are at least four socioeconomic requirements favoring the emergence and maintenance of democracy, namely, the degree of urbanization, the level of industrialization, the degree of education, and per capita income. However, Lipset warns against believing that democracy can be considered consolidated in the absence of a political culture made up of attitudes of tolerance, acceptance of dissent, and criticism of the rulers. See Lipset, *Political Man*, 15.
188 See Lipset, *Political Man*, 135, 136n3, with reference to Harold Lasswell, "The Psychology of Hitlerism," *The Political Quarterly* 4 (1933): 374.
189 Cf. Karl Polanyi, *The Great Transformation* (New York: Farrar and Rinehart, 1944); Martin Trow, *Right-wing Radicalism and Political Intolerance: A Study of Support for McCarthy in a New England Town* (New York: Arno, 1980).
190 Cf. Fritz Thyssen, *I Paid Hitler* (New York: Farrar and Rinehart, 1941); Louis P. Lochner, *Tycoons and Tyrants: German Industry from Hitler to Adenauer* (Chicago: Henry Regnery, 1954).

and Lipset could be seen as early scholarship that paved the way for post-Holocaust sociology.

Looking back at nationalism, it is presented as an opportunist phenomenon, able to grasp the contradictions of Weimar modern society and then turn them to its favor. During the years 1928–33, the NSDAP seems to have been a defense against existing institutions and arose as a "reactionary" fascist party compared to industrial capitalism and the Marxist Left. In fact, Lipset examines the electoral support that parties obtained in the regions of Lower Saxony, Schleswig-Holstein, and Bavaria. These regions are areas of Nazis feuds and constitute a representative sample. These regions are similar to the fiefs of medieval times: they are veritable feuds over the support of Nazis. The first two regions were on the borders of Germany, not in the least irrelevant in the Nazi political agenda. But the Bavarian case is different. Lipset examines the election results of the right-wing Liberals (DVT), of the Left (DDP), of the *Wirthschaftspartei*; of the Conservative Party (DNVP), of the center-Catholic party; of the Socialists (SPD), Communists (KPD), and, finally, of the NSDAP. These are the electoral votes of thirty-five election districts, which come from that crucial year of 1932, when the balance of consensus shifted and leaned in favor of the NSDAP. This recalls what Cesarani stated, namely, that there was an evolution of anti-Jewish policy in the 1930s.

The variables, causing an increase of the electoral consensus for the NSDAP are, for Lipset, essentially of four types. These are mainly (1) socioeconomic factors, which have to do with the processes of industrialization and modernization. Then, of an (2) ideological type, which means that voters hostile to Marxism vote more favorably for the NSDAP. Also, of a (3) political-nationalist kind: persons who are not in favor of the process of Prussianization or Berlin-centric positions, by autonomist positions, vote for the National Socialist Party.[191] Finally, the dependent variable of a (4) religious nature shows how Protestants are more favorable to the rise of the NSDAP.

---

191   This is the voice of federalists: the support comes from border regions.

1.6.2. Lipset's Election Analysis

Lipset is best known as a passionate teacher and scholar at many universities (from Stanford to Harvard, Columbia to Toronto, to cite a few). He is celebrated in many realms and noted for numerous works, but his name is not considered when speaking of the Holocaust: and yet his *Political Man* concerns the Jewish question. For instance, one of his biggest Italian critics, Gianfranco Pasquino, although he presents the work as controversial, but also emphasizing its profound subtlety, does not cite Lipset's attention to Jewish matters. To Pasquino, Lipset (influenced by Adorno's famous study on the "authoritarian personality") goes in search of social conditions that favor authoritarianism. The authoritarian tendencies he identifies depend on a low level of education; lack of political participation of political organizations or voluntary associations; social isolation resulting from the type of activity; economic insecurity; and, finally, the authoritarian footprint of the family life. Pasquino finds this list debatable, because the listed factors are inappropriate to the working class, organized in trade unions or political parties: namely, the components share a subculture of community work. A second discrepancy concerns relationship between religion and democracy: Lipset's hypothesis does not seem reliable, says Pasquino, since the various and numerous varieties of Protestantism provide the first impetus to the democratization.

This provides Lipset with a comprehensive framework: the studies on Protestant reformism and relationship of these high-level officials with Hitler and his followers should be kept in mind.[192] This examination of Lipset's analysis helps to comprehend the failure of Prussian policies and politics, the Nazi ideology, their ability to create political networks in the society, obtaining the social consensus to the power rise. In 1960, such a political analysis as this, and directly connected with the Holocaust theme, was without precedent.

---

192 Cf. Gianfranco Pasquino, "Democrazia ed eccezionalismo," review of *Istituzioni, partiti, società civile*, by Seymour M. Lipset, *New York Review of Books*, March 2010, accessed May 2, 2010, http://www.larivistadeilibri.it/2010/03/pasquino.html.

The first thing Lipset did was to count how many voters the mentioned parties lost and how many votes the NSDAP gained due to their decline. In this manner he could demonstrate that as votes in favor of the NSDAP grew, the percentage of votes in support of liberal parties decreased proportionally. The parties in this period that lost votes were the Catholics, the Marxist Left, and the nationalist conservative right wing, for example, the DNVP. The result of the analysis is particularly significant as it indicates that the Nazis were supported by former liberals, according to Günther Franz, a German political scientist, in conclusion to analysis on voting trends in Lower Saxony, a state in which the Nazis were very strong. He reported similar patterns: in other words, in the main Nazi voters had bourgeois center parties as their origin.[193] Nevertheless, Lipset became a larger-than-life figure in post-Holocaust sociology for having shown that deserter voters belonged to liberal parties. He sums the votes that the NSDAP obtained and establishes a connection between the number obtained and losses incurred by electoral parties: the percentage result achieved was 0.46 percent. Then he estimates the relationship between the votes obtained by the Nazis and the losses suffered by the DNVP: the result that emerges is 0.25 percent. From a comparison of the two percentages it is evident that the voters who left the DNVP for the NSDAP are less than voters abandoned the liberal party. This analytical element on generations of politicians and scholars acquainted with politology was immense, but unfortunately it did not affect sociologists studying the Holocaust.

In dealing with the conceptual category of border (*limen*), Lipset examines the border regions and states, and through an analysis of electoral votes, as in the period 1928–33, he shows that the electoral success of the Nazis was greater in those regions. It thus appears that these regions were among the most conservative and nationalist and, finally, the most resistant to the Treaty of Versailles. This signifies that not only the liberal parties lost many voters, but also the federalist parties of the middle classes or autonomous regional parties. At the base of defection, as in Lower Saxony and Schleswig-Holstein, there was above all the disapproval of the process of national unification. In the same regions, it is possible to

---

193 Lipset, *Political Man*, 143, with reference to Günther Franz, *Die politischen Wahlen in Niedersachsen 1867 bis 1949* (Bremen-Horn: Walter Dom Verlag, 1957).

observe middle-class discontent, especially in cities and in rural areas, because of modern bureaucratization and industrialization. The National Socialist policy was the mouthpiece of all these forms of social discontent, promising regional autonomy, decentralization, and the end of economic insecurity. The autonomist tendencies (it is no coincidence that regionalist parties' programs were inspired by the same economic values pursued by the Nazis) meet the favor of social strata threatened by liberal and monopolist capitalism. In the wake of the Chicago School, Lipset recalled the spatial relationship between the environment, the economic sectors in which they develop, and typical cultural characteristics, explaining how in the border regions, on the edge of national territory, the sense of social and economic insecurity increased together with the possibility of being conquered. Already in 1893, the historian Frederick J. Turner had indicated the meaning of "the frontier" as a passable border to be overcome for American history and at the base of two of the nation's founding values, namely, those of democracy and individualism.[194]

Albeit in a completely different context, the Nazis turned those borderlands of high ethnic nationalism into conquerable ideological lands, in which to pass the new National Socialist ideology of power, that not only denied but also went against national unification of Germany, with Berlin at the center. In the light of what Heberle had written before— "The craftsman [artisan] has to be protected on the one hand against capitalism, which crushes him by means of its factories, and on the other hand against socialism, which aims at making him a proletarian wage-laborer. At the same time the merchant has to be protected against capitalism in the form of the great department stores, and the whole retail trade against the danger of socialism"[195] Interesting is the fact that these phrases are a speech by a farmer named Iversen-Munckbrarup at Rendsburg. It was released on January 21, 1921. The language of the National Socialist movement with its lack of coherence and clearness was, Heberle stated, in 1945, "itself a sociologically significant phenomenon."[196]

---

194   Cf. Frederick J. Turner, *The Frontier in American History* (Tucson: University of Arizona Press, 1986).
195   Heberle, *From Democracy to Nazism*, 47, quoted in Lipset, *Political Man*, 145.
196   Ibid., 47n45.

Lipset emphasizes the close relationship between the regionalist ideology, opposing centralization, and the special interests of small business, especially by parliamentary alliance of the two most important regional parties, the *Deutschland-Hanoverischen Partei* of Lower Saxony and the *Bauern und Mittelstansbund* of Bavaria, with the *Wirtschaftpartei* as the party representing small business. There were at least three main aspects of their programs: first, an aversion to Prussian policy; second, the refusal to consider Berlin as the center of German culture; and, finally, the privileges to residents of the place in recruitment of labor. Behind the disapproval of Prussian policy hid the hostility to industrial capitalism; in the 1924 elections, the regionalist parties, which were responsible for these programs, were preparing the way for National Socialism. From the election results, Lipset notes that the NSDAP obtained the most votes, especially in small rural communities or communities not very urbanized, jealous of the development of large cities. The environment of the small communities, like the narrow rural environments and the National Socialist circles, was more conducive to NSDAP policies, because it was contrary to the modernization accomplished in large urban areas. Lipset arrives at the claim that the lower part of the middle class, composed of small landowners in rural areas and of the urban petty bourgeoisie, supported the Nazis.

What follows is a significant statistical correlation concerning the numerical density of population and the percentage of Nazis votes. This relationship was being studied in 1932, when, following the outcome of the election ballots, in German cities with more than 25,000 inhabitants it was found that the percentage of Nazis votes was inversely proportional to the number of people present in the urban area. This means that in cities with more than 25,000 inhabitants, the NSDAP reached a lower percentage of votes than the Catholic Party and the DNVP, which received, on the contrary, the most votes.

The only exception, and here the religious variable came into play, was the city of Berlin, a large conurbation, but also with a unique Protestant election district, where the Nazis, in July 1932, won less than 25 percent of the votes, which explains how Nazi theory clashed with the positions in favor of Berlin. A further correlation concerns the middle class of wage earners or of small owners: as the index of economic crisis increased, the percentage of votes in favor of the Nazis rose in direct proportion, while the percentage in favor of liberal parties decreased, always in a direct and proportional way. Still, Lipset noted here that men voted more than women.

He also studied the "percentage of the members" of the Nazi Party in relation to the rest of the German population, divided by categories. From the comparison conducted in 1933, one can see that it was the skilled working class, independent workers, and domestic staff who supported the Nazis, as they had been ideologically influenced by the family in which they lived. So, as Abel did in 1938, Lipset prepared the Nazi ideal-type voter of 1932: "a middle-class self-employed Protestant who lived either on a farm or in a small community, and who had previously voted for a centrist or regionalist political party strongly opposed to the power and influence of big business and big labor."[197]

Small wonder that not every Nazi voter possessed all the features put together: as each party undertook to procure votes, the NSDAP also strove to reconcile interests within the electoral district. This signifies that among Nazis voters were both the middle class and the unemployed. Additionally, Lipset presents Nazism not as a class movement, using a variable from Bendix's studies: it was the abstainers, the uninterested in politics, young voters, and, again, those who had never voted or had unclear political positions who increased the percentage of the Nazi vote:

> Geiger, Bendix, and others who concluded that the Nazis derived their early backing from traditional nonvoters based this opinion on the overall election figures which showed an enormous increase of Nazi votes simultaneous with the sudden participation of over four million previous nonvoters.[198]

Lipset's lesson concerns the pivotal role of democratic organizations. Lipset investigates authoritarianism of the middle class, particularly

---
197 Lipset, *Political Man*, 149.
198 Ibid., 151. Recall that Bendix's opinion changed later. Cf. ibid., 150n32.

its causes and its origins and the fact that extremism is a choice. Specifically, he refers to the workers organizations with liberal positions belonging and opposed to communism and demonstrating in favor of a democratic regime:

> In Germany, the United States, Great Britain, and Japan, individuals who support the democratic left party are more likely to support civil liberties and democratic values than people *within* each occupational stratum who back the conservative parties. Organized social democracy not only defends civil liberties but influences its supporters in the same direction.[199]

In his research, many times the categories of election and electoral participation recur to clarify the importance of the election at the base of democratic life of a country. Moreover, "a number of sociologists in pre-Hitler Germany suggested that the concept of the 'generation' had to be added to such structural categories as class or ethnic group to explain political behavior."[200] It can said that fifty years after the publication of *The Political Man*, Lipset's text is still new in some respects.

1.7. "GOOD PEOPLE AND DIRTY WORK": HUGHES

Now, let me introduce one of the central works under consider in my study here. That in a factory the division of labor is combined with the rationalization of time was a well-known truth to Everett C. Hughes, author of two misunderstood essays, "Good People and Dirty Work," written in 1948 and only published in 1962, and "The Gleichshaltung of the German Statistical Yearbook" at the end of 1955. In the form of a letter, in "Good People and Dirty Work" he dealt in an early way with the banality of evil, during a seminar at McGill University, while the scenarios of World War II were still in everyone's eyes, and an intense revival of

---

199 Ibid., 128.
200 See Lipset, *Political Man*, 265n2. Age also constrains the type of voting or preference, an analytic factor considered previously by Abel.

sociology was underway.²⁰¹ It is interesting to notice that, whereas "Good People," relating to the Holocaust, was neither published nor discussed in the academic media, "The Gleichshaltung," concerning the Third Reich and highlighting political manipulations of the Reich in the compilation of statistical yearbooks of the German Departmental Offices, was indeed published but not adequately disseminated among scholars.²⁰² This latter essay did not meet any delay in publication, above all because the title does not address political issues and the methodology was consistent with the teachings of U.S. academic positivism. Nevertheless, it did not receive critical attention. In a postwar Europe, the title of the piece, "Good People and Dirty Work," was too close, from a political point of view, to the Jewish question. This strongly influenced the reception of his work, delaying its publication for fourteen years. Therefore, the critical review of his study is scarce and quite recent.

"Good People" may be considered a work inaugurating post-Holocaust sociology has more than one reason. First, in the essay, published in *Social Problems*, social causes lead good people (specifically the German SS and the common people) to practice or simply to allow the dirty work—the social dirty work of exterminating the Jews—and these are analyzed in a very early way, in 1948. Second, among the key issues are the legitimacy of the German National Socialist government; the internal administration of the SS; and the social dirty work, which includes both organized and divided labor in the concentration camp, and the work of single individuals, morally

---

201 See Hughes Papers at Boston College, Burns Library, classified as BC Faculty Papers (private-familiar documents, manuscripts, acts of government), and at the Regenstein Library in Chicago. Hughes archive must be visited, because in 1938-61, in conducting his research on the Jewish question and teaching in Chicago, he could not publish his results. About Hughes as father of the category of banality of evil, see Subseries 6, Manuscripts, Box 109 Folder 4 "Good People and Dirty Work," 1948-1963; Series X Oversize, Box 145-147, last accessed March 8, 2016, https://www.lib.uchicago.edu/e/scrc/findingaids/view.php?eadid=ICU.SPCL. ECHUGHES#idp151097072. See further Arendt papers at the Library of Congress, Manuscript Division in Washington, DC, last accessed March 8, 2016, https://memory.loc.gov/ammem/arendthtml/arendthome.html, to compare the years in which both Arendt (1963-75) as professor and visiting lecturer, and Hughes (1938-61) taught in Chicago.

202 "The wissenschaftliche Soldaten or 'soldiers of science,' as the Third Reich dubbed statisticians, neither conceived nor were responsible for Nazi policy, but they were its instrument" (Traverso, *The Origins of Nazi Violence*, 43).

separated in society. Properly, this dirty work of violence and indifference against Jews is defined as "social" by Hughes: it means that the destruction was possible because that society was devoid of moral obligations.

To illustrate the operation of the National Socialist state, Hughes uses the concepts of "division of labor," "modern industry," and "alienation." His categories of "dirty work" and "good people" are directly borrowed from industrial environments of the city of Chicago and recall the mainstream of the Chicago School.[203] Concerning the "dirty work," Hughes reveals, in the National Socialist state, a specialized division of tasks among the structures of the army, Nazi Party, bureaucracy, and economic apparatus, which immediately recalls the dirty work practiced in modern industry, based on the principle of rational and uniform organization of labor. As for the "good people," there is a lot in common between the good people of the National Socialist society and that of the modern factory, where the craftsperson ceases to exist: instead of him, in contemporary industry, there is a wage-earning mass, unqualified and always replaceable. Apropos of this idea, Traverso speaks of an "intelligent gorilla,"[204] of a worker without intellectual autonomy and one able to perform merely standardized actions. Thus, in this environment there is only room for a man without a brain or imagination, who, because of the delegation of functions and obedience to a head, resulting from the division of labor, loses any responsibility and accountability for his actions. Good people are thus shaped: subject to a social division of labor in the factory, they also experience a moral division in everyday and social life. Such are the good people of the National Socialist state: common people, banal, indoctrinated, and terrorized, but also uncritical and unreflecting, who obey the leaders and perpetrators of violence, all driven by extreme anti-Semitic hatred.

1.7.1. Beyond the Banality of Evil

When I argue that post-Holocaust sociology might have commenced with "Good People," I put into evidence a worthy aspect concerning the

---

203 See Subseries 6, Manuscripts, on unpublished articles about the problems of sociology: especially, Box 108, Folder 20–21, Special articles and lectures, list, manuscripts, 1926–1961; Box 109, Folder 5, Race, unpublished manuscripts, lectures, 1948–1964.
204 Traverso, *The Origins of Nazi Violence*, 39.

academic status of sociology and its increase of publications, that is, with the stages of research and the time and manner of publication of sociological works. This may be perceived as a kind of a normative symbolic system of power into which several sociologists were placed and indeed invested: this signifies that, if "Good People" had been published right away, it would have been counted in post-Holocaust sociology, inaugurating therefore this strand of Holocaust Studies.

The case of Hughes is significant. During a seminar at McGill University in 1948, he discussed normal people, concentration camps, and the dirty work of extermination, in the presence of a very attentive audience. But his paper was only published in a scientific journal about fourteen years later: the summer of 1962, in *Social Problems* (it would be presented again, in the winter of 1963, with even greater emphasis in a conference).[205] At that date, Hughes received little critical notice for his studies related to the Jewish question: attention that he has finally obtained for his Holocaust research is not only recent but scarce. Even when it was published, scholars undervalued its aims and targets. This argues for a sociological delay in the study the Holocaust, but it misses an important point about the roles of sociologists.

In the early 1960s, his shift toward publication of "Good People" was linked, first, to the English-language version of Elie Wiesel's *Night* (1961), and then to the advent of the trial of Adolf Eichmann. However, there is another reason, too: it deals with the contemporary politics of John F. Kennedy and the movement for civil rights for blacks. Nevertheless, Hughes's recognition among scholars came in the 1970s, when a set of his sociological works were gathered and published together under the name of *The Sociological Eye* (1971): a direct result of the Six-Day War and other political events changing civil and cultural world scenarios. These were the years in which the Holocaust could have been conceived of in a different way and related to other events. Moreover, in those years, the

---

205 See Subseries 5: Visiting Seminars and Lectures; in particular, Box 83, Folder 16, McGill University, Post War Housing and Community Planning Lecture Series, lecture, March 14, 1944 (it contains data on the postwar period at McGill University where he teaches a course of study on the Holocaust under a different name, as evident from Box 77, Folder 1, Sociology, 325, "What's in a Name?" lecture, notes, correspondence, 1950). See also Box 87, Folder 11, War propaganda, publications, 1940–41.

thought of Fackenheim, who shaped theoretically the relation between the Holocaust and the State of Israel, emerged as a milestone: ideas issued originally in 1974 and reproposed in the 1997 edition of *God's Presence in History*.[206] It was a theoretical watershed in which the Jewish philosopher strongly noticed the importance of the peace among the Jews and in Israel to account for what happened to the Jews during the World War II. It was a landmark work that cleared the ground for Holocaust thought in general.

The starting point for Hughes's reflection was a trip to Germany in 1948, when on a train full of people, back to Frankfurt after a hike in the Taunus Mountains on the occasion of the Feast of the Ascension, a woman standing beside him said, "But, Mein Herr, you are not an average American; that is, racially. I would have said an Englishman or a man from Hamburg."[207] The thought, repeated several times and expressing much more than a simple impression, drove him back to the subject of racial prejudice and the consequence of such ideas as "the Nordic ideal." He had already denounced the strength of the ideology of race as the cause of social disintegration in modern industrial environments of the early twentieth century in "The Knitting of Racial Groups in Industry." This essay of 1946 puts together the themes of industrialization, division of labor, and racial prejudice and was a preparatory work to "Good People," especially because Hughes deals with two consequences of racial prejudice:[208] the isolation between individuals of the same society, regardless of organic solidarity, and then social anomie, which slowly leads to the unjust social division of labor. What he stresses is precisely how racial attitudes and predispositions assume specific connotations in industrial

---

206 Cf. Richard L. Rubinstein and John K. Roth, *Approaches to Auschwitz, Revised Edition: The Holocaust and Its Legacy* (Louisville, KY: Westminster John Knox, 2013), 446n69.

207 Everett C. Hughes, "Innocents Abroad, 1948, or How to Behave in Occupied Germany," *Sociologica* 2 (2010): 1, accessed March 28, 2012, doi:10.2383/32715. See Series II, Correspondence; Series IV: Writings and Research Material, Subseries 1: Travel Diaries and Memoranda, Box 96 Folder 4-8 (to comprehend political events in 1948–58); Subseries 2, Research Materials, Box 99 Folder 23, Germany, Frankfurt diary, Spring 1948 (to acquaint better with his stay in Germany: this diary served as the basis for the conference on the banality of evil then became the essay "Good People"); Box 100, Folder 7, Germany, "Innocents Abroad, 1948, or How to Behave in Occupied Germany," 1948.

208 Everett C. Hughes, "The Knitting of Racial Groups in Industry," *American Sociological Review* 11, no. 5 (1946): 512–19. See Box 100, Folder 9, Committee on Human Relations in Industry, Race Relations in Industry, notes, manuscripts, 1944–1945.

environments. In 1946, when Hughes wrote (while the World War II dead were still being counted), employee rights and workplace safety were not fully established, and they were by no means a certain eventuality. In an environment where guaranteed rights or medical insurance coverage were rare, it is obvious that workers felt increasingly threatened and, for that reason, they tended to coalesce with their peers (by age, gender, or race) against those perceived as different.

At the time that Hughes returned to reflecting on the strength of racial prejudice, the extermination of the Jews, the product of the ideology of the Aryan race, was very recent. Hughes warned that racial prejudice, once rooted, takes deep root and is difficult to dislodge. It had already resulted in the destruction of the Jews, but in postwar Germany after the Holocaust, it continued to live. On that train to Frankfurt, Hughes realized for the first time that the extermination had not only been practiced by those who directly killed the Jews. It was and would be made possible by all those "good people" who used to nickname the Jews "Kikes" in a derogatory way, and that with their manners they had consented and still consented in making them a subrace to be exterminated.

Hughes tackled the operating mechanisms of prejudice and especially its method of deployment that, if at in the first instance it led to the Holocaust, it would subsequently lead to a lack of accountability, by making those who had not directly taken part in the killing feel like strangers to the extermination and thus innocent. In 1945, Karl Jaspers focused attention on the "question of German guilt." For Hughes, the temptation to feel, on that train, "without fault," namely, unconnected with the facts, in the same way that Peter denies knowing Jesus ("the Peter temptation is there"), was strong.[209] However, the American world in which he lived and where prejudice against blacks was strong drove him, at the end of the 1940s, to denounce the consequences of racial prejudice.

As a sociologist observing the social reality contemporary to him, Hughes addressed what happened to the Jews. What led him to study such a delicate issue were incidents of racism occurring in his American context

---

209 Hughes, "Innocents Abroad, 1948," 4.

and familiar to him: he wanted to prevent other "good people" behaving towards blacks in the United States in the same way that banal persons had behaved towards the Jews in Europe. It can be said that Hughes's sociology is a metasociology in the sense that, through the notions of anti-Semitism and racism, he explains the Holocaust in order to denounce the new forms of American racism against blacks, Japanese, Canadians, and others.

Hughes, half American and half French, was a scholar with a dynamic personality and multifaceted training,[210] and, often on the road to Germany, he wrote a piece that may be defined "by many issues." In his study, questions of great value (which would be recovered and analyzed with greater passion by other authors in subsequent decades) arose. The three central aspects in "Good People" are (1) the role of the German National Socialist government, since without a legitimate government there would be no mass extermination; (2) the army of the SS; and (3) the social dirty work, which included not only organized and divided labor of the concentration camp, but also that practiced by individuals in modern society without moral obligations, in step with the rhythms and times of industrial capitalism *sine ira ac studio*: "Max Weber realized that moral indifference constituted an essential feature of modern bureaucracy, which was specialized and therefore irreplaceable, but separated from the means of work and unaffected by the final outcome of its actions."[211] This social dirty work of annihilation, indifference, and violence against Jews was indeed social since it was only possible because in Nazi society the universe of moral obligations was untied to, and without any moral cogency of, the individual.

The short but intense eight pages of "Good People" describe how the persons were unable to control the process of their actions in the same way as factory workers, for whom only the principles of calculation and segmentation of skills counted. In similar environments, conditions increasing phobias against enemies (to be eradicated) develops easily. Therefore, it was in late

---

210 Although known as a Chicago sociologist, he taught in a number of universities, from McGill University to Boston University, passing through the Chicago School (1938–61) and Brandeis University (1961–68).
211 Traverso, *The Origins of Nazi Violence*, 42.

nineteenth-century France that Édouard Drumont was among the first to oppose the "Israelite" merchant, "cerebral, and calculating," to the "Aryan" farmer, heroic and creative.[212] The context in which the Nazi belief took root formed a fertile ground for modern phobias and stereotypes. Under the Nazi violent terror, the population easily accepted the messianic promises of the ideology with its mythical traits and reassurance for the fortunes of Germany. The society of good people is the society in which the individual believes, wrongly, that the other is dangerous. This dichotomous definition between Aryans and Jews constitutes the basis of nationalist culture, based on the construction and negative stigmatization of the other, considered an enemy, which first resulted in the persecution of the "other-Jews," and ended with the phases of ghettoization, concentration, and extermination. The distinction "we–they," between "ingroups" and "outgroups," is the initial ring of nonexistent solidarity among individuals of the same society and passes for a denied identity called racism.[213]

According to Hughes, and unlike that affirmed later by Bauman, the action of the single individual matters greatly in anti-Jewish policy: virtuous and individual cruelty (possible because of the ideology of racial superiority and purity) has to be adjoined to extermination practices in the gas chambers. To understand the nature and roots of prejudice, Hughes writes that it is necessary to go through the issue of guilt. His reflection is essentially this: Is the population in postwar Germany able to come to terms with what has happened and with the prejudice? At the base of the work, he places witnesses' experiences (specifically, he asks if "they knew something") and traditional concepts of sociology, such as the division of labor and organic solidarity.

In the early 1930s, Hughes had already visited Germany, the land of the fathers of sociology. During his stay in 1948, he publicly reflected on the causes that led ordinary citizens to share the work of extermination, in modern society, in accordance with the rules and rhythms typical of the modern factory. Especially, he wondered why the Jews, who were German

---

212 Ibid., 131.
213 See Arnold M. Rose, "Comment on 'Good People and Dirty Work,'" *Social Problems* 10, no. 3 (1963): 285–86; Renate Siebert, *Il razzismo: Il riconoscimento negato* (Rome: Carocci, 2003).

citizens, were not defended or protected by their fellow compatriots. When Hughes uses the term "good people," he refers both to those who practiced the work of extermination in *Vernichtungslagers*, easily willing to exercise a power legitimized by violence, and to those who perpetrated the killing from a distance, leaving it to be done without intervening or ever entering the death camps. Focusing on the reasons pressing good people to conduct extermination or to allow others to do it, he deliberately ignores the presence in Germany of an age-old anti-Semitism, atavistic and stubborn, a thesis instead widely supported in the following decades by other authors, such as Daniel Goldhagen.

The witnesses with whom Hughes talked, and thanks to whom he sustained his own thesis, were very different from each other: he found himself faced with individuals who had made an admission of guilt (albeit quickly), ones who had removed everything violent from their recollections, completely ignored the reality of genocide, or were silent. Finally, he talked with people who claimed to know nothing or who did not believe, at the time of National Socialism, that the Nazi extermination program could actually be realized. Faced with these cases, Hughes questioned if they knew the truth:

> The architect: "I am ashamed for my people whenever I think of it. But we didn't know about it. We only learned about all that later. You must remember the pressure we were under; we had to join the party. We had to keep our mouths shut and do as we were told. It was a terrible pressure. Still, I am ashamed. But you see, we had lost our colonies, and our national honour was hurt. And these Nazis exploited that feeling. And the Jews, they *were* a problem. They came from the east. You should see them in Poland; the lowest class of people, full of lice, dirty and poor, running about in their Ghettos in filthy caftans. They came here, and got rich by unbelievable methods after the first war. They occupied all the good places. Why, they were in the proportion of ten to one in medicine and law and government posts!"[214]

---

214 Hughes, "Good People and Dirty Work," *Social Problems* 10, no. 1 (1962): 5, http://www.jstor.org/stable/799402.

What is interesting is that he introduces, for his own study, the interview method, a clear novelty in post-Holocaust sociology of the 1940s and a common sociological device for the Chicago School. In his dialogues with witnesses, he can stress that among the factors pushing for the "dirty work" of extermination in Nazi society, there was above all the strength of racial prejudice. Einstein said many times that "it is more difficult to break a prejudice than an atom."[215] Hughes realizes the terror practiced for years (degenerated into collective guilt, removed at the end of the war) only when one of his witnesses, an architect, suddenly stops talking and goes into confusion:

> He continued: "Where was I? It is the poor food. You see what misery we are in here, Herr Professor. It often happens that I forget what I was talking about. Where was I now? I have completely forgotten."[216]

On one side the forgetfulness shows how the human mind struggles to accommodate some situations, while on the other it reveals the stubbornness of "those who have seen" in not admitting the truth. Jaspers has also acknowledged that it was easier to remove everything that they could not accept or that for which they did not want to take responsibility: "How hard it is to believe that men will be as bad as they say they will. Hitler and his people said: 'heads will roll,' but how many of us—even of his bitterest opponents—could really believe that they would do it."[217]

There are also those who, like the professor in the interview, were willing to publicly break the silence about Nazi atrocities with articles or speeches at seminars. Hughes, however, ignores the number of people ready, like him, to tell the truth or the way in which the events actually happened. For him, every society has some good people when the power falls into the hands of fanatics, and social order is constructed on the basis of false promises. It is not a radical evil against which nothing can be done. Rather, faced with the irresponsibility of the "good people," Hughes

---
215 See Albert Einstein, *Ideas and Opinions* (New York: Random House, 1954).
216 Hughes, "Good People and Dirty Work," 5.
217 Ibid., 6.

suggests encouraging the formation of public opinion capable of sharing the same values, weaving networks of solidarity among people, a concept (that of solidarity) that Hughes mainly derives from *Der SS-Staat* by Eugen Kogon. Here it is possible to notice the influence of functionalism of historians and their thought and the mechanisms through which the morality of the individual and the moral solidarity of society are destroyed within the camps. These aspects, introduced by Hughes, would also be studied by Arendt, Fein, Bauman, and Gamson at a later time.

1.7.2. The Theory of Flow and Empirical Evidence at the Basis of Hughes's Thinking

Going beyond his multiple-level reading, Hughes observes critically the social reality and builds a new sociological knowledge through which he explains historical phenomena. It is an *in situ* observation, which is both a sociological concept and an analytical method. This emerges when, for instance, he employs some sociological categories (such as class, division of labor, career, ethnicity, institution, function) to explicate other notions. In "Good People," he uses the concepts of division of labor, modern industry, and alienation: his aim is that of illustrating the structure of the National Socialist state. This means we have to consider two levels of interpretation: namely, the immediately sociological signifier (i.e., modern industry) —the container of the discourse—and then the "meaning" of the signifier (i.e., the sociological notions to which Hughes wants to refer). Behind the "dirty work" and the "good people" of the modern industry (two conceptual moments that refer to different situations) there are obviously modernity, industry, the division of labor, and the alienated class of the factory, but there is above all the "dirty work" and the "good people" of the National Socialist state. The "good people" are the normal people, ordinary and common, while the concept of "dirty work" results from the entire reference model of Hughes, who combines the classical ecology of Park with functionalism and the structuralist interactionism. The sociological institution of a "going concern" and dealing with human ecology shapes his approach and his work on the Holocaust.[218] The "dirty work," a term that in Hughes's studies translates the concept of division of labor, represents a dynamic institution, which evokes, on the one hand, the concept of struggle and competition for survival, and, on the other, it refers to the tensions that are generated in the modern factory. It is this "dirty work," namely, this struggle for survival in the working environment of the modern factory, that creates the "good people" (normal and banal) performing simple mechanical work without reflecting on their actions. To illustrate his thesis, Hughes refers to the environment of modern industrialization in which the division and specialization of labor in the factory generate moral and social division, especially between those belonging to diverse sex, social class, and ethnic backgrounds. In this context, the organic solidarity among similars, and of which Durkheim speaks, disappears or thins out because of the absence of solidary norms, typical of modern society divided morally before and socially after. Hughes's theoretical assumption, which comes from the environments of modern industry of the city of Chicago, constitutes his sociology as a practice of thought that is at once both "interpretative and ecological." At the basis of the essay there is his sociological eye and investigation of reality in a critical way: he analyzes social phenomena within the institutional scenarios and across social processes. In other words, the individual empirical case is just the starting point for addressing more general issues, which are mutually comparable: for example, Hughes moves from the definition of the individual situation towards an institutional scenario. His observation operates on two levels interacting with each other, namely, subjective-individual and institutional, where the subject is placed. The individual is conditioned by the institution, which in turn influences the same

---

218 Rick Helmes-Hayes, who has recovered many of Hughes's works along with his several fragments, gives this reference model the name of interpretative institutional ecology. Any institution is constantly changing and is called a "going concern" and has, or rather is made up of, tasks and roles established in constant flux. Institutional change is due to the interaction between people within the institution and in the struggle waged by these in order to survive. The struggle for survival with all its consequent adaptation takes the name of "human ecology."

individual. To interpret the Nazi state, Hughes, able to grasp the dynamics that exist between the various institutions, relates the individual self with the personal institution, nested in a competitive ecosystem, explaining that good people exist because mechanisms of competition are created within the society. Analyzing the practices of the division of labor in which he encounters situations of rivalry between individuals, he introduces the modern industrial society as the ideal laboratory and, at the same, as the perfect sociological concept for describing the nature of the National Socialist state. The general division of labor of the modern factory affects the social and intimate sphere of the common people, their principles of moral solidarity: it is related to the struggle for social survival and has several repercussions among individuals, producing social anomie as a result. This society, modern and industrialized, exhibits new social phenomena, such as extracontinental immigration, the influx of a new workforce belonging to different ethnic groups, and minorities.

What Hughes stresses is that the new realities are perceived as social threats to be fought immediately as insidious and dangerous; and the Jews are depicted as the biggest target of social hate: this explains the speed with which the totalitarian ideology of a better and perfect society, which legitimates genocidal practices, takes root.

Hughes's methodology, in many aspects "Simmelian," equates the "micro" establishment of divided labor of the factory with the "macro" establishment of the division of political labor in society. "Good People" comes from an empirical background, when he gives birth to the concept of "moreso" and studies labor relations of racial and ethnic type. It reflects a competitive ecosystem that dominates structures and affects common habits. A significant concept he adopts is that of "moral-spatial competition." When I argue that his essay is a *chef d'oeuvre* in post-Holocaust sociology, I refer also to his methodology in understanding a social fact, that is, when he combines an empirical case. It is a set of concepts with the mind of a marginal man (called by him "outsider") who observes, working for associations in a free manner, but who is always guided (without getting caught) by absolute theories. In this manner, the theory is not the mere result from combined data and ends with producing others: on October 19, 1977, at the Round

Table at the University of Toronto, Hughes expounded the methods of this sociological process. In the author's eyes, it worked well in Nazi society.

1.7.3. Halfway between Modern Industry and National Socialist Society

Is it proper to say that dirty work is an immoral division of labor? Hughes pools factory work with the dirty work of the National Socialist state, and the workers of the modern factory with the people who live under the Nazi regime. Affiliating the ecological aspect of institutions and the sociopsychological features of collective behavior, he prepares a theoretical transposition with a double meaning, already explicit in the title. Consisting of two parts, it contains the metaphor of the dirty work of the factory and that perpetrated by the Nazis. The concept of division of labor that lies behind the expression "dirty work" is primarily a social institution ("a going concern").

Hughes uses the institution of factory work category because this concept is meaningful sociologically and important to his aim of explaining how Nazi society works with its various offices and specialized division of tasks and functions. This guarantees the order and control of economic production, and it also produces people-merchandise, employed persons whose interests are not clear even to themselves. For Hughes, the social division of labor in the factory reproduces alienated people who do not have a consciousness of their own in society and whose benefits are mantled by ideologies that justify existing relations, represented as carriers of universal interests, finishing with legitimating forms of social command and control of the totalitarian type. Similarly, the Nazi state, based on fundamental structures, such as the army, the NSDAP, bureaucracy, and the economic apparatus, organizes the economic life and every other aspect of society, of both a political and cultural nature, thanks to a specialized division of tasks and charges.

Clearly, if the city of Berlin inspired Georg Simmel to write *Die Grosstädte und das Geistesleben*, the conditions of modern industrial Chicago stimulated Hughes in the late 1940s to talk about the social disorder of the Nazi state, through the ideal laboratory of the dirty work of the factory. He explained, first during his lectures in 1948, and then in his writing, how in the Third Reich's society the division of labor was a process used to build a totalitarian state. In other words, Hughes through the explanatory model of the modern factory (which he knows and sees as similar to that of Nazi modern society) is able to describe how the totalitarian society arose in Germany. In essence, the realm of the modern factory constitutes an organized and structured system where things become more efficient and, in a sense, more controlled by instrumental logic, according to which the superiors have to be followed. Environments exposed to threats and therefore in dangerous conditions voluntarily predispose people of these places, alienated from the working practices and set aside economically and socially, to a struggle for social survival against foreigners, immigrants, or, more simply, against those who do not share the same cultural heritage. The alienation of labor affects the moral solidarity among individuals who live in the same town. The competitive mechanisms or pressures of a selective nature leading these wage earners, who are normal and common people, to be willing to do anything to count for something and deserve some greater social recognition, are not few. It is a social instinct that regulates survival and that Hughes calls the "ecology of modernity."

Normal and ordinary were people indoctrinated by the Nazi myth that promised the creation of a perfect society. Once the bonds of solidarity between counterparts loosen, people are easily more willing to follow leaders and to agree to be part of a system that monitors and ensures public order. Unable to develop their own vision of the facts that are antagonistic to that of the ethical state to which they belong, they are more easily indoctrinated. Banal people slowly educated to hate practice extreme acts of violence. The Third Reich existed and survived thanks to the good people too: some societies, such as Nazi society, arose by performing tasks of organizational rationality and producing a collective will compliant in their work, like that of the good people. At the same time that strategies for social adaptation are adopted, particularly genocidal practices by the state to solve issues of public importance, conceived in terms of human ecology, make people feel protected. This means that concepts such as "natural selection," "survival of the fittest," of "adaptation of the best species" to the environment are transferred in the social field and filled with political content. Therefore, a rational selection organized by the state replaces the natural selection of the best.

As wage workers compete with each other and fight for social survival owing to the contingent conditions of insecurity, similarly, for Hughes, in the pre-Nazi society there were situations that threatened the existence of the Germanic culture, issues of human ecology that led ordinary persons to fight among themselves. In this totalitarian society, where social order alienates ordinary people, acting without thinking and obeying only the authorities, they practiced hate crimes.

Starting from the study of special collections of Hughes's Papers, at Regenstein Library at the University of Chicago and the J. J. Burns Library at Boston College, Helmes-Hayes sheds light on the peculiar nature of Hughes's "sociological eye," which exceeds the purely naturalistic, descriptive, ethnographic explanation of interactionism and absolutely does not ignore the ecological dynamics of interinstitutional relations.[219]

1.7.4. "Good People" according to Critical Essays and Reviews

To comprehend what Hughes elaborates sociologically, we should analyze what scholars understood about it and how his work affected the academic realm, that is, how his sociological knowledge of the Holocaust was reached in scholarship. By reading "Good People" through the academic critical reviews—an expedient approach in post-Holocaust sociology—it is possible to handle the contemporary assumption of the sociological delay.

First, criticism of "Good People" can be divided into two distinct blocks: that of immediate criticism, following the publication of the piece, and that of distant criticism, which instead comes much later. The initial discovery of this author begins in 1971, after the republication of some of his essays into a single volume titled *The Sociological Eye*. At this point, it is important to underscore that the early 1970s were for sociology fruitful years characterized by a kind of a reawakening of the discipline in which

---
219 Let me thank Rick Helmes-Hayes for some relevant information about Hughes's papers; Helmes-Hayes, e-mail message to author, September 17, 2011.

along with the sociological researches there gradually developed relevant sociological reviews and journals. It is in this renewed context, cultural and political, that Hughes's work was revalued.[220] In several fields of knowledge, mostly what unlocks the broad silence for the accounting for the Holocaust is, first, the fear for another destruction after the 1967 Six-Day War, when another Holocaust seemed to be possible again, this time in Israel. Second, as a result of the war, the attention that the Jewish philosopher Fackenheim was able to channel into the Holocaust. His 614th commandment—"Thou shalt not give Hitler a posthumous victory"[221]—would always mark his thought in general: it is going to kick off a new period, paving the way for free thought, and that would not cease, especially, after the end of the Vietnam War, when the image of a democratic America changed.

As Fackenheim said in 1968, "Only after many years did significant Jewish responses begin to appear. Little is and can be said even now."[222] In the words of Amos Kenan, "I want peace peace peace peace, peace peace peace," written immediately after the war in "A Letter to All Good People." Both statements were heard clearly.[223]

Looking back to Hughes, perusing of the academic journals means examining the appreciation for his work. Among the criticism is the positive kind, which commends Hughes's work of putting collective behavior at the center of the study of the Holocaust; and the negative kind, which, on the contrary, regards "Good People" as too anecdotal and with an inadequate thesis. Hughes is criticized for having excluded from among the Holocaust's causes the thesis according to which in Germany there was an atavistic racism. At the time that he talks of "good

---

220 *The Sociological Eye* contains the sociologist's masterpieces and accounts for his methodological choices. From a perusal of reviews on the EBSCO database, it may be noted that there are more critics after 1971: after that date I found more reviews than those following the 1962 edition.
221 See Emil L. Fackenheim, *The Jewish Return into History: Reflections in the Age of Auschwitz and a New Jerusalem* (New York: Schocken, 1978), 23–24; Fackenheim, *To Mend the World: Foundations of Post-Holocaust Jewish Thought* (Bloomington: Indiana University Press, 1982); Rubinstein and Roth, *Approaches to Auschwitz*.
222 Fackenheim, *Quest for Past and Future*, 18.
223 Fackenheim, *God's Presence in History*, 91, 103, fns. 50 and 54. See http://circle.org/jsource/a-letter-to-all-good-people-by-amos-kenan/ (accessed, February 13, 2016).

people" who act without thinking and on behalf of their own interests, he creates a gap between his assumption and traditional theory. For instance, Arnold M. Rose, the first scholar who wrote a comment on this essay, in *Social Problems* in the winter of 1963, shows his considerable misgivings. For him, the thesis of *racism in reverse*, anticipating in some respects what Goldhagen will make his own in 1990s, is instead fundamental in the sense that anti-Semitic racism is a specificity of Germany and has a national character. For Rose, who argues that the highest levels of anti-Semitism were recorded in Germany just after the Napoleonic period, the national-German racism is at the base of the Holocaust: it means that the thesis of atavistic anti-Semitism functions well. However, Hughes's thesis does not affect Rose's way thinking or that of later scholars: for most of them, the Holocaust was the result of a millennial German anti-Semitism. Moreover, to Rose, Hughes's assumption is easily confutable.

The Montreal businessman Rose's question, "Why don't we admit that Hitler is doing to the Jews just what we ought to be doing?," leads Hughes to demonstrate that even in America there was a strong feeling of anti-Semitism, but for Rose it is not very significant.[224] Rather, what he praises of Hughes is the combination of psychological tools with specific issues of sociology, such as the authoritarian personality, racial ideology, and nationalism: these elements inaugurate, in 1948, a new path in Holocaust Studies. Nevertheless, many sociologists were disappointed in the interpretations of Hughes. In part, the success of Bauman's *Modernity and the Holocaust* can demonstrate this.

Hughes replies in a very simple way to the criticisms raised by Rose: that racial and anti-Semitic hatred, atavistic and stubborn, leads to the destruction of an entire people, through a state law that legalizes mass killings within a country. In Germany this occurred at the end of the Great War and during the crisis of the Weimar Republic. Thanks to the public/academic dialogue between Rose and Hughes, the dangers of a racial ideology returning became evident. In the United States during World War II, racism against blacks in its various forms (from defamatory

---

224 Rose, "Comment on 'Good people and Dirty Work,'" 285.

campaigns to lynchings) urged Hughes to rediscover the racism of the National Socialist Germany: he sadly discovered that "the today" and "the yesterday" are not different—"so things are."[225]

Looking at the second block of criticism (termed "distant"), there was a series of reviews following the publication of *The Sociological Eye* of 1971, which is really a collection of "selected papers," fifty-eight to be precise, written between 1927 and 1969, mostly essays "reworking" important issues, including the social conflicts between different ethnic groups. About a year later, in September 1972, a book review by Arlene Daniels appeared in *Contemporary Sociology*: here she sees in Hughes's "sociological third eye" a view beyond the ordinary and usual "on" and "toward" the society. She stresses the intuition of Hughes, who adopts the division of labor as an analytical category for understanding the Holocaust.[226] Hughes—Daniels explains—tries to measure the level of social integration, which, for him, is possible because of the study of the practices, tasks, and rituals in a society. For example, "dirty work" indicates that in the post–Great War Germany, there were some dysfunctions at a political level that blew up moral solidarity or social responsibility: Jews, despite being integrated citizens, were regarded as a rival group that could not enjoy the solidarity of other fellow citizens. It is important to ask how the National Socialist society was held together. In the society of dirty work the groups that maintain order are no longer based on values such as universal citizenship, but on purely biological elements (specifically, the Aryan race). The National Socialist leaders who exercised a totalitarian power over the rest of the people personified them. Hughes considers the National Socialist government as the starting point of his discourse. Next to these leaders, then, the lower part of society places itself.

Daniels asks if it would have been possible to avoid the "dirty work," and what did not occur that instead should have occurred. Hughes reflects

---

225 See Everett C. Hughes, "Rejoinder to Rose," *Social Problems* 10, no. 4 (1963): 390.
226 Richard Robbins refers to "the third eye" by borrowing a famous metaphor of Reike, who, however, spoke of a "third ear"; see Theodor Reike, *Listening with the Third Ear: The Inner Experience of a Psychoanalyst* (New York: Farrar, Straus, 1948); Richard Robbins, review of *The Sociological Eye: Selected Papers*, by Everett C. Hughes, *British Journal of Sociology* 23, no. 3 (1972): 362-3. Cf. Arlene K. Daniels, review of *The Sociological Eye*, by Everett C. Hughes, *Contemporary Sociology* 1, no. 5 (1972): 402–9.

on the conditions allowing the break of universal solidarity: for example, the SS man's desire for having advancing his own career and obtaining honors.

Also in September 1972 another critique appeared: a positive comment by Richard Robbins, who revaluates "Good People," highlighting how there is an analytical combination of "race and work" at the base of the Hughes's sociology. Robbins stresses that Hughes peruses statistical yearbooks—a theme to which we will return to later. Indeed, the aspect is notable because his examination opens a view to a comprehensive frame of Nazi policies, given that they oversee every aspect of daily life, from art to culture, from the economy to education, and so on. Without forgetting that such consultation of a statistical yearbook helps Hughes measure the level of democracy in Nazi society.

In the wake of Robbins's positive opinion, a series of reviews came out in 1972. Ida H. Simpson and Ely Chinoy, who reevaluated most of Hughes's work, finally proposed a rereading of them through new analytical keys and edited them.[227] Just as Durkheim did, Simpson, after focusing on decisions and intentions of central power, quickly highlights how the category of moral order is at the center of the essay: every society maintains itself on the basis of specific institutions and thanks to the moral division of work and consensus ("satisfaction of people's wants"). The immoral work ("dirty") instead is established from above and is managed according to the rules of the head people, specifically, the Nazi leaders that defined Jews as different people, "outgroups," depriving them of citizenship rights, and that institutionalized an immoral division of labor ("dirty work"), which destroyed any form of opposition by means of terror and indoctrination practices.

When Simpson writes that dominant groups conceive ideologies to maintain their power, she also sheds light on the behavior of the SS, which acted like a secret society, in the sense that, when they were placed at higher levels, they justified themselves in behaving irrespon-

---

227 See Ida H Simpson, "Continuities in the Sociology of Everett C. Hughes," review of *The Sociological Eye*, by Everett C. Hughes, *Sociological Quarterly* 13, no. 4 (1972): 547–58; Ely Chinoy, review of *The Sociological Eye*, by Everett C. Hughes, *Sociological Quarterly* 13, no. 4 (1972): 559–65.

sibly, precluding normal people from any possibility of rebellion. By analyzing the social relationships between individuals, or among groups, Simpson notes that in societies where dirty work is practiced, the system is amoral, that is, the groups are geared toward themselves: the social dirty work is possible because there are barriers to organic solidarity or cracks within citizenship bonds of an economic or political nature.

On the one hand, an adaptation of institutions to an immoral division of work took hold, on the other, there was no growing awareness of the situation by good people, who were unable to organize forms of resistance or develop groups of organic solidarity ("alter-ego interaction model"). Simpson's study on Hughes is very special because she does not only review the essay, but she even tries to delve into the issue of the society of dirty work. In her opinion, against terror and indoctrination there have to be responsible people who are able to remove institutional barriers imposed from above. What is interesting is that Simpson identifies the thread passing through Hughes's works, recovering, for example, several elements that join "Good People" and "The Gleichshaltung," where Hughes explains how National Socialism flattened every aspect of social life in the light of totalitarian principles.

Ely Chinoy was another participant in the symposium of critics on Hughes, if it can be defined it in this way. For him, the dirty work society is an unfree society: only a "free association" is the basis for a healthy development of social institutions, and it can take hold only if the individual is capable of self-determination under the presence of a "moral constitution." Unlike Hughes, according to whom good people are not deviant, but normal, Chinoy thinks instead that "bastard institutions" lead to the destruction of society.[228]

Reviewer David S. Davis returned in 1984 to the pathogenic nature of moral institutions in Nazi society: by departing from the approach proposed by Hughes, he conceives dirty work and good people just like degeneration cases. His consideration results from his reflection on the immoral division of

---

228 See Series III: Course Material, Subseries 2: University of Chicago, 1938–1961, box 79, folder 1, Sociology 350, "Bastard Institutions," lecture, 1951.

labor. Placing employment at the center of his analysis, Davis introduces dirty workers as workers who toil, slave laborers and socially isolated, corrupted, and often men who provide lower services for others ("bail bondsmen"). These good people practice dirty work that becomes a kind of release from the condition of social inferiority with which they are faced and an escape from such situations. However, Hughes, unlike Davis, does not believe that dirty workers are deviants, but, rather, that they are people well integrated into society. What Davis aims to state is evident from the title, "Good People Doing Dirty Work." His review deserves more attention.[229]

Bernard Goldstein's 1986 article also belongs to the second stage of criticism. The scholar immediately defines *The Sociological Eye* as a set of writings closely linked between them ("paperbound edition"). In his review published in *AJS*, Goldstein emphasizes the concept of the banality of evil and how dirty work is repeated over time in society:

> Hughes developed the concept of "dirty work" in his analysis of work and occupations; he put it to good use in "Good People and Dirty Work." It becomes a perspective from which to understand both the Germans who did the dirty work in the death camps and the good people who permitted them to do it. Under appropriate circumstances and relevant incentives, any society will yield people willing to do its dirty work—incarcerate Japanese-Americans or cause Argentinians to disappear. The banality of such dirty work is illuminated in the movie *Shoah*, which in turn underlines the relevance of this essay written more than 30 years ago.[230]

For Goldstein, at the base of Hughes's essay are the role of the self and the concepts of work-self, emergency, and routine, which show how the immoral division of work, among citizens of the National Socialist society, was the result of arrested development of the consciousness of the individual. In the wake of Simpson, Goldstein also intercepts a subtle

---

229 See David S. Davis, "Good People Doing Dirty Work: A Study of Social Isolation," *Symbolic Interaction* 7, no. 2 (1984): 233–47, doi:10.1525/si.1984.7.2.233.
230 Bernard Goldstein, review of *The Sociological Eye: Selected Papers*, by Everett C. Hughes, *American Journal of Sociology* 92, no. 2 (1986): 459, doi:10.1086/ajs.92.2.2780158.

connection between Hughes's texts: both in "Good People" and in "The Gleichshaltung" the totalitarian power of the National Socialist government makes good people terrified and easily indoctrinated.

Following the publication of "Good People" in *Classical Tradition in Sociology* (1997), a critique finally appeared, written by Anselm Strauss, who highlights the Hughes's mission. Hughes, interested, like Park, in the complexity of social relations (especially between different ethnic groups), industrial labor relations, or urban space, puts in writing, with an informal linguistic style, important concepts regarding the destruction of European Jews.

At the conclusion of this brief critical overview, one can make two observations: first, the criticism came late; second, reviewers often reversed the contents of Hughes's researches. What is certainly curious is the delay in publishing his essay, because between 1938 and 1961, Hughes conducted his own research while at the Chicago School. Why didn't he publish his work in those years? This is a crucial question, especially because Hughes's work broke the stereotype of the "backwardness of sociology" in the study of the Holocaust: if it had been published in 1948, it could have paved the way for a long series of works about the Jewish question.

1.7.5. "The Gleichshaltung"

"The Gleichshaltung" appeared in *The American Statistician* in December 1955. By reading the article, it is possible to understand what there is behind a name[231]—first, because Hughes dealt with the Jewish question according to a different approach from that used in "Good People"; second, because the research was not issued in the official review *The American Journal of Sociology*, published by the University of Chicago.

The work starts casually when Hughes looks at the first page of the *Statistical Yearbook of the Third Reich* (1941–42), the last statistical yearbook published by the National Socialist regime, and the table titled "Racial Classification of People Who Married in 1938." After perusing the classic publication of the Statistical Office of the State reporting the social

---

231   See note 205, above.

and economic life of the German *Nation*, based on an enormous amount of statistical data collected in areas subject to survey, Hughes unveils how important a statistical yearbook is that relates numbers and percentages, and how statistical data provides information on the social, political, economic, and cultural life of a people or the quality of life of a state. "The Gleichshaltung" is a kind of news where facts and events are transformed into numbers to be easily measured and read. It received a greater scientific consensus than "Good People" would later receive, in 1962, and this is because of the title.

"What changes did the statistician of the German Reich have to make in his official Yearbook when the Nazis came to power?"[232] Ten years after the end of the World War II, in the middle of the Cold War, Hughes accessed documents of the National Socialist state, and published during the Thaw era, in 1955, the results of his research in the quarterly of the American Statistical Association in Washington, DC. Although at the beginning Hughes does not adopt a quantitative approach for his research and escapes from the principles of sociological positivism and statistical research of the early century, at the end he does not only choose the statistical way, to deal with the Jewish question, but he is also interested in methodological discipline. "What we count" and "how" can be very important. Hughes uses statistical tools to describe some of his theories that otherwise he would not have been able to explain. Through numbers, he elaborates a new way to tell the reality, and it proves that he is a pioneer in sociological studies on the *Shoah*. The main goal of his work is to emphasize the nonindependence of scientific research. Particularly, he denounces each time data are not reported accurately because of the dependence of the Department of Statistics on the government. Before 1933, terms such as "Jew," "Jewess," and "Jewish" did not appear in any yearbook. In 1934, a census was conducted according to criteria that were never used before. Especially, a series of tables to record the place of birth of the Jews and the percentage of those who had German origin was prepared: everything needed to take the census of "persons belonging to the religion of Israel." In that occasion, the locution *Glaubensjuden*, "Jew

---

232 Hughes, "The Gleichshaltung of the German Statistical Yearbook," 8.

by faith" (a phrase that would acquire a racial meaning with legal value as of the Nuremberg Laws), appeared in the yearbook. The Third Reich developed its own language because it changed the meaning of terms, creating new meanings with different intentions for political use. Jews were a race, not a religious group. German statistical segregation was also complete. Jews were seen nowhere in tables as simply another category of people, which included other Germans.[233]

In essence, the statistics of the Third Reich had to put Hitler's regime in a good light, showing progress in the economic field together with territorial conquests: in the yearbooks, the *Endlösung*, or "project," to liberate Germany from "Jewish blood" was never mentioned (neither in a graph nor in a table of contents). For Hughes, consulting the yearbooks of the Nazi dictatorship is useful to explain that German "good people" were *gleichgeshaltet*, "coordinated." From his perusal, two important issues emerge. First, both the Catholic and Protestant churches, considered by the Party as moral enemy agencies, were silenced, albeit with partial results. The Catholic Church underwent a minor reduction in its obedience to the pope; while the Protestant church, divided into different denominations, partially aligned with the NSDAP with the creation of the "Protestant Reich Church, headed by Ludwig Müller. Second, the policy of *Gleichschaltung* refers to a leveling policy, of equalization, synchronization, and coordination, which, having as its goal that of putting every type of institution (political, religious, and so on) under Nazi authority and control, deleted all kinds of specificity, both national and cultural.

In many ways, "The Gleichshaltung" and "Good People" can be considered as a single work. "Most of what follows was written after my first postwar visit to Germany in 1948," Hughes writes in his "Good People."[234] In reviewing the salient years of his academic activity and the tradition of the Chicago School, one may argue that Hughes's writings (especially if "Good People" would have been published on time) show that speaking of the "delay of sociology" in Holocaust Studies is inappropriate.

---

233   Ibid.,10.
234   Hughes, "Good People and Dirty Work," 3.

At this point, it is decisive to count the works conducted by Hughes and the Chicago School on the destruction of the Jews and then analyze in which years these researches were published and in which reviews. To place them in the most general view of sociological studies on the Holocaust, I measured the productivity of authors writing about the Holocaust and the degree of appreciation for their works. I considered two broad periods—(1) after 1945 to the present day and (2) the years before World War II—in order to examine as well as I could all the publications that, at least once, contained in the title of the article or book review terms related to the Jewish question. The aim was to measure "the speed of publication" of Hughes's research, his scientific impact, and his productivity, specifically, Hughes's visibility. In 1948, upon his return from Germany, Hughes put his experience in writing, introduced in the form of a seminar at McGill University:

> Shortly after my return from my first visit to Germany since 1932, a student asked me whether a certain German, who was to be one of the first to visit the University of Chicago after the war, was a good man. I said I was sure he was, but wanted to know why she asked. Her answer: "Well, he's still alive, isn't he?" I replied rather sharply that although quite a number of Negroes had been lynched in this country that year, she appeared in good health and unruffled. My answer was as much an accusation of myself as of her. The effect of visiting Germany was not to make me—at the moment—inquire why the Germans did what they did, but to marvel at the fact we have not quite done likewise and to ask what any of us does to prevent it.[235]

After a decade, 1928–38, spent at McGill University, Hughes worked at the Chicago School until 1961, and then moved to Brandeis University as a professor of sociology until 1968, when he arrived at Boston College. In the years of the Chicago School, which provided publication of research on contemporary society in *AJS*, the bimonthly founded by Small in 1895 (the same year in which Durkheim founded the *Année sociologique* in

---

235 Hughes, "Rejoinder to Rose," 390.

France), the essay "Good People" was never proposed for publication there, not even during the years of Hughes's stints on the editorial board, from 1952 to 1957, and again from 1959 to after 1960.[236] In 1943, Glenn E. Hoover wrote that there were about a dozen writings on political issues that had been accepted by top journals to be circulated, addressing the difficulties, for some academic researches, of being published. He dealt with the content of the research, its time of dissemination, and the media used to spread the topic in question, referring to a close connection between politics and society, academia and media.

Hughes was studying the Holocaust in 1948, but his essay was published only in 1962 and not in *AJS*, but in *Social Problems*, a quarterly that, starting from June 1953, on behalf of the University of California Press, officially published the works of the Society for the Study of Social Problems, founded in 1951 by Elizabeth Briant Lee and Alfred McClung Lee. *Social Problems* followed the bimonthly of the Chicago School in both its issues and methodology.[237] When "Good People" was published,

---

[236] William Rainey Harper, president of the University of Chicago from 1891 to 1906, wanted the *AJS* to disseminate the research of the sociological discipline. This journal, which thus founded sociology itself, publicized research activities, promoted organizational elements, and founded the resources to start research, legitimizing the discipline in the eyes of the public. It played a cultural hegemonic role in American sociology, especially until 1936, year of foundation of the *American Sociological Review*.

[237] In 1962 the director of *AJS* was Peter Blau (1960–66). *Social Problems* offered space to research on conflict, action, and social change, on poverty, inequality, and ethnic minorities. It has only recently been surveyed by JSTOR. Herbert Blumer was director of *Social Problems* in 1954–55, when Hughes was instead at the head of the *AJS*. The Society for the Study of Social Problems (SSSP) was presented as a community of scholars, lawyers, and students interested in studying the problems of society in a critical, scientific, and humanistic manner. Blumer dealt with the Jewish question. In this period, but also in subsequent years, in which both the comment and the debate of "Good People" were reported, Marshall B. Clinard (1961–62) of the University of Wisconsin, Marvin B. Sussman (1962–63) of Western Reserve University, and Jessie Bernard (1963–64) of Pennsylvania State University supervised the editing of articles. To verify the reasons for the surrender of Hughes in publishing his work, which was irreconcilable with traditional academic thinking and the positivist quantitative approach, see the Hughes manuscripts on labor relations with the *AJS* and policies internal to the University of Chicago and Brandeis University. Also see Neurath, *The Society of Terror*, 286. To understand better his studies in the postwar period in Germany, see lectures, lecture notes, syllabi, course profiles, mimeographed leaflets, diaries of courses, memoranda, manuscripts of other authors and students, reprints, newspaper clippings for instance in Series II: Correspondence, Box 4, Folder 9; Box 19, Folder 17; Box 68, folder 6-11; and of Series III: Course Material, "Subseries 2: University of Chicago, 1938–1961."

the direction of *Social Problems* was supported by scholars not engaged with the ideal of the progressive and reformist "good deal," which interested the Chicago School.

According to my perusal conducted in EBSCO, "Good People" received some comments and opinions from some critics, but all were concentrated in the first years following publication of the article. Although this "Good People" broke the sociological silence concerning the Holocaust, it did not earn huge acclaim from academics.

What deserves more attention is the title of the article. Let me say that it is credible that its nonpublication in 1948 and the carelessness of the work in 1962 depended on the choice of the title, which with Arendt found its fortune. Despite being an important member of the Second Chicago School, in 1948 Hughes presented a title that clashed with the positivist orientation of American sociology of the 1930s and 40s, a discipline also imbued with practices of anti-Semitism. Nevertheless, Hughes's interest in the Jewish question was not curbed by the missed issuance of "Good People": between 1948 and 1962, he published a remarkable paper with a "more agreeable" title based on an analysis of a quantitative kind. When Rose, wrote in 1963 in *Social Problems* that Hughes had some hesitation in publishing the piece of 1948, he also highlighted how his thesis would have overturned traditional literature of historians and psychologists.

More curious is that the works subsequent to the publication of Hughes's essay did not confront his statements, but only rehashed academic stereotypes. For instance, Goldhagen did not consider the novelties introduced by Hughes, especially, the condoning of Nazi massacres: the dirty work of Nazis. "Good People" was only published in the Chicago School review in 1997, eight years after the fall of the Berlin Wall, in the second volume of *Classical Tradition in Sociology*, when the entire body of Hughes's works, his sociological tradition, following a new study of the Chicago School, had begun to be revisited, thanks to Helmes-Hayes.

1.7.6. A Self-Coördination Case

Hughes's research on the banality of evil was published at the beginning of the 1960s, when the thinking of critical sociology changed, that is, when the legacy of positivism was at its end. A series of things varied and pierced or, better, uncovered the limits of some of the ideologies that dominated the world. While the limits of Soviet ideology were emerging, the limits of American individualistic ideology were also coming to light. In addition to the Korean War (1950–53) or the arrest of Eichmann in Buenos Aires, on May 11, 1960, or other events that might come to mind, it is crucial to remember that the Thaw started with Stalin's death in 1953, and was propelled on February 25, 1956, in the Twentieth Party Congress of the Communist Party of the Soviet Union with the denouncing of Stalin's crimes by Khrushchev. Nevertheless, what modified profoundly the situation was the Vietnam War. Thanks to a complex variety of circumstances, the publication of "Good People" became possible. Hughes's publication was helped by these all events and coincided with the release of Arendt's articles on the Eichmann trial for *The New Yorker*, and then collected in book form the following year in *The Banality of Evil*: the two texts, that of Hughes and that of Arendt, meet on many points. Fairly similar in content (in that the people of whom the two texts speak are "good" or "banal," both are concerned with "normalcy" or the "ordinary being"), both essays conceive the evil perpetrated under the Nazis not as radical, but as a thing of the everyday, not of a faraway world: it belongs to the ordinary people, is common, and is practiced among neighbors. If, on the one hand, the meaning behind the phrase "good people" is not immediately clear, on the other hand, Hughes seems with his focus on banality to argue for the absence of anti-Semitism in Germany. However, more disconcerting, upon publication of "Good People," was his movement away from the methodological positivism that had characterized the Chicago School, which had begun in the second half of the 1920s with William Ogburn. To better understand the situation, it is relevant to remember that in the late nineteenth century, but especially at the beginning of the twentieth century, under the influence of American progressivism, sociology, founded as a secular religion to study the problems of modern American society, tended to become for all intents and purposes a positive discipline. Meanwhile, numerous quantitative researches with a positivist approach, able to give an account of economy and finance in American society, were subsidized by some philanthropic foundations, such as the Rockefeller Foundation and the Russel Sage Foundation. For instance, in 1923, Rockefeller funded the University of Chicago, a private school and with a liberal tradition, as Edward A. Shils noted.

> If a university did the research a foundation wanted because it wanted the money, clearly the foundation is setting the agenda—but universities did not only do the research the foundations wanted, when they did have clear wants, because of the money. The University of Chicago is an interesting case because it has been accused of being unduly dependent on Rockefeller money.[238]

Thanks to the provision of a large amount of funds for research, the Sage or the Rockefeller philanthropic foundations ensured the development of American sociology as a discipline and as an academic corpus. In the United States of the 1930s, when the ideology of progress and scientific achievements of the natural sciences went hand in hand with the devastating effects of the 1929 economic crisis, for sociology, the need to mimic the positive or natural sciences became more urgent than ever, and this required a specifically methodological approach. Sociology did not only tend to become a science in all respects, but, especially, it also aimed at finding solutions to the long list of new modern social problems. Positivist teaching had a long-term effect on U.S. academic research. Its echo can be clearly seen in Parsons, the "towering figure in the social sciences," as defined by the *New York Times* in his obituary, "who was responsible for the education of three generations of sociologists," especially in the decade 1950–60, and after that the limits of the legacy of American positivism came to light.[239] In 1946, two years after becoming director of the Department of Sociology at Harvard University, Parsons transformed it into the Department of Social Relations, remaining director there for many years. As recalled by Marco Santoro, there "were assigned to the Department, during the first ten years of its life, eighty doctoral positions, most of them to students of the same Parsons, who thus sees his social capital growing tremendously, i.e. the network of rela-

---

238 Platt, *A History of Sociological Research Methods in America, 1920–1960*, 173–74.
239 *New York Times* obituary quoted in http://biography.yourdictionary.com/talcott-parsons (accessed March 28, 2012).

tionships on which he could count in the American academic world."[240] It was another way to create consensus to present sociology in accordance with political and governmental ideas.

Some attitudes and practices in academia led Hughes, in 1948, not to publish his essay. In 1943, the scholar Glenn Hoover wrote that "questions are never settled until they are settled right."[241] Hoover shows the complicated relationship between scientific research, social and economic sciences, and the dissemination of their findings: he centers on the difficulties encountered while writing a research paper and publishing it. To Hoover, the research does not always receive proper editorial attention from the scientific community, for various reasons. In essence, from Weber onward the values-free method became an indispensable prerequisite to ensure scientificity in research, and under the wave of positivism it marked American sociological reflection for nearly three decades, from the 1920s to the 1950s. As remembered by Enzo Trapanese, it was combined with ameliorism: a kind of ideology that aspires to achieve the status of scientificity for American sociology (as natural sciences) and the perfect social order, a golden age for American society. In 1938, Shils spoke of the nonautonomy of research. Professor of Social Sciences at the University of Chicago, in *Limitations on the Freedom of Research* Shils provided data and information on the restrictions to which scientific research is subject for reasons of political or cultural interest and about sanctions against scholars, whose scientific writings run "counter to the evaluations dominant in their institution or in the wider community."[242]

When Hughes, in 1948, seemed to be reticent about the publication of his essay and, in the end, decided to not submit it for publication, he avoided those penalties commonly practiced in academic circles. Shils had exposed the deeply rooted conflict in the culture of his time between the positivist scientific model and society, with its ethnic relations and riven by racism. Shils shed light on the contradictions of the social

---

240 Parsons, *Professioni e libertà*, 123 (my translation).
241 Glenn E. Hoover, "The Failure of the Social Sciences," *American Journal of Economics and Sociology* 3, no. 1 (1943): 91.
242 Shils, "Limitations on the Freedom of Research and Teaching in the Social Sciences," 144.

sciences, for example, when reporting the statement of Louis Levine related to "the prohibition against publication of his taxation study":

> Chancellor Elliott did not claim that his new policy gave him the right to forbid me to publish my monograph privately. He argued with me that it would be better for me not to publish it. He told me that "The Interests" were determined to crush out all liberal thought, and that if I published the monograph, an attack would be made on me generally: that the newspapers of the State would not give me a fair hearing.[243]

An atmosphere of tension enveloped the researchers who did not follow the orthodoxy of the department, and discarded works continued to remain as such for a long time while sanctioned researchers remained marked. Hughes was aware of the forms of obstruction to research that mainly occur during campaigns for research funds: especially when the department is in financial straits or in more precarious institutions, that is, those in which the need for money is higher and the directors are obliged to protect the interests of those who funded the research. Between 1919 and 1953, U.S. government funding was mainly addressed to guarantee social policies for solving practical problems after World War I, and then came the New Deal programs in the 1930s, and thereafter, in relation to these projects, the collaboration between state agencies and universities multiplied. As Jennifer Platt notes, the agencies dealing with the collection of funds for research projects were power entities, and the universities had a big weight in society: "The foundations did play a significant role in the funding of quantitative work, and of the development and diffusion of quantitative methods."[244] In the face of intimidation and threats, several researchers left their research ("self-intimidation") or abandoned it to teach other topics ("*coördination*").[245] However, both the dismissal itself and the threat of being expelled from

---
243 Ibid., 155, with reference to the newspaper *The New Northwest* (Missoula, Montana), March 14, 1919.
244 Platt, *A History of Sociological Research Methods in America, 1920–1960*, 189.
245 See Shils, "Limitations on the Freedom of Research and Teaching in the Social Sciences," 161.

the academy served as a wake-up call. That is what Hughes highlighted, in 1955, about German universities.

Hughes's case might be an instance of self-alignment ("*self-coördination*"), in 1948, when he decided not to publish his work, because it was irreconcilable with traditional academic thinking and because it was absolutely "new" at a methodological level, that is, far from the quantitative positivist approach, he avoided the restrictions or penalties that could have been inflicted on him. From the 1930s to the 1950s, American sociology underwent a paradigmatic conflict between a human ecology almost at sunset and a Parsonsian functionalism in its infancy. These two interpretative models of reality bracketed other theories, such as symbolic interactionism and Freudianism. Hughes lived in this very eclectic stage for the academy.

1.7.7. Hughes's Delay Roots in the American Sociological Tradition

More can be said about Hughes's delay. It was not only an academic self-alignment: as I was able verify, starting from Halpert's study, Hughes's delay was prepared in several academic realms where topics related to Jews were undervalued. The reasons why Hughes did not publish his essay in 1948 may be found in the first decades of the twentieth century, when sociology was established as an academic discipline.

In the introduction, I said that after reading Halpert's article, I started to examine the academic realm of sociology and themes related to Jews, especially because the primary goal of Halpert was to understand the failure of the social sciences in the study of the Holocaust, which led him to study the history of American sociological thinking, focusing on the early years of academic research in the United States. Specifically, Halpert's article highlights social change and the development of industrial-urban Chicago at the turn of the century, together with the role played by the academic, political, economic, and military elite in society. He explains how in those years academic research was "permeated" by ideologies, such as Christian Reformism (a movement that had taken root in the best universities on the U.S. East Coast of between 1905 and 1930) and sociological positivism. When research was not conducted according to the canons of positivist thinking or not characteristic of Protestant Christian values, it was discarded.

It is proper to recall, even if briefly, that faced with disruptive modernization and its consequent problems, the founding fathers of American sociology, from Lester F. Ward to Charles Horton Cooley, from Franklin H. Giddins to Edward A. Ross, were distinguished then for the belief they held, a kind of "Social Gospel," which promoted Christian principles in sociological environments; and which had, ultimately, as its aim that of making modern America better at the turn of the century. Among the Christian moral values, oriented to reforming America, there was also that of considering the Jews as enemies, because they were god-killers:[246] "Considering Jews to be 'insoluble clots,' Ross wanted to cleanse America of these people, thereby creating a racially pure country composed of the descendants of early settlers and Nordic immigrants."[247]

Let me summarize what Halpert underscores. When Hitler came to power, Ross argued the doctrine of racial superiority. These anti-Semitic sentiments were widespread in the Northeast, where most of the population was from Northern Europe. National Socialism was regarded positively across the ocean and thought able to boost the economy. The founding fathers of American sociology of the 1920s had a phobic and ethnocentric approach in solving the problems produced by modernity: hence, the ease with which they built, in many ways, a Social Gospel characterized by stereotypical fears and prejudices. This acontemporary and apolitical procedure, far from real social problems, prevented them from recognizing the roots of National Socialism. There were few who identified Nazism as a totalitarian political phenomenon. The 1929 financial crisis and the rise of Hitler were linked with the phase of the demagogues who spread their anti-Semitic feelings in a period of economic and military downturn. A large majority of Americans were against the increasing the number of German Jews resettling in

---

246 To examine the question further, see Anders Gerdmar, *Roots of Theological Anti-Semitism: German Biblical Interpretation and the Jews, from Herder and Semler to Kittel and Bultmann* (Leiden: Brill, 2008). I would like to thank Giuseppe Veltri for the reference.
247 Halpert, "Early American Sociology and the Holocaust," 9.

the United States. This explains the ease with which news that there was a Jewish conspiracy at an international level (which also had the aim of de-Christianizing America) spread and took root. Hitler's policy of ethnic cleansing, built to solve the problem of the Jewish question, was looked upon with favor in anti-Semitic areas of the United States. Under Hitler, anti-Semitism in Germany attained its acme. Halpert argues that American sociologists' fallback towards positivism was used only to cover their anti-Semitism. It is important to consider that in the 1940s and 50s a majority of American sociologists were entrenched in a deep cultural oblivion, while those who tried to deal with the Jewish question, such as Hughes, were unable to do so. Several presidents of the associations of sociology showed anti-Semitic leanings, and few scholars contradicted them. Halpert reports the instance of Robert K. Merton, president of the ASS, who recognized in 1957 the danger of science "in service" or "in the hands" of the state—as occurred in Germany with Hitler.

Looking back, according to the hitherto known literature, the topic remained vague until, in the 1960s, sociology opened itself to themes no longer positivist. It was the end of the Parsonian era, and for the issue of the Holocaust there was still plenty of space, as for Hughes's article, which was not commented on in a timely manner by the international critics. Actually, Hughes opted for a historical reconstruction of sociological sources, which forced him to examine society by trying to capture those social arrangements that led to the Holocaust in the German *Gesellschaft*. When I argue that Hughes was influenced not to publish any writing directly related to the Holocaust, I recall that his other writings were published on time. Hughes conducted other research in those years that was published and in several academic journals. By perusing the official review of the Chicago School, some of his speeches on the issue of racism emerge. For instance, the name of Hughes appears for the first time in *AJS* as the reviewer of *Modern Industry* by Ernest L. Bogart and Charles E. Landon in 1928.[248] To give an answer to the question of who writes what on the Jewish question and when, we can make a distinction in broad

---

248 See, for example, Hughes, review of *Race, Nation, Person: Social Aspects of the Race Problem: A Symposium,* by Joseph M. Corrigan and G. Barry O'Toole, *American Journal of Sociology* 50, no. 4 (1945): 320–21.

terms on the basis of visibility given to the research over the years in *AJS*. One can read articles with a positivist bent and essays on topics related to the race question and eugenics, such as *Making the Fascist State* by Herbert W. Schneider, reviewed by Charles A. Ellwood—or reviews of some studies on anti-Semitism.

At the end of the war, there were only three reviews on the Jewish question. The most exciting work appeared in January 1957, *Status, Authoritarianism, and Anti-Semitism.* Written by Walter C. Kaufman according to the quantitative approach, the book relates the phenomena of "social-state," "authoritarian personality," and "anti-Semitism" through precise parameters or scales of sociological methodology.

A historical turning point in the post-Holocaust sociological literature occurred after the arrest and trial of Eichmann, namely, after 1961, a period in which the theme of Jewish resistance also began to be enhanced. The word "holocaust" appears for the first time among the titles of *AJS* in 1983, in *The Holocaust and the German Elite*, while "Good People" continued to be ignored. Instead, journals such as *American Sociologist* or *Social Problems* housed Hughes's discussions.

Hughes is well known as an exponent of the Chicago School, but he is hardly ever remembered as one of the earliest sociologists to study Nazi Germany.

The problem of the ghettoization of the Jews crosses the centuries. In 1928, thanks to Louis Wirth, one could read *The Ghetto*: the first attempt to address the sociological history of the Jewish people and one of its specific situations. If Hughes's work is explained by the division of labor, *The Ghetto* instead places categories of isolation, of physical distance, and, therefore, of social distance at the center of reflection. The isolated individuals belonging to different ethnic groups are classified as dangerous "outsiders" from whom it is necessary to defend oneself, and legitimized, according to Wirth, is the physical distance, which, in turn, promotes and legitimizes the cultural one, until it becomes social discrimination. The mechanism of self-engulfment or self-phagocytization that is set in motion slowly erodes the organic solidarity among individuals of the same society. This distance, analyzed in *The Ghetto*, starting from the definition of "outsider," reaches its culmination in the Nazi society that destroyed the Jews in

Europe. Moreover, the physical distance serves to legitimize the practice of discrimination and violence perpetrated by neighbors, making them normal. Moreover, the distance described in *The Ghetto* allows the banality of the actions of "good people," their "dirty work." Through the analysis of the social function of the ghetto, compared to the areas that form it, the differentiation of modern urban interests in the community and then the corresponding function of the "division of labor" appear. This means that the category of the social division of roles, first, in *The Ghetto* and, then, in "Good People," is a normal category, close to the thought of the Chicago authors: indeed, they assume that starting from the reality of the city it is possible to tell what happens to its inhabitants. And it is possible to comprehend the modern home of Jewish immigrants in the Western world. On the one side, it is an institution, on the other, it is a process; however, both aspects emphasize the *modus vitae* of ethnic groups.

The establishment of the ghetto returns over time and space along with the stereotype of the Jew who lives separately from other citizens. Between *The Ghetto* and "Good People" one can draw a thin line. In the first work, the Jewish question is addressed, but the war had not started yet. In the second, this view is instead filtered through the extermination of the Jews, a topic not easily treated at an academic level in the postwar period. The two works can be seen as a sort of continuum in the sense that *The Ghetto* prepares the theoretical level for what then happens with "Good People" in dealing with the completion of the "discrimination-ghettoization" foretold in *The Ghetto*. That is to say, in time and space the aptitude of nonthinking is prepared by unclean legal practices, that is, by dirty social work.

However, Hughes's ideas were never taken into account in Holocaust Studies. I have tried to demonstrate that here. But, at this point, it is proper to ask whether the evil is really banal. What exactly does it mean to be a superficial person and practice death? Is not evil radical? What are its roots, and where are they? In other words, why does a person decide—if he does indeed decide—to stop thinking and commit crimes? Hughes's case leads us to ask what is good and what is evil in human beings.

It is pertinent to introduce how attention to Hughes's studies (especially to "Good People") can move scholarship on the subject forward.

Recently, the last trial concerning whether evil is banal or radical was a debate of a historical-philosophical nature between the historian Richard Wolin and the American philosopher of Turkish origin Seyla Benahbib, in the *Jewish Review of Books*, and added to the English edition (2014) of the original German *Eichmann vor Jerusalem* (2011) by Bettina Stangneth.[249] Stangneth studies the period before the Eichmann trial (exile notes combined with the German Nazi Willem Sassen interviews). From her examination (of the unpublished and previously never seen writings of Eichmann, written during his exile), an anti-Semitic Eichmann who plans the extermination of the Jews arises, a fanatical believer in extermination rather than simply an unthinking bureaucrat. In this manner, Stangneth dismisses the concept of banality of evil and trounces Arendt's theory. Hughes's case provides us with the reexamination of the banality of evil question posed by Arendt, especially after the calling into question of her theory. After having done numerous readings and reviewed several criticisms, I underline a research space that will allow those types of strands of thought to flourish. Meantime, the discovery of Hughes restores value to the thesis of a banality of evil not committed by monsters.

Hughes was a social observer contemporary to events when he elaborated his thesis: he observed what happened during and after the war. (Hughes based much of his work on his own experience in Germany.) So, if on one side, the eight pages written by him appear few compared to those of other sociologists, in reality, the speed with which he analyzed the Holocaust and conceived the category of banality of evil—which was affirmed in the scholarly literature after the Eichmann trial and with Arendt's book—put sociology onto the study of the Holocaust.

Let me be precise in a last point. When Hughes speaks of the banality of evil, he refers exactly to banality of evil. It is not of a signifier (banality of evil) that alludes to another meaning. At times, it happens that the same categories may be used to signify others: this is not the case here.

---

249 See Richard Wolin and Seyla Benhabib, "Eichmann, Arendt, and 'The Banality of Evil,'" *Jewish Review of Books*, accessed November 2, 2014, https://jewishreviewofbooks.com/articles/1317/eichmann-arendt-and-the-banality-of-evil/. See also Bettina Stangneth, *Eichmann before Jerusalem: The Unexamined Life of a Mass Murderer* (New York: Alfred A. Knopf, 2014 [2011]).

Like Bauman and Fein, Hughes earned his pariah status within the field of the Holocaust Studies. Nevertheless, unlike them, there has never been any attempt to reassess soberly Hughes's work. This consideration can highlight how the category of the banality of evil returns in certain historical periods and how scholars use it to read and interpret current events of contemporary world. With the fall of the Berlin Wall, the opening of the archives of the East, and the outbreak of civil war in ex-Yugoslavia (1991–95), a return was made in philosophical-historical academic discussions to the causes of the genocide of the Jews (and therefore of all genocides): again, is evil banal or radical? In addition, Hughes's research calls into play a number of concepts that open the way to further research (a rethinking of the Holocaust and the postwar period and the modern labeling of contemporary violence). Especially, it leads scholars to return to the archives. In 1963, when *The Banality of Evil* by Arendt was published, there were many public and conflicting critics both in Israel and in the United States.[250] It was a debate that divided the thinking of politicians, philosophers, historians, and sociologists, involving the international media (*New York Times*, *Der Spiegel*, and so on) in addition to academic journals, the educated public, and the more casual observer. The controversy sometimes seems to have been extinguished for certain periods (1966–69; 1970–77; 1978–85) but then reignited in crucial periods, leaving the dispute without a definitive answer. For instance, in the functionalist-intentionalist debate in the 1960s, the functionalists found support for their thesis in the category of the banality of evil.

The Arendt controversy was rekindled in something like a trial or "question-and-answer" mode just after the fall of the Berlin Wall, when the banality of evil lent itself as a historical category to explain genocides and wars in the Balkans.[251] Again scholars are forced to take the side of Arendt and to reconsider the final solution, the concentration camp system. Or they openly oppose the scholar's thesis, as did Goldhagen, who

---

250 See Leora Bilsky, "The Arendt Controversy 2000: An Israeli Perspective," *Arendt's Newsletter* 5 (November 2001): 41–46; Michael Ezra, "The Eichmann Polemics: Hannah Arendt and Her Critics," *Democratiya* 9 (2007): 141–65.
251 See Richard Cohen, "Arendt Controversy," in *Encyclopedia of the Holocaust* (New York: Macmillan, 1990), 1: 80–81.

opened further debate in 1996.[252] At the beginning of the millennium, in the context of an increasingly globalized world, the controversy persists under a different guise: the question of a radical or a banal evil is used to interpret the concepts of international political responsibility.[253]

The debates for and against Arendt continue, and innovate research sheds light on the World War II in a broad sense. Historians rethink the Third Reich's anti-Semitism, for instance. Through the category of "good people" they revisit the genocides of the twentieth century, and in a comparative way. In the first decade of the twenty-first century, the positions of Lozowic and Cesarani led to the abandonment of the previous argument in favor of Arendt and a total reconsideration of the banality of evil.[254]

Here, Hughes's case can demonstrate how the ongoing debates opened around the banal or radical nature of evil serve to further reconsider such concepts as modernity, atomization, and mass society, all inherent in the Holocaust and generating in turn other thinking tools to read the postwar period. Additionally, it demonstrates the polysemic capability of this category, which in relighting durable diatribes opens new archives or reopens old ones. The category of the banality of evil returns in various studies for reading contemporary events and, in particular, new contemporary violence. At this point, it is essential to follow the scholars Ulrich Herbert and Bettina Stangneth for having tried, through their studies, to give in-depth answers, which can only emerge after consulting the archives, by allowing a dialogue between disciplines, such as history, sociology, and philosophy. It is decisive to return to the Arendt and Hughes archives. In bringing to light unpublished works, rediscovering Hughes's researches, and reflecting on the reception of these works, it updates the various currents of the Chicago School by reconsidering the overall history of sociology and

---

252 See Daniel J. Goldhagen, *Hitler's Willing Executioners: Ordinary Germans and the Holocaust* (New York: Alfred A. Knopf, 1996); Israel Gutman, "Goldhagen—His Critics and His Contribution," *Yad Vashem Studies* 26 (1998): 329–64; Avraham Barkai, "German Historians Confront Goldhagen," *Yad Vashem Studies* 26 (1998): 295–328.

253 Cf. Idith Zertal, *Israel's Holocaust and the Politics of Nationhood*, trans. Chaya Galai (Cambridge: Cambridge University Press, 2005).

254 See Yaacov Lozowick, *Hitler's Bureaucrats: The Nazi Security Police and the Banality of Evil* (London: Continuum, 2002); David Cesarani, *Becoming Eichmann: Rethinking the Life, Crimes, and Trial of a "Desk Murderer"* (Cambridge, MA: Da Capo, 2006); Deborah Lipstadt, *The Eichmann Trial* (New York: Schocken, 2011).

academic policies revolving around the research. As Helmes-Hayes told me in an e-mail on March 8, 2012, in speaking of the Hughes papers, "It is truly a treasure trove of materials." For example, the rediscovery of ignored correspondence with Goffman unearths that Hughes had a dispute with his disciple because of the category of "total institution," which Goffman had appropriated from him.[255]

In the same way, the category of the banality of evil, which affected the research paths and historiography of World War II, in general, is still attributed to Arendt. Hughes's case can rebuild the so-called Arendt controversy and explain how scholars resort to it to understand precise political situations, ranging from state crimes to events of new violence to international politics.

To sum up, in 2010 Bernard Wasserstein and David Satter inaugurated the debate on evil and whether it was "banal or radical." Both Wasserstein and Satter wondered if Arendt's concept was still relevant. The debate has had positive results because it renews the discussion with Stangneth, whose research using the archives of the German state, which had never been consulted before, allowed her to systematically and thoroughly study a number of other issues related to the Holocaust, leading to sensational truths (the open letter of Eichmann to Adenauer, the reluctance to sue him in Germany because of the Nazi past of Globke, director of the German Chancellery in 1953–63), forcing scholars to begin other investigations (the 3,400 folders on Eichmann stored by the German Intelligence Service [BND] have yet to be declassified) and to review certain issues that have reopened unresolved cases (international networks that protected Eichmann, the communist threat, and relations between Israel and Germany, for example).

---

255   See Everett C. Hughes, "Memorandum on Total Institutions, *Sociologica* 2 (2010): 1–5, accessed March 28, 2012, doi:10.2383/32719; Philippe Vienne, "The Enigma of the Total Institution: Rethinking the Hughes–Goffman Intellectual Relationship," *Sociologica* 2 (2010), 1–5, accessed March 28, 2012, doi:10.2383/32720; Vienne, "Introduction to Everett C. Hughes' 'Memorandum on Total Institutions,'" *Sociologica* 2 (2010), 1–5, accessed March 28, 2012, doi:10.2383/32718. For a detailed study on the sociology of Everett C. Hughes, see Richard Helmes-Hayes, "Studying 'Going Concerns': Everett C. Hughes on Method," *Sociologica* 2 (2010): 1–27, accessed February 23, 2016, doi:10.2383/32714. I would like to thank Richard Helmes-Hayes for directing me to the articles about Hughes in *Sociologica* edited by Marco Santoro and him.

Hughes's thesis shows that the extermination of the Jews was possible thanks to the "grey-collar" class, as Allen explains, starting from 1997, reopening a debate in sociology. They have a "gray" collar because as blue collars they practice a manual work that is dirty; because they execute—they put in practice, into execution—a work directed from above, on the part of leading persons, white collars, who order the dirty, gray work, that is, of practicing the injustice and committing the death. In this way, they can be labeled as gray collars. Their attitudes are also gray, and recall the color gray, because they are not well defined, they are not clear in themselves: their attitude is not white, but it is not perfectly black, it is gray, a color as confused as their action, mixed in a way that evokes death or gray ashes. It is gray, intermediate between white and black, indeed, it is good people.

1.8. SUMMARY

Contrary to general opinion, it was not the Frankfurt School alone that approached the Jewish question. In this chapter, I have recalled the main sociological traditions, especially the Chicago School, and have tried to give an account of post-Holocaust sociology until the 1960s. Next, I analyzed with which categories and sociological devices they reached the objective of publicizing and publishing studies on the Holocaust. One could reflect on which factors (structural, political, academic) led to the delayed publication of these works; and we saw the factors (anti-Semitism, political agendas) that set up the famed sociological delay. This chapter has tried to demonstrate that this delay did not exist—as the Parsons, Hughes, Hartshorne, and Neurath cases, for instance, demonstrate. Meantime, it sought to prove the factors that did create this delay and which elements led to people to speak of the delay of sociology in approaching the Holocaust. The attention to historical facts and the consideration with which they were approached accounted for the trials and troubles post-Holocaust sociology experienced. In this chapter, Traverso's lesson in dealing with Auschwitz and intellectuals and Nazi violence is evident.

CHAPTER 2

The Destruction of the Jews in a Sociological Perspective during the 1970s

> Do not do unto thy neighbor what thou wouldst not like to have done to thyself. The rest is commentary.
> —**Hillel**
>
> Do not harm your neighbour and, if at all possible, save him … What doomed that experiment to fail was the fact that the Nazi mind had not considered the possibility of psychological resistance in extremity or the various forms of struggle and solidarity in self-defense.
>
> …
>
> Conspiratorial organizations in Auschwitz were closely linked to clandestine organizations outside the camp and historians will have to give their views (as precisely as the documents that have been preserved will allow) on how the foundations of organized conspiracy in the camp were laid.
> —**Anna Pawełczyńska, 1973**

2.1. PREFACE

The echo of the Third Arab–Israeli War, and above all the image of Jerusalem bombarded on June 5, 1967, continued to resound in the world during the 1970s. The fear of another Holocaust, after only twenty years, scared, unnerved, and impelled people to stand up against another destruction: "At Auschwitz in the 1940s, and at Jerusalem in 1967, Jews were singled out and alone."[1] Especially the Jews, but all humans, are called to remember what the Holocaust was and to hold it tight in memory: "Today, no Jew, however deeply involved in universally human concerns,

---

1 Fackenheim, *Quest for Past and Future*, 3.

can go on pretending to himself that he is a man-in-general. The universal and the particular are inextricably intertwined; he cannot be present at Selma and Hiroshima unless he is present at Auschwitz and Jerusalem."[2] In 1968, when the Jewish thinker Fackenheim said these words, he revealed in advance what Levy and Sznaider would elaborate in the 2000s, namely, the cosmopolitanism of the Holocaust. Under the ringing of deaths in Vietnam, "the commanding voice of Auschwitz bids Jews, religious and secularist, not to abandon the world to the forces of Auschwitz, but rather to continue to work and hope for it."[3] In any here and now. In these years, "a commanding voice is heard, and that is being heard with increasing clarity."[4] The post-Holocaust commandment, the so-called 614th commandment by Fackenheim, slowly took its shape: "For two long weeks in May 1967 the world-wide Jewish community perceived the spectre of a second Jewish holocaust in a single generation.... In May 1967 Jews heard the commanding voice of Auschwitz."[5] In the summer of 1967 it was clear that "Jews are not permitted to hand Hitler posthumous victories."[6] In protecting Jews from another extermination, increasing attention, or, rather, open attentiveness, was reserved for the Holocaust. The issue began to be dealt with more freely and without reserve in more scholarly disciplines. "The Commanding Voice of Auschwitz"[7] as a shofar summoning the Hebrews to battle or worship, seemed to be a political-moral warning that opened the brackets in which the Holocaust, and its discourse, had been put. It seemed to be the needed gate to the Holocaust question in the academy. It became a daily matter of discussion, for instance, when, at the University of Michigan in 1970s, Fackenheim presented in a seminar to Jewish students the question of the memory of 6 million Jews killed in the Holocaust. Fackenheim's discourses prepared new thinking grounds in general environments.

---

2 Ibid., 4.
3 Fackenheim, *God's Presence in History*, 87.
4 Fackenheim, *Quest for Past and Future*, 20.
5 Ibid., 24–25.
6 Ibid., 20. See Emil L. Fackenheim, "Jewish Values in the Post-Holocaust Future: A Symposium," *Judaism* 16, no. 3 (1967): 266–69.
7 Fackenheim, *God's Presence in History*, 67.

Looking at the overall development of post-Holocaust sociology between 1970 and 1979, it is striking how profoundly it changed in little less than a decade. These years can be described as a period of public "awakening" in the sense that the sociology profession as a whole updated itself on this topic. For many years, the Holocaust could not be prominent on the agenda of academic sociologists, and this delayed the spread of influential studies. What happened at the international level, resulting also from Willy Brandt's genuflection at Warsaw on December 7, 1970, was a rebound in sociological studies. Both historical works and sociological research, even if in a parallel way, sought the same aim: the accounting for what occurred in Europe to the Jews. These approaches could be made sociologically, since in the 1970s sociology was called to new challenges in passing to new developments as an academic discipline. This discourse varied from country to country, but what matters is that it was always far from functionalist assumptions. Above all, the Vietnam War with its oppositional dynamics between a liberal and socialist world ricocheted in sociological thought, leading to conflict sociology, a neo-Marxist view. Sociology of the 1970s also went through a phase of divisions within the discipline as a result of interdisciplinary influences, leading sociology to sectorialize itself in more strands and to the birth of new fields of sociology. Particularly, in this period emerged the importance of the sociology of organization and movements of social stratification, which resulted also from the historical movements of 1968 and the early 1970s that changed the history of many countries. However, primarily, general conflict theory—evident in the studies of Anna Pawełczyńska, Celia S. Heller, Barrington Moore, and Helen Fein, the outstanding researchers of Holocaust scholarship of the 1970s—allowed the reestablishment of the critical theory of the Frankfurt School. Principally, the negative conclusion of the Vietnam War for the United States, that is, the defeat for liberalism and the liberal world, permitted the termination of an era of liberal optimism sustained by functionalist thought. Meanwhile, the increasing specialization of sociology in several areas, concerned with methodology and approach (of gender, race, and so on) had as a result the introduction/revaluation of sociological journals, such as *Social Forces* or *Social Problems*, academic reviews perused for the occasion of rethinking post-Holocaust sociology.

In the 1970s, attention to microsociological issues came to dominate post-Holocaust sociological issues: they dealt with the *Shoah* and addressed basic sociological tools, such as movement, organization, group, mass, solidarity, ethnos, obedience, and revolt. A broad-ranging work on the Nazi concentration camp system appeared in 1973, coinciding with the outbreak of the war on Yom Kippur, the holiest day in the Jewish calendar. Meanwhile, as a result of the international economic crisis, the growing sociological shift toward research related to economic and government data, or attention to econometric devices and statistical methods, was seen in *Accounting for Genocide* by Fein in 1979. A concrete knowledge of the Holocaust became ever greater in the subsequent years.

2.2. AUSCHWITZ IN THE LIGHT OF ANNA PAWEŁCZYŃSKA: FROM VIOLENCE TO VALUES

To acquaint us better with the topic, my examination of post-Holocaust sociology follows a chronological order. At this point, it may be said that *Values and Violence* by Pawełczyńska inaugurated the post-Holocaust sociology of the 1970s. Being a work on post-Holocaust sociology was twice as great a charge as being a simple sociological piece. Starting from her original research and from what violence and values meant at Auschwitz for her, it is possible to delineate the prominence that sociological concepts such as movement and organized group have:

> While observing the shapes of the chimney smoke from the crematory, and without losing one's identification with those who died, one might envision little angels in flight and imagine the shape that one would take oneself at the appropriate time. Such a defense mechanism helped to lessen the camp terrors and the feeling of guilt toward those perished, as it also set a limit to Nazi power: what more can you do to me—I'll fly out through the chimney. So what?[8]

---

8 Anna Pawełczyńska, *Values and Violence in Auschwitz: A Sociological Analysis*, trans. Catherine S. Leach (Berkeley: University of California Press, 1979), 132; Polish edition is *Wartości A Przemoc: Zarys socjologicznej problematyki Oświęcimia* (Warsaw: Państwowe Wydawnictwo Naukowe, 1973).

Pawełczyńska, a political prisoner at Auschwitz-Birkenau, described the structure of the largest death camp, the *Vernichtungslager* of Auschwitz, correctly and in a timely manner. "The writing of this book," she commences in *Values and Violence in Auschwitz*, "needed the perspective of thirty years. Only historical distance, long reflection, and the calm of approaching old age made it possible to consider the concentration camp in objective categories."[9] Her written work is the careful, factual account of a witness who experienced Auschwitz; it is not the result of a process of revision of the collective memory. Despite being the result of a subjective experience ("a writing of memory [that] needs loneliness to account for the desolation of the lived experience"),[10] Pawełczyńska's analysis does not present smudges whatsoever attributable to imprisonment in the camp. This is due essentially to Stanisław Ossowski's teachings, which allow her to reach, starting from personal experience, a global perception of the concentration camp system.[11]

---

9   Ibid., 1.
10 See Traverso, *Auschwitz e gli intellettuali*, 20.
11 Stanisław Ossowski's sociological theory contributed significantly to the drafting of *Values and Violence*. He completed his studies in Warsaw, Paris, and Rome, and under the influence of Jan Łukasiewicz and Tadeusz Kotarbiński's Polish School of Logic. At the end of the World War II, he taught at the University of Łódź, eventually to hold, from 1947 onwards, the chair of sociology at the University of Warsaw. In 1957, he established the Polish Association of Sociology, of which he was president until his death. His masterpiece, *Struktura klasowa w społecznej świadomości* (1957), represents one of the most important attempts to compare the theoretical positions of Marxism with those of non-Marxist sociology.
Cf. Stanisław Ossowski, "Prawa 'historyczne' w socjologii," *Przegląd filozoficzny* 37 (1935): 3–32; Ossowski, *Struktura klasowa w społecznej świadomości* (Łódź, Wrocław: Zakład narodowy imienia Ossolińskich, 1957); Ossowski, *O osobliwościach nauk społecznych* (Warsaw: PWN, 1962). As Catherine Leach notes in her introduction to Pawełczyńska's book: "From Ossowski, Pawełczyńska learned to combine a precise conceptual framework and expository style with rigorous inductive analysis, and to view the results from a broad historical and cultural perspective. This method has made it possible for her to come to grips with a problem few scholars have been able (or willing) to tackle. It has enabled her to present the problems of the concentration camp in social categories familiar to everyone, while the richness of documentation (see Polish edition), which includes specialized scholarly studies, guarantees that her experience of the facts can be compared and expanded to the point where generalization becomes possible. What sets her study apart are the precise distinctions on which she bases her judgements—her analyses, for example, of spatial factors and communications, of the role of small groups, of the behaviour of the Muselmänner, of the function of the camp market. Through her complete avoidance of naturalism (which, by

Applying the lessons of "Prawa 'historyczne' w socjologii" (*The Laws of Historical Sociology* (1935) by Ossowski, she especially combines theoretical concepts and an analytical explanation typical of sociology with the inductive process, according to a perspective that takes account of events in general. This method not only allows her to confront problems that few scholars had been able to deal with,[12] but more importantly it helps to represent the environment and the situations of the concentration camp with categories familiar to readers, while the wealth of sources, especially in the Polish edition, is a guarantee of the quality of her research. Thus, when, thirty years later, Pawełczyńska put in writing and into perspective her own personal experience, that of a political prisoner, she transformed herself into a scholar of resistance:

> Pawełczyńska herself soon became a member of the Resistance and acted as a carrier for the underground press and also as a liaison for one of the officers of the Home Army in the Warsaw district. In addition she attended clandestine study sessions to prepare for her final examinations. Such illegal educational activity was carried on at great risk by school and university authorities throughout the occupation. While the author was taking her exams, the Gestapo arrested the group of instructors.[13]

Born in 1922 to a Polish family belonging to the middle class, soon after the German invasion of Poland in 1939, Pawełczyńska organized a

---

sparing the mind the paralyzing effects of horror, enables it to penetrate to inner laws) and her perspective as a cultural anthropologist, she succeeds in viewing the concentration camp in the context of the most basic values of European culture (or 'Western civilization'). And thus she brings her subject out of its isolation and neglect into the realm of contemporary social awareness" (Pawełczyńska, *Values and Violence in Auschwitz*, xxi).

See also Miroslaw Chałubiński, "The Sociological Ideas of Stanisław Ossowski: His Life, Fundamental Ideas and Sociology in Polish and World Science," *Journal of Classical Sociology* 6, no. 3 (2006): 283–309, accessed November 24, 2010, doi:10.1177/1468795X06069679.

12 Cf. Olga Wormser-Migot, *Le système concentrationnaire nazi (1933–1945)* (Paris: PUF, 1968); Falk Pingel, *Häftlinge unter SS-Herrschaft : Widerstand, Selbstbehauptung und Vernichtung im Konzentrationslager* (Hamburg: Hoffmann & Campe, 1978); Jane Caplan and Nikolaus Wachsmann, eds., *Concentration Camps in Nazi Germany: The New Histories* (London: Routledge, 2010).

13 Pawełczyńska, *Values and Violence in Auschwitz*, xiv.

program of humanitarian aid to the Polish soldiers wounded in war. Her very timely reaction to the invasion helps us understand how she was part of that generation of young people who glimpsed a further confirmation of the tragic history of Poland in the outbreak of the conflict and a return to foreign domination and dependence.

Values and Violence in Auschwitz is a sociological masterpiece, almost a treatise on sociology, through which it is possible to read the history of Poland. In the text, the echoes of the master Ossowski are noticeable: Pawełczyńska makes each historical and political background not just a digression or presentation of knowledge, but a rich source of information to explain how the events at Auschwitz have to be put into relation with the Polish past. In this way, important and original aspects on the Jewish question are highlighted.

Pawełczyńska did not write about Auschwitz during the war or even at its end, but only after thirty long years of silence, during which she acquired the basic concepts of sociology, criminology, and history:[14] "It was my friend and colleague Stanislaw Kłodziński, of Krakow, who encouraged me: he said that to write down my experience not only would help me to rearrange my life, but it would also serve others: a 'story for the whole society,' he meant it in this way, and that is a sociological lesson after Auschwitz; on his insistence I convinced myself to do it."[15]

---

14 The author spent the Stalinist years completing various studies "in the field," in particular dealing with juvenile delinquency. In this regard, she was part of a research team in the Criminology Section of the Polish Academy of Sciences' Institute of Legal Studies. In 1956, the so called Thaw year, she was in France as a visiting sociologist at the Institute of Demography and Public Opinion Research. This latter Institute resulted from the strong development sociology had in France after 1945. Through her multifaceted training, she was also an expert in statistics, ecology, and urban studies (her works on the relationship between the environment, society, and territory are remarkable), and together with the scientific activities in the field of empirical social research and public opinion, she was able give a sociological explanation of Auschwitz, putting aside the way of religious naturalism; see Pawełczyńska, *Values and Violence in Auschwitz*, xxi–xxii.

15 My interview (Warsaw, December 20, 2011) with Anna Pawełczyńska, "Nel campo di Auschwitz," *Free Ebrei: Rivista di identità ebraica contemporanea* 4, no. 2 (2015), http://www.freeebrei.com/anno-iv-numero-2-luglio-dicembre-2015/nel-campo-di-auschwitz-a-cura-di-adele-valeria-messina; republished with further presentation in *DEP* 30 (2016): 202–26, http://www.unive.it/nqcontent.cfm?a_id=200057. I particularly thank Hanna K. Ulatowska for the translation from Polish into English during the interview.

When Pawełczyńska joined the underground army against the Nazis, her political objectives were, like those of all other resistant Poles, strongly characterized by feelings of a patriotic nature, focused on the fight for the independence of the country. After her arrest, on August 15, 1942, she found herself locked up for nine months in Pawiak prison.[16] Resistant to torture during interrogation and, although she did not receive any condemnation, she was sent, on May 13, 1943, to Auschwitz-Birkenau, where she was recorded as a political prisoner, number 44764. From May 1943 to October 1944, she remained in Auschwitz and took part in the resistance movement inside the camp, being part of the command of the women's camp. Particularly, she profited from favorable situations that arose when, together with some prisoner detachments, she went to work in the subcamps outside of the main camp. As the result of a disease, she was then housed in the "sick bay for prisoners" until the late fall of 1943.

As a political inmate, she was in a privileged position to analyze the functioning of the *Lager* and the changes within it. Along with Zofia Brodzikowską-Pohorecka, Janina Tollik, Zarzycka Anna (Eva Agapsowicz), and Maria Mazurkiewicz, she put her own life at risk to fill in secret lists of women and children transported to Auschwitz in August and September 1944, following the repression of the Warsaw Uprising.[17] These lists are, in many cases, the only documents that can prove the presence of an individual at Auschwitz. She was transferred at the end of October 1944, in Dresden, to one of the Auschwitz subcamps at the Flossenbürg factory of the Zeiss-Ikon group, then in April 1945, during the evacuation of the subcamp, while she was close to the front, she fled from the marching columns and found refuge in the forests, where she remained until May 7. From here, and throughout the month of June, she prepared an assistance program for Poles returning home.

At the end of the war, like many survivors, or rather like all those who passed through the experience of Nazi totalitarianism, Pawełczyńska also

---
16 Cf. Julian Hirshaut, "Paviak Memoirs," in *Anthology on Armed Jewish Resistance 1939–1945*, ed. Isaac Kowalski (Brooklyn, NY: JCPH, 1991), 493–506.
17 Pawełczyńska speaks of it widely in the interview with me mentioned above.

fed her desire to work towards a better society.[18] She realized this aspiration through the study of society. Back in Warsaw, in fact, she attended sociology courses with Stanisław Ossowski and Maria Ossowska and Jan Strzelecki, and, in 1960, she obtained her doctorate under the supervision of Ossowski, from whom she inherited the refusal of a rigid Marxism and mechanical assimilation of Marx's axioms.

Values and Violence in Auschwitz: A Sociological Analysis is the literal translation of the Polish *Wartości a przemoc: Zarys socjologicznej problematyki Oświęcimia*.[19] This was the first sociological analysis of the Nazi concentration camp system—after Abel's analysis of the concentration camps (1951)—centered on its social organization, relations between prisoners, strategies of survival, and inner resistance.[20] Values and violence are construed as social forces that coexist with each other, albeit in the opposite way, in the *Lager*. In many ways it also appears as a study of philosophy, politics, law, medicine, and psychology, of great importance because the author was a survivor, who moreover addressed the issue of resistance practiced in the camps at a time when it was not discussed at all, not to say that it was explicitly denied.[21] In 1973, when during the Yom Kippur War the vulnerability of Israeli army led to the collapse of the myth of an ever-victorious Israel, in the collective thought the ideology of military force began to slowly crack, giving rise to a new idea of resistance, in which weapons or physical force lost their centrality.[22] In this sense, it spoke of a change of perspective from armed resistance to unarmed resis-

---

18 Cf. Pawełczyńska, *Values and Violence in Auschwitz*, xviii–xix. Bauman belongs to Ossowski's school too.
19 The first English edition translated in place of "violence," "coercion," and proposed as a subtitle *An Outline of the Sociology of Auschwitz* instead of *A Sociological Analysis*. See Pawełczyńska, "Values and Violence Sociology of Auschwitz," *Polish Sociological Bulletin* 3 (1976): 5–17.
20 Cf. Theodore Abel, "The Sociology of Concentration Camps," *Social Forces* 30, no. 2 (1951): 150–55, doi:10.2307/2571626.
21 She received the Book Award in the field of Scientific and Popular Research of Modern Polish History in 1974 and won the prize dedicated to Ossowski (Stanisław Ossowski Award) by the Polish Sociological Association. The American edition appeared in 1979, and the German, *Werte gegen Gewalt*, in 2001.
22 See Jeffrey C. Alexander et al., *Remembering the Holocaust: A Debate* (New York: Oxford University Press, 2009), 182–83, 191.

tance. The picture offered by Pawełczyńska did not find a receptive international audience: it was not possible to conceive any action of resistance within the Auschwitz camp, and this especially because, in the period in which the scholar published, there was still a tendency to think of resistance as only armed resistance.[23]

2.2.1. Inside the Time and Space of Auschwitz

Every manifestation of resistance, even though reprisals (and guilt by association) threatened those who took part in it, cracked the structure of terror, proved to those who had lost hope that hope existed, showed that there were indeed ways out of a dead-end situation, and they were various. Every method of opposition—no matter whether it increased the survival odds for a group of prisoners or a particular person, or was the immediate cause of death for the resister—expressed a protest against violence.

Every manifestation of loyalty and cooperation was proof that terror liberates the strength to resist and produces attitudes of self-reliance. This self-reliance was expressed not only through the struggle for life but also through independent choice of the type of death. This struggle for life and self-reliance was also waged in the sphere of values. Every gesture of loyalty, of sympathy, and of organized resistance was an externalization and a defense of the basic values of European civilization against the terrorism of those who denied the existence of those values.... This common system of values united

---

23 On resistance without weapons, see Henri Michel, *The Shadow War: European Resistance 1939–1945* (New York: Harper & Row, 1972); Bruno Bettelheim, *Surviving and Other Essays* (New York: Knopf, 1979); Vittorio E. Giuntella, Il nazismo e i Lager (Rome: Studium, 1979); Jacques Sémelin, *Senz'armi di fronte ad Hitler: La Resistenza civile in Europa, 1939–1943* (Turin: Sonda, 1993); Abraham J. Edelheit and Hershel Edelheit, *History of the Holocaust: A Handbook and Dictionary* (Boulder, CO: Westview, 1994); Antonio Parisella, *Sopravvivere liberi: Riflessioni sulla storia della Resistenza a cinquant'anni dalla Liberazione* (Rome: Gangemi, 1997); Dan Michman, *Pour une historiographie de la Shoah: Conceptualisations, terminologie, définitions et problèms fondamentaux* (Paris: In Press Éditions, 2001); Howard Blum, *La brigata: Una storia di guerra, di vendetta e di redenzione* (Milan: il Saggiatore, 2002); Robert Rozett, "Jewish Resistance," in *The Historiography of the Holocaust*, ed. Dan Stone (New York: Palgrave Macmillan, 2004), 341–63.

prisoners and their nations and strengthened their resistance, thanks to the sense of support. The Germans who resisted the turning of their government into a terroristic Nazi gang during the period 1933–39 did not have such support.[24]

Values and Violence constitutes another piece refuting the thesis of the sociological delay. In some ways, reading *Values and Violence* means to enter the Auschwitz camp, the life of the community of prisoners. The book is divided into twelve chapters that provide an in-depth analysis of the reality of Auschwitz, focusing on the relationship between the physical place and natural body of any inmate. The object of research is the group-community of prisoners, with its determinants and especially the relationships that are formed among the residents in that delimited space and at that time. *Values and Violence* highlights, on the one hand, the values that are at the basis of human behavior, which are also found in Auschwitz, and on the other, it emphasizes the consequences of Nazi violence.

Pawełczyńska, concerned about placing Auschwitz geographically, establishing where it is and what there is outside of it, presents the outside world, in its position and in its structure, before investigating the inner camp. In the wake of the Chicago School, the concepts of space (physical and social) and of time are central from the beginning. The constant reference to the physical-spatial element is needed to consider the attitudes assumed by the inmates and to assess their chances of survival. Her intensely factual written account almost seems like an autopsy examination, which captures the subtle relationship between environment and person, exploring in depth the community of prisoners and mechanisms of functioning of the Auschwitz system.[25] Blocks, barracks, crematoria: all places dominated by the same principle of closure and total control of space and time. This is the first definition that the author gives about Auschwitz: it is primarily a

---

24 Pawełczyńska, *Values and Violence in Auschwitz*, 121–22.
25 See Hans G. Adler, "Ideas toward a Sociology of the Concentration Camp," *American Journal of Sociology* 63, no. 5 (1958): 513–22; Christian Fleck and Albert Müller, "Bruno Bettelheim and the Concentration Camps," *Journal of the History of the Behavioral Sciences* 33, no. 1 (1997): 1–37, doi:10.1002/(SICI)1520-6696(199724)33:1<1::AID-JHBS1>3.0.CO;2-Y.

concentration camp. Now, in the physical sciences, the camp is a region of limited space, under observation, where physical quantities behave as forces. For Pawełczyńska, inside the Auschwitz camp two types of forces, interacting in the opposite view to each other, unfold. On the one hand, a destructive force, to which the author gives the name of violence (*przemoc*), a term consciously adopted in the singular. On the other, a defense mechanism, always a force that reacts to violence, a reactive force made up of bonds of solidarity, which takes the name of values (*wartości*), a term used in the plural and placed first in the title of the volume, almost emphasizing the victory of good over evil. The reference is clearly to Durkheim, who explained several times in his writings that holding a society together is a set of values, which he called "morals."

As regards the Nazi terror and violence, Pawełczyńska, a Polish intellectual and against any kind of totalitarian power and knowing well the consequences in her country that resulted from the suppressing of the Prague Spring, when the Polish People's Army participated in repressing the 1968 democratization process of Czechoslovakia, in her book stresses the relevance of communities of solidarity to pierce and fight totalitarianism. And in *Values and Violence* she reports the cases in which certain moral values prevailed among the prisoners that led to the formation of communities of solidarity: through small and "stubborn" acts of resistance and friendship, prisoners at Auschwitz fought against the authority of the legitimate terror and against all forms of demoralization. The contemporary political facts of her native Poland helps her account for her past in Auschwitz, and her past in Auschwitz allows her to denounce Polish totalitarian power and limits of socialism with a human face. *Values and Violence* is almost in a way written to fight communism and to stop totalitarian power. Nevertheless, some events helped set the stage for her work: in December 1970, Willy Brandt knelt down at the monument to victims of the Warsaw Uprising, asking forgiveness for Nazi crimes. This public asking for forgiveness and reconciliation, and the treaty with West Germany, initiated five years earlier with a "Letter of Reconciliation of the Polish Bishops to the German Bishops," in 1965, supported her return to her past in Auschwitz, in accounting for what happened in a Poland of the 1970s, building positive relations with Germany. To construct a human society in post-Holocaust Poland, to build a democratic liberal future between the two countries, it was crucial to return to the past and step-by-step to recognize publicly what had occurred: including guilt and accountability. For Pawełczyńska, encouraged by her friend Klodziński, the time to write her experience had arrived.

Returning to the construct of "camp," and even more the general meaning of "field theory," it provides insight into the specifics of a social phenomenon. One can understand in what sense Pawełczyńska conceives Auschwitz as a social phenomenon thanks to what Durkheim said, when, in his *Les règles de la méthode sociologique*, he defines the social fact as any attitude, fixed or not, capable of exercising on the individual an external constraint, or as any general manner within a given society, since it has its own existence, independently by individual events.[26] Focusing attention on the adjective "social," meaning a phenomenon (social), an anonymous and impersonal end that stands above all particular consciousness and therefore can serve to unite them, one may understand how Pawełczyńska explains the constitution of community of solidarity in Auschwitz. Actions, beliefs, values, languages, patterns of behavior, in Durkheim's language "facts" or "social phenomena," in *Values and Violence* are all reinterpreted on the basis of a fundamental norm:

> In every camp situation there would be prisoners forming into groups—though continually fragmented by the camp system—uniting together in the practice of the basic norm, "Do not harm your neighbour and, if it at all possible, save him," even in the most oppressive conditions. It was the prisoner's most important field of battle.[27]

"Do not harm your neighbour and, if it at all possible, save him" was the moral norm that had supported in the Auschwitz system small solidarity groups of an organic type, ensuring the continuation of human society.[28] For this reason, the camp in her work is dominant. It is a dynamic system in which laws do not hinge on the individual characteristics of the elements

---

26 See Émile Durkheim, *Les règles de la méthode sociologique* (Paris: F. Alcan, 1895).
27 Pawełczyńska, *Values and Violence in Auschwitz*, 144.
28 Cf. Ferdinand Tönnies, *Gemeinschaft und Gesellschaft* (Berlin: Karl Curtius, 1912).

involved (in the specific case, of individuals), but on the configuration and the movements of the forces acting on its inside. Because the events that occur in a given area and at a given time do not have another explanation than that which arises from the properties of the field itself, the configuration and properties of Auschwitz allow the deployment of two types of forces that, in their interacting, determine a phase of equilibrium:

> Prisoners' individual reactions, their reactions as members of small spontaneously formed (and frequently fragmented) groups, and their organized reactions were expressions of their outlook on life and their values, which changed under the influence of the relations and conditions in the camp.... Every prisoner had his own "neighbors." In the midst of the fight against a world of hatred, as a reaction to a degenerate system of terror, a world of friendship came into being. And precisely in this sense, regardless of prisoner conduct that did not harmonize with the standards of free societies, the concentration camp established a basic norm, the observance of which is everywhere indispensable, and it created a new moral value: that bond with the wronged which demands the greatest renunciations.[29]

In accordance with the principle of temporal causality, she moves towards an explanation of the facts that focuses on the dynamics of the system and that puts together all the elements involved, namely, the inner world (subjective) of inmates with that outside. This approach conflicts with the principles of Nazi totalitarian politics, which tend to atomize individuals and make them an amorphous and total whole. Cognitive, emotional, and environmental factors, in their interdependent system, clarify which laws govern life in a concentration camp, ensuring its subsistence.

2.2.2. The Hodological Space in the Structure of Terror

Extremely complex issues are presented in a simple way, as evidenced by the substantial bibliography in the original Polish edition, which accounts for a

---

29 Pawełczyńska, *Values and Violence in Auschwitz*, 101, 144.

debate and a school of thought, which was largely unknown to German- or English-speaking readers. The examination is original, first because the author is an Auschwitz survivor, an eyewitness to what happened. Second, she had been deported for having joined the Home Army (*Armia Krajowa*). Finally, in the book published in Poland in 1973, for the first time she introduced sociological categories that helped to analyze the specific fate of women, an issue that until then had nearly no place in Holocaust Studies.

Inside the camp, intended as "a totality of social facts coexisting in their social interdependence," Pawełczyńska identifies some subfields of study corresponding, in the physical space of Auschwitz, to four subsections.

(1) A "living space" where the individual prisoner moves: the physical environment in which he lives and the psychological one with which he perceives things. This living space includes needs, motivations, moods, fears, goals, ideals, and the reactions of those who find themselves within the camp. "Yes, the humor: for me it was vital; I have felt that it was the only way to survive," she says in an interview in Warsaw in December 2011.[30] (2) The multiplicity of processes that unfold in the physical and social world of the major camp. (3) The third zone is not well defined and it is called "boundary." It is one in which the individual prisoner builds her own camp structure (hence the extensive and very detailed analysis by the author of maps, photos, measurements in height and width) and absorbs the social processes that develop. In this frontier space each force converges: the physical world, social phenomena, and the nervous structure. Here the behavior of inmates unfolds as an extension of the relationship between environmental factors, camp conditions, and values of a personal kind. However, above all, in this area with uncertain borders, the individual has the opportunity to start resistance defense mechanisms against terror. (4) The perceptual process determined by external physical stimuli, that is, by that part of the physical world that directly affects the sense organs; it is closely connected to the world of interpersonal relationships among prisoners and determines the execution of action.

Pawełczyńska, faithful to Weber's idea of social action motivated by and oriented to the attitude of other individuals, seeks to outline what

---

30 See note 15, above.

type of social action has been produced in Auschwitz.[31] As Floyd H. Allport already wrote in 1924, the meaning of social behavior is the same as the nonsocial;[32] in this case, for Auschwitz prisoners, biological individual maladjustment determines social action.

However, the study of a dynamical system understandably includes environmental factors and social facts but also strictly individual elements, such as the nervous structure of a person. Pawełczyńska focuses just on the system of physical-social relations that unfold in the *Lager*, on all the factors that come into play, and they are related in the same physical space. Therefore, she proposes a particular idea of social camp to appreciate how social phenomena not hinging on single individuals were deployed in Auschwitz.

This camp is seen as an experimental field, a social experiment that requires, like physical-mathematical sciences in the early stages of testing, submission to precise physical laws in order to ensure the success of the experiment in progress. In the *Lager*, the major law is the ideology of physical and mental terror, applied through technology and social engineering. In essence, obedience and willing acceptance prevail. On the limits of Auschwitz's space, Pawełczyńska elaborates a very precise, refined, almost geometric, analysis.

Auschwitz is a historical fact, a social phenomenon and a physical reality: it is a structured space, finished and at the same time composed of parts infinitely divisible into several subcamps, yet spaced among them. Pawełczyńska, partly conditioned by her past as a member of the Resistance requiring a specific knowledge of a topological nature and a practical expertise typical of topography, represents the most likely spaces and times of Auschwitz as an "hodological space." Namely, she alludes not only to the geometric characteristics of the place, but also to the type of relationships that take shape inside the same, among prisoners (analysis from the individual-social point of view) or among several subcamps (from the systemic-spatial point of view)[33]:

---
31   See Weber, *Economy and Society*.
32   Cf. Floyd H. Allport, *Social Psychology* (Boston: Houghton Mifflin, 1924).
33   See Kurt Lewin, *Field Theory in Social Science* (New York: Harper & Row, 1951); Pawełczyńska, *Values and Violence in Auschwitz*, 24–43. Pawełczyńska describes the plan of Auschwitz I, but she also presents the photographs, the internal divisions, geographical

The dimensions of concentration-camp space: the length of the road to work, the size of the subcamps, the barracks, and the bunks and "roosts," were radically transformed in the consciousness of the prisoners living in that space. Because of the prisoners' physical deterioration, the way to work felt like a march many dozens of miles long—the onerousness of that walk was intensified by shoes that were suited neither for such purposes nor for the prisoners' foot sizes. The subcamp seemed like a large city divided up by a main artery and side streets.[34]

Not surprisingly, the paragraph of the third chapter of "Living Space" (*Przestrzeń do Życia*) begins with the words "At home" (*W domu*), which, in a lapidary way, refer to how totalitarian power penetrates into the inner personal life of the individual, transforming Auschwitz into a daily environment where intimacy, made public, loses any value. The choice of the term "home" rather than "house" (stressing the family environment rather than the brick building, the building itself), on the one hand, accounts for the pervasive and total power of Nazi coercion that encroached upon family life, and on the other, it highlights the opposite meaning. Namely, that in Auschwitz even forces of solidarity and solid ties of friendship, typical of a warm environment and family, unfold. In explaining the dynamics of opposed social forces, Pawełczyńska, when introducing the categories of opposites ("open-inner/open-closed" and "whole–part"), lets *Values and Violence* become a treasurable work in Holocaust Studies.

The first category of "open-inner" dominates the entire first chapter, "The World outside the Camp," (*Świat poza obozem—Układy odniesienia*) where the *Lager* is presented as an organized structure of power according to the bureaucratic model of the German state. The author speaks of the world outside Auschwitz always referring to the German state system

---

locations, the site of the Auschwitz II-Birkenau, the size of bunk beds, roosts, the sketch plan of the crematory III in Auschwitz II-Birkenau, the distances to work sites outside the camp in kilometers, and, finally, some photos from the archives. What is striking is her perfect description.

34 Pawełczyńska, *Values and Violence in Auschwitz*, 41–42

that allowed Nazi violence. Hodological opposition space, based on "inside–outside" directions, recalls the concept of relationship among individuals belonging to the inner world and those forming part of the outer world. Particularly, "external" direction among inmates refers to their thoughts, which lead them to escape, at least in dreams, from the camp. This is not a simple removal from reality but, rather, a complex defense mechanism that serves to enter life within the camp. Through the binomial of the opposites "whole–part," she refers instead to how, facing the total system of terror, the part of values unfolds. The tension between the "whole" of terror and the "part" of values clearly causes an unbalanced situation. Faced with the threat of terror, the strength of resistance, applied to violence, increases: "natural need" spreads the bonds of solidarity also, and, as Pawełczyńska says, "the mechanism of individual and organized resistance in extremity—the inner resources which man, under extreme conditions, is capable of bringing to bear against crime."[35] It is also in the wake of concepts of social distance, ecological space, and border from the Chicago School that Pawełczyńska provides her description of Auschwitz:

> If one interprets the site of the main camp, the subcamps, the construction and use of the residential dwellings in spatial terms, then considering the function served an analogy can be made with certain types of colonial settlements. The subcamps numbered, on the average, several tens of thousands of prisoners; they formed peculiar city-states set apart by boundaries, the crossing of which was prohibited to their inhabitants and carried penalties similar to those attached to an illegal crossing of national boundaries.
> Lengthier contacts, in situations where men and women were working in close proximity or where a work crew under the supervision of an SS officer was sent onto the grounds of another subcamp, made possible not only the exchange of information but also the transmittal of things. In this way the crisscrossing of two divisional systems extended living space by breaking through the

---

35 Ibid., 2.

boundaries of isolated city-states and creating a system of communication among them.³⁶

2.2.3. Resistance as Defense of the Dimension of Life by Group Dynamics

Resistance can be expressed in many ways. Not every situation affords the chance to give open battle, or even to make a passive protest. Under the circumstances at Auschwitz, maximum adaptation had to be achieved. Resistance was expressed in the constant effort to maintain inner freedom while outwardly adapting. In the battle for this freedom prisoners gave each other mutual assistance.³⁷

Pawełczyńska's book is significant for post-Holocaust sociology since it addresses the discourse of resistance in a period, the 1970s, in which this topic was not well known or discussed. Let me focus, here, on what Pawełczyńska refers to when she tackles the theme of resistance. For her, "to resist" essentially means "to rescue," that is, an act of defense of human life. This type of social action that puts everything into play, even the possibility of losing one's own life, brings to mind the concept of "sanctification of life" usually attributed to Yitzhak Nissebaum, the rabbi of the Warsaw ghetto, but it dates back to earlier times and is used to define Jewish survival. Beyond characteristics and definitions, she clearly returns to the theme of the *Amidah*, which, in this context, can be translated as "upright," meaning that "to resist" basically means "to stand." How did they remain standing at Auschwitz? How was sanctification of life possible? The Jews undertook to continue a civil life under conditions imposed upon them by a force that had abandoned all previous humanistic tradition, an effort based on an instinctive impulse to move forward, both through the traditional way of life based on religion, in most cases, and through the most ancient traditions combined with modern humanism, liberalism, or socialism.³⁸ When this occurred, either individually or through solidarity acts by the

---

36 Ibid., 30, 42.
37 Ibid., 127.
38 See Bauer, *Rethinking the Holocaust*, 119–66.

group, the Jewish community managed to survive Auschwitz. "These were the most strenuous tests of human feelings; they were ultimate decisions—love or death," which explains the basic meaning of social action in the eyes of Pawełczyńska.[39] Many forms of resistance in the *Lager* are possible, because a bond of feeling (an "optimistic bond among prisoners" that makes them a unified group) unites many inmates.[40] At stake is not armed victory, but the triumph of humanity in front of an inhuman world.[41]

At the root of every act of resistance are found elements of love and compassion: "No one ever knew the price that might have to be paid for such an act of friendship, of solidarity, of duty, and many a time we paid very dearly. Yet this, too, was taken into account."[42] Pawełczyńska emphasizes a specific form of awareness, linked to what happened on September 1, 1939, when the Germans entered Poland: from that time, a history of violence and attacks on national independence began for Poland. Facing the threat of invaders, several situations of cohesion, circumstances, and places of unity arose; and the first clandestine organizations of resistance and underground movements took shape. Experiences from outside the camp, before Auschwitz, therefore made the building of unbreakable bonds possible within the camp, where Tönnies's *idem* feeling, which unites individuals against Nazi terror and against the loss of national independence, in spite of the atomization that German policy, resounded as "an unbreakable bond":

> Every show of aid counteracted the prisoners' isolation, which formed a necessary part of the Nazi plan of extermination. The need to minister to those in prison broke every ideological barrier and created a platform for organized cooperation between the various groups of the Polish Resistance. Those who took part in relief

---

39 Pawełczyńska, *Values and Violence in Auschwitz*, 96.
40 Ibid., 97.
41 See Pawełczyńska, *Values and Violence in Auschwitz*, 6, with reference to Tadeusz Strzembosz, *Odbijanie i uwalnianie więźniów w Warszawie, 1939–1944* (Warsaw: PWN, 1972).
42 Ibid., 13. Pawełczyńska recourses to Strzembosz's testimony to better explain the risks of those who decided to resist: "Every camp, every prison in Poland was surrounded by a similar atmosphere of fraternal support. Prices for those acts of friendship and loyalty were paid on both sides of the barbed wire; both the givers and the receivers perished in Nazi reprisals" (ibid., 14).

actions—underground organizations, families and friends of prisoners, local residents in the vicinity of camps situated on Polish territory—were people not indifferent to misfortune, who risked their lives neither for fame nor reward but in simple response to a heart that was sensitive to pain and the dimensions of that pain. A broadly-based moral community grew up, bringing together people of various social strata, people in various life situations; the awareness of this community constituted a great strength which made it possible for prisoners to mobilize various defense mechanisms to resist Nazi terror. Regardless of what form the relief actually took—from gestures of friendly greeting to aid in organizing escapes—every bit of help from the outside bolstered not only the physical stamina of a concrete individual, but helped many prisoners to muster their psychic forces, something that would have been beyond the means of a person deprived of hope and support.[43]

Between the inside and the outside of the camp there is a continuous line exceeding the barbed wire and connecting the world of the *Lager* with civil society. If, in the totalitarian Nazi order the same social groups and aggregates of people present in the traditional civil society are suggested, within the camp any element of distinction between an individual and the other is cleared, in particular national identity, with the last consequence of deleting any form of social differentiation, and then the person itself:

> This badge marked people of Jewish origin, regardless of their citizenship or national sentiments. Culturally many of these prisoners were incomparably closer to prisoners who came from the same country as themselves than they were to the mass of prisoners marked with the yellow triangle. This symbol was worn by people transported from Poland, Hungary, Slovakia, Greece, Austria, and Germany, and no criteria exist (but the Nazi) that would enable all of them to be treated as a homogeneous group.[44]

---

43   Ibid., 12.
44   Ibid., 91.

At the base of national identity there are common values among individuals, such as language and culture. Although the Nazi violence tended to destroy national groups, inside the camp the various national identities are involved in the same social actions: driven by the same need to resist the terror, they cooperate with each other in front of the totalitarian whole. Pawełczyńska also proposes an ethnogenic analysis. Where are the places to practice solidarity and to shape homogeneous groups? To prepare for resistance there are, first, social adaptation, as a reduction of material needs, self-control of goods, food, and clothing, which the author calls "inner resistance":

> Inner resistance took various forms. One could eat the desired piece of bread immediately. Or one could, though feeling hungry, keep part of it in one's pocket, conscious of freedom won: I am not eating it all, because I choose not to. This form of self-defense, however, was related to the tolerance of hunger, which varies widely among individuals.[45]

Second, knowledge of *Lager* laws is essential: the understanding of inner mechanisms of the camp helps to move with ability, facilitating resistance acts. The inmates who are in the same subcamp for a long time have better knowledge of the SS-functionaries' (*Posten*) action and break times, their spaces and turnovers. The control under the spaces and times of the camp means to be aware of all possible movements, opportunities, and hidden dangers; for that reason prisoners are subject to continuous transfers.[46] Similar to what happens in an experimental field, even in Auschwitz, similar conditions for survival are created in order to resist. Here, it is possible to retrieve an echo of the justice and suffering theory resulting

---

45 Ibid., 128.
46 Cf. ibid., 119, 134. At Auschwitz two types of criteria were used in dividing prisoners into groups: on the one hand, the criterion of residence, which served to form "residential groups" subject to constant change, on the other, that of the place, which served to divide the place of residence and then the prisoners: "Crossing a camp section from one end to the other was perceived as a distance crossed on foot in a rather large city—in the prisoner's mind that distance was increased by the swampiness of the terrain, which added to the effort of getting around" (ibid., 42).

from iniquity, according to which the prisoners come together to act together as a united body, starting from a similar conception of justice, by the same social suffering:

> In this gamble for life over which the prisoners had no influence, fate, like a roulette ball, would come to rest on the black or on the red—the red meant living to see the end of the Nazi era and realizing one's dreams of a normal life; the black meant the end of one's own life and the chance for others to survive.[47]

2.2.3.1. Resistance as Communication

Pawełczyńska's work is extraordinary because in 1973 she introduced the notion of resistance in post-Holocaust sociological literature in an unprecedented way. She specifies a series of unusual places where detainees practice resistance acts. For instance, in bunk beds (places where prisoners belonging to the same ethnic or social origin often found themselves), it is easier because they speak the same language. It is in these "bed places," which become common spaces since inmates share similar experiences, that a first collective feeling is made, one that motivates prisoners to communicate with each other and form collaborative groups. These places are unique opportunities to pass information about forms of resistance they want to arrange. Since these areas are beyond the total control of the SS, there are many suspects. For these reasons, the guards repeatedly practice continuous transfers of detainees, from barrack to barrack, in order to limit any kind of collaboration, break the bonds of solidarity, and prevent any forms of community survival.

For Pawełczyńska, another place of resistance is the space between the barracks; actually, it is an artery of communication, still subject to the Nazi guards' control, but to a lesser extent than the main road of the camp. In this place, the prisoners can build bonds of friendship or business, but, more importantly, they can also exchange information or consult regarding resistance initiatives.

---

47 Ibid., 132.

The bathrooms are also points of contact and communication where news and alerts can be passed along. Next to the barbed wire, which isolates the subcamp of women at Birkenau, there is a narrow strip of bare earth, called the "meadow." It is a space of relative rest and a meeting place where prisoners, forcibly brought from the barracks for disinfestation, can communicate. There is also a railway platform, enclosed by barbed-wire cordons, placed at the center of the subcamp of women and of a section of the subcamp of men: "During periods of relaxed supervision people could meet their loved ones at this spot, letting themselves be seen, and in this way telling them that they were still alive."[48] However, the prisoners are put in that condition to prepare their defense actions mainly thanks to a ban (the so-called *Blocksperre*), which prevents them from leaving the barracks. Precisely in virtue of this prohibition, they learn the selection times for gas chambers. If, at first glance, this refusal to leave the barracks seems to interrupt communication lines, it actually informs about internal events in the camp. In other words, the *Blocksperre* functions as a sentinel, warning the prisoners and alerting them to different times of events in the camp: from the arrival of new transports to every possible destination.

Another time or place in which resistance can be organized is in food transportation.[49] Nevertheless, it is mainly the work camps that provide daily spaces where inmates can transmit news and receive information:

> The work sites, besides consolidating the work crew, performed still another function (thanks to the prisoners' heightened ingenuity) which had nothing to do with the work performed. All cracks and holes, sometimes even larger hiding-places, could serve to keep various necessaries with which prisoners could increase their chances of survival (e.g., food, clothing, medicine) and the crews' occupational contacts constituted a communication network used for transmitting these things to other prisoners, or for exchange. Things connected with the organized resistance movement in the camp could also be kept in these hiding-places.[50]

---

48 Ibid., 35.
49 Cf. ibid., 69.
50 Ibid., 40.

Even the work teams become places to pass information. If the division "for teams" and that "for barracks" are specially designed to break the links between prisoners, continuously limiting their ability to form any kind of relationship, the continuing divisions among prisoners facilitates lines of communication as they widen contact points between different prisoners, by passing information along a larger number of prisoners. The information then passes through the organized labor of prisoners:

> After some time, thanks to the organized work of prisoners, certain key points in the camp's framework of terror began to crack; the doctors were able to obtain by "illegal" means some medicine and nourishment for the prisoners—minimal, of course, in relation to the need—and they also received necessary information for saving the sick from other forms of terror.[51]

The same travel conditions are excellent opportunities to form identities and bonds of organic solidarity: prisoners traveling in the same carriage easily aggregate into small groups to exchange news and facts. Finally, an unusual form of resistance comes from the power that some prisoners are able to acquire from their superiors. This strategy allows them to overcome the barrier that separates prisoners from the camp authorities, but it is especially conducive to the development of various forms of organized resistance: "It is a little what happens to Martha and Liza, the protagonists of *Pasażerka*: the strong personality of Martha, Polish political prisoner in Auschwitz, influences Liza, the German SS, who, indubitably, does not want to save Martha. Rather than using the carrot and the stick, she aspires to become an accomplice of her crimes and to keep her a slave obedient and submissive."[52]

> The prisoners, who were usually more intelligent than their overseers, knew how to observe and make use of their supervisors' weaknesses

---

51 Ibid., 73.
52 My interview with Zofia Posmysz-Piasecka, Warsaw, December 19, 2011. I particularly thank Hanna K. Ulatowska for translation from the Polish in English.

like laziness, desire for advancement, greed, desire to insure their family's material well-being, desire for great riches, fear of other SS officers, desire for a professional approval of their performance from a superior.[53]

2.2.3.2. The Market as Defense Mechanism Par Excellence

Pawełczyńska's work deserves attention especially for her sociological ability to examine some situations in Auschwitz in an unpredictable manner: starting from elements typical of ordinary life, like the market, she describes forms of resistance entering life at Auschwitz:

> At Auschwitz the prisoners, or at least some of them, won greater real chances for survival from the moment when the "market" began to function and, together with it, the laws of the marketplace.[54]

Within the camp, there are spaces, circumstances, or situations in which prisoners can exchange goods. Marketplaces are used to keep morale up and to break the order of terror of the concentration camp, emanating out from the place of concentration. In addition to being a psychological mechanism of self-defense, a form of survival, it is a true economic exchange whose intensity depends on the influx of goods, while prices obviously vary, hinging on the amount of available goods:

> Collective defense also depended on the influx of various goods to the camp market and on certain symptoms of demoralization among the camp officials and functionaries that could be used to the prisoner's advantage, such as the lack of solidarity, greed, bribe-taking and, in the criminal groups who lacked inner cohesion, specific enmities and accounts to settle between members and jealousy over the distribution of profits.[55]

---

53 Pawełczyńska, *Values and Violence in Auschwitz*, 71.
54 Ibid., 101.
55 Ibid.

Like any market, even that of Auschwitz takes place in a space where actors exchange goods: on the one hand, there are prisoners who offer food rations (obviously not those appropriated for personal use, but rather expropriated or surplus food), on the other, there are prisoners who request it:

> Simultaneously, farm crops (raw potatoes, carrots, etc., depending on the season of the year) acquired by the crews working out in the fields came on the market. Some prisoners were bold enough to eat their acquisition during work hours; some dared to bring it through the camp gates (risking severe penalties) in order to trade it for something else, or for a friend who lacked such possibilities.[56]

The market helps inmates to survive: the so-called talk business among prisoners or with the SS allows for the retrieval of traits of humanity; the rules of the market, of which Simmel and Weber spoke, allow prisoners to resist anonymity.[57] Meantime, these exchange places create all the necessary conditions for a material type of resistance: prisoners exchange all kinds of information on actions to be undertaken. Behind the initial exchange of goods and commercial speculation of products, first, it is possible to identify areas in which prisoners communicate, make plans, and turn the situation to their advantage; moreover, to discover the birth of a social opinion, which involves both the prisoners and the SS. In fact, the market—as Simmel noted in *Die Großstädte und das Geistesleben*—in addition to being the place that blurs differences between goods (allowing everything to become exchangeable, due to economic interest situations that are created), it is also the place where they can break down the barriers between the supervised and guards. It makes the prisoners, in some cases, superiors able to exert some authority:

> In this way some of the SS officials came to depend on prisoners, who could in turn skillfully make demands of their own. A currency strong enough to buy the services of SS officials and prisoner-functionaries had made its appearance inside the camp. New groups of interests

---

56 Ibid., 102.
57 See Max Weber, *Die Börse*, 1894, accessed February 15, 2012, http://www.zeno.org/Soziologie/M/Weber,+Max/Schriften+zur+Soziologie; Georg Simmel, *Die Großstädte und das Geistesleben* (Dresden: Petermann, 1903).

arose, linking particular officials with prisoners who were no longer anonymous.... This activity considerably weakened the effectiveness of some SS officers. For many of them getting rich had become their main objective, and striving toward it consumed some of the energy which had formerly gone into winning a promotion in the official hierarchy.[58]

Alongside the terror system, different struggles for power coexist in the camp. It is possible to distinguish a first phase, that of taking advantage, from a second, in which cooperation among prisoners leads to the formation of pressure groups; the latter, by pressing directly on prisoner-functionaries, limits the actions of violence towards their fellows. The pressure groups, however, continue to involve the same SS, sometimes even making the prisoner become the ally of the SS officers, and thus breaking the boundary between the human and the inhuman:

> And with this the prisoners further extended their influence to having a say in the filling of camp functions with prisoners who were capable of resistance. At a certain point the stage was set for the operation of an organized resistance movement, which had already acquired a certain influence inside all the separate subcamps. The mechanisms of self-defense began to function, not only in the formal structure of the resistance movement but also through the energetic behavior of informal prisoner groups loyally cooperating with each other. In spite of the continuing terror and violence, a unique double authority became operative, as a result of which prisoners in a certain area (though a relatively small one) were able to resist....
>
> Outside help—contacts with the resistance movement outside the camp and with the population who lived in the vicinity—was part of the odds favoring the resistance movement, as was the awareness that the era of concentration camps had to end, regardless of who would be granted individual survival. The vision of another life—a free, normal life—injected energy....
>
> A corruptible guard, or an SS officer who represented a higher authority (and thus offered more possibilities), was often very useful

---

58 Pawełczyńska, *Values and Violence in Auschwitz*, 105.

for the prisoners' organized resistance. They could "sell" their real knowledge about dangers within the camp and about the political situation....

The business arrangements which made many SS officials dependent on prisoners had further consequences: there were cases where the sense of community with other SS colleagues clearly broke down and confidence in a prisoner (or prisoners) known from everyday contacts took its place.[59]

2.2.3.3. Resistance as Movement and Organization

What does it mean when Pawełczyńska defines "resistance" as a spontaneous movement but also she speaks of organized resistance? To ask if resistance is a movement or an organization is not naïve because, in the sociological literature, the use of the first category rules out the second. Here is the novelty of Pawełczyńska's work contributing to the status of sociology in Holocaust Studies. Studies of movements (from Durkheim's and Marx's classic contributions to the contemporary theories by Alberto Melucci, Alessandro Pizzorno, Francesco Alberoni, or Alain Touraine) define them, in general, as forms of innovative solidarity, of a collective kind, and essentially spontaneous due to their fluid form. They aim at changing a given historical situation and the existing institutional apparatus, in such a way as to replace the traditional values with those experienced in the new group.[60] A common feeling upon which a different collective identity forms is typical of movements, which act to achieve specific objectives. "Incipient state," for Alberoni, or "society *in nuce*," according to Pizzorno, in any case, means that a movement ceases to exist when it is being institutionalized. In Auschwitz, forms of resistance exist with all the features of a social movement: according to these

---

59 Ibid., 108–10.
60 See Alaine Touraine, *Production de la société* (Paris: Éditions du Seuil, 1973); Francesco Alberoni, *Movimento e istituzione* (Bologna: il Mulino, 1981); Alessandro Pizzorno, *Le radici della politica assoluta e altri saggi* (Milan: Feltrinelli, 1993); Alberto Melucci, ed., *Fine della modernità?* (Milan: Guerini Studio, 1998).

definitions, the actors of the "resistance movement" are the inmates. What is at the base of this "spontaneous" aggregation among prisoners are the three principles of *identity, opposition,* and *totality*, proposed by Touraine. In essence, the actors-detainees, first, are able to self-define; second, able to give a name to their opponent, specifically the SS-Nazis, and to enter into conflict with them; finally, both the inmates and the Nazi guards, who occupy opposing positions, contend for control of the domain.

Faced with the necessity for common defense, prisoners aim at rescuing the life of their own fellow prisoner in order to bear witness to the nature of violence deployed in Auschwitz.[61] For Pawełczyńska the movement is spontaneous because the prisoners spontaneously decide to unite and fight together to change the existing apparatus of terror. However, in Auschwitz, there are also already existing forms of resistance, such as that of Polish political groups, imprisoned because they belong to a conspiratorial organization.[62]

The term "organization" means a set of actors who act in a rational and structured way in the name of certain goals.[63] This concerns a community with specific purposes, formal, in the sense that rules governing actors' behavior are formulated in a precise and explicit manner. Pawełczyńska speaks of "resistance as an organized movement" in reference to formal organizations of resistance and types of inmates' cooperation of conscious, deliberate, and coordinated nature with precise aims to gain.[64]

---

61 Cf. Pawełczyńska, *Values and Violence in Auschwitz*, 113.
62 Cf. Józef Garliński, *Fighting Auschwitz: The Resistance Movement in the Concentration Camp* (London: J. Friedmann, 1975).
63 Cf. Peter M. Blau and W. Richard Scott, *Formal Organizations: A Comparative Approach* (Stanford, CA: Stanford University Press, 2003).
64 Cf. Chester I. Barnard and Kenneth Thompson, *Organization and Management: Selected Papers: Early Sociology of Management and Organizations* (London: Routledge, 2003). See Herbert A. Simon, "A Behavioral Model of Rational Choice," *Quarterly Journal of Economics* 69, no. 1 (1955): 99–188, doi:10.2307/1884852; Simon, *Administrative Behavior: A Study of Decision-Making Processes in Administrative Organization* (New York: Free Press, 1976); James G. March and Herbert A. Simon, *Organizations* (Cambridge, MA: Blackwell, 1993). According to Amitai Etzioni, organizations are social units that are deliberately constructed and reconstructed to achieve specific purposes; see Amitai Etzioni, *The Monochrome Society* (Princeton, NJ: Princeton University Press, 2003).

152 | American Sociology and Holocaust Studies

For reasons that it is necessary to explain briefly and for which it is possible find many justifications, Poles mainly become part of the collective resistance. Since 1939, in Poland, there were organized forms of resistance against the Nazi invasion and for the fight in favor of national independence to the extent that, as Pawełczyńska recounts, the existence and function of Polish conspiratorial organizations in Auschwitz deserved a separate chapter in a reconstruction of the battle against Nazism. For Pawełczyńska, an organized resistance movement is a community whose participants share an interest, namely, the survival of the system, and they engage in informally structured collective activities to achieve this goal.[65] From this point of view, the organized resistance movement is similar to the "natural system" proposed by Alvin Gouldner in 1959.[66] At Auschwitz, the prisoners are rooted in the environment with which they interact or to which they adapt; however, they form communities that are trying to survive, creating activity systems. Finally, Pawełczyńska stresses how in the *Lager* there is an organized resistance due to its geographic position: "That Auschwitz was situated on Polish territory (and the Poles living in the vicinity of Auschwitz were not all deported) gave to prisoners of Polish nationality the best chance to make contacts outside the camp; and to the conspiratorial organizations in Poland it gave the best chance to get through to their imprisoned comrades. At the same time the organizational structure of some of clandestine groups advocating Polish independence (e.g., the Polish Home Army) enabled information to be transmitted to countries or territories not occupied by the Nazis."[67] By speaking of the organized resistance movement, Pawełczyńska alludes to the role of conspiratorial organizations in Auschwitz and their links with clandestine organizations outside the camp:

> For certain, the activities of the organized resistance consisted in establishing all contacts with organizations outside the camp and transmitting documents through them that communicated what was going on in the camp; also, the collecting, transferring

---

65 See W. Richard Scott, *Le organizzazioni* (Bologna: il Mulino, 2005), 45.
66 See Alvin W. Gouldner, ed., *Studies in Leadership: Leadership and Democratic Action* (New York: Garland, 1987).
67 Pawełczyńska, *Values and Violence in Auschwitz*, 114.

and delivering of these documents were organized activities, as were the frequently successful destruction or falsification of documents directly threatening to the life of individual prisoners. Their activities also included operations requiring great skill and coordination on the part of their members living in the various subcamps: such as, for example, the planning of a strategy for defense in the event of all-out danger, or the revolt of the *Sonderkommando*—long in preparation but prematurely set in motion—that resulted in the destruction of two crematories and an attempted mass escape. The same coordination and careful preparatory work (which required making connections with local residents and conspiratorial organizations outside the camp) were also indispensable for arranging escapes from the camp. Information concerning the existence and functions of the Nazi concentration camp, including partial lists of prisoners, was transmitted to countries not occupied by the Nazis, thanks to the activity of the camp organizations. Red Cross intervention and the packages streaming into the camp in response to that information sowed panic among the planners and administrators of the extermination camps, because their strictly secret operation had been exposed.[68]

It is very difficult, if not impossible, to clearly distinguish resistance as a "spontaneous movement" from resistance as "an organized form." The two forms run into a block of resistance, sometimes unique, against the system of terror and violence in the camp; and this union is revealed as perfect, since the first is able to move better than the second:

> Doubtless they will never enable all the phenomena of conspiratorial work in the camp to be established with complete precision, much less the phenomena of spontaneous resistance among people loyally working together in response to specific situations.[69]

---

68   Ibid., 115. I have omitted the author's in-text citations.
69   Ibid., 114–15.

This is because resistance functions as structured groups, due to the action of people who are in interaction with one another with continuity, according to relatively stable schemes. It provides the passage of news and information from one part to another of the camp. This happens in the case of the formation of small groups that transmit received information. Each group is appointed to receive data, according to which it is informed about the action that must be completed. It is important that each group follow the provided instructions to ensure the success of the action. In this human chain of information, the element of trust between prisoners and between groups of prisoners engaged in resistance is essential. Gradually, a structure in resistance action comes about: a hierarchy between those who resist, with rewards and greater privileges to those who contribute to conspiracy forms or who have experiences of clandestine activities.

2.2.4. The Institutions of the Criminal State

In the years in which New Deal legislation, in general, grew, along with the increasing request for social-democratic rights, especially starting from 1970, contemporarily, there developed a sociological interest in juridical or legal issues. This is evident in *Values and Violence* too. What matters is the attention that Pawełczyńska reserves for themes dealing with law or constitutional rights. What is more is the way she adopts, by speaking of crime, a new analytical category in the 1970s for Holocaust sociology. In essence, for Nazi leaders, several economic logics justified the genocide. What was prepared and perpetrated by National Socialist policy, she defines it as an organized power structure. The camp of Auschwitz existed only because the Third Reich existed. It operated because of a legal system that ensured totalitarian plans of government through bureaucratic institutions placed under its orders and through a military system in charge of complying with them. Moreover, the bureaucracy organized the application of the Nuremberg Laws, the census of Jews, and *Mischlinge*, expropriations against them in the context of the measures of Aryanization of the economy, their ghettoization and then their deportation, and the management of concentration and extermination camps. This multifaceted bureaucracy was one of the cornerstones of the execution of Nazi crimes.[70]

Like the modern bureaucratic state in Weber, the Third Reich was a modern state in which power passed through legal and rational channels, and it only worked because there was an apparatus performing certain offices. However, Auschwitz was not only the result of projects by political circles, but it was possible due to the mentality and attitudes of good people. When, in her second chapter, Pawełczyńska speaks of "Institutions of State Crime," (*Państwowe Instytucje Prezestępcze*) all structures of extermination are presented, which operated at several levels. Particularly, she focuses on the bureaucratic structure, the military establishment, and the economic system. For her, the genocide of the Jews was a state crime, made legal by laws prescribed and guaranteed.[71]

What matters is that Nazi organizations are defined as criminals in the same way Hartshorne did thirty years earlier.[72] In *Values and Violence* the topic of the composition of the Nazi Party returns: it is made up of border people, squads, and of people belonging to the upper classes:[73]

> It must be clearly emphasized that every successively higher link in the chain of command, up to the top leadership of the Nazi party and government, was part of that group responsible for these crimes and that this group included numerous tycoons of industry and their subsidiary organizations, as well as some members of the health-care field. Besides this, some parts of German society at large performed functions which contributed to the existence and operation of

---

70 See Traverso, *The Origins of Nazi Violence*, 42–44.
71 See note 15, above.
72 See Hartshorne, *The German Universities and National Socialism*; Hartshorne, "The German Universities and the Government," *Annals of the American Academy of Political and Social Science* 200 (1938): 210–34.
73 Cf. Karl O'Lessker, "Who Voted for Hitler? A New Look at the Class Basis of Naziism," *American Journal of Sociology* 74, no. 1 (1968): 63–69; William I. Brustein, "Who Joined the Nazis and Why?" *American Journal of Sociology* 103, no. 1 (1997): 216.

concentration camps, and some consciously enjoyed advantages from the continuous criminal activity carried on in the camps.[74]

Referring to the studies of the Chicago School on juvenile delinquency, Pawełczyńska defines the followers of the Nazis as a social "gang" because of the methods used and above all for their moral bearing: they belong to the organized proletariat or simple working class, and, in any case, these people consciously obey the orders of the German machine, supported by a sizable part of society:

> The SS functionaries employed in the camp were recruited from various social milieu and, on close examination, can be seen to have reflected a cross-section of society. Although persons from the lower classes with lesser education predominated, we also encounter among the SS in Auschwitz, and among persons who worked closely with them, people who rank very high on the level of education and training (e.g., doctors, school teachers, and even university professors).[75]

The one thing that really moves the wires of the criminal state is the authority of terror, which found, in the crisis of modern society, a fertile ground especially among young people: lacking in a strong moral identity, they are easily indoctrinated. Symbolically Auschwitz represents the suicide of German society.[76] According to Pawełczyńska, who examines how criminal the military establishment operating at Auschwitz was, the stages of Nazi criminal institutionalization are at least five. First, the Nazis violate the principles of international law. Second, Nazi power is not based on laws that take into account the needs of the German people. Third, the Nazis destroy the evidence of their crimes, and the criminals erase the evidence of their felonies.[77] Fourth, in occupied

---

74 Pawełczyńska, *Values and Violence in Auschwitz*, 22.
75 Ibid., 20.
76 Cf. Friedrich D. Weil, review of *The Holocaust and the German Elite: Genocide and National Suicide in Germany, 1871–1945*, by Ranier C. Baum, *American Journal of Sociology* 89, no. 3 (1983): 751–54.
77 Cf. Pawełczyńska, *Values and Violence in Auschwitz*, 83. "Owing to the secret nature of the majority of directives, concentration-camp personnel are obliged to falsify general reports and the records pertaining to the causes of prisoners' deaths" (ibid., 17).

countries, National Socialist activities are considered "criminal actions."[78] Finally, this gangster state, to function, needs institutions applying the genocidal program:

> An attitude of this sort inclined the functionary to take advantage of privileges either within the bounds established by regulation or outside of those bounds, all the while maintaining caution and restraint lest excesses diminish one's opportunities.
>
> Acceptance of the job itself in Auschwitz for its special advantages—it was a shelter from military service at the front; it was secure; for those who stuck to the rules it furnished a large number of opportunities; for those who did not, it provided the chance to thieve on a grand scale and, thanks to this, a life that was alluring while on the job plus considerable material resources for the future. Such a motivational pattern arose out of the need for physical security (an escape from the danger threatening combatants) and the ambition to acquire the greatest number of material goods, assuring a prosperous and comfortable life in the future.[79]
>
> ...
>
> There also exists detailed documentation on the way in which the victims' possessions were plundered; these goods were viewed as the property of the Third Reich and were sorted by prisoner work crews.... Some of the victims' property, useless in camp, but possessing great value in the categories of a free society, will end up in prisoners' hands and will serve to bribe the SS and their functionaries.[80]

The exchange of goods and economic institution in the broadest sense guarantees the exercise of totalitarian power within the camp. If, on the one hand, the advantages that Nazis reached by their criminal actions atrophy prisoners' morale, on the other, the tendency to identify with the

---

78 Ibid., 47: "The terror and physical violence which accompanied the performance of work was also an element of this system, as was the murdering of those prisoners who were not up to the work, or upon whom the overseers vented their sadism."
79 Ibid., 19.
80 Ibid., 78, 80.

aggressor (with the Nazi state, at every level of the pecking order), contributes to the perfect terror system. The prisoners, classified and numbered, distinct in social classes, are forced to become an appendix of the work and bureaucracy machine of the German system within the camp. In this regard, the author speaks of "degeneration of authoritarian power": some prisoners are assigned typical tasks of leadership, or are given higher powers than other inmates. But the detainees often turn these special functions to their own advantage, allowing the "higher" prisoners to help their fellows: "Despite their complete submission to the existing power structure and their choice of the Nazi value system, many of them did not banish all human responses; these they expressed by aiding the few prisoners who aroused those feelings in them."[81] Such a division of labor always involves the organization of forms of terror. It is crucial to think again about the detainees who are entrusted with the execution of a part of the genocide, namely, the task of accompanying other prisoners to the gas chambers. This is the extreme form of terror: the division that the Nazis establish not between "fellow-prisoners" and "killers," but between the "powerful" as such and the defenseless.[82] "At the extreme of this terror," explains Pawełczyńska, "there is just the élite, the one mentioned by the sociologist Vilfredo Pareto."[83]

The establishment of industrialized mass murder is the finest structure of the organization of terror in the camp. The actors of this organization, both bureaucratic and industrial at the same time, do not control the process as a whole, but they execute orders without having to be accountable for their actions. For Weber, moral indifference is a constitutive feature of modern bureaucracy, and thus Pawełczyńska is able to explain—reformulating the concept of organization—the system of the death factory at Auschwitz:

> The operation of industrial genocide was familiar to the inmates of the camp. Only the appearances of secrecy were maintained in front

---

81 Ibid., 50.
82 Ibid., 49. "Besides the organized terror, another, more elemental terror came into being: of the stronger over the weaker. This was the inevitable consequence of the whole camp situation" (ibid., 66).
83 Pawełczyńska, my interview.

of the prisoners. As a rule the women prisoners in camps a and b at Auschwitz-Birkenau (separated from the men's camp by two bands of electrically-charged barbed wire, between which ran the railroad platform used for unloading the transports and the road leading to crematories II and III) and the men in the camps on the other side of the platform were witnesses to the process of selection for the gas chamber. The road leading to crematories IV and V separated two men's camps in Birkenau, and the prisoners in these camps could see it. All the prisoners in Auschwitz-Birkenau saw the crematory chimneys, and they knew what the smoke from those chimneys meant.[84]

2.2.5. Auschwitz as Modern State

Throughout her account, Pawełczyńska continually states that Auschwitz, in the same way as a modern nation-state, is marked by well-defined national boundaries, by a political community, the detainees, and by sovereignty exercised in a total and concentrated way by Nazi authority. Like in the modern Weberian state, there is a monopoly of violence, and power is organized and operated thanks to an administration based on the principles of specialization, calculus, segmentation of responsibilities, and distribution of tasks in a variety of activities, apparently autonomous but actually coordinated. Within the two types of state, the concentration camp and the modern, lies an indistinct mass of individuals. Undoubtedly, the two cases have many differences, but what they obviously have in common is that both the members of the modern nation-state and the prisoners of the concentration-camp state are individuals alone, placed close together from the point of view of time and space, but, ultimately, people in their own right, foreign, and, therefore, nicknamed "atoms." Briefly, the process of national unification in the modern age is born from the need to create an entity state based on the commonality of language and cultural values of the inhabitants. The major difference is that in the modern nation-state, individuals, concentrated, all belong to the same country, speak the same language, and

---

84 Pawełczyńska, *Values and Violence in Auschwitz*, 79.

share the same culture, while inside the concentration camp the national identity is barely scratched. The distinction according to nation is deleted at the same time that prisoners belonging to different nationalities are confused with each other and put together without distinction. Only rarely are the prisoners divided according to national ethnic group: this is visible when a letter is affixed to their uniforms, in addition to the numbers tattooed on arms and representing an identification code, a sort of anonymous name, impossible to pronounce and, more importantly, it does not consider the personality of the prisoner. Since in the same space there is a very diverse mix of people, who share neither language nor beliefs nor, again, belong to the same nation, prisoners are prevented from communicating with each other. In fact, language is a social phenomenon, even before an analytical category, which creates identity, bonds of solidarity; in order to avoid the formation of chains of solidarity, capable of defeating terror, the prisoners are precluded from any form of communication.[85] Let me, finally, focus on the last point distinguishing Pawełczyńska's book. Like every modern state, the camp of Auschwitz is based on a statute, that is, it provides a regime of governance. In Auschwitz, there is an order of values, a "common law," in which the old principles of equality, fraternity, and liberty are revisited and the Ten Commandments are readapted to the camp. The "do not harm," "do not bear false witness," or "do not steal" are words or norms, the author explains, that have to be revisited in the context of a new totalitarian state. The reinterpretation of moral standards is performed on the basis of a minimum of morality, one that let Auschwitz survive and tell the truth, namely, "Do not harm your neighbour and, if at all possible, save him" is the adaptation of the principle of universal brotherhood and the most profound "love your neighbor as yourself."[86] The final lesson of the author, a witness and survivor, claims a philanthropic obligation: both ordinary citizen and the most complex institutional political structure must keep civil society alert against any breach of human rights.

---

85   Cf. David Rousset, *L'univers concentrationnaire* (Paris: Éditions de Minuit, 1946).
86   Cf. Pawełczyńska, *Values and Violence in Auschwitz*, 140–44.

2.3. JEWS IN POLAND

Always keeping in mind chronological order, in this reconsideration of post-Holocaust sociology, it is crucial to explain the novelty of Celia S. Heller's contribution. Let me articulate the fundamental points of her work. When the scholar, after several works on Polish society and its historical development (attempting to understand the differences and similarities between diverse cultures in Poland), published *On the Edge of Destruction*, in 1977, the genocide of the Jews was a little more than thirty years old.[87] The term "edge," which immediately recalls the limit, a territorial division, in other words, the edge of a border, highlights the central theme of her book, which, for the author, is the main cause of the destruction of the Jews in Poland—Polish nationalism or, better yet, the national claims of various ethnic groups present in the area. To the Polish sociologist, the origins of the genocide were in the national boundaries and ethnic pride of the Poles. The physical destruction of about 3,000,000 Jews in Poland, who were approximately 10 percent of the population and represented the oldest Jewish community in Europe, did not have Nazi ideology or German racism as the only reason. As Heller explains, in the eastern region there was no need to educate Poles in hatred of the Jews: genocide was not only the product of National Socialism, it was also the result of an ancient local anti-Semitism. Nazism just completed, refined, and extended existing anti-Semitic practices and policies and, finally, put in place one of the major targets of the same Polish nationalism, that is, the end of the Jews and their influence in Poland.[88] This is very evident from the "Poland in 1938" map on the expansionist aspirations of the country reported by Heller.

In 1937, Otto D. Tolischus, correspondent of the *New York Times*, denounced the dangers of modern anti-Semitism, which, in his opinion, would result in a tragedy of huge proportions: "Turning the recurrent Jewish tragedy in that biggest Jewish center in the world into a final

---

87 See Celia S. Heller, *On the Edge of Destruction: Jews of Poland between the Two World Wars* (New York: Columbia University Press, 1977).
88 Cf. David Cymet, "Polish State Anti-Semitism as a Major Factor Leading to the Holocaust," *Journal of Genocide Research* 1, no. 2 (1999): 169–212.

disaster of truly historic magnitude."[89] Concerning his prophecy, or, more simply, his ability to read the present, Heller speaks of Tolischus as a "sentinel of the night" who guards the society in crisis caused by major changes and a world war of which it was still possible to count the ruins. If there were other observers like him, maybe the destruction could have been avoided.

Trained as an ethnologist, Heller especially explores social, political, and cultural aspects of the Jews in Poland between the two world wars: she involves herself in the study of kinship, social structures, traditions, customs, rituals, religion, and even the Polish adaptation to the environment, from food to clothing, for her interest in the assimilation of the Jews.[90] Hence, her ten interviews with assimilated survivors. Then there are diaries, memoirs, autobiographies. Through newspapers broadly distributed in Yiddish and in Polish, she is also able to make a type of census of the Jews, recording the places where they live. The assumption from which Heller starts is that the majority of Poles, as Catholics, treat Jews, a minority group, in the same way that blacks were treated in Mississippi before the civil rights movement. When the author writes of the cultural and national history of Poland in the period before the Great War, she also focuses on the situation of the Jews, particularly, on how they were socially defined (as Bolsheviks, the enemies of Poland). In the Polish territory there coexisted positions in favor of the Jews and an irreducible anti-Semitism: tolerance and hatred (for the latter a party is even organized) become hopelessly mixed.[91]

If, in the first chapter, Heller is essentially concerned with bringing together all the violent attacks suffered by the Jews, in the second, she instead describes their political activism, or, rather, when they demonstrate for claims of Jewish equality against the nationalist positions of fellow Poles. The pattern of oppression legitimated by a gradually increasing popular support advances on a very simple fact, namely, that the Jews were foreigners since their arrival

---

89 Otto D. Tolischus, "Jews Face Crisis in Eastern Europe," *New York Times*, February 7, 1937, quoted in Heller, *On the Edge of Destruction*, 10.
90 See Celia S. Heller, *Mexican American Youth: Forgotten Youth at the Crossroads* (New York: Random House, 1966).
91 Cf. Heller, *On the Edge of Destruction*, 83, 133.

in Poland. Nevertheless, if at first they are considered outsiders because they belong to a different religion and culture, then later they are labeled as *extra*-individuals (*obcy*), outside the Polish culture since they do not share blood (*krew*) with the Polish people. The element of blood is of great importance, even at the basis of the concept of nation, and comes before, in many ways, the other constituent factor, that of ground or soil (*ziemia*).

Using surveys conducted on the activities of the Polish workers and their distribution in urban and rural areas, Heller notes that the sense of belonging to the same lineage is strong enough to limit the development of values and cultural beliefs among Polish residents of different ethnicity. Thus, in retracing the period subsequent to the Piłsudski regime (1926–35), in the third chapter, "The Heirs of Piłsudski," she immediately addresses the issue of inequality of power and political instability, then the question of official anti-Semitic ideology and economic policies against the Jews, and, finally, the role of the Church.

As Hartshorne and Hughes had highlighted in their works, the place where anti-Semitism grew and was fed was the university, a hotbed of anti-Jewish ideology, while at the beginning its fountainhead was mainly the national intelligentsia. How the Jews reacted when faced with organized terror is mainly discussed in the fourth chapter. Between tradition and assimilation, Polonization and secularization, Heller analyzes the status of Orthodox Jews steadfast in the cultural tradition; the role of Agudat Israel, the umbrella party for almost all Haredi Jews in Israel; the meaning of *Kehilla*, the Jewish organizational structure, secular and religious, and elected by its members. Despite oppression and anti-Jewish measures, these communities and organizations develop and carve out a space within the Polish society, by creating a system of political institutions, at the local, regional, and national levels; communities and organizations, including socialist, Zionist, Orthodox positions in addition to those in favor of assimilation, that present no minor problems both in terms of cultural profile and in terms of national identity. For Heller, who admits that she does not fully explore the issue, Polonization (*polonizacja*) passes for a phase of acculturation through public schools, considered as the social agency able to guarantee Jews the acquisition of elements of Polish culture.

What distinguishes this work is also the secularization question addressed by Heller in the 1970s. Let me be precise, in studying secularization, she identifies the "generational conflict" and the "mother's role" as analytical categories in the years between the two world wars. The latter, in fact, is more determinative than the father's role to the values and the culture of the country. In this way in the family, the mother happens to play the role of mediator between the traditional authority of father over children, who must be educated in the new modern context. As the school has the task of transmitting Polish culture in society, similarly the mother transmits national culture at home. In the context of assimilation, the times and places resisting oppression emerge.

As main forms of resistance, Heller indicates, there are the appeal to Poles' leftist political parties and to the Zionist movement, the Bund's initiatives, and, finally, the ability to migrate to Palestine, *Eretz Yisrael*. However, the disappointment of Jewish policies within the Polish parliament are not late in coming. In light of the cultural and historical context, the roots of the Holocaust in Poland are in the same Polish culture.[92] The Kielce, Cracow, Chelm, and Rzeszów pogroms testify that, at the end of the war, the Jews who returned home were denounced as hostile and violent or were killed. Those who, "facing the extreme," remained, either because they believed the promises of a socialist Poland, or because they wanted to contribute to a better society, did not consider themselves of Polish citizenship but of Polish nationality.[93]

Gershon C. Bacon stresses how important the categories of Heller, both historical and sociological, are in Holocaust scholarship. Above all is the distinction between the period in which Jews were welcomed by Poles and the one in which, at the time of Poland's independence and democratic constitution (after the Great War peace treaties), they became the object of persecution.[94] What is more important is that Heller destroys the idyllic

---

92 See Norbert Elias, *The Germans: Power Struggles and the Development of Habitus in the Nineteenth and Twentieth Centuries* (Oxford: Polity, 1996 [1989]); Dunning and Mennell, *Elias on Germany, Nazism and the Holocaust*.
93 Cf. Cvetan Todorov, *Face à l'extrême* (Paris: Éditions du Seuil, 1991).
94 See Gershon C. Bacon, review of *On the Edge of Destruction: Jews of Poland between the Two World Wars*, by Celia S. Heller, *Journal of International Affairs* 31, no. 1 (1977): 143–45.

myth of the "happy life" that Jews would lead in Poland, showing how events related to assimilation generated conflicts between fellow compatriots.[95] She does this in 1977. Heller remembers the times that Jews tried to enter public life and raise their concerns in parliament, with negative outcomes. Emblematic is the excerpt reported below and regarding four rabbis—Kanal, Perelman, Langleben, and Fajner—who, on a visit to the cardinal of Warsaw, Kakowski, June 7, 1934, asked for immediate action against youthful outbursts of anti-Semitism, invoking the moral authority of the high Catholic prelate to save the Jews victims of violence:

> Your Eminence!
> In the name of the rabbinate of the Polish Republic we turn to you in the following powerful matter. In Germany in the land of the Teutonic knights, from time immemorial Poland's enemy, a horde of barbarous pagans has recently come to power warring against all the laws of God, trampling upon all the important principles of the Christian faith, persecuting all adversaries with cruelty unknown in human history, especially to the descendants of the land of Israel. The whole civilized world, and the princes of the Catholic Church, has condemned the monstrous actions of the Nazis in Germany. Unfortunately in Poland the land with the greatest number of God-fearing Catholic Christians, a certain faction, especially youth, is troubling us. Shamefully, calling themselves Polish nationalists, they modeled themselves after the example of the pagan Nazis. They attack defenseless people walking on the streets of Poland's cities because they look Jewish. Without pity they bully, beat and injure them. Sometimes these ruffians encounter resistance from their innocent victims and they react with even more fury bringing shame to Poland's old reputation for tolerance and God. We are convinced, Cardinal, that no true Polish Catholic can be utterly corrupt, that these youth have been momentarily deluded by the slogans of foreign enemies. At

---

95 See Marta Petrusewicz, "Fine della Polonia innocente: Analisi di un dibattito," *Passato e Presente* 20, no. 56 (2002): 153–66.

an appeal by their senses and certainly cease the persecution of the Jewish people which defames Poland's good name. In the name of the Rabbis and Jews of this illustrious Republic, we entreat you, Cardinal, to issue a pastoral appeal about this to all Poland Catholics. Then peace and order will reign again in the land beloved by us all. May grace flow upon it. Amen.[96]

It could be asked how modernization was linked with the destruction of the Jews. Between the two world conflicts, the Jews were a highly urbanized group in a predominantly rural country. Heller comments that they were easily visible and distinguished not only because of their religion, but above all for their modern manners and customs. At least in five of the largest Polish cities, Jews accounted for between a quarter and a third of the population, while in smaller towns they constituted the majority. They had philanthropic institutions, an active political life, and publishing houses—they engaged in the publication and dissemination of news in Yiddish, Polish, and Hebrew.

What were the causes that led to the disappearance of the Jewish community in Poland? Heller's book closes with a picture of a tombstone, a memorial of what happened to the Jews between the two wars. The image of the plaque commemorating the destruction of the Jews is also observable in a historical book on anti-Semitism in Poland dedicated to the destruction of the Jewish community in Jedwabne by fellow Christians. Here also the myth of the good and innocent Poland is debunked.[97] Nevertheless, because of numerous inaccuracies, insufficient documentation, or absence of a bibliography, Heller's work is

---

96 Ronald Modras, *The Catholic Church and Anti-Semitism in Poland, 1933–1939* (Chur, Switzerland: Harwood Academic Press, 1994), 348, quoted in Feigue Cieplinski, "Poles and Jews: The Quest for Self-Determination, 1919–1934," *Journal of History* (2002), accessed November 24, 2010, http://www2.binghamton.edu/history/resources/journal-of-history/poles-and-jews.html#_ftn1.

97 See Gross, *Neighbors*, 114. On the debate surrounding Gross's book, see Joanna B. Michlic, *Coming to Terms with the "Dark Past": The Polish Debate about the Jedwabne Massacre* (Jerusalem: SICSA, 2002); Petrusewicz, "Fine della Polonia innocente"; Antony Polonsky and Joanna B. Michlic, eds., *The Neighbors Respond: The Controversy over the Jedwabne Massacre in Poland* (Princeton, NJ: Princeton University Press, 2004).

not considered of great importance.⁹⁸ For most critics the research lacks a comparative perspective and reflects an inappropriate use of sociological concepts. Indeed, it cannot be inserted into any of the traditional strands of literature. It has to do with the inability of contemporary scholars to understand a work opening up completely new perspectives for Holocaust scholarship: Heller addresses issues that only after 1989 are going to have more room in Holocaust Studies, as with the analysis of the public nature of genocide and the involvement of local collaborationist populations.⁹⁹

"*Przepraszam, Jedwabne*," in this way the president of the Republic of Poland, Kwasniewski, began his speech of July 10, 2001, before the notable personalities at the ceremony of the sixtieth anniversary of the massacre in Jedwabne. Nobody knew of the Polish town until Jan T. Gross, a Jewish scholar of Polish origin, in *Neighbors*, recounted the story of 1,600 Jews (i.e., the entire resident Jewish community) who were herded into a barn to be burned alive on July 10, 1941. However, no Germans perpetrated the massacre but, rather, a group of Polish inhabitants of Jedwabne itself: they were neighbors. A new plaque, in place of the old Jewish cemetery, commemorates the Jews of Jedwabne, without mentioning the number of deaths or the names of the guilty. The themes of innocence and martyrdom, founding myths of the historical Polish identity, began to be questioned: it was the "end of innocent Poland," thanks to Gross, who, in the spring of 2000, delivered to the public, in the native language, his complaint book. Although he had resided in the United States since 1969 and despite having regularly published in the English language, he decided to tell the story of Poland in Polish, allowing his fellow citizens to face the inconvenient truth. Nevertheless, the issue, rather than stirring the Polish consciousness, a feeling of shared responsibility, and a joint assumption of guilt, created a

---

98 Cf. Bacon, review of *On the Edge of Destruction*, 143–45; Dank, review of *On the Edge of Destruction*, 129–30.
99 See Omer Bartov, "L'Europa orientale come luogo del genocidio," in *Storia della Shoah*, ed. Marina Cattaruzza et al. (Turin: Utet, 2005), 2:419–59; Andrea Graziosi, "Rivoluzione archivistica e storiografica sovietica," *Contemporanea* 8, no. 1 (2005): 57–85; Antonella Salomoni, *L'Unione Sovietica e la Shoah: Genocidio, resistenza, rimozione* (Bologna: il Mulino, 2007); Salomoni, "L'Europa orientale: Transizioni, stabilizzazioni, nuove identità," in Ridolfi, *La storia contemporanea attraverso le riviste*, 149–64.

long intellectual, and even media, debate, expressing the fatigue of Poland to take on a collective crime.

Rich in captioned photos, Heller's book presents itself as a pioneering work in the field of post-Holocaust sociology. In fact, questioning the historical tradition of an innocent Poland, it anticipated courses of study, undertaken later in Eastern Europe when, since the early 1990s, the new historiographical practices put in doubt the position of the modernity of the Holocaust resulting from the publication of *Modernity and the Holocaust* by Bauman. This was possible thanks to the opening of archives in Eastern Europe, which had remained inaccessible for a long time. As Bacon stresses, "a particularly poignant example is the quotation from the diary of a young girl who witnessed the execution of the rabbi of Plock on trumped-up charges of espionage."[100] Not all critics are superficial. According to Barry Dank, it is a work firing up interest in the Jewish question.[101] While reading Heller's book, one gains access to a pronounced sociological study: she was among the first researchers to examine collections of autobiographies, diaries of young Jews gathered in Poland in Wilno (now Vilnius, Lithuania) in the 1930s, by the Jewish Scientific Institute (JIVO), established in 1925, now in New York:

> For other aspects which required primary research, I have examined some of the Jewish daily press (written in Yiddish and Polish). I have also analyzed census data. My greatest find was the autobiographies and diaries of young Jews; they had been collected in Poland during the 1930s by YIVO, the Jewish Scientific Institute in Vilno. Over 600 such documents were in the possession of YIVO before the war broke out. When the Nazis occupied Vilno, they removed them to Germany. After the war, 302 of these were found near Frankfurt. With the aid of the U.S. State Department and Military Government, they were brought to YIVO in New York, where its headquarters had been transferred in 1940.

---

100 Bacon, review of *On the Edge of Destruction*, 144. See Heller, *On the Edge of Destruction*, 53.
101 Cf. Dank, review of *On the Edge of Destruction*.

I consider myself fortunate to have had access to these and am grateful to YIVO for its generosity. Reading these documents was like hearing voices recalled to life. In analyzing these documents, however, I was careful to discern fact from fancy. These autobiographies supplied illustrations for findings derived from other data. I quote from these autobiographies and diaries (which I translated from the Yiddish and Polish in which they were written), as well as from the interviews I conducted, in order to bring some of the fleshless findings to life.[102]

2.3.1. Twenty-one Years after Celia Heller

Tadeusz Piotrowski, the Polish-born American sociologist, dedicated his book in 1998 to the 6 million "Polish citizens" who perished during World War II. His research begins with these words: "After 123 years of partitions by its imperialistic neighbors Russia, Germany (Prussia), and Austria, Poland finally regained its independence in 1918. In the years following World War I, two major problems confronted this young republic: the problem of its forever-straying borders, and the problem of its minorities."[103] Thus, Piotrowski introduces at once two primary issues: on the one hand, the recurrent problem of a redefinition of territorial boundaries, on the other, the issue of ethnic minorities.[104] For approximately 123 years, the empires of Russia, Austro-Hungary, and Germany took turns on Polish territory until, at the end of the Great War, with the collapse of the three great powers, Poland could formally declare its freedom from foreign

---

102   Heller, *On the Edge of Destruction*, 9–10.
103   Tadeusz Piotrowski, *Poland's Holocaust: Ethnic Strife, Collaboration with Occupying Forces and Genocide in the Second Republic, 1918–1947* (Jefferson, NC: McFarland & Company, 1998), 3.
104   See the document *Decision of the Conference of Ambassadors, March 15, 1923, on the Subject of the Frontiers of Poland*, in Stanisław Skrzypek, *The Problem of Galicia* (London: Polish Association for the South-Eastern Provinces, 1948), 74–75, quoted in Piotrowski, *Poland's Holocaust*, 263. According to the decision, a new Poland emerged from the maps of Europe: it included some of the territories that had belonged to the First Republic of Poland before the partitions, and other territories: the province of Wilno, a large part of Belarus, the western part of Volhynia, the whole of eastern Galicia, the Polish Corridor, a part of Upper Silesia, a slice of East Prussia, and some of the disputed territories along the Czechoslovak border.

powers and, as a result of independence (November 11, 1918), a number of economic, political, and identity problems were reborn. As Feigue Cieplinski explains, "Poland became an independent nation against all odds in the interwar period and retained her sovereignty from 1919 to 1939; hence the concept [of] "interwar Poland." The vicissitudes of her existence earned her the name of "God's Playground."[105] Mentioned by me here as a substudy of Heller, Piotrowski's work can be read as an independent study on the Holocaust in Poland, which focuses on the problem of the multinational composition of the Polish state and considers Jews victims as "Polish citizens." In the years of the Second Polish Republic (1918–47), for Piotrowski, the Holocaust includes ethnic strife between different ethnic groups living together in the same territory, local collaboration with occupying forces, and, finally, the total genocide. This is accompanied by a description of the behavior of different ethnic groups or nations, in those years, against the Jews. Evident, following in the steps of Heller's piece, is the echo of ethnographic theories of communities of Warner and Lynds. When she describes the different ethnic groups living on Polish soil at the end of the Great War, she stresses that they assumed radical nationalist and separatist attitudes and, claiming the primacy of their own nationality, prevented the formation of a Polish national unitary state: "Thus, the yearnings for an independent 'greater Ukraine' a reunited Belarus or a Jewish state within the Polish one smoldered relentlessly."[106] They were ethnically diverse and mixed lands, which looked for some time to bring out their peculiarities and to carve out an autonomous territorial space where they could transmit their culture. Piotrowski underlines the need for the Poles to be distinguished from other nations in the area and seems to borrow sociological categories of social and spatial distance and geographical mobility typical of the Chicago School.

From a sociological point of view, this means the institutionalization of social distance between the nation of Poland and other ethnic realities,

---

105 Cieplinski, "Poles and Jews," with reference to Norman Davies, *God's Playground*, vol. 2 (New York: Columbia University Press, 1982).
106 Judith Olsak-Glass, review of *Poland's Holocaust: Ethnic Strife, Collaboration with Occupying Forces and Genocide in the Second Republic, 1918–1947*, by Tadeusz Piotrowski, *Sarmatian Review* 19, no. 1 (1999): 1, last accessed March 28, 2011, http://www.ruf.rice.edu/~sarmatia/199/glass.html.

and finally the institutionalization of new political entities. This process providing for formation of defined geographical areas and delimitation of a geographically distinct *limen*, which coincides with the political formation of the nation-state, requires significant transformations and border changes beyond the local level. In fact, the phenomenon of geographical mobility (to, through, and outside a specific territory) is accompanied by a profound cultural change, often not accepted, especially by countries that, in the process, are damaged or lose large portions of territory, with negative implications in terms of demographic policy.

The peculiar aspect of this work is that Piotrowski illustrates the social problems that Polish society faced. For instance, he reports that, according to the 1921 census, more than 30 percent of all Polish citizens were ethnic minorities—more than 15 percent were Ukrainians/Ruthenians, 8 percent Jews, 4 percent Belarusians, 3 percent Germans, with a low percentages of Lithuanians, Russians, Czechs, Tatars, and even small groups of Gypsies, Kashubians, and Karaites. Two years earlier, on June 28, 1919, when the Minorities Treaty was signed, in accordance with chapter 1, article 7, an attempt was made to ensure equality for all inhabitants of Poland before the law without distinction of race, language, or religion. Instead, chapter 1, article 2 declaimed: "Poland undertakes to assure full and complete protection of life and liberty to all inhabitants of Poland without distinction of birth, nationality, race or religion." The 1921 Polish Constitution arose to protect against all forms of discrimination and to ensure peaceful coexistence between the various minorities. Article 109, paragraph 1 established that any citizen had the right to preserve his nationality, to speak his language, and keep his national qualities.[107] Piotrowski accounts for all these preventions and legal measures, especially because, despite them, Polish prejudice against ethnic minorities continued, and mainly in the eastern regions.

Let me stress another point on which he reflects. When, in 1934, the Treaty for the Protection of Minorities was unilaterally abrogated by Poland, Polish nationalism was publicly legitimated and every effort to ensure rights and protection was extended only to residents of Polish

---

107 Cf. "Excerpts from the Minorities Treaty of June 28, 1919," in Piotrowski, *Poland's Holocaust*, 263 and "Excerpts from the Polish Constitution of 1921," in ibid., 264.

nationality. This was at the origin of public recognition of a Polish state inhabited by Poles. In many regions of eastern Poland, these minorities, taken collectively, constituted the majority of Polish citizens in those regions. The constitution of 1921 was a more than valid document, but its application proved to be unsteady, accompanied by the impatience of minorities expecting a timely and immediate justice and rights from the new republic. To all this must be added the strong waves of nationalism that, thanks to the action of some leaders, always found more space, promoting the idea of national independence and reunification of ethnic territories. There were breakaway trends among the Ukrainians, for example, that moved in favor of an independent Western Ukraine. Then, there were aspirations of Lithuanian nationalists for a return of the Lithuanian Republic; of Jewish nationalists and Zionists who looked to Palestine, but in the meantime wanted to be treated as a national minority in Poland; of Belarusians, who were also in favor of reunification and independence. This very precarious situation continued, albeit intermittently, but still was able to control ethnic tensions until the outbreak of war in 1939, when the newly established democratic institutions were no longer able to maintain such a temporary and uncertain balance. The aspirations of the radical nationalist groups and oppressed ethnic minorities took over the governing class. For Piotrowski, in the aftermath of World War I, ethnic conflict exploded in Poland, while pillars of democracy were more fragile. As Aleksander Smolar, an intellectual Polish Jew, recalls, with the beginning of the war Poles found themselves faced with two enemies at once: Germany and the Soviet Union.[108] For ethnic minorities, the situation was good and was exploited to achieve their independence aims: so rather than helping Poland, these minorities, although they had obtained Polish citizenship, preferred to stand and cooperate with the Soviet Union, or with Germany, and to see their nationalist dream realized.

2.3.1.1. Polish Nationalism during the Soviet Occupation

Irina and Jan Gross state, "The arrival of Russians in Poland was sad, and joyful. For some Jews, Byelorussians, and Ukrainians it was joyful. And

---

108 Cf. Aleksander Smolar, "Jews as a Polish Problem," *Daedalus* 116, no. 2 (1987): 38.

for the Poles it was sad and hard."[109] That is, few Poles welcomed the Soviet invasion. Piotrowski follows an accurate scheme: he presents the situation in Poland or, better, of all Polish citizens (and thus also of minorities) in the period between the two world wars, distinguishing the years of the Soviet occupation from those of the German. His goal is to show who collaborated with whom, according to the period and situation, showing the unceasing change of alliances: "It is precisely these incomprehensible, changing, complex collaborations among military and quasi-authoritarian regimes surrounding Poland, Piotrowski argues, that made these horrifying events on Polish soil possible."[110]

In the wake of the Polish historian Władysław Bartoszewski, Piotrowski tells how the Jews were constantly in danger. They lived with the continuous threat of being caught by not only German police or extortionists deliberately recruited from the dregs of Christian Polish and Ukrainian police, but also by Jewish confidence men, who, seduced by false hopes and promises, often helped the Germans to hunt out fellow Jews who lived hidden in Aryan Warsaw:[111]

> Of course there were Polish policemen who rounded up Jews and Poles, who blackmailed Jews whom they recognized as such ... But who of the Jews survivors does not know ... that there were also Jewish blackmailers, some of them even quite famous by name, outside the Ghetto, who were neither better nor worse than the Polish ones, and also Jewish policemen in the Ghetto whose duty in the first weeks of the extermination of summer 1942 was to deliver, each of them a specified number, Jewish victims to "be sent" to extermination.[112]

---

109 Irena Grudzińska-Gross and Jan T. Gross, *War through Children's Eyes: The Soviet Occupation of Poland and the Deportations, 1939–1941* (Stanford, CA: Hoover Institution Press, 1985), 56, quoted in Piotrowski, *Poland's Holocaust*, 48. See Tadeusz Piotrowski, *Vengeance of the Swallows: Memoir of a Polish Family's Ordeal under Soviet Aggression, Ukrainian Ethnic Cleansing and Nazi Enslavement, and Their Emigration to America* (Jefferson, NC: McFarland, 1995).

110 Lisiunia A. Romanienko, review of *Poland's Holocaust: Ethnic Strife, Collaboration with Occupying Forces and Genocide in the Second Republic, 1918–1947*, by Tadeusz Piotrowski, *Humanity and Society* 24, no. 1 (2000): 99, doi:10.1177/016059760002400110.

111 Cf. Piotrowski, *Poland's Holocaust*, 75; Władysław Bartoszewski, *The Warsaw Ghetto: A Christian's Testimony* (Boston: Beacon, 1987), 89. See also Garliński, *Fighting Auschwitz*.

112 Israel Shahak, "'The Life of Death': An Exchange," *New York Review of Books*, January 29, 1987, quoted in Piotrowski, *Poland's Holocaust*, 75.

And: "We have done very little to condemn Jewish collaboration with the Nazis. When, after the war, I demanded that those who had abused their office in ghettos or concentration camps be removed from Jewish committees, I was told that 'this would diminish the guilt of the Nazis.'"[113]

Taking advantage of ethnic tensions, both Germany and the Soviet Union obtained their military and territorial objectives. Piotrowski accounts for how, for each region, interests and actors were different and therefore the attitudes towards fellow Poles differed. For example, during the Nazi occupation of Belarus, three different groups appeared on the scene: the Soviet partisans, who obeyed Moscow, with 143,000 members by June 1944; Belarusian pro-Nazis; and the anti-Nazi nationalists, who aspired to a unified and independent Belarus. For Lithuania, however, the emblematic case was represented by the change of the name of Vilnius: *Wilno* in Polish, *Vilnius* in Lithuanian, *Vilna* in Russian and Belarusian, *Wilna* in German. Moreover, for the Jews, Wilno was the Jerusalem of culture, the historical capital of the Grand Duchy of Lithuania, where the YIVO archive was created. At the beginning of 1942, the Ukraine undertook a campaign of ethnic cleansing. The formal letter addressed to Hitler by the head of state, signing with the "Seal of the Ukrainian State," on April 7, 1941, explains the nature of interest of relations unfolding during the conflict:

> To the Führer and the Chancellor, Berlin
> 7/4/41, Lvov, Ukrainian Government, No 2/41
> Your Excellency:
> It is with an overwhelming feeling of gratitude and admiration for your heroic army which has covered itself with new glory in battles with Europe's worst enemy—Moscow Bolsheviks—that we are hereby sending Your Excellency, on behalf of the Ukrainian people and its government which has been created in liberated Lvov, our heartfelt wishes for complete victory in your struggle.
> The triumph of German arms will enable you to extend your planned construction of new Europe also to her Eastern part. You

---

113 Simon Wiesenthal, *Justice Not Vengeance* (London: Weidenfeld and Nicolson, 1989), 231, quoted in Piotrowski, *Poland's Holocaust*, 75.

have thus also given an opportunity to the Ukrainian people as one of the full and free members of the family of European nations to take an active part in the implementation of this great plan in its sovereign Ukrainian state.

On behalf of the Ukrainian government,

Yaroslav Stetzko,

Head

(Seal of Ukrainian State).[114]

Nevertheless, Hitler later arrested the leaders and dissolved the Ukrainian government, attacking all over nationalist Ukraine. The Ukrainian context was very difficult to handle: if the relationships between Poles and Lithuanians created tensions just for the city of Vilnius, those between Poles and Ukrainians were strained in approximately four of the eastern provinces of Poland. The Ukrainian nationalists were armed and supported by the Germans against the Poles. It was a civil, fratricide war, started in 1919, and in addition an "ethnic cleansing."[115] The author explains how Poland was divided and occupied in accordance with war plans. To Piotrowski, the first nationalist Ukrainian document can be traced back to 1900, when Mykola Mikhnovskyi published the history of independent Ukraine. It was a real call to arms, which urged Ukrainians to take up arms against the foreigners in their own land and to defend the nation, following the motto "whoever is not with us is against us." Thus a group identity was slowly formed. At the Congress of Vienna (January 28–3 February 3, 1929), the first real meeting of the organization of Ukrainian Nationalists (OUN), the ideology was translated into a proclamation addressed to all Ukrainians with the aim of adopting a resolution on the issue:

> **Proclamation**: Only the *complete removal* of all occupants from Ukrainian lands [*povne usunennia vsikh okupantiv z ukrainskykh zemel*—i.e., ethnic cleansing] will create the possibility for an expansive development of the Ukrainian people in the borders of

---

114 "Captured Nazi War Document no. 145," in B. F. Sabrin, *Alliance for Murder: The Nazi Ukrainian Nationalist Partnership in Genocide* (New York: Sarpedon, 1991), 51, quoted in Piotrowski, *Poland's Holocaust*, 211–12.

115 Piotrowski, *Poland's Holocaust*, 177.

their own nation ... In its internal political activity, the Ukrainian nation will strive to attain borders encompassing all Ukrainian ethnographic territories.

Resolution: The *complete removal* of all occupants from Ukrainian lands [*povne usunennia vsikh zaimantsiv z ukrainskykh zemel*—i.e., ethnic cleansing], which will follow in the course of a national revolution and create the possibility for an expansive development of the Ukrainian people in the borders of their own nation, will be guaranteed by a system of our own military formations and goal-oriented political diplomacy.[116]

The repetitions in the two texts clearly emphasize the strength of the nationalist spirit with its fanatical attitudes. In the totalitarian ideologies, if the iterations, the sentences repeated several times, on the one hand, reflect the poverty of language, then, on the other, they tend to inoculate some truth in an unconscious way. They can indoctrinate the population without it noticing it, bringing it to internalize expressions and concepts that, again unconsciously, lead to the adoption of attitudes corresponding to the principles of nationalist ideology.

At the second major conference of Ukrainian Nationalists (VZUN, *Velykyi Zbir Ukrainskykh Natsionalistiv*) held in Rome on August 27, 1939, the same concepts were repeated, but in an even more dramatic way, ending with the adopting, five days before the invasion of Poland, of the Nazi solution of "blood and iron." As stressed here, "Ukraine for Ukrainians. We will not leave one inch of Ukrainian land in the hands of enemies and foreigners ... only blood and iron will decide between us and our enemies."[117] When, on September 1, 1941, in Volhynia, Ulas Samchuk notified Ukrainians that the "element" (i.e., Jews and Poles, deliberately "made a thing" in the singular form to cancel personality) that occupied their cities should completely disappear, the Jewish problem was already in a resolution phase. It started a practice that would result in a general reorganization of the New Europe. At the end

---

116 Ibid., 242–43, and fn. 473.
117 Ibid., 243, and fn. 474.

of the war, the beneficiaries should be, for Samchuck, the true owners of the land, who the Ukrainian people:

> This OUN editor knew full well that by September 1, 1941, "the element… brought here from outside the Ukraine" was already in the Gulag.
>
> The Galician Ukrainian Nationalists said, "*Smert lakham, zhydam i moskalam*" ("Death to the Poles, Jews, and Russians"), and when their territories were Judenfrei, they said: "We have finished with the Jews, now it's the Poles' turn." They then began on their long-talked-about and planned program of the "complete removal" (*povne usunennia*) of all occupants for the sake of their "free, independent, united" (*vilna, samostiina, soborna*) "Ukraine for Ukrainians" on all "Ukrainian ethnographic territories" under the rule of the "initiative-minority," the superior people of the OUN.[118]

In August 1943, when the organization of Ukrainian nationalists led by Stepan Bandera, the OUN-B, after the First World Conference of Ukrainian Nationalists (VZUN), began to make its own democratic principles and to pursue a progressive social program, going against Nazi and fascist positions to promote a system of free peoples and independent states as the best solution to the problems of international order, the killings of foreigners in most of western Ukraine continued unabated.

2.3.1.2. Polish Collaboration during the German Occupation

As reported by Faye Schulman, a "partisan" and a "woman of the Holocaust," hundreds of Jews were killed by Soviet partisans:[119]

> In 1941 the partisan movement was struggling. Spies, traitors and Nazi collaborators among the populace abounded. Many partisans were ambushed and killed. In frustration, the commander of the Pinsk partisan units issued an order to kill every stranger in the woods who was not attached to a partisan group.

---

118   Ibid., 243, and fns. 476, 477.
119   See next note.

Unaffiliated strangers were immediately shot. Most were Jews who escaped from ghettos or camps and were hiding in the woods. They did not belong to any combat unit because the partisans did not want them. How cruel that those lucky enough to have escaped from the Nazis into the forest survived only to be shot as spies. Hundreds were killed before the commander realized his error; he was targeting innocent Jews and not Nazi spies. By the time he called off the order, it was too late for too many.[120]

According to the valiant fighter Oswald Rufeisen, the Soviet partisan units did not kill Jews for anti-Semitic reasons alone: there were the so-called laws of the jungle, those that let the strongest survive. At the beginning, the Russian partisans were not very organized, and among the Jewish fugitives there were many elderly people, children, and women, seen as obstacles to the underground army. The Russians also feared that, once captured by Germans, the Jews could reveal their location of hiding in exchange for safety. Faced with this danger, to save their skin it was necessary to deprive Jews of any help, security, and, especially, weapons, if not even to kill them. For Rufeisen, this was the law of the jungle.[121] Moreover, the new regime and communist ideology regarded them as class enemies to be eliminated since they were enemies for Poland. Marek Edelman, the last survivor of the leaders of the Warsaw Uprising, helps us understand the situation: "We didn't get adequate help from the Poles, but without their help we couldn't have started the uprising. You have to remember that the Poles themselves were short of arms."[122]

What matters here is how Piotrowski seeks to document, thanks to witnesses' voices, all aspects of Polish collaboration, but also "assistance to Jews." Through Zofia Kossak-Szczucka's speech or, better, through her

---

120 Faye Schulman, *A Partisan's Memoir: Woman of the Holocaust* (Toronto: Second Story Press, 1995), 104, quoted in Piotrowski, *Poland's Holocaust*, 105–6.
121 Cf. Piotrowski, *Poland's Holocaust*, 106; Nechama Tec, *In the Lion's Den: The Life of Oswald Rufeisen* (New York: Oxford University Press, 1990).
122 Piotrowski, *Poland's Holocaust*, 107, fn. 172, with reference to Sheldon Kirshner, "Warsaw Ghetto Commander Forgives Tormentors" (an interview with Marek Edelman), *Canadian Jewish News* (Toronto), November 9, 1989. Cf. Marek Edelman, *Getto walczy: udzial Bundu w obronie getta warszawskiego* (Warsaw: Nakladem C. K. "Bundu," 1945).

eloquent protest, Piotrowski first documents then condemns social action reduced to silence in the face of the extermination: "He who remains silent in the face of murder becomes an accomplice of the murderer. He who does not condemn, condones."[123] Instead, through Emmanuel Ringelblum's words, Polish assistance to the Jews is heard: "No one will accuse the Polish nation of committing these constant pogroms and excesses against the Jewish population. The significant majority of the nation, its enlightened working-class, and the working intelligentsia, undoubtedly condemned these excesses, seeing in them a German instrument for weakening the unity of the Polish community and a lever to bring about collaboration with the Germans."[124] These are words that resound as criticism that the famed historian of the Warsaw ghetto says to the Poles for not having done enough to help the Jews. Among those who did not remain indifferent to the conditions of the Jews and hid their children in Christian monasteries, finding a safe refuge, there were even old anti-Semites whose ideas had been held for decades, who had favored the end of Polish Jewry: "The fault is entirely theirs that Poland has given asylum at the most to one per cent of the Jewish victims of Hitler's persecutions."[125] In an economy destroyed by the Great War, many ethnic nationalisms led to the final solution for the Jews in Poland:[126]

> Motivated perhaps, as a response to recent scholarly denunciation of the role of Polish people in the horrors that occurred upon Polish soil during World War II, Tadeusz Piotrowski attempts to set the historical and sociological record straight in *Poland's Holocaust*. Using a strategy of combining ethnographic, demographic, policy, and archival data drawn from primary and secondary sources extracted through government documents, eye witness accounts, and interviews conducted in several languages and across several continents; Piotrowski's book is one of the most comprehensive,

---

123 Smolar, *Jews as a Polish Problem*, 36, quoted in Piotrowski, *Poland's Holocaust*, 112.
124 Emmanuel Ringelblum, *Polish-Jewish Relations during the Second World War*, ed. Joseph Kermish and Shmuel Krakowski (Evanston, IL: Northwestern University Press, 1992), 53, quoted in Piotrowski, *Poland's Holocaust*, 112.
125 Ibid., 113.
126 Cf. Olsak-Glass, review of *Poland's Holocaust*, 1.

well documented, multimethodological contributions to scholarly work in the area.[127]

Solid and informative, for critics, says Romanienko, in "focusing the analysis to events that occurred within and around Poland's borders," Piotrowski's work represents a bulwark in Holocaust Studies, above all because he calls Polish behavior and attitudes into question during the conflict years in "identifying the changing face of Poland's perpetrators, as well as a clarification of her victims."[128] It is relevant to notice when his work was issued: his reflection arrived at the end of Bosnian conflict (1992–95), that is, of an ethnic cleansing. His research inquiries into the roles ethnic minorities played in the end of the Republic of Poland and in the cruel acts that happened under the occupying troops. It carefully looks at the Polish government's response to increasing ethnic tensions in the prewar years and its conduct of the war effort. This is not the first work in this regard: the historian Gross in previous years wrote on the role of Polish society during the German and Soviet occupations and on deportations of Jews. The researches of Piotrowski, Heller, and Gross may be read as a set of works forming the outline of a fairly exhaustive frame of what the Holocaust in Poland was.[129] Additionally, one can recall the work on the anti-Semite Polish state by David Cymet (1999), who indicates anti-Semitism as a major cause of the Holocaust.[130] In some respects, Piotrowski's book seems to be a foretaste of what historically Gross would bring to bear in *Neighbors* about the massacre of the Jewish community in Jedwabne, perpetrated by Christian collaborators. Like Heller, he places the question of social evil,

---

127 Romanienko, review of *Poland's Holocaust*, 99.
128 Ibid.
129 See Jan T. Gross, *Polish Society under German Occupation: The Generalgouvernement, 1939–1944* (Princeton, NJ: Princeton University Press, 1979); Gross, *Revolution from Abroad: The Soviet Conquest of Poland's Western Ukraine and Western Belorussia* (Princeton, NJ: Princeton University Press, 1988); Tadeusz Piotrowski, *Ukrainian Integral Nationalism: Chronological Assessment and Bibliography* (Toronto: Alliance of the Polish Eastern Provinces, with the Polish Educational Foundation in North America, 1997).
130 Cf. Cymet, *Polish State Anti-Semitism as a Major Factor Leading to the Holocaust*. See also Pawel Korzec, "Antisemitism in Poland as an Intellectual Social and Political Movement," in *Studies on Polish Jewry, 1919–1939*, ed. Joshua A. Fishman (New York: Yivo Institute for Social Research, 1974), 12–104.

which legitimized genocide policies, at the base of his work. As Aleksander Wat wrote in 1977: "In the end I had read a bit of history and I knew that evil takes one incarnation or another in every epoch. And I thought that in the twentieth century evil had incarnated itself in history and that Bolshevism was the devil in history."[131] And further concerning Piotrowski:

> To that end, the book is organized not by chronological events, aggregations of villains, typologies of blame, or ethnographic tales of sole surviving heroes; but simply of cultural coordination or collaborations among ethnic groups. This approach demands that the reader keep focused on complex relations among and across nation-states, and avoids the reductivist tendency toward binary vilification (i.e. good guys/bad guys) as well as anti-Semitic agenda setting recently evident among media-savvy sociologists breaking into holocaust scholarship.[132]

This lets Piotrowski highlight the role Ukrainians, Russians, Germans, Poles, Lithuanians, and Belarusians played in the extermination of the Jews, when their social action did not correspond to common sense. He focuses on this social diversity and moral incapacity: for instance, when some Poles informed the Germans of other fellow Poles who had been interned in the concentration camp of Rembertow; or when some poor Jews provided the SS with other rich Jews' identities to profit from them; or when Lithuanian police killed Polish people because they spoke in their national language; or, finally, when Russian volunteers picked up thousands of Jews in one day, at the request of the Orthodox Church, to assist the Germans in their reprisals of genocide (according to some estimates, approximately 40,000).[133] As Lisiunia A. Romanienko underscores, "The author further suggests that historic animosity against the Polish people was used by some ethnic groups to substantiate aggressive acts and policies

---

131 Aleksander Wat, *My Century: The Odyssey of a Polish Intellectual* (Berkeley: University of California Press, 1988), 225.
132 Romanienko, review of *Poland's Holocaust*, 99.
133 Cf. Piotrowski, *Poland's Holocaust*, 8, 16, 67, 104, 155.

of excessive violence (i.e., infamous Ukrainian guards at Treblinka concentration camp). In other documented instances, barbarity against Polish people was used to foster nationalism and purity among perpetrators (i.e., winter expulsion of Belorussian Poles to Siberia by the Russians)."[134]

Almost by way of bulletins, the text accounts for the ethnic tensions that exploded during World War II, under Soviet terror (in the first chapter) and under the Nazis (in the second chapter). What matters is the space Piotrowski gives to the voice of some witnesses to reactions of the people in the provinces of Białystok, Lwów, and Tarnopol under Soviet power.[135] The peculiar character of the problem he sociologically reports is the question of responsibility for what happened during the war. Moreover, he points out very important matter, namely, "the children of these nations… have to come to terms with the 'sins of their fathers.'"[136] In explaining what collaborating with the occupiers means, Piotrowski deals with the documents on cooperation in the years between the two world wars, under the first Soviet occupation, then German, and in the immediate aftermath of the war, of Poles, Belarusians, Lithuanians, Ukrainians, and Jews themselves. He devotes a chapter to each.[137]

2.4. INJUSTICE IN THE EYES OF GERMAN WORKERS

In 1978, Barrington Moore published *Injustice*.[138] The central question posed in his book is whether a society can be defined as healthy without social justice. This was not the first time that Moore, who had been publishing a number of works, called for an understanding of social justice. But at the end of 1970s his vision became compelling, after a series of political events and while sociology as a discipline was undergoing several interdisciplinary influences and academic subdivisions. Between 1939 and

---

134 Romanienko, review of *Poland's Holocaust*, 99.
135 Cf. Piotrowski, *Poland's Holocaust*, 17–18.
136 Ibid., 6.
137 Four maps and twenty-five didactic tables offer a kind of summary of the work: table no. 15 represents "National Minorities in Poland, 1995"; no. 16, the "Ethnic Structure of Poland, 1931"; no. 17, the "Number of Poles Resettled or Evicted Between 1939 and 1944 in German-Occupied Poland."
138 Cf. Barrington Moore, *Injustice: The Social Bases of Obedience and Revolt* (White Plains, NY: Sharpe, 1978).

1945, Europe experienced unprecedented destruction. In asking how this was possible, Moore, an American sociologist and famed policy analyst for the government and on staff at the Department of Justice after a period in the OSS, tries to give an answer by taking the "German working class" as his analysis key. This choice may seem misleading, but the subject proposed by Moore and, more broadly, the social division of labor and the relationships among workers, helps to us to understand a human's disposition to bear social relations of an oppressive nature. Other scholars, such as Edward P. Thompson and Carl E. Schorske, had pointed out the feelings and the history of the working masses in a different manner, highlighting their life conditions but especially their attitudes in the face of power.[139] But now Moore tries to fathom, through the notion of the "German working class," the reasons why some men rebel, when laws are violated or equality claims are avoided, while others accept oppression and degradation: "This is a book about why people so often put up with being the victims of their societies and why at other times they become very angry and try with passion and forcefulness to do something about their situation."[140] His approach is significant because it starts from an attitude or a political tool that recurs in 1970s, namely, politicians and the elite keep workers divided and undercut their attempts in organizing. In this way the author is able to discuss the roots of totalitarian power.

After his *Soviet Politics* (1950) and *Social Origins of Dictatorship and Democracy* (1966), the Harvard scholar Moore, focusing on the particular case of Nazi Germany, moved with increased interest toward those who were the "social bases of obedience and revolt."[141] His intent was to study "those who have obeyed" an unfair power and "those who," instead, "have challenged authority," trying, in the latter case, to trace the social causes that led to the rebellion.

---

139 See Carl E. Schorske, *German Social Democracy, 1905-1917: The Development of the Great Schism* (Cambridge, MA: Harvard University Press, 1955); Edward P. Thompson, *The Making of the English Working Class* (London: Gollancz, 1963).
140 Moore, *Injustice*, xiii.
141 Cf. Barrington Moore, *Soviet Politics—The Dilemma of Power: The Role of Ideas in Social Change* (Cambridge, MA: Harvard University Press, 1950); Moore, *Social Origins of Dictatorship and Democracy: Lord and Peasant in the Making of the Modern World* (Boston: Beacon, 1966).

By "basis of society" Moore means individuals at the base (or at least near the base) of the social order, and "social order" refers to three institutions (authority, division of labor, and market or distribution of goods and services) that serve to keep society cohesive. As a result, the bases of society are all those people who have little power or authority, limited assets, insufficient incomes, scarce resources, or who are devoid of any material means or social advantage:

> The moral order of a society consists, among other things, of a sense of corporateness. This sense is embodied in symbols (e.g., the flag), rituals (e.g., inaugurations), and representatives (e.g., officials) who speak and act as agents of the collectivity. In large measure, these symbols, rituals, and representatives themselves define and reaffirm the corporate character of a society.[142]

These individuals, by virtue of the fact that they have little power and scarce resources, should be the first in the society to feel a sense of injustice, to perceive, for instance, when authority becomes abuse of power, when goods and services are not distributed fairly. Under these circumstances, they should also be among the first to rebel and seek by every means to do something to change the situation. The question is, therefore, why the "social bases" of German society did not rebel against Nazi totalitarianism, an extreme case of social injustice, and, on the contrary, actually supported it:

> Nevertheless it is worthwhile observing that for very many human beings, especially the mass of human beings at the bottom of the pyramid in stratified societies, social order is a good thing in its own right, one for which they will often sacrifice other values. They detest violent and capricious interference with their daily lives whether it comes from brigands, religious and political fanatics, or agents of the powers that be. People will generally support, even if

---

142 Robert Wuthnow, "On Suffering, Rebellion, and the Moral Order," *Contemporary Sociology* 8, no. 2 (1979): 213.

partly frightened into it, a political leader who promises peace and order, especially when he can do so under some color of legitimacy as defined in that time and place.[143]

In the light of what happened in Nazi Germany, Moore tries to comprehend if Hitler's advent was inevitable or if in post–World War I Germany liberal conditions or democratic institutions, capable of preventing the fall of the Weimar Republic, existed. After examining the problems faced by the Social Democratic coalition government, he develops his own thesis: the explosion of a strong social resentment, silenced for many years, inflamed the downfall of Weimar; this "repressive aspect of moral outrage" was finally channeled into the Nazi ranks.

To Moore, the origins of this sense of injustice or moral outrage date back to 1848 and persisted until 1920. They stemmed from the period when Germany evolved from a system of craft production to an advanced capitalist industrial system. Through a sociological survey also based on autobiographies and questionnaires, he analyzes the way of thinking, acting, and the life conditions of the German workers. Both popular nationalism and class claims, for the author, were already present in 1848, when conflicts between principles based on birth and attribution and those based on merit and achievements, next to the first forms of nationalism among workers in urban centers, started to appear in the social hierarchy. At that period, the German claims on Schleswig-Holstein, then under Danish sovereignty, had been made, but without success, by the Prussian armies; at the time of the Truce of Malmö, a violent popular uprising exploded, fueled by discontent of workers with low social status.

For Moore, the suppression of this antibourgeois and antiliberal current, developed among the lower classes of urban centers and outside parliament, and the inability of the Assembly of Frankfurt to meet popular demands, let a popular nationalism grow, albeit slowly. This nationalism sought to define the ideal type of German, with negative consequences in the long term: "The most one can assert with confidence therefore is that

---

143 Moore, *Injustice*, 22n13.

the seeds for a working-class nationalism, as well as its contradictions and dilemmas, were already present. They would have plenty of time to grow."[144]

2.4.1. AN OBEDIENT PROLETARIAT

The object of Moore's study is the "social action" of the German working class in different historical phases: from 1848 to the period prior to the Great War, from the reformist revolution (1918–20) to the revolt of the Ruhr. In each of these periods, the working class was facing, although in different ways, a breach of the social contract. Despite their rights and expectations being damaged, the social protests were, however, limited or had no effect: few put together all the grievances and arranged them into a revolutionary program. In essence, the workers did not challenge the existing power because they did not have definite opinions on the obligations and duties of the authority, and they lacked a historical consciousness.[145]

At the outbreak of the Great War, there was a large industrial proletariat, which posed a strong threat of revolution in Germany. Particularly, in the Ruhr, a symbol of industrial production where the precarious conditions of work were more evident and the wages lower than any in other European country, neither the coal miners nor steelworkers rebelled against the oppressive forms of power. The first because they were embedded in a system of corporate paternalism, the second because they were incapable of managing collective action:

> Subject directly or indirectly to the disciplinary paternalism of the highly status-conscious mine officials (*Bergbehörde*), the miners were granted exemptions from certain taxes and feudal dues. Their working conditions were under state protection. According to prevailing legislation, "loyal and obedient mining *people*" (*not* "workers": a term that when used later was regarded as an insult) were to have their names inscribed in the *Knappschaftsregister* and

---

144 See ibid., 171–72.
145 In this regard, Moore suggests a Chinese tale that shows how to lead a people to revolt: it is Fang-La, leader of the rebels, who mobilizes the population against the Sung dynasty; cf. ibid., 27.

had the right to receive from a collective fund specified amounts in case of illness or accident.[146]

Those who worked in the coal mines found a common culture on which to draw: the miners had their *Gedinge*, their *Knappschaften*, and their *Berggesetz*, social institutions that distinguished them from other workers and that enhanced forms of collective protest. Nevertheless, the wage concessions they obtained delayed tensions without bringing any recognition of rights: they were mainly intended to build consensus among workers. Additionally, the patronizing attitude of the industrialists, benevolent and authoritarian at the same time, did not help social-democratic initiatives. For ironworkers, instead, the situation was different: because of technological innovations, they worked in displaced areas or in different areas of the factory that were not conducive at all to everyday personal relationships. As Moore underscores, "A smelter and a man who helped to operate the flying shears were not likely to have as much in common as the various grades of coal miners, making collective action more difficult."[147]

Since the steel industries were more technologically advanced compared to the mining industry, they required, and created at the same time, a more diverse workforce and often imported labor from other regions of Central Europe: for example, many Poles were working with the Germans without sharing similar values. The absence of a shared past, social fragmentation in the workplace, and the lack of a tradition of informal collective bargaining, such as the *Gedinge*, did not promote the formation of a common sentiment, which must be the basis of collective action. Although, in the Ruhr, the growth of big industry had created a substantial working class, the elite of this proletariat had fractures within its ranks, while the mass of workers pursued minimum targets. Furthermore, the general trauma of the war, with especially its political and economic consequences, the end of the monarchy, and the discrediting of strata and dominant institutions in German society, contributed to the industrial workers lack of cohesion into one revolutionary force. What is noticeable is that issues

---

146 Ibid., 234.
147 Ibid., 271.

related to revolutionary forces were common and usual in political agendas of the 1970s, especially because episodes breaking the status quo or promoting political revolution, by involving a complete change, after 1968, were frequent. Moore stands out in post-Holocaust sociology for this attention to the political scene: he approaches the theme of Nazism and the consensus in favor of the NSDAP through contemporary sociological devices, mirroring what was happening around him in the 1970s:

> In the chaos following Germany's defeat, workers took to the streets, fought against the authorities, and formed representative councils. Unfortunately, the leaders of the labor movement were afraid to use these energies to effect a liberal revolution that might have destroyed the old order and formed the base for a democratic state, the leaders' failure helped to evoke a "radical thrust" which culminated in the rising of the Red Army in the Ruhr during the spring of 1920, put down by reactionary forces fighting on behalf of the moderates.[148]

Moore accounts for the difficulties of German society, which was prostrated on the economic plan and deeply divided by the social plan, with high unemployment at the end of the Great War. In the cities, worker and soldier councils occupied companies and newspaper offices, requisitioned food to be distributed to the population, among demonstrations and riots. Seeking to leverage this situation was the extreme Left, gathered around the Communist Party, which, even after the failure of the Spartacist uprising and the Republic of Bavaria, continued to propose revolution as a solution to the country's problems.

The situation was similar, in some respects, to that of Russia in 1917, but, in reality, there were many differences, and several obstacles to revolution: a mobilization of the rural masses was lacking, and, more importantly, there were various power relationships within the labor movement. The German Social Democrats, willing to form an alliance

---

148 James J. Sheehan, "Barrington Moore on Obedience and Revolt," *Theory & Society* 9, no. 5 (1980): 729–30.

with moderate forces, and in no way intending to dismantle the military and civilian structures of the old order, were able to prevent a general revolution:

> The first wave of the revolution that had begun in Kiel in November, 1918, with the sailors' revolt had been predominantly a "people's" revolution, with limited liberal objectives. It was a general popular upheaval directed almost entirely against the military, the monarchy, and anything that smacked of the continuation of wartime discipline, suffering, and sacrifice. Though the workers played a major role, those who sought to turn the popular revolution into a radical or proletarian one were a small and scattered minority. Had not Ebert and his colleagues forestalled them by taking power in Berlin, they might have mounted a coup but hardly a revolution. The local workers' and soldiers' councils that sprang up spontaneously after the Kiel uprising might have become the organs of a popular democracy, or at least agents to break the institutional hold of the dominant classes—the Junkers, big business, the higher levels of the judiciary and the bureaucracy. But this did not happen. One obvious reason is that the reformist leadership of the SPD was afraid of letting it happen, lest the movement get out of hand and turn into a socialist revolution, which they believed would have disastrous consequences for all of Germany, including the industrial workers. Another reason why nothing resembling a democratic dictatorship emerged from the council movement is the fact that by and large the peasants would have nothing to do with the councils.[149]

The sailors' rebellion of the German fleet gave impetus to a revolutionary process that ended with the fall of the empire of William II and the proclamation of the Republic in November 1918:

> The revolt in the Ruhr, in reaction to the Kapp Putsch, the abortive rightist coup of March 13–17, 1920, was the most significant uprising

---
149 Moore, *Injustice*, 316–17.

by industrial workers that has so far taken place in any modern industrial country. Within a few days the Ruhr workers managed to improvise a Red Army. With this army they managed to capture Dortmund and Essen, major cities in Germany's industrial heartland, and several smaller ones.[150]

In the Ruhr, the industrial process transformed the structure of employment, dramatically driving up the proportions of the proletariat. There, the lack of decent and humane treatment, withholding of pay, and the arbitrary pay scales creating conflicts between employees without encouraging the cooperation to form revolutionary groups, together with the lack of safety at work and the continuous possibility of dismissal without just cause, all increased discontent that could no longer be contained. Friedrich Ebert's political choices, the implicit suppression of a socialist alternative implied by the Social Democrats' compromises with the existing power structures to maintain social order, helped to channel discontent progressively towards National Socialism.[151] In the context of a lost war, of growing inflation, of scattered territories or slices of German nationality, the moral outrage of workers, previously repressed, had to lead somewhere. The attention Moore devotes to the National Socialist German Workers Party, which, by promising an end to social injustice, harnessed this political disappointment. The NSDAP, with its propaganda based on the concept of national community and on the abolition of class alliances, recruited Germans from all sectors of the population. Of an anti-Marxist and interclassist matrix, it elaborated a propaganda line tending to attribute the responsibility for the defeat of Germany in the Great War to the "anti-national elements," a term by which Marxists and Jews were designated. Through this policy, the reason why the Nazi Party was born returned: workers and impoverished petty bourgeois, threatened by massive Czech immigration in areas inhabited mainly by Germans in the Sudetenland, sought to protect the rights of the German majority of that region. The sudden increase in unemployment and inflation produced

---

150   Ibid., 328.
151   Cf. Charles Tilly, *From Mobilization to Revolution* (Reading, MA: Addison-Wesley, 1978).

anxiety, especially among the middle classes and the urban underclass. Taking advantage of the discontent of the petty bourgeoisie and the unemployed, of the political instability of the Republic, and the errors of the moderate parties, already during the election campaign of 1930, the NSDAP was able to act as a force that could propose solutions for salvation, winning about 6,500,000 votes and 107 deputies.

2.4.2. "Was du für Volk und Heimat tust, ist immer recht getan!"

The National Socialist program of February 24, 1920, responded to the needs of frustrated workers and an exhausted Germany: among its points was primarily the concern of uniting all Germans and forming a greater Germany, as evident below from documents reported by Walther Hofer:

> 3. We demand fields and lands (colonies) to feed our people and for the settlement of our surplus population.
> 4. Citizen of the State (*Staatsbürger*) can only be one who belongs to the popular community (*Volksgenosse*). Volksgenosse can be only one who is of German blood, without any regard to religious affiliation. Therefore, no Jew can be Volksgenosse.
> 7. If it is not possible procure the necessary foods for the entire population of the State, the members of foreign nations (who are not citizens of the State) must be expelled from the Reich.
> 8. We demand that all non-Germans, who immigrated to Germany after 2 August 1914, be forced to leave the Country immediately.[152]

To evaluate the extent to which the Nazi Party was a workers' party, and the number of those who instead belonged to the lower middle class, Moore resorts to *Parteistatistik*, a study conducted in secret by the leadership of the Nazi Party (*Reichsorganisationsleiter*) in 1935, which became available only after the end of the war. The three volumes collecting data,

---
152 Walther Hofer, *Il nazionalsocialismo: Documenti 1933–1945* (Milan: Feltrinelli, 1964 [1957]), 25–28 (my translation).

actually, could not be disclosed outside of the internal personnel office of the *Reichsleiter* without written permission, and they had to be kept in a safe place.

Abel, Gerth, Heberle, and Lipset had already largely dealt with the social composition of the Nazi Party.[153] Moore adds another statistical source to previous research: the results of the general census of employment in 1933, carried out simultaneously with the general census of June 1933, five months after the rise of Hitler.[154] Until that time, the Nazis had not exercised any control over the Central Statistical Service, as Hughes explains in "The Gleichshaltung." Moore shows how it is possible to obtain useful information from data. For instance, based on the census of employment and the *Parteistatistik* it is possible to determine the percentage of those enrolled in the NSDAP in many professional groups of German society. He notes that 94.5 percent of the NSDAP members were male and that the total number of Party members equaled 2,493,890, representing 7.7 percent of the labor force, which had about 32,296,496 people; of these a little less than two-thirds were male, or 20,817,033. According to 1935 data of the Party and official census in thousands, Moore presents a table with professional groups who joined the NSDAP. By the intersection of the two data sources, it appears that from 1930 to 1935 the percentage of industrial workers and agricultural laborers increased by 4 percent, as opposed to that of employees, who suffered a decline of 4.6 percent. There are three groups of occupations appearing in the table: the first group includes a series of lower-middle-class professions; the second contains the manual workers of the city and the countryside, while the rich, retirees, and housewives constitute the third group. His sociological correlations are impressive—let me recall the consideration sociology as a discipline reserved for statistics in 1970s—in examining the role of NSDAP. For example, Group 1 contains small holders with difficulties in placing their goods on the market or retailers grappling with competition; the old middle class (as rural owners but with mortgage debt and craftworkers out of the market) and new middle class (now made

---

153 Cf. Richard F. Hamilton, *Who Voted for Hitler?* (Princeton, NJ: Princeton University Press, 1982).
154 For census data Moore consults *Statistik des Deutschen Reichs* (SDR), Band 453, Heft 2 (Berlin, 1936), 6.

up of civil servants, salaried workers, and teachers, who constituted the profession with the highest percentage of subscribers to the NSDAP). Moore emphasizes the correlation between a limited level of education and the influence of the charisma exercised by the NSDAP. So, the lower-middle class forms all of Group 1. There were some resentments feeding the Nazi movement. They were those of the "'little man' angry at the injustices of a social order that threatened or failed to reward the virtues of hard work and self-denial as these personal efforts became crystallized in the merchant's store, the peasant's plot, the craftsman's manual skill, the white-collar job, and the technician's and journalist's gifts. Here was one possible outcome of the labor theory of value."[155]

Manual workers, especially industrial workers, form Group 2. Although the data highlight that, in 1935, there was not a massive shift into the Nazi ranks by these workers, the Nazis managed to infiltrate and gain more than half of their number. Moreover, as Moore underlines, in 1918, specialized metalworkers were the major source of combative and even revolutionary impetus.

Group 3 is made up of the wealthy, retirees, and housewives, on the edge of the productive system, according to Moore, who nourished a "rather desperate resentment" for their conditions, considering the fact that they represented one-twelfth of Party members.

This is why Moore stands out—his sociological analysis of these three groups, socially frustrated and resentful because of the work that was not paid a just wage or, as in the case of the unemployed, because they could not find a job. It was a frustration going back to a strong work ethic, the historical precursor of a popular reactionary movement. In doing so, Moore illustrates how the NSDAP, to the majority, was the "center and promoter of the resentment type and moral fury." Then who were the Nazis?

Moore elaborates in a more specific second table the social composition of the NSDAP in 1935. The first distinction he explains is concerned with "manual" and "non-manual" labor, and then with that between the "lower-middle" and "middle-upper" class. This analysis shows that the

---

155   Moore, *Injustice*, 406.

principal organized expression of resentment came from the lower-middle class, with industrial workers accounting for slightly more than a quarter but no more than half of its members. The Party was made up of ordinary people: over three-quarters of members belong to this fluid category. It seems to be a national community, which, in some ways, recalled life conditions in the trenches, where the common good must come before individual utility. According to Moore's surveys, the strength of the Party was, therefore, represented by the lower-middle class (i.e., by self-employed craftsmen, clerks, small businessmen, civil servants, teachers, but also by many industrial workers).

2.4.3. The Early Nazists for Abel, Merkl, and Moore

The autobiographical accounts of Nazi militants, collected by Abel in 1934 and examined by Merkl and Moore in the 1970s, testify that the first in Germany to feel the tension among conservatism, liberalism, and revolutionary radicalism were the workers, especially young workers, who were raised on values of honesty, obedience to authority, and fatigue. What is interesting is that Moore, looking back at or starting from *Nazi Movement* by Abel, underscores their values and when they begin to feel threatened. Here are two examples:

> Troops were once again returning to the Fatherland, yet a disgusting sight met their eyes. Beardless boys, dissolute deserters and whores tore off the shoulder bands of our front-line fighters and spat upon their field gray uniforms. At the same time they muttered something about liberty, equality, and fraternity. Poor, deluded people! Was this liberty and fraternity? People who never saw a battle field, who had never heard the whine of a bullet, openly insulted men who through four and a half years had defied the world in arms, who had risked their lives in innumerable battles, with the sole desire to guard the country against this horror.
>
> For the first time I began to feel a burning hatred for this human scum that trod everything pure and clean underfoot.[156]

---

156   Abel, *The Nazi Movement: Why Hitler Came into Power*, quoted in Moore, *Injustice*, 413n14.

And:

> My most urgent task in 1919 was to make my business a going concern once more. This was the more difficult since throughout the long years of the war no one had had the time to concern himself with it.
>
> After much effort I finally succeeded in getting some orders. All my hopes, however, were dashed. The inflation put an end to my endeavours … Hunger and privation once more held sway in my home. I cursed the government that sanctioned such misery. For I was convinced at the time that the inflation was not necessary on the scale on which it had been carried out. But it had served its purpose: the middle class, which still had some funds, and which had steadily opposed Marxism without actually combating it, was completely wiped out. The only way out of our misery was to find a man who might succeed in uniting all Germans who still had some regard for honor.[157]

The NSDAP members viewed the serious economic situation in moral terms. Moore cites among the main reasons for Hitler's followers' enrollment the disappointment in the solutions that other parties, such as the *Deutschnationale Volkspartei*, a reactionary monarchist party supported by Junker and big industry, had suggested in such a difficult situation:

> How different from this was the daring proposition that sprang from Hitler's warm sympathetic heart! His idea was not to use the resources of the state to help industrialists and land owners, but to take advantage of them immediately to relieve the misery of millions of unemployed Germans![158]

Nazi ideology offered real and salutary solutions, without cost in terms of conflict and suffering, to the social workers, who felt themselves morally outraged by the existing social order and victims of the

---

157 Ibid., 414n16.
158 Ibid., 416n22.

liberal capitalism of the Weimar Republic. Merkl, another sociologist, in *Political Violence under the Swastika*, analyzes the 581 case studies collected by Abel in 1934 and elaborates some social profiles for different subgroups.[159] His study shows a generalized hostility toward any authority. Merkl's research, richer in statistical data than Moore's, demonstrates that for the majority of Abel's interviewees the experience of camaraderie in the trenches, the defeat, the revolution, the exposure to foreign occupation, and the situation in border areas were the decisive factors in joining the Nazis in the name of *Volksgemeinschaft*.

Abel reports how, many of them, in 1930–32, were stoned or stabbed in the street by blends of organized groups of the Left: factors that sharpened the sense of persecution and reinforced the feeling of loyalty to Hitler. The greatest curiosity emerging from Merkl's study regards the violence of the young Nazis, which was inversely proportional to anti-Semitic prejudice, a factor that leads him to outline a typology of anti-Semitic prejudice. Nevertheless, Abel reports that 60 percent of interviewees were not anti-Semitic, unlike Merkl, who found that only 25 percent were not anti-Semitic. According to Moore, those who adopted violent attitudes showed a lower verbal violence, but such an interpretation, in reality, only reveals the discordance between data. What is noticeable is then the statistical influence in Merkl's piece, in which statistical methods and econometrics are evident. It is an influence involving the sociology of any country, in general, for reasons related to national economic needs, resulting from the international economic crisis of 1973. Both works represent a reinterpretation (that of Merkl in a statistical key, that of Moore in a historical key) of Abel's sociological survey. That Merkl updates the personal stories of the earlier Nazis by emphasizing a theme, that of the social composition of the NSDAP, which had often been sidelined but deserves the greatest emphasis. Nevertheless, both authors point out that the lower-middle class that supported and represented the NSDAP was not a homogeneous mass. Although criticized by his disciples, such as Charles Tilly,

---

159 Cf. Merkl, *Political Violence under the Swastika*.

Moore's work stands out in post-Holocaust sociology for another element. Namely, it focuses on the theme of human suffering, or on the social causes of human suffering, a highly recurring question between the 1970s and 1980s in sociology (Bauman would also deal extensively with this question) in rereading the nature of political power.[160]

2.4.4. Surrender to Authority in Concentration Camps

That Moore's work is also a historical piece is evident in studying the power of concentration camps. It seems he is influenced by the pioneering works of Kogon, Adler, and Bettelheim.[161] This emerges by examining those social and psychological mechanisms that led some prisoners to accept the moral authority of their oppressors. There seem to be two main causes of these attitudes. First, a number of prisoners, like German patriots, shared Nazi values and ideology since the beginning. At this point, Moore remembers, "When Bettelheim in 1938 asked more than a hundred old political prisoners if they thought the story of the camp should be reported in foreign newspapers, many hesitated to agree that this was desirable. Nearly all the non-Jewish prisoners, he asserts, believed in the superiority of the German race and took pride in the so-called achievements of the National Socialist state, especially its policy of expansion through annexation."[162]

Second, within the camp, social pressures fall on the individual who wants or tends to resist the moral authority of the oppressor: heroic deeds, in fact, threaten not only the lives of those who resist but also those of the group to which he belongs. Assuming that cruelty and suffering are imposed on prisoners through violence and coercion, Moore tries to

---

160 Cf. John P. Fox, review of *Political Violence under the Swastika: 581 Early Nazis*, by Peter H. Merkl, *International Affairs* 53, no. 2 (1977): 304–5; Tilly, *From Mobilization to Revolution*; Albert Schweitzer, review of *Political Violence under the Swastika: 581 Early Nazis*, by Peter H. Merkl, *Contemporary Sociology* 7, no. 4 (1978): 460–61.
161 Cf. Eugen Kogon, *Der SS-Staat: Das System der deutschen Konzentrationslager* (Munich: Alber, 1946); Hans G. Adler, *Theresienstadt 1941–1945: Das Antlitz einer Zwangsgemeinschaft* (Tübingen: Mohr, 1955); Bruno Bettelheim, *The Informed Heart: Autonomy in a Mass Age* (Glencoe, IL: The Free Press), 1960.
162 Moore, *Injustice*, 74n64.

explain how capitulation to moral authority of the oppressors, especially by members of the middle class, is attained.

In the first case, the victims feel that the suffering is not divorced from moral authority and, therefore, what seems inevitable is somehow right. This attitudinal acceptance of oppression sometimes leads some of them to identify with the SS, imitating, as far as possible, the uniform. In analyzing this, one should ask which practices the Nazis carry out in order to exercise totalitarian power in the camps. All social constraints and any kind of relationship among the camp inmates are broken. By reducing the possibilities for communication and collaboration among them, it is possible to guarantee total disintegration, denying any type of social agreement aimed at overturning the power within the field. Citing the elements contributing to isolating the individual, Moore gives special importance to the welcoming ceremonies, really traumatic rites, which degrade the subject, destroying self-esteem and respect. The degrading equalization of the inmates, marked by an equal uniform or by a tattooed number, is the initial step of destruction, namely, the beginning of a regime that deprives prisoners of everything. In this total institution, SS control pervades every moment of prisoners' lives, to the point of granting them minimum time to defecate, urinate, or sleep. Moore glimpses into this a kind of social relation that is atypical and one-way.[163]

These social factors cause an increase of the instinctual drives of hunger and other bodily needs, accelerating adaptation processes and encouraging the habituation to oppression and fear, while the desensitization feeling generates uncertainty and discomfort in the prisoner. According to the "definition of the situation" (at the basis of social action) by Merton, it is clear that the uncertainty of the situation in the camps caused both the inability to act and the submission to SS moral authority.[164] Clearly, at the basis of obedience to moral authority of injustice there was social

---

163 Cf. Howard S. Becker, "The Art of Comparison: Lessons from the Master, Everett C. Hughes," *Sociologica* 2 (2010): 1–12, accessed March 25, 2012, doi:10.2383/32713; Hughes, "Memorandum on Total Institutions"; Vienne, "Introduction to Everett C. Hughes' 'Memorandum on Total Institutions'"; Vienne, "The Enigma of the Total Institution."

164 Cf. Robert K. Merton, *Social Theory and Social Structure: Toward the Codification of Theory and Research* (Glencoe, IL: The Free Press, 1949).

disintegration, resulting from some elements that contributed to the atomization process among prisoners. First, mutual suspicion, created specifically by the SS (thanks to the presence in the camp of outlaws or criminals) undermines any form of collaboration between prisoners by making the exercise of power more invisible. Second, the theft or the fear of being robbed removes the element of trust at the base of solidarity action for revolts against authority. Finally, the different historical and social experiences of the prisoners prevent forms of collaboration and common strategies of survival. Moore many times stresses how the heterogeneity of the prison community makes solidarity and resistance impossible:

> There was also prisoners from different ethnic backgrounds between whom there was often violent hostility, even among Jews from different nationalities. In Theresienstadt Czech Jews frequently hated German Jews. At one point the Czech Jews said, "Now the Germans will see what 'transport' means!" (Transport was the euphemism for shipping prisoners out to an extermination camp.) Czech Jews also fought with the Zionists.[165]

Nevertheless, the political atomization of inmates leaves to prisoners some spaces of minimal freedom: since the authority needs prisoners' cooperation to carry out the daily routine, it sometimes does not come into the dorms or other spaces, allowing the formation of informal networks of cooperation among the prisoners. Several of them react by creating space for survival and response to authority. Reparaphrasing Bettelheim, Moore explains that those who survive in the camps are mostly political communists, who, faced with unfair moral authority, do not falter. Rather, they use to their advantage the power of the SS, with whom they must cooperate. The minimum cooperation with the SS, however, leads to defilement, in the sense that they end up exercising power over other prisoners in the camp, especially over direct enemies, namely, the criminals.[166] Obviously, within the camp the politicians on the Left constitute an elite (*Prominten*),

---

165   Moore, *Injustice*, 67n44.
166   See ibid., 70.

the ruling class (the one that Gaetano Mosca called "of managers," as they are used to exercising power in society).[167] Now, for the fact in itself that these prisoners, compared to the others, had a greater chance of survival, they were privileged in the sense that, when they decided whom to let live or let die, they exercised an arbitrary power, like the SS, in the camp. Belonging to this elite are especially the elderly prisoners, who hinder the chances of survival of the newcomers as they, being alien to the culture or the rules of the camp, could upset the precarious balance between the prisoners.[168] Apolitical, rich, or wealthy classes instead fail to define or understand their situation: they accept it as a mistake. The inability to process this generates self-pity, not allowing thinking or reaction to injustice. Muslims represent the extreme form of capitulation: they abandon any form of class action, renounce their feelings, and after ceasing to act at all, they die.[169] As concerns the middle class, a factor weakening the ability to resist is the attachment to the familiar routines before camp life, as Moore reports in referring to Bettelheim's experience:

> In Buchenwald Bettelheim asked many German Jewish prisoners why they had not left Germany beforehand because of the utterly degrading conditions to which they had already been subjected in 1938. Their answer was to the effect that they could not leave because it meant giving up their homes and places of business.[170]

2.5. HOW MANY VICTIMS OF THE HOLOCAUST?

In the shadow of international revolutionary facts, such as the Soviet invasion of Afghanistan in late December 1979 or the 1979 Iranian Revolution with its consequences for real life, public opinion, and the societal change set in motion, for sociologists there started a phase focusing on their attention on micro-questions. The previous "theory building" continued to develop within specialty fields under the influence

---

167   See Gaetano Mosca, *Elementi di scienza politica* (Turin: Bocca, 1923).
168   Zofia Posmysz-Piasecka returns to this aspect during interview cited above.
169   Cf. Primo Levi, *Se questo è un uomo* (Turin: Einaudi, 1958).
170   Moore, *Injustice*, 68.

of other social sciences, particularly political science and economics. By 1970, the attention to case studies, status variables, economic analysis, and statistical data became increasingly more profoundly relevant in sociological research.

While there was an ever more evident period of segmentation in sociology (accompanied sometimes by a reduction or decadence for theory building), a sociological touchstone in Holocaust scholarship was issued in the form of *Accounting for Genocide* (1979) by Helen Fein. In reading the book, one seems to find the mathematical and statistical influences characterizing the state of sociological studies of the period. Indeed, if one decides to start to identify and number the victims of the Holocaust (when looking at post-Holocaust sociology), the mind immediately runs to *Accounting for Genocide*. Nevertheless, the major reviews written about this book presented it as a kind of macabre bulletin for its attention to how many victims and where deaths have been.[171]

When analyzing her work, one can notice how Fein creates a much more complex research, far from a simple statistical analysis on the number of victims for any country of Europe. For instance, the sociometrical theory by Jacob L. Moreno resounds in the piece as does the methodological preferences of sociology of the 1970s: what is original is that she deals with all this by addressing the destruction of the Jews. As stressed by Benjamin M. Ben-Baruch, "her application of statistical controls to factors influencing historical processes affects the agenda for future research."[172] Meanwhile, the influence of the intentionalist Dawidowicz is glimpsed in her research.

A set of historical events coincided with her work, which received less attention than they should have. As Fred Crawford says, "this analysis of itself guarantees Fein's work a place as a timeless scholarly classic dealing with a human problem of such magnitude that few social scientists have

---

171 Cf. Fein, *Accounting for Genocide*; Irving L. Horowitz, "Bodies and Souls", review of *Accounting for Genocide: National Response and Jewish Victimization during the Holocaust*, by Helen Fein, *Contemporary Sociology* 9, no. 4 (1980): 489; Helen Fein, "Reduction by Review," *Contemporary Sociology* 10, no. 2 (1981): 168; Irving L. Horowitz, "Reply to Fein," *Contemporary Sociology* 10, no. 2 (1981): 170.
172 Benjamin M. Ben-Baruch, review of *Accounting for Genocide: National Response and Jewish Victimization during the Holocaust*, by Helen Fein, *Theory & Society* 10, no. 3 (1981): 461, http://www.jstor.org/stable/657477.

ever considered it—the Holocaust."[173] In essence, her work (arranged into 12 chapters and with 468 pages that recount in a new way what happened to the Jews of Europe) followed the lead, on May 26, 1972, of SALT I, the international treaty between the United States and the Soviet Union on nuclear weapons. The event, in the midst of the Cold War, together with the conclusion of the Vietnam War in 1973–75 and the Camp David Accords, on September 17, 1978, between Israel and Egypt, opening a new phase in the Middle East, opened the way to account for, in a novel manner, the destruction of the Jews of Europe. To this context, one can add the social movements and antiwar protests in 1970s along with the role of the women's rights and civil rights movements. All these events started to address a new democratization process and to pierce again, and above all publicly, the politics of the Iron Curtain.

Thirty-four years after Hitler's death, Fein emphasizes the concept of nation-state by specifically questioning how nation-states behave when faced with the destruction of the Jews. What matters more is that she breaks the categories of historical and traditional analysis, especially because her comparative and statistical examination reevaluates and reconsiders those factors leading a nation-state to practice genocide and how a particular group becomes vulnerable and subject to the genocidal process. When she compares the Turkish massacre of the Armenians and the extermination of the Jews in the chapter opening the book, she explains in what way groups occupying peripheral positions in the world system are easily vulnerable in respect to other young rising groups.[174] Among the most exposed to discrimination, persecution, massacres, and extermination are communities that do not hold strong ties with the dominant political group and are therefore excluded from the nexus of power and other strong bonds. In addition, by abandoning the traditional analytical categories of victims and bystanders, she focuses on political communities under the Nazi domain. For instance, when speaking of

---

173 Fred R. Crawford, review of *Accounting for Genocide: National Response and Jewish Victimization during the Holocaust*, by Helen Fein, *Social Science Quarterly* 61, no. 1 (1980): 179.

174 Cf. René Lemarchand, Disconnecting the Threads: Rwanda and the Holocaust Reconsidered," *Journal of Genocide Research* 4, no. 4 (2002): 499–518; Paul Bartrop, "The Relationship between War and Genocide in the Twentieth Century: A Consideration," *Journal of Genocide Research* 4, no. 4 (2002): 519–32.

"strong bonds" or "value consensus," she refers to the juridical situations dealing with the acquisition of civil and political rights (and those that recall citizenship concepts) and relations of goods exchange, remembering the relevance of moral solidarity by Durkheim or *idem sentire* of Tönnies. What she underlines is that both relationships, referring to political competition between groups (for polity and resources address), produce asymmetry among subjects opposed to each other.

If the sociological notions underpinning the work are those of nation-state and national solidarity, the concepts with which Fein elects to explain the genocide of the Jews are the "intensity of German control" over occupied European states, in satellite or allied states, and the "level of anti-Semitism" present in the same territories in the period before World War II. Fein, in a vast geopolitical space that draws on and shows the speed of the destruction of the Jews of Europe as it occurred, addresses these two last variables.

For Ben-Baruch, one of Fein's biggest critics, the possibility of genocide arises when, in a country isolated from international context, a vulnerable group does not create, for various reasons, alliances or relationships of any kind with the group able to bypass or circumvent the danger. This detachment caused by a lack of "moral solidarity" among fellow countrymen degenerates into relational anomie, so that the minority group is left to itself or, worse, led to the final solution. When Fein states that political national behavior, in front of the National Socialist totalitarian ideology, changed from nation-state to nation-state, she alludes to the fact that those countries depended on the type of political competition that is the struggle of power present in each state. This means that different countries of Europe reacted differently to Nazism. Specifically, they took different positions and adopted distinct public policies that made the difference between the genocide of Jews perpetrated in Poland and that in Romania, in Holland, and so on: the public policies that varied from state to state enlighten the reasons for the different numbers of Jewish victims from a particular country.

What distinguishes Fein's sociological work is that she does not consider Europe as a single large and indistinct territorial block where the extermination was perpetrated: rather, she illustrates that Europe is made up of several states and acknowledges the cultural specificities of each country. At a time when she analyzes the number of deaths for each part of the genocide, she gives them a nationality, a specificity, rebuilding their history and their emancipation stages. In this sense, thanks to her work, sociology made room, in an early way, for studies giving importance to identification of any victim of the *Shoah* (a process that in historical works would be evident only when the archives of the former Soviet Union were finally opened). Reliable data on the former Soviet Union through new research began to appear only after the collapse of the Berlin Wall in 1989 and afterwards, when the archives, which had been kept secret or hidden for years could be opened and the darkness of Europe could be pierced.[175] Let me underline a point. If in the East the archives were opened after 1989, in the West, after 1989, it was possible to unearth unnoticed sociological writings and disseminate them. I refer to Gerhardt's edition of Parsons's works on National Socialism in 1993, to Neurath's study edited by Fleck and Stehr in 2005, and, finally, to Hartshorne's researches, uncovered by Gerhardt and Karlauf in 2009. All this was possible only after the end of communism.

Another central aspect of her examination concerns the power relations between groups arising during the formation of nation-states within the international context. Following Immanuel Maurice Wallerstein (the founder of the world-system theory) and Theda Skocpol (the American sociologist who used the historical approach for her thinking on state autonomy), Fein explains the ways in which the international system intervenes, or rather interferes, with the small structures of national power.[176] As Ben-Baruch notices, Fein highlights the close link between political relationships that unfold between different groups within a state and the rapport that the same state has with other countries,

---

175 See Mark Mazower, *Dark Continent: Europe's 20th Century* (New York: Knopf, 1998); Barbara Curli, "Il dopoguerra lungo: L'Europa indivisa di Tony Judt," *Contemporanea*, 12, no. 3 (2009): 581–97, accessed March 10, 2016, doi:10.1409/29975.

176 See Andre G. Frank, *The Development of Underdevelopment* (New York: Monthly Review Press, 1966); Immanuel Wallerstein, *The Modern World-System* (New York: Academic Press, 1974), 347–57; Amin Samir, *Imperialism and Unequal Development* (New York: Monthly Review Press, 1977); Giovanni Arrighi, *La geometria dell'imperialismo* (Milan: Feltrinelli, 1978); Theda Skocpol, *States and Social Revolutions: A Comparative Analysis of France, Russia, and China* (New York: Cambridge University Press, 1979).

which is often influenced by geographical location. By analyzing social groups and their networks, behaviors, attitudes, and bonds of solidarity, she enlightens the disintegration of those ties and the establishment of a context favorable to genocidal practices: the "weak ties" among groups inner to a society enlarge the angle (the *gonos*, from ancient Greek γόνος) of social and political discrimination, favoring a power competition.[177] The groups most vulnerable to genocide are those intermediaries who, by birth, do not enjoy political rights and duties (*they lack a native political base*). Especially, Jews are numbered as an "interstitial nation," that is, a sovereign nation but without a state territory, which is why, from the outset, they are excluded from the national universe of juridical obligations. By performing these obligations, the subjects are obliged to fulfill positive performance, that is, enjoy and exercise rights or discharge negative services or practice corresponding legal situations of duty. Fein stresses how genocide plays a significant role in the constitution of the order-national state. For Fein, who considers several genocide examples by making a comparison among distinct cases, the final solution was possible because the rapport of organic solidarity was weakened and failed within each state of Europe. This was due to weak bonds, not so indissoluble between Polish Jews and Polish Catholics, for example.[178] Fein wonders why the Germans did not become alarmed by the progressive disappearance of the Jews, while the killing of Poles forced Hitler to revise the initial plans. She sees foreshadowed the beginnings of the Holocaust in the loss of democratic power, in the midst of an economic and liberal crisis following the Great War, when the formation of totalitarian states became possible.

2.5.1. Within a Statistical Framework

Accounting for Genocide shows how important the statistical approach and data collection were in sociology by the 1970s, when statistics and

---

177 See Giuseppina Pellegrino, "Introduction: Studying (Im)mobility through a Politics of Proximity," in *The Politics of Proximity: Mobility and Immobility in Practice*, ed., Giuseppina Pellegrino (Aldershot: Ashgate, 2011), 1–14. Let me cite also the international workshop conducted by PIC-AIS, "Cultures of Mobility: Proximity, Displacement, New Media," University of Calabria, March 12–13, 2010.
178 Cf. Fein, *Accounting for Genocide*, 4n7, 84–88.

econometrics were appearing more and more in sociological researches. The relevant point is that this novelty is evident with Fein explaining the destruction of the Jews.

Born in 1934 and with a background in history studies, Fein investigates the aspects and properties of political communities within which genocide has been perpetrated: the percentage of a particular country of Jewish victims directly or indirectly killed or interned in concentration camps presents a broad reference range—from 95 percent in Poland to 1 percent in Finland. Through an analytical model of statistical regression, the sociologist describes the variability of these rates. For example, she compares two or more groups of data, or compares the variability within groups with the variability between groups: everything she needs to determine under which conditions genocide had a strong success. Fein explains the destruction of the Jews with the measurement of variability. This sociological approach allows for data values (i.e., y-dependent variables and x-independent variables) that are statistically significant in the sense that to each numerical data a given social phenomenon corresponds and can therefore be explained.

Her study plays a pivotal role in the development of post-Holocaust scholarship. It includes all the countries of Europe during the Nazi era—twenty-two states and political units (except the Soviet Union, due to the unavailability of data at the time of the research, and countries, such as Luxembourg, with a low density of Jews), in the period before the World War II. She juxtaposes to it the time variable, specifically, the period that extends from the rise of the Nazis to the end of the war. The main causes, for Fein, accounting for the destruction of the Jews were Nazi control exercised in occupied territorial areas and anti-Semitism present in the same countries before the war. These two reasons alone account for about 86 percent of the difference in the rates of Jewish victims in Europe: prewar anti-Semitism determined the number of victims, in any country, and in the countries where Nazi control was greatest, mortality rates were higher.

Into her analytical model, however, Fein enters other variables depending on the type of political competition in every state and the influence in the genocidal process. (Among these variables are the reception mode of National Socialist directives for each state, Jewish responsiveness before anti-Jewish policies, national collaboration, and so on.) Fein's model on the genocidal process can therefore be considered as a good framework within which to place and rethink previous works about the Holocaust. The exclusion of the Jews from the national universe of juridical and political bonds, indicated by the success of the prewar anti-Semitic movements and the absence of a strong government capable of protecting the civil rights and political liberties of the Jews, elucidates why states cooperated with the Nazis, allowing anti-Jewish policies to flourish. In fact, in areas that were already fully subjected, the Nazis leveraged the help of local governments: where the bonds of national solidarity were weak, the state encouraged collaboration with the occupying forces and allowed the social segregation of the Jews, including their isolation in the ghettos.[179] Fein's presentation, which, for experts in statistics, might resemble a diagram in ascending values, allows a revisiting of all the stages of the extermination.[180] As Ben-Baruch remembers, under Nazi power the anti-Semitic countries launched actions against the Jews that were more violent than those started before the conflict.

What distinguishes Fein work is that, on the one hand, she considers genocide committed in any state of Europe, but, on the other, she also presents the factors decelerating cooperation with the Nazis in each state and that somehow hindered the stages of discrimination, increasing the chances of survival for the Jews. The protests of the churches and the initiatives of half of the Jews, such as resistance movements or actions of the leaders in exile, lowered percentage indices of the victims, at least in areas where Nazi control was not very high. The effects of these factors can be found in the outstanding examples of the Netherlands and Romania, carefully studied by Fein. Despite the low level of anti-Semitism in the Netherlands, the rate of victimization was almost 80 percent: promoting the success of genocidal practices was, in fact, the high level of cooperation on the part of the Dutch bureaucracy, which mechanically carried out orders given from above. The Dutch social institutions at the

---

179 Cf. Hilberg, *The Destruction of the European Jews*, 43–174, 257–308, 555–619.
180 About state "willingness" to segregate and isolate the Jews, see figure B-1, "Chain Illustrating How Cooperation of Jewish Agents and Rank of Jewish Victims Are Linked to Isolation of Jews during the Holocaust," in Fein, *Accounting for Genocide*, 354; Hilberg, *The Destruction of the European Jews*, 31–39.

beginning even promoted the Nazi occupiers, while the Dutch Reformed Church or the government in exile did not use their leadership to put a stop to collaboration. On the other side, the one of the victims, the situation was no better: the movements for Jewish social defense required and found the cooperation of networks (of social defense) poorly organized or not made up of Jews; this situation persisted even after half of the Dutch Jews were deported.[181] In the other case, that of Romania, anti-Semitism allowed the extermination of the Jews: the liquidation of the Jews had begun even before the Nazi order was explicitly given, and only when Germany started to lose did Romania change cooperation policies, trying to extricate itself from the Axis. This belated resistance was supported by both the state and the churches and had as its objective that of minimizing the revenge of the winners after the war. The number of victims in Romania was below 60 percent.[182]

Accounting for Genocide is a meaningful sociological work, especially because Fein sheds light on the actions of single citizens interacting within the public sphere. These findings link, and at the same time cross, the private and public dimensions: Fein's ability lies in tying and braiding the behavior of the individual with the future of the national subject. For these reasons, she never separates her *Heimat*, both intimate and personal, from the universal and public. The extent of the action of the individual has to be considered in the context of the status of the nation and in no case is separate from the national political context. This action is inseparable from the experience of what Simmel calls *Wechselwirkung*; and this reciprocity between public and private actions remembers the "being in the world" of Arendt: alien to herself many times, but bound and attached to the world *of* and *from* which she could not be felt as a foreign. For her the social action was "an acting together with the other," transferring private moments and situations in the public sphere:

---

181 In accordance with Hilberg's subdivision, the Netherlands falls in the west of Europe. Cf. Hilberg, *The Destruction of the European Jews*, 363–381; Fein, *Accounting for Genocide*, 262–89, 458–59.

182 Hilberg makes a distinction, in the Balkans, among "Military Area Southeast," "Satellites par Excellence," and the "Opportunistic Satellites," such as Romania, by analyzing their collaborationist political behavior; see Hilberg, *The Destruction of the European Jews*, 432–554.

When finally the "before" of childhood became a memory that stood behind the great wall of the Second World War, Hannah Arendt began to talk about …in 1964 …until the end of her life, her Heimat, her home and her homeland, so to speak, was a political fact …was also a way of not remembering, or remembering only indirectly, that her childhood had been cut in two. To cut it in two was the death of her father, even if the trauma was not sudden …what is most striking in this work is a kind of nostalgia, a vision of that sense of community that St. Augustine called "the love of the next" …in 1933 with the rise to power of Hitler …"the love of neighbor" was something that was to become concrete and practical.[183]

In the 1970s, which were characterized by political revolutions in favor of democratization processes, Fein came to combine two human dimensions, one private and one public, transforming a highly emotional field (concerning the destruction of the human life of 5.1 million Jews) into field operations. Undoubtedly, this is an accurate measurement from a statistical analysis of the Holocaust, with the numbers of victims expressed as a percentage for each country in Europe:[184] "The essential focus is on the differences, in the response to genocide against Jews, of European states and regions occupied by or allied to Germany in World War II."[185]

2.5.2. Space and Time as Coordinates

Divided into two parts, Fein's text describes and analyzes the behavior of the Jews faced with extermination, showing how the victims, in the places

---

183　Elisabeth Young-Bruehl, *Hannah Arendt, 1906–1975: Per amore del mondo* (Turin: Bollati Boringhieri, 1990), 29–31 (my translation).

184　Here the term "operation" or "process of operationalization" alludes to the observation and the subsequent measurement of a social phenomenon through the use of statistical and sociological variables, both dependent and not. The study in question is therefore regarded as a system. Concerning the number of victims, see Brunello Mantelli, "Campi di sterminio," in *Storia della Shoah: La crisi dell'Europa, lo sterminio degli ebrei e la memoria del XX secolo*, ed. Marina Cattaruzza et al. (Turin: Utet, 2005–2006), 2:536–59; Horowitz, "Bodies and Souls," 489.

185　Leo Kuper, review of *Accounting for Genocide*, by Helen Fein, *Ethnic & Racial Studies*, 3, no. 2 (1980): 238–39.

most exposed to destruction, recognized the danger and reacted to it.[186] The first part, with a quantitative approach, traces the structure of social forces (explaining the circumstances that influenced, controlled, or simply facilitated the genocide), while the second reconstructs some case studies (in particular, where the territorial contexts of Warsaw, the Netherlands, and Hungary are analyzed). Acute issues such as international indifference towards the extermination, the behavior of the churches, and the role played by the Jewish Councils are also highlighted.

In the first part, for four long chapters, Fein explores a huge volume of dates: she inspects, nation by nation, the numbers of Jewish victims, examining the differences in the numbers of victims. Deep inequalities emerge from the intersection of space and time variables: they are translated into numbers, percentages, and statistical data and concern the independent causes that led to the different numbers of deaths for each country in Europe. To understand the reasons for these numerical differences, Fein sets certain statistical correlations: in the first part, she specifies which factors, forces, or sociopolitical conditions contributed to these results, as far as to draw and read significantly, in a statistical way, the percentage of the variance of the numbers in question. Fein, who, in many ways adopts the methods of social mathematics, tries to understand the statistical correlations existing between the independent and dependent variables.[187] As Ben-Baruch shows, her reflection on the percentage difference of the victims, "variance" as she calls it, depends not only on geographical space but also on the temporal dimension, that is, the time when the Nazis ascended to power and their dictatorial control expanded from Germany to Europe. In his words, "Fein's sociological model of a process occurring over time explains both the general pattern and the exceptions because she accounts for variation in the crucial intervening processes."[188]

With a 360-degree eye carefully looking at the international political system, Fein does not fail to consider the behavior of the Jewish

---

186 For Hilberg, Hungary falls in the area called "the opportunistic satellites"; cf. Hilberg, *The Destruction of the European Jews*, 473, 509–54.
187 Fein's sociology could be defined a "between sociology," midway between the mathematical sciences and historical knowledge.
188 Cf. Ben-Baruch, review of *Accounting for Genocide*, 459.

communities in Europe and the United States. Also, she does not forget to examine the attitude of Christians; the role of Pope Pius XII during World War II; Allied policies; the reasons for not bombing the concentration camps; and, finally, the functions of the Jewish Councils. It is relevant to stress that Fein adds other statistical indexes to the crucial variables preparing, regulating the extermination.

Maps, charts, themed figures, and dates both explain and illustrate the social relations that gradually disintegrated in Europe, allowing the collapse of national social solidarity and the decimation of the Jews. In a perfect way, Fein illustrates how genocidal policies were favored and anticipated from the training and development of anti-Semitic movements in the period preceding World War II. Thanks to a mass of documents and considering the density of the Jews for each specific region of Europe, Fein is able to theorize her correlation and, explicitly, show that prewar anti-Semitism and control of the SS, in 1941, explain approximately 86 percent of the number of Jewish victims in Europe.[189] By gradually considering the factors analyzed by Fein, it becomes clear that anti-Semitism is a sensitive measure to gauge because one is unable to predict or anticipate the results of the war period. Thanks to the presence of strong bonds of national solidarity in countries such as Denmark, located in what Hilberg calls the "semicircular arc," where there was a low percentage of anti-Semitic movements, the number of deaths reported was not high. Before 1936 in Denmark, the success of the anti-Semitic movements occupies, in the table prepared by Fein, a "low" level: in fact, the Danish Nazi Party (DSNAP), but also that of the Netherlands (NSB), were the only ones to spread anti-Semitic propaganda.[190] From the analysis of tables 2.3, 3.5 and figure 3.4, it is evident how, between the two variables (prewar anti-Semitism and Nazi control) the prewar anti-Semitism is assessed more precisely. When the level of prewar anti-Semitism is high while Nazi control is low, the number of deaths recorded is disproportionately higher than when prewar anti-Semitism is lower and Nazi control is instead higher. Certainly, anti-Semitic practices or attitudes play a significant role in extermination, but it is clear that these factors alone cannot explain the destruction of the Jews of Europe:

---

189   Cf. Horowitz, "Bodies and Souls," 490.
190   See tables 2.3, 3.5, and figure 3.4 in Fein, *Accounting for Genocide*, 45, 80–81.

> Fein has little to say about how anti-Semitism among non-dominant political actors (including both ethnic groups and churches) affected the fate of Jews. France, for example, is classified a "low" anti-Semitic state (similar to Denmark, Belgium, and Finland) because prewar governments acted against anti-Semitic movements. Nevertheless, the advent of the Vichy government certainly provided new opportunities to traditionally anti-Semitic political actors.[191]

Far from being simple, the research presents many complicated aspects. For instance, the variable of national anti-Semitism (measured for each country) cannot alone account for the Holocaust if not crossed with other independent variables, such as that of the control or dominion exercised by Nazi forces. Certainly, there is no mechanical connection between the number density of the Jews in a country and the high number of victims. Fein does not observe a high percentage of victims in areas where the concentration of Jews was low: in her presentation, which exceeds the elementary factors of pure demographics, the victims, produced by each nation-state, do not depend on the number (quantum) of Jews surveyed: "Fein also rejects historical interpretations claiming that Jewish demographic characteristics, such as their percentage of the population, absolute size, or extent of concentration in urban areas, are causally related to the victimization rate."[192]

Demographic characteristics do not offer an extensive explanation of the variable rate of victims. Fein focuses more attention on the social position of the Jews and the organizational nature of their communities, especially, the relationships between the Jewish and non-Jewish organizations and institutions of their communities represent a set of variables to be studied. How a state practiced discriminatory measures against Jews depended on the type of competition that existed between ethnic groups residing in a given territory and the position that Jews occupied among these within the same social structure. For example, in the Balkan countries, isolated by the collapse of the Ottoman Empire, the Jews constituted only one of the numerous ethnic groups (Armenians, Greeks, and Syrian

---

191 Ben-Baruch, review of *Accounting for Genocide*, 462.
192 Ibid., 461.

Christians), and as a group, Ben-Baruch explains, they were also less suited to becoming the first social target to be hit. The Jews lent money with interest: to governments for their armies, or in the exercise of their functions, to the upper classes, but also to craftsmen and peasants; they were intermediary actors in society, responsible for a public service. Returning to political competition between groups, the nature of discrimination against the most vulnerable is highly dependent on international relations that a state is able to establish with others. Fein does not renounce considering the impact of the international economic crisis and the influence of financial capital system on the states, which were at the base of violent anti-Semitic waves that occurred during the two world wars.[193] According to her, the structure of the Jewish community and specific relationships between groups (although they are variables of a dependent nature) deserve consideration rather than demographic factors. In fact, the low percentage of victims was related to the ability of the leaders of the Jewish Councils, who were able to mobilize resources and networks of social defense and cooperation with allies.

2.5.3. Moral Solidarity

To comprehend the relevance of Fein's work in relation to the development of Holocaust scholarship, it is crucial to illustrate the central issues of her thesis. My choice for analyzing chapter by chapter is related to the following aim: by addressing the sociological concepts she adopts in explaining the genocide, it is possible to clarify that Fein's interpretation and her sociological devices pave the way for a resolution to the question of the delay of sociology. The reason is linked to the 1970s, years in which sociology woke up as discipline.

The first chapters, "The Calculus of Genocide" and "The Bonds that Hold, The Bonds that Break," represent a *unicum* in Holocaust sociology. These chapters, in which the social reality is explicated in a clinical manner and with microscopic details, develop an original model and method in comprehending the "Jewish victimization," considering the nationality of

---

193 See Richard J. Overy, *The Inter-War Crisis, 1919–1939* (London: Longman, 1994).

the victims without creating a unique discourse, that is, without universalizing the extermination.

In "The Calculus of Genocide," Fein sums up genocide. She tries to explain the manner according to which the Jewish communities were systematically disintegrated by those social systems by which they should have been protected, and she does it by adopting three theories: namely, that of solidarity, of Nazi control, and of value-consensus. The first theory, the one that puts the category of solidarity at the center of the reflection, is that of verifying the exercise or practice of resistance opposed to the violence perpetrated against the Jews. Since Jews belong to a universe of common bonds, Fein asks what had or had not allowed their nationals to act on their behalf, ensuring the cohesion of society.[194] "How is society possible?" was the question that Simmel, author of several excursus, had posed to himself.[195] Societal cohesion depends on a number of devices. For example, to maintain cohesiveness between individuals there is a system of obligations, such as the law. For Fein, under the National Socialist power, organic solidarity was interrupted—encouraging the elimination of those shared norms that allowed the compatriots of the Jews not to intervene in their defense against extermination. She explains how "before the war, Jews were members of the nation-state, accepted within the universe of obligation by other natives."[196] Before the war, there were anti-Semitic environments in which it was easy for the Nazis to take power and ensure the end of solidarity ties of a political nature, such as citizenship and civil rights, and of economic order, such as the relation of economic exchange:

> Their acceptance as members of the nation-state with equal rights was inversely related to the achieved success of anti-Semitic movements.

---

194   In the light of *Values and Violence in Auschwitz* by Pawełczyńska, Fein often returns to the notion of solidarity and thus the importance of holding strong bonds to contrast and limit any extermination initiative: "The author's principal stress is on how prisoners maintained solidarity, at the small group level principally, to show how bonds and values are related to survival"; see Helen Fein, "The Holocaust and Auschwitz: Revising Stereotypes of Their Victims," *Contemporary Sociology* 9, no. 4 (1980): 496. For a sociological theory of morals, see the categories of "social proximity," "moral responsibility," and "social production of distance" in Zygmunt Bauman, *Modernity and the Holocaust* (Cambridge: Polity, 1989), 169–200.

195   Cf. Georg Simmel, *Soziologie: Untersuchungen über die Formen der Vergesellschaftung* (Leipzig: Duncker & Humblot, 1908).

196   Fein, *Accounting for Genocide*, 35.

The extent of states' resistance to or cooperation with German-instigated or -imposed anti-Jewish policies during World War II was a function of the extent of value consensus between Germany and occupied states, satellites, and colonies. State authorities' policies reflected the maximal earlier success of anti-Semitic movements.[197]

What led to the end of national solidarity and ensured that states cooperated or collaborated with Germany depended on what Fein defines as "anti-Semitic humus." It was powered during the formation of modern nation-states, when a series of historical and political circumstances, by intervening on the bonds of solidarity between fellow countrymen, represented anti-Semitism with a quite unusual role, which was, in fact, modern:

> The emancipation of the Jews in Europe generally accompanied the consolidation of the modern nation-state because, [as] Salo Baron asserts, the grant of citizenship to all and annulment of special statuses was a logical need of those states. If Jews also became integrated following their inclusion—assuming the presence of other conditions mediating integration—the degree of integration should be positively related to the stage's age.... The state's accession to demands for disemancipation of the Jews would signify the destruction of the nation-state's constituent assumptions. An attack upon the Jews was an attack upon the integrity of the nation: it was best realized and defined as that in Denmark, the oldest of the most solidary states. To protect the nation, one must also protect the Jews.[198]

Fein puts into play an important argument concerning when Jews were granted rights of a political nature or other guarantees. This coincides with one of the phases of the modern nation-state and deals with one of

---

197 Ibid., 35–36.
198 Ibid., 86–87n41. The reference is to Salo W. Baron, "The Modern Age," in *Great Ages and Ideas of the Jewish People*, ed. Leo W. Schwartz (New York: Modern Library, 1956), 317. Fein subsequently will reconsider the strong solidarity ties of the state. Cf. Fein, *Accounting for Genocide*, 114–15, 144–46.

the greatest achievements of modernity. It recalls *iure soli*, a principle of national sovereignty, namely, the conditions in which the struggle and the competition between established groups and minorities for the management and allocation of political and economic resources easily took root. This is one of the contradictions of modernity:

> If we take the encapsulation of minorities within the nation-state as a given condition, the implication of the Holocaust is that the life and liberties of minorities depend primarily upon whether the dominant group includes them within its universe of obligation; these are the bonds that hold or the bonds that break.[199]

At the end of the Great War, when the old empires crumbled and nationalist claims emerged with greater force, the level of solidarity cohesion between residents of a territorial state was lowered, allowing social disintegration to reach high levels. Without overgeneralizing the discourse, Fein, by seeking to identify the differences of extermination rates of the Jews in European countries, brings into play a number of variables, such as the density or visibility of Jews in the population of a state and the "warning time," that is, the period in which the threats of the Nazi danger begin; the attitude of the national and local governments and their characteristics before the conflict; the response of the Jewish community; the actions of the righteous, the rescuers who work to save Jews; and the opportunities for local residents to practice genocide:[200]

> Thus the territories ranking highest in the annihilation of Jews fall in the areas the author lists as the zone of domination (Austria, Germany, the Protectorate of Bohemia-Moravia) and the zone of extermination (Estonia, Latvia, Lithuania, Poland and Serbia).[201]

---

199 Fein, *Accounting for Genocide*, 92.
200 See the codebook, notes, and the methodological tables in ibid., 327–57.
201 Kuper, review of *Accounting for Genocide*, 239. In Estonia, Latvia, Lithuania, and Poland extermination was to ensure living space (*Lebensraum*) for the German nation. All of these countries before World War II had strong anti-Semitic movements and perpetrated the massacre without the German control. "Auxiliaries from the Baltic States served in the

Fein uses the time variable to relate the place where genocide was practiced with the phases of deportation and then extermination. In this way, she obtains a regional analysis of the Holocaust: the so-called warning time for a region, that is, the time the deportations and the destruction phase commenced, depended on the extent of control exercised by the SS in that region and on the level of anti-Semitism. Deportation and extermination were accelerated by the presence, in any region, of prewar anti-Semitism, while the number of victims, in any region, grew proportionally with the increase of the control of the SS: under Nazi control did extermination became possible.

Faced with the domination practiced by National Socialist forces, three kinds of attitudes arose: some states, while adapting to new conditions, used the time at their disposal to prevent Jews from being deported; others did not make use of the time available; and some countries facilitated or accelerated the stages of the final solution.

Commenting on the construction of a superior race, Fein shows that anti-Semitism was not the socialism of fools, but the policy of a totalitarian system, in the sense that the aversion for the Jews had become a cathartic moment to redeem the conflicts of race even before those of class.[202] This "-ism," considered as a "discursive practice" or "set of relationships" (Simon Levis Sullam remembers that it became the "ideology of Party and State, transforming itself into a political program, and finally into action"), aimed at hitting the Jews in place of another larger community:[203]

> The German nationalist ideologies united romantic nationalism with anti-Semitism and modern racism. They assumed an underlying mythic identity or homogeneity among the German people, or *Volk*, based on "blood." The Jews were not *Volk*, but aliens to whom the

---

killing-centre operations, and we know from other sources that in the euphoria of liberation, the Poles instituted pogroms against the few, small, surviving remnants of Jewry" (ibid.).
202 Cf. Bauer, *Rethinking the Holocaust*, 31–38. See Charles H. Stember et al., *Jews in the Mind of America* (New York: Basic Books, 1966); Paul W. Massing, *Rehearsal for Destruction: A Study of Political Anti-Semitism in Imperial Germany* (New York: Fertig, 1967).
203 Cf. Horowitz, "Bodies and Souls," 491; Simon Levis-Sullam, *L'archivio antiebraico: Il linguaggio dell'antisemitismo moderno* (Rome-Bari: Laterza 2008).

Germans owed no obligation. This was explicit in the Nazi party program of 1920. While the Germans belonged to the Aryan race, whose supremacy over the Slav and nonwhite races they unhesitatingly asserted, the Jews, according to the Nazis, were nonhuman; blood-suckers, lice, parasites, fleas, bacilli.[204]

As Dawidowicz and Salomoni evidence in their works, the date June 22, 1941, was crucial and groundbreaking. Starting from that date, when Germany invaded the Soviet Union, anti-Semitism and Nazi control were echoed by the absence of an authority or a popular answer, or something else in opposition to Nazi power.[205] Because in a political system practicing a genocidal policy passive acquiescence facilitates the final solution of the races considered as inferior, Fein glimpses the lack of organic solidarity between fellow citizens in the majority who did not intervene. Thus, her question is about the deterioration of national solidarity and the factors that contributed to the process. It can sound like a strange method, but it is far from it if we consider, in Fein's work, the fourth to seventh chapters, constituting the central part of the text where problems and specific issues are addressed in a linear and extensive manner.

For example, in her chapter 4, "The Keepers of the Keys," the role of the churches and their attitudes (which differed from country to country) in the promotion, or not, of genocidal practices are analyzed: the arguments in question appear complicated from the outset. A distinct difference exists between the indulgence of Pius XII and the militant opposition of the metropolitan of the Orthodox Church of Bulgaria. Fein interrogates herself on the diversity of behaviors assumed, and tries to comprehend if this sort of discrepancy has to do with political issues or rather is dependent on the control exercised by the Nazis in a particular area. The Bulgarian Orthodox Church belonged to the regional context of the East. Following map 2.1 showing the intensity of Nazi control (during the phases of deportation or direct physical extermination) reported by Fein in the second chapter, we can observe that while Bulgaria, from March 1943, was located in the

---
204 Fein, *Accounting for Genocide*, 20.
205 See Dawidowicz, *The War against the Jews*; Salomoni, *L'Unione Sovietica e la Shoah*.

"colonial zone—least control," the Roman Catholic Church instead lay in the "command zone—more control" and had done so since October 1943. From the analytic regression developed by Fein, it is clear that the behavior of the churches varied considerably according to the extent of the Nazi control, the role of national churches (especially that dominant in a state), the vicissitudes of state policies, and the spread of anti-Semitism.[206] For instance, the Roman Catholic Church compared to the Orthodox and Protestant churches was less willing to fight against Nazi practices when faced with a domination of their local institutions.

Fein discovers a high correlation between anti-Semitism and profession of Catholicism. First, protests of the churches were totally absent in countries with a Catholic predominance and with high anti-Semitism. Second, the non-Catholic churches were able to let their voice be heard, especially in states where the anti-Semitic movements, prior to World War II, had little success. Croatia and Slovakia represent a special case because they were Catholics states created by the Nazis during the conflict. The forms of clerical protest, analyzed by Fein, are important because they reduced the extent of state cooperation with the Nazis and facilitated the spread of "social defense networks for Jews," to the point of influencing mortality rates.[207] Beyond the specific analyses, Fein opens a crucial issue in Holocaust research and is concerned with the political aspects of neo-Catholic states.

In her chapter 5, "The Judenräte and Other Jewish Control Agents," Fein explores the role of the Jewish Councils and other Jewish institutions established to foster the isolation of Jews and accelerate the stages of destruction.[208] In this manner, she contributes to the international academic debate on the effects of cooperation of the Jewish Councils in relation to the fate of the Jews. If Arendt had emphasized the cooperation of the Jewish Councils with the Nazis because they "rounded up" as many Jews as possible for the extermination camps, Fein focuses instead on the reasons for the

---

206 See Ben-Baruch, review of *Accounting for Genocide*, 459.
207 Cf. Fein, *Accounting for Genocide*, 341–42.
208 On the stages of destruction, see the classification prepared in 1996 by Gregory H. Stanton, "The 8 Stages of Genocide," on the occasion of the Yale Program in Genocide Studies, accessed March 24, 2010, http://genocidewatch.net/2013/03/14/the-8-stages-of-genocide.

cooperation of the *Judenräte*, in some ways, considered as appendages of the modern rational process of destruction. Specifically, in analyzing the causes and consequences of this cooperation, during deportation phases, she describes the ways in which the Jews became victims in any state. For example, in Italy, if there were conspiracy networks, the likelihood that a Jewish Council was established or collaborated with the Nazis was lower than in regions where the bonds of organic solidarity between Jews and Italians were frayed:

> The principal intervening factor accounting for the extensiveness of Jewish victimization during the Holocaust was the isolation of the Jews, which was not attributable to German control alone but is best accounted for by state cooperation to segregate Jews that was not checked by native resistance. State cooperation is principally accounted for by the degree of legitimation of anti-Semitic movements by 1936. German control, the choice of tactics, and the time the state was occupied account for the establishment of *Judenräte*, social control organizations designed to further isolate the Jews and facilitate their annihilation.[209]

According to Fein, who verifies with data in hand how the cooperation of the Jewish Councils, in the final stages of the solution, actually increased the number of victims, Arendt excessively emphasized the role of Jewish institutions in the process. By distinguishing the actions of *Judenräte* between a "before the deportations" and an "after," Fein underlines that, after ghettoization, they did not have a significant impact on the increase of the number of victims. Rather, the cooperation of the Jewish Councils, before the deportations began, prevented single Jews or those in the group from creating organizations or networks of resistance at an international level.

It seems that *Accounting for Genocide* challenges Arendt's thesis and at the same time the majority of other studies focusing attention on the *Judenräte* in Eastern Europe, which are certainly valuable in understanding

---

209 Fein, *Accounting for Genocide*, 141.

the life of the ghetto, but they do not help to determine the causes of the so-called variability of victims' rates.

Chapter 6, "Forging the Bonds That Hold," is located in the middle of the book and appears to be a studied and thoughtful response to the third chapter, the one on the ties of national solidarity that remained or were interrupted during the genocidal process.[210] At the same time, this chapter anticipates and prepares for the second part of the book, which presents the "victims' view" and case studies of the Netherlands, Hungary, and the Warsaw ghetto.

Fein's chapter 7 is instead centered on the behavior of forces external to the German orbit. Specifically, "The Role of the Allied Governments" investigates the passivity of the U.S. and British governments in putting an end to the genocide and the inadequate responses of the American and English Jewish communities, addressing what responsibility a state has towards its own citizens. This is a topic reconsidered in 1980s in the journal *Genocide Studies*, as we will see with Horowitz and Kuper in the next chapter.

2.5.4. Jewish Victims

Several distinctions are useful. In this manner of thinking, the peculiar feature about a book is not in the structure that it constructs, but in the theory that supports it. Thus, Fein's work is a determining moment in post-Holocaust scholarship for her attention, in 1979, to Jewish victims: with her chapter 8 (with which the second part of the work begins), she shifts the focus from the macrosociological lens to the everyday world of the victims.[211] *Accounting for Genocide* interprets the destruction of the Jews as a result of European history, on the basis of statistical correlations for which she provides a "codebook" at the end of the work, a sort of instruction booklet to understand the meanings of the statistical measures taken. The

---

210 Cf. Fein, *Accounting for Genocide*, 262–89; Suzanne Vromen, "Collective Memory and Cultural Politics: Narrating and Commemorating the Rescue of Jewish Children by Belgian Convents during the Holocaust," in *Sociology Confronts the Holocaust*, 134–53.
211 The "victims' view" allows for the punctual retracing of the particular type of "*resistors*: the partisans, ghetto fighters, organizers of death camp revolts, and soldiers in the Red Army" (Porter, "The Holocaust as a Sociological Construct," 186).

set of data collected by Fein also contains the tabular material in the appendix in order to verify the assumptions, procedures, and outcomes of the same research: it is material operationalized by correlation coefficients, and that assumes the cooperation of the state, organizations of the Jews, phase segregation, and the number of victims as variables.[212] In addition to the masterpiece of the book, there are more than forty-eight pages of notes explaining in detail the key points of the twelve chapters, and also forty-eight pages of bibliography, an index of names, and one of themes. Behind Fein's work we can see a new alternative hypothesis in the comprehension of the *Shoah*. She anticipates the discourse of several historians, evident especially after the fall of the Berlin Wall, when the archives were opened and the end of communism and the Iron Curtain gave names to forgotten victims. Fein avoids homogenizing the different regions of Europe: she captures the specific conditions that led the Jews to become victims in any particular country. "Communists erect monuments to victims-of-fascism-in-general-depriving the dead of Auschwitz of their Jewish identity even in death,"[213] Fackenheim has declaimed.

2.5.5. International Debate after Publication

In 1980, one year after the publication of *Accounting for Genocide* (described by the director of the National Jewish Resource Center, Irving Greenberg, on the back cover of the book, as "a pathbreaking work in Holocaust Studies"), the first criticisms regarding Fein's work appeared. They were not all positive. Among many comments, ranging from its textual elegance to banality, its innovation to sociological imagination and methodological pedantry, there was that of "ambiguity of its ubiquity."[214] In essence, two of her most critical commentators, Horowitz and Kuper, help us understand the meaning of this expression. After admitting to having reviewed the book with great difficulty, they comment that it is, for them, both excruciating and "agonising."[215]

---

212   Horowitz, "Bodies and Souls," 492.
213   Fackenheim, *Quest for Past and Future*, 17.
214   Cf. Horowitz, "Bodies and Souls," 489.
215   Cf. Kuper, review of *Accounting for Genocide*, 238.

The debate, which I researched using online reviews, is reported here to show how scholars, like Kuper and Horowitz, were affected by her piece, especially by her interpretation of genocide. A little further on, I will address their subsequent Holocaust researches, very important not only for post-Holocaust sociology but also for Holocaust Studies in general. It can be said that this lively debate paved the way to Holocaust sociology of the 1980s. In addition, Horowitz's criticism regarding the statistical approach of Fein helps to show that sociology, in its segmentation in 1970s, was increasingly influenced by economics and statistics. If some scholars had looked at Fein's book with more attention, maybe the assumption Bauman made about how sociology woke up in 1989 would not have had so much influence in the discipline.

The first criticism concerned the very title and subtitle, or the choice of the words, *Accounting for Genocide* and *National Response and Jewish Victimization*. These terms were completely cut and sifted in a very meticulous manner by the critics. It is Kuper who started the criticism in April 1980, according to whom the expression "accounting for genocide" implies that the general theory of genocide is improper. This because Fein had not considered the defining work on the genocidal process, begun in 1943 with the definition by Lemkin, and then reused by the UN to approve the text of the Convention on Genocide on December 9, 1948.[216]

Apart from some positive comments, for Kuper, who published his *Genocide* a few years later, Fein's book shows some genocide examples without elaborating the massacres perpetrated in the course of the twentieth century in the theoretical part: brief references are only reported by Fein about the genocide committed by the Turks against the Armenians and about the destruction of the Gypsies:

> The sociological study of genocide has been almost a taboo subject, and Helen Fein's book is an important contribution in the attempt to gain more adequate knowledge of the process. It is all the more significant, since genocide is so prevalent in our own era, and the

---
216 Cf. Leo Kuper, *Genocide: Its Political Use in the Twentieth Century* (New York: Penguin, 1981): 210–14. About Lemkin's definition see the next chapter in this book, section 3.2, "The Significance of Genocide."

United Nations, charged with its prevention and punishment, hardly attains the level of the almost silent diplomacy of the Vatican during the period of Nazi ascendancy.[217]

After a few months, in July 1980, Horowitz published his doubts surrounding the choice of the verb "accounting for" in *Contemporary Sociology*—it is mainly a cause of ambiguity because it reduces reflection upon the extermination to a simple reporting, based on the rational principle of "costs/benefits," even though this was not Fein's intention.

Additionally, Horowitz criticizes the analytical research method used by Fein, and he accuses her of having examined and studied a dense topic, full of suffering and worthy of compassion, with cold estimation: she had counted "bodies and souls." For these critics, the Holocaust topic cannot be reduced to a mere computation that measures statistical relationships between the various causes that led to the destruction of the Jews of Europe. However, in my reading, Fein's "analytical framework" the bodies are not just counted: people are not forgotten nor are the tragic or moral issues transformed into pure technology or into problems of social engineering, since ample space is given to the notion of "subject":

> There is intellectual risk in reducing the Holocaust to strictly sociological proportions. The Holocaust is an issue that has gripped historians, theologians, and every human soul concerned with questions of human survival in an atmosphere of official homicide. If the attempt to render the Holocaust in statistical terms is warranted, its results must perforce be limited.[218]

Concerning the unsuitable choice of the title, Horowitz continued by pronouncing against the use of the term "victimization" and transforming the criticism into a real academic diatribe. The initial question concerns to whom and to what the term "Jewish victimization" refers. Horowitz explains that the English noun "victimization," utilized by

---

217 Kuper, review of *Accounting for Genocide*, 240.
218 Horowitz, "Bodies and Souls," 489.

Fein, does not simply translate the noun "victim" but also alludes to the action of "victimizing." Actually, it brings into play the rendering of someone as a victim and being a victim, thus placing the one who victimizes (victimizer) and the victimized on the same level. However, for Horowitz, the term "victimization" cannot distinguish the victims from victimizers: a subtitle, such as "Victims and Survivors of the Holocaust," would have clarified the matter.

The critics then dealt with the approaches of the second part of Fein's treatment, "which are interesting but irrelevant to the genocidal outcome. This latter section, analyzing the victims' views, is largely derivative and not particularly innovative."[219] According to Horowitz, there is a consequential logic disordered between the two parts of the book. Briefly, for Horowitz, at the end of the reading of *Accounting for Genocide*, the reader who intends to comprehend the history of the Holocaust remains confused: if the first part claims that the Jews who resisted were unable to reach a change of Nazi genocidal policies, the second part instead detects actions and behaviors inconsistent with the first. Namely, considering Fein's work, one fails to understand if the reactions of the Jews really had a significant effect or not during the genocidal process. Therefore, Horowitz questions why one would tell a second story that contradicts the first.

Finally, according to Horowitz, Fein seems not to refer to the specific issues of the history of the Jews, for example, to the Zionist tradition. In reality, the second part of the book, which puts emphasis on the victims' point of view and the theme of resistance, recalls the concepts of socialism and Zionism:

> Between Zionism and socialism, neither of which dominated Jewish thinking, was the bourgeois vision of an integrated enlightenment that created the foundations for the survival of Jews in liberal states. But the elimination of basic forms of political democracy invited the elimination of Jewish communities. One feels the weakness of a functional analysis divorced from political analysis. The daily struggles of the Jewish communities of Europe were not simply in terms

---

219   Ibid.

of participation in civil service bureaucracies or in terms of Jewish community life as a relatively vague secular act, but rather they were struggles of Jews with each other.[220]

The idea of a self-emancipation of the Jews as a nation, outside of the European continent, reveals just how precarious the process of national integration of the Jews of Europe was. Under Nazism, this integration completely failed. "In the eyes of the anti-Semite," Hilberg writes, "the Jews therefore became a 'race,'" an *Unterasse* in society.[221] "This took place at a time when Jewish communities did not have the capacity for national self-defense."[222]

When Hugo Bettauer, in the early 1920s, eleven years before Hitler's rise, published *Die Stadt ohne Juden*, he stressed that Vienna could not do without the Jews. Certainly, in front of a "State without Jews" the inert attitude of the Allies makes even more evident the absence of a same national feeling:[223]

> A uniform solution and integrated annihilation would be made possible by pressuring those areas where resistance was strongest or those areas in which anti-Semitism was weak in an early warning period. I realize that this is grotesque rendering of Fein's data, but it is a conceivable end.[224]

Horowitz's criticism does not only concern the numerical or graphical representations developed by Fein.[225] Horowitz thinks it is not highly

---

220 Ibid., 491–92. On Zionism see Vincenzo Pinto, *I sionisti* (Milan: M&B Publishing, 2001).
221 Hilberg, *The Destruction of the European Jews*, 13n31. The reference is to Konrad Dürre, "Werden und Bedeutung der Rassen," in *Die Neue Propyläen Weltgeschicte* (Berlin 1940), 89–118.
222 Horowitz, "Bodies and Souls," 492.
223 Hugo Bettauer, *Die Stadt ohne Juden*, quoted in Raul Hilberg, *The Destruction of the European Jews*, 17.
224 Horowitz, "Bodies and Souls," 492.
225 "The captions are proper, but the maps are not" (ibid., 492). In particular, Horowitz noticed some errors in map 2.1 ("Intensity of German Control over European States at Time Deportation of Jews or Direct Physical Extermination Began"); in map 2.2 ("Development of Political Anti-Semitism up to 1936 in European States Occupied by and/or Allied with Germany during the Holocaust"); in chart 3.2 ("Relative Size and Visibility of Prewar

appropriate that Fein uses statistical tools in interpreting the Holocaust: even if she is brilliant in using categories of statistics, he questions the statistical method in itself. To Horowitz the statistical approach is not the best way to comprehend the genocide of the Jews.

The collection of material "nation by nation," optimal places for research on Jewish resistance, is misleading because of the lack of a link between description and explanation or between correlation and causation. It is undoubtedly a publication "apart" that represents a sociological bastion, truly, the only report of mass murder perpetrated against the Jews of Europe in the twentieth century.

2.5.6. An Intellectual Diatribe: Horowitz and Fein

Unconsciously, this debate came to set the discipline of sociology in a respectable place in Holocaust scholarship, greatly refuting the notion of its so-called delay in approaching the Holocaust. Fein responded in March 1981 to five criticisms advanced in July 1980 by Horowitz in *Contemporary Sociology*.[226] Particularly, "While I stand accused of reductionism, it is the reviewer who is disinterested in understanding the meaning of the victims' behavior for its own sake who dismisses Part II—"The Victims' View" (not views)—which essentially complements Part I and restores the unity of their experience."[227]

"The Victims' View," singular, rather than "views," plural, is an essential and basic aspect of her research. In fact, it serves to define the situation of victims and to appreciate their humanity. Fein highlights that certainly several Holocaust researches had been conducted before *Accounting for Genocide* but that these works mostly focused on blaming the Nazis or defending the victims without periodically defining the historical situation. In regard to the second part of the research, which is for Horowitz "derivative and not particularly innovative," Fein writes that this is the result of an

---

Jewish Population in European States Occupied by and/or Allied with Germany during the Holocaust"); and in map 3.3 ("SS Grip over European States in September 1941"). Cf. Fein, *Accounting for Genocide*, 39, 46, 59, 79).
226 Fein, "Reduction by Review," 168.
227 Ibid., 169.

intensive work based on the memoirs and diaries of Jews living in the Netherlands, Hungary, and in the Polish city of Warsaw, where a high number of victims were recorded. This part is then used to reconstruct the perceptions, attitudes, and the "responsiveness" of the victims. Far from summarizing *Sepolti a Varsavia* by Emmanuel Ringelblum or building new theoretical structures, Fein aims at bringing to light what had been hidden or forgotten.[228]

In support of her discourse, she speaks of the last pages of the chapter "Implications," specifically, those in which she has analyzed collective behavior of the mass of the Jews, answering those accusations according to which she would fail to interpret Jewish strategies as part of the genocidal process.

To Horowitz, who criticizes her neglect of Jewish ideologies, she instead replies that those details are discussed in both the fifth and seventh chapters.[229] With regard to the allegations about the contradiction between the two parts of the book, Fein defends herself by saying clearly that her critics, after all, disregard the conclusions of the book.[230] The cases of Western countries, such as Belgium and the Netherlands, with low anti-Semitism and low control by the SS, compared with those of the East, Romania and Hungary, with high anti-Semitism and Nazi high control, prove an irrefutable reality: even if "the Jewish responses" did not produce clear effects against Nazi policies, the active role of Jewish leadership would have increased the possibility for Jews to survive.[231] Thus in the last pages of *Accounting for Genocide* we read:

> However, the effectiveness of defensive strategies undertaken by Jewish leaders depended on the magnitude and timing of the threat to the Jews and the extent of sympathetic response by native leadership. Where SS control was at its most intense earliest and anti-Semitism was high, scarcely any strategic response of Jews affected the outcome. But in states where these conditions did not

---

228 Cf. Horowitz, "Bodies and Souls," 489; Emmanuel Ringelblum, *Sepolti a Varsavia: Appunti dal Ghetto* (Milan: il Saggiatore, 1965).
229 Cf. Horowitz, "Bodies and Souls," 491–92.
230 Cf. Fein, "Reduction by Review," 169.
231 Cf. Fein, *Accounting for Genocide*, 45–53, table 2.3.

prevail simultaneously, the ability of Jewish leaders to anticipate and mobilize against threats could make a difference.[232]

Concerning the critique about prewar anti-Semitism, according to which it is represented as a constant of Western societies, a mechanism of state power, Fein specifies that Horowitz advances only fatuous generalizations, ignoring what is shown by her in the first part. She then emphasizes that anti-Semitism is indexed by the political success of anti-Semitic movements from 1936 and must be interwoven with the anti-Jewish policies from 1939 to 1945.

As evident from figure 3.3, anti-Semitic movement is a crucial variable that accelerates the process of extermination.[233] The probability of the Jews becoming victims just depends on the level of anti-Semitism, a factor on which the choice of the individual state to segregate and isolate the Jews is based, making their defense or escape less easy. In any particular country, when the individuals perceived the Jewish problem as the natural result of their actions over the centuries, it was obvious that a feeling of aversion towards them had taken deep root. This fact undermined the moral bonds of solidarity among fellow citizens and reduced the possibility of resistance to Nazism. In the opposite case, the possibility of collaborating with the Nazis increased. Fein in her chapter "Direct Causes of Jews' Vulnerability to Victimization" defines all these elements.

Certainly, when Fein writes that "nowhere did I say anti-Semitism necessarily accounted for each outcome," she does not yield to any generalization; rather, in illustrating the exceptional cases of the Netherlands and Romania she sheds light on a number of factors involved in the genocidal process.[234] For instance, in the Netherlands, in spite of the long history of civic inclusion of the Jews, the cooperation of the state facilitated their segregation and their extermination, even though prewar levels of anti-Semitism were low.[235] In Romania, the government was pressed to prevent segregation and the concentration

---

232 Ibid., 325.
233 Cf. ibid., 65, fig. 3.3.
234 Cf. Fein, "Reduction by Review," 170.
235 Cf. Hilberg, *The Destruction of the European Jews*, 365–81.

of Jews despite the triumph of prewar anti-Semitism and the collaborationist government. This element is correlated with the impact of the Jewish leadership, but it does not assume a statistical significance.

Interesting is that this intellectual diatribe clarifies how difficult and harsh research on the Holocaust can be. Fein does not try to reexplain her theoretical positions already asserted; rather, she asks Horowitz, "How long, O Irving, how long must I wait to integrate?"[236] since he had previously written that "the author [Fein] unfortunately is not yet at an intellectual stage at which an integrated result can issue from study of this subject in cross-cultural or cross-national terms."[237]

Their heated debate, which did not end with these two pieces, invited a resumption of research. Horowitz's reply always starts off on the same note: "Let me begin my reply to Helen Fein with the same point with which I opened my review of *Accounting for Genocide*. This is a very difficult book to review."[238] The critic in appreciating Fein's study wishes to replicate the points that, according to him, have aroused his wrath.

Contrary to Fein's assertions, Horowitz claims to have read the book "from cover to cover" on three different occasions for a period of four months. Additionally, he states that his charge of reductionism starts from thesis of Fein, who presents the "size of Nazi special task forces in place" as the sole cause of the extermination at the outbreak of hostilities. Moreover, for Horowitz, Fein has not established any statistical tie or any correlation between this variable and prewar anti-Semitism and the number of victims. Horowitz continues to speak of reductionism in relation to Fein's discourse on Jewish leadership. His reasoning is more or less as follows: although this leadership had the chance to secure the Jews, Fein, in demonstrating this, has not shown any significant correlation between their autonomy and capacity for survival of the Jewish communities.[239] Briefly, for Horowitz, *Accounting for Genocide* is a mechanical juxtaposition of numbers that do not tell of, but rather cloud,

---

236 Fein, "Reduction by Review," 170.
237 Ibid.
238 Horowitz, "Reply to Fein," 170.
239 Cf. Edward S. Herman and Noam Chomsky, *Manufacturing Consent: The Political Economy of the Mass Media* (New York: Pantheon, 1988).

some factors that would have been interesting to analyze, but yet they are ignored in the book.

This diatribe is more important for another point: in the article Horowitz comes to speak of racism of whites in the United States. For him, the presence of a constitution (albeit unequal) and a civil society that does not become the *speculum* of a totalitarian state would have prevented the genocide of blacks. In other words, in the United States, borrowing Fein's words, "the bonds that hold" occur. Instead, in Germany during the crisis of liberal democracy there developed the mythical worship of a community of people, *Volk-Gemeinschaft*, although (as Horowitz says) the explanations about the difference between *Staat* and *Gesellschaft* are not read. Finally, he criticizes Fein's inability to integrate her work with other researches conducted at the international level on the fault or defense of the victims. In closing the article, he therefore calls for continuing the research on the Holocaust, using Fackenheim's midrashic words:

> The deed is done, but it has not yet come to men's ears. If a few feel differently, it is because their ears have heard, if indeed they are not survivors who have seen with their own eyes. These few will not enter the madhouse of their own accord. Never! They must not enter the madhouse. The post-Holocaust universe is in need of them. It needs them if man is to become, not a superman replacing God, or a "last man" replacing man, but rather, after what has happened, once again human. Yes, it is necessary for we who are not survivors to become heirs of their witness in this world and beyond.[240]

2.5.7. Ben-Baruch's Position

Ben-Baruch raised one different criticism on the concept of nation-state. According to him, in *Accounting for Genocide* much space is devoted to the attitudes of/between groups, although the explanation about competition for power and resources is omitted. Indeed, power and resources are notions at the basis of the juridical concept of the modern nation-state,

---

240 Horowitz, "Reply to Fein," 171, with reference to Emil Fackenheim.

namely, when a nation exercises its sovereignty on the basis of established legitimate powers and of certain resources on a given territory. Although Fein focuses on the universe of the obligations of a state, she does not consider nation-states as arenas in which groups compete for resources. Through her approach, it is possible to see how anti-Semitism has led some states or groups with strategic locations within a country to cooperate with the Nazis, outlining dynamics of cooperation and conspiracy networks. However, for Ben-Baruch this model superficially describes the causes of the cooperation of states or the conduct of the churches.

2.5.8. Accounting for Genocide and the Sociological Tradition

Horowitz says he notices a discrepancy between the first and the second part of *Accounting for Genocide*, and, indeed, his view opened a new path of research on the Jewish question in 1980s. Unknowingly, his criticisms highlight an aspect neglected by previous sociological works, namely, "the victims' view," which was original in the literature of Holocaust Studies. In the early 1960s, some historians especially analyzed the way in which the National Socialist state had prepared and finalized the annihilation of the Jews of Europe. These reflections gave rise to works on the perpetrators of the crime, all based on German documents and with a methodological perspective of a global type. Prior to Fein, nobody had studied the victims' point of view in sociology. Moreover, in her discourse she does not speak of their viewpoint in general: the choice of the plural "victims' view" should serve to unify the voice of all the victims in a unique *idem* feeling as if they were a single organic body that is the community, which, during the crisis of liberal democracies, had frayed. Through the history of the Jewish victims, Fein recovers the solidarity that was broken versus the necessity of preventing the destruction of 5.1 million Jews. Nevertheless, the novel contribution of the research is her focusing on the category of nation-state. By moving the center of attention from the role of victims and perpetrators to community policies and their attitudes faced with National Socialism, Fein examines variables such as prewar anti-Semitism and Nazi control, which, in correlation with geopolitical space, allow for the analyzing of local collaboration, a new element compared to the previous sociological literature. Her processing is original, combining the social, political, and structural aspects of the state with those of the genocide. The relationship she outlines between the state and genocide in some ways anticipates the sociological studies on the genocidal state inaugurated by sociologists like Kuper and Horowitz in the 1980s: "Holocaust scholars will have to treat seriously her findings and inferences and thus begin to incorporate the sociological perspective into their work."[241]

Fein is executive director of the Institute for the Study of Genocide at the City University of New York and always puts the issue of genocide at the center of academic debates. In this way, in 1994, together with Israel W. Charny, Robert Melson, and Roger Smith she established the International Association of Genocide Scholars, of which she became the first president. She was convinced that it was possible to prevent genocide only through a network of scholars, intellectuals, Holocaust survivors, and journalists, who were able to teach nonhatred and nonviolence. For her, the inclusion of educational proposals that emphasized the weak boundary between the violation of human rights and the genocidal act itself into political programs and of teaching was almost obligatory. The creation of solidarity networks and the involvement of as many people as possible in research programs or comparative studies on new genocidal cases would help to build a picture as exhaustive as possible and to fight the violence on multiple fronts.

At this point, one can question, as Ben-Baruch does, why such a serious and significant work had not been applauded, as it should have been. Particularly, in reference to the thoughts of Horowitz, according to whom sociology profanes or desacralizes a tragic experience with its quantitative and qualitative analyses:[242]

> Is it because the primary sources are hidden in the mysterious corners of archives where historians have staked their territorial claims? Is it because those historians uniquely qualified because of their mastery

---

241 Ben-Baruch, review of *Accounting for Genocide*, 462.
242 When Horowitz's article was published, several studies on the Holocaust had yet to be fulfilled, for example, the so-called *Historikerstreit* and the wide and lively debate among historians in Germany in 1986–89.

of several European language are not trained in sociological methods? Only partly.[243]

For Ben-Baruch, Fein is able to hear, penetrate into, and open a trauma hiding in time. It is a metasociological book showing the ways to enter into tragic historical events and human suffering by using statistical elements that bring order out of chaos with "a historical methodology ... essentially a discussion on the proper way to interpret the surviving sources."[244]

2.6. SUMMARY

We have seen how, especially, women sociologists, such as Pawełczyńska, Heller, and Fein, stood out in the post-Holocaust sociology of the 1970s. I described the structural conditions making the extermination of weaker groups possible and the factors allowing its practice within a nation-state. Starting from the category of solidarity, a new sociological concept of resistance was theorized. Thanks to Fein's book, the sociological discipline, in the 1970s, distinguished itself for the attention reserved to an individual victim, and not just for victims in general. Sociology, as a discipline, saw a time of entry into a number of sociological subfields, resulting from the influence of other social sciences, and post-Holocaust sociology saw a fertile period. The influence of econometrics or mathematical analysis was visible in the works of Fein, Merkl, and Moore. I analyzed the Yom Kippur War (the 1973 crisis), neoliberalism phases, and other political facts that led to this influence. For authors of these years, anti-Semitism was the hotbed of the Jewish genocide. For a better view of the sociological lesson of the 1970s, one should read several excerpts, especially related to Polish nationalism. How history and sociology can dialogue emerged from studies by Pietrowsky and Heller.

---

243 Ben-Baruch, review of *Accounting for Genocide*, 462–63.
244 See Arnaldo Momigliano, *Sesto contributo alla storia degli studi classici e del mondo antico* (Rome: Edizioni di storia e letteratura, 1980), 1:14 (my translation).

CHAPTER 3
Toward a Sociology of Genocide, 1980–1989

> Genocide is pre-eminently a government crime and governments can hardly be expected to plead guilty.
> —Leo Kuper

3.1. GENOCIDE AS A GOVERNMENT SOLUTION DURING THE 1980S

It is not a mistake to assert that a new interpretation of the Holocaust was outlined in sociology scholarship of 1980s. In 1979, Israel W. Charny, Shamai Davidson, and Elie Wiesel—Leo Kuper also deserves mention—established the Institute on the Holocaust and Genocide in Jerusalem. Just three years after its foundation, in 1982, for the first time, a multidisciplinary conference on the Holocaust and genocide—perpetrated over the centuries—was organized at an international level. The forum was a success despite the obstacles created by some national governments attempting to hinder its satisfactory outcome, as the *New York Times* and other newspapers reported.[1]

Post-Holocaust sociology, in the 1980s, constituted a sort of moral reaction in the face of massacres and atrocities of a nationalistic nature committed in many countries and noted by mass media. This led to a continuous raising of consciousness to what was and is genocide, an awareness that, in various ways, paved the way toward the cosmopolitan memory of the Holocaust in the early twenty-first century. In the 1990s, ethnic cleansing in the Balkans and the return of nationalism and fundamentalism in Europe and the United States revealed the negative aspects of civil progress in modern states: there was a new kind of

---

1 Israel W. Charny, *Fascism and Democracy in the Human Mind: A Bridge between Mind and Society* (Lincoln: University of Nebraska Press, 2006).

challenge, a kind of regeneration after communism and sectarian wars, after the 1992–96 civil war in Bosnia, for example.

In 1994, Mike F. Keen, with some quotations in *American Journal of Sociology*, recalled the intuition of Parsons, who, before 1947, had spoken of "the challenges of modernity" in referring to conflicts with difficult resolutions.[2] For many sociologists of the 1980s, such as Kuper, Baum, and Horowitz, historical texts, the experience of the witnesses of the Holocaust, and, above all, the Maya Indians genocide (1981–83), the Sikh genocide of 1984, and Burundian genocide that started in 1972 and ended only in 1993, all raised provocative questions scholars of society could not ignore. It can be said that in the 1980s there started a new consciousness in sociology—the twentieth century was the century of genocides. What all these sociologists, having studied records of the Nuremberg trials, the Convention on Genocide adopted in 1948 by the UN, and the role of the International Criminal Court, seemed to agree on was the concept of "genocide committed by the state." In the light of this new interpretation, their path of thought, which they inaugurated, rendered them, in many ways, the sociologists of the "genocidal state" because of their ability to reconstruct the history, processes, and development, together with the causes and circumstances of the destruction of the Jews. Meanwhile, their studies constituted a welcome start for a typical approach of criminology that, in theorizing the genocide and addressing the issue of the Holocaust, leveraged the question of civil and criminal liability.[3] It is relevant to stress how these approaches explain unusual devices within post-Holocaust sociology in general. Although several scholars do not agree with this, it was a new current seeking to enlighten people on the responsibility of states that exterminate their own citizens. What mattered to these scholars was that of eliminating genocide from the political agenda, often used as a political tool and adopted by national governments to solve problems of public order. Behind their efforts was the desire to end further human destruction.

---

2 See Keen, review of *Talcott Parsons on National Socialism*, 1359–61.
3 Cf. Woolford, *Making Genocide Unthinkable*.

What happened to the Jews has no historical precedent. Its exceptionality derives—as Wolfgang Sofsky (one of the researchers in this current of studies) stresses in *The Order of Terror*—not from the manner or methods of extermination, but from the fact that genocide was perpetrated "with the aid of an experienced bureaucratic administration, a civil service for extermination. The setting up of death factories, to which an entire people, from infants to the aged, were transported over thousands of kilometers to be obliterated without trace and 'exploited as raw material' was not just a new mode of murder; it represented a climactic high point in the negative history of social power and modern organization."[4] As Antonio Cassese says, these atrocities "have been made possible, in their immense proportions, by the modern state, with its enormous bureaucratic apparatus, the centralization of power and the monopoly of economic and military resources. And, indeed, in both cases, the policy of genocide, devised and planned by the central authorities of the State, was performed through the use of modern mass of communication (for example, by trains for deportations)."[5] In the wake of these studies, the political scientist Rudolph J. Rummel, after a long collection of data on collective violence and war, coined the expression "democide," which was meant to describe actual murder committed by a government of its people that was not covered by a juridical definition of genocide.[6]

---

4 Wolfgang Sofsky, *The Order of Terror: The Concentration Camp* (Chichester, West Sussex: Princeton University Press, 1997 [1993]), 12.

5 Antonio Cassese, *I diritti umani oggi* (Rome-Bari: Laterza, 2010), 146 (my translation).

6 Cf. Raphael Lemkin, *Axis Rule in Occupied Europe: Laws of Occupation, Analysis of Government, Proposals for Redress* (Washington, DC: Carnegie Endowment for International Peace, 1944); Horowitz, *Taking Lives;* Frank Chalk and Kurt Jonassohn, *The History and Sociology of Genocide: Analysis and Case Studies* (New Haven, CT: Yale University Press, 1990); Helen Fein, *Genocide: A Sociological Perspective* (Newbury Park, CA: Sage, 1993); Steven T. Katz, *The Holocaust in Historical Context*, vol. 1, *The Holocaust and Mass Death Before the Modern Age* (New York: Oxford University Press, 1994); Rudolph J. Rummel, *Death by Government* (New Brunswick, NJ: Transaction, 1994); Stanton, *"The 8 Stages of Genocide";* Samuel Totten, William S. Parsons and Israel W. Charny, eds., *Century of Genocide: Eyewitness Accounts and Critical Views* (New York: Garland, 1997); Leighton C. Whitaker, *Understanding and Preventing Violence: The Psychology of Human Destructiveness* (Boca Raton, FL: CRC Press, 2000); Stephen T. Davis, ed., *Encountering Evil: Live Options in Theodicy* (Louisville, KY: Westminster John Knox Press, 2001); John G. Heidenrich, *How to Prevent Genocide: A Guide for Policymakers, Scholars, and the Concerned Citizen* (Westport,

Literally, "killing of δημος (*démos*), i.e. of people," actually, the locution "democide," for Rudolph Rummel, is the "assassination of any person or a community committed by a government": among cases examined, Rummel distinguishes between genocide, political murder, and mass murder: for him genocide is a specification of wider democide.[7] After noting that a precise term is lacking with the meaning of the destruction or the intention of destroying entirely (or in part) specific individuals belonging to a given group, he invents the notion of democide. The new term would help to solve this conceptual problem. Indeed, the deaths caused by a government for political reasons do not constitute instances of genocide. The author does not include in his statement those who die during armed reprisals against civilians, in protests or riots, and those sentenced to the death penalty. According to his research, during the twentieth century, the number of people killed because of democide was six times higher than for victims of all the wars of the century.

Starting from the assumption that democracy is the form of government that is less likely to kill its own citizens, Rummel marks as democide examples, along the course of history, Stalin's purges in the Soviet Union, the deaths caused by the colonial policies in the Congo, and those caused by the famine that followed Mao Tse-tung's Great Leap Forward. In all these examples, the victims were not selected on the basis of their race, but were victims of government policies. As demonstrated by his research, as the basis of recent Holocaust studies, we find the idea that there is a close correlation between the degree of a people's freedom and the possibility that a government can practice democide.

Kuper, Baum, and Horowitz, in different ways, account for the fact that genocide may increase in the case of conflict, when a state is faced with inner disorders or needs to avert threats to its own government policies. Obviously, there is a series of steps, one of which is genocide, allowing national governments to eliminate not only the members of a hated or envied group, but also to reap security benefits, both economic and material, by massacres,

---

CT: Praeger, 2001); Konrad Kwiet and Jürgen Matthäus, eds., *Contemporary Responses to the Holocaust* (Westport, CT: Praeger, 2004).

7 See Rudolph J. Rummel, *Democide: Nazi Genocide and Mass Murder* (New Brunswick, NJ: Transaction, 1992).

by the appropriation of victims' goods, or by replacing them in commercial activities. Then it is relevant to consider the basic ideology behind the genocide, that is, the belief, in common opinion, that the national, ethnical, racial, or religious group "chosen for the extermination" is contemptible because it does not participate in the "community of values" of the dominant group. It is necessary to highlight above all that the actions are all aimed at the destruction of the "protected group." This means that the groups who have been "voted for extermination" are intentionally destined for destruction, which is never, therefore, the indirect consequence of an action intended to accomplish a different goal. Moreover, the choice of the verb "to destroy," as stressed by all these authors in their works, is not arbitrary: on the contrary, it points out a gap between a general massacre and that committed instead with the intention of eliminating even only one person. In the 1980s, the researches of these sociologists were joined by studies by Nechama Tec and Bauman. Tec, especially, introduced a new concept of Jewish resistance, starting from her *Defiance*.[8]

3.2. THE SIGNIFICANCE OF GENOCIDE

On December 9, 1948, the United Nations adopted the Convention on Genocide (in force since January 12, 1951) according to which (art. 2) genocide is defined as "any of the following acts committed with intent to destroy, in whole or in part, a national, ethnical, racial or religious group."[9] The Jewish Polish jurist Raphael Lemkin, a scholar of international law, coined the term "genocide" in 1944. A refugee in Sweden in 1939 after the German occupation of Poland, between the end of 1942 and beginning of 1943, Lemkin fled to the United States, where he persevered, first, at the School of Military Government at the University of Virginia and, then, at the War Department in adopting an international convention on genocide, even though he had already formulated the concept during a conference held in Madrid in 1933. On that occasion, he presented a paper in which he recalls attention to the destruction of racial or religious groups over the centuries,

---

8   See Bauman, *Modernity and the Holocaust*; Nechama Tec, *Defiance: The Bielski Partisans* (Oxford: Oxford University Press, 1993).
9   Accessed May 8, 2010, http://www.preventgenocide.org/genocide/officialtext.htm.

wishing for an agreement that, similar to the one against slavery and piracy, condemns all acts aiming at the destruction of specific groups as "international crimes." With reference to these crimes, Lemkin had initially adopted the expression "acts of barbarism." However, dissatisfied due to its too general definition, and because it had not been adopted in subsequent international law, some years later he created the neologism "genocide."

Professor of law at Duke and Yale towards the end of the war, Lemkin published *Axis Rule in Occupied Europe* (1944), where for the first time he advances the notion of genocide as a "practice of extermination of nations and ethnic groups." Additionally, he proposed its regulation at the international level. Nominated four times for the Nobel Peace Prize, Lemkin played an important role in the trials against Nazi war criminals before the International Military Tribunal at Nuremberg. Equally important was his contribution in the debates on genocide in the United Nations, culminating in General Assembly Resolution, 1946 96 (I), according to which "genocide is a crime under international law which the civilized world condemns, and for the commission of which principals and accomplices—whether private individuals, public officials or statesmen, and whether the crime is committed on religious, racial, political or any other grounds—are punishable."[10]

Beyond the contradictions that emerged from the terminology, which important scholars have extensively debated, what matters is the irrefutable element that is at the center of the discourse (genocidal) and that makes genocide a specific type of murder, distinguishing it from all other forms of murder. Its essential feature is "the destruction of the foundations of the life of certain national groups, in order to eliminate the groups themselves."[11] The same etymon of the word helps to understand the specifics of the crime. It includes two relevant meanings. On the one hand, there are the Greek words γένος (*ghénos*) and γίγνομαι (*ghignomai*) that translate the sense of "to be born," "to originate," "to be," and, above all, the meaning of

---

10   Accessed May 8, 2010, http://archive.adl.org/education/curriculum_connections/spring_2005/spring_2005_lesson2_resolution.html; see Rudolph J. Rummel, "Genocide," *Enciclopedia del Novecento*, III Supplement, 2004, accessed May 8, 2010, http://www.treccani.it/enciclopedia/genocidio_(Enciclopedia-del-Novecento)/.

11   See Bauer, *Rethinking the Holocaust*, 9, see 276n13; Lemkin, *Axis Rule in Occupied Europe*, 79–81; Michele Sarfatti, *La Shoah in Italia: La persecuzione degli ebrei sotto il fascismo* (Turin: Einaudi, 2005), 8.

"generating" (in its noun form, "generation"); on the other hand, the final suffix -*cidio* refers to the Greek word κτείνω (*ktéino*), which means "to kill." In other words, the term "genocide" literally renders the phrase "killing life." This is the last sense lying in Lemkin's statement "destruction of the foundations of the life" of a race, that is, the killing of all the aspects or elements that contain life and serve to pass on the *ghénos* of a nation, including its culture. Faced with such an essential definition, the annihilation of the foundations of the life of a nation embraces the destruction of economic and religious institutions, the decay or degradation of the moral fiber, the demolition of the educational system, and the mass murder of selective sectors of the population.[12] According to article 2 of the Convention, genocide refers to (1) killing members of the group; (2) causing serious bodily or mental harm to members of the group; (3) deliberately inflicting on the group conditions of life calculated to bring about its physical destruction in whole or in part; (4) imposing measures intended to prevent births within the group; (5) forcibly transferring children of the group to another group.[13]

From the reading of these points, the specific procedural aspect of genocide emerges. The process of genocide includes a series of events and issues that are interrelated and in conjunction with one another, with the aim of destroying step-by-step any form of life: not only physical (within a genocidal project, for example, the aim is the annihilation of structures and institutions responsible for the allocation of economic resources, functional to reproduction), but also spiritual and moral. For this reason, here, it is proper to speak of the "genocidal process" rather than "genocide," stressing the procedural aspect, in a series, total, of the destruction of life.

3.3. WHEN STATES SPONSOR GENOCIDE

Leo Kuper fully understood what discrimination, segregation, and collective mass massacres meant only when the Nationalist government of South

---

12 Bauer briefly presents two formulations on genocide developed by Lemkin: the first is "a radical and murderous denationalization accompanied by mass murder, which destroys the group as an entity but leaves many or most of the individuals composing it alive"; the second is, instead, the "murder of every single individual of the targeted group" (Bauer, *Rethinking the Holocaust*, 9).
13 Accessed May 8, 2010, http://www.hrweb.org/legal/genocide.html.

Africa banned some of his works concerned with the cruelest aspects of his country's policies. Nevertheless, he preferred a passive resistance to revolutionary violence, guided by liberal principles and cooperation.

Born in Johannesburg on November 24, 1908, Kuper was one of the few who, along with Nelson Mandela and Desmond Tutu, laid the foundations for a concrete peaceful transition to democracy in South Africa after Apartheid.[14] In the midst of a politics of violence in his country, Kuper obtained a degree in law and conducted a legal practice until the outbreak of World War II, and thus he was able to obtain a certain mastery in law and a penchant for juridical texts, allowing him to approach the notion by Lemkin.

Motivated by the desire to denounce crimes committed in his own South Africa and willing to promote an education rejecting nationalist or genocidal violence, Kuper began to think the about category of genocide and elaborate a broader consideration of the Holocaust. In this sense Kuper was the sociologist who, starting from the UN Convention on Genocide, inaugurated a new interpretation of the Holocaust, according to which the extermination was primarily designed as a "genocide committed by the State." Obviously, this had previously been an unexplored concept in sociology, but one to which many scholars remain devoted today.

Kuper began his training in sociology in 1948, first at the University of North Carolina and then with Charles Madge at the University of Birmingham, where he prepared a sociological masterpiece in urban planning entitled *Living in Towns* and based on research conducted in the city of Coventry, England. His attention to genocidal studies resulted also from his marriage to the anthropologist Hilda Kuper, who brought him closer to genocidal reality from a theoretical point of view. Their home in Westwood Village became a kind of cultural paradise, a leisure center where many scholars and intellectuals, but also friends of their children,

---

14 Cf. Desmond M. Tutu, *No Future without Forgiveness* (New York: Doubleday, 1999). During 1980s, Desmond Mpilo Tutu, the South African Anglican archbishop, was committed to making his country a democracy. At the end of Apartheid, he led the Commission for Truth and Reconciliation, an important institution and a new event at the international level for transparency and methods of appeasement adopted against injustice and massacres of the dictatorial regime's past. Tutu's philosophy of action, attentive to others, was based on the idea of *ubuntu*, an African concept according to which society is without divisions. Tutu received the Sidney Peace Prize in 1999.

could take refuge to think. As a staunch supporter and activist for the assertion of rights in South Africa, Kuper transformed himself into a theorist of peace against any genocide in 1953, when he returned to South Africa as a professor of sociology at the University of Natal in Durban. During this period, he published two classic studies on South African society, *Passive Resistance in South Africa* and *An African Bourgeoisie*, both banned by the government, and in 1958 he prepared a study of racial ecology with two colleagues of Durban.[15]

When the Nationalist Party required entry tests to matriculate at universities, having as one selection criterion that of race, Kuper wrote a scathing satire on new "tribal" colleges, but, despite calls by his friend Alan Paton to leave the country, he decided not to emigrate. In 1961 he agreed to move to the University of California, where he remained until his retirement, while also performing the functions of manager at the Center for African Studies for four years. His commitment to a peaceful transition, a kind of obligation for the future, was mandatory and adamant, especially after 1963, when his brother, a judge in South Africa, was killed. It was then that Kuper underwent a profound change: he started with a long series of studies on theories of race and ethnic relations in societies, then moved on to the question of genocide.

3.3.1. Between Nation-State and International Law: The Role of International Organizations

In *Genocide* (1981), Kuper outlined the history of genocidal violence. On the cover of the book are the years in which the genocides of Armenians, Jews, Bangladeshis, and Hutu occurred, with the corresponding number of victims. Together with *The Pity of It All* and *The Prevention of Genocide*, *Genocide* constitutes an extensive analysis of the genocides during the twentieth century, describes the factors leading a society toward violence

---

15 Cf. Leo Kuper, P. Sargant Florence, and C. Madge, eds., *Living in Towns: Selected Research Papers in Urban Sociology* (London: Cresset, 1953); Kuper, *Passive Resistance in South Africa* (New Haven, CT: Yale University Press, 1957); Kuper, *An African Bourgeoisie: Race, Class, and Politics in South Africa* (New Haven, CT: Yale University Press, 1965).

and extermination, and identifies the social forces, such as international organizations, committed to preventing it.[16]

In the mid-1980s, with help of Michael Young, Baron Young of Dartington, Kuper established International Alert, a nongovernmental organization aimed at defending human rights. This agency, together with the International Center for Transitional Justice instituted in 2001, was engaged in adopting political strategies to recompose or recast, within states, those social cleavages causing ethnic conflicts. Both institutions were committed to the peace process between states. The International Center especially aspired to identify people involved in crimes against humanity.[17] For more than twenty years, Kuper personally followed the cases of genocide in a ceaseless work of complaint, as objectively as possible, with the conviction that only accurate information about events can face up to the evil in society. His inexorable inquiry had a wide international resonance, particularly with regard to Central Africa. For example, by studying massacres of Tutsis and Hutus in Rwanda and Burundi in the 1960s, he came to the bitter conclusion that the intervention of international agencies and foreign governments had caused a higher number of deaths than they had managed to prevent. When, in the preface to *Genocide*, Kuper states that the United Nations responds with indifference to genocidal violence and that even their attitude legitimizes violence when they defend the rights or sovereignty of the individual state, his position of open condemnation towards the current international system of protection of human rights is clear. In this way he calls the role played by different countries during the Holocaust into question. Kuper repeatedly explains how, in the course of the twentieth century, genocide had been used by national governments as a screen to maintain internal order or national sovereignty over a specific territory. When he affirms that "the word [genocide] is new," but "the crime ancient," he means exactly this: genocide has always unfolded in the presence of social

---

16   Cf. Kuper, *The Pity of It All: Polarisation of Racial and Ethnic Relations* (London: Duckworth; Minneapolis: University of Minnesota Press, 1977); Kuper, *The Prevention of Genocide* (New Haven, CT: Yale University Press, 1985).

17   Cf. Sara Dezalay, "Des droits de l'homme au marché du développement," *Actes de la recherche en sciences sociales* 174, no. 4 (2008): 68–79.

and ethnic divisions. For this reason, he defines multiethnic societies as "plural" and "divided."[18] Genocide is an "anodious scourge" that returns and is encouraged when the international community intervenes to protect state sovereignty:[19] the United Nations condones genocidal violence when it defends or restores the rights of the individual state, while civil societies foment the return of genocidal holocausts.

During the debate on the Convention on Genocide at the UN General Assembly, the representative of the United Kingdom, Sir Hartley Shawcross, denounced these limits. For him, it was disappointing that the security of a state depends on a UN convention—behind which there is always the rule of law and thus the sovereignty of a nation—and on the decrease of dangers and threats of racial and religious persecution.

Kuper's researches are important because they explain how the extermination of the Jews rendered possible the recognition of genocide as a crime in international law. Thanks to Lemkin's studies, it is possible to comprehend that genocide is not only the immediate killing of a community but also a coordinated plan of different actions aiming at the annihilation of the essential foundations of the life of national groups, with the goal to destroy them and to avoid, in the long term, the regeneration of the protected nation.

It should be noted that Kuper's and other sociologists' contributions first developed the category of genocide, first, as the outcome of the conflict between racial, national, ethnic, or religious groups, and, second, as an event intimately related to the wars of a political nature and to the division of the territory between nations. In other words, characteristics specific to the modern nation-state. After examining various genocide theories, Kuper identifies which social structures determine it. Genocidal massacres take root in "plural societies," those in which there are some fractures between ethnic groups and religions present in the same area, resulting from colonial domination, on the one hand, and the phases of decolonization and succession to power, on the other. In these multiethnic

---

18 Kuper, *Genocide*, 11; Kuper, *Race, Class and Power: Ideology and Revolutionary Change in Plural Societies* (London: Duckworth, 1974). See Arend Lijphart, *The Trauma of Decolonization: The Dutch & West New Guinea* (New Haven, CT: Yale University Press, 1966).
19 Kuper, *Genocide*, 11.

societies, the difference has not been processed or, if it has, the process of social reconstruction has not reelaborated the diversities. As Kuper stresses, this notion is found "in a tradition deriving from J. S. Furnivall, to describe societies with persistent and pervasive cleavages between these sections."[20]

Other factors leading to genocide are the old religious differences concentrated in a region, the lack of political participation, economic inequality, and migration. Nevertheless, what is most relevant in Kuper's analysis is what he says about social evil by alluding to the process of dehumanization and exclusion of "protected groups" from the human community—genocide is the political instrument that breaks moral obligations among fellow countrymen, classifies people into heterogeneous categories, requires from them a designation, or demonizes them.

The categories of this process were the concepts returning in the post-Holocaust literature in 1980s: (1) reduction of man to an object; (2) the destruction of a group or collectivity as such; and (3) the denial of it later. Since the specificity of genocide is the killing of a *ghénos*, in order for that to happen, the act must be legitimate in everybody's eyes. If, in the common mind prevails the idea that the group in question is a bacillus (it represents a cancer to society, such as the Jews to the Nazis), genocidal ideology succeeds in its intent. In genocide the concept of carcinogen evil is thus *in nuce*. This is the reason for which the genocide is designed and adopted as a policy solution, with biological connotations, to solve the social evil. High ideals of social order, within a national system, often serve to put a genocidal act into practice. However, Kuper shows his disagreement with the definition of the UN Convention on Genocide since it does not consider as cases of genocide either the destruction of a political group or the cancellation of the culture of a human group.[21] In Kuper's consideration of the genocide of the Armenians, and that of the Jews, evident is the functionalism of Hilberg's and Reitlinger's thought, especially when Kuper contemplates genocide as "a gradual process" characterized by typical stages, such as the legal

---
20   Ibid., 57.
21   Cf. ibid., 39.

definition, expropriation, and concentration of the victims.[22] The most complex part of Kuper's thesis is that in order for the state to maintain territorial sovereignty (the national law within its borders) it invokes the right to genocide. In this way, a burning issue is posed and a theoretical reflection of no small value is required, since in the UN convention's intentions there is the need to protect from genocidal massacres, but, in its effort to ensure the principle of national sovereignty principle, the UN consents to genocide. So Kuper asks what we have to do when the state rather than defending its own citizens turns against them; and when the system of international law, which should protect citizens from a country with genocidal goals, instead does not intervene, and lets the massacres happen. Later Donald Bloxham noted, "Modern States are, in normatively neutral terms, particularly well-suited to large tasks, including mass murder, because of their control over sophisticated and powerful organs of administration and coercion."[23]

The problem is also to understand what really happened to the Jews who were European citizens. The state is constituted by three elements: those of people/nation, its territory, and sovereignty. When the state practices genocide (it kills the nation), it provides only two factors: namely, the sovereignty and territory. This means that the state itself, from a formal point of view, fails.

For Kuper, the extermination of European Jews, like all genocides, was not the outcome of a conflict. Rather, it resulted from flawed integration policies, typical of societies in which ethnic, racial, or religious minorities, not long before recognized as subjects of civil and political rights, are dismissed. Kuper's theory of genocide appeared in 1985 with *The Prevention of Genocide*, where he distinguishes between domestic genocides, that is, those caused by inner divisions within society, and genocides that instead explode as an outcome of an international state of war.[24]

---

22 Ibid., 137.
23 Donald Bloxham, "Organized Mass Murder: Structure, Participation, and Motivation in Comparative Perspective," *Holocaust and Genocide Studies* 22, no. 2 (2008): 203, doi:10.1093/hgs/dcn026. See Anthony Giddens, *The Nation-State and Violence* (London: Polity, 1985).
24 Cf. Paul R. Bartrop and Steven L. Jacobs, *Fifty Key Thinkers on the Holocaust and Genocide* (New York: Routledge, 2011), 164–68.

3.4. A GENERAL THEORY ON STATE-SPONSORED GENOCIDE: BAUM AND HOROWITZ

"Zeolites"—"stones that boil," from ancient Greek ζέω (*zéo*), "boil," and λίθος (*lìthos*), "stone"—are minerals characterized by an enormous amount of empty volume. If heated, they expand by releasing steam from water trapped in inner cavities. More or less Kuper's plural and divided societies function in the same way: because of their own internal cleavages, if inflamed by some event, they can ignite conflicts degenerating into genocides.

During the 1980s, sociologists trying to understand the destruction of the Jews through the category of genocide were faced with a great challenge: the concept, not purely sociological, was born in a juridical context and was used in anthropological sciences. In some ways, Kuper revolutionized the model of the UN Convention on Genocide when he defined genocide sociologically: especially because he evidenced the failures of this Convention, inasmuch as genocides continue in the world.[25] When the German sociologist Baum published *The Holocaust and the German Elite*, in 1981, he put the end of moral values among elites, after Wilhelmine unification, at the center of the discussion, meaning that the ruling political class and elite thinking (both economic and military) cannot create a critical and public opinion. In studying the Holocaust, Baum adds or introduces a new concept to Kuper's thought: that of "national suicide." The upholders of the killing of the German nation were in fact the Germans themselves.[26]

Baum presents an echo of the functionalism of Hilberg: the German sociologist rejects both the idea according to which the Nazis had committed murder to steal the wealth and property of the Jews (a theme addressed, later on, by Horowitz and still later on by Götz H. Aly, according to whom the Nazis came to favor persecution for economic reasons). Here we can see similar thought in both sociology and history—it all boiled down to Hitler's charismatic charm.[27] For Baum, the Holocaust was, first, the product of a bureaucratic plan, developed to relieve Germany of excess

---

25   Cf. Cassese, *I diritti umani oggi*, 150–55.
26   See Baum, *The Holocaust and the German Elite*.
27   Ibid., 150.

population; second, it was made possible thanks to moral the indifference of elites, by which, following Simmel's tradition, he means the loss of moral sense; but beyond the elites, he refers to all those who held goods, power, or knowledge in the Holocaust years.

When Baum argues that the Junkers had lost their positions within the body of the army after the Treaty of Versailles, or that teachers, priests, artists, civil servants, and military officers had been underpaid since the establishment of the Second Reich and that their situation had become more and more aggravated until the outbreak of the Great War, he alludes to the fact that these elites had been gradually downgraded. Additionally, he explains that the elites, from Wilhelm II to Hitler, had a one-dimensional nature and were antithetical to each other, because among them there was no open channel able to facilitate communication. In other words, the elites, though holding great resources, did not hold the power nor did they occupy prestigious positions in universities, while those who exercised power were not rich nor did they possess strategic positions in academia, and so on. However, mostly they were not blended together because they did not share the same values or the same common opinions: they were morally divided. For Baum, this social cleavage dated back to the same time that the elites were formed. It is important to remember that Germany became a modern nation-state rather late, only in 1871, and it was industrialized, albeit unevenly across regions, during the same period in which it became a nation-state. This double process of modernization led to a destratification of traditional society and a reversal of traditional values: when the new German nation was established, an industrial revolution was in progress and led to the replacement of traditional values with the new ones of the city and modern industry. Since modern development produced different circumstance, the process of national unification was very complicated and was not based on a single national value. Among the many fundamental values, finally, those of the Prussian ruling class gained the upper hand. The moral division mentioned by Baum can be better understood in the light of the fact that the values (in accordance with Durkheim's morality) of the Prussian dynasty were different from those of the emerging industrial class. The new German nation, in asserting its own territorial sovereignty, was then looking for a living space: here Nazi ideology found a fertile ground in the new state, where the idea that sovereignty belongs only to the German nation took root, and that those who are part of another *ghénos* (aliens or foreigners) have to be sent away, especially the Jews.[28]

The problem, for Baum, was therefore in the process of naturalization of the Jews recently undertaken. Paradoxically, the nation-state, which provides for a population that exercises sovereignty over a territory, contemplates genocide: it finds its *raison d'être* exactly in the nation-state since a nation must make room over a territory to exercise sovereignty, removing all other ethnic groups. More precisely, genocide is the destruction of "protected" nations.

Both in *Genocide* (1976) and in *Taking Lives* (1982), Horowitz underlines that genocide is a fundamental mechanism of the modern state. According to the author, the state that "robs" human lives, taking them away from their own territorial boundaries, commits an abuse of power. In some aspects, Horowitz recalls the short but intense history of blasphemy with which Norman Cohn, in *Warrant for Genocide* (1967), explains how a myth, and that is the strength of ideology or conspiracy theory, can lead to the rise of nonliberal powers and the construction of genocidal states. Pre-Hitler Germany and Europe were not free of responsibility for what happened. May a state—Cohn will wonder some years later on, as part of a research on the preconditions of persecutions and genocides—commission death?[29]

Centered on the exercise of power by the modern nation-state, *Taking Lives* is an essential work in the history of sociological literature that has as its object of study the genocide and the Holocaust, since it rebuilds, starting from 1945, the social and political context of genocidal states. As Horowitz clarifies in his research, genocide is not a sporadic event, rare or unusual, nor it is necessarily linked to economic development and social

---

28 Cf. Daniel Tollet, review of *The Holocaust and the German Elite: Genocide and National Suicide in Germany, 1871–1945*, by Ranier C. Baum *Annales. Économies, Sociétés, Civilisations* 39, no. 4 (1984): 734–36. Tollet writes that an alien (*allogène*) is one who belongs to another *ghénos*.

29 See Norman Cohn, *Warrant for Genocide: The Myth of the Jewish World Conspiracy and the Protocols of the Elders of Zion* (New York: Harper & Row, 1967); Irving L. Horowitz, *Genocide: State Power and Mass Murder* (New Brunswick, NJ: Transaction, 1976); Horowitz, *Taking Lives*.

progress, rather, it is a mass destruction carried out with the consent of the state apparatus.

Here a new course of study opened up that was to find fortune in later years, especially in the field of Holocaust and Genocide Studies. At the center of this thought, there is the concept of bureaucracy, namely, of men in charge of accomplishing the genocidal massacre. They are men paid to execute certain orders: they, like white-collar workers, are employees or have managerial positions, and, the same as blue-collar workers, they do jobs that are of second order or manual. For this, they escape from their ambivalent feature—they are beyond the specific essence of blue collars and white collars: the work they do is a dirty job, gray, which involves the administration of death. It precedes an ordinary, banal evil. These people are the new workers with a "gray collar"—the "grey-collar workers," as Allen calls them.

In this period, as a result of German historical studies, begun in the late 1980s and producing important contributions to the end of the 1990s, Brustein returned to the structure of the National Socialist Party, analyzing the documents of 40,000 members of the NSDAP. The material constitutes a representative sample of German society. In 1998, data on how economic interests led individuals to militate in the NSDAP emerged.[30]

3.4.1. The Holocaust as Crime of State in Sofsky

One reason to keep reconsidering *The Order of Terror* (*Die Ordnung des Terrors*) by Sofsky is that he so vigorously demonstrates that post-Holocaust sociology addressed the problem of the Holocaust in unexpected ways. When Sofsky writes that "a new species of absolute power was unleashed

---

30 See Charles W. Mills, *White Collar: The American Middle Classes* (Oxford: Oxford University Press, 1951); Norbert Elias, *Humana conditio* (Bologna: il Mulino, 1987 [1985]); Michael T. Allen, "The Banality of Evil Reconsidered: SS Mid-Level Managers of Extermination Through Work," *Central European History* 30 (1997): 253–94; Allen, "Grey-Collar Worker: Organization Theory in Holocaust Studies," *Holocaust Studies: A Journal of Culture and History* 11, no. 1 (2005): 27–54; William I. Brustein, *The Logic of Evil: The Social Origins of the Nazi Party, 1925–1933* (New Haven, CT: Yale University Press, 1998); Brustein, "The Nazi Party and the German New Middle Class, 1925–1933," *American Behavioral Scientist* 41, no. 9 (1998): 1237–61. On Allen, see the end of subsection 1.7.7 of this book.

that shattered all previous conceptions of despotism or dictatorial brutality," he refers to the metamorphosis of the concentration camp "from a locus of terror into a universe of horror."[31] And this is crucial.

Göttingen scholar Sofsky (born in Kaiserslautern in 1952) brings to light "the business-like annihilation of human beings." It is a rational explanation without losing sight of human suffering, as Ralf Dahrendorf comments. *The Order of Terror* continues the discourses of Baum, Kuper, and Horowitz as concerns the courts' acquiescence in applying expected legal rules against genocide. Not quite knowing how to underline the novelty of this sociological piece, we accentuate primarily that the study is focused on the removal strategies and improper language of defining the Holocaust simply as a "crime against humanity," as if the only Nazi fault was that of not having had humanity. "The ideology of disburdenment, of "safe disposal" (*Entsorgung*), has penetrated public discourse, leeching the lexicon," explains Sofsky. "It diminishes the significance of facts and takes flight into sanctimonious moralizing, although no form of traditional religious or political morality can adequately grapple with the enormity of the atrocity."[32] When Sofsky states that "any attempt to engage in a theoretically guided investigation runs up against two reservations: the topos of the basic incomprehensibility of the camps and the notion of singularity, the incomparability of that welter of crimes subsumed under the name of Auschwitz,"[33] he deals with the comprehension of the camps through cognitive categories. Can the concentration camp system be conceived of as an extreme form of power and modern organization?

Sofsky is a scholar who revisits the testimonies of those who passed through the camp, while his work, concerned with Adler's texts, does not belong to an analysis typical of the functionalist approach. Namely, Sofsky does not explain "the external history of the system."[34] The originality of this research is the questioning of the role of the sociological discipline pursuant to the institutionalization of the concentration camp system. Sociology has always been careful to interpret society in the light of the

---

31 Sofsky, *The Order of Terror*, 5.
32 Ibid., 7.
33 Cf. ibid., 8–9.
34 Ibid., 10.

concepts of social action, reciprocity, labor and power, and common opinion—the fundamental elements of society. For Sofsky, the reality of the concentration camps led to the disappearance of all of these categories (absent in the institution-*Lager*), determining the end of the same society and then of sociology, a discipline that is based on its study. Strange to say, since, for him, the camp is "at the margins of sociality":[35] however, at the base of his theory there is the concept of society, even before that of absolute power and organized terror.

Like Simmel, Sofsky posits social relationships (taking shape in the recurring behaviors of men) as the foundation of society. Moreover, of these relationships he studies the particular form of power that, in his view, in the *Lager* becomes absolute, one "that has broken free, fundamentally and totally, from the familiar forms of social power."[36] Sofsky identifies some analytical categories of absolute power, explaining how the concentration camp (a place in which terror and destruction are pursued through organizational instruments) is an invention of the twentieth century. The absolute power of which Sofsky speaks, developed in Nazi concentration camps, had nothing to do with the common types of domination and was not be confused with the usual forms of government, namely, asymmetrical relationships of exchange or unequal abilities to distribute sanctions. It could not even be compared with modern disciplinary power or with relations of hegemony based on obedience. Typical processes of this power went far beyond the exploitation, the monopoly of penal force: they contemplated the ability to manipulate space, time, and sociability among men. The universe of the *Lager* was much more than a rational system, equipped with clear and specific purposes. Between administrators and guards, collaborators and victims, beneficiaries and camp-work employees, it unfolded as a system of relations made of dependence and antagonism. The concentration camp was an entity isolated from the rest of society, where a watchdog group dominated prisoners. It was—in accordance with "social systems closed theory" that experienced a particular development in 1980s—a

---

35   Ibid., 9.
36   Ibid., 10.

kind of terror zone situated on the edge of human society.[37] Finally, this power, using terror, broke the structures of common sense (namely, those of time and place mentioned by Alfred Schütz) to disorient isolated individuals, as Pawełczyńska highlighted in *Values and Violence*.

In what way the concentration camp had its own routine, that is, its own normality, transferring absolute power into a particular configuration of power, emerges from Sofsky's work, based on extensive historical research, but mainly on inmates' memories, on administrative documentation of *Lager* commands, and on the acts of the Nuremberg trials. As he underscores, "The concentration camp cannot be integrated into the history of despotism, slavery, or modern discipline. Organized terror cannot be mapped onto a continuum of domination. The differences are not gradual, staggered along a line of coercion, but fundamental."[38] For example, it did not renounce any kind of violence, which, thanks to the different ways of organization, it started to implement where the terror of tyranny ended. Under such conditions, blind obedience or loyalty to discipline did not protect anyone from the most terrible consequences, because of the absolute uncertainty. In this situation, victims became a mass of unequal individuals to whom systems of control and maltreatment were applied. This type of terror was not the result of the infringement of rules: it was unleashed anywhere and at any time. It did not restrict freedom: rather it annihilated it; did not guide action, but destroyed it.

Kuper's sense of genocide as "the destruction of every aspect of human life" returns in Sofsky, or it finds in *The Order of Terror* an interesting development. It is crucial to stress that this power is organized (in its structures the typical characteristics of the organization can be found, such as the hierarchy of command, the division of labor, and discipline for subordinates) and absolute, that is, free from every constraint. "Absolute," from the Latin *ab-solutus* and the Greek λύω (*lùo*=to dissolve), refers to a type of independent power and is, as such, irresponsible. In fact, the bureaucracy of the SS did not require an automatic or mechanical reaction, but, rather, the kind of personal

---

37 Cf. Franco Crespi, *Evento e struttura: Per una teoria del mutamento sociale* (Bologna: il Mulino, 1993).
38 Sofsky, *The Order of Terror*, 16.

initiative that does not obey orders blindly. This action is flexible and varies depending on the mechanisms of corruption, of personal rivalry and camaraderie. In the *Lager*, it was dominated by the principle according to which responsibility belongs to the doer. Under these conditions, to predict SS behavior was quite impossible: it was the initiative of the authorities, which increased the sense of uncertainty in action, disorientation, free will, all of which factors, naturally, generate terror. What Sofsky means is that in the camp there were rules, but to each of them the inability of the individual prisoner to follow them corresponded. This allowed the watchdog group to act in a discretionary manner: paradoxically, the rules were created especially to be disregarded and to enhance the terror. Behind his expression "the order of terror," we must understand that the rules did not serve to limit the exercise of power, but they were the institution that provided the "terrorist will."

3.4.2. The Organization of Work

As noted by Baum, Kuper, and Horowitz, this absolute power subverts the principles of social classification and destroys society. Free from space and time conditions, it is omnipresent and unlimited. It is more evident when through the mechanism of delegation of power some victims are converted into complicit agents of the Nazis. Additionally, since this power is absolute, it does not need ideological consensus to be established and maintained. Sofsky emphasizes that the personal guard of the camp was made up of careerists, criminals, and corrupt men who did not share the elitist pride professed by leaders of the SS. The work was a tool of oppression and terror, and absolute power had no other basis than itself. In the *Lager*, there was not the rationality of capitalism of which Weber spoke, namely, a rational action of purpose. Only in the final stages of the war, when workers fit for production were becoming fewer and fewer, did the objective of economic rationality become a priority. It was a work of attrition and harassment, of a complete power that also abolishes the symmetry inherent in the most basic violence, one that provides for the possibility of a man to kill another, or the possibility of suicide, and then to exercise power over oneself. For Sofsky, the concentration camp system instead disabled all these opportunities. It was a laboratory of violence functioning with the brute violence that unchains among its enclosures, within the "triple barbed-wire fence," a ruthless struggle for survival. Inside the prisoners did not die from wounds directly suffered, but as an outcome of a slow sinking into degradation, starvation, exhaustion, and disease. When Sofsky explains how absolute power did not kill immediately but created a sort of no-man's-land between life and death, he refers to the production of "living skeletons" as "genuine inventions" of concentration camps: in this sense, the extermination was organized in different phases.[39] Sofsky is well known for his powers of reasoning, and it is noteworthy to stress the main theme of this work: absolute power in its deployments and the structures from which it draws strength. The space controlled by impassable boundaries, characterized by a strong physical densification and standardized times, changeable in an arbitrary manner, created social areas where time was warped and the victims were no longer capable of perceiving its flow. Sofsky's analysis, as that of Pawełczyńska, does not seem to be of the institutional type. Rather, he enumerates the autonomous dynamics of terror processes. In this sense, there is a continuum, of a sociological kind, between the work of both authors. Resulting from Sofsky's sociological research (and, for that reason, very significant), *The Order of Terror* is a book offering a complete reconstruction of the concentration camps, from the first camp established in 1933, Dachau, to the end of the war. What has to be stressed is the sociological representation of the concentration camp system, providing one with the devices to comprehend what a "total institution" is.[40]

3.5. THE SOCIOLOGICAL FRAME OF KATZ

New was a post-Holocaust sociology dealing with the modernity and un-modernity of the Holocaust, and Katz addressed that in 1982.

---

39 Ibid., 25.
40 Cf. Cornelis J. Lammers, review of *The Order of Terror: The Concentration Camp*, by Wolfgang Sofsky, *Organization Studies* 16, no. 1 (1995): 139–56, doi:10.1177/017084069501600107; John Torpey, review of *The Order of Terror: The Concentration Camp*, by Wolfgang Sofsky, *Contemporary Sociology* 26, no. 6 (1997): 719–20; Paul Rock, review of *The Order of Terror: The Concentration Camp*, by Wolfgang Sofsky, *British Journal of Sociology* 49, no. 1 (1998): 159–60 (see note 255, above, chapter 1), about "total institution"); Renzo Gubert and Luigi Tomasi, eds., *Teoria Sociologica ed investigazione empirica: La tradizione della Scuola sociologica di Chicago e le prospettive della sociologia contemporanea* (Milan: FrancoAngeli, 1995).

Katz takes note of details about the causes leading to the extermination, such as anti-Semitism and nationalisms, the consequences of the Great War, and the destruction practices perpetrated against the Jews. With his "Sociological Perspective to the Holocaust," published in the journal *Modern Judaism*, Katz was among the first sociologists sustaining concepts such as routinization and bureaucratization during the extermination phases. He revisits several times the categories of the routinized banality of evil and incremental process of extermination in his research. Especially, he was the very first scholar to be faced with the role of the *Einsatzgruppen* in the Nazi policies of destruction, or in the immediate phase, which involved the immediate killing of Jews in the occupied territories of the Soviet Union—a theme that would emerge strongly in historical scholarship after the fall of Berlin Wall. Some years later, in 1993, he reproposed the question by dealing the banality of evil.[41]

When it is argued that his sociology is of a synoptic type, this alludes to the fact that Katz addresses a number of relevant topics, such as the sociological debate on the alleged silence regarding the Holocaust. He explicitly criticizes, at the opening of his essay, those who deny the contribution of sociology in the study of the Holocaust: "To a sociologist Dawidowicz' book strikes a timely note. Sociologists, too, have been reluctant to study the Holocaust. Not long ago it was noted in a sociology journal that 'there is no sociology of the Holocaust.'"[42] Katz opposes the contributions of Fein and Horowitz, who, in his view, mark positively the post-Holocaust sociological literature.

Despite his concise contribution, Katz identifies a combination of factors leading to the destruction of European Jewry. What made him an innovator in post-Holocaust sociology were his sociological concepts and the manner in which he used them to rethink the Holocaust. In part, they were already known (such as the concept of banality of evil by Hughes and Arendt) and in part were entirely new. When he says, "In this paper I want to take a step in this sociological direction by discussing the Holocaust as a way of routinizing monstrous behavior. ... The vast scale on which the

---

41 Fred E. Katz, *Ordinary People and Extraordinary Evil: A Report on the Beguilings of Evil* (Albany: SUNY Press, 1993).
42 Katz, "A Sociological Perspective to the Holocaust," 273n2.

Holocaust operated means that, to a considerable extent, the killings and torture were routinized,"[43] he anticipates concepts used later by other scholars, for instance, the notions of bureaucratization and routinization in the definition of modern extermination proposed by Sofsky in 1993. Nevertheless, it is right to say that his theoretical combination of routinization and the banality of evil was a novelty in Holocaust sociology. When one can read, "One feature of the routinization process that is especially important is that relatively 'ordinary' people participated in the murderous Nazi bureaucracy, and did so with enthusiasm and innovativeness,"[44] it appears that Katz presents the Holocaust as a product of modern bureaucracy, highlighting sociological concepts that express something else about the modernity of extermination:

> Much of the Holocaust was carried out as part of the "ordinary" day-to-day routines of government machinery. Much of it became part-and-parcel of "ordinary" career patterns of civil servants, of military personnel, and of many persons in the civilian, private sector of European nations. Much of it relied on a specially trained staff of concentration camp administrators, persons who were human extermination specialists.[45]

What we can appreciate here is that, first, he introduces the concept of "appendage of the machine," which Bauman will use later, and second, that in the wake of Hughes, he explains how the work of the specialists of death is very similar to the work of the employees in the assembly line, where it is not the production of a commercial product at stake but, rather, human death.

3.5.1. Individuals and the Factory System

At this point, we can ask what it is that makes us think about piece of Sofsky's piece in a new way. Surely, his crucial problem is that of

---
43 Ibid., 273–74.
44 Ibid., 275.
45 Ibid., 274.

comprehending how the destruction of Jews became a routine. For him, the ways in which the death camps functioned as factories for the production of death are vital. According to the sociological concept of routinization, the fulfillment of complex social goals, such as education or learning, involves the development of phases and organizational forms. The fundamental role in the process is played by bureaucracies present in a state and that follow the rules. What matters is the achievement of the goal, which requires obedience to rational and legal rules imposed by an authority that must be obeyed. Specifically, bureaucracy obeys and accomplishes the orders given by the state without reflecting on the performance in progress—the necessary actions do not require a responsible reflection. The most important element in modern bureaucracy is the achievement of objectives regardless of moral sense of the action. Here the transition from routinization of actions to their mechanical execution becomes crucial.

For Sofsky, the workers in charge of destruction were an appendix of the bureaucratic machinery of the annihilation: they were employed on an assembly line that performed standardized actions prescribed for certain purposes. For Katz, these men, specialists of death, were officials performing the command to kill in a systematic and planned process of elimination. Thanks to the category of "no responsibility for their actions" (used later on by Bauman), Katz explains the ways in which it passed from a modern administrative system to a bureaucratic system of death, or an extermination system. Death was administered through a corps of bureaucrats in charge of the chain of murder and obedient to authority. At the base of the process were the notions of the repetition of actions, modern specialization of functions, and obedience to legal-rational authority:

> The possibility that one's actions may be evil is often beyond the day-to-day level of awareness. So it comes about that when the bureaucrat organizes the transportation of Jews (and Gypsies and others deemed undesirable) to extermination camps, or arranges for the "efficient" use of slave labor in the Ruhr's munitions factories, the immorality of killing people is not taken into account. Morality or immorality may simply be outside the bureaucrat's range of concern.

Technological issues—the availability of trains, for example—are apt to prevail.[46]

According to Katz, there were no government leaders or charismatic leaders within the bureaucratic chain or within the average levels of the Nazi hierarchy. It seems Katz opposes the absurd positions of some sociologists, who, in saying "we are all Nazis, so what to do?" elude or block the responsibility question.[47] Differently from Bauman, Katz does not consider the Holocaust as only the product of industrial modern rationality and administrative technique. When he speaks of a process of destruction (in the wake of Hilberg), defining it as "incremental," he takes the "personal participation"—not contemplated in notions of modern bureaucracy—of German officials into account. According to Weber, in fact, bureaucracy and offices should not be of a personal nature, nor should the properties of the individual. What is more important is that Katz, in his understanding of the Holocaust, deals with sociological concepts typical of the modern age, putting in evidence their limits. When he defines the destruction process as a set of developed and packaged actions, he evidences an aspect that has nothing to do with the ideal type of modern bureaucracy posited by Weber, according to whom the orders and the functions to be carried out must be clear and precise.

Therefore, Katz addresses the question of the ordinariness of evil linked to personal autonomy. Nevertheless, this factor collides with the canonical concept of modernity of the Holocaust, as expressed some years later by Bauman, according to whom there are not decisions of personal nature, but only orders to be executed in a mechanical way and precisely. Looking back to the element of autonomy, the discretionary behavior of bureaucrats, especially of the Nazi officials, makes an incredible comeback. Even if these are hints by Katz, it emerges at the moment he refers to the work of the *Einsatzgruppen* in the occupied Soviet areas, when he addresses the different ways of killing on the Eastern Front: an extermination of a nonsystematic kind, but personal and of a public and dramatic nature.

---

46   Ibid., 274.
47   Ibid., 275n11, quoting Hans Ashkenazy, *Are We All Nazis?* (Secaucus, NJ: L. Stuart, 1978).

Katz's first part is of a theoretical nature, but the second part of the essay deals with the specific case of Rudolf Höss, the commandant of Auschwitz. Katz centers on an important point, and he does this handling Höss's case: when he addresses Höss's horror faced with brutality committed in Auschwitz, Katz readdresses the question of the banality of evil and how ordinary evil is "transformed into the *extraordinary*."[48]

3.6. TEC AND SOCIOLOGICAL CATEGORIES OF GENOCIDE

"Behind me was Lublin, the city in which I was born—a city now *Judenrein*."[49] In this way, Nechama Tec starts to account for her "lost childhood." Tec, in her first steps addressing the destruction of the Jews, analyzes the death process in telling her own personal history in *Dry Tears* (1984). Her story is an example of a wider theme: resistance acts conducted in the midst of evil, which she terms "light." In her eyes, resistance was essentially a flame that "pierced" the darkness.[50] Although Tec's works explain different stories, they are quite similar. Their common interpretive notion, a turning point in post-Holocaust sociology, is the unexplored concept of resistance. It is a repeatedly addressed theme: in *When Light Pierced the Darkness* (1986), Tec considers Christians who rescued Polish Jews; in *The Lion's Den* she tells the story of a Polish Jew, who, under a false Christian identity, used the knowledge and power in his hands to save other victims of Nazism. Nevertheless, *Defiance* (1993)—where she describes how some Jewish partisans, the Bielski brothers, fought the Nazis and survived, rescuing other Jews—represents a revolutionary sociological piece in Holocaust scholarship:

> Like most charismatic leaders, Tuvia [Bielski] was spontaneous. He felt free to pursue an agenda that required him to save as many of the doomed Jews as possible. ...

---
48 Katz, "A Sociological Perspective to the Holocaust," 282.
49 Nechama Tec, *Dry Tears: The Story of a Lost Childhood* (New York: Oxford University Press, 1984), 43.
50 Cf. Tec, *When Light Pierced the Darkness: Christian Rescue of Jews in Nazi-Occupied Poland* (New York: Oxford University Press, 1986); Tec, *In the Lion's Den*.

No matter how a woman arrived, no matter who she was, when she reached the Bielski otriad she could automatically become a member.[51]

When Tec refers to "Tuvia's policy of unconditional acceptance of every Jew, man, woman, and child, no doubt accounts for the high proportion of women, a proportion that fluctuated between thirty and forty percent,"[52] she puts victims' behavior at the center of her studies, demolishing the image of "Jewish passivity." For Tec, passivity and, additionally, the complicity of the Jews in their own destruction, seems to absolve the perpetrators from their accountability for crimes committed, and she gives visibility to the history of the righteous, to persons who worked to save Jews from mass extermination. In the introduction to *When Light Pierced the Darkness*, she underlines how everybody knows the story of Anne Frank, but they ignore the history of those who had saved themselves or the reasons that led these people to risk their lives to save their family. Her aim is to reflect on the ordinariness of good—"small goodness"—through an original research dealing with "case histories."[53]

Based on published personal stories, statistical data, archival collections, and extensive interviews with survivors (rescued, rescuers, and bystanders), *When Light Pierced the Darkness*—whose final ten pages are a sort of postscript on Tec's methodology—emphasizes how sociology needs to work together with history, especially when she stresses issues such as the extermination and Nazi propaganda, sadism and indifference of the Poles, and the silence of other nations: "The world looks upon this murder, more horrible than anything that history has ever seen, and stays silent."[54]

Interesting is that, first, in her works, Tec always takes time to answer frequently asked questions, such as "Why did the Jews go like sheep to their slaughter? Why did they not stand up to the Germans? Why did they

---

51   Tec, *Defiance*, 109, 158.
52   Ibid.
53   See Tec, *When Light Pierced the Darkness*, 3–4; Enrico Deaglio, *La banalità del bene: Storia di Giorgio Perlasca* (Milan: Feltrinelli, 1991); Salomoni, *L'Unione Sovietica e la Shoah*, 182–91.
54   Tec, *When Light Pierced the Darkness*, 111.

refuse to fight?"[55] Second, thanks to unpublished written works, personal stories, and interviews, she gives voice to the witnesses. Her research speaks of both the saved and the rescuers (several times, the author asks herself questions: Who were the saviors? Alternatively, what did they feel in saving other Jews?), and she speaks of persons who were indifferent to the destruction. She clearly evokes the question of guilt. What is new is her articulate manner in dealing with these topics.[56] To understand her sociological approach, we can stress that at the basis of *When Light Pierced the Darkness* we find her personal story of Jews rescued by fellow citizens of the Christian religion, the description of the environment of Gentiles in which she grew up, and the analysis of the world insensitive to the extermination.[57] Tec examines how minorities are persecuted anywhere at any time. Among the multitude of persecutors, there were also people willing to help the persecuted:[58] even in Nazi-occupied Poland, where the chances of rescuing Jews were reduced to the extreme, there was moral solidarity. For Tec, the Poles who risked their lives to save those of their fellow citizens were "altruistic helpers," while most of those who could intervene and did not—the author also includes heads of state in this category—are defined as "uninvolved" persons. Among the saviors, there were also those who saved lives on payment, "paid rescuers," but the focus is mainly on the righteous among the nations.

What matters is the newness with which she addresses the issue of anti-Semitism and the role that ideology played in the extermination process. When she speaks of the "Polish antisemitic rescuer," she refers to residents in Poland who, before the outbreak of the war, nourished sentiments of anti-Semitism, but who, during the Nazi occupation, aided

---

55 Nechama Tec, *Jewish Resistance: Facts, Omissions, and Distortions* (Washington, DC: Research Institute of the United States Holocaust Memorial Museum, 2001), 1. See Michel, *The Shadow War*; Israel Gutman and Shmuel Krakowski, *Unequal Victims: Poles & Jews during World War II* (New York: The Holocaust Library, 1986).
56 Cf. Karl Jaspers, *La questione della colpa: Sulla responsabilità politica della Germania* (Milan: Cortina Raffaello, 1996 [1946]).
57 Cf. Carol Rittner, Stephen D. Smith, and Irena Steinfeldt, eds., *The Holocaust and the Christian World: Reflections on the Past, Challenges for the Future* (New York: Continuum, 2000).
58 Cf. Celia S. Heller, review of *When Light Pierced the Darkness: Christian Rescue of Jews in Nazi-Occupied Poland*, by Nechama Tec, *American Journal of Sociology* 93, no. 1 (1987): 221–22, http://www.jstor.org/stable/2779692.

the Jews. For example, in the "Protest!" of 1942—a manifesto of the Catholic Front for the Rebirth of Poland (*Front Odrodzenia Polski, FOP*), a document of protest, an official proclamation, created in Warsaw to establish an illegal unit in saving the Jews and whose greatest exponent was Zofia Kossak-Szczucka—stated that one who would not help the Jews was not a true Catholic or even an authentic Polish citizen.[59] In the document, the nationalist creed and the image of Jews as defenseless victims are evident. The anti-Semitic saviors were devout Catholics and ardent nationalists who were elites on the social scale. Many of those interviewed by Tec were committed actors who could not remain silent when faced with Nazi atrocities, and for that reason they opposed the totalitarian regime, as evidenced by the activity of the Council for Aid to Jews, starting from the end of 1942.

3.6.1. The Meaning of Resistance

In *Defiance*, written while traveling between the United States, Israel, and Poland, Jews are treated as a special category of victims, those who rebelled against oppression and took part in the resistance, by which term Tec means (referring to Roger S. Gottlieb's formulation) a series of activities motivated by the desire to limit and stop the exercise of oppression against the oppressed.[60] Her assumption is simple: the resistance is conceived as a reaction to oppression; hence, the different forms of resistance, including armed resistance, spiritual, urban, rural, and so on. Fascinating is the motivation. There is a certain link between resistance and oppression: the stronger the oppression, the greater the need to oppose it; however, the more intense the oppression, the lower the possibility of reacting to it effectively. Tec considers that revolutions are always carried out by those who are less dominated by power and that, therefore, they become the organizers of resistance groups.

---

59 For more details, see "Protest!" in Collection: Jan Karski, Polish History Museum, accessed July 19, 2016, https://www.google.com/culturalinstitute/beta/u/0/asset/WgEHPjyKIluslA.

60 Cf. Tec, *Jewish Resistance*, 2, 4, 25–26; Roger S. Gottlieb, "The Concept of Resistance: Jewish Resistance during the Holocaust," *Social Theory and Social Practice* 9, no. 1 (1983): 31–49.

Tec's studies cross through different conceptions of resistance, from those of Bettelheim to Hilberg, passing through Arendt, questioning or at least inviting us to reframe the surrender of the Jews faced with the oppressor and the role of the Jewish Councils. Tec focuses on the moral effects and positive results that the acts of resistance produced as much as on those who performed them and, more generally, on victims. That is what she intends to show. When Yitzhak Zuckerman, deputy commander of the Warsaw Uprising, on the commemoration of the twenty-fifth anniversary, claimed not to know "if there is a yardstick to measure all this," she refers to the strength shown by the young Jews who, after years of submission, challenged their executioners, knowing very well that they would face death.

Tec's sociological mission is to rethink the history of the destruction of the Jews through sociological questions in the spirit of the sociological tradition. She seems to be worried about rehabilitating the real image of European Jewry during the war.[61] In doing this, affected by Ringelblum's and Friedman's historical studies, she focuses more on the victims than on the perpetrators of Nazi crimes. Her researches become institutional places to reconsider, without omissions of any kind, the most heroic and the most obscure actions. Only in this way is it possible to refute the alleged passivity of the Jews or their alleged complicity in their destruction. For instance, when she defines the Bielski otriad as a community in the forest, she highlights the moral strength of the partisan unit, which challenged the Nazi policies of destruction.

To break down some prejudices, Tec reports some selfless efforts of the otriad members, aimed at protecting their fellow Jews and asserting traditional moral values. They are examples of resistance without weapons. When a partisan unit assisted the persecuted and individuals groups, women and sick people (offering them a refuge or ensuring their survival), a series of compassionate activities, more often illegal and not violent, were put into practice.

---

61 Cf. Philip Friedman, *Roads to Extinction: Essays on the Holocaust* (Philadelphia: Jewish Publication Society of America, 1980); Norman Davies, *Rising '44: The Battle for Warsaw* (New York: Viking, 2003).

The heart of Tec's analysis takes into account different actions of the partisans, within humanitarian action, in favor of their compatriots: acts of resistance. Her methodology, going beyond the specific resistance movements, emphasizes the relevance of a comparative approach. For instance, she focuses on the activities of the Jewish resistance movements in the occupied areas of Europe, where wooded and mountain areas became inaccessible shelters, theaters of struggle and combat. Additionally, Tec elaborates on the linkage between organization and resistance in the face of danger. In 1942, after the Nazis gave greater impetus to their annihilation policies, large masses of people were deported from Western to Eastern Europe. In 1943, almost all the ghettos were emptied. In this period, Jewish resistance movements developed their own strategic base of operations, studying the spaces within which to move, favoring mobility and movement, and creating a balance between the reduced number of rebels and the scarcity of weapons. What arouses one's curiosity is that Tec poses some relevant issues, such as the active leadership that made the difference, as in the case of the Bielski brothers:

> The existing leadership gap was filled in part by the young heads of the local branches of the various youth organizations. Most of these underground commanders were idealistic, and eager to protect and fight for the Jewish people. Also, as in most periods of social upheaval, during the German occupation there appeared a few charismatic leaders such as Tuvia Bielski. All of these new leaders, though anxious to relieve the Jewish plight, were inexperienced. As we have already seen, at times their idealism coupled with inexperience curtailed their effectiveness.[62]

At this point, we recall what Israel Gutman writes apropos of the leaders during the Warsaw Uprising, that they were "idealists with no battle experience, no military training. With but a few weapons and limited ammunition, they knew that they had no chance to succeed. Their choice was ultimate: not whether to live or to die, but what choice to make as to

---

62 Tec, *Jewish Resistance*, 17.

their death."⁶³ In reading Tec's treatment, what is without precedent in post-Holocaust sociology is that the Bielski otriad is introduced as a typical Jewish resistance movement, different from national resistance movements in which Jews were active fighters or from movements, also national, in which Jews fought while hiding their identity. The Bielski otriad was a unit of partisans taking refuge in the forests of Belarus, with a common goal: to save as many human lives as possible. When, in 1942, rumors began to circulate about the presence of partisans in the forests, the possibility arose for many Jews in the ghettos to join partisan fighters: "One might attempt to reach and join the partisans."⁶⁴ The Jewish partisan network continually sent guides (in ghettos still active) with lists of people to whom to propose escape (usually friends or relatives of people already in the forest) and aimed at saving the lives of as many Jews as possible and resisting when faced with evil. Tec stresses how "Tuvia, for example, sent an invitation to his friend Chaim Dworecki, his wife, and his two teenage daughters. The Dworeckis were forced into the Lida ghetto during the liquidation of the Iwje ghetto. In his letter Tuvia wrote, 'It does not interest me if you have a gun or not, you are coming with your wife and children. Nothing is important. Just come.'"⁶⁵

Bielski otriad, a community with rules mediated and directed by its leader, Tuvia, always tried to elude the enemy.⁶⁶ However, primarily—as the sociologist Einwohner put in evidence in the 1990s—it was possible to combat and resist thanks to information or *correct* information about what was happening. The partisan unit was kept informed of what was happening outside the woods. Good information allowed the otriad to react and to plan resistance actions. In 1943, towards the end of July, the otriad learned of a German document, dated July 7, 1943, which spoke of the operation *Unternehmen Hermann* aimed at attacking the Nalibocka forest to defeat the partisan movement. The Bielski partisan unit, like other detachments, refused to remain passive and organized a coordinated

---

63 Israel Gutman, *Resistance: The Warsaw Ghetto Uprising* (Boston: Houghton Mifflin Company, 1994), xii.
64 Tec, *Jewish Resistance*, 8.
65 Tec, *Defiance*, 97.
66 Ibid., 42, 174, 233.

and extensive collective action along entry points into the forest. Thereafter, the Bielski otriad was officially included in the Soviet army's Kirov brigade.

What Tec aims at in telling the story of the Bielski brothers is the complex organizational structure of this partisan unit, especially during the last phase (1943–44) spent in the Nalibocka forest. The otriad included a general district under the command of Tuvia Bielski, with a leader of the combatants, a deputy commander, a staff officer, a commissioner, platoon and section leaders, a chief doctor, and more. It also had different workshops, ranging from a bakery to a public bath, from transport management to an Orthodox butcher: the entire life of members was organized and designed to ensure survival hopes outside of the ghetto. In the Bielski otriad, community life of the ghetto could continue:

> I was amazed at what Tuvia did. I saw the workshops, the children [cries] … I saw an orthodox Jew pray. People worked, they fixed watches, made shoes, they made leather from cowhide. People from all the surrounding areas came there to have things fixed.[67]

3.7. "THE HOLOCAUST AS THE TEST OF MODERNITY"

When Bauman says that "having read Janina's book" he starts to think about what he did not know "properly," he realizes that he did not comprehend what had occurred—in his words, "in that 'world which was not mine.'"[68] Analyzing, in this place, his approach to the Holocaust, it is not only important for the reasons already introduced (because his *Modernity and the Holocaust* is considered by most as the work that woke up post-Holocaust sociology), but this also helps to ask what happened to Holocaust sociology, in general. First and foremost, we must know his past: this means understanding the story of the scholar who made his exile from Poland a fascinating choice and point of strength in accounting for what was happening in 1960s, even in sociology. Additionally, my look

---

67 Ibid., 138, referring to an interview with Zorach Arluk.
68 Bauman, *Modernity and the Holocaust*, vii.

at Bauman provides a much needed look at his work, even though this excursus does not seem to be coherent with the rest of my treatment in this book. Instead it is useful to clarify how Bauman developed his thinking, or how he began to speak of the Holocaust in starting from the notion of human suffering.

Primary, the Holocaust, for the Polish Bauman, who began to study the extermination of the Jews only after his forced emigration to England in 1968, was not an aberration or a cancerous growth within civilized society and was not a deviation in the midst of civilization, nor did it constitute a millennial anti-Semitism episode. What he underlines is that Holocaust literature, seeing the destruction of the Jews as a hiccup, had not considered the internal logic of modernity as it developed in the West and had not called into question the "normal condition of society."[69] This is one of the central points for Bauman. As he says, "The Holocaust was a unique encounter between the old tensions which modernity ignored, slighted or failed to resolve—and the powerful instruments of rational and effective action that modern development itself brought into being."[70] In other words, the phenomenon cannot to be inscribed within the framework of national states where the legal definition of citizenship is relevant; rather, it should be placed between the social mesh and fluctuation resulting from a series of processes, such as modern rationalization and bureaucratization.

3.7.1. Between England and Poland

Both Fein and Bauman have recourse to the concept of the nation-state in trying to understand the Holocaust, even if in different ways. Each has his own way of showing new insights into the relationship between the rationality of the modern world and the political life characterizing the heart of Europe in the first half of the twentieth century.

Zygmunt Bauman was born in Poznań in 1925. When Poland was invaded by German troops in 1939, he was forced to flee with his family to the Soviet Union, where, instead of joining the ranks of physicists, he

---

69 See ibid., viii–xiv.
70 Ibid., xiv.

enlisted in a Soviet military unit. At the end of the war, he returned to Poland to study sociology at the University of Warsaw with Julian Hochfeld and Stanisław Ossowski. After studies at the London School of Economics, during which he prepared his dissertation on British socialism, he published, in 1959, the work that opened the doors of academia to him (even though since 1954 he had been a professor at the Faculty of Social Sciences in Warsaw). On March 25, 1968—while social rights movements filled up the American academies and streets, Bauman was removed from the chair of sociology at the University of Warsaw as consequence of a new wave of anti-Semitism detonated by Polish authorities.[71] His expulsion from the ranks of academics was not a random event: on the contrary, it was prepared and planned. Already in 1953, the author experienced some anti-Semitic purges: as a Jewish officer, he was expelled from the Polish army due to the "nationalization of the executives," which required the removal of all Jews from leading positions. In 1968, this dejudaization policy was intensified and touched all the intellectuals who headed or organized the 1968 student protests: among these organizers, there was also Bauman:[72]

> After leaving Poland I was inundated with offers to join all sorts of "sovietologist" establishments, and with invitations to write for their journals. I was one of the "Warsaw six"—the "dissident" professors of Warsaw University who were demoted and expelled on 25 March 1968 on the accusation of fomenting student riots—and the case was widely publicized in the Western press. I refused the offers. I had no intention of living the second half of my life off the first (as things looked then, I could live quietly and happily ever after out of my "dissident past").[73]

---

71 See Peter Beilharz, "Modernity and Communism: Zygmunt Bauman and the Other Totalitarianism," *Thesis Eleven* 70 (2002): 98.

72 Cf. Keith Tester, *Il pensiero di Zygmunt Bauman* (Gardolo: Erickson, 2005 [2004]), 14–15.

73 Keith Tester and Michael H. Jacobsen, "Bauman before Exile—A Conversation with Zygmunt Bauman," *Polish Sociological Review* 3, no. 155 (2006): 273. Actually, this conversation appeared for the first time in Keith Tester and Michael H. Jacobsen, *Bauman before Postmodernity: Invitation, Conversations and Annotated Bibliography, 1953-1989* (Aalborg: Aalborg University Press, 2005).

After several attempts to move to Israel and Australia, in 1971 Bauman obtained a new academic position at the University of Leeds, where he taught until 1990.[74] This period—of English exile begun on March 25, 1968, and far from Poland—paved the way to *Modernity and the Holocaust*.

The two European countries, England and Poland, mark his life, even if Bauman always takes care to qualify the "similarities" in order to avoid any kind of generalization in not considering the specifics of each nation.[75] When he arrived in England in 1971, it was a time of political, social, and cultural change in the history of England and Poland, and the days of student radicalism: there was a collective fermentation and mobilization abroad at international level and on others fronts. The new British Left, the revolution of the socialist proletariat in Britain, and the completely political reality of Polish '68 affected his life: after these events, and primarily resulting from the English exile, he wholly changed his own social theories. Starting from 1971, he no longer wrote in Polish, but almost always in English, and he himself translated his previous works into English. It was a new route between England and Poland, similar and parallel, but absolutely not identical.[76]

3.7.2. From *Memories of Class* to *Modernity and the Holocaust*

At the end of the war, Bauman continued his military career in communist Poland—he reached the rank of captain—having as his project building a Poland free from any totalitarian horrors and any kind of misery and discrimination, in other words, towards a respectable life.[77] World War II had not yet finished when Bauman glimpsed, in the actual Polish socialism, those elements able to eliminate all inequality and all forms of anti-Semitism,

---

74 Cf. Tester, *Il pensiero di Zygmunt Bauman*, 15.
75 Cf. Tester and Jacobsen, *Bauman before Exile*, 274. See also Karel Kosík, *La nostra crisi attuale* (Rome: Editori Riuniti, 1969).
76 See Beilharz, "Modernity and Communism," 94–95. Regarding the difficulty of translation from Polish to English—in some respect it reflects national Polish problems—and the choice of writing directly in English, see Tester and Jacobsen, *Bauman before Exile*, 268.
77 Cf. Tester, *Il pensiero di Zygmunt Bauman*, 14; Zygmunt Bauman and Keith Tester, *Conversations with Zygmunt Bauman* (Cambridge: Polity, 2001); Beilharz, "Modernity and Communism," 88.

underdevelopment, backwardness, poverty, social differences, and power conflicts among classes. Designed as a universal dream, socialism, especially for its economic and political features, seemed to be the impeccable solution against discrimination and therefore suffering in general in capitalist and industrial society. As Peter Beilharz writes, by focusing on the relationship between modernity and all types of totalitarianism, "communism survives, as a ghost, as it ghosts us all, those on the left or who came from it."[78] Prior to his English exile, Bauman never referred to the Jews in his studies: only in 1989, when the communist ideology symbolically collapsed on a universal level, did he publish *Modernity and the Holocaust*, when a set of historical circumstances (political and economic) intervened. Among these was, for instance, the Demjanjuk trial that ended in April 1988 in Jerusalem. One may ask what led him to move his sociological thinking towards the *Judënfrage* and, above all, why he dealt with the social suffering of the Jews only at the end of the 1980s.

His turning point of thought came from his wife, Janina Bauman, who had experienced the Holocaust firsthand, and she recounted what the Holocaust was for her in *Winter in the Morning* in 1986.[79] She was a Jewish girl and experienced the Nazi occupation of Poland. Her statement on those days and the years during which (together with her mother and sister) she succeeded in avoiding deportation to Auschwitz or Treblinka with the help of some fellow countrymen, expresses the plight of remaining human in inhuman conditions more than the dramatic experience being of and in the ghetto. Even in her story, situations of courage and moral integrity are opposed to cruelty and the depravity of some men. She clearly puts human suffering and the experience

---

78 Ibid. Cf. Ferenc Fehér, Agnes Heller, and Gyorgy Márkus, *Dictatorship over Needs* (Basingstoke: Palgrave Macmillan, 1983). A symposium was organized on this work. It dealt with a power vigilant of bodies, souls, and needs. Cf. Zygmunt Bauman, *Memories of Class: The Pre-History and After-Life of Class* (London: Routledge & Kegan Paul, 1982); Beilharz, "Modernity and Communism," 91.

79 Tester, *Il pensiero di Zygmunt Bauman*, 142. See Michael H. Jacobsen and Sophia Marshman, "The Four Faces of Human Suffering in the Sociology of Zygmunt Bauman—Continuity and Change," *Polish Sociological Review* 161, no. 1 (2008): 9–10. Cf. Janina Bauman, *Winter in the Morning: A Young Girl's Life in the Warsaw Ghetto and Beyond, 1939–1945* (New York: Free Press, 1986).

of pain at the center of the discourse: "I belong to the Jews. Not because I was born one or because I share their faith—I never have done. I belong to the Jews because I have suffered as one of them. It's suffering that has made me Jewish."[80] Janina's words in retelling the story of the ghetto experience and that of a Jewish youth lived in uncertainty gradually made Zygmunt feel she really was Jewish and understand the meaning of human suffering, which was central notion in his thought.

The choice of being Jewish did not happen causally but came at a time when he felt the unfinished tragedy of Jewish persecution, as when the anti-Semitic campaigns restarted in Poland in 1967–68, while the reality of Polish socialism vanished into the ideal of utopia.[81] Before 1967, his Jewish identity did not count for much in his life:

> It was I who was mistaken, grossly and totally. In the quasi-totalitarian quasi-Soviet regime, sociology as I saw it could only be an alien body and treated as the enemy's fifth column. And the rulers understood it before I did. It took me a few more years to catch up with their wisdom.[82]

It was this identity change resulting from the Polish anti-Semitism of 1960s, a rather late change of attitude for Bauman, that brought him closer to Hebrew reality. The personal pain he felt caused by his expulsion from the University of Warsaw, for the fact of being one of the most active intellectual "Jewish dissidents," woke up him and showed him the suffering

---

80 Bauman, *Winter in the Morning*, 181. Cf. Jacobsen and Marshman, "The Four Faces of Human Suffering in the Sociology of Zygmunt Bauman," 9.
81 Cf. Tester, *Il pensiero di Zygmunt Bauman*, 141. The first time that the sociologist realized he was a Jew happened at the explosion of anti-Semitism in Poland in 1967. See Zygmunt Bauman, *Intimations of Postmodernity* (London: Routledge, 1992); Harald Welzer, "On the Rationality of Evil: An Interview with Zygmunt Bauman," *Thesis Eleven* 70 (2002): 100–12. "The Soviet system is an acid test for the enlightenment utopia, for it sets the idea of a social rationality against that of individual rationalities by substituting state order for individual autonomy. Its failure indicates the hiatus of all socialist utopia" (Beilharz, "Modernity and Communism," 91–92). Cf. Jacobsen and Marshman, "The Four Faces of Human Suffering in the Sociology of Zygmunt Bauman," 9; Carmen Giaccardi, and Mauro Magatti, *La globalizzazione non è un destino: Mutamenti strutturali ed esperienze soggettive nell'età contemporanea* (Rome-Bari: Laterza, 2001), 150.
82 Tester and Jacobsen, "Bauman before Exile," 270.

endured by the Jews under the Nazis, and moved him towards an understanding of human suffering in general. It is useful to remember that in postwar Poland, the communist regime often used the theme of anti-Semitism in an instrumental way in order to face and easily overcome periods of instability and crisis.[83]

However, the topic of human suffering began to become a recurring and cyclical argument in his sociological writings and it became even deeper because of his experience of exile. The personal choice of feeling Jewish turned into a kind of challenge that Bauman chose to attack by creating a whole new critical sociology, a type of "human creative practice": in light of this, human suffering developed into a social category by which he explained, starting from his own evil, the pain in society. Following his Polish teachers, Hochfeld and Ossowski, he built a critical sociology, modeled on humans and making reference to humans.[84] As he retold it in 1992, "The Jewish experience had a special significance for understanding the logic of modern culture."[85] Again, it was mainly the Polish anti-Semitic campaigns of 1967–68 that led him to think critically and in a completely new way about society and humans *in* and *of* society. When he connected his own individual discomfort with that of the others, he translated his experience and the phenomena of society into sociological thought and literature.[86] Like him, Arendt, Hochfeld, and Mills had correlated their private world with the public, being able to transfer and place the particular experience of their private affairs within the public sphere. To reelaborate unpleasant experiences, a narrative community arises where language mediates: with and through the language it is possible to review the past (*monstrum*) through the mirror of distance. This reflects some sociological strands of the 1970 and 80s when a reflexive sociology was

---

83 Cf. Michael Checinski, *Poland: Communism, Nationalism and Anti-Semitism* (New York: KarzCohl, 1982); Tester, *Il pensiero di Zygmunt Bauman*, 14; Jacobsen and Marshman, "The Four Faces of Human Suffering in the Sociology of Zygmunt Bauman," 11.
84 Cf. Tester, *Il pensiero di Zygmunt Bauman*, 143.
85 Bauman, *Intimations of Postmodernity*, 228.
86 See Peter Beilharz, *The Bauman Reader* (Oxford: Blackwell, 2001). The text reports an interview prepared for Bauman, published in *Critical Theory* in 2001, even if the article, in which Todorov's thinking resounds, was written ten years before; see Cvetan Todorov, *Les abus de la mémoire* (Paris: Arléa, 1995).

affirmed because of postmodernity (and this discursive sociology of the postmodern period was evident when Bauman approached the Holocaust). He was a citizen-writer who found his homeland, in exile, through narration.[87] If the Polish anti-Semitism in 1968 and the experience of exile changed his sociological perspective, modifying his thinking on social suffering, then it is pertinent to comprehend what Bauman meant by suffering. What pushed him to *Modernity and the Holocaust* was indeed the ideal category of suffering even before the concept of nation-state. So, what was suffering for Bauman?

3.7.3. Suffering in Society

The concept of social suffering, inherited from Hochfeld and Mills (like Mills, Hochfeld is aware that the persons can suffer),[88] is a moral evil born in and caused by social relationships and therefore not attributable to natural phenomena, against which men are powerless. On the contrary, in the case of social suffering, men can intervene, indeed they must do so to limit the effects of suffering caused by their own interactions and relationships in communication.[89] Bauman, in a period in which sociology as academic discipline focused mostly on economic inequality and social suffering (after the fall of Berlin Wall, i.e., with the collapse of the communism), was in step with the sociology introducing the reflection on a bygone industrial period, namely, dealing with postindustrial doctrines. Bauman particularly questioned what type of social relationship generates social suffering, and he dealt with this when tracing a historical parable of human suffering that goes from solid to liquid modernity—reflecting the

---

87 Cf. Beilharz, "Modernity and Communism," 97; Paolo Jedlowski, *Il racconto come memoria: Heimat e le memorie d'Europa* (Turin: Bollati Boringhieri, 2009).
88 Cf. Tester, *Il pensiero di Zygmunt Bauman*, 55.
89 Cf. ibid. "Morality is not a product of society, but is rooted in the human condition of 'being with others' and is manipulated by society;" see Moishe Postone, review of *Modernity and the Holocaust*, by Zygmunt Bauman, *American Journal of Sociology* 97, no. 5 (1992): 1522, the reference is to Levinas. "That is, according to Elias, what we have come to call "morality' is not 'innate' but socially produced and variable through time and space" (Dunning and Mennell, "Elias on Germany, Nazism and the Holocaust," 340).

postindustrial principles of postmodern sociology following a period of an intense sociological growth.

For Bauman, human suffering changed over time in society and assumed different faces (from *The Flawed Producers in Crisis-Ridden Capitalistic Society* to *The Jews and Modern Adiaphorized Genocide,* from *The Others and the Strangers* to *The Human Waste of Liquid Modernity*).[90] He distinguishes four stages, or he speaks of four faces of human suffering, which I will introduce one by one.

The transformation of social relations of an economic and political kind, in modern society, generates social change that disrupts the orders of the new era, causing deep divisions and transformations. In accordance with the topological scheme of Stein Rokkan, these cleavages (center–periphery, church–state, industry/city–countryside, and work–capital) result from the two major changes that occurred during the nineteenth century—the political and the industrial revolutions—and reflect the relational asymmetries of forms of power present in a society. These new imbalances create social suffering. In his retracing the human relationships that determine it—in the wake of Vilfredo Pareto—he raises the concept of the "power social forces." The first human relationships of suffering that Bauman investigates are, in fact, work relationships and the bonds forming between the working class and the capitalist class. These relationships become the object of his interest since they produce alienation, which in turn generates suffering episodes of stigmatization and marginalization.[91] In his own approach, or for the coalescence of Marx's and Weber's theories that Bauman uses, it seems Bauman reflects the neo-Marxism phase of sociology from the 1960s to 1990s. Thus, every face essentially coincides with a historical period. Michael H. Jacobsen and Sophia Marshman give a name to each of these faces—Marxian, Modernist, Moral, and Mosaic. And following their schema, let me here repropose the question.

---

90 Cf. Jacobsen and Marshman, "The Four Faces of Human Suffering in the Sociology of Zygmunt Bauman," 3–4.
91 See Richard Kilminster and Ian Varcoe, "Appendix: Sociology, Postmodernity and Exile: An Interview with Zygmunt Bauman," in Zygmunt Bauman, *Intimations of Postmodernity*, quoted in Jacobsen and Marshman, "The Four Faces of Human Suffering in the Sociology of Zygmunt Bauman," 5.

The first phase is the one in which the Marxian echo spreads. Already from Bauman's early writings, from 1956 to 1968, emerge issues concerning the alienation, social injustice, and the struggle of the working class in the light of Marx's thought. These works, mentioned in the first years of his study, criticize the situation of the post-Stalinist society. Thanks to Bauman, a Polish sociology, free and open, results: "And it had to stand up against the new injustices and inequalities that the new powers spawned in profusion in the course of extirpating the old ones."[92]

To report how the imbalance of the socioeconomic relationship between the capitalist class and the labor force is reflected in forms of power within the society, he studies with great thoroughness the miserable condition prevailing in the working class, the proletariat of the rags of the late-capitalist society mentioned by Marx. The working class, not owning what it produces, finds itself understructured compared to the owning elite or those with managerial functions in society. Briefly, Bauman highlights that it is "ejected" from the sphere of political decisions. Since real socialism proposed itself in its plan to eradicate all forms of social injustice and inequality, it becomes, in Bauman's eyes and not only, one of the historical alternatives to capitalism: indeed, after the Great War it was the only alternative to capitalism.[93] Nevertheless, over time, he no longer considers the suffering of the working class as the universal symbol of all suffering and finds quite a different symbolic equivalent, another category of suffering universally accepted and legitimized by historical events.

There were a succession of historical political and economic situations that let Bauman no longer look at the suffering of the working class but at that of the Jews. Over the passage of years, concrete facts revealed fresh forms of inequality and modern practices of authoritarianism, but, above all, he saw the lack of freedom triggered by real socialism and then the fallacy of the cause for which Bauman initially stood up. The anti-Semitism episode that broke out in Poland at the end of the 1960s, and which led to his expulsion from academic positions, highlighted all the so-called αλλαί

---

92 Tester and Jacobsen, "Bauman before Exile," 271.
93 Cf. Marcello Flores, "Autoritarismo, totalitarismo, comunismi," *I Viaggi di Erodoto* 22 (1994): 237; Beilharz, "Modernity and Communism," 91.

("others"), other forms of social inequality and imbalance no longer linked to the relations of capitalist production. The issue of anti-Semitism at this point became central in the life of Bauman, who, in his writings, reviewed the Polish real socialism dear to him previously. Bauman is the one who transforms the criticism of real socialism into a discursive practice and represents the academic person who, at a theoretical and cultural level, subdues many buttresses of the communist ideology.

He refused to equate the working class with universal suffering, and stated it at the center of his discourses, because of a sequence of political events. There was the failure of actual socialism and the collapse of Stalinism (in 1956 there was the condemnation of war crimes during the Twentieth Congress of the Communist Party of the Soviet Union (PCUS),[94] and a revisionism of a cultural kind that criticized the failure of socialism and the Polish political system for failing to put an end to social injustice.

If the renunciation of the centrality of the working class had already been announced at the beginning of the 1970s with the crisis of the system of Fordist production and the loss of the central role of the working class in the system of the world economy, it was now Bauman who revealed the true face of real socialism. In the early 1970s, the crisis of Fordism, a key element of modernity, was accompanied by the change of the positions of cultural systems of values or, rather, the crisis of social regulation and hence the crisis of the welfare state, the bureaucratic hierarchical model, and the analytical approach of pluralism. It is obvious that if the working class loses its importance, the universal social suffering (resulting from the rapport between the capitalist class and the working class) can no longer coincide with the particular suffering of the working class: it must be replaced by something else.

Bauman reflected on the fact that actual socialism had offered solutions to the problem of human suffering represented symbolically by the working class, and he asked by whom or by what human suffering could be represented, when real socialism fails in its objectives, creating

---

[94] "The Polish regime only emulated Soviet Stalinism into the 1950s, losing its impetus by 1953 and ending with Beria's death in 1956. The 'Polish Road to Socialism' emphasized differences, rather than similarities with the USSR. As a result, there was little synchronization of the political histories of the two countries. The Polish regime prided itself as Polish, western, over the Russian eastern ways" (Beilharz, "Modernity and Communism," 95–6), (author's in-text citations omitted).

even more alienation. To sum up, thanks to, and after, the failure of socialism in Poland, whereby the political limits of a totalitarian system were unmasked (this system was intended to conceal them through anti-Semitic practices), it was clear that social suffering, personified by the working class, could not be the only one. Namely, there was other suffering in addition to that of the "the proletariat of rags."

In the 1980s, his thought could no longer reflect the suffering elaborated in the so-called Marxist phase, since real socialism created the same alienation caused by the capitalist system, both economic systems used the same modern utilitarianism typical of managerialism.[95] When, as a result of exile, Bauman abandoned the cause of real socialism, he found himself examining a humanity dominated by the strong utilitarianism typical of the capitalist Fordist system and of the communist economic model, based on state planning of investments and on heavy industry. For him, it was necessary overcome the liability of the two modes of production: the problems attributed by Marxism to the market economy reappeared in real socialist regimes. Real socialism and capitalism missed the mark in solving the agitations between the market and state.[96]

The traditional concept of sociological imagination relative to the working class went into crisis in the 1980s, and this "modernist phase" coincided with the age of neoliberalism: the years of UK prime minister Margaret Thatcher and U.S. president Ronald Reagan, at the end of the so-called golden age or welfare state.[97] In his continuous attempt to universalize suffering, Bauman had to consider new economic policies and postindustrial culture, the structural increase of unemployment, inflation, turbulence of consolidation of the welfare state and the exhaustion of labor movements, and, finally, the two systemic crises that capitalism suffers.[98] A first time when there is a change and transformation from the

---

95 Cf. Tester, *Il pensiero di Zygmunt Bauman*, 109–63.
96 See Beilharz, "Modernity and Communism," 93–94.
97 Cf. Tester, *Il pensiero di Zygmunt Bauman*, 53–79; Giaccardi and Magatti, *La globalizzazione non è un destino*, v.
98 See the "Winter of Discontent" at Brixton, Toxteh, in 1978–79. For a general overview, see https://libcom.org/history/1978-1979-winter-of-discontent (accessed July 20, 2016). Cf. Jacobsen and Marshman, "The Four Faces of Human Suffering in the Sociology of Zygmunt Bauman," 7.

rural, feudal, and premodern world to the organized world of modern factories (this is the so-called period of solid modernity), and a second time when, in the last part of the twentieth century, society was gradually transformed from a producer society to a consumer society. It was the latest crisis to affect Bauman: in this society, new deprivation, social injustice, and alienation were born, which ills were no longer attributable to the capitalist system of production in which the workforce is underdeployed. This shift resulted from "solid modernity"—in Bauman's words—that generates a social progress fast enough to create new spaces for new poor: the latest poor are marginalized and are not part of the working class.

For Bauman, there was a historical parable of suffering beginning with the working class and ending with the consumers of the modern age. Already in 1982 in *Memories of Class*, he had understood that the social suffering of the working class was not enough to represent the universal suffering of the whole society: it lacked a "between" or a link, and at there was a void to be filled.

The events of socialist Poland during the Cold War, the anti-Semitic incidents that happened to him personally, the issue of *Winter in the Morning*, and, the failure of real socialism led him to change to the subject of alienation. It is passed from the working class of modernity to the marginalized unemployed and those unable to find a job in the era of late capitalism.[99] Thus, *Memories of Class* has to be read as a revision of Marx's orthodox theory: all those who are deprived of power in society and who are not protected are the victims of this new suffering.[100] When Bauman universalized the particular suffering endured by the Jews, he had precisely this in mind, namely, that of talking about the history of the new social suffering and the new ghettos formed unintentionally and in which those who are left out of the economic production live (flawed producers).[101] Characterized by an uninterrupted deprivation, which accumulates over time all those who do not participate in the game of production and consumption are the new losers of the society, labeled as the sponges of the welfare state and late capitalism. In the so-called moral phase (or that of values, in accordance with Durkheim's meaning)

---

99 Ibid.
100 Ibid. Cf. Bauman, *Memories of Class*, 170.
101 Cf. Jacobsen and Marshman, "The Four Faces of Human Suffering in the Sociology of Zygmunt Bauman," 8.

during the 1990s, the protagonists of suffering were the "otherness," while in the new millennium there were the "wasted lives": namely, the underclass of consumers spoiled by liquid modernity.[102] These unwelcome people (immigrants or asylum seekers) constitute the "just arrived" faces of social suffering, determined this time by social causes not modern. Then the question concerns which modern solidarity was lacking in time:

> What happens to these superfluous and useless people? First of all, they are physically isolated in involuntary ghettos—out of sight and out of mind of the rest of society. Second, they are made responsible for their own misfortune and thus barred from complaining, asking for help or even demanding solidarity or moral concern from those lucky enough to escape such misfortune. Finally, they are informed that they are alone in their suffering when being told that their suffering is *their* suffering, *their* problem, *their* fault.[103]

In the so-called liquid society of the last millennium, in which the producing class disappears, that of consumers emerges, and in which the conditions alienating individuals increase, it is necessary to find new symbolic equivalents that reflect suffering. In this society, there is no more space for the weeds but only for the waste.

3.7.4. The Holocaust as a Product of Modernity

It matters that Bauman, while approaching solid modernity, used the category of the Holocaust, choosing the metaphor of "perfect garden." He points to the suffering endured by the Jews during World War II as a universal symbol of human suffering, able to assume any kind of misery. His is a new sociological imagination of his post-exile life. While analyzing the route of the European Jews, he opens up an original critical perspective on human reality.[104]

---

102 See Zygmunt Bauman, *Wasted Lives: Modernity and its Outcasts* (Cambridge: Polity, 2004).
103 Jacobsen and Marshman, "The Four Faces of Human Suffering in the Sociology of Zygmunt Bauman," 14.
104 Cf. Tester, *Il pensiero di Zygmunt Bauman*, 140.

The very first book of his critical sociology of post exile was *Memories of Class*, which anticipated, in some respects, *Modernity and the Holocaust*. The *trait d'union* between the two works is human suffering. "I assumed that the Holocaust," the author writes "was, at best, something to be illuminated by us social scientists, but certainly not something that can illuminate the objects of our current concerns."[105] Inspired at the end of the 1980s by reading *Winter in the Morning*, Bauman shifted the object of social suffering from the tension between the working class and spoiled producers to that of Jews who experienced the Holocaust and to a critique of the modern and "adiaphorized" genocide of the Jews. While *Modernity and the Holocaust* marked the transition from the Marxian phase to the modern phase in sociology, in post-Holocaust sociology it was focused on the role that modernity had played in the destruction of the Jews of Europe. In the 1980s, in the years in which he criticized all the modern trends of totalitarianism and the ways in which modernity had not only generated the civil progress but also the suffering of millions of Jews (persecuted and killed during World War II and beyond), Bauman rediscovered his Jewish roots, his identity never recognized before. He especially binds modernity to the process of adiaphorization, referring, first, to the emptying (in actions) of moral content and, second, to the establishment of a chain of command and execution of mediated orders in which no actor is responsible for his own actions.

For Bauman, this system remembers what happened in a Western space during World War II. This mechanism of adiaphorization was started and maintained by modernity itself and, in its unfolding, remains trapped in its same modern devices, by finishing in engulfing itself and destroying the freedom for which it was set in motion.[106] The concept is central for understanding in which way the two ideologies, capitalism and socialism, are explained by the category of modernity. Bauman does that.

Both capitalism and real socialism, aspiring to achieve a rational purpose, work towards a goal that is realized only in the indefinite future,

---

105   Bauman, *Modernity and the Holocaust*, viii.
106   Cf. Ulrich Beck, *I rischi della libertà: L'individuo nell'epoca della globalizzazione* (Bologna: il Mulino, 2000); by selected essays, *Riskante Freiheiten* (Frankfurt: Suhrkamp, 1994), chap. 1; *Kinder der Freiheit* (1997), chaps. 2–5; *Modernität und Barbarei* (1996), chap. 6.

and both end up turning the world into a tool.[107] Both deliver the idea of a perfect society: in the case of capitalism, manageable through the market, and, in the case of real socialism, through the state. At the base of the two ideologies, there is the modern totalitarian project of the perfection of society. The real socialism pursuing rationality in respect to value tends to ensure a perfect future in the same manner as modern capitalism. For example, the *Gulag* ensured death in the name of values and this happened due to real socialism; while the *Lager* (in Bauman's version it is the result of capitalist modernity) promised death in the name of instrumentality. In other words, the Holocaust was instrumental in ensuring an order able to eliminate any kind of disorder: clearly, both ideologies moved from the desire to create order in future times.[108] In *Legislators and Interpreters*, Bauman examines the modern order in which the state is compared to and behaves as a gardener careful to weed out all the weeds that can infest his garden. In this sense, the one who orders exercises and practices power.[109] Next there are also other officials in charge behaving like this gardener. This happens because they take care to treat their state as if it were a garden, where only a few plants are to be grown and within certain limits, in a precise area, and in a manner appropriate to the gardener and his helpers.[110] The state is this gardener ordering and not allowing any spontaneous growth unauthorized by him: namely, in such state-garden no disorder or disproportion is possible. The will and management of perfect order coincide with a totalitarian context of ideas: in this way, Bauman explains sociologically the Holocaust as a product of modernity.

Modernity as a project subsumes the metaphor of the "state-gardener": and genocide can be conceived as a work of gardening, while the state, considering its own society as a garden, destroys all forms of weeds, eliminating any element that haunts its garden. In this perspective, the action of eradicating (i.e., the genocide) becomes a creative and

---

107 Cf. Tester, *Il pensiero di Zygmunt Bauman*, 140.
108 See Beilharz, "Modernity and Communism," 92–93 and see also Zygmunt Bauman, "Dictatorship over Needs," *Telos* 60 (1984), 263, quoted in Beilharz, "Modernity and Communism," 91.
109 Cf. Zygmunt Bauman, *Legislators and Interpreters: On Modernity, Post-modernity, and Intellectuals* (Cambridge: Polity, 1987).
110 Cf. Tester, *Il pensiero di Zygmunt Bauman*, 147; Bauman, *Modernity and the Holocaust*, 91–93.

nondestructive work. However, in modernity, to order also signifies to be able to determine what is harmful and what is harmless: the power to sort by name, according to instrumental and precise purposes, answers to the rationality of the existence of the modern state. The taxonomizing, classifying, differentiating, segregating, and collecting in classes, by limiting possibilities for grouped items to escape from that class, in some respects evokes the supervising action exercised by a state on the society.[111] Nothing should be missed by the gardener-state that cares to structure and allocate the subjects of its own society in a particular class.[112]

Another important point on which Bauman focuses is this: the groups not classifiable as ambivalent belong to more classes and consequently they seem to be not controllable like Jews, homosexuals, and Gypsies, who make imperfect and uncontrolled, according to totalitarian ideologies, the social garden of modernity. In accordance with totalitarian ideology, they must be eliminated. Now, the ambivalent class par excellence is the one made of foreign persons physically close, but spiritually and culturally distant. Their physical proximity frightens and threatens the established order. The Jews appear as the "foreigners par excellence," who, one day, in the modern period, arrive and do not leave.[113] Their presence serves as a reminder of the fallacy of any nationalism or, rather, its incompleteness and thus the limits of any national project. The questions are where these groups should be inclosed and how they should be classified for the public good. Namely, in what garden may they be? The problem lies in that they cannot be confined anywhere, because they are extraneous to any classifiable national identity. It is therefore a trial for the Jews by the modern nation-state, which lets their unit (faced with their interstitiality) disappear or be lost. The modern project of classifying national identities leads to Auschwitz. For Bauman, who in his analysis deals with the category of rationality, the modern nation-state or the ambivalence of the modern state leads to genocide. One of the reasons he chooses the category of

---

111   See Mary Douglas, *Purity and Danger: An Analysis of the Concepts of Pollution and Taboo* (London: Routledge & Kegan Paul), 1966; Michel Foucault, *Surveiller et punir: Naissance de la prison* (Paris: Gallimard, 1975); Tester, *Il pensiero di Zygmunt Bauman*, 151.
112   Cf. Tester, *Il pensiero di Zygmunt Bauman*, 122–25.
113   Cf. ibid., 152.

modernity to account for the Holocaust coincides with the crisis of solid modernity, with its social consequences and the effects of capitalism. In essence, Bauman connects the Holocaust to the phase of the maximum deployment of modernity, which, according to him, coincides with its crisis. As Silverman notes, "the rediscovery of the Holocaust is symptomatic of the crisis of modern France and Western modernity as a whole."[114] Faced with this social crumbling, in finding an answer, Bauman reconsiders the suffering endured by the Jews.

At this point, it is important to remember the different theories of modernity: only by taking in mind what modernity means, in the main scholars' eyes and over the time, can one understand Bauman's interpretation of the Holocaust. One of the many ways is to define—as in a glossary—the species of modernity, ordered according to the peculiar characteristics of modernity and the reference categories of space and time. For this purpose, let me introduce here thirteen definitions of modernity in referring to Bauman's approach to the Holocaust. Specifically, let me attribute to the category of modernity an adjective referring to its specific historical context and then match an exponent or a scholar representative of each of these qualified categories. For instance, one can consider the *aesthetic* modernity of Charles Baudelaire, the *capitalist* modernity of Marx, and the *rational* modernity of Weber. Moreover, one can speak of the economic modern analysis of Simmel's or Durkheim's sociological analysis, or the lesson of the Frankfurt School, or a definition of modernity in Parsonian expressions.

Behind this discourse, there are the ideas of progress, the limits of modern liberties, and the exercise of accountability. Nevertheless, what is modernity? *Modus* and *modernus* are Late Latin terms that, translating the expressions "now," "last," and "more recent," allude to incessant change, which creates instability and uncertainty, typical aspects of modernity. The element of "always new" features the polysemic category that appears in the discourses of several scholars and that unifies the temporal dimension of the "present-time" with that of the space-qualitative of "last-recent."

---

114 Max Silverman, *Facing Postmodernity: Contemporary French Thought on Culture and Society* (London: Routledge, 1999), 13.

A present is always new, based on the maximum autonomy of the individual. Augustine had marked the caesura between the pagan and Christian world through the term *modernus*.[115] Like a key, modernity opens the closure of a flexible society: the elements of "here" and "now" distinguish modernity from the traditional elements of an unmodern society. According to this sociological interpretation, modernity coincides with the physical and political space of the West, and, as in a mirror, the geopolitical space is Eastern and amodern. To define modernity, it is suitable to modify the noun with several qualifiers, such as historic, political, socioeconomic, and philosophical. The result is an elementary dictionary with many voices individuating one or more representative scholars for any definition.

The study of structural and procedural characteristics of modern society problematizes the tradition of the new: from a sociological examination, a status of crises emerges. The Greek verb κρίνω (*krino*), "to choose," underlines the moment of the transition from traditional societies, economically and socially static, to those that are dynamic and in continuous progress. Studying *Modernity and the Holocaust* one may see what makes a society modern. Namely, behind the work is a wonderful sociological piece related to modernity and the categories that identify it. A digression about modern society in considering classical and contemporary theories of sociological literature can help to understand the reasons why several scholars, including Bauman, chose to explain the destruction of the Jews through the category of modernity. Here, I will not focus on modernity characterized by the capitalist system of production that transforms the economic and social relationships in a modern way. Rather, I will consider the category of instrumental rationality as a feature of modernity. In the steps of Weber, the origins are in the practical implementation of the Protestant ethic. In 2000, Peter Beilharz highlighted what Weber had bequeathed to Bauman, especially, the dominance of a formal and a-reflexive rationality. What matters is that it can legitimize any social action and degenerate into genocidal practice.[116] It can be added that the notions of modern Western capitalism, bureaucracy, and legal-rational authority

---

115 William Outhwaite et al., eds., "Modernità," in *Dizionario delle scienze sociali* (Milan: il Saggiatore, 1997), 440.
116 Cf. Kuper, *The Pity of It All*.

that characterize modernity certainly constitute a good analytical basis for *Modernity and the Holocaust.* It recalls in turn the economic, social, and political sphere.

Specifically, modernity coincides with the modern national state: capitalist, bourgeois, and that which develops in the West. In essence, for Weber, the social action of an economic capitalistic kind, that is, oriented to constant increase of capital, results in a continuous growth of new elements. Thus, he considers modern society as a capitalistic society whose conditions are rational organization, development of open markets, so-called rational-legal authority, formally ruled, and the separation of family from trade. The end of *gubernaculum* emphasizes that within the state, the obedience to a command or a monopoly of legitimate violence over a given territory is necessary: "When nation states begin to assert themselves against medieval universalism, …the nominalist conception of the individual is prepared, which will become a second nature in all further development."[117] In other words, in Weber modernity is essentially the formation of nation-states. To protect markets and prevent conditions of abuse or oppression on the part of companies, the modern national state assumes the responsibility of protecting its citizens. In this modern state also the exercise of power is rationalized. Its implementation requires an administrative apparatus, that is, a rational organization of the work according to five principles: (1) the presence of services and expertise regulated by legislation; (2) a functional hierarchy; (3) impersonal appropriation of the charge; (4) recruitment on merit; and, ultimately, (5) wages for state officials. From these five points, the sense of office—the instrumental rationality and the end of personal individuality in the performance of the role—emerges. What Bauman takes from it, for his discourse, is that the rational organization in political, legal, and economic settings reduces, however, so-called discernment, in the sense that the individual is no longer required to evaluate his own actions. The sphere of options and values gives way to pure instrumental rationality: when the

---

117 Horkheimer and Adorno, *Lezioni di sociologia*, 52 (my translation). The sense of *individuum* is always present in the modern context. Furthermore, the locution *individuum* is the Latin translation of Greek ἄτομον ("atom"), from Democritus: in the *humus* of modern individualism the doctrine of free competition flourishes.

moral practice of action stops working, it performs the end of reason mentioned. This withdraws in front of the hypertrophic development of the intellect.[118] But, above all, all this can degenerate into irresponsible actions.

The calculation of means and ends becomes the goal of modern social action aimed at perfection. What is happening to society is quite similar to what happens to a body in which antibodies are higher than normal, a sort of hyperattentiveness. As in an immune system where the excessive number of antibodies ends up engulfing parts of the body itself, in a modern society those rational elements, the symbol of the liberation from superstition and fear, a legacy from the medieval age, degenerate into irrationality and loss of meaning (of actions) and freedom of individuals.[119] It is the process Weber defines as *Entzauberung*, "progressive disenchantment," faced with which the only solution seems to be refuge in the irrationality of myth and a charismatic leader, which become secure anchors against the iron cage of formal rationalization incumbent on every relational system. In its deployment upward, the *logos rationale* staggers into *sur*-ratio, regressing at irrational times. Thus, Horkheimer notes in *Eclipse of Reason*: "Society would be deprived of any intellectual means of resistance to a bond that social critiques have always denounced."[120]

3.7.5. His Sociological Lesson

Can we write a history of *Modernity and the Holocaust*? Until Bauman, the Holocaust was basically conceived as an event that happened to the Jews, an episode of the long history of anti-Semitism or some sort of aberration or deviation in and from the progress of civilization.[121] In the wake of the

---

118   Cf. Simmel, *Die Großstädte und das Geistesleben*.
119   Cf. Jay, *The Dialectical Imagination*; and see Horkheimer, *Eclipse of Reason*.
120   See ibid., 50 and Horkheimer and Adorno, *Lezioni di sociologia*, 108.
121   Cf. Bauman, *Modernity and the Holocaust*, viii–ix; Halpert, "Early American Sociology and the Holocaust," 7. See also Postone, review of *Modernity and Holocaust*, 1521; Robert van Krieken, "The Barbarism of Civilization: Cultural Genocide and the 'Stolen Generations,'" *British Journal of Sociology* 50, no. 2 (1999): 297–315; Tester, *Il pensiero di Zygmunt Bauman*, 154–55.

master Ossowski, Bauman recuperates typical concepts of the sociological discipline and thinks about a new sociology of the Holocaust, since, according to him, traditional sociology had failed in its task. Postone wrote, "Bauman claims that sociology has not adequately confronted the challenges raised by the Holocaust, in part because sociology participates in the same scientific culture of modernity, shares its emphasis on technique, its propensity for social engineering, and its understanding of rational action.... Bauman contravenes this view and calls for a reconsideration of modernity and of the nature of sociological thought."[122]

After an excursus of private and personal research, Bauman does not choose the usual image of "victim, perpetrator (inhuman) and viewer." He does not even opt for the conception of a cancerous formation occurring in the course of modern civilization. Rather, he explains the Holocaust through modern societal dimensions. Modernity and the Holocaust are quite exceptional terms, which the scholar connects in an original way, forming a multifaceted union. In fact, the concept of modernity is polysemous and extends beyond historical trends. For this reason, the bond with the Holocaust, a phenomenon more specifically historical, is perfect. This unusual verbal couple arouses the interest in Holocaust scholars, who return, after his publication, to rethink it.

Bauman's sociological lesson attracts scholars because, on one side, he considers modernity the primary historical cause of the destruction of the Jews, and on the other, he makes the Holocaust modern. Now, for a detailed analysis of Bauman's construct, it is necessary to identify the traces of the Holocaust in modernity and also understand the modernity of the Holocaust. According to Bauman, the question concerns which historical and sociological conjunction links modernity with the Holocaust. Certainly, it is the rationality principle, even if the deeper lesson is in the combination of two inventions of modernity, namely, the bureaucratic apparatus is used to implement the ideological project of a perfect social order, which

---

122 Postone, review of *Modernity and Holocaust*, 1521; see also Bauman, "Sociology after the Holocaust," 469–97; Tester and Jacobsen, *Bauman Before Exile*, 267–74.

demands and legitimates contemporarily the instrumental purpose for the destruction of the Jews. The Holocaust is modern because it is given by a combination of modern factors:[123]

> No doubt the Holocaust … bore features that it did not share with any of the past cases of genocide.… Like everything else done in the modern—rational, planned, scientifically informed, expert, efficiently managed, co-ordinated—way, the Holocaust left behind and put to shame all its alleged pre-modern equivalents, exposing them as primitive, wasteful and ineffective by comparison.… It towers high above the past genocidal episodes in the same way as the modern industrial plant towers above the craftsman's cottage workshop, or the modern industrial farm, with its tractors, combines and pesticides, towers above the peasant farmstead with its horse, hoe and hand-weeding.[124]

3.7.6. A Samizdat Phenomenon

When Bauman elaborates his critique on Western modernity, he carries with him the experience in Poland, that which happened in the heart of Europe in the years of late socialism. As in the Frankfurt School, his thinking criticizes totalitarian power, even though his design is quite different:[125]

> The question of Soviet modernity and the status of the Polish experience of which Bauman was part need to be placed alongside the more famous critique of the Holocaust, which can be more readily aligned with Horkheimer and Adorno's views in *Dialectic of Enlightenment*.[126]

---

123 The concepts of "house in order" and "perfect garden" respond to the public policy of social hygiene of the Third Reich, according to thesis of Habermas on the project of modernity.
124 Bauman, *Modernity and the Holocaust*, 88–9.
125 Cf. Beilharz, "Modernity and Communism," 89.
126 Ibid., 88.

The hope for a real change after the death of Stalin in 1953, and the following condemnation of his crimes at the Twentieth Congress of the Communist Party of the Soviet Union with Khrushchev's secret speech on February 25, 1956—for several intellectuals a kind of window of free expression of thought—was short-lived. The trials against intellectuals returned by giving a new start to a long season of dissent.

Bauman, no longer willing to waive the rights enshrined in an official way at the Helsinki Conference in 1975—which would characterize the subsequent history of the Soviet Union, Czechoslovakia, and Poland—opened his own conflict, ideal and real, between the political regime and civil society. He wants primarily to express his deep disapproval towards the politics of real socialism and the fallacy of the communist system in *Modernity and the Holocaust*.[127] As several intellectuals did between the end of 1950s and the beginning of 1960s in order to circulate their texts or ideas that did not conform to official canons, he adopted a *samizdat* strategy: a clandestine publishing industry, which requires, especially in the early stages, only the copying and distribution of banned texts. The reference to this Russian term *samizdat*, which literally means "self-publishing," in this case reminds us of the author's attempt to disseminate his thoughts about communist ideology in an indirect way. His text was published in 1989, when totalitarianism of the Left symbolically fell with the fall of the Berlin Wall.[128] Bauman disagrees with a state, the real socialist Poland, which in politics contradicts its own ideological *pre*/promises. He undoubtedly alludes to difficulties or the impracticality of a free and critical literature in Eastern Europe, where cultural dissent is being denied: the anti-Semitic purges of senior or academic positions confirm this. Thus, in *Modernity and the Holocaust* totalitarianism assumes a symbolic dimension that is new for academic sociology, namely, that the totalitarian experience is not just the prerogative of the National Socialists: in the

---

127 Cf. Peter Beilharz, *Zygmunt Bauman: Dialectic of Modernity* (London: Sage, 2000).
128 Valentina Parisi, "Samizdat: Problemi di definizione," *eSamizdat* 8 (2010–2011): 19–29, accessed March 28, 2012, http://www.esamizdat.it/rivista/2010-2011/index.htm.

history of totalitarianism it is necessary to also include the Bolsheviks and consider communism as modern:[129]

> Bauman reintroduces the frame of modernity and after. Communism was socialism in overdrive, socialism in a hurry, the younger, hot-headed and impatient brother. Lenin's political impatience led to a sociological rupture. Lenin redefined socialism (or communism) as a *substitute for*, rather than a *continuation of*, the bourgeois revolution. Communism would be modernity without the bourgeois revolution, without bourgeois democracy or a public sphere of any kind. Communism was an image of modernity one-sidedly adapted to the task of mobilizing social and natural resources in the name of modernization.[130]

Furthermore *One-Dimensional Man* by Marcuse and *Dialectic of Enlightenment* by Adorno and Horkheimer indicate how the Bolshevik and Nazi experiences, despite their distinctions, must be compared in order to obtain a picture as complete as possible about the age of totalitarianism.[131] However, for Bauman, any modernity is totalitarian, including real socialism.[132] According to Beilharz, both the Frankfurt School and Bauman (apropos of totalitarianism) agree on the limits of the Enlightenment when rationality is bridled and self-phagocytes its raison d'être:

> The relation of National Socialism to the rebellion of nature was complex. Since such rebellion, though "genuine," always involves a

---

129 Cf. Beilharz, "Modernity and Communism," 89; see also Beilharz, *Zygmunt Bauman*.
130 Beilharz, "Modernity and Communism," 96.
131 The sociologist subsumes Nazi and Soviet totalitarianism under a single analytical category. Cf. Beilharz, "Modernity and Communism," 92. "Forty years ago, writing in *One-Dimensional Man*, Herbert Marcuse suggested that 'domination [now] ... extends to all spheres of private and public existence, integrates all authentic opposition, absorbs all alternatives.' Today, his thesis seems justified, as the historic decline of critical social movements, the absorption of countercultural elements into consumer capitalism, and the continued erosion of the public sphere make it ever more difficult for society to acknowledge even the possibility of an alternative to the status quo"; John Sanbonmatsu, "The Holocaust Sublime: Singularity, Representation, and the Violence of Everyday Life," *American Journal of Economics and Sociology* 68, no. 1 (2009): 122 (author's in-text citations omitted).
132 Cf. Beilharz, *Zygmunt Bauman*; Beilharz, "Modernity and Communism," 89.

regressive element …In modern fascism, rationality has reached a point at which it is no longer satisfied with simply repressing nature; rationality now exploits nature by incorporating into its own system the rebellious potentialities of nature. The Nazis manipulated the suppressed desires of the German people.[133]

And, "Anti-Semitic behavior is unleashed in situations in which blinded people, deprived of subjectivity, are let loose as subjects."[134]

In any case, the Enlightenment is revealed as a utopia, a "no place" both in the Soviet system, organized according to a rational state, and in the modern National Socialist state, which replaces the state order with individual rationality.[135] Both systems can be defined as "modern":

> For the Bolsheviks did violence to their people in their own name. The murders were done in the name of noble ends. Where the Final Solution was rational in its own terms, a murderous solution to a Nazi-imposed Jewish problem, the ethics of communism were worse than those of fascism, for the Bolsheviks were prepared to commit murder for noble rather than ignoble ends. Thus the irony of the fellow-travelling insistence that Stalinism was superior to Nazism because it sought to improve Humanity. Unlike the Nazis, the Bolsheviks meant well; this is supposed to be some kind of compensation for their victims.[136]

At a time when control over society fails, human behavior is exploited and objectives are pursued with determination and efficiency without moral approval from those who pursue them. The result is the destruction of the

---

133 Horkheimer, *Eclipse of Reason*, 82.
134 Horkheimer and Adorno, *Dialectic of Enlightenment*, 140.
135 Cf. Beilharz, "Modernity and Communism," 92.
136 Ibid., 90. See Julian Hochfeld, "Poland and Britain: Two Concepts of Socialism," *International Affairs* 1 (1957): 2–11; Leszek Kolakowski, "A Pleading for Revolution: A Rejoinder to Z. Bauman," *Archives Europeenes de Sociologie* 12, no. 1 (1971): 52–60; Zygmunt Bauman, *Stalin and the Peasant Revolution: A Case Study in the Dialectics of Master and Slave* (Leeds: University of Leeds Department of Sociology, 1985).

Jews: the Holocaust and real socialism are, for Bauman, ideal-typical experiences of the modern project:[137]

> A condition in which the actor sees himself as executor of the wishes of another person.[138]

3.7.7. Some Literary Critics

To see with what happened after *Modernity and the Holocaust* came out, I'll summarize the principal content of the main criticisms in order to understand why Bauman's thesis works well among scholars.

Essentially, most public reviews were favorable towards the work, celebrating it as unique in the sense that, for the mainstream of scholars, it was going to break the professed silence in post-Holocaust sociology and because it seemed to surpass the gap between functionalist theories and those of intentionalists in the historical field. Before analyzing the leading critiques, we must underline one point[139]—that the book appears "thought-provoking," as Postone notes, for having put the category of modernity in progress. Meantime, it seems like a "puzzling" work[140] and "fails to say enough about Germans and Jews."[141] It is relevant to notice that reviewers such as Banton, Beilharz, Dunning, and Mennell are scholars who, in their works, reevaluate the notion of modernity, starting from the categories of civilization and genocide. This is evident from review of academic journals online. As we saw in the first paragraphs of this chapter, the civilizing process involves genocidal practices. According to anthropological studies, genocide is a system of relationships between people having nothing to do with the so-called primitive societies. For postcolonial historians, genocides are perpetrated with instruments of

---

137 Cf. Tester, *Il pensiero di Zygmunt Bauman*, 170.
138 See ibid., 157. Cf. Beilharz, "Modernity and Communism," 96.
139 To criticisms by Natan Sznaider and Arne Johan Vetlesen, I will devote a separate study. Now, for additional features, see Natan Sznaider, *Jewish Memory and the Cosmopolitan Order* (Cambridge: Polity, 2011).
140 Postone, review of *Modernity and the Holocaust*, 1523.
141 Beilharz, "Modernity and Communism," 97.

violence of a higher evolution of military technology. Thus, they have to be considered as outcomes of Western modernity.

In essence, immediately after the publication of *Modernity and the Holocaust*, Michael Banton, of the University of Bristol, was among the first to review the book. Banton, who published his review in March 1991 in *British Journal of Sociology*, recalling both Lemkin's discourse and the text of the UN Convention on Genocide, appreciates Bauman's work in a positive manner.[142]

Michael Freeman, instead, philosopher of social sciences at the Government Department of University of Essex, has quite a different critical look: because of his works on the genocide, he considers that Bauman's arguments upset the orthodox theories of sociology, ethics, and politics. Briefly, Bauman seems not to reflect on the history of genocide and not focus on the specifics of the national history of Germany, unlike Elias, who considers instead the civilization as a pacification process of borders:

> Lemkin did not develop the concept in order to comprehend the event we now know as "the Holocaust." His purpose was to document German war crimes. He came to the view that these crimes were so barbarous that they went beyond the acts that had been rendered criminal by the framers of the relevant international law. This body of law assumed that war was fought between *states*. However, the German state, under the influence of Nazi ideology, was waging war against *nations*. It was for this project that Lemkin coined the term "genocide." The original conception of "genocide," therefore, was that of the waging of war by a state in order to destroy nations.[143]

Now, to come back to Freeman's critique, for this scholar Bauman "misses" an important aspect, namely, "what was not modern in that genocide." He fails for not having collocated "the Holocaust in the more general theoretical consideration of genocide."[144] In this sense Freeman is close to a relevant

---

142 Michael Banton, review of *Modernity and the Holocaust*, by Zygmunt Bauman, *The British Journal of Sociology* 42, no. 1 (1991): 164.
143 Freeman, "Genocide, Civilization and Modernity," 209.
144 Ibid.

matter, that Bauman, in choosing modernity as unique explaining key of the Holocaust, fails to offer a complete lesson of the event; that, in his effort to understand the Holocaust through the category of modernity, Bauman cannot recognize the specificity of the Holocaust; by locating the destruction of the Jews in a Western space, he does not take into account (and this is the main failure) the public massacres perpetrated in the East by means of unmodern practices.[145] It is linked to the fact that slaughters executed in the Soviet territories are unknown to scholars: first, because the Soviet archives were closed until the fall of Berlin Wall; second, because they are voluntarily dismissed under the Cold War ideologies. His failure is more evident when Freeman highlights the difference between Lemkin's assumptions and Bauman's, which are totally opposed to Lemkin's. For example, according to Lemkin, the Nazi case constitutes a return to barbarism despite the practice of high-tech and modern methods. But for Bauman, the Holocaust is the full manifestation of the modern age and civilization and not at all a moment of return to barbarism. This point distances and moves from genocidal practices committed in the Soviet territories and that fit in the Holocaust. This element opens on to new reflections in comprehending the Holocaust in the East related to the recent theories on the genocide.[146] As Freeman says, "The values of

---

145   Cf. Chalk and Jonassohn, *The History and Sociology of Genocide*; Gross, *Neighbors*; Bartov, "L'Europa orientale come luogo del genocidio". See John Mueller, "Changing Attitudes towards War: The Impact of the First World War," *British Journal of Political Science* 21 (1991): 1–28.

146   See Steven L. Jacobs, "The Papers of Raphael Lemkin: A First Look," *Journal of Genocide Research* 1, no. 1 (1999): 105–14; Dan Stone, "Modernity and Violence: Theoretical Reflections on the Einsatzgruppen," *Journal of Genocide Research* 1, no. 3 (1999): 367–78; Øystein G. Holter, "A Theory of Gendercide," *Journal of Genocide Research* 4, no. 1 (2002): 11–38; Matthew Lippman, "A Road Map to the 1948 Convention on the Prevention and Punishment of the Crime Genocide," *Journal of Genocide Research* 4, no. 2 (2002): 177–95; Bartrop, "The Relationship between War and Genocide in the Twentieth Century"; Jeffrey S. Morton and Neil V. Singh, "The International Legal Regime on Genocide," *Journal of Genocide Research* 5, no. 1 (2003): 47–69; Jacques Sémelin, "Toward a Vocabulary of Massacre and Genocide," *Journal of Genocide Research* 5, no. 2 (2003): 193–210; Akio Kimura, "Genocide and the Modern Mind: Intention and Structure," *Journal of Genocide Research* 5, no. 3 (2003): 405–20; Linda M. Woolf and Michael R. Hulsizer, "Psychosocial Roots of Genocide: Risk, Prevention, and Intervention," *Journal of Genocide Research* 7, no. 1 (2005): 101–28; Stuart D. Stein, "Conceptions and Terms: Templates for the Analysis of Holocausts and Genocides," *Journal of Genocide Research* 7, no. 2 (2005): 171–203.

our society require that we develop such a sociology."[147] It requires a retracing of the genesis of the genocide. Moreover, this is a new field of research for sociology and history in the post-Holocaust years that has to do with the state establishment. For Freeman, genocide is both a manifestation of modern civilization and a return to barbarism.

Let us look at, even if briefly, another critique, by Dunning and Mennell, published in 1998, which puts at the center of its response "how the German historical experience" explains "its occurrence or peculiar features."[148] They do this while reconsidering *The Germans* by Elias, and their piece confronts Bauman's and Elias's statements.

Published in the same year as Bauman's *Modernity and the Holocaust*, Elias's *The Germans* agrees partly with Bauman, specifically, when it points out that the planned extermination of the masses does not fall outside of the mass society. Instead, Elias opposes Bauman as regards the theory of the civilizing process at the basis of the rise of totalitarian power.[149] According to Elias's interpretation, the civilizing process is especially the pacification of the borders for national and individual security from all forms of predatory incursion or incivility. Unlike Elias, who puts the specificity of the German national history at the basis of his work, Bauman neglects the social forces that unfold during the process of democratization in Germany.[150]

The specificity of the Germany history is instead rather crucial: the process of German civilization, translated with the term *Kultur*, explains better the sense of the struggle for power or control and falls in the last stage of imperialism. From 1871 to 1918, the *Kaiserreich* was a society guided by a code of honor (*satisfaktionsfähige Gesellschaft*). Nevertheless, the unification of Germany included a process of brutalization, in the sense that the aristocracy and the middle class found themselves in the new unified Reich, but without sharing the same cultural background and national levels—the middle and working class ignored the rules of the code of honor of the aristocracy, that is, when Germany was founded, at

---
147 Freeman, "Genocide, Civilization and Modernity," 222.
148 Cf. Dunning and Mennell, "Elias on Germany, Nazism and the Holocaust," 342.
149 Elias, *The Germans*.
150 Cf. Dunning and Mennell, "Elias on Germany, Nazism and the Holocaust," 344–45.

the end of the nineteenth century, it had unnationalized masses: there was no any merger of values and national ideals common to the majority of the middle and working classes.[151] There was no nation. What is also crucial, for Dunning and Mennell, is that the international context of the Great War deserves more attention. *Freikorps* were educated in a climate of violence and barbaric national mythology full of prejudices, which slowly led to Hitler's rise:

> Germans in general did not develop a habitus and conscience attuned to the give-and-take of parliamentary rule. On the contrary, they developed a pattern dependent on external, authoritarian control expressed through such concepts as *Kadavergehorsam*—"corpse-like obedience." Hans Frank, the *Reichsminister* and Governor-General of occupied Poland, for example, recast Kant when he wrote that: "The categorical imperative of action in the Third Reich is this: act in such a way that the *Führer*, if he knew of your action, would approve of it." Consistent with this was the metaphor of the *Radfahrermechanismus*—the "cyclist mechanism"—which referred to a lust for submission to those in power and the displacement of the resultant hostilities onto those below.[152]

In the bourgeois aristocracy ethos, the military component and the ethos of the honor code (*satisfaktionsfähige*) were very important. Discipline, honor, and sense of duty were essential, while hierarchy, discretion, social distance, and formality characterized social relations:[153]

> The brutalization of leading sections of the German middle classes and their absorption of a militaristic code thus formed, according to Elias, one of the preconditions for the process of barbarization in Germany which helped pave the way for Nazism. In short, Elias stresses how a peculiar conjuncture of circumstances arose in

---

151   Cf. ibid., 350, 352–53.
152   Ibid., 351–52; the reference is to Elias, *The Germans*.
153   Cf. ibid., 349; the reference is to Stephen Kalberg, "The German *Sonderweg* De-Mystified: A Sociological Biography of a Nation," *Theory, Culture and Society* 9, no. 3 (1992): 111–24.

German history and social development, combining to produce a resurgence of warrior values when a more unilinear theory—of the kind which Bauman and Burkitt wrongly interpret Elias as having proposed—might have led to an expectation of their decline.[154]

The *Kaiserreich* society aimed at maintaining the characters of the German aristocracy and the character of the German Aryans. It is relevant to remember what Jeffrey Herf says, "The reactionary modernists insisted that the *Kulturnation* could be both powerful and true to its soul. As Joseph Goebbels repeatedly insisted, this was to be the century of *stählernde Romantik*, steellike romanticism."[155]

As pointed out by Dunning and Mennell, for Elias, National Socialism inherited the characteristics of the dynastic Prussian state: those of a strong German Aryanism. (The *Kaiserreich*, in its formation, combined rapid industrialization with the structures of the Prussian dynasty, leaving little room for political and economic liberalism.) These conditions did not result in a state embodying a nation with which the mass of the population identified. Rather, in the modern *Kaiserreich* the transcendental myth of Aryan beauty and the belief that from the best fathers are born the best children unfolded. In this context, Elias sees all those conditions that allow the engraftment of Nazi ideology leveraging on the Aryan race, and that creates the premises of biological anti-Semitism: *Blut und Boden*.[156]

What Dunning and Mennell's piece unearths, in confronting Elias's and Bauman's works, is that in Nazi society were those characteristics specific to the society of honor code, where the masses do not enter into the state and where the state does not include their social claims. In essence, they stress that at the basis of Elias's discourse there is a mass "not nationalized" and that the "non-nationalization," during the process of modernization in Germany, in some ways, stopped civilization: when, for instance, this mass did not come into politics. The preserving of the aristocratic German tradition, rather than modern progress, interpreted

---

154 Ibid., 349–50.
155 Herf, *Reactionary Modernism*, 3.
156 See Dunning and Mennell, "Elias on Germany, Nazism and the Holocaust," 349, 352–53.

as a degeneration of values, was a return to barbarism. It was a process opposite to that of civilization, called "de-civilization" by Elias.

What Dunning and Mennell underscore is, first, the role of National Socialism, which offered a vision of a society reassuring to the conservative classes: a society that would allow economic development without putting at risk social boundaries and national traditions. Second, that at the origins of nonnationalization of the mass were political instability and tensions between the house of Hohenzollern and Habsburg in the more general context of the Weimar Republic years.[157] Namely, following the second industrial revolution, several changes occurred, especially for the emergence of the working class: its role became crucial in the rise of National Socialism and the Holocaust. It is well outlined by Elias:[158]

> One thing, though, has to be said in favour of Bauman compared with Elias: he does develop a stimulating explanation of why the Holocaust was directed mainly against Jews. Despite his own Jewish origins, that is an issue on which Elias was relatively silent.... Ultimately, however, his attempt to transcend Elias fails because he does not realize how crucial the concept of "functional democratization" is to Elias's theory. Nor does he appreciate the fundamental role attributed by Elias to middle-class groups.[159]

Looking at the other reviews, we should highlight that in the 1990s the resonance of *Modernity and the Holocaust* was felt in Australia, where, after the 1968 Polish anti-Semitic purges Bauman had spent a period of study. Robert van Krieken of the Department of Sociology of Work, Social Policy and Sociology at the University of Sydney, on the basis of the concept of social suffering, dear to Bauman, started to approach the Holocaust to explain additional exterminations. He tells of new massacres, genocides, starting from the accounting for the Holocaust. For instance,

---

157 Cf. ibid., 346–50; George L. Mosse, *Die Nationalisierung der Massen: Politische Symbolik und Massenbewegungen von den Befreiungskriegen bis zum Dritten Reich* (Frankfurt: Campus, 1993).
158 Cf. Dunning and Mennell, "Elias on Germany, Nazism and the Holocaust," 350–54.
159 Ibid., 354 (authors' in-text citations omitted).

he explains the social suffering of indigenous children in Australia, looking at the systematic removal of indigenous children from their families, mostly for reasons of social engineering, with the aim of systematically annihilating the cultural identity of the Aborigines.[160] This is central for seeing how the Holocaust as a phenomenon can become a social/sociological category—this element will be more evident in my next chapter—to explain disorders in society in the form of deviation, annihilation, and crime.

For Krieken, *Modernity and the Holocaust* becomes a kind of theoretical basis to compare contemporary historical situations, in which similar events to those that happened to the Jews occur. In this way, in Bauman's aim, the suffering endured by the Jews is emblematic of all suffering. This is possible thanks to the end of the Cold War, when there started, systematically, a more open vision towards what happens in the world. Although Krieken has recourse to the category of modernity, he deviates from Bauman's general theory. Foremost because he focuses on questioning what kind of modernity is one that leads to the genocidal practice, stealing entire generations. Nevertheless, what does it mean to be a modern citizen?

Starting from these elements, Krieken evidences that modern culture has ambivalent aspects and that behind the genocidal policies or practices there is the process of civilization:[161] modernity includes a barbaric civilization that refers to the perpetration of genocide as a means of solving political problems. What is remarkable in reading Krieken's critique is that, by criticizing *Modernity and the Holocaust*, genocide appears in its essential nature, namely, as a system of relationships between populations not at all primitive. Modern societies become barbaric in their unfolding, in their civilizing process. In the modern world, barbarity is accomplished—this is the ambivalence of modernity. Moreover, the discourse would become more evident with the explosion of the civilian wars in the Balkans during the 1990s.

Right in this period, in 1992, an important critique of *Modernity and the Holocaust* was published. Postone, of the University of Chicago, puts in the center of discussion why Bauman cannot simply explain

---

160 Krieken, "The Barbarism of Civilization," 297.
161 Cf. ibid., 309. See Dunning and Mennell, "Elias on Germany, Nazism and the Holocaust," 339–57.

the story of the Holocaust with the concept of anti-Semitism. After a synthetic presentation of the work, Postone reflects on the failure of sociology in the study of the Holocaust. A few years earlier, in 1986, in *Anti-Semitism and National Socialism*, he had explained the reasons why the Jews are considered both the source of financial capitalism and of international communism.[162] For him, the main reason lies in the status of the same subject, in the sense that sociology, in assimilating the positive sciences, forgets the content and the proper tools of sociological analysis, underestimating important categories, such as that of Durkheim's moral solidarity.[163] Postone, who reconsiders the entire conceptual notions and sociologists referring to Bauman, devotes much space to his methodology. He reflects on the issue of cooperation of the victims with National Socialism. Nevertheless, the more important factor is that, for Postone, the kind of relationship that Bauman traces between anti-Semitism and modernity is unsatisfactory. According to this explanation, modern anti-Semitism would be the expression of phobias *versus* modernity. Finally, "Although Bauman's position parallels central aspects of that of the Frankfurt school, they differ fundamentally as regards the issue of society and morality. Bauman does not appropriate their sophisticated attempts to consistently regard humans as culturally, socially, and historically constituted by socially grounding both conformist and oppositional worldviews."[164]

When *Modernity and the Holocaust* was disseminated in France, the country came to terms with one of the many contradictions resulting from modernity: the destruction of the Jews of Europe was interpreted as a unique event in the Western culture. Michael Bernstein to this end talks about obsession for "issues raised by the Nazi genocide":[165]

---

162 See Moishe Postone, "Anti-Semitism and National Socialism," in *Germans and Jews since the Holocaust*, ed. Anson Rabinbach and Jack D. Zipes (New York: Holmes and Meier, 1986), 302–14.
163 Cf. Halpert, "Early American Sociology and the Holocaust"; see also Hoover, "The Failure of the Social Science," 89–96.
164 Postone, review of *Modernity and the Holocaust*, 1523.
165 Cf. Silverman, *Facing Postmodernity*, 13

In France this obsession epitomizes a country ill at ease not only with its own involvement in genocide but also with the very ideals of modernity which France upheld.[166]

The reception of *Modernity and the Holocaust* in France coincided with a kind of awareness at the national level that allowed reflection on its historical specificity, especially, on the responsibilities that the Vichy regime had in the destruction of the Jews. However, the reflections on the Jewish question were only possible after the death of Charles de Gaulle:

> At the beginning of the 1970s, the death of Charles De Gaulle (1969) and the challenge to the great resistance myth that he personified—epitomized by Marcel Ophuls's documentary *Le Chagrin et la pitié* (1971) and Robert Paxton's book (1972) on Vichy France—opened the way to a reappraisal of the question of anti-Semitism and the relationship between Vichy and the "final solution."[167]

In the France of the 1970s, the Holocaust entered into public discourse and began to be regarded as the genocide of the Jews. All this happened in a period that followed the Eichmann trial, as the era of witnesses who survived the Holocaust that had just begun.[168] However, in France, Holocaust Studies were postmodern and closer to the positions of the Frankfurt School than the theory of Bauman, since they regarded the Holocaust as a decline and not a product of modernity.[169] In essence, the reflection of French scholars on the Jewish question went hand in hand with the crisis of modernity, when it started an animated cultural debate resulting from a series of circumstances—from the Yom Kippur War to the oil crisis, from the end of Fordism to the decline of the welfare state, passing through the collapse of public management and, theoretically,

---

166 Ibid.
167 Ibid., 12.
168 Cf. Annette Wieviorka, *L'era del testimone* (Milan: Cortina, 1999); Silverman, *Facing Postmodernity*, 12.
169 Cf. ibid., 20, 24, 31–32; Paul Gilroy, *The Black Atlantic: Modernity and Double Consciousness* (London: Verso, 1993).

through its deconstruction by Derrida, who criticizes the modern Western tradition.[170]

3.7.8. An Open Problem on the Modernity Thesis

The thesis of the modernity of the Holocaust argued by Bauman seemed to fail or, certainly, was put into discussion after the publication of *Neighbors* by Gross. Here arises a reevaluation of Bauman's book for the role that anti-Semitism and Polish nationalism ideologies played in the destruction of the Jews. This analysis seems to be crucial to confront the thesis of both authors. It is important to ask (and the question remains open) why Bauman, who escaped from Poland and became a refugee in England, after Australia, and Israel, due to Polish anti-Semitism, in his book explaining the Holocaust, sets apart anti-Semitism. He outlines instead modernity as the primary cause of the Holocaust. By asserting that it is a question in progress, the mind runs to the inevitability for Holocaust scholars to confront with it. One reason why his thesis fascinates and attracts numerous scholars (from historians to theologians, from politologists to anthropologists, and not only sociologists) even so far to define his book as the work wakes up the Holocaust sociology, might have to do with the political obligation European governments have had to face after the opening of Eastern archives, after 1989. In other words, that opening changed the entire situation by compelling an assumption of responsibilities for what happened. In addition, we can highlight that it deals with the anti-Semitic experiences of Bauman. Specifically, other scholars who experienced anti-Semitism dwell on it, but Bauman does not put it at the center of his thinking. Rather, he is for thought *sine ira ac studio*, avoiding explanations filled with too much personal meaning. Moreover, following the thinking of social sciences of 1960s onwards, he avoids monocausal explanations of phenomena. Hence, his modern devices that embrace and call for many other causes.[171] Bauman is aware of this scholarly opinion and is brilliant

---

170 Silverman, *Facing Postmodernity*, 17. Cf. Gillian Rose, *Judaism and Modernity: Philosophical Essays* (Cambridge, MA: Basil Blackwell, 1993).
171 Let me thank Giuseppe Veltri for having discussed the matter with me.

in arguing the modernity thesis in a better way: he does this speaking of the human suffering in society.

That the modernity thesis, as neutral, is purposeful in academic realms is evident in stressing further how it is an outcome of sociological thinking of 1980s. It reflects the political and economic changes of the period: the end of the welfare state and the beginning of globalization period, when an intensification of demands for rights is developed.

In saying that Bauman puts in progress the category of modernity, I refer also to the fact that modernity is a powerful tool: it calls politicians and politologists to a new politics, economists to a new economy, and so on. However, this notion fails to find the real roots of the Holocaust and to find those responsible for it. It misses in defining the perimeters of who perpetrated the Holocaust, failing, as a consequence, the coming to terms with penalties assessed against the perpetrators of the Holocaust. Paradoxically, but the line of reasoning is thin, it returns what happened during the Cold War, or its effects—that of the deresponsabilization, of not paying for crimes committed (government by government, country by country).

At the same time, the modernity thesis is neutral because it is not going to disturb anyone and it does not open extra halls of shame for the governments of the Cold War period, but, above all, it does not put anyone on trial, in the sense that modernity has no personal face, an individuality. By assuming the theory of modernity as source and cause of the Holocaust, circuitously, it happens that scholars attribute any accountability to modernity, in general. Strange to say, but people stop finding the guilty party, and it means, according to the law, that there is no unequivocal and definite condemnation of the individual guilty. And thus a destruction of people can always happen. As Neumann remembers, the Holocaust was not born with Nazism. Rather, it belongs to worldwide anti-Semitism.[172]

Generally, the category of ideology, literally "science of ideas," thanks to Destutt de Tracy, helps us better comprehend the power of destruction that the anti-Semitic ideology brings. The social construction of situations not corresponding to the truth, but assumed as real, hardly leans towards a

---

172   Cf. Neumann, *Behemoth*.

justice of the facts. In addition, it finds its legitimacy in scientific rhetoric and social engineering.

Reconsidering the thesis of modernity of the Holocaust, in some ways, means to compare the sociological approach with the historical one. It also can be argued that modernity as notion is meaningful, for Bauman, because in Poland, and in other communist countries, the passage to modernity had been much slower.

Bauman, in presenting modernity as the real cause for what happened to the Jews, does not contemplate the registration of acts committed. Namely, the so-called criminal responsibility for the mass murder cannot deal with the modernity of the Holocaust. For their specificity, the legal inquisition or the celebrations of the proceedings cannot admit the rationality of evil or pure evil as the main indicator of Nazi crimes. The criminal responsibility with the attribution of committed crimes, the clarification of the offense, and the definition of the offender have the practical utility of recognizing the offense, avoiding a possible prescription or its nonexistence. This is because it brings legal justice with it. At the head of a bureaucratic office, there is a juridical person, one who centralizes power relations, mediates directives received, or performs the final operations, and who is juridically responsible. Thus, to ensure the accountability for the action, it is feasible that any public courtroom can see and accuse the rationality of evil or the ideological-totalitarian regime. The modernity of the Holocaust removes instead the personal assumption of blame, in the sense that, if one imputes the Holocaust to modernity, "the empty dock" finishes in disregarding the evil done and even denying the Holocaust. Bauman unexpectedly risks obtaining this effect. Furthermore, the responsibility question defines the civil liability within a state when it recalls the element of territoriality, that is, the place where a crime is committed.[173] The accusing of single individuals, at fault in Nazi fascist crimes, is the duty imperative, necessary to break the rational, bureaucratic, and industrial chain set in motion by the Nazis; then, the execution of service orders, which reproduce the leadership command and imply the hierarchy of skills.

---

173 Cf. Silverman, *Facing Postmodernity*, 34.

In essence, *Modernity and the Holocaust* is a work that opened up a significant debate, among sociologists and historians, and that inevitably intersected with the reality of modern society, social devices, and national structures that facilitated or controlled extermination by fellow citizens. Both history and sociology, as academic disciplines, have to reconsider the practices and theoretical categories of modern anti-Semitism on the genocide in Eastern Europe: the matter lies in the appropriating of the specific (cultural, historical, and political) notions and tradition of those territories.[174]

Rereading the event through the category of modernity is certainly a fruitful exercise, but considered alone it resizes and flattens the reality.

Modernity and the Holocaust is presented in a postmodern world: it results from the post-1968 era and comes up between German philosophy, French sociology, and English beliefs. Bauman knows this. After his publication, or after 1989, a number of factors have to be considered instead: into the Holocaust fit not only the victims of death and concentration camps, but also the Jews who died in the forests or were killed in the Soviet territories with the help of local people, supporters, ordinary people *(anashim tovim)*. One cannot forget the akcjas, or pogroms, against the Jews that followed, in rapid succession, until after the end of the war, as evidenced by the massacres of whole communities perpetrated in Eastern Europe due to the anti-Semitic feelings. As Bauer notices, the same Bauman recognizes the scope of the anti-Semitism in *Endlösung*,[175] although in the work he then disassociates its determinant role.

At one point, Bauman writes that historian Martin Broszat has synthesized compelling results from a historical point of view:

> "In those cities and towns where Jews formed a large segment of the population, the relations between the Germans and the Jews were, even in the first years of the Nazi era, for the most part relatively good and hardly hostile." Nazi attempts to stir up antisemitic feelings and to re-forge static resentment into a dynamic one (a distinction

---

174 See Bauman, "On the Maturation of Socialism," *Telos* 47 (1981): 48–54; Augusta Dimou, *Entangled Paths towards Modernity: Contextualizing Socialism and Nationalism in the Balkans* (Budapest: Central European University Press, 2009).
175 See Bauer, *Rethinking the Holocaust*, 68–83.

aptly coined by Müller-Claudius)—i.e. to inflame the non-Party, ideologically uncommitted population into acts of violence against the Jews or at least into an active support of SA displays of force—foundered on the popular repugnance of physical coercion, on deep-seated inhibitions against inflicting pain and physical suffering, and on stubborn human loyalty to their neighbours, to people whom one knows and has charted into one's map of the world as persons, rather than anonymous specimens of type.[176]

However, this historian had been a member of the Nazi Party.

What matters is that Bauman overlooks the concept of citizenship: although Jews are citizens, they are perceived by their compatriots as a foreign body to be eliminated or as enemies to be fought as a threat to the health of the nation.[177] If stateless and without rights, like the Jews, as mentioned by Arendt in 1951, instead for Bauman the new pariahs are all those who live on the margins of a society that has dismissed the bonds of solidarity.[178] What was lacking, in the construction process of the modern state, the so-called nationalization, was a process of policies of integration for foreigners or policies for citizenship. When the achievement of certain rights had occurred or a change of balance in power relations had taken place, some social groups and existing hierarchies felt undermined: what Gérard Noiriel calls "déclassement" happens and that degenerates into forms of rejection against certain persons.[179] The protection of rights is largely dependent on the level of democracy present in the institutions, while their violation (the Nuremberg Laws or the waves of anti-Semitism) is linked to specific times of political and social crisis.[180] The Jews were foreigners and nationals at the same time.

---

176 Bauman, *Modernity and the Holocaust*, 186, see 223n10.
177 Cf. Enzo Traverso, "Immigrazione, antisemitismo e razzismo: Una sola storia?" *Contemporanea* 12, no. 1 (2009): 204; the author refers to Michael Foucault, *Bisogna difendere la società: Corso al Collège de France* (Milan: Feltrinelli, 1998 [1977]).
178 Cf. Bauman, *Modernity and Ambivalence*.
179 Cf. Traverso, *Immigrazione, antisemitismo e razzismo*, 205–6; see also Gérard Noiriel, *Immigration, antisémitisme et racisme en France (XIX–XX siècle): Discours publics, humiliations privées* (Paris: Fayard, 2007).
180 Cf. Luciano Morlino, *Democrazie e democratizzazioni* (Bologna: il Mulino, 2003).

It can be said that a series of very complex factors made the Holocaust possible: it is proper to consider all of them to avoid rendering the phenomenon incomprehensible or mysterious. Let me stress, here, that the failure of the modernity thesis or arguing for the amodernity of the Holocaust can be fertile. Bauman's thesis provides, for example, scholars with the analytical tools for starting new research in the areas of the former Soviet Union. In addition, it, indirectly, leads the same scholars to readdress the responsibility question: the accountability that any individual has (and for which he must pay the penalty) for having committed genocide.

3.8. SUMMARY

In this chapter, we have seen that post-Holocaust sociology engaged with issues of genocide traditionally located outside the realm of conventional sociology. My focal point was the sociological reworking of the concept of genocide, at a time when the bonds of national solidarity were continuously destroyed by a continuous proliferation of genocides. This new sociological shift at work was particularly visible in the 1980s. I delineated the ways in which the discipline arrived at the term "sociology of genocide" and came to speak of "genocidal states." By offering new studies that investigated what is meant by the order of terror as total institution or by dealing with the contradictions of modernity placed sociology of the 1980s in a noteworthy light. Sociology combined well with history in handling questions such as resistance and the banality of good. Much space was dedicated to the concept of social suffering: thanks to Bauman, who had repersonified human suffering in making the Jews the emblem of all the oppressed, in line with the social sciences of the 1980s. Also seen was the significance of the opening of the Eastern archives after the collapse of the Soviet Union. Whether Bauman's book did indeed wake up post-Holocaust sociology was also put into question.

CHAPTER 4
The Problem of the Holocaust after 1989

Why women? Why should a book on the Holocaust—which targeted all Jews for annihilation irrespective of their sex or age or any other social characteristics—focus on women?
—**Dalia Ofer and Lenore J. Weitzman (1998)**

Another political factor that contributed to the bracketing of the Holocaust was the rhetoric of the Cold War (during which the old enemy Germany had become an ally, and the Soviet Union, the old ally, had become the new enemy) and its conceptual foundation, the theory of totalitarianism. In this context there was no space for a particularistic version of the Holocaust. Instead the victims of concentration camps were primarily depicted as political prisoners.
—**Daniel Levy and Natan Sznaider (2002)**

Birnbaum attributes the rise of modern anti-Semitism to popular reaction against the strong state. Where a strong state is perceived as having imposed on society the emancipation of the Jews, anti-Semitism tends to be strong (for example, Germany and France). On the other hand, where the state is relatively weak and Jews obtained equal rights through society rather than the state, anti-Semitism tends to be muted (for example, the USA and Great Britain).
—**William I. Brustein and Ryan D. King (2004)**

4.1. AFTER THE FALL OF THE BERLIN WALL

Holocaust sociology after 1989 is important, especially because, for this discipline, the 1990s were characterized by an experimental unceasing period of subdivision into original interminable substrands. Therefore, it is important to try to understand how these different substrands approach the topic with their typical devices. This chapter is concerned with the sort of scientific contagion of sociology with other social sciences: mostly, politology, statics, and demography. It seems that sociology went in different directions, and post-Holocaust sociology followed this trend. This new approach was possible after 1989, the year in which the collapse of the Berlin Wall marked the end of bipolarism and signaled the start of a long series of political transformations, and everyone understood that the Iron Curtain dividing the world was no more. From that event it becomes possible to account for, step-by-step, any nation's story and any national Holocaust history in a manner that was either not admissible or unthinkable under communism.

The resonance of these political events and, especially, the power to reproduce and disseminate durable representations of these important changes are prominent in post-Holocaust sociological studies. Scholars were now able to elaborate the past without the shadow of Cold War ideas. As well stressed by Daniel Levy and Natan Sznaider, "The end of the Cold War has led to a fundamental change in the parameters of collective memories in Europe and made possible attempts to produce shared cosmopolitan memories."[1]

In this period, *Modernity and the Holocaust* attained universal approval: in essence, everyone welcomed it, and it was an enchanting book. Bauman's sociological interpretation marks Holocaust Studies in general: historical, politological, and philosophical researches seemed like they could not do without it. This is because of his key reading of the "rationality of the Holocaust," which has fascinated scholars ever since.[2]

As we saw in the previous chapter, the category of modernity is not going to disturb any conscience or any government. It is neutral, perfectly scientific, as the postindustrial era requires. Nevertheless, the efficiency of this category is questioned by recent historiography (possible after the end of bipolarism), as demonstrated by the debate resulting from the publication, in 2000, of Gross's volume on the massacre of the Polish Jewish community in Jedwabne on July 10, 1941.[3]

---
1 Levy and Sznaider, "Memory Unbound," 100.
2 Cf. Postone, review of *Modernity and the Holocaust*, 1521–23.
3 See notes 97, 99, above (chapter 2). Consider Simcha Epstein, "From Anti-Semitism of 19th Century to Nazi Anti-Semitism," paper presented at Yad Vashem, Jerusalem, August 22, 2011.

"The Cold War," Levy and Sznaider write, "was an alliance of values as much as of interests."⁴ The opening of archives allowed a review of the history of former Soviet satellites and, consequently, an accounting for the number of dead Jews in the Soviet territories and the extermination methods adopted. The huge difference compared to other parts of occupied Europe was in the public nature of the genocide and the collaboration of local people in the slaughters. By the beginning of the 1990s, there was a profound conversion in historiographical practices, after decades during which the Holocaust and its memory was off limits in the Eastern communist territories. The archives in Eastern Europe were opened to historians, and a new phase of historiography commenced, revising and openly placing previous results into question, but the historical overview of sociological studies of this period instead presents several difficulties. As Antonella Salomoni writes, "At the stage in which historians prevail, however, the pressure of sociologists arises because of their ambition to offer a kind of overall story of the Holocaust, shaping it as a specific line."⁵ Nevertheless, the end of bipolarism constituted a watershed that overturned the established systems of thought:

> When the uniting interests and values of anti-communism vanished, international cooperation had to be reorganized on a new basis. The attempt to articulate and organize around new values has been a conscious one over the last ten years. And it is no accident that the Holocaust has come to play a major role in that reorganization. It has emerged precisely because of its status as an unquestioned moral value on which all people can supposedly agree.⁶

The theme of the Holocaust, because of the influences upon sociology, started to be analyzed and mixed with supplementary issues, such as migration to Israel, the birth of the State of Israel, and the experience of second-generation survivors. Furthermore, it is relevant to stress that while the globalization process reached its peak, some sociologists (like Levy and Sznaider, in the wake of Beck and Alexander) began to show

---

4 Levy and Sznaider, "Memory Unbound," 96.
5 Salomoni, *I libri sulla Shoah*, 4 (my translation).
6 Levy and Sznaider, "Memory Unbound," 96–97.

some sensitivity towards aspects of the global society, so much so that the concepts derived by observing this phenomenon were placed at the center of their analysis on the Holocaust. In other words, their works constituted a new current of sociological strand and a new path for Holocaust sociology because of the original analytical categories they introduced.

Thus, in the last twenty years, Holocaust sociology has differed from the earlier tradition, both in perspective and in research methods. The works of this period, elaborated in the most intense moment of the globalization process, have been affected by the global dimension, which has been ever-present. This means that they present a multidimensional view not referring to a physical space and having no ties with a specific territory. Because, after 1989, the Holocaust has sometimes been studied in a confusing manner, let me here try to put some order to it by examining some major conceptual themes and recalling what Gerson and Wolf have already synthetized in *Sociology Confronts the Holocaust*.[7] Those themes are *collective memory*, *gender*, and *collective action*, which can be found in the general discourse of sociology of the period, given that they constitute the principal notions introduced and recurring in sociological debates.

4.2. FROM COLLECTIVE NATIONAL MEMORY TO COSMOPOLITAN MEMORY

It is crucial to retrace what "collective memory" means. First, it is assumed that no human life can be rebuilt outside of its territory, alluding to the deep connection between the "reinterpretation of experienced sense" and the physical location where the event or object of the narrative reelaboration occurs:[8] "Halbwachs never provides a clear definition of *collective memory*. Synthesizing several of his formulations, I would say that the collective memory of a group is, for Halbwachs, a set of representations of the past that are stored and transmitted among its members through their interactions.

---

7 See Gerson and Wolf, *Sociology Confronts the Holocaust*, 3–37.
8 Carlo Socco, "Landscape, Collective Memory and Cultural Identity," paper presented at the forum Italian Landscapes for the Government of Transformations, organized by Benetton Foundation, Castelfranco Veneto, May 26–29, 1999; see also Eugenio Turri, *Il paesaggio come teatro: Dal territorio vissuto al territorio rappresentato* (Venice: Marsilio, 1998).

Sets of events and concepts mentioned, it is also a common way to interpret them."[9] Thus, the collective memory as a set of traces of the past that one social group transmits from one generation to the next, in connection with own traditions and history, constitutes the expression of the identity of a group.

According to Nora, starting from the 1990s, a new era commenced for Holocaust sociology, marked deeply by the weight of collective memory.[10] As Traverso stresses, the extermination of the Jews became a central event in the contemporary world, but only when Nazism started to belong to a distant past. In the 1940s, "it was unimaginable to begin a university career preparing a thesis on the extermination of the Jews—Raul Hilberg's memories are eloquent in this regard—but now this issue has turned into a real scientific discipline." In addition, for the edition of his book, he writes that it is "inevitably indebted to a *Zeitgeist*, that of the current turn of the century. Thirty years ago it would have been inconceivable."[11] What has led to this shift, up until the contemporary and ever-increasing attention, is a matter of considerable interest, as Traverso points out. There have been several factors, such as the persistence of anti-Semitism in different realms and in postwar international politics, in the removal or omission of the memory of what happened to the Jews:

> The immediate aftermath of the Second World War was marked by a silence concerning the destruction of European Jewry, which at that time did not even have a name yet. It was broadly subsumed under the atrocities of the war. The idea of the Holocaust did not spring full-grown from the facts. And yet, surprisingly perhaps, all

---

9   Paolo Jedlowski, *Memoria, esperienza e modernità: Memorie e società nel XX secolo* (Milan: Angeli, 2002), 50–51 (my translation).
10 Cf. Pierre Nora, "Mémoire collective," in *La nouvelle histoire*, ed. Jacques Le Goff, Roger Chartier, and Jacques Revel (Paris: Retz, 1978), 398–401.
11 Cf. Traverso, *Auschwitz e gli intellettuali*, 227–28, 237–38, see note 4 (my translation). On the difficulties concerning the publication of studies dealing with the Jewish question, reconsider Neurath's case or Hughes's story. Apropos of the powerlessness of pursuing a university career by studying the subject of the Holocaust, see Halpert, *Early American Sociology and the Holocaust*, 6–7, and again the case of Hughes, who held a course on the Holocaust at McGill University but with a different name; see note 205, above (chapter 1).

the "facts" were there in the beginning. The Nuremberg trials were held in November 1945, where the highest Nazi officials still alive and under guard were accused of killing 5.7 million Jews as part of a conscious plan. Calling up the original document on the Internet reveals a 226-screen-long document. But only three are taken up with the extermination the Jews. And that is a fairly graphic representation of how the Holocaust was originally conceived: as one in an almost endless list of Nazi crimes. It was perceived as part of a larger practice of war crimes. To be sure, Auschwitz was certainly addressed by intellectuals and others, but the Holocaust did not permeate public discourse nor was its commemoration institutionalized.[12]

The Cold War diverted many things from their proper course. It modified, in Central and Eastern Europe, and worldwide, the methods and means for telling about the past. Here, let me borrow Traverso's thinking: that, at the end of the conflict, the Western bloc overlooked that Germany was the successor country of Nazism. The Federal Republic was part of the Atlantic Pact; it was going to constitute a free trade asset for the Western world in contrast to Soviet totalitarianism:[13]

> Germany, Israel and the USA had different motivations for being silent about this past, but there were also nation-transcending commonalities that informed the postwar references to the Holocaust.
> … An acknowledgment of political responsibility for the "crimes committed by a small murderous gang of Nazis in the name of Germany" was not only marked by this kind of linguistic distancing but also confined to a few voices. References to the Holocaust were frequently articulated in the broader context of war atrocities and as a measure of German suffering.[14]

---

12   Levy and Sznaider, "Memory Unbound," 93–94 (authors' in-text citations omitted).
13   Cf. Traverso, *Auschwitz e gli intellettuali*, 231–32.
14   Levy and Sznaider, "Memory Unbound," 94.

The competitive coexistence and, especially, the equivalence between Nazism and communism "puts in brackets" the story of the Holocaust, making it a Nazi regime product.[15] When I began work on this book, I had only some notions about the Iron Curtain and post-Holocaust memory. My goal was to awaken sleeping consciences by returning to the discourse about denazification, which had decelerated the practice of collective memory and the process of accountability for what happened. It was necessary to create a context for the Holocaust victims and for the lives around them. The denazification program betrayed proposed expectations, such as those of permanently and totally removing Nazism from Germany. As Traverso explains, Adorno's formula, according to which the real danger was the survival of fascism, was concrete in post-Holocaust governments:[16]

> Talk about a "European Civil War"—a term that later would become a code word for historical revisionism in Germany—was a pervasive rhetorical strategy among leading politicians and other public figures. … The Cold War, together with a focus on the *Wirtschaftswunder* (economic miracle) provided Germany with a universal frame of reference. Modernization, both in economic and cultural terms and as a paradigm for sociological analysis, dominated the public imagination.[17]

Because of a series of political events that promoted increasingly broader reflections, starting from the 1960s (contemporary to the initial processing of collective memory) what happened to the Jews of Europe in the twentieth century became progressively visible. Here, what is relevant is remembering that "Europe" and "twentieth century" constitute two central categories: of space and time. They have been used to identify a given phenomenon within precise boundaries. Why is this important? Because such spatial-temporal demarcation uses the same elements (time and space) utilized to define conceptually the modern nation-state.

---

15   Cf. Traverso, *Auschwitz e gli intellettuali*, 227–37.
16   Ibid., 231–32.
17   Levy and Sznaider, "Memory Unbound," 94. The success of the category of modernity arises in this context.

Additionally, the same categories have led the scholars Levy and Sznaider to speak, at the beginning of the twenty-first century, of national collective memory. The specificity of this analytical tool (which involves the concepts of memory, society, and nation) is that of focusing on something (in our case it is the trauma of the Holocaust) that occurs in a given time and within well-established national boundaries.

What makes new and original Levy and Sznaider's Holocaust discourse is that "the conventional concept of 'collective memory' is firmly embedded within the 'Container of the Nation-State.'"[18] This means that the notion of national collective memory goes hand in hand with (or derives from) the concept of the modern state, to which drafting the element of territorial borders contributes. Based on the fact that the modern national state exists if there are elements of territory, people (residing on the same territorial space), and sovereignty, the national collective memory arises when the same community that dwells in the same territory, which has the same culture and speaks the same language and so on (i.e., it belongs to the same country), shares and then reprocesses the same event.

In Levy and Sznaider's words, "the nation is the basis for authentic feelings and collective memory."[19] This requires that the fact itself has as its subject and addressee of the memory only those who belong to the same national reality: it is not legitimate to go beyond that. And thus in this sphere of memory, the boundaries of the nation are not exceeded: they constitute the inner element of the modern state. What sociologist Maurice Halbwachs says about social memory and collective memory helps to better understand Levy and Sznaider's discourse. Briefly, in the first case, Halbwachs means the memory of things, to which one, or the group to which one belongs, has a personal and direct experience. It is the story itself that is, before it becomes history, celebrated and relived through the memorials from the group that has had the experience: in our case, for instance, the social memory of the Holocaust belongs to and is limited to the generation that lived during the war period. In the second case, namely, in historical

---

18 Ibid., 88.
19 Ibid., 90–91.

memory, Halbwachs includes the memory mediated by books, movies, and so on.[20] In this discussion, the persons concerned are, on the one hand, the Germans, as the perpetrators of mass murder, and on the other, the Jews, as victims. In the modern nation-state, Jewish people are considered interstitial, that is, a nation in between spaces.[21] Other individuals seem (and are) cut off, since they do not appear to fall within the national sphere of Jews or German Nazis. According to that, the persons involved are the Jews, as victims, and the Germans, as guilty of genocide. It means that only those who are linked to the event, due to the national factor, and belong to this collective memory, which, in turn, identifies them, are required to commemorate and to reprocess their trauma or their faults.[22] This means that the memory remains within national boundaries in which the event has occurred. To summarize, we may speak of national memory when the event (which has to be remembered) recalls the same schema that defines the nation-state: if modernity is concerned with the border issue, territorial *limen*, and it results historically in the construction of the nation-state, then in the same way the collective national memory coincides with the elements of modernity, with national borders. However, what is innovative is that this issue—the modern collective memory—constitutes another way to define modernity itself:

> The Holocaust, or rather the representations that produce shared memories, is a paradigmatic case for the relation of memory and modernity. Modernity, until recently one of the primary analytic and normative frameworks for intellectual self-understanding, is itself questioned through memories of the Holocaust. On this view, the mass murder of European Jews by the Nazis is not considered as

---

20 See Maurice Halbwachs, *La Mémoire collective* (Paris: Presses universitaires de France, 1950); Olimpia Affuso, *Il Magazine della memoria: I media e il ricordo degli avvenimenti pubblici* (Rome: Carocci, 2010).
21 See Irena Steinfeldt et al., *How Was It Humanly Possible? A Study of Perpetrators and Bystanders during the Holocaust* (Jerusalem: Yad Vashem, 2002). On the political construction of foreigners, see Beck, *I rischi della libertà*, 167–95.
22 Cf. Levy and Sznaider, "Memory Unbound," 88; see also Anthony D. Smith, *Nations and Nationalism in a Global Era* (Cambridge, MA: Blackwell, 1995).

a German-Jewish tragedy but as a tragedy of reason or of modernity itself.[23]

When Levy and Sznaider say that the Holocaust "was not perceived as a timeless and de-territorialized measuring stick for good and evil, but instead as a terrible aspect of a particular era,"[24] they explain how the theory of modernity of the Holocaust justified the silence about the Holocaust in the context of the Cold War. However, this remains a good open question.

During the 1990s, after the collapse of frontiers of the bipolarism era, it became common among scholars to speak of nation and national memory. In addition, exactly when national limits fell, as a product of globalization process (i.e., when the nation as nation-physically and conceptually), several Holocaust scholars started to deal with nation and memory issues in their reflections. Here, let me mention a few cases to introduce the context. For instance, *The War After* by Karpf, a writer of the second generation who tells the experience of personal pain of parents in the light of the collective experience of the entire Jewish people, and *Genre Memories and Memory Genres* by Olick. Both works, though in a different way (Karpf's piece puts the role of victims into the foreground—she traces the lives of her family, their marginalization in the Nazi era, and their obsession with death after the Holocaust—while Olick's research focuses on the perpetrators), confine the extermination of European Jews to the specific context of the twentieth century. In this manner, they make the memory exclusive to people who directly or indirectly lived through that experience.[25] It can be said that their works became part of the thinking of national collective memory. Among scholars, the idea of conceiving the Holocaust as trauma came to the fore.[26] This means that it did not coincide

---

23 Levy and Sznaider, "Memory Unbound," 88.
24 Cf. ibid., 95.
25 Cf. Anne Karpf, *The War After: Living with the Holocaust* (London: Heinemann, 1996); Jeffrey K. Olick, "Genre Memories and Memory Genres: A Dialogical Analysis of May 8, 1945 Commemorations in the Federal Republic of Germany," *American Sociological Review* 64 (1999): 381–402.
26 Cf. Alexa R. Kolbi-Molinas, *The Secret of Redemption. Memory and Resistance: A Lesson for the 21st Century* (New York: The Elie Wiesel Foundation for Humanity, 2000); Alexander et

exclusively with the extermination perpetrated by the Nazis against the Jews: it was something more. A trauma crosses consciences universally, taken as a reference model for further traumatic events. Unknowingly, this original conceptualization paves the way to the cosmopolitan memory, which recalls the concepts of accountability and responsibility:

> As the same Cassin had said in a report to the French government at the beginning of the works, in February 1947: "If men want to be protagonists of the whole of human society against arbitrariness, they must assume in exchange, as citizens of the world, their duties and their responsibilities."[27]

For the same reasons, in more recent years, the concept of anti-Semitism has been primarily due to Brustein, who delineates the anti-Semitic phenomenon in *Roots of Hate*, as we will see at the end of this chapter. Episodes of contemporary anti-Semitism acquaint scholars with the Holocaust matter.[28]

4.2.1. Levy and Sznaider in the Wake of Ulrich Beck

The postcommunism years have been experiencing a collective memory boom. Two scholars, Daniel Levy and Natan Sznaider, especially, are distinguished in collective memory studies of the Holocaust,[29] because the past, remembering Halbwachs's words, "is not preserved, but it is

---

al., *Cultural Trauma and Collective Identity*; Olimpia Affuso, "Jeffrey C. Alexander—il processo del trauma culturale," in *M come Memoria: La memoria nella teoria sociale*, ed. Teresa Grande and Olimpia Affuso (Naples: Liguori Editore, 2012), 215–43.

27 Zappalà, *La tutela internazionale dei diritti umani*, 29 (my translation).
28 With King, Brustein wrote an essay on anti-Semitism. Helen Fein measured anti-Semitic phenomena in different European countries (Great Britain, France, Germany, Italy, and Romania) from 1899 to 1939. Cf. William I. Brustein and Ryan D. King, "Anti-Semitism in Europe before the Holocaust," *International Political Science Review* 25, no. 1 (2004): 35–53, doi:10.1177/0192512104038166.
29 Levy and Sznaider, "Memory Unbound"; Daniel Levy and Natan Sznaider, "The Institutionalization of Cosmopolitan Morality: The Holocaust and Human Rights," *Journal of Human Rights* 3, no. 2 (2004): 143–57, doi:10.1080/1475483042000210685.

reconstructed starting from the interests of the present."[30] For both authors, in the global age, or at a time that nation-states are no longer considered as the primary actors in political, social, and economic life, it is crucial to build a collective memory crossing state boundaries to reach a full moral responsibility and political accountability about the extermination of the Jews.

International criminal law, born from the Nuremberg trials and Tokyo tribunals, has suffered almost immediately "the paralyzing effects of ideological opposition."[31] And, "global media representations, among others, create new cosmopolitan memories, providing new epistemological vantage points and emerging moral-political interdependencies."[32] The transformations that have occurred in the last twenty years, linked to the transition from modernity to globalization, give rise, in a broad sense, to the need for a new form of universalism, in the political and cultural sphere, focusing on the multidimensional nature of the events.[33]

Levy and Sznaider, trained in the school of Ulrich Beck (professor of sociology at the Ludwig-Maximilians-Universität, in the heart of Munich, at the Fondation Maison des Sciences de l'Homme (FMSH) in Paris, and at the London School of Economics), think of modernity as a project in accordance with the essential current of German social philosophy from Habermas onwards. The originality the two disciples of Beck (famous for his studies on modernity and for the concepts of "second modernity" and "theory of risk") deals with the process of modernization. It is a reflexive thought that opens towards fresh political and social scenarios. In essence, from Beck's theory revolving around the concepts of risk, individualization, and subpolitics, Levy and Sznaider take into consideration, in contemporary Holocaust sociology, primarily the third aspect, that of subpolitics. On this, which Beck calls "risk society" (where the places, times, and media of politics continuously change), or "second modernity," especially by the mid-1980s, Levy and Sznaider focus their attention in comprehending the Holocaust memory. In fact, in the new

---

30 Affuso, *Il Magazine della memoria*, 21.
31 Zappalà, *La tutela internazionale dei diritti umani*, 120.
32 Levy and Sznaider, "Memory Unbound," 87.
33 See Bertarnd Badie, *La Fin des territoires: Essai sur le désordre international et l'utilité sociale du respect* (Paris: Fayard, 1995).

contemporary space, democratic rights and obligations, along with private interests related to work, ask for a reconsideration. For instance, if the rules of profit, on the one hand, lead to an expansion of national markets on a global scale, then, on the other, they lead to new forms of political participation that break the boundaries of traditional politics, putting into play additional institutions outside of parliaments, governments, and national political parties. The result is a completely changed political and moral dimension. What matters is that, according to Levy and Sznaider, the studies on the collective memory of the Holocaust have to be rethought in the light of globalization phenomenon, since globalization restructures social life in a plurality of spaces and times. Subsequent to 1989, what the two authors investigate is very innovative. While new historiographical practices—resulting from the opening of archives in Eastern Europe—call into question Bauman's thesis, Levy and Sznaider wonder if the thesis of the modernity of the Holocaust (linked to the concept of the modern state) is still valid in a historical-political context in which the modern national state is in crisis and loses its centrality. Additionally, they ask if it is more appropriate to find new sociological categories for the study of the Holocaust:[34]

> Can this event be memorialized by people who do not have a direct connection to it? At the beginning of the third millennium, memories of the Holocaust facilitate the formation of transnational memory cultures, which in turn, have the potential to become the cultural foundation for global human rights politics. This nation-transcending dynamic stands at the center of our sociological analysis.[35]

Levy and Sznaider identify original means and procedures to investigate the phenomenon within works on collective memory in the age of globalization. In addition, once identified, their main objective becomes that of analyzing these different forms of memory.[36] In a globalized society, even memory

---

34 See David Harvey, *The Condition of Postmodernity: An Enquiry into the Origins of Cultural Change* (Oxford: Blackwell, 1989); Joseph E. Stiglitz, *Globalization and Its Discontents* (New York: W. W. Norton, 2002).
35 Levy and Sznaider, "Memory Unbound," 88.
36 See ibid., 87–88.

changes and transcends national boundaries. What is important now is to see in which way Levy and Sznaider analyze how the transition happens from the national to the cosmopolitan memory.[37] At the time that the states begin to be traversed by the flow of goods, capital, ideas, information, and, not least, human beings, even cultural dimensions fluctuate and, in our case, the memory of the events related to a nation mutate.[38]

When Levy and Sznaider speak of cosmopolitan memory, they reelaborate Beck's principle of cosmopolitanism, which overcomes the dualisms of global/local and national/international. Based on this thought, they conceive the end of a memory relegated to national borders, that is, defined according to the categories of physical modern space, geometric and unidimensional, and the practice of a memory always exercisable and present, even in regions with boundaries, which are definable in a conventional way.[39] Clearly, this thought, when it puts aside the assumptions of nationalism, according to which the individual regional differences are incorporated and lost in a wider territorial-national context, which historically takes the form of the nation-state, nullifies the specificities of a nation. In the past, the process of modern national unification has canceled those ethnic and national singularities on the territory forming the nation-state. However, it is crucial to remember that the modern state, while achieving the nationalist project, establishes some limits with other nation-states through so-called state boundaries.

Levy and Sznaider aim at moving towards a memory unbound, that is, not bound by national borders. Especially, their category of cosmopolitanism, in the sense of beautifying—from the Greek κοσμέω ("to order")—the inhabited world, "combines appreciation of difference and alterity with attempts to conceive of new democratic forms of

---

37 Cf. Benedict Anderson, *Imagined Communities: Reflections on the Origin and Spread of Nationalism* (London: Verso, 1983).
38 About the despatialization and respatialization of geographic borders, see Arjun Appadurai, *Modernity at Large: Cultural Dimensions of Globalization* (Minneapolis: University of Minnesota Press, 1996); Appadurai, ed., *Globalization* (Durham, NC: Duke University Press, 2001).
39 Cf. Daniele Archibugi, David Held, and Martin Köhler, eds., *Re-imagining Political Community: Studies in Cosmopolitan Democracy* (Cambridge: Polity 1998).

political rule beyond the nation-State."[40] It refers to a process of globalization or extension of the confines that transfers categories or social phenomena from a global to a local community. The same process creates interdependencies among morality (inner *forum*), politics, and the public life of persons, building a bridge between the spheres, which exceeds delimited margins. The authors investigate "what happens when an increasing number of people in Western mass-consumer societies no longer define themselves (exclusively) through the nation or their ethnic belonging?" They ask, "Can we imagine collective memories that transcend national and ethnic boundaries?" What leads to a "transnational memory" is the recognition of otherness, which is the basis of Beck's principle of cosmopolitanism. In addition, there is a concept of opposites: good and evil. In this manner, they do not conceive the Holocaust as something specific typically of the Jews of Europe, but as an event that must belong to every inhabitant of the world, "a formative event" that offers "the foundations for a new cosmopolitan memory, a memory transcending ethnic and national boundaries,"[41] as a part of the national identity of every man:

> The so-called responsibility to protect is the last frontier of national sovereignty. The fundamental idea is to impose on States the obligation to defend its citizens and to ensure their safety and respect for the most basic rights, preventing the State from massacring its civilian population; the shield of sovereignty falls. National sovereignty becomes responsible sovereignty, as the final document of the Summit of the UN General Assembly in 2005 stated, when the state protects its population from genocide, war crimes, ethnic cleansing and crimes against humanity. This responsible sovereignty leads to prevent such crimes, incitement to commit them by means of strategies, appropriate means to do that.[42]

---

40 Ulrich Beck and Edgar Grande, *Cosmopolitan Europe* (Cambridge: Polity, 2007 [2004]), 12.
41 Levy and Sznaider, "Memory Unbound," 88. Cf. Levy and Sznaider, "The Institutionalization of Cosmopolitan Morality," 152; Elihu Katz and Ruth Katz, "Life and Death among the Binaries: Notes on Jeffrey Alexander's Constructionism," in Alexander, *Remembering the Holocaust*, 156–70.
42 Zappalà, *La tutela internazionale dei diritti umani*, 132.

This is possible when the Holocaust is taken as a paradigm of all tragic events. In 2011, Raphael Vago, during a seminar, spoke, as Bauer did, of the uniqueness of the *Shoah*. According to the Vago, of Tel Aviv University, the globalization of the Holocaust translates a very important idea: that every person can be a potential victim, perpetrator, or bystander. In this way, the interpretation of the Holocaust does not belong only to the first generation of survivors, but it transcends national borders of Europe: hence the concept of globalization of the Holocaust. This reinforces Bauer's thesis, who speaks of the unprecedented nature of the Holocaust. This new interpretation returns, once again, a specific identity, a name (*yad vashem*) to the victims.[43]

The goal of Levy and Sznaider is that of universalizing knowledge by creating a public discourse that does not take the boundaries of the nation-state into account. Along these lines, the categories of space and time, at the basis of modernity, cease to be linear: from their relation the physical quantity (speed) that accelerates the bonds and the possibility of meeting among many societies spreads. The relations generated are of two kinds: they can have a reticular form or continuous streams that, in any case, do not consider limits or established conventions. The speed transforming space into temporalized dimensions and making time spatialized comes out from the rapport of space above time. Namely, it allows individuals belonging to different places to associate themselves with events occurring in the same time.[44]

The collective memory of the Holocaust no longer involves only the direct actors (the Jews, affected by the genocide, and the Nazis, perpetrators of the crime): Jews become universal victims, and, as such, they belong to all the territories in which genocide is perpetrated, while the Nazis become

---

43 Cf. Bauer, *Rethinking the Holocaust*, 14–67. The talk in question was "Shoah and Genocide," paper presented at the International School for Holocaust Studies for the ICHEIC Program for Holocaust Education in Europe, Yad Vashem, Jerusalem, August 28, 2011. See Fackenheim, "Jewish Faith and the Holocaust"; Fackenheim, *Quest for Past and Future*, 17–20; Fackenheim, *God's Presence in History*, 87–88.
44 For the time–space compression, see Stephen Kern, *The Culture of Time and Space, 1880–1918: With a New Preface* (Cambridge, MA: Harvard University Press, 2003); Gabriella Paolucci, ed., *Cronofagia: La contrazione del tempo e dello spazio nell'era della globalizzazione* (Milan: Guerini, 2003).

the perpetrators par excellence of the crime. In thinking this way, the social evil assumes a cosmopolitan dimension that allows not taking into account the specificity of the victims or perpetrators at a given time and in a given spatial context:[45]

> Even though the Holocaust and the fate of the Jews remained a neglected aspect of the Nuremberg trial, it formed the backdrop for its universalistic message. The struggle at Nuremberg was conceived as one between civilization and barbarism. Civilization was the victim, Nazi barbarism the perpetrator. And this is how we initially got from the Holocaust to the concepts of "humanity" and of "crimes" against them. The Jews were there, but they were standing in for "humanity as a whole." This version then guided the legal argumentation, as indicated in the following statement by the chief American prosecutor at Nuremberg, Supreme Court Justice Robert H. Jackson: "The crime against the Jews, insofar as it is a crime against humanity and not a war crime as well, is one which we indict because of its close association with the crime against peace."[46]

As Levy and Sznaider underline, this interpretation brings substantial benefits to sociological theory, since it rethinks the phenomenon of the Holocaust with categories taken from contemporary social reality, and the universalization of the genocide of the Jews allows for recognition, in a global society, of the same conditions that permitted the Holocaust. Levy and Sznaider pave the way to recognizing these dangers that may reoriginate the genocide. The universalization process of the Holocaust does not lead to a loss of recognition of the specific event: on the contrary, the Jews are assumed to be universal victims, and the Nazis (and those who support them) to be universal criminals. This procedure of reprocessing memory has the positive claim to identifying all the victims of all genocides and the perpetrators of the corresponding crimes, because, as both authors stress, "One of the central questions relates to the 'right' or 'appropriate' form to commemorate

---

45 Cf. Levy and Sznaider, "The Institutionalization of Cosmopolitan Morality," 152–53.
46 Ibid., 149 (author's in-text citations omitted).

the event. Who does the Holocaust 'belong' to in the global age? Can it only belong to the Jewish victims of the German perpetrators?"[47]

By reflecting on this, the solidarity of which Durkheim spoke (at least this is the intention of Levy and Sznaider's lesson) is no longer national. It transcends territorial boundaries, moving towards a universal consciousness in the sense that the event or the location of a genocide belongs to everyone, even to those who do not reside in that place, or, rather, who do not belong to that place at that time. That is, the authors address a cosmopolitan collective responsibility that makes each victim or perpetrator of crimes a citizen of the world and no longer only of the state where genocide happens—all citizens of the world, in the name of universal citizenship, are called to act against the violation of universal rights. The price of required responsibility is very high, since it strains and speeds up, in the same way as the globalization process, the timing of intervention.[48]

4.3. BETWEEN MEMORY AND POLITICAL ACTING: THE HOLOCAUST IN GLOBAL SOCIETY

> The term Holocaust has passed from an abstract universal, to a set of very particularistic and/or national meanings, back to what we have elsewhere referred to as cosmopolitan memories. The Holocaust is now a concept that has been dislocated from space and time precisely because it can be used to dramatize any act of injustice, racism, or crime perpetrated anywhere on the planet.[49]

Beck repeatedly stresses that we cannot undisputedly accept the distinction between national and international after the end of bipolarism, by the breaking of the East–West conflict. In this way, entirely original dimensions are introduced in the historical space of Europe. This means that the Nazi

---

47 Levy and Sznaider, "Memory Unbound," 92–93.
48 See Immanuel Wallerstein, "Citizens All? Citizens Some! The Making of the Citizen," *Comparative Studies in Society and History* 45, no. 4 (2003): 650–79; cf. Zappalà, *La tutela internazionale dei diritti umani*.
49 Levy and Sznaider, "The Institutionalization of Cosmopolitan Morality," 156.

horror, extermination of the Jews, and ethnic persecution can no longer be investigated according to traditional categories of a national perspective, but only in accordance with "methodological nationalism."[50]

Levy and Sznaider use the analytical category of globalization (which is, we can say, procedural-methodological) to speak of cosmopolitan memory issues. By virtue of the unfinished broaching of boundaries that widen the spaces of memory, albeit for a short while, both scholars try to outline a history of representations of the Holocaust, in the last fifty years, and take the area of three countries as an explanatory model—the United States, Germany, and Israel. In addition, the authors divide the globalization process of memory into three chronological stages on the basis that every historical process, and therefore the social construction of memory, is prepared by a number of events. They are the postwar phase, the period of the Cold War, and the years following the Cold War. Here, let me briefly report what Levy and Sznaider investigate to stress better their lesson in post-Holocaust sociology or in the Holocaust sociology of the globalization age.

They consider the first postwar years as the founding stage of the process of memory based on three key events: the Nuremberg trials, which established the "legal notion of crimes against humanity,"[51] the UN Universal Declaration of Human Rights (UDHR), and, the UN Convention on Genocide, which set up "the foundation of human rights regimes."[52] Our authors reflect on this UDHR in a period after the end of the Cold War. As Beck highlights, the Nuremberg trials, their internationality, led to the formation of juridical categories and of a court that go beyond state sovereignty to ensure justice for citizens whose rights have been violated by their own state. In accordance with article 6 (c) of the constitutive act of the International Military Tribunal at Nuremberg, "any civilian population"[53] refers to the end of the principle of nationality according to which the imputation is made within certain boundaries. Another new juridical

---

50   Cf. Beck and Grande, *Cosmopolitan Europe*, 132.
51   Levy and Sznaider, "The Institutionalization of Cosmopolitan Morality," 149.
52   Ibid., 143.
53   United Nations, Charter of the International Military Tribunal—Annex to the Agreement for the Prosecution and Punishment of the Major War Criminals of the European Axis ("London Agreement"), August 8, 1945, accessed March 17, 2010, http://www.refworld.org/cgibin/texis/vtx/rwmain?docid=3ae6b39614.

principle was established, one of cosmopolitan responsibility. This was designed to safeguard the civilian population from violence perpetrated by states or enemies, but also, primarily, it protected individuals from acts of violence committed arbitrarily by sovereign states against their own citizens. This underscores Beck's lesson: he defines a "criminal state" and stresses how crimes against humanity are not simply war crimes that can be judged and whose perpetrators can be sentenced within the boundaries of a nation-state. In this way, Beck creates a different order of juridical moral priorities among nations. He explains how juridical cosmopolitan morals supersede those of national laws: based on what happened historically, the crimes against humanity erase the principles of national legislation and the statal jurisprudence in the sense that they question the essence of a state as a defender of human rights. Beck's reflection goes further: if the traditions are European from which the Holocaust, nationalism, and genocide arise, it is clear that the legal and moral measures used to judge them are also European. The initial requests of the victors, Churchill and Stalin, of condemning the perpetrators of Nazi terror in accordance with martial law, were set aside, and they allowed the trials of these men in national courts, as happened in the Eichmann trial in Jerusalem or in the Auschwitz trials in Germany. In the face of the degeneration of national law, the European tradition of recognition of the other was called in.[54] In the name of global memory, by placing the Holocaust as a paradigm of universal suffering, the Polish Jew Raphael Lemkin defined genocide:

> The term "genocide" was coined in 1946 by Raphael Lemkin, a Polish Jew. No doubt the example of the Holocaust was the trigger for Lemkin's efforts to warn the world about systematic attempts to annihilate specific groups. In his mind, however, genocide was by no means synonymous with the extermination of the Jews. Instead, Lemkin justified his project with references to genocidal activities that took place before and after the Holocaust. He was eager, as were so many others, not to present the Holocaust as an exclusive threat

---
54 See Levy and Sznaider, "The Institutionalization of Cosmopolitan Morality," 150.

for European Jewry, as is made clear in the following passage: "The Nazi leaders had stated very bluntly their intent to wipe out the Poles, the Russians; to destroy demographically and culturally the French element in Alsace-Lorraine, the Slavonians in Carniola and Carinthia. They almost achieved their goal in exterminating the Jews and Gypsies in Europe."[55]

In the years of bipolarism, the globalization of memory was built starting from the Eichmann trial, which became the very first stage of the construction of collective memory, because, during the process, as Arendt argues, for the first time, witnesses reached a public visibility. This court case led to an open representation of the Holocaust, not as an "unprecedented crime of genocide" but, on the contrary, as the oldest known crime: it "constitutes an important moment in the nexus of memory and legal narratives ... it paid to the voices of the victims." But, especially, what emerged from the Eichmann trial was that its "elements are recovered and reinterpreted three decades later in the context of the Balkan wars and the ongoing war crimes tribunals beginning in the 1990s."[56] This is important because the third phase of which Levy and Sznaider speak is characterized by conflicts that erupted in the Balkans in the 1990s. As they explain, "It was the historical backdrop of the Balkan crisis and unsuccessful demands for NATO intervention in Bosnia that helped establish the link and thus the centrality of the Holocaust as a measuring stick for international human rights politics." The Holocaust became "a global icon ... through a number of mass-mediated events,"[57] which contributes to spread Beck's lesson. To develop collective memory, at a cosmopolitan level, the mass media are available to present at a local level what happens at a distance:[58] the local/global dimension and "televised images" set the so-called Holocaust iconog-

---

55 Ibid., 150–51.
56 Ibid., 152. See David Bankier and Dan Michman, eds., *Holocaust Historiography in Context: Emergence, Challenges, Polemics and Achievements* (Jerusalem: Yad Vashem; New York: Berghahn, 2008).
57 Levy and Sznaider, "The Institutionalization of Cosmopolitan Morality," 152.
58 Levy and Sznaider explain how the film *Schindler's List*, directed by Steven Spielberg, and the establishment of the Holocaust Museum (1993) in Washington, DC, contribute to this

raphy that can produce an identification with others.[59] This identification process is possible by virtue of the connection between the global and the local element, which, ultimately, provides an analysis transcending the nation-state. When it is said that the memory of the Holocaust crosses borders, it means that the victims (Jews) and executioners (Nazis) do not belong only to the borders of Germany or Europe. Rather, the victims and perpetrators are repeated in time and space. This aspect establishes the element of decontextualization of the Holocaust (always falling in the globalization process of the phenomenon), in other words, the memory of the Holocaust in the globalization age outlines and structures a "new rights culture."[60] Highlighting this awareness or, better, this shift in the theoretical paradigm were the genocide in Kosovo, to such an extent that Levy and Sznaider coined the term "Kosovocaust," and the Stockholm Conference in January 2000. The two events are seen as benchmarks.[61] When Levy and Sznaider stated that "slowly over the course of the Bosnian conflict the U.S. public came to identify the Serbs with the Nazis,"[62] they helped to deterritorialize and detemporalize any suffering, recognizing all the victims of any ethnic nationalism. "As a Jew I say that we have to do something to stop the bloodshed in this country (Bosnia). People fight and children die. Why? Something, no matter what, must be done."[63]

What deserves attention is that the Balkan crisis and NATO's intervention built a bridge between the past of the victims par excellence, the Jews, and the new victims of the Balkans—once again, in the heart of Europe. This link provides the basis for international policies different from those previous and for a transnational system of values that is based

---

social construction. Cf. Levy and Sznaider, "The Institutionalization of Cosmopolitan Morality," 152.
59 Cf. Levy and Sznaider, "Memory Unbound," 92, 99; Levy and Sznaider, "The Institutionalization of Cosmopolitan Morality," 153.
60 See ibid., 155–56; cf. Howard Rheingold, *The Virtual Community: Homesteading on the Electronic Frontier* (Boston: Addison-Wesley, 1993).
61 Cf. Iain Chambers, *Migrancy, Culture, Identity* (London: Routledge, 1994); Levy and Sznaider, "Memory Unbound," 97–102.
62 Levy and Sznaider, "Memory Unbound," 97–98.
63 Ibid., 99, quoting Elie Wiesel, who in his speech "on the day of the museum's inauguration directly turned to President Clinton."

on human rights and condemns all forms of genocide.[64] It has moved the perspective from a Kantian universalism to a more contextualized cosmopolitanism, where the watchword has become "Nuremberg now." In February 1993, the UN Security Council requested the establishment of an International Tribunal to prosecute persons responsible for violations of humanitarian law in the former Yugoslavia (based on the model of Nuremberg) and thus institutionalized the globalization of memory. It could be said that the reception of the Kosovo conflict constituted the end of supremacy of "nation-centered memories." Human rights became the new yardstick for measuring global politics while there arose new transnational solidarities that corresponded to new levels of power, superseding or putting in second order state authority. This reinforced the institutionalization of cosmopolitan memory.[65] At this point, let me reflect on what Beck and Grande say reproposing Arendt's thought:

> Not only God must grant forgiveness; human beings must forgive each other, and publicly, because only in this way can they recuperate the ability to act. Although this is true in general, it is particularly true in view of the monstrous crime of the destruction of the Jews. What is important for Hannah Arendt is that human beings can begin *anew* and not remain prisoners of the past. That is what forgiveness means. Only through the ability to forgive, which nobody can demand as a right, can action, which is more urgent than ever, regain its political efficacy.[66]

In January 2000, while Levy and Sznaider discussed the importance of a Europe unified by common values, but above all the need, in the wake of Adorno's categorical imperative, to prevent another Holocaust and other genocides in Europe, historical conditions arose to decontextualize the Holocaust and institutionalize universal memory. This culture of prevention became a kind of universal *memorandum* for European civilization: "A closer look at the final declaration of the

---

64 Cf. ibid., 98–99.
65 Cf. ibid., 100.
66 Beck and Grande, *Cosmopolitan Europe*, 133.

Stockholm Forum illustrates the institutionalization of an emerging European cosmopolitan memory."[67]

In view of this responsible type of political sovereignty, which provides a response to any genocide with the aim of preventing it, we can see the universalization of the Holocaust: "It can happen to anyone, at any time, and everyone is responsible."[68]

> However, institutionalized cosmopolitanism appears to be the most viable answer to the horrors of the 20th century, which apparently will continue in the future. The Holocaust, or rather the collective memories that have sprung from it during the last six decades, is a paradigmatic case for the political and cultural salience of cosmopolitan sentiments.[69]

In some ways, the cosmopolitanism of the Holocaust represents the realization of the Enlightenment project, which if, on the one hand, it has given the universal values of freedom, unity, and equality to society, then, on the other, it has triggered the process of the construction of nation-states, legitimizing national peculiarities. In the current globalization phase, the Enlightenment represents itself as a "civilizing project," which places human rights at its core.[70] It is relevant to note that during this age of globalization post-Holocaust sociology has increased its presence.

Globalization cancels territorial distances by a spatialization of time that allows long distances to be connected in the shortest possible time. By virtue of highly refined technological devices, we reach what is called a "cancellation of space" and the annulment of national borders, and, in a broader sense, of national, ethnic, and other differences.[71] The geographical contemporary landscape outlined by Appadurai marks the end of

---

67 Levy and Sznaider, "Memory Unbound," 101. See Raymond Aron, *Paix et guerre entre les nations* (Paris: Calmann-Lévy, 1962); Ulrich Beck, *What Is Globalization?* (Cambridge: Polity, 2000); Zygmunt Bauman, *In Search of Politics* (Cambridge: Polity, 1999).
68 Levy and Sznaider, "Memory Unbound," 101.
69 Levy and Sznaider, "The Institutionalization of Cosmopolitan Morality," 155.
70 Ibid., 145. See Hannah Arendt, *On Revolution* (New York: Viking, 1963).
71 Cf. Mike Featherstone, *Global Culture: Nationalism, Globalization and Modernity* (London: Sage, 1990); Luciano Gallino, *Globalizzazione e disuguaglianze* (Rome-Bari: Laterza, 2000).

organic society based on Durkheim's moral norms: gradually, we are witnessing the end of stability and the beginning of moral uncertainty. In this context of perpetual movement and fluidity, there is a need to have some certainty, a "moral touchstone" to cling to.[72] This stone is precisely the phenomenon of the Holocaust that becomes an irreplaceable moral security, but also indissoluble and with dual characteristics: it is a solid phenomenon, it cannot fail, and it is mobile, in the sense that it is able to cross national borders, according to the logic and timing of globalization. It exceeds territorial *limina* and goes beyond state boundaries, and it creates links between the states themselves becoming a certainty in a world of uncertainty.

As Beck states, a universal historical perspective has to seek the global in the local and at the same time cross borders, even conceptually and methodologically. The aspect of localization is the other side of the coin of the globalization process. It is important because, when a state prepares and elaborates its own discourse on the Holocaust according to the historical events that occurred in its own national context, the representation of the Holocaust (the *pro* of the state) returns its national specificity to the event. Paradoxically, the process of the globalization of memory, in global society, constitutes national specificities (the *quid* of the modern state). The two phenomena of globalization and localization represent what Bauman calls "glocalization" and that now, in the representation of the Holocaust, is to be rethought.[73]

I have provided a kind of review of the sociological literature on cosmopolitan memory because it deals with an important aspect: as a public discourse, the Holocaust serves as a narrative memory in post-Holocaust sociology. In other words, it creates community narratives in a globalized society. In essence, for Beck and for Levy and Sznaider, the process of globalization of memory leads to the assertion of universal rights and the constitution of identity no longer based on the concept of state, nation, or the founding myths of a race, but on the unique sharing of human suffering. The cosmopolitan memory of the Holocaust becomes

---

72 Levy and Sznaider, "The Institutionalization of Cosmopolitan Morality," 155.
73 Zygmunt Bauman, "On Glocalization: or Globalization for Some, Localization for Some Others," *Thesis Eleven* 54 (1998): 37–49; Levy and Sznaider, "Memory Unbound," 93.

a warning against the eternal modernization of violence, which in the years 1914 to 1945 had seen the state and the nation, quoting Traverso, in "fire and blood."[74] This could suggest that it urges a rethinking of Levy and Sznaider's concept of cosmopolitan memory. The entire conceptualization leads to a debate in social theory, namely, whether or not it has to take leave from postmodernity. Nevertheless, this question still remains open.[75]

4.4. ALEXANDER AND DURKHEIM: "WHAT HOLDS SOCIETY TOGETHER?"

At this point, one can ask how integration occurs in a global society. If, in 1895, Durkheim wondered in *Les règles de la méthode sociologique* what guaranteed the unity of a society, today Jeffrey Alexander wonders if there is something that holds the global society together. A society where there are a few absolute truths and those that seem like confirmed convictions (such as the distinction between the sexes, the rejection of violence, and so on) are continually put into question, with the result that everything is confused and nothing is stable. When Alexander writes, "If progress is to be made, morality must be universalized beyond any particular time and place,"[76] he aims at providing an intellectual and practical therapy for society. As a remedy for the evils of contemporary society and progress, which have produced the wars in the Balkans, the genocide in Rwanda and Burundi, and the destruction of humanity in the broadest sense, Alexander offers the social construction of universal values that lead individuals to the common good. For this reason, it is crucial to understand how morality is socially constructed. In this sense, Alexander proposes the eternal conflict between

---

74   Cf. Daniel Levy and Natan Sznaider, *Erinnerung im globalen Zeitalter: Der Holocaust* (Frankfurt: Suhrkampf, 2001); Ulrich Beck, Daniel Levy, and Natan Sznaider, "Erinnerung und Vergebung in der Zweiten Moderne," in *Entgrenzung und Entscheidung: Wast its neu an der Theorie reflexiver Modernisierung?* ed. Ulrich Beck and Christoph Lau (Frankfurt: Suhrkampf, 2004); Enzo Traverso, *Fire and Blood: The European Civil War (1914–1945)* (London: Verso, 2016).
75   Beck and Grande, *Cosmopolitan Europe*, 134. Levy and Sznaider, "Memory Unbound," 103–4; Daniel Levy and Natan Sznaider, "The Cosmopolitanization of Holocaust Memory: From Jewish to Human Experience," in Gerson and Wolf, *Sociology Confronts the Holocaust*, 313–30.
76   Alexander, *Remembering the Holocaust*, 35.

good and evil as indisputable truth, valid everywhere.[77] For him, as for Durkheim, a moral sentiment binding each of the members of society to the society itself (a pattern of values in which the individual can be identified) guarantees societal unity and therefore its cohesion and reproduction over the time. Identity and memory, morality and solidarity are the notions to which he refers in his theoretical model, whose center is the cultural construction of trauma. In other words, at the basis of society Alexander puts a collective identity that arises when "members of a collectivity feel they have been subjected to a horrendous event that leaves indelible marks upon their group consciousness, marking their memories forever and changing their future identity in fundamental and irrevocable ways."[78] Alexander looks for a trauma, a historical injustice, which, in a global society, can become a "transnational paradigm of collective identity," the universal symbol of human suffering. World War II, an unprecedented historical event, hit all of humanity and the entire world by showing the Holocaust as a "global icon of evil." In a world of uncertainty, in what Beck calls the "risk society," the destruction of the Jews represents a traumatic reality that cannot be denied and whose elaboration can serve to establish bonds of solidarity among individuals.[79] Alexander reports the attention to the historical past of the Holocaust, tracing its roots, and he posits the event as a paradigmatic moral reality, which must be understood in order to live in society, so that humans will no longer be destroyed and human rights will no longer be violated under the name of progress, violence, and modern technology.

  As a sociologist of culture, Alexander is aware that the meanings of the social world are constructed from relationships between human beings and groups. After having analyzed society and identified a number of problems to solve, he identifies historical categories and social phenomena that can turn into sociological concepts able to solve those same social problems. Alexander deals with the function the Holocaust has in society: it is first and foremost a historical phenomenon, called upon to form a culture, norm, morals to transmit (as in Durkheim's

---

77 Cf. James Waller, *Becoming Evil: How Ordinary People Commit Genocide and Mass Killing* (Oxford: Oxford University Press, 2002).
78 Alexander et al., *Cultural Trauma and Collective Identity*, 1.
79 Cf. Alexander, *Remembering the Holocaust*, 174–75, 185.

thought) and, therefore, is seen as a useful sociological category to read contemporary reality, particularly, to avoid further human rights violations:

> How did a specific and situated historical event, an event marked by ethnic and racial hatred, violence, and war, become transformed into a generalized symbol of human suffering and moral evil, a universalized symbol whose very existence has created historically unprecedented opportunities for ethnic, racial, and religious justice, for mutual recognition, and for global conflicts becoming regulated in a more civil way? This cultural transformation has been achieved because the originating historical event, traumatic in the extreme for a delimited particular group, has come over the last fifty years to be redefined as a traumatic event for all humankind. Now free-floating rather than situated—universal rather than particular—this traumatic event vividly "lives" in the memories of contemporaries whose parents and grandparents never felt themselves even remotely related to it.[80]

Alexander's sociology, political and cultural, contributes conceptually to the explanation of which effects cultural facts produce on the moral life of persons and society; how a universal morality is constructed when a suffering that unites individuals provides for the basis of the collective identity. Especially, Alexander conceives the Holocaust as a trauma (τραυμα) in accordance with the meaning of the ancient Greek, which is both a personal injury and a defeat or destruction of a community. In order to become a cultural fact or norm, it has to be represented: it must become a social representation, a drama or, more precisely, a tragedy.

4.4.1. Τραγῳδία as Interpretation of the Human Condition

The idea of the tragic is a kind of consciousness that man has of himself, his realm, of the world. When Thespis, in 534 B.C., staged the first tragic

---

80 Ibid., 3.

performance in Athens, something special happened: it dealt with the witness. In the invention of tragedy, there was a basic step, namely, that of exiting from one's own personal identity to play a role. In this novel condition, which is indeed that of the actor, in a time dimension that equates the past with the present, he presented himself as protagonist of a reality whose imitative power attracts those who view it, making them part of the action totally and immediately. In Alexander's words, "this transcendental status, this separation from the specifics of any particular time or space, provided the basis for psychological identification on an unprecedented scale."[81] Thanks to this transformation from the individual to the collective, the fundamental transition from representation to action occurs—from the "song of the goat," τραγῳδία (*tragoidia*), to the drama (δραμα), which, according to Greek verb δράω (*drao*), "to act" and "to do" (in some versions also "to run"), is no longer narrated but lived. In line with the Dorians' tradition, the sense of action is visible in the word "tragoidia" from the root άγω, "act." Briefly, both drama and tragedy translate the sense of an action represented mimetically. The terms "tragedy" and "drama" in Greek share the same root stem, δρ-, dental plus liquid, consonants that onomatopoeically render the idea of action.

Faced with the irreconcilable conflict between good and evil, faced with the horror of the evil that undermines the basis of human life, the action (in the sense of "what should we do?") the drama, becomes the natural vehicle of expression, the conceptual discourse through which persons can reflect and the value framework to which one can refer—not as a system of abstract formalisms, but as a mentality, a norm of practice, a dynamic acceptance of a common tradition, which returns and evolves into a single creative act.

Tragedy, when it was born, was a literary genre that addressed a community of men and women in a visual-auditory way, and this fact demanded a specific reference system to facilitate receipt of the staged message. This discourse is clearly present in the thought of Alexander, who wants to make the trauma a drama, visible and audible since it is both alive and real. The observation of social real problems leads, in an Aristotelian

---

81   Ibid., 32.

sense, first, to a recognition of the error, αμαρτία (*amartia*), and then to action. The purpose of trauma-drama is that the single social individual, who hears and sees, assumes, as a tragic hero, the accountability for his own fate and the moral responsibility to fight against evil in society. Alexander perceives urgently the need to address the problems dealing with the fate of man and his existence in the world. The tragedy, for its character of collective experience in which there are moral and political instances, constitutes an ideal venue to meditate on reality, involving the society as a whole. As for Aeschylus, in the sixth century B.C., so for Alexander tragedy is a device able to investigate and express a world of values. The Holocaust was a tragic event, and tragedy, as it is conceived, is a literary genre that allows reality to be criticized. Considering the ethical and didactic usefulness of tragedy, he resorts to the tragic event because an existential interpretation is subtended by it. Just as in Sophocles's tragedy, the absolute protagonist of the tragedy is the individual man, who suffers on the stage the fate of all humanity and who has to seek the meaning of his experience and accept his responsibilities, in the same way the dramatic action brings the individual of the global society to bear the weight of human condition. More than being Sophoclean, Alexander moves closer to Euripides's tragedy, as an expression of human relationships and choices. The Greek tragedian entrusts the fate of man to human reason. For Euripides, the rules and structures of society are valuable. In this sense, tragedy has a pragmatic value, that is, it becomes a symbol of something and a frame of values within which to move. Zofia Posmysz-Piasecka recalls:

> When I heard by chance some German voices next to me, I was in Paris, the voice of one of them took me back immediately to Auschwitz; that voice seemed the same of a SS. It was a trauma. Then I wrote a radio drama in 1959, which was broadcast in the same year. It was called *Pasażerka z kabiny 45* (*Passenger from Cabin Number 45*). It became a television drama thanks to Andrzej Munk, between 1961 and 1963, and the friend and colleague Witold Lesiewicz, who after his death, in the middle of production, during an automobile accident in 1961, continued the production of the film with a group of filmmaker friends. Then Aleksander Medvedev wrote a booklet in

Russian and Miecyzslaw Weinberg made it a play in 1968. But for years the work was banned by the Soviet authorities. The opening play, directed by David Pountney, was in Bregenz last summer.

Theater is a necessity. The orchestra is the symbol of the world: there is a total identification of the public, which makes its own a reality that has already existed, symbolically placed in the center: at that time the space is at the center of the orchestra of the world.[82]

Given that the social construction of universal values is a social process that occurs in steps, at the time that a historical event becomes a cultural thing, there is a critical passage to cross, namely, the trauma experienced by the victims has to become trauma for the community. This ritual of identification, empathy, or compassion helps man in the global society. Martha Nussbaum explains that a cultural trauma is built by dramatizing an event: to make it tragic essentially means to propose it again with its victims, its perpetrators, and its consequences. The representation of trauma in its entirety lets the scene be internalized, makes it possible to acquire it and to acquire it as a mental habit.[83] It is a catharsis that makes it possible: "We seek catharsis because our identification with the tragic narrative compels us to experience dark and sinister forces that are also inside of ourselves, not only inside others."[84] Since among the purposes of tragic representation is that of touching suffering, and evil in society, the tragedy itself, the trauma-drama for Alexander becomes a kind of moral code that prescribes what should not happen. Thus, all those who have internalized the trauma may recognize evil and be able to choose correctly when faced with it:

> The project of renaming, dramatizing, reifying, and ritualizing the Holocaust contributed to a moral remaking of the (post)modern (Western) world. The Holocaust story has been told and retold in

---

82 See note 52, above (chapter 2).
83 See Martin L. Hoffman, *Empathy and Moral Development: Implications for Caring and Justice* (Cambridge: Cambridge University Press, 2000); Karsten R. Stueber and Hans H. Kögler, eds., *Empathy and Agency: The Problem of Understanding in the Human Sciences* (Boulder, CO: Westview, 2000); Marta Nussbaum, *The Fragility of Goodness: Luck and Ethics in Greek Tragedy and Philosophy* (Cambridge: Cambridge University Press, 2001).
84 Alexander, *Remembering the Holocaust*, 33.

response not only to emotional need but also to moral ambition. Its characters, its plot, and its pitiable denouement have been transformed into a less nationally bound, less temporally specific, and more universal drama. This dramatic universalization has deepened contemporary sensitivity to social evil. The trauma-drama's message, like that of every tragedy, is that evil is inside all of us and in every society. If we are all the victims and all the perpetrators, then there is no audience that can legitimately distance itself from collective suffering, either from its victims or from its perpetrators.[85]

4.4.2. Trauma Theory: From Cultural Trauma to Universal Value

"From bad to good" and "good from evil" are some expressions that are read repeatedly in Alexander about the construction of universal values. When Durkheim speaks of culture, he alludes to the norms and social institutions that guide the single choices of the individual. When Alexander presents the genocide of the Jews as a cultural trauma, he refers to the break that a civilization suffers. A society that has been wounded clearly suggests that it is vulnerable, in the social structure. So, what was wrong in society prior to the Holocaust? More to my point, Europe's democratic system—for example, Weimar Germany—was a political reality in progress, characterized by untested democratic reforms. At the same time, a particular cultural efflorescence was intersecting with the nationalization of masses. Europe saw these masses fighting for liberal guarantees, modern entitlements, and rights. The citizenship rights requirements dealt with the state-building process, but, this nation-formation has not been simple: nations came into being by means of bloody and cruel acts, with proper policies lacking or incongruous, and saw the collapse of four empires at the end of the Great War. Modernization as system of ideas and ideals failed: political theory was turned into successful economic policies or democratic governance. By the end of the Treaty of Versailles, a common political language was missing, a political deal made of reforms that also would lead, ultimately, to a democratic

---

85 Ibid., 35.

"polite" Europe, in peace and without hostility toward the other citizens that were considered to be foreign.

For Alexander, once the war ended, what happened to the Jews tended to have a series of representations that were called "atrocities," or "man's inhumanity to man," but no one said the word "Holocaust":

> In the beginning, in April 1945, the Holocaust was not the "Holocaust." In the torrent of newspaper, radio, and magazine stories reporting the discovery by American infantrymen of the Nazi concentration camps, the empirical remains of what had transpired were typified as "atrocities." Their obvious awfulness, and indeed their strangeness, placed them for contemporary observers at the borderline of the category of behavior known as "man's inhumanity to man."[86]

Certainly, in the collective imagination, they were inhumane and brutal events. Holocaust survivors were rarely mentioned in interviews with their first names or their identities were only sporadically revealed: they were instead presented as an indistinct mass. This depersonalization made the identification of trauma by the community more difficult and slower. As noted by Halbwachs, most prominent among things in rethinking the past by a community are interests and projects of the present. Following Halbwachs, who died in Buchenwald in 1945, Alexander emphasizes the constrained construction of social memory.

As concerns the victims, it is important to recall that they were often subjected, on the part of the Allies, to the same mistreatment suffered during the war under the Nazis, as the case of General Patton, reported in the *New York Times* in October 1945 following the inspection by Earl Harrison at the behest of President Truman: "American and British administrators felt impatient with many Jewish survivors, even personal repugnance for them, sometimes resorting to threat and even to punishing them."[87] As he noticed, this failed recognition of their status as victims depended very much on the Allies' behavior. For example, it depended on

---

86 Ibid., 3.
87 Ibid., 6. See "The Case of General Patton," *New York Times*, October 3, 1945, 18.

the U.S. government policy of establishing national quotas for the immigration emergency plan at the end of the war, when misplaced German citizens were the first to be marked in the lists, while the Jewish survivors were the last.

I have spent some time on the sociology of Alexander because it explains how post-Holocaust sociology changed during the globalization age. Indeed, he does something more: starting from the study of the Holocaust, in a sociological way, he provides sociology with fresh devices. In this manner, starting from a subfield, substrand, like post-Holocaust sociology, he brings innovation to the discipline in general, demonstrating also how the numerous subsections of sociology work under globalization. This is evident when Alexander explains how the control of the meanings of symbolic production is at the basis of the social construction. Who tells of the event, and in what way, builds the collective memory that is the constitutive element of the same identity and, therefore, in Durkheimian terms, of its cohesion. Alexander wonders what would have happened if the Allies had not won the war. This is a relevant question, because the Holocaust may never have been noted or remembered.

Looking back at Alexander's method, to become a historical trauma in cultural fact, it is essential that the event be identified and marked (Where did the event happen? Who were the victims, and who were the perpetrators?) in its entirety. Then it has to be reconstructed as it occurred in order to be "told and shown," in the sense of Edmund Husserl and Alfred Schütz.[88] The performance of tragedy is a cultural structure that allows for the giving of a name to the suffering, for calculating its weight in time and space, for identifying the protagonists-victims (the good) and the antagonists-persecutors (the evil). As in the Greek theater, Alexander explicates that the suffering is transferred: in light of what Aristotle said, this closeness/distance from the

---

88 Cf. Edmund Husserl, "Ideen zu einer reinen Phänomenologie und phänomenologischen Philosophie. Erstes Buch: Allgemeine Einführung in die reine Phänomenologie," in *Jahrbuch für Philosophie und phänomenologische Forschung* (Halle: Max Niemeyer Verlag, 1913), accessed September 8, 2012, http://www.freidok.uni-freiburg.de/volltexte/5973/pdf/Husserl_Ideen_zu_einer_reinen_Phaenomenologie_1.pdf; Alfred Schütz, *The Phenomenology of the Social World* (Evanston, IL: Northwestern University Press, 1967).

scene transforms the pain, the irreversible end of the tragedy, in τέλος (*telos*), namely, in the end of the drama itself.[89]

If, in Greek tragedy, Sophocles wanted to educate the citizens of the *polis* to civic commitment, in the same way Alexander's spectators, the persons of any society, after having identified themselves with the general suffering, are called to become actors: they must work to ensure that the perceived evil is not repeated. In doing so, they become morally responsible and the Holocaust rises to the archetypal, mythical state of evil. The tragedy is, therefore, a mental attitude, a method that brings each victim to recognize personally within himself his secret identity: in tragedy everyone has his own name:

> This personalization brought the trauma drama "back home." Rather than depicting the events on a vast historical scale, rather than focusing on larger-than-life leaders, mass movements, organizations, crowds, and ideologies, these dramas portrayed the events in terms of small groups, families and friends, parents and children, brothers and sisters. In this way, the victims of trauma became everyman and everywoman, every child and every parent.[90]

In shedding light on the social origins of this mental reality, Alexander seeks to understand what lies behind the social construction of the Holocaust and asks what are the "social frameworks of reference," according to Halbwachs, between the two world wars, in Europe and in the United States. This is relevant since they prepare its codification at the end of the war. Nazism, considered the absolute evil, a symbol of ethnic violence, racial, and religious hatred, leads one to interpret the Holocaust essentially as a product of Nazism itself. *Kristallnacht*, for example, in the United States engenders reactions of bitter condemnation against a dictator and his highest expression of anti-Semitism. This assimilation between Nazism and anti-Semitism obviously makes the opponents of Nazism the sympathizers of the Jews. The social construction or image is

---

89 Alexander, *Remembering the Holocaust*, 32.
90 Ibid., 38.

this: those who fought against the Nazis defended the Jews and were not anti-Semitic. Nevertheless, this cultural attitude together with the attitude of the Allies deviates from grasping the reality of anti-Semitism and deciphering the Holocaust, which is told as a warfare story.[91] What matters is that this does not help to provide people theoretically with the right means, conditions, and so on to recognize the events as they happened.

The conditions for recognition of the Holocaust as genocide and for a construction of a cultural trauma missed, because, by the end of the war until the 1960s, the image of a democratic America, bearer of values and sacrifice in fighting Nazism, was the most prevalent: "The goal focused not on the Holocaust but on the need to purge postwar society of Nazi-like pollution."[92] The United States was the country that further participated in the construction of a new moral order on the ruins of the old world without forgetting that in this nonprocessing of the Holocaust, anti-Semitism of half a century before played a big role. It has meant anti-immigration: when American Jews did not want to be reidentified with this old story, they did not want to match again their identity with that reality.

To break the ideal of a perfect America that always stands up for any democratic cause were the Eichmann trial, Stanley Milgram's research on obedience to authority, which began three months after the beginning of the Nazi war crimes trial, and, finally, the study by Christopher Browning about the commonplaceness of persons. Thanks to these events, the circle of perpetrators was enlarged, putting into question conceptions such as radical evil and evil as social. Until that time, Alexander enlightens how, for the entire American society, the Nazi Holocaust was a Nazi product that had to be placed within precise territorial and temporal boundaries: Europe during World War II. It was still not a cultural and universal fact, and the Allies fighting against each specter of Nazism were considered heroes. However, when in the mid-1960s, the Vietnam War started, the fate of the social representation of the Holocaust changed, bringing about its universalization. Vietnam showed how the United States was not the

---

91 See ibid., 16.
92 Ibid., 27.

keeper of goodness and not faultless. The suffering and the social evil that they caused in Vietnam led to the end of their monopoly on the production of symbolic meanings: of the social representation of good and evil. Since the United States was committing war crimes, other democratic societies did not have any guarantees against the dangers of another mass murder. When Alexander writes, "as America became 'Amerika,' however, napalm bombs were analogized with gas pellets and the flaming jungles of Vietnam with the gas chambres," it is quite clear that the Holocaust was taking the form of a trauma returning: a structural aspect of the tragedy.[93]

The Vietnam War thus led to rethinking the past of the Allies in the 1970s, "suggesting that the anti-Semitism of Roosevelt and Churchill and of American and British citizens had prevented them from acting to block the mass killings."[94] Moreover, another event of deconstruction of the facts and of symbolic inversions contributed to rendering the Holocaust universal. Let me remember Alexander's statements. When, on September 27, 1979, the chair of the Commission of the Victims of the Holocaust, during construction work at the Holocaust Museum in New York, underlined that the institution had the task of remedying the indifference of the American nation to the extermination of the Jews, clearly, a first step toward public admission of guilt was taken. This means that they moved towards a broadening of responsibility, that the fault was not only that of the Germans, but also of the spectators who did not intervene. For these reasons, an inner bridge to a tower whose rooms show artifacts of the camps connects the third floor of the museum, filled with images of the death camps. As soon as the visitor approaches the bridge, in the middle of the representation of evil, one sees a wall photo of Auschwitz-Birkenau, taken by U.S. Air Force intelligence on May 31, 1944. As recalled by the ethnographer of the museum project, Edward Linenthal, the photo caption states that it was the day in which large-scale death of the Hungarian Jews, who had just arrived in the camp, was to begin. At the top of the photo, the fourth crematorium is visible. This public admission of guilt, first, recalls Arendt's thought about the necessity of public accountability and pardon. The admission of guilt

---

93   Ibid., 45.
94   Ibid., 46–47.

for not taking action against what happened to the Jews ("an artifactual indictment of American indifference" for Linenthal; "the effective alignment of Allied Armies with Nazi perpetrators" for Alexander) reduces the idea of a Nazi specificity of the Holocaust. It meant that the genocide was not only the actions of Germans in Europe, and not only a product of Nazism in Europe.[95] It can be added that it is possible to recognize a lost generation if persons who have not been educated to face the past honestly. In other words, the violence can be repeated. This introspective catharsis on the past, by leading to a recognition of responsibilities, corresponds to the moral conscience of which Habermas spoke: publicly admitted, it is the basis of political culture. The Vietnam War revealed in which way evil is nested in society. For Alexander, the Holocaust becomes the metaphor par excellence of the representation of evil, which acts as a bridge between the suffering of every age and condition. The obstruction of evil generates the universalization of the Holocaust. For example, one can consider expressions like "nuclear holocaust," the Balkan wars as a "new holocaust," or the term "Kosovocaust" coined by Levy and Sznaider.

Looking around, the postcommunist world is experiencing a museum, ritual, and memorial boom. When Alexander remembers a comic strip of *Non Sequitur* by Wiley that shows a young girl who ignores the significance of the number tattooed on the arm of a survivor with whom she speaks, he proposes one of the steps of the construction process of collective identity. This is more evident especially at the end of the strip: the now elderly victim tries to explain that the tattooed number serves to remind not only him of what the Holocaust was, but to remind every person. The girls asks: "So you kept it to remind yourself about the dangers of political extremism?" He answers: "No, my dear. To remind you."[96] Surely, the representation of the Holocaust differs from country to country.

It is important to reflect on Israel's representation of the Holocaust. Thanks to Alexander's lesson, it is possible to understand some points better. For instance, in Israel the universalization or cosmopolitanization of the Holocaust (going beyond the borders of the Jewish state and the

---

95 Ibid., 47.
96 Ibid., 173–74.

categories of modernity, since that memory no longer belongs exclusively to the Jewish survivors arrived in the country) began when the army of the Jewish state barely managed to avoid a military catastrophe in 1973.[97] Israel seemed to meet the reality of defeat, of the myth of infallibility of its army, or of an always victorious Israel. This loss of importance for the military aspect itself and the discrediting of militant Zionism shifted attention to suffering in general, highlighting the suffering of Palestinians and Israel's expanding national borders to all victims of every nation. This event was reflected in post-Holocaust sociology. It started a sociology that thinks, considers, or puts into reflection the tortures of the victims in the camps and ghettos, and shows that resistance can be not only active and military but also passive and spiritual.

Important in the consideration of these sociological studies is that the cosmopolitanism of the Holocaust, or rather the cosmopolitan sociology of the Holocaust, involves the gradual abandonment of the typical categories of modernity by which the Holocaust has hitherto been studied. This occurred, at least in Israeli society, just at the time that the image of one of the major factors of modern national states, the Israeli army—one of the two major collective references of Zionism (after the *kibbutz*)—is undermined. In this context, Israeli perception of the Holocaust changed: it ceased to be typical of the Jews, by ensuring that all human suffering has neither territory nor nation. Its universalization was clearer when Alexander recalls as an instance Ronit Lentin's study on the death of Palestinians, during the Lebanon War, told with Holocaust notions and images.[98]

4.5. GENRE STUDIES AND THE JEWISH QUESTION

Up to this point, I have tried to focus on the collective memory and topics related to cosmopolitanism. But my interest in Holocaust sociology after 1989 led me to other topics concerned with the theme. After the collapse

---

97 In Weber's sociology, the monopoly of legitimate violence is a crucial notion: it is at the base of the modern state.
98 Cf. Michael Brenner, *Breve storia del sionismo* (Rome-Bari: Laterza, 2003 [2002]); Ilan Greilsammer, *Il sionismo* (Bologna: il Mulino, 2007 [2005]), 99. Let me thank Guido Bartolucci for the references. See also note 104, below.

of the Berlin Wall and the end of communism, Holocaust Studies continued to grow, and several approaches raising new questions to/about the issue arose. Among the different disciplines approaching the problem, without interruptions or reversals, there was indeed Holocaust sociology. By the end of the 1970s, the division of sociology into many sociological subfields was more evident than previously, because of outside influences of different disciplines of the social sciences. The sociology of social movements and of organizations, the sociology of stratification, the sociology of religion, and others were born in this period. They were linked to or resulted from the turmoil following 1968. In other words, a dissemination/proliferation of sociology (that coincided with its subdivision into multiple subdisciplines) happened along with the development of civil rights battles and Vietnam War protest movements.

As regards post-Holocaust sociology, among the various approaches to the destruction of the Jews among the several subfields of sociology, stood the sociology of gender. To be more precise, the sociology of gender approached the Holocaust theme in 1990s, to the point that we could speak of the "post-Holocaust sociology of gender." We can see this thanks to the valuable study by Robin Linden.[99] This study is considered the first work to break a scholarly taboo, according which the category of gender is pointless in the study of the Holocaust (in the sense that it leads only toward a banalization of the event). Second, the book shows the trauma of some women survivors interviewed by the author.[100] It is relevant to stress that the method of interviews with the Holocaust survivors is another consequence of the division of sociology into several subfields.

Gender Studies deserve attention in their approach toward the theme of the Holocaust. In essence, this field became part of post-Holocaust sociology only in the 1990s because of a previous scholarly preconception that the category of gender would trivialize the Holocaust. The work published by Renate Bridenthal, Atina Grossman, and Marion Kaplan in 1984 was the exception.[101]

---

99 Robin R. Linden, *Making Stories, Making Selves: Feminist Reflections on the Holocaust* (Columbus: Ohio State University Press, 1993).
100 See Ayşe Gül Altınay and Andrea Pető, "Europe and the Century of Genocides: New Directions in the Feminist Theorizing of Genocide," *European Journal of Women's Studies*, 22, no. 4 (2015): 379–85, doi:10.1177/1350506815608325.
101 Cf. Renate Bridenthal, Atina Grossman, and Marion Kaplan, eds., *When Biology Became Destiny: Women in Weimar and Nazi Germany* (New York: Monthly Review Press, 1984).

However, the taboo was formally broken by Linden, who, thanks to the categories of postmodernism, also explains the extermination experience of a few survivors in *Making Stories* in 1993, the same year in which the question of the banality of evil was reproposed by Fred E. Katz in *Ordinary People and Extraordinary Evil*.[102] An additional work, edited by Dalia Ofer and Lenore J. Weitzman, explored the better chances women had, compared to men, of surviving the Holocaust.[103] Especially in the third part of the book, devoted to resistance and rescue, and in the fourth section, consecrated to labor and concentration camps, the two scholars explain how the division of labor was crucial for women's survival. First, because women, destined for domestic work, had been less exposed to the public environment and consequently it was easier for them to escape Nazi control; and second, because Jewish women, not bearing the mark of circumcision, as men did, were less distinguishable from other women and therefore more easily able to mix in secular and Christian environments. Above all, Ofer and Weitzman highlight the active role of women in resistance organizations, putting aside the stereotype according to which they were passive actors or, at most, were supportive to the men. Their dealing with the resistance topic contributed to improving Holocaust Studies in general.

Other works with a gender perspective come from Lentin, who examines the role of the Holocaust and its representation in Israeli society, and from Wolf, who deals with the slight attention paid to personal care within the camp, especially among men, in a survey conducted through the personal story of the survivor Jake Geldwert.[104]

---

102 Cf. Katz, *Ordinary People and Extraordinary Evil*; Judith T. Baumel, *Double Jeopardy: Gender and the Holocaust* (London: Vallentine Mitchell, 1998).
103 See Sheila F. Segal, *Women of Valor: Stories of Great Jewish Women Who Helped Shape the Twentieth Century* (West Orange, NJ: Behrman House, 1996); Dalia Ofer and Lenore J. Weitzman, eds., *Women in the Holocaust* (New Haven, CT: Yale University Press, 1998); Brana Gurewitsch, ed., *Mothers, Sisters, Resisters: Oral Histories of Women who Survived the Holocaust* (Tuscaloosa: University of Alabama Press, 1998); accessed September 8, 2011, http://www1.yadvashem.org/yv/en/education/newsletter/18/couriers.asp; Joan B. Wolf, review of *Women in the Holocaust*, by Dalia Ofer and Lenore J. Weitzman, *American Journal of Sociology* 105, no. 1 (1999): 296–97.
104 See Ronit Lentin, *Israel and the Daughters of the Shoah: Reoccupying the Territories of Silence* (New York: Berghahn, 2000); Gerson and Wolf, *Sociology Confronts the Holocaust*, 29–31.

Resilience and Courage by Tec also was very important. Dealing with Nazi policies and brutalization to which Jews were subjected, Tec photographed the attitudes and reactions of men and women, underlining their strategies for survival in the ghetto and the camp. From the reading of the text emerges the courageous behavior of women in the camp and their alternation in typically male functions. In addition, Tec poses the concept of division of labor at the center of her study, not a mere coincidence since this concept by the end of 1980s in sociology had become a category of study. As in her previous studies, Tec gives ample space to the witnesses, such as Eliszewa/Elza Binder, a twenty-one-year-old woman, and Juliusz Feuerman, a war veteran and member of the Jewish Council with Zionist positions, who gives valuable information about the liquidation of the Stanisławów ghetto in Ukraine that began on February 23, 1943. Elza Binder started to write her story on December 23, 1941, and completed it on July 18, 1942, during a reprisal. From her diary, it is possible to reconstruct the ghetto conditions. Feuerman's story is slightly different: after the liquidation of the ghetto, in February 1943, he was imprisoned along with twenty-two other Jews to finish the work and projects of the Gestapo:[105]

> Feuerman remained alive at least until February 1944. While in prison, Feuerman wrote several texts intended for his son, Lonek (b. 1917), which he addressed to Dr. Benedict Lieberman in Nahariya in British Mandate Palestine. He smuggled the texts out several pages at a time through a friendly Pole who had worked for him before the war and was now a Gestapo employee. Lonek survived the war in the Soviet Union; when he returned to Stanisławów in search of his family, he met this man, who gave him Feuerman's papers. Lonek — now Mr. Arieh Ogen of Bonn, Germany—donated his father's papers to Yad Vashem.[106]

---

105 Rachel F. Brenner, "Voices from Destruction: Two Eyewitness Testimonies from the Stanisławów Ghetto," *Holocaust and Genocide Studies* 22, no. 2 (2008): 320, doi:10.1093/hgs/dcn028.
106 Ibid., 325.

Binder's and Feuerman's writings are significant, first, because they offer a precise description of the work of the Jews in the ghetto or life in prison; second, because they account for the behavior of the leaders of Gestapo.[107]

Finally, two very special works complete the framework of post-Holocaust sociology of gender. The first is an ethnographic research on the collective memory of the Holocaust in Eastern Europe written by Janet L. Jacobs in 2004: in the wake of Harold Garfinkel's ethnomethodological studies, and through the categories of genre, genocide, and ethnos, which had never been combined together before, she conceives the Holocaust as a genocidal phenomenon.[108]

The second is the work of Suzanne Vromen, who, in 2008, reconstructed from interviews the story of several Jewish children saved by Belgian nuns.[109] According to her reviewer, Alan Berger, it is "a welcome addition to the literature dealing with hidden Jewish children and their rescuers during the Holocaust. She focused on Belgium, and interviewed 28 former hidden children (16 women and 12 men); eight nuns and one priest who hid them; two surviving members of the Belgian resistance; the President of the Association of the Hidden Children; and various persons involved in commemorations. The result is a new appreciation of the complexity of rescue as well as the lasting trauma of those whose lives were saved. Her interviews with the nuns, a group typically omitted from this research, is especially significant," and these precious notes or suggestions result from book reviews, perused online and whose importance it has been stressed more times.[110]

---

107   Some writings attributed to Binder and Feuerman were not written by them, but by other comrades. Cf. ibid; *Holocaust Encyclopedia*, United States Holocaust Memorial Museum, accessed September 9, 2011, http://www.ushmm.org/wlc/en/article.php?ModuleId=10007305. See Nechama Tec, *Resilience and Courage: Women, Men, and the Holocaust* (New Haven, CT: Yale University Press, 2003), 336–39.

108   Cf. Harold Garfinkel, *Studies in Ethnomethodology* (Englewood Cliffs, NJ: Prentice-Hall, 1967); Janet L. Jacobs, "Women, Genocide and Memory: The Ethics of Feminist Ethnography in Holocaust Research," *Gender and Society* 18 (2004): 233–38.

109   Suzanne Vromen, *Hidden Children of the Holocaust: Belgian Nuns and Their Daring Rescue of Young Jews from the Nazis* (Oxford: Oxford University Press, 2008).

110   Alan L. Berger, review of *Hidden Children of the Holocaust: Belgian Nuns and Their Daring Rescue of Young Jews from the Nazis*, by Suzanne Vromen, *Studies in Christian-Jewish Relations* 5, no. 1 (2010): 1.

In essence, the work traces a completely new path in the reprocessing of collective memory, especially since the Jewish children (the saved victims) and some women (the righteous) are put at the center of reflection. Particularly, among these women, there are common persons accompanying children from their families up to the convents of nuns, keeping them hidden, saving them from extermination.[111] The reconstruction by Vromen highlights an aspect of resistance underestimated by the sociological literature.[112] In telling the manner in which this specific type of resistance unfolded, Vromen first identifies the institutions involved, namely, the Independence Front and the Jewish Defense Committee, and devotes ultimately a part of the work to the hierarchy of the Catholic Church. As well stressed by Berger, "*Hidden Children of the Holocaust* also sheds light on the patriarchal nature of the Church." Indeed, the fact that the nuns, as women, were undervalued "had a great impact on post-war commemorations," and "women were sometimes seen as inferior by Church leaders." This delays their recognition (as righteous) for having saved the Jewish children, unlike the immediate recognition for priests, men.[113] In this sense, as several book reviewers notice, Vromen's piece is relevant. She also highlights how "rescue efforts were part of the broader resistance to the Nazi occupation of Belgium," and she stresses "the importance of women in this process."[114] These rescue actions constituted a manner of resistance challenging the institutionalized power of the higher clergy. What matters is that, thanks to the category of "institutionalized and cultural power," Vromen explains how the Belgian nuns saved Jewish children in convents: since in the hierarchy of the Catholic Church, they occupied "the lower clergy," and they could challenge authority because they were not subject to controls. Nevertheless, this could have happened only in Belgium, in an area that, like France, constituted a "Romanic" region—in Hilberg's words—and not therefore destined to

---

111 Although the context is different, see the personal story of Irena Sendler, righteous among nations. Accessed September 9, 2011, http://www.yadvashem.org/yv/en/righteous/stories/sendler.asp.
112 See Vromen, "Collective Memory and Cultural Politics," 134, 148–49, 153.
113 Berger, review of *Hidden Children of the Holocaust*, 2.
114 Ibid. Cf. Vromen, "Collective Memory and Cultural Politics," 150.

become an administrative part of the Third Reich.[115] It seems that Vromen adopts a procedure typical of cosmopolitan memory in giving space and voice to the victims of Nazism by using witnesses. In doing so, it is possible to discover that the nuns decided, in the name of the right to life, not to take the ethnic or religious origins of children into account. Vromen underscores that their actions went beyond national borders:

> She was also a nun. Sister she was called, she was a nurse, and I will not forget her. She loved the children very much. I remember one day I had to undress because I had boils and I was very much ashamed. I was afraid that she should see that I am Jewish, so she told me: you can undress, and you have nothing to fear from me … and I adored her. Not only I, all the children.[116]

Monasteries, the object of the research, were symbolic places, the spaces par excellence of Catholicism, which, under the Nazi occupation, housed Jewish children in a challenge to the power of the Third Reich.[117] In addition, Vromen explores the baptism question and what happened to these children, at the end of the conflict, and what it meant for her to be annihilated twice:

> The book is a valuable resource for those wanting to know more about the experiences of Jewish children hidden in places that were historically and theologically hostile to Judaism. Vromen intelligently touches on theological matters in this regard.[118]

Finally, Vromen accounts for the anti-Semitism in religious circles: she discovers the apprehension of nuns who were very friendly and very willing to rescue Jewish children, but she also records the behavior of religious people who openly expressed their dislike. Vromen brings to

---

115 Cf. Hilberg, *The Destruction of the European Jews*, 383.
116 Vromen, "Collective Memory and Cultural Politics," 138.
117 The appendix contains the names of 52 nuns, of whom 19 were mother superiors who are today commemorated by Yad Vashem as "The Righteous Among the Nations," accessed September 9, 2001, http://www.yadvashem.org/yv/en/righteous/index.asp.
118 Berger, review of *Hidden Children of the Holocaust*, 1.

light the continuous effort of the mothers superior to convince hesitant nuns to protect and hide Jewish children from the Nazis: the thoughts and words of these righteous sisters were constantly aiming at understanding that God's desire was not to convert Jewish children to Christianity, but simply to save them.[119]

4.6. THE POST-HOLOCAUST SOCIOLOGY OF THE SOCIAL MOVEMENTS

Closing symbolically *ha-Shoah* in the last few years was the research activity conducted by Rachel L. Einwohner. At the beginning of the third millennium, post-Holocaust sociology, thanks to some sociologists, like this scholar, who introduced new concepts or, better, used them in a new way, was reinvigorated. And thus sociology in general was updated.

Einwohner can be seen as a pioneering theorist of Jewish resistance from the explanations she provides sociology. In September 2000 she introduced her ideas at the Noon Lecture and Discussion Series of the Jewish Studies Program at Purdue University. In essence, she studied the reality of the Holocaust, particularly, the phenomenon of the Jewish resistance, through the concept of social movement.[120] In her words: "My contribution toward a sociology of the Holocaust is to use research findings from the field of social movements to present a more distinctly sociological analysis of Jewish resistance. In fact, I argue that a sociological lens proves particularly useful for illuminating the dynamics of Jewish resistance, especially the participation in collective resistance."[121] It was a turning point, a result of the sociology of political movements, established following the trade union movements of the 1980s in Europe and in the United States. The need to study the destruction of the Jews with different

---

119 Cf. ibid., 1–2.
120 In 2001, her paper was presented at meeting of the Pacific Sociological Association in San Francisco, and it was published in *AJS* in 2003. See Rachel L. Einwohner, "Opportunity, Honor, and Action in the Warsaw Ghetto Uprising of 1943," *American Journal of Sociology* 109, no. 3 (2003): 650.
121 Rachel L. Einwohner, "Availability, Proximity, and Identity in the Warsaw Ghetto Uprising: Adding a Sociological Lens to Studies of Jewish Resistance," in Gerson and Wolf, *Sociology Confronts the Holocaust,* 277.

categories occurred at the beginning of the twenty-first century, at the gradual end of the theory of modernity of the Holocaust when, contemporarily, the awareness that contributions of some sociologists had improved the Holocaust literature in general grew among scholars. In effect, this application of concepts related to the theory of social movements, such as social interaction, collective behavior, social group, group dynamics, or social construction of group identity, will be fruitful.[122]

4.6.1. The Warsaw Ghetto Uprising as Social Movement

My discussion focuses on the Warsaw Ghetto uprising of 1943, the best-known and perhaps most revered instance of Jewish resistance during the Holocaust. I pose two questions about this case: who participated in the uprising, and what was the motive for their actions? In doing so, I hope to illustrate just one of the ways that the discipline of sociology can contribute to academic analyses of the Holocaust.[123]

Many questions and issues arise when considering the resistance that unfolded in the ghetto or district (*Wohnbezirk*) of Warsaw. From a sociological point of view, its representation as social movement seems to be undoubtedly an innovation.[124] Here, I will not reflect on the history of the ghetto and episodes of riots and insurrection, since my goal is to spotlight how Einwohner's sociological perspective explains what happened in Warsaw in a different mode. Primarily, she debunks the traditional

---

122 Cf. Rachel L. Einwohner, "Gender, Class, and Social Movement Outcomes: Identity and Effectiveness in Two Animal Rights Campaigns," *Gender and Society* 13, no. 1 (1999): 56–76, http://www.jstor.org/stable/190240; Deborah A. Abowitz, "Bringing the Sociological into the Discussion: Teaching the Sociology of Genocide and the Holocaust," *Teaching Sociology* 30, no. 1 (2002): 26–38. According to the United States Holocaust Memorial Museum in Washington, DC, the resistance took place in about 800 slums in so-called Nazi-occupied Eastern Europe, accessed 21 July, 2016, https://www.ushmm.org/search/results/?q=resistance.
123 Einwohner, "Availability, Proximity, and Identity in the Warsaw Ghetto Uprising," 277.
124 The Warsaw Uprising is the best documented and most symbolic example of Jewish resistance. Cf. Joseph Kermish, *To Live with Honor and Die with Honor!: Selected Documents from the Warsaw Ghetto Underground Archives "O.S." [Oneg Shabbath]* (Jerusalem: Yad Vashem, 1986); Rachel L. Einwohner, "The Need to Know: Cultured Ignorance and Jewish Resistance in the Ghettos of Warsaw, Vilna, and Łódź," *The Sociological Quarterly* 50 (2009): 407.

stereotype according to which Jews were "sheep led to slaughter," which is necessary for reframing the event correctly.[125] Although Einwohner's choice to represent the Warsaw Uprising as a social movement could appear strange (because the classical theory of social movements is based on elements that seem to be absent in this uprising), it turns out to be strategic in many ways. Starting with the basic definition, social movements are conceived as innovative forms of solidarity. Since they are fluid in form, they exist to change preexisting manners of relationship between inner members. At the same time, they are thought as actions that clash with the existing institutional apparatus, in order to subvert it, by swapping the founding values with those experienced in the group. Thanks to Einwohner's studies (in comprehending the Holocaust) it is possible to resume or retrace the main steps of traditional sociology dealing with social movements and organizations. For instance, it is possible to come back to Marx, referring to social movement at the time that the transition from "class in itself" to "class for itself" is realized; or to Alain Touraine, a classical theoretician of social movements who emphasizes the element of conflict.[126] Einwohner's works do not only distance themselves from these specifications, but they also rely on fresh elements, resulting from a recent line of research that investigates social movements and collective action:[127]

> This case is of substantial importance to the study of social movements for two reasons. First, it extends current theory and research to

---

125 See Yitzhak Arad, Israel Gutman, and Abraham Margaliot, eds., *Documents on the Holocaust: Selected Sources on the Destruction of the Jews of Germany and Austria, Poland, and the Soviet Union*, 8th ed., trans. Lea Ben Dor (Lincoln and London: University of Nebraska Press, Jerusalem: Yad Vashem, 1999), 433–34, doc. 196, *Proclamation by Jewish Pioneer Youth Group in Vilna, Calling for Resistance, January 1, 1942*; and 459–60, doc. 209, *Proclamation by the F.P.O. Calling for Revolt in Vilna, September 1, 1943*; Bauer, *Rethinking the Holocaust*, 119–42; Einwohner, "Opportunity, Honor, and Action in the Warsaw Ghetto Uprising of 1943," 650–65; Havi Ben-Sasson and Shlomit Dunkelblum-Steiner, *Resistance: Spiritual Resistance, Revolt, Partisans, and the Uprising in the Death Camps* (Jerusalem: Yad Vashem, 2004), 66, 86.
126 See Touraine, *Production de la société*; Vincenzo Bova, *Solidarność: Origini, sviluppo ed istituzionalizzazione di un movimento sociale* (Soveria Mannelli: Rubbettino, 2003).
127 Cf. James M. Jasper, *The Art of Moral Protest* (Chicago: University of Chicago Press, 1997); Einwohner, "Opportunity, Honor, and Action in the Warsaw Ghetto Uprising of 1943."

a new terrain. As scholars are increasingly recognizing the limitations of a research literature based mainly on the study of protest in contemporary Western democracies, an analysis of collective resistance that took place in a nondemocratic context during World War II offers a useful test of the applicability of dominant theoretical concepts to a broader range of cases. Second, as stated above, this case presents an important challenge to one of the explanatory factors offered by these theories; namely, the concept of political opportunity.[128]

Einwohner's piece shows how the sociological approach is important for Holocaust Studies. The phenomenon of resistance that took place in Warsaw presents some unusual details for the traditional sociology of social movements. Einwohner's study refers to very recent research, which sees Melucci among major representatives and which puts the concepts of collective identity and honor at the center of the theory of collective action:[129]

Thus, framing their resistance as a fight for honor may have been compelling because, by doing so, the ghetto fighters made a statement about who and what Warsaw Jews were: strong and proud people, not the weak "subhumans" portrayed by Nazi ideology. Resistance was therefore the enactment of an identity.[130]

The main ideal type of social movement of which Melucci speaks and to which Einwohner refers is based on the concept of the *idem* feeling, or organic solidarity: concepts that evoke the categories of moral and collective consciousness of Durkheim. Einwohner deals with the phenomenon of Jewish resistance in the Warsaw ghetto through the concept of collective

---

[128] Einwohner, "Opportunity, Honor, and Action in the Warsaw Ghetto Uprising of 1943," 651 (authors' in-text citations omitted).

[129] Melucci was trained at the school of Alain Touraine. On the concept of "honor," see Arad, Gutman, and Margaliot, *Documents on the Holocaust*, 315–16, doc. 145, *The Last Letter from Mordecai Anielewicz, Warsaw Ghetto Revolt Commander, April 23, 1943.*

[130] Einwohner, "Opportunity, Honor, and Action in the Warsaw Ghetto Uprising of 1943," 668.

identity, considered as a moral glue that can hold together individuals and encourage them to revolt: "They saw armed resistance as a way to act with dignity and honor."[131]

In the *Wohnbezirk* of Warsaw, collective action was possible due to a social context or frame that was based on honor.[132] In the wake of Horowitz's and Bourgois's studies, by "honor," Einwohner means the respect for the law in a society. It is an analytical key that allows her to explain the reasons that led to the uprising in the ghetto. In fact, the concept of honor itself is based on moral norms, which ensure a common *idem* capable of uniting social actors in an action-resistant milieu.[133] This means that collective action took place in Warsaw because in the ghetto the conditions demanding respect for the law had been established: this demand pushed the population of the ghetto to react. Here, the concepts of honor and dignity are what Goffman and Schütz call a "motivational framework of reference."[134] In contrast with what the classical theory of social movements supports, for which a social movement is born at the moment that there are social conditions that pave the way for action (the status quo of Alberoni and one that has to be changed to obtain a new reality), Einwohner considers other conditions leading the community to act, specifically, to resist.

Following Ian Clark, according to whom these conditions are given by incentives of solidarity, or from social situations that press on the group, stimulating elements of belonging and identity, Einwohner emphasizes that these incentives in Warsaw (of identity or solidarity) were refiled under the form of honor, but political opportunities were absent.[135] This latter expression refers to all possible forms or relational power abilities able to manage the contradictions that arise from the

---

131 Einwohner, "The Need to Know," 416.
132 See Arad, Gutman, and Margaliot, *Documents on the Holocaust*, 276–77, doc. 125, *Call to Armed Self-Defense, from an Underground Publication*.
133 See Ruth Horowitz, *Honor and the American Dream: Culture and Identity in a Chicano Community* (New Brunswick, NJ: Rutgers University Press, 1983); Philippe Bourgois, *In Search of Respect: Selling Crack in El Barrio* (Cambridge: Cambridge University Press, 1995).
134 See Schütz, *The Phenomenology of the Social World*; Erving Goffman, *Asylums: Essays on the Social Situation of Mental Patients and Other Inmates* (New York: Anchor, 1961).
135 See Ian Clark, *Globalization and Fragmentation: International Relations in the Twentieth Century* (New York: Oxford University Press, 1997).

relationship between prescriptive time and complexity of action. This ability to manage contradictions between power poles in favor of resistance in the ghetto—for example, the *Jewish Fighting Organization* (ŻOB) and the *Jewish Military Union* (ŻZW)—and outside of it—such as the *Armia Krajowa (Home Army* or *Polish Military Underground* and the Polish government in exile in London)—is equal to zero. This is because relationships between the centers of power were lacking. The underground Jewish military organization, ŻOB, was constituted in the Warsaw ghetto on August 28, 1942, thanks to the Zionist youth movement, which included three pioneering movements: *Ha-Shomer Ha-Tsa*ir*, *Dror*, and *Akiva*. Several times the name *Dror* ("Freedom") appears. It was a left-wing Zionist youth movement, associated politically with *Poalei Zion* ("Workers of Zion," a Zionist party of the Left), and *Hechalutz* ("The Pioneer"), an umbrella organization of communities for agricultural training. Most of the underground movements and political parties in the ghetto—Zionists, Bund, and the communists—then joined in October and November 1942 as the underground organization of ŻOB. The other clandestine military body, ŻZW, prepared by a revisionist movement, did not ever integrate with the ŻOB.[136] On the basis of this power vacuum, the population of the ghetto, in accordance with the principle of opposition theorized by Touraine, developed a resisting force, which had as its goal the establishment of an entity different from other centers of power with decision-making power:[137]

---

136 Cf. Ben-Sasson and Dunkelblum-Steiner, *Resistance*, 69–70, 72, 75, 82–83.
137 Ibid., 30, 62; Einwohner, "The Need to Know," 416; Arad, Gutman, and Margaliot, *Documents on the Holocaust*, 303–4, doc. 139, *Call for Resistance by the Jewish Military Organization in the Warsaw Ghetto, January 1943*; William A. Gamson and David S. Meyer, "Framing Political Opportunity," in *Comparative Perspectives on Social Movements*, ed. Doug McAdam, John D. McCarthy, and Mayer N. Zald (Cambridge: Cambridge University Press, 1996), 275–90; Jeff Goodwin and James M. Jasper, "Caught in a Winding, Snarling Vine: The Structural Bias of Political Process Theory," *Sociological Forum* 14 (1999): 27–54; Jeff Goodwin, *No Other Way Out: States and Revolutionary Movements, 1945–1991* (Cambridge: Cambridge University Press, 2001); Jeff Goodwin, James M. Jasper, and Francesca Polletta, *Passionate Politics: Emotions and Social Movements* (Chicago: University of Chicago Press, 2001); Jeff Goodwin and Steven Pfaff, "Emotion Work in High-Risk Social Movements: Managing Fear in the U.S. and East German Civil Rights Movements," in *Passionate Politics*, ed. Jeff Goodwin et al., 282–302.

In fact, collective resistance emerged precisely *because* Jews recognized there was no way out of the ghetto. This awareness helped create collective action by allowing a particular motivational frame to take hold: one that equated resistance with honor. An analysis of this case therefore goes beyond recent discussions of structural and perceived opportunity to show how framing processes can facilitate collective action even in the absence of political opportunity. It also suggests that some of those contingencies to which Goodwin and Jasper refer can include genocide and the belief among participants that their deaths are inevitable, contingencies that fit Goldstone and Tilly's concept of threat. Finally, as I explain in the conclusion, this case points to the need for empirical research on a greater variety of cases—especially those in situations of extreme powerlessness—to continue to refine our understanding of the emergence of collective action.[138]

Looking back at the Jewish resistance, one can see in this community action an orientation toward a belief of the Weberian ideal type that, in this case, coincides with the desire to die with dignity. Furthermore, Einwohner enlightens the concept of field of action within which opposing factors unfold under the control of Nazi forces. Since the collective action in Warsaw occurred by virtue of the absence of a series of political opportunities, one can consider the Weberian concept of social interactions.[139] When the society of the Warsaw ghetto realized that there were no political opportunities, only then numerous interactions were established between the residents of the ghetto; there was a social action among inhabitants.[140]

The resistance movement in Warsaw was distinct from traditional social movements also for other reasons. While traditional social movements are born with clear objectives to be pursued (they are against-societies or societies

---

138 Einwohner, "Opportunity, Honor, and Action in the Warsaw Ghetto Uprising of 1943," 654 (author's in-text citations omitted).
139 See William A. Gamson, *Talking Politics* (New York: Cambridge University Press, 1992).
140 The concept is at the basis of social movements theory. In accordance with Latin meaning, the verb *moveo* translates the same sense of Latin *ago* from which the Italian word action originates.

in nuce aiming at changing the existing status in which they are formed), the Warsaw Uprising was instead a movement that did not aim at the overturning of the status quo. Actions were purely motivated and oriented towards the value of resistance in itself, as an act of dignity and reaction to Nazi evil. Faced with the threat and the awareness of being exterminated, only people of the ghetto retained the human dignity continuously subtracted through violence. In Warsaw to resist meant the ability to reject evil:[141]

> What distinguishes this case from others is not simply that the ghetto fighters risked death, but that they believed they were *certain* to die; further, they felt that they would die *regardless of their decision to resist*.[142]

Starting from July 1942, the situation began to plummet due to deportations. This factor pushed the inhabitants of the ghetto to redefine their situation and to move to the stage of armed resistance. Precipitating factors joined the existing social tensions. For Neil J. Smelser's theory of value-added, these elements lead to the breaking of the balance. In other words, the movement of resistance arises when collective consciousness and mobilization arise, by changing the status quo of social conflict and redefining the social action:

> If Warsaw Jews had the option of either resisting or continuing to live in the ghetto under German occupation, perhaps the uprising would not have taken place; indeed, the fact that no collective resistance took place before July 1942 supports this conclusion. Yet with an attribution of threat so great that they believed their deaths to be inevitable, resistance—framed in terms of an honorable death—became preferred.[143]

After July 1942, Einwohner explains that an organic action of solidarity unfolded in Warsaw: she elaborates this, following *Les règles de la méthode sociologique* by Durkheim.

---

141 See Touraine, *Production de la société*; Pizzorno, *Le radici della politica assoluta e altri saggi*. On right of resistance, see Angela De Benedictis and Valerio Marchetti, eds., "Resistenza e diritto di resistenza: Memoria come cultura," *Quaderni di Discipline Storiche*, 15 (Bologna: Clueb, 2000).
142 Einwohner, "Opportunity, Honor, and Action in the Warsaw Ghetto Uprising of 1943," 670.
143 Ibid.

4.6.2. The Conditions of Collective Action

One of the main questions is "why *did* Jews resist?" after all.[144] Einwohner asks herself how it was possible that Jews resisted under the Nazi totalitarian power. The term "to resist," which she essentially translates in her vocabulary with "to move" or "to act," concerns two questions: Who resisted? Against whom or what? Obviously the ones who resisted were the residents of the ghetto, whose social action had as its goal the fundamental act of resistance in itself. Einwohner explains that "collective action need not always require opportunity."[145] The theory she conceives, in rethinking the Holocaust, is completely innovative for sociology. This is important because some scholars, like her, in reconsidering the Holocaust contribute to improving sociological thought in general: "This case therefore illustrates how framing processes can mediate structural conditions to produce collective action in the absence of opportunity. It also points to the need for additional research on protest and resistance in nondemocratic settings."[146] The resistance in question is form of political participation since it presees an adhesion of collective kind.[147] In fact, social movements constitute a specific type of political participation. Einwohner clarifies the success of this collective endeavor (in this way Herbert Blumer defines the social movement) through the sociological concepts of "availability," "proximity," and "identity," borrowed from the Chicago School.[148]

Availability is further specified with the concept of activism, which is closely linked to that of proximity. Individual activism, thanks to social proximity, turns into a social movement. To clarify, when any single resident of the ghetto felt the need to act, the action of the individual became the act of everyone. This was possible because residents shared with each other the same physical space: they were forced to live concentrated in

---

144   Ibid., 651.
145   Ibid., 650.
146   Ibid.
147   Cf. Einwohner, "Availability, Proximity, and Identity in the Warsaw Ghetto Uprising," 277; Pizzorno, *Le radici della politica assoluta e altri saggi*.
148   See Herbert Blumer, "Social Problems as Collective Behavior," *Social Problems* 18, no.3 (1971): 298–306.

small areas, which helped to make them similar, if not identical. How the population of Chicago tended to be distributed geographically according to social class was well explained in 1925 by Robert E. Park, Ernest W. Burgess, and Roderick D. McKenzie in *The City*. The authors illustrated how it is possible to locate, in the urban space, some natural areas corresponding to social classes of individuals (the spatial distance is used to reflect the social distance between individuals belonging to different classes). Now, reversing the situation, moving from physical-spatial distance to physical-spatial proximity, we can apply this way of thinking to the Warsaw ghetto: in *Wohnbezirk* physical and territorial proximity created bonds of solidarity among persons forced to live crowded together.[149]

Thus, the individual activism, due to social proximity, becomes a moral solidarity, which leads, in turn, to a social movement: the element of identity, the third constituent of a social movement, holds the individuals who participate in resistance actions together. Einwohner's explanation refers to a vast literature that lets identity be the basic concept of the nature of social movements and that puts the process of group identity at the basis of participation in a movement:

> A strong sense of "we" is a necessary component of collective action frames or the subjective assessment that make activism possible. Some scholars go so far as to suggest that collective action is the enactment of identity in that individuals participate in protest because doing so is a reflection of who and what they understand themselves to be.[150]

In short, individual activism, social proximity, and collective identity were the concepts defining the dynamics of social action in Warsaw, in which women and young people also took part, since, in the ghetto the force of moral solidarity canceled gender differences.[151]

---

149 In Chicago School theory, physical distance is used to translate the social distance with the function of establishing a distance of a moral kind among the residents of the city. Cf. Louis Wirth, *The Ghetto* (Chicago: University of Chicago Press, 1928).
150 Einwohner, "Availability, Proximity, and Identity in the Warsaw Ghetto Uprising," 280 (authors' in-text citations omitted).
151 See Baumel, *Double Jeopardy*; testimony no. 5469.O.3, Yad Vashem Archive, Jerusalem. On the role of the couriers, see instead Vladka Meed, *On Both Sides of the Wall: Memoirs*

The memories of Jack Klajman (2000), who was a ten-year-old boy in Warsaw in 1941, mention a young female fighter:

> So many courageous young people were taking part in the uprising—women as well as men. I remember one of the people who dropped into our hideout was a woman who seemed particularly stoic. She was proudly wearing a German helmet. I asked her where she got it. "This is a souvenir of a stinking Nazi I killed," she said. "I grabbed his gun and his helmet." I asked her if I could kiss her on her cheek for her bravery. Laughing, she granted me permission. I grasped her hand and told her I hoped she would survive the war and save that helmet to show her grandchildren one day. I could see the tears forming in her eyes. "I don't think so," she said. "I don't think I will ever see that day. I'm ready to die any time, at any moment, and I'm happy that I was able to be a part of this movement to take revenge on the Nazis." I knew they were preparing for another attack so I wished her well and told her to come back in one piece. She never returned.[152]

Einwohner notices the role played by female couriers moving inside and outside the ghetto in providing and obtaining information, weapons, food, and so on. They were called *kashariyot*, from the Hebrew *Kesher* ("connection"), especially because they ran from one ghetto to another bringing into contact people in crucial moments so that a real link had been established for survival of the Jewish community's identity. In addition, they had the special feature of enduring more than the men did under the Nazi terror. Einwohner, in proposing

---

from the Warsaw Ghetto (New York: Holocaust Library, 1979); Tzivia Lubetkin, *In the Days of Destruction and Revolt* (Tel Aviv: Beit Lohamei Haghetaot, 1981); Arad, Gutman and Margaliot, eds., *Documents on the Holocaust*, doc. 111, *The Girl Couriers of the Underground Movement*, 239–40; Bronka Klibanski, "In the Ghetto and in the Resistance: A Personal Narrative," in *Women in the Holocaust*, ed. Dalia Ofer and Lenore J. Weitzman, 186, accessed July 17, 2011, http://www1.yadvashem.org/yv/en/education/newsletter/18/couriers.asp.

152 Einwohner, "Availability, Proximity, and Identity in the Warsaw Ghetto Uprising," 284, with reference to the memoirs of Jack Klajman.

this type of social resistance movement, leads scholars to review important topics in sociology.

4.6.3. Leadership Question: Three Cases in Comparison

Who symbolized the power in the *Wohnbezirk* of Warsaw and in the Vilna and Łódź ghettos? Well, if in the first case the resistance was planned and realized, in the Lithuanian case, instead, although it was prepared, it did not take place. In the third example, then, the resistance was not scheduled and consequently not even established. Faced with the three cases, Einwohner tries to develop a theory starting from the notions of leadership and authority:

> In many ways, the study of social movements is synonymous with the study of leadership. Scholarly accounts of movement activity nearly always mention the actions of movement leaders, and most of the documents and events that serve as the empirical sites for movement analyses bear the imprints of leaders' decisions. Furthermore, although a focus on organizations is still prevalent in the research literature, it is often difficult to think of many social movement organizations without those groups' leaders also coming to mind.[153]

From Lenin onwards there was a widespread awareness that a revolutionary movement could not exist without a strong organization of leaders capable of guaranteeing continuity. In the light of Weber's theories, the term "authority" means the ability to receive obedience to the orders given. But it also means charismatic power when a person exercises above all other individuals a certain charisma or charm, which helps the person only by grace (χάρις) to find obedience and consent.

---

153 Rachel L. Einwohner, "Leadership, Authority, and Collective Action: Jewish Resistance in the Ghettos of Warsaw and Vilna," *American Behavioral Scientist* 50, no. 10 (2007): 1306, doi:10.1177/0002764207300160. See Aldon D. Morris, *The Origins of the Civil Rights Movement: Black Communities Organizing for Change* (New York: Free Press, 1984). Cf. Einwohner, "The Need to Know," 423–25. There is a new sociology of social movements based on the category of leadership.

I would like to evidence how Einwohner in studying the different points of these three ghettos is able—and it does not always happen—to combine or conjugate the main Holocaust historiography with sociological thought. When she reelaborates the works of Arad, Gutman, Corni, Hilberg, and Unger, she demonstrates, in 2000s, that a dialogue between history and sociology is possible.[154] In addition, the phenomenon of ghettoization analyzed by Einwohner sheds light on the nature and functions of the Jewish Councils: from simple intermediaries between Nazi officials and the ghetto populations (they had to provide for the recruitment of labor and organization of community), they became a real bureaucratic administration, sometimes, as in Warsaw, a municipal hall. For example, Czerniaków received the title of mayor. From the time that the simple council turned into a bureaucracy responsible for the housing problem or for that of public health, it had been constituted as a civil service, an apparatus with counselors, also remunerated, which perfectly reflected Weber's model of bureaucracy.[155]

Warsaw, always considered as the center of Jewish culture in Europe, during World War II went down in history especially for the events that occurred in its ghetto and for the forms of resistance that unfolded. On the basis of the category of social movement, Einwohner believes that the resistance had been prepared and carried out, in the ghetto, thanks to the collective action of the resident population.[156]

Einwohner gives the name of "authority work" to the coordinated center of power that plans armed resistance: organized work that confers authority to the resistance group and to ensure its success. The positive result of the decision-making power of the ŻOB and of the ŻZW was also attributable to the fact that, in the Warsaw *Wohnbezirk*,

---

154 Einwohner, "The Need to Know," 412–13.
155 Cf. Hilberg, *The Destruction of the European Jews*, 234.
156 Cf. Arad, Gutman and Margaliot, eds., *Documents on the Holocaust*, doc. 101, *From a Lecture on the Steps Leading to the Establishment on the Warsaw Ghetto, January 20, 1941*, 222–28. See Einwohner, "The Need to Know," 413: "In Warsaw, small children were most likely to be the ones to smuggle food in from outside the ghetto walls (the 'Aryan side') because they were small enough to slip through holes in the wall and to evade the guards" (authors' in-text citations omitted).

the *Judenrat* leader Czerniaków was not considered a "legitimate" authority.[157]

In other words, Einwohner focuses her attention on the leadership question, a relevant topic in sociology. Since Czerniaków did not enjoy consensus within the community, his orders were not heard; consequently, ŻOB and ŻZW, the organizations that Einwohner defines as authority work in sociological terms, found a wider listening space to organize the resistance. Einwohner illustrates how fundamental in the ghetto the role of the leader was, and to what extent the possibility of revolt against Nazi power depended on him, with the suicide of Czerniaków, when mass deportations began in July 1942. From that time, the Warsaw insurrection took place and was successful: the decision-making power was going to concentrate in the hands of the authority work, which was organizing the resistance. Finally, the economic nature of the ghetto based on private endeavor ensured the power of the resistance groups. This aspect was not secondary since the outputs from the ghetto for work reasons created and facilitated communications and relations between the world outside and the inside and the resistance organization.[158] For the Lithuanian ghetto of Vilna, things went differently.[159] Although there had been a resistance movement capable of planning the action of revolt, a real resistance itself never took place:

> As noted earlier, plans for resistance in the Warsaw Ghetto emerged in response to the receipt of information from Vilna, where mass killings of Jews began in summer 1941. Somewhat ironically, however, while the actions of resistance fighters in Vilna were central to the emergence of resistance in the Warsaw Ghetto, those

---

157 See Einwohner, "Leadership, Authority, and Collective Action," 1324, see note 4.
158 Cf. Arad, Gutman, and Margaliot, *Documents on the Holocaust*, doc. 102, *The Smuggling of Food into the Warsaw Ghetto*, 228–29; ibid., doc. 102, *The Dilemma of Jewish Self-Help*, 232; ibid., doc. 107, *Ringelblum on Cooperation Between Jewish Political Parties in the Underground*, 234; ibid., doc. 108, *"Oneg Shabbat," The Jewish Underground Archives in the Warsaw Ghetto*, 235; *Shoshana Baharir's testimony about the preparations and the Warsaw Ghetto Uprising*, Testimony no. 5469 O.3, Yad Vashem Archive.
159 See Einwohner, "The Need to Know," 416.

same activists were unable to achieve their goal of a sustained armed uprising in Vilna.¹⁶⁰

The actions of the United Partisans Organization (*Fareinikte Partizaner Organizatsie, FPO*) did not result in a real resistance and did not lead to the destruction of the ghetto. The answer lies in the fact that, in Vilna, unlike Warsaw, there was a strong leader, Jens Jacob, in charge of the council. He was able to counteract resistance actions since he believed that the economic and productive activity of the ghetto was helpful to the Germans and that, for these reasons, they would not ever proceed to a mass murder. For him, the clandestine activities of opposition to the Nazis constituted a clear threat to the life of the Jews. His speech of May 15, 1943, about the dangers relating to the introduction of weapons into the ghetto was clearly significant and shows all his disappointment in the manner of operation of the FPO: "From an economic point of view the ghetto is very valuable, but if you are going to take foolish risks and if there is any question of security, then I will wipe you out."¹⁶¹

Einwohner explains how, in the case of Lithuania, the authority work and charismatic power of the FPO could not substitute for the authoritarian power of the head of the Council.¹⁶² As for the ghetto of Łódź, in the years 1940–44, it showed a power structure different from the previous ones. As Hilberg writes, "measured in its powers to regulate and interfere with the life of the inhabitants, the Jewish bureaucracy of the Łódź ghetto was probably the most totalitarian of all ghetto bureaucracies":¹⁶³

> The ghetto in Łódź was the first major ghetto in Poland; it was established in February 1940 and mostly liquidated by August 1944.

---

160 Ibid.
161 Arad, Gutman and Margaliot, eds., *Documents on the Holocaust*, doc. 205, *Address by Gens on the Danger of Bringing Arms into the Vilna Ghetto, May 15, 1943*, 453–55; cf. ibid., doc. 206, *From an Article in "Ghetto News" on the Importance of Industry and Work in the Vilna Ghetto*, 455–56.
162 Ben-Sasson and Dunkelblum-Steiner, *Resistance*, 28–31.
163 Hilberg, *The Destruction of the European Jews* (New York: Holmes & Meier, 1985), 86.

In contrast, the ghettos of Warsaw and Vilna were more short-lived: the Warsaw Ghetto was established in October 1940 and destroyed in May 1943, while the ghetto in Vilna lasted from its establishment in late August 1941 until its liquidation in September 1943.[164]

If one looks at the economic life of the ghetto, the totalitarian power of leadership was unquestioned. In Łódź, the Jewish Council directly managed trade and industry: hence, the dictatorial authority of the Council and especially of its head:

> While food shortages characterized all three ghettos, hunger appears to have been the worst in Łódź, where food smuggling was nonexistent and where ghetto leader Mordechai Chaim Rumkowski, the Nazi-appointed "Eldest of the Jews," maintained strict control over the meager food rations provided by the Germans.[165]

In addition, other aspects confirm the authoritarian characteristics of such power. As Hilberg noted, the administrative apparatus of the Łódź ghetto went even further than its Nazi prototype, its sole judicial office was incorporated in the police.[166] Considering that the ghetto was the largest in number density, among those near Warsaw, and that it was a kind of "holding place" where all the Jews coming from the western regions (Vienna, Prague, etc.) arrived, it was normal to find there, among residents, someone who had experience of political participation. From this point of view there were no differences between the population of the Łódź ghetto and the population of those of Warsaw and Vilna: what differed among the activists in Łódź and other activists was that the residents of the Łódź ghetto did not feel called upon to fight or react against the Nazis.[167]

For Einwohner, there are three explanations. First, it is necessary to take the type of power present in Łódź into account. Second, it is central to remember that the control exercised by the Nazis on the ghetto was

---

164   Einwohner, "The Need to Know," 412.
165   Ibid., 413 (authors' in-text citations omitted).
166   See Hilberg, *The Destruction of the European Jews*, 155n118.
167   Cf. Einwohner, "The Need to Know," 418.

greater than that exercised in the other two ghettos due to its geographical position. The possibilities of organization decreased from the isolation produced: "Furthermore, unlike the case in Warsaw and Vilna, it is notable that the primary data from Łódź display few claims about genocide, suggesting that Jews in Łódź were mostly unaware of the massacres happening in other ghettos. This lack of awareness stemmed in large part from the ghetto's relative isolation."[168] And third, it is essential to consider carefully the charismatic figure of Chaim Rumkowski, head of the Council:

> Rumkowski countered some of their protests with the use of force (applied by the ghetto's Jewish police force) and others with public speeches warning of even greater repression from the Nazis if factory work was disrupted. For instance, in a speech made at the conclusion of a workers' strike in January 1942, he said, "Had the strike attempts that recently took place here come to the attention of the authorities, the snow would have been red with blood.... I am certain that if the ghetto does its work in earnest and does it well, the authorities will not take repressive steps."[169]

In the wake of Berger and Luckmann's studies, Einwohner stresses that the social construction of reality in Łódź influenced totally the actions of individuals: the communication of distorted news avoided armed resistance in the ghetto.[170] Despite the skills and ability to organize collective action, since several political activists lived in the ghetto, the false building of reality prevented residents of Łódź from resisting. Additionally, the position of the ghetto, vital for the Reich's actions, compelled it to endure continuous control by Nazi forces: it was completely isolated. The geography of the ghettos was conceived and designed precisely to impede communication and common action among individuals: the physical distance, under control, generated a kind of moral distance among

---

168 Ibid., 418–19.
169 Ibid., 418 (authors' in-text citations omitted).
170 Cf. Peter L. Berger and Thomas Luckmann, *The Social Construction of Reality: A Treatise in the Sociology of Knowledge* (Garden City, NY: Anchor, 1966).

individuals. As in Łódź, this favored "incredibility."[171] Thus, individuals found it hard to believe the truth, or remain in "ignorance." Consequently, what happened was not recognized. This uncertainty, or, rather, this undefined situation, as in the Łódź community, did not create collective action, since, in the community's imagination, all those social forces leading to a revolt were silenced:

> A memo written by the members of the Jewish National Committee in May 24, 1944, read in part, "Despite our many efforts to make contact with the Łódź Jews ... we have failed to make our way into the ghetto. It is an island, totally cut off from the rest of the world." Without knowledge of the killings of Jews elsewhere in Europe, Jews in the Łódź Ghetto had no reason to believe that a similar fate would befall them; correspondingly, members of the community directed their efforts toward surviving the harsh ghetto conditions rather than resisting against the Nazis.[172]

By reading Einwohner's articles, two important issues arise. The first is with the power itself: the different forms of social life and organization forms among the residents of the ghetto depended on the kind of power exercised in the ghetto. The second issue concerns the power structure: personal, as in the case of the chief of the Council, or of a collective nature, as in the case of authority work, which organized the resistance.[173] Thanks to Einwohner, it is also possible to construct mentally a kind of conceptual matrix with two crossed variables on the nature of power. On the horizontal axis, there are the power structure (individual/collective) and the type of power (charismatic/authoritarian). On the vertical axis there are the times starting from which the political opportunities to resist Nazi power diminished, that is, from 1942, when the deportations began.

---

171 Einwohner, "The Need to Know," 410.
172 Ibid., 419 (authors' in-text citations omitted).
173 Cf. Peter Bachrach and Morton S. Baratz, "Two Faces of Power," *American Political Science Review* 56, no. 4 (1962): 947–52.

Taking these data into account, one can hypothesize that, in Warsaw, the stronger type of power, the one that received obedience to its own commands, was charismatic and exercised by the authority work (ŻOB, ŻZW, *Oneg Shabbat*), which allowed for the formation and actions of resistance in the ghetto.[174]

In Vilna, instead, the kind of power that found greater obedience was that of the authority of the chief of the Jewish Council, and, contrary to the actions of revolt, his power impeded the real deployment of resistance. Einwohner shows how power exercised in Łódź reveals that authoritarian power of the *Judenrat* and that exercised by the Reich coexisted.

Finally, Einwohner focuses on the relationship between the structures of the territory, or rather on the geographic location of the ghetto, and the political regime to which it is subjected. The Third Reich was organized in power layers that made it unique. The type of power exercised in the ghettos hinged on the geographical location of the ghetto itself. For instance, in the case of Warsaw, placed in the general government, the influence of the Reich was lower than that in Łódź, a city almost in the heart (from a geographical point of view), of the control policy of Nazis, since it was located in the *Wartheland*. Instead, Vilna, located in the territories to the east, belonged to those occupied areas of German influence in which the totalitarian power unfolded mainly in the second wave of massacres that began, in the Baltic area, in the autumn of 1941 and went on to increase the following year in all occupied territories. Thus, while the second was unleashed in the north, the first was still in progress at the south. For the Łódź ghetto, its geographical location, in the territory of Poland and incorporated into the Third Reich after Germany's invasion in 1939, was fatal, because "the resulting isolation not only contributed to the physical suffering of the ghetto inhabitants (i.e., by restricting the

---

174 See Avraham Milgram, Carmit Sagui, and Shulamit Imbar, eds., *Every Day Life in the Warsaw Ghetto, 1941* (Jerusalem: Yad Vashem, 1993), 54–57; Einwohner, "Opportunity, Honor, and Action in the Warsaw Ghetto Uprising of 1943," 655, see note 4.

available food supply) but also severely curtailed the transmission of information from other ghettos."[175]

4.6.4. The Geography of Resistance in Warsaw, Vilna, and Łódź

The collective action was not the same in Warsaw, Vilna, and Łódź. Einwohner tries to account for this geography of resistance by conceiving a new sociological category. In the wake of the studies of Schwartz, speaking of structured ignorance, and of Snow and Benford, who speak of empirical credibility, she coins the sociological notion of "cultural ignorance."[176] This concept was conceived for the occasion of understanding the Holocaust, but it is useful for sociology in general. Einwohner emphasizes that resistance was possible in Warsaw and that at the time Jews were able to obtain information on the Nazis' genocidal plans, and only when such information had become credible in the collective consciousness.[177] In essence, in the case of Vilna, the action of the chief of the Council impeded resistance efforts. Instead, in Łódź (where ignorance about genocidal news was institutionalized, that is, the false news was constructed as true to become credible in the public opinion of residents), credence was not given to reports regarding massacres: the ignorance became value-binding for individuals and slowly turned into a legitimate cultural ignorance:

> I use these concepts to examine what Jews knew about their situation (i.e., the extent to which they knew about the Nazis' genocidal plans) and to explore the role of this knowledge in their decision to resist. I find that while ignorance and knowledge help explain action (or the lack thereof) in each ghetto, these cases also reveal that "ignorance" has cultural as well as structural components. I use these findings to draw

---

175   Einwohner, "The Need to Know," 419 (authors' in-text citations omitted).
176   Cf. Michael Schwartz, *Radical Protest and Social Structure: The Southern Farmers' Alliance and Cotton Tenancy, 1880–1890* (Chicago: University of Chicago Press, 1976); David A. Snow and Robert D. Benford, "Ideology, Frame, Resonance, and Participant Mobilization," in *From Structure to Action: Comparing Social Movements Research across Cultures*, ed. Bert Klandermans, Hanspeter Kriesi, and Sidney Tarrow (Greenwich, CT: JAI Press, 1988), 197–218.
177   See Einwohner, "The Need to Know."

broader implications for future research on social movements and collective resistance.[178]

Structured ignorance is a social process that starts a much more complex and serious cultural ignorance. While the first restricts or precludes knowledge of the facts to individuals, the second is based on interpretative binding practices that act as rules and intervene on decision-making and emotional acting of the same.[179] In this way, the flow of the news becomes a social phenomenon that is useful to study. In Warsaw, the resistance was only possible because there was knowledge rather than ignorance. Collective action in Warsaw did not begin in the fall of 1940, when the ghetto was built for the first time: "Notably, these discussions began in response to news from Vilna, where mass murders of Jews had occurred in the nearby woods of Ponar the previous summer and fall and where young activists were organizing for resistance."[180] The possibility of action started to be discussed only after January 1942, namely, when information on the massacres perpetrated in Vilna arrived in the ghetto. And the action became concrete from July 1942, when deportations from the ghetto began.

Instead, in the ghetto of Vilna the phenomenon of cultural ignorance only led to a plan of resistance since the attitude of the chief of the Council triggered the mechanism of noncredibility, of what was not possible:

> Interestingly, the news about the massacres in Vilna was not interpreted in the same way by all members of the ghetto community in Warsaw. While young activists in the Warsaw Ghetto argued for resistance, older community leaders countered them by saying that attempts at collective resistance would only bring greater hardships upon the ghetto community. Describing one community meeting at which the topic of resistance was discussed, Vladka

---

178 Ibid., 408.
179 See Karen A. Cerulo, *Never Saw It Coming: Cultural Challenges to Envisioning the Worst* (Chicago: University of Chicago Press, 2006); Lee Clarke, *Worst Cases: Terror and Catastrophe in the Popular Imagination* (Chicago: University of Chicago Press, 2006); Einwohner, "The Need to Know," 410–11.
180 Ibid., 415 (authors' in-text citations omitted).

Meed (who became a member of the ŻOB) wrote, "The Jewish leaders did not want to assume the responsibility of risking the lives of those who still hoped to survive. The prevailing opinion still was that no more than, say, 60,000 or 70,000 people would be deported and that the rest would survive. Under the circumstances, how could anyone find it in his heart to jeopardize the lives of the entire Warsaw ghetto for the sake of active resistance? ... The illusion that one was bound to survive drowned out voices of warning."[181]

The construction of reality weighs on this past: faced with the existence of the facts the power of imagination prevails, in the sense of a false image duly constructed by power in force. Escapism was then evident in the ghetto of Łódź, where the false construction of reality and false hopes, combined with the voice of the head of the *Gettoverwaltung*, Biebow, were more convincing than the army and extreme self-defense. The choice of resisting in Łódź was made too late to change the common sense view, of which Schütz wrote in 1953—it was too strong among the residents of the ghetto to be discontinued:

> Notably, the isolation of the Łódź Ghetto prevented residents from obtaining information about roundups and deportations in other ghettos. Without being able to pool information with Jews in similar circumstances, Łódź residents failed to recognize the genocide and therefore failed to launch resistance efforts against the Nazis. In contrast, the physical construction and daily operation of the ghettos of Warsaw and Vilna, which made it easier for Jews to slip out to the "Aryan side," were more facilitative of inter-ghetto communication. In accordance with the concept of structured ignorance, these structural features made it possible for Jews in those ghettos to learn about what was happening elsewhere, thereby reducing the ignorance that acted as a barrier to collective action.[182]

---

181 Ibid.
182 Ibid., 420.

4.7. ANTI-SEMITISM IN BRUSTEIN

William Brustein's *Roots of Hate* (2003) tackles the question of anti-Semitism in an original way: Brustein measures the intensity of the phenomenon in time and space. Nevertheless, some of the reviewers of the book, especially Jeffrey K. Olick, present some negative critiques of the sudden historicity with which the author recounts the events. Brustein puts in evidence the huge links among National Socialism, anti-Semitism, and the Holocaust. He explains the spread of anti-Semitism, recalling Goldhagen's political and cultural thesis, the modernization theory, the scapegoat notion, and the position proposing a strong state.[183]

In essence, in the first case, Brustein calls into question the idea of an eliminationist anti-Semitism of a long tradition in Germany, which is unable to explicate the diverse waves of the phenomenon at different times in the history of country. He states that the Holocaust was a direct consequence of Hitler's rise to power and not an inevitability of history and Germanic culture. In other words, it cannot be understood only as an outbreak of brutal violence or as a radicalized extreme form of *deutsche Sonderweg*. This challenges the thesis of a German national program that considered the Holocaust as the inevitable result of a national pathology by which Germans, as prisoners of an atavistic belief, believed the Jews were worthy of death. Brustein's approach to the Holocaust integrates a combination of factors (religious pressures, economic instability, elements of racism, political crisis) that degenerated in Weimar Germany, into one

---

[183] Cf. Goldhagen, *Hitler's Willing Executioners*; William I. Brustein, *Roots of Hate: Anti-Semitism in Europe before the Holocaust* (Cambridge: Cambridge University Press, 2003); Brustein and King, "Anti-Semitism in Europe Before the Holocaust," 35–53; Jeffrey K. Olick, review of *Roots of Hate: Anti-Semitism in Europe before the Holocaust*, by William I. Brustein, *American Journal of Sociology* 111, no. 3 (2005): 945–48. Anti-Semitic attitudes and behavior reported in "American Jewish Yearbook" and in articles published in the five countries mentioned in the years 1899–1939, with events that pertain to the long period 1870–99, are the basis of Brustein's study.

narrative that enlightens the threshold level of anti-Semitism.[184] His sociological method seems to be uncommon: one that cannot be used to read the studies linking European anti-Semitism to the modernization process, that is, to liberalism and capitalism, which are important factors in political, social, and economic emancipation of the Jews.

One reason for this is that their social mobility and then the social mechanism of competition reinforced feelings of fear and hostility resulting in anti-Semitic attitudes and passions among non-Jewish countrymen. Although this theory expounds the growth of anti-Semitism after 1870, it cannot account for the changes, sometimes even reductions, of levels of anti-Semitism starting from 1890.[185] It is not able to explicate why anti-Semitism in Europe increased significantly during the decade 1880–90, fell sharply between 1900 and 1914, and then climbed steeply in the early 1920s and in the mid-1930s. Finally, it does not clarify why the level of anti-Semitism was higher in Romania and Germany than in Britain and Italy.

With regard to the scapegoat theory, Brustein points out that, in times of national crisis, people instinctively seek groups on which to transfer anxieties or social concerns. The presence of the Jewish immigrant, dispersed in many countries, was used to solve several problems: he became the scapegoat on which to project the contradictions of modernity. Nevertheless, this theory, by making manifest the sociopsychological irrational pulses of a society in crisis, fails when it cannot explain why in certain societies where there were a number of Jews, they are not the only victims—other social groups were also victims of violence.[186]

---

184 Cf. Traverso, *The Origins of Nazi Violence*, 136–48.
185 See Anthony Giddens, *Modernity and Self-Identity: Self and Society in the Late Modern Age* (Stanford, CA: Stanford University Press, 1991); Alberto Martinelli, *La modernizzazione* (Rome-Bari: Laterza, 2004).
186 Cf. Sigmund Freud, *Das Unbehagen in der Kultur* (Vienna: Internationaler Psychoanalytischer Verlag., 1930); Norbert Elias, *Über den Prozess der Zivilisation* (Basel: Verlag Haus zum Falken, 1939); Zygmunt Bauman, *Modernity and Ambivalence* (Cambridge: Polity Press, 1991). This theory, based primarily on Freudian assumptions, revisits also Elias lesson. The civilizing process includes the sublimation of destructive impulses and the progressive elimination of all forms of violence, historically inveterate with the monopoly of legitimate violence of the modern nation-state in order to ensure public order and the defense industry.

Ultimately, Brustein undermines the theory of a strong state proposed by Pierre Birnbaum in 1992, according to which anti-Semitism was a reaction of the people against the state imposing the emancipation of the Jews. This thesis illustrates well the variation of levels of anti-Semitism in several European countries: specifically, it is strongest where the state imposed emancipation, as in France and Germany, weak where the emancipation was a gradual phenomenon that started from the bottom through society, as in the case of Britain. The weaknesses of the theory, for Brustein, concerns the times of anti-Semitism, since Birnbaum does not clarify the causes carrying a strong anti-Semitism in France in the period 1890–1930, within which there was a phase of weak anti-Semitism in the years 1904–30.[187]

In recent decades the Holocaust question has been addressed by many crosscutting topics not always directly related to the Holocaust: for instance, it has been studied within the framework of collective memory research or migration matters. Namely, there are tendencies of mixing the Holocaust with other events in the 2000s. Let me recall that these authors and their works were introduced and noticed by Gerson and Wolf in 2007.[188]

4.8. SUMMARY

In this chapter we have seen how post-Holocaust sociology changed during globalization. The merits of sociologists studying the phenomenon, along with the categories typical to examining the globalization process, that is, with the categories going beyond modernity features and borders, were examined. We also described the different types of memory, the main notion of these years, so that we can now understand the passage from a collective memory to a cosmopolitan memory to a sociological representation of the Holocaust in society. Readers can see how important this is for sociology as academic discipline. The result is a new sociology

---

[187] Cf. Pierre Birnbaum, *Anti-Semitism in France: A Political History from Léon Blum to the Present* (Oxford: Blackwell, 1992); Brustein and King, *Anti-Semitism in Europe before the Holocaust*, 37.
[188] See note 7, above.

of the Holocaust but also, above all, a new sociological thinking related to globalization: in other words, sociologists who study the Holocaust starting from globalization finish with the study of globalization itself in a new sociological way, providing sociology with new approaches. We glimpsed at the post-Holocaust sociology of gender in that 1990s and how it led to a new reprocessing of categories such as resistance and anti-Semitism as consequence of the decadency of the American myth, a discourse that has returned in the last decade.

Conclusions: The Alleged Delay

This book has tried to fill a gap in the literature of sociology and Holocaust Studies. Sociology as a discipline will, I hope, benefit from it: by the perusal of the sociological literature, conducted with Internet archives, databases, and online academic reviews, using which, to the best of my possibilities, it was perhaps possible to rewrite the history of the sociology of the Holocaust and, and the same time, sociology itself.

The usefulness of this book is that it questions and puts into discussion the sustained thesis—reaffirmed among scholars at the 2001 conference at Rutgers University—of the so-called delay of sociological scholarship on the Holocaust. Contrary to the assumption of a delay, I have attempted to demonstrate that sociology has not absolutely been on delay. The event of the Holocaust and its related themes were not considered by scholars for a series of reasons. By sifting sociological works and sources, I have discovered—and tried to evidence in the book—that several sociologists approached the Holocaust, and not only after 1945, but even during World War II itself. The reader will note Parsons's writings and his entire case outlined in Chapter 1. However, for a set of pragmatic reasons, the sociologists who approached the Jewish question were not given credence in the academic realm; their writings were unnoticed, as evidenced by the works of Neurath, Hughes, or *Anti-Semitism* by the Frankfurt School. By dismissing these primary works that paved the way for a sociology of the Holocaust, the scholarship and a sociological tradition on the Holocaust is missed.

Indeed, by looking at any paper, nay, by perusing the record paper by paper, article by article, I discovered a series of circumstances (political, academic, and cultural) that led to this sociological delay and gave rise to a tradition of scholars missing in post-Holocaust sociology. The Cold War must take precedence among the salient factors: the world lived under the fear of the well-known Red menace, while the pragmatic and functional sociology of Parsons, far from Simmel's interests and qualitative approach, enjoyed his fortune in the academy. In the postwar years, political institutions, foundations funding scholarships, research centers, and the same academic realm preferred or opted for a-evalutative theories that did not put in discussion what happened and did not ask questions about what occurred, avoiding in this way a possible change of the status quo or of what was wrong in society. This a-evalutative thinking, removed from reality, is the opposite of what Arendt called "political thinking" and found in Parsons its major exponent and theorist. To some extent, as I have attempted to show, Parsons's theories were politically aroused and generated—they were necessary in the political environment of that period. Moreover, Parsons was driven by a set of events, personal and not, to elaborating and conceiving an a-evalutative sociology, removed and detached from real society: conceptual and suitable for postwar policies.

This does not mean that there were not sociologists who developed other, different thoughts in sociology. For example, as stated in Chapter 1, Hughes and Sorokin represent some exceptions. They faced a not few problems with the power of the academy. However, Parsons's theories worked well and unflinchingly because they were in harmony with the contemporary political thought of a pragmatic America and in accordance with interests of foundations funding research in the postwar years. After World War II, most research was financed with the aim of combating communism—hence, Harvard University established the American Russian Research Center, which was active in discovering any source of the Soviet threat or useful related information.

It should be remembered that in the postwar years an important link between sociology, the science of society, and political life was created, and I sketched a brief outline regarding the academic life of Harvard University. I repeat, the academy privileged those issues that did not deal with certain political or burning questions, namely, that of the eternity of evil, supreme evil, or with topics of a moral nature, theorized by the Frankfurt School or about which it had speculated. Political and educational institutes or foundations preferred to focus their research attention on apolitical themes or those related to a methodological research of quantitative kind. There were not a few conflicting positions that rose among scholars with different opinions: for example, between MacIver and Lynd within the Department of Sociology at Columbia University in 1940s, as seen in Chapter 1.

The question of supreme evil and the eternal evil, echoing Frankfurt School thoughts, was shunned for an a-evaluative thinking, which wanted to sustain a pragmatic society in the United States, thought to be socially mobile, oriented to the individual, and capable of resolving any problem—this was the spirit after World War II. This led to a rejection of any "metaphysics of being," any scientific philosophy of the spirit. Any topic dealing with metaphysical thinking and not with logic was materially false, logically not sustainable, and thus without sense. It was necessary to reject any metaphysical proposition because it did not offer a solution to fundamental problems (the postwar economic crisis, migration, etc.). Thus moral and ethical issues concerning eternal evil were not inscribed into American pragmatism and in support of the ideology of a perfectly functional America, most concerned with avoiding in any way the Red menace. Hence, the continuous efforts to finance research and promote foundations and collaborators intending to do it, such as the Harvard Russian Center. Different discourses were not considered; they were simply dismissed. This continued until the limits of American pragmatism emerged in the 1960s, when a series of events of various natures (political facts and the cultural order) encountered one another repeatedly throughout the era and determined the end of pragmatism. Better still, the limits of this theory became visible to all and the paradigm of sociology, Parsonsism, and the structural-functional prominence underwent a change. The changes came in the years after Stalin's death in 1953, the Thaw era, the Congo crisis of 1960–65, the Six Days' War in 1967, and up to the end of the Vietnam War. At that time, conflict theory in sociology in its extreme form led to a revival of the critical theory of the Frankfurt School, which after World War II had been abandoned for the sociological theories of the time aiming at maintaining the *status quo*. And even history as a discipline was underestimated and was losing importance in academics in those years (hence the relevance of the first publication of Hilberg's historical research in 1961).

This book is important because it argues for a presence of post-Holocaust scholarship in the postwar years. Therefore, if the thesis of the delay is to be given credence to this day, the delay has to be modified to a "intended delay," especially as it pertains to the timing of publication, as put in evidence by the Hughes and Neurath cases and by the unpublished Parsons letters. The delay was *intended* by the academies, universities, and funding centers of research. That is, it is possible to speak of a kind of *delayed memory*: Hughes decided to not publish his piece in 1948, even if he had taught a course on social movements, referring to National Socialism and what came to be known as "Hughes on the Nazis" at McGill University in 1930s. There was a delayed memory for scholars who were going to approach the destruction of the Jews, and there was a problem inside the academy, namely, that of anti-Semitism, a pervasive factor that influenced the whole issue.[1] First, prejudice denied the authors a chance to examine Jewish matters honestly; second, it hindered, at Harvard University, academics and scholars in tackling the Jewish question and, specifically, the genocide of the Jews. The anti-Semitism harbored in the prewar period obstructed scholarly opportunities to stand against Hitler's regime.

Thus, I hope that this book has challenged us to review the stereotype according which Bauman "woke up" post-Holocaust Sociology. By my sociological perusal, some works, in particular Hughes's "Good People and Dirty Work," broke the stereotype of the so-called delay of sociology by revealing that Cold War policies had put into brackets the discourse on the Holocaust. In other words, sociological research on the extermination of the Jews was being written, but out of the limelight. Coming back to Hughes's and Neurath's studies, they were not published soon after their drafting because of conflicts with the political concerns of academy and with the interests of private and government funding of research. Or publishers were not available, in the case of Neurath, to print such studies. The destruction of the Jews was a political issue, and political issues and moral matters were not being promoted by the academy, but only topics suitable for interests and government policies in favor of a pragmatic, functionalist America. To make the issue clearer, I repeat that the climate of Cold War created an iron curtain upon the research world: so any argument not dealing with the Red menace—it was a kind of anxiety—was

---

1 Halpert, "Early American Sociology and the Holocaust"; Norwood, "Legitimating Nazism."

dismissed until the 1960s and after, when a series of events of historical and political capacity, and some currents of thought, not only sociological, initiated, at least theoretically, caused a tear in this iron curtain.

WATERSHED EVENTS

Sociological interest in the Holocaust started to come back in the early 1960s, as shown by my perusal of online reviews, which do not replace or supplant paper or printed journals, but support them, permitting us to have a wider range for analysis. Without this scientific and scholarly literature available online, I couldn't have written this book. After analyzing sociological texts, private writings, and letters, it is evident that some studies, such as *The German Universities and National Socialism* (1937) by Hartshorne or *Anti-Semitism* conducted by the Frankfurt School in 1944–45, were unnoticed: they have largely been forgotten, even by many scholars of the field. Small wonder that the above disinterest coincided with the end of the functionalism era in sociology. It is important to sum up events or circumstances that led to the demise of functionalism America in the 1960s.

First and foremost, I have mentioned the Eichmann trial of 1962, which strongly focused attention on the question of evil: starting from that event, one can continuously ask how people and a society become evil. The Eichmann process put on the scene the banality of evil, echoing the importance of moral issues and how important it was that humankind use its faculty of thinking. In this book, I have explained that the banality of evil notion was invented and utilized in 1948 by a sociologist, Hughes, and then used again by Hughes in 1962, and by Arendt in the same year. Since then many scholars, such as Michael T. Allen and James Waller, have used it.[2] Additionally, the publication of *Eichmann in Jerusalem: A Report on the Banality of Evil* by Arendt, first in serial form in 1962 and then in a book in 1963, and the earlier release in the United States in 1961 of the *The Destruction of the European Jews* by the historian Hilberg broke definitively the scholarly silence on the Holocaust.

---

2   See note 201, above (chapter 1).

To put an end to the *delayed memory* in sociology were the Six Days' War (*Milhemet Sheshet Ha Yamim*) and the Jewish philosopher Fackenheim's theories. Jews feared another Holocaust in 1967. Fackenheim recalled scholars and thinkers to the task of addressing and tackling the question of supreme evil. Two years later, in 1969, the philosopher stated that "the Nazi Holocaust is totally present, contemporary, and non-anachronistic. The passage of time has brought it closer rather than moving it farther away."[3] The question of the moral issue, abandoned after World War II in favor of a functionalist and pragmatic sociology, now returned. The fallacies of American functionalism emerged at that time: the AGIL paradigm of Parsons did not sufficiently work anymore, as it did during the postwar years when his theory was useful for sustaining the political ideas of a government principally worried about preventing and avoiding a communist takeover. Indeed, the Six Days' War shifted the attention onto what occurred to Jews during World War II. And again another conflict, that of Yom Kippur War in 1973, and the military victory for Israel led to a more proper and open approach to the Holocaust. Moreover, the near military defeat for Israel focused attention on the theme of spiritual and not armed resistance. It meant that a strong army started to lose importance in favor of more peaceful endeavors. In this period, I do not know if it is a pure coincidence, I could not verify, in Poland an important sociological text, and eyewitness account, by Pawełczyńska, not related to armed resistance, appeared, in a time that scholars were not yet discussing resistance and while the theme was unknown.

To point out the limits of American pragmatism and the end of the American positivistic remnants of the 1920s–30s were the years of the Vietnam War (1954–75) and its tremendous human cost. This war, called by the Vietnamese the "War against the American to Save the Nation," saw U.S. combat units introduced in 1965 and reached the worst human costs in 1969. One may read between the lines the fallacy of the choices in favor of a functionalist America. Evidence for this was clear at the end of the

---

3 Debóra Dwork and Robert Jan van Pelt, *Holocaust: A History* (New York: W. W. Norton, 2003), 386n38, 428.

war, with the defeat of the United States and the nonaligned movement established in 1961 in Belgrade. Pragmatism, first, and functionalism, after, did not lead to anything good. Faced with the victims of Vietnam, there was a rethinking: this time on the side of the victims. The attention moved towards real problems that led humankind to reflect and ask: What comes now? The military strategy of containment was going to be reviewed. In the meanwhile, there were also the social earthquake of the civil rights struggle in the early 1960s and the 1968 movements for an America free and civil to pave the way in the addressing the question of evil. The writings by the sociologist Sorokin and philosopher Fackenheim reported the attention on the eternal evil, an undervalued issue in the postwar years because of the Cold War.

Without the perusal of well-qualified online reviews, several sociological studies mentioned in the book would be forgotten. If this approach is used by scholars in the future, readers will be able to deal with post-Holocaust sociology in a more specific way: this book aspires to inaugurate a sociological scholarship able to retrace post-Holocaust sociology country by country and in the language of the country considered. I smile at the prospect.

Cui prodest? I hope this book can be a kind of sociological key to rethinking the Holocaust using sociological tools. It is appropriate now to divide the sociologists who have distinguished themselves for their researches on the Holocaust, at least into two large types of researchers: sociologists "of the first hour," namely, those who from Hitler's rise until the crisis of modern society used in their works, although in different ways, similar analytical categories, and those "of the last hour," belonging to the age of globalization and tending to coin new concepts after having approached and combined more theories.

In the first group, the studies of Heberle, Merkl, and Lipset are especially significant: working at different times, they were standing for the way in which, starting from the idea of "political group" (*Politischer Verband*), to analyze the Nazi regime. Then, let me add to this group Shils and Janowitz, who investigated instead—on the basis of the concept of "primary group"—the characteristics and influence of German militarism. It is also possible to include in this group Moore and Bauman: starting from conditions of alienation and discomfort of the working class, these scholars addressed the issue of social suffering, conceiving the Holocaust as an evil product resulting from interpersonal relationships in a context in which the economic or political power failed to allocate resources.

In the second group, it seems that the framework of research has been constantly progressing and, in recent years, particularly innovative. This is the case, for example, of Allen, who, in 1997, in describing the importance of bureaucracy in genocidal action, refers to both "white-collar"—the middle class of which Mills spoke—and blue-collar workers, manual labors. On the occasion he introduces the category of the "grey-collar worker," workers who practice a dirty job, gray and ordinary, which substantially consists in the administration of the death.

Following the studies of Schwartz about "structured ignorance" and of Snow and Benford on "empirical credibility," the scholar Einwohner instead has recently conceived the notion of "cultured ignorance," alluding to the negative effects that the lack of knowledge of the facts has upon society when this ignorance becomes part of the culture. Moreover, Einwohner and Pawełczyńska developed a new conception of Jewish resistance. Einwohner goes against the traditional theories of sociology in presenting the resistance as a social movement and organization, typical concepts of sociology, examining three historical cases: Warsaw, Vilna, and Łódź. Pawełczyńska, in proposing her original theory of resistance, allows us to significantly enrich our knowledge about the forms of spiritual resistance, *Amidah*.

Finally, Levy and Sznaider have prompted research into new directions, presenting the Holocaust as a social representation of absolute evil.

On the one hand, tracking the status of sociology, as a discipline and as an academic corpus, when faced with the extermination of the Jews, meant having a particular device to reinterpret and reread the phenomenon of the Holocaust, on the other hand, such an approach might make the same genocidal event an analytical tool with which to retrace post-Holocaust sociology.

This signifies that, in the light of the phenomenon of the Holocaust, it has been possible to reformulate the history of sociology, by perusing unknown texts, and even now unreleased (for instance, the writings of Parsons on National Socialism and his "mysterious" letters), by using ignored categories (such as "rationalization of terror," designed precociously by Gerth in 1940), or improperly attributed to scholars different from the original ones: the concepts of the "banality of evil" and "total institution" developed by Hughes, for example, were assigned to Arendt and Goffman, respectively.

There was a need for an editing or a correction of some stated theoretical points. Hence, I hope my study provides motivations and incentives for scholars to engage in new research that brings scholars back into the archives. We need more work on this kind of research: because only by entering into the archives, only by rereading, to some extent, of some papers or "missing letters," only through a critical analysis of texts, it is possible to get close to an in-depth truth.

Now, since, in the beginning of this work there was a question: Is it necessary to determine if *Modernity and the Holocaust* really was the first or only work that led sociologists to reflect on what had happened to the Jews of Europe? Hence, the perusal of the entire sociological literature with key concepts recalling or related to the destruction of the Jews, not driven by concentration camp phases, as stated many times in the book and explained by Hilberg in *The Destruction of the European Jews* or by David Cesarani. Thus, the preliminary question was if there were, before Bauman, other sociologists who, with specific categories of discipline, had approached the genocidal phenomenon. Traverso, in 1997, in his *Histoire déchirée*[4] wrote of the indifference of intellectuals faced with the extermination of the Jews. With regards to sociology, this assertion is not at all proper (or it deserves to be reformulated), in the same way in which it is quite incorrect to speak of "sociological silence." Disagreeing with what several authors argued in the conference of 2001, I state that sociology was not delayed in studying the Holocaust. Kirchheimer, Hartshorne, Neurath, Hughes, and Parsons were among the first to denounce the Nazi socialist reality and the risks to which it would lead.

They were muses who "did not listen" or were "nonaligned," sometimes "silent," despite their innovative analysis in respect of the sociological

---

4   Cf. Traverso, *Auschwitz e gli intellettuali.*

tradition.[5] The writings that have remained unnoticed for years or buried in the archives are not few—those of Hartshorne and Parsons, for example—as long as other scholars have not unearthed them more or less randomly. This happens behind the policies of objectivity and neutrality dictated by the contingency of the times—of World War II, first, and of the Cold War, after.

Sociologists have long been hindered in spreading their opinions on what they saw. However, these sociologists were perhaps the only ones who, as privileged observers of society, and representatives of elite thought, had the tools and knowledge necessary to disclose the great catastrophe that would be unleashed on European society at the end of the long process that began with the fall of the Old Regime and led the West to trigger the continuous process of national integration. When this process of integration, in the shadow of imperialism, was broken, negating the possibility of a balanced and peaceful coexistence among different nations, it also broke the development of the "bonds of organic solidarity," of a political or economic nature.

On March 6, 1927, in Vilsbiburg, Hitler stated that "when the nations are in a state of necessity, they do not refer to legal rights. One question arises: Does a people have the right to conquer the land and the land that it needs?"[6]

Thus, if "rethinking" the genocide of the Jews means to do justice to the facts, through the sociological discourses and practices typical of the discipline, this book has aimed at inviting us to rethink how antimodernist ideas, the idea of the nation, and the myths of the Aryan race and blood were met with technological progress on German soil. In a passage from *The Seventh Million*, Tom Segev expresses better towards which truths a scholar has to tend:[7]

---

5 See note 70, above (chapter 1).
6 Neumann et al., *Il nemico tedesco*, 458. For Hitler's speech, see *Völkischer Beobachter*, March 8, 1927, quoted in *Hitler's Words*, ed. G. W. Prange (American Council on Public Affairs, 1944), 17.
7 Cf. Enzo Traverso, ed., *Insegnare Auschwitz: Questioni etiche, storiografiche, educative della deportazione e dello sterminio* (Turin: Bollati Boringhieri, 1995). Tom Segev, *The Seventh Million: The Israelis and the Holocaust* (New York: Henry Holt, 2000).

On the way to Auschwitz one of the teachers read a few lines from Viktor Frankl's *Man in Search of Meaning* into the bus's loudspeaker. Frankl was much quoted during the trip; the Viennese psychiatrist had survived Auschwitz. "It seems that man is able to endure suffering, humiliation, fear, or anger thanks to the image of a loved one that he preserves in his heart," Frankl wrote, "or thanks to religion or a sense of humor, or even thanks to a glance at the people imprisoned with him, or thanks to his belief that in the end all will be well."[8]

But, according to Segev, Frankl had not discovered the sense of life in Auschwitz, as his publisher wanted the reader to believe, but long before being arrested. The sufferings of Auschwitz, however, had demonstrated the validity of his theory.[9]

---

8 Ibid., 496–7.
9 See ibid. The reference is to Segev, "Is It Worth Living?" *Haaretz* (supplement), June 11, 1981, 12–14.

Bibliography

Abbott, Andrew. *Department and Discipline: Chicago Sociology at One Hundred*. Chicago: University of Chicago Press, 1999.

Abel, Theodore. *Why Hitler Came into Power*. Cambridge, MA: Harvard University Press, 1938; reprinted as *The Nazi Movement: Why Hitler Came into Power*. New York: Atherton, 1966.

———. "The Sociology of Concentration Camps." *Social Forces* 30, no. 2 (1951): 150–55. doi:10.2307/2571626.

Abowitz, Deborah A. "Bringing the Sociological into the Discussion: Teaching the Sociology of Genocide and the Holocaust." *Teaching Sociology* 30, no. 1 (2002): 26–38.

Adam, Uwe D. *Judenpolitik im Dritten Reich*. Düsseldorf: Droste, 1972.

Adler, Hans G. *Theresienstadt 1941-1945: Das Antlitz einer Zwangsgemeinschaft*. Tübingen, Mohr, 1955.

———. "Ideas toward a Sociology of the Concentration Camp." *American Journal of Sociology* 63, no. 5 (1958): 513–22.

Adorno, Theodor L. W. *Minima Moralia: Reflexionen aus dem beschädigten Leben*. Frankfurt: Suhrkamp, 1951.

———. *Negative Dialektik*. Frankfurt: Suhrkamp, 1966.

Adorno, Theodor, Else Frenkel-Brunswick, Daniel J. Levinson, and R. Nevitt Sanford. *The Authoritarian Personality*. New York: Norton, 1950.

Affuso, Olimpia. *Il Magazine della memoria: I media e il ricordo degli avvenimenti pubblici*. Rome: Carocci, 2010.

———. "Jeffrey C. Alexander—il processo del trauma culturale." In *M come Memoria: La memoria nella teoria sociale*, edited by Teresa Grande and Olimpia Affuso, 215–43. Naples: Liguori Editore, 2012.

Alberoni, Francesco. *Movimento e istituzione*. Bologna: il Mulino, 1981.

Alexander, Jeffrey C. *La costruzione del male: Dall'Olocausto all'11 settembre*. Bologna: il Mulino, 2006.

Alexander, Jeffrey C., Ron Eyerman, Bernhard Giesen, Neil J. Smelser, and Piotr Sztompka. *Cultural Trauma and Collective Identity*. Berkeley: University of California Press, 2004.
Alexander, Jeffrey C., Martin Jay, Bernhard Giesen, Michael Rothberg, Robert Manne, Nathan Glazer, and Elihu Katz, and Ruth Katz. *Remembering the Holocaust: A Debate*. New York: Oxford University Press, 2009.
Allen, Michael T. "The Banality of Evil Reconsidered: SS Mid-Level Managers of Extermination through Work." *Central European History* 30 (1997): 253–94.
———. "Grey-Collar Worker: Organisation Theory in Holocaust Studies." *Holocaust Studies: A Journal of Culture and History* 11, no. 1 (2005): 27–54.
Allport, Floyd H. *Social Psychology*. Boston: Houghton Mifflin, 1924.
Altınay, Ayşe Gül, and Andrea Pető. "Europe and the Century of Genocides: New Directions in the Feminist Theorizing of Genocide." *European Journal of Women's Studies* 22, no. 4 (2015): 379–85. doi:10.1177/1350506815608325.
Aly, Götz H. *Hitler's Beneficiaries: Plunder, Racial War, and the Nazi Welfare State*. New York: Henry Holt, 2005.
American Philosophical Society. "Symposium on the Totalitarian State." *Proceedings of the American Philosophical Society* 82, no. 1 (1940): i–vi, 1–102.
Anderson, Benedict. *Imagined Communities: Reflections on the Origin and Spread of Nationalism*. London: Verso, 1983.
Anheier, Helmut K., Friedhelm Neidhardt, and Wolfgang Vortkamp. "Movement Cycles and the Nazi Party: Activities of the Munich NSDAP, 1925–1930." *American Behavioral Scientist* 41 (1998): 1262–81.
Appadurai, Arjun. *Modernity at Large: Cultural Dimensions of Globalization*. Minneapolis: University of Minnesota Press, 1996.
———, ed. *Globalization*. Durham, NC: Duke University Press, 2001.
Arad, Yitzhak, Israel Gutman, and Abraham Margaliot, eds. *Documents on the Holocaust: Selected Sources on the Destruction of the Jews of Germany and Austria, Poland, and the Soviet Union*. 8th ed. Translated by Lea Ben Dor. Lincoln and London: University of Nebraska Press, and Jerusalem: Yad Vashem, 1999.
Archibugi, Daniele, David Held, and Martin Köhler, eds. *Re-imagining Political Community: Studies in Cosmopolitan Democracy*. Stanford, CA: Stanford University Press, 1998.

Arendt, Hannah. *The Origins of Totalitarianism*. New York: Harcourt, Brace & Co., 1951; German edition: *Elemente und Ursprünge totaler Herrschaft*. Frankfurt: Europäische Verlags-Anstalt, 1955.

———. *The Human Condition: A Study of the Central Dilemmas Facing Modern Man*. Chicago: University of Chicago Press, 1958.

———. *Eichmann in Jerusalem: A Report on the Banality of Evil*. New York: Viking, 1963.

———. *On Revolution*. New York: Viking, 1963.

Aron, Raymond. *Paix et guerre entre les nations*. Paris: Calmann-Lévy, 1962.

Arrighi, Giovanni. *La geometria dell'imperialismo*. Milan: Feltrinelli, 1978.

Askenazy, Hans. *Are We All Nazis?* Secaucus, NJ: L. Stuart, 1978.

Avineri, Shlomo, Richard Bernstein, Jonathan R. Cole, Hans-Peter Krüger, and Alan Ryan. "Universities under Conditions of Duress: Question and Answer Session." *Social Research: An International Quarterly* 76, no. 3 (2009): 959–62.

Bachrach, Peter, and Morton S. Baratz. "Two Faces of Power." *American Political Science Review* 56, no. 4 (1962): 947–52.

Bacon, Gershon C. Review of *On the Edge of Destruction: Jews of Poland between the Two World Wars*, by Celia S. Heller, *Journal of International Affairs* 31, no. 1 (1977): 143–45.

Badie, Bertarnd. *La Fin des territoires: Essai sur le désordre international et l'utilité sociale du respect*. Paris: Fayard, 1995.

Bahr, Ehrhard. "The Anti-Semitism Studies of the Frankfurt School: The Failure of Critical Theory." In *Foundations of the Frankfurt School of Social Research*, edited by Judith Marcus, and Zoltán Tar, 311–21. New Brunswick, NJ: Transaction, 1984.

Bankier, David, and Dan Michman, eds., *Holocaust Historiography in Context: Emergence, Challenges, Polemics and Achievements*. Jerusalem: Yad Vashem; New York: Berghahn, 2008.

Banton, Michael. Review of *Modernity and the Holocaust*, by Zygmunt Bauman, *The British Journal of Sociology* 42, no. 1 (1991): 164.

Barkai, Avraham. "German Historians Confront Goldhagen." *Yad Vashem Studies* 26 (1998): 295–328.

Barnard, Chester I., and Kenneth Thompson, *Organization and Management: Selected Papers. Early Sociology of Management and Organizations*. London: Routledge, 2003.

Bartoszewski, Władysław. *The Warsaw Ghetto: A Christian's Testimony*. Boston: Beacon, 1987.

Bartov, Omer. *The Eastern Front, 1941–45: German Troops and the Barbarisation of Warfare*. New York: St. Martin's Press, 1986.

———. "L'Europa orientale come luogo del genocidio." In *Storia della Shoah: La crisi dell'Europa, lo sterminio degli ebrei e la memoria del XX secolo*, edited by Marina Cattaruzza, Marcello Flores, Simon Levis-Sullam, and Enzo Traverso, 2:419–59. Turin: Utet, 2005–2006.

Bartrop, Paul R. "The Relationship between War and Genocide in the Twentieth Century: A Consideration." *Journal of Genocide Research* 4, no. 4 (2002): 519–32.

Bartrop, Paul R., and Steven L. Jacobs. *Fifty Key Thinkers on the Holocaust and Genocide*. London: Routledge, 2011.

Bauer, Yehuda, *The Holocaust in Historical Perspective*. Seattle: University of Washington Press, 1978.

———. *The Jewish Emergence from Powerlessness*. Toronto: Toronto University Press, 1979.

———. *Rethinking the Holocaust*. New Haven, CT: Yale University Press, 2001.

Baum, Ranier C. *The Holocaust and the German Elite: Genocide and National Suicide in Germany, 1871–1945*. Totowa, NJ: Rowman and Littlefield, 1981.

Bauman, Janina. *Winter in the Morning: A Young Girl's Life in the Warsaw Ghetto and Beyond, 1939–1945*. New York: Free Press, 1986.

Bauman, Zygmunt. "On the Maturation of Socialism." *Telos* 47 (1981): 48–54.

———. *Memories of Class: The Pre-History and After-Life of Class*, London: Routledge & Kegan Paul, 1982.

———. *Stalin and the Peasant Revolution: A Case Study in the Dialectics of Master and Slave*. Leeds: University of Leeds Department of Sociology, 1985.

———. *Legislators and Interpreters: On Modernity, Post-modernity, and Intellectuals*. Cambridge: Polity, 1987.

———. "Sociology after the Holocaust." *British Journal of Sociology* 39, no. 4 (1988): 469–97.

———. *Modernity and the Holocaust*. Cambridge: Polity, 1989.

———. *Modernity and Ambivalence*. Cambridge: Polity, 1991.

———. *Intimations of Postmodernity*. London: Routledge, 1992.

———. "On Glocalization: or Globalization for Some, Localization for Some Others." *Thesis Eleven* 54 (1998): 37–49.

———. *In Search of Politics*. Cambridge: Polity, 1999.

———. *Community: Seeking Safety in an Insecure World*. Cambridge: Polity, 2001.

———. "Categorical Murder, or: How to Remember the Holocaust." In *Representing the Shoah for the Twenty-first Century*, edited by Ronit Lentin, 25–40. New York: Berghahn, 2004.

———. *Wasted Lives: Modernity and its Outcasts*. Cambridge: Polity, 2004.

Bauman, Zygmunt, and Keith Tester. *Conversations with Zygmunt Bauman*. Cambridge: Polity, 2001.

Baumel, Judith T. *Double Jeopardy: Gender and the Holocaust*. London: Vallentine Mitchell, 1998.

Beck, Ulrich. *The Reinvention of Politics: Rethinking Modernity in the Global Social Order*. Cambridge: Polity, 1996.

———. *What Is Globalization?* Cambridge: Polity, 2000.

———. *I rischi della libertà: L'individuo nell'epoca della globalizzazione*. Bologna: il Mulino, 2000; by selected essays: *Riskante Freiheiten*. Frankfurt: Suhrkamp, 1994, chap. 1; *Kinder der Freiheit*. Frankfurt: Suhrkamp, 1997, chaps. 2–5; *Modernität und Barbarei*. Frankfurt: Suhrkamp, 1996, chap. 6.

———. *La società cosmopolita: Prospettive dell'epoca postnazionale*. Bologna: il Mulino, 2003.

Beck, Ulrich, and Edgar Grande. *Cosmopolitan Europe*. Cambridge: Polity, 2007.

Beck, Ulrich, Daniel Levy, and Natan Sznaider. "Erinnerung und Vergebung in der Zweiten Moderne." In *Entgrenzung und Entscheidung: Wast its neu an der Theorie reflexiver Modernisierung?* edited by Ulrich Beck and Christoph Lau, 440–68. Frankfurt: Suhrkamp, 2004.

Becker, Howard S. *Outsiders: Studies in the Sociology of Deviance*. New York: The Free Press, 1963.

———. "The Art of Comparison: Lessons from the Master, Everett C. Hughes." *Sociologica* 2 (2010): 1–12. Accessed March 25, 2012. doi:10.2383/32713.

Beilharz, Peter. *Zygmunt Bauman: Dialectic of Modernity*. London: Sage, 2000.

———. *The Bauman Reader*. Oxford: Blackwell, 2001.

———. "Modernity and Communism: Zygmunt Bauman and the Other Totalitarianism." *Thesis Eleven* 70 (2002): 88–99.

Ben-Baruch, Benjamin M. Review of *Accounting for Genocide: National Response and Jewish Victimization during the Holocaust*, by Helen

Fein. *Theory & Society* 10, no. 3 (1981): 456–63. http://www.jstor.org/stable/657477.

Bendix, Reinhard. *From Berlin to Berkeley: German-Jewish Identities.* New Brunswick, NJ: Transaction, 1986.

Ben-Sasson, Havi, and Shlomit Dunkelblum-Steiner. *Resistance: Spiritual Resistance, Revolt, Partisans, and the Uprising in the Death Camps.* Jerusalem: Yad Vashem, 2004.

Bensoussan, Georges. *Auschwitz en héritage? D'un bon usage de la mémoire.* Paris: Éditions Mille et une nuits, 1998.

Benz, Wolfgang. *Der Holocaust.* Munich: Beck, 1995.

Berenbaum, Michael. Review of *Sociology Confronts the Holocaust: Memories and Identities in Jewish Diasporas*, by Judith M. Gerson and Diane L. Wolf, *Journal of Contemporary History* 45, no. 2 (2010): 505–7. doi:10.1177/0022009410045002 0110.

Berenbaum, Michael, and Abraham J. Peck, eds. *The Holocaust and History: The Known, the Unknown, the Disputed, and the Reexamined.* Bloomington: Indiana University Press, 1998.

Berg, Mary. *Warsaw Ghetto: A Diary.* New York: L. B. Fischer, 1945.

Berger, Alan L. Review of *Hidden Children of the Holocaust: Belgian Nuns and Their Daring Rescue of Young Jews from the Nazis*, by Suzanne Vromen. *Studies in Christian-Jewish Relations* 5, no. 1 (2010): 1–3. http://escholarship.bc.edu/scjr/vol5.

Berger, Peter L., and Thomas Luckmann. *The Social Construction of Reality: A Treatise in the Sociology of Knowledge.* Garden City, NY: Anchor, 1966.

Berger, Ronald J. "It Ain't Necessarily So: The Politics of Memory and the Bystander Narrative in the U.S. Holocaust Memorial Museum." *Humanity & Society* 27, no. 1 (2003): 6–29. doi:10.1177/016059760302700102.

———. Review of *Sociology Confronts the Holocaust: Memories and Identities in Jewish Diasporas*, ed. Judith M. Gerson and Diane L. Wolf. *Shofar: An Interdisciplinary Journal of Jewish Studies* 27, no. 1 (2008): 151–2. Accessed October 2, 2009. doi:10.1353/sho.0.0275.

Bernard, Jessie. *American Community Behavior.* New York: Dryden, 1949.

Bettelheim, Bruno. *The Informed Heart: Autonomy in a Mass Age.* Glencoe, IL: The Free Press, 1960.

———. *Surviving and Other Essays.* New York: Knopf, 1979.

Betton, John, and Thomas J. Hench. "'Any color as long as it's black': Henry Ford and the Ethics of Business." *Journal of Genocide Research* 4, no. 4 (2002): 533–41.

Bilsky, Leora. "The Arendt Controversy 2000: An Israeli Perspective." *Arendt's Newsletter* 5 (November 2001): 41–46.

Birnbaum, Pierre. *Anti-Semitism in France: A Political History from Léon Blum to the Present.* Oxford: Blackwell, 1992.

Blakeslee, Spencer. *The Death of American Antisemitism.* Westport, CT: Praeger, 2000.

Blau, Peter M., and W. Richard Scott. *Formal Organizations: A Comparative Approach.* Stanford, CA: Stanford University Press, 2003.

Bloxham, Donald. "Organized Mass Murder: Structure, Participation, and Motivation in Comparative Perspective." *Holocaust and Genocide Studies* 22, no. 2 (2008): 203–45. doi:10.1093/hgs/dcn026.

Blum, Howard. *La brigata: Una storia di guerra, di vendetta e di redenzione.* Milan: il Saggiatore, 2002.

Blumer, Herbert. "Social Problems as Collective Behavior." *Social Problems* 18, no. 3 (1971): 298–306.

Bodemann, Y. Michal. "The State in the Construction of Ethnicity and Ideological Labor: The Case of German Jewry." *Critical Sociology* 17 (1990): 35–46.

———. *A Jewish Family in Germany Today: An Intimate Portrait.* Durham, NC: Duke University Press, 2005.

Borowski, Tadeusz. *This Way for the Gas, Ladies and Gentlemen.* London: Cape, 1967 [1959].

Bottomore, Thomas B. *The Frankfurt School.* London: Tavistock, 1984.

Bottomore, Thomas B., and Robert A. Nisbet. *A History of Sociological Analysis.* New York: Basic Books, 1978.

Boudon, Raymond, and François Bourricaud. "Storia e Sociologia." In *Dizionario critico di sociologia*, edited by Lorenzo Infantino. Rome: Armando, 1991.

Bourgois, Philippe. *In Search of Respect: Selling Crack in El Barrio.* Cambridge: Cambridge University Press, 1995.

Bova, Vincenzo. *Solidarność: Origini, sviluppo ed istituzionalizzazione di un movimento sociale.* Soveria Mannelli: Rubbettino, 2003.

Bracher, Karl Dietrich. *The German Dictatorship: The Origins, Structure and Effects of National Socialism.* New York: Praeger, 1971.

Braham, Randolph. L. *The Politics of Genocide: The Holocaust in Hungary.* New York: Columbia University Press, 1994.

Breitman, Richard. *Official Secrets: What the Nazis Planned, What the British and Americans Knew.* New York: Hill and Wang, 1998.

Brenner, Michael. *Breve storia del sionismo.* Rome-Bari: Laterza, 2003.

Brenner, Rachel F. "Voices from Destruction: Two Eyewitness Testimonies from the Stanisławów Ghetto." *Holocaust and Genocide Studies* 22, no. 2 (2008): 320–39. doi:10.1093/hgs/dcn028.

Bridenthal, Renate, Atina Grossman, and Marion Kaplan, eds. *When Biology Became Destiny: Women in Weimar and Nazi Germany.* New York: Monthly Review Press, 1984.

Browning, Christopher R. *Ordinary Men: Reserve Police Battalion 101 and the Final Solution in Poland.* New York: HarperCollins, 1992.

Brustein, William I. "Who Joined the Nazis and Why." *American Journal of Sociology* 103, no. 1 (1997): 216–21.

———. *The Logic of Evil: The Social Origins of the Nazi Party, 1925–1933.* New Haven, CT: Yale University Press, 1998.

———. "The Nazi Party and the German New Middle Class, 1925–1933." *American Behavioral Scientist* 41, no. 9 (1998): 1237–61.

———. *Roots of Hate: Anti-Semitism in Europe before the Holocaust.* Cambridge: Cambridge University Press, 2003.

Brustein, William I., and Ryan D. King. "Anti-Semitism in Europe before the Holocaust." *International Political Science Review* 25, no. 1 (2004): 35–53. doi:10.1177/0192512104038166.

Bulmer, Martin. *The Chicago School of Sociology: Institutionalization, Diversity, and the Rise of Sociological Research.* Chicago: University of Chicago Press, 1984.

Burkitt, Ian. "Civilization and Ambivalence." *British Journal of Sociology* 47, no. 1 (1996): 135–50.

Burrin, Philippe. *L'antisemitismo nazista.* Turin: Bollati Boringhieri, 2004.

Buxton, William. Review of *Talcott Parsons on National Socialism*, by Uta Gerhardt. *Canadian Journal of Sociology* 19, no. 3 (1994): 425–27.

Cajani, Luigi, and Brunello Mantelli, eds. *Una certa Europa: Il collaborazionismo con le potenze dell'Asse 1939–1945: Le fonti.* Brescia: Fondazione Luigi Micheletti, 1994.

Camurri, Renato, ed. "L'Europa in esilio: La migrazione degli intellettuali verso le Americhe tra le due guerre." *Memoria e Ricerca: Rivista di storia contemporanea* 16, no. 31 (2009): 5–187.

――. Introduction to "L'Europa in esilio: La migrazione degli intellettuali verso le Americhe tra le due guerre," edited by Renato Camurri. *Memoria e Ricerca: Rivista di storia contemporanea* 16, no. 31 (2009): 5–11.

――. "Idee in movimento: L'esilio degli intellettuali italiani negli Stati Uniti (1930–1945)." In "L'Europa in esilio: La migrazione degli intellettuali verso le Americhe tra le due guerre," edited by Renato Camurri. *Memoria e Ricerca: Rivista di storia contemporanea* 16, no. 31 (2009): 43–62.

Caplan, Jane, and Nikolaus Wachsmann, eds. *Concentration Camps in Nazi Germany: The New Histories*. London: Routledge, 2010.

Cassese, Antonio. *I diritti umani oggi*. Rome-Bari: Laterza, 2010.

Cattaruzza, Marina, Marcello Flores, Simon Levis-Sullam, and Enzo Traverso, eds. *Storia della Shoah: La crisi dell'Europa, lo sterminio degli ebrei e la memoria del XX secolo*, vols. 1–4. Turin: Utet, 2005–2006.

Cerulo, Karen A. *Never Saw It Coming: Cultural Challenges to Envisioning the Worst*. Chicago: University of Chicago Press, 2006.

Cesarani, David. *Becoming Eichmann: Rethinking the Life, Crimes, and Trial of a "Desk Murderer."* Cambridge, MA: Da Capo, 2006.

――. *Final Solution: The Fate of the Jews, 1933–1949*. London: Macmillan, 2016.

Chalk, Frank, and Kurt Jonassohn. *The History and Sociology of Genocide: Analysis and Case Studies*. New Haven, CT: Yale University Press, 1990.

Chałubiński, Mirosław. "The Sociological Ideas of Stanisław Ossowski: His Life, Fundamental Ideas and Sociology in Polish and World Science." *Journal of Classical Sociology* 6, no. 3 (2006): 283–309. Accessed November 24, 2010. doi:10.1177/1468795X06069679.

Chambers, Iain. *Migrancy, Culture, Identity*. London: Routledge, 1994.

Chapoulie, Jean M. "Everett Hughes and the Chicago Tradition." *Sociological Theory* 14, no. 1 (1996): 3–29.

――. "Using the History of the Chicago Tradition of Sociology for Empirical Research." *AAPSS* 595 (2004): 157–67.

Charny, Israel W. *Fascism and Democracy in the Human Mind: A Bridge between Mind and Society*. Lincoln: University of Nebraska Press, 2006.

Checinski, Michael. *Poland: Communism, Nationalism and Anti-Semitism*. New York: KarzCohl, 1982.

Cheyette, Bryan, and Laura Marcus, eds. *Modernity, Culture and "the Jew."* Stanford, CA: Stanford University Press, 1998.

Chinoy, Ely. Review of *The Sociological Eye*, by Everett C. Hughes. *Sociological Quarterly* 13, no. 4 (1972): 559–65.
Cieplinski, Feigue. "Poles and Jews: The Quest for Self-Determination 1919–1934." *Journal of History* (2002). Accessed November 24, 2010. http://www2.binghamton.edu/history/resources/journal-of-history/poles-and-jews.html#_ftn1.
Clark, Ian. *Globalization and Fragmentation: International Relations in the Twentieth Century*. New York: Oxford University Press, 1997.
Clarke, Lee. *Worst Cases: Terror and Catastrophe in the Popular Imagination*. Chicago: University of Chicago Press, 2006.
Cohen, Elie A. *The Abyss: A Confession*. New York: Norton, 1973.
Cohen, Naomi W. "Anti-Semitism in the United States." *American Jewish History* 71, no. 1 (1981): 5–9.
Cohen, Richard. "Arendt Controversy." In *Encyclopedia of the Holocaust*, 1:80–81. New York: Macmillan, 1990.
Cohn, Norman. *Warrant for Genocide: The Myth of the Jewish World Conspiracy and the Protocols of the Elders of Zion*. New York: Harper & Row, 1967.
Collomp, Catherine. "La Scuola di Francoforte in esilio: Storia di un'inchiesta sull'antisemitismo nella classe operai americana." In "L'Europa in esilio: La migrazione degli intellettuali verso le Americhe tra le due guerre," edited by Renato Camurri. *Memoria e Ricerca: Rivista di storia contemporanea* 16, no. 31 (2009): 121–40.
Corni, Gustavo. "I ghetti e l'Olocausto." In *Storia della Shoah: La crisi dell'Europa, lo sterminio degli ebrei e la memoria del XX secolo*, edited by Marina Cattaruzza, Marcello Flores, Simon Levis-Sullam, and Enzo Traverso, 2:461–91. Turin: Utet, 2005–2006.
Coser, Lewis A. *Refugee Scholars in America: Their Impact and Their Experience*. New Haven, CT: Yale University Press, 1984.
Crawford, Fred R. Review of *Accounting for Genocide: National Response and Jewish Victimization during the Holocaust*, by Helen Fein. *Social Science Quarterly* 61, no. 1 (1980): 179.
Crawford, William R., ed. *The Cultural Migration: The European Scholar in America*. Philadelphia: University of Pennsylvania Press, 1953.
Crespi, Franco. *Evento e struttura: Per una teoria del mutamento sociale*. Bologna: il Mulino, 1993.

Crow, Graham P., Graham A. Allan, and Marcia Summers. "Changing Perspectives on the Insider/Outsider Distinction in Community Sociology." *Community, Work and Family* 4, no. 1 (2001): 29–48.

Curli, Barbara. "Il dopoguerra lungo: L'Europa indivisa di Tony Judt." *Contemporanea* 12, no. 3 (2009): 581–98. Accessed March 10, 2016. doi:10.1409/29975.

Cymet, David. "Polish State Antisemitism as a Major Factor Leading to the Holocaust." *Journal of Genocide Research* 1, no. 2 (1999): 169–212.

Czerniakòw, Adam. *The Warsaw Diary of Adam Czerniakow: Prelude to Doom*, edited by Raul Hilberg, Stanislaw Staron, and Joseph Kermisz. New York: Stein and Day, 1979.

Dadrian, Vahakn N. "The Determinants of the Armenian Genocide." *Journal of Genocide Research* 1, no. 1 (1999): 65–80.

Daniels, Arlene K. Review of *The Sociological Eye*, by Everett C. Hughes. *Contemporary Sociology* 1, no. 5 (1972): 402–9.

Dank, Barry M. Review of *On the Edge of Destruction: Jews of Poland between the Two World Wars*, by Celia S. Heller. *Contemporary Sociology* 8, no. 1 (1979): 129–30.

Davie, Maurice R. *Refugees in America: Report of the Committee for the Study of Recent Immigration from Europe*. New York: Harper, 1947.

Davies, Norman. *Rising '44: The Battle for Warsaw*. New York: Viking, 2003.

Davis, David S. "Good People Doing Dirty Work: A Study of Social Isolation." *Symbolic Interaction* 7, no. 2 (1984): 233–47. doi:10.1525/si.1984.7.2.233.

Davis, Stephen T., ed. *Encountering Evil: Live Options in Theodicy*. Louisville, KY: Westminster John Knox Press, 2001.

Dawidowicz, Lucy S. *The War against the Jews: 1933–1945*. New York: Holt, Rinehart and Winston, 1975.

———. *The Holocaust and the Historians*. Cambridge, MA: Harvard University Press, 1981.

———. *What Is the Use of Jewish History?* New York: Schocken, 1992.

Dawson, Nelson L. "Louis D. Brandeis, Felix Frankfurter, and Franklin D. Roosevelt: The Origins of a New Deal Relationship." *American Jewish History* 68, no. 1 (1978): 32–42.

Deaglio, Enrico. *La banalità del bene: Storia di Giorgio Perlasca*. Milan: Feltrinelli, 1991.

De Benedictis, Angela, and Valerio Marchetti, eds. "Resistenza e diritto di resistenza: Memoria come cultura". *Quaderni di Discipline Storiche, 15*. Bologna: Clueb, 2000.

Deery, Philip, and Mario Del Pero. *Spiare e tradire: Dietro le quinte della guerra fredda*. Milan: Feltrinelli, 2011.

Derrida, Jacques. *Perdonare: L'imperdonabile e l'imprescrittibile*. Milan: Cortina, 2004.

Dezalay, Sara. "Des droits de l'homme au marché du développement." *Actes de la recherche en sciences sociales* 174, no. 4 (2008): 68–79.

Diamond, Sigmund. *Compromised Campus: The Collaboration of Universities with the Intelligence Community, 1945–1955*. Oxford: Oxford University Press, 1992.

Diefendorf, Jeffry M., ed. *Lessons and Legacies VI: New Currents in Holocaust Research*. Evanston, IL: Northwestern University Press, 2004.

Dimou, Augusta. *Entangled Paths towards Modernity: Contextualizing Socialism and Nationalism in the Balkans*. Budapest: Central European University Press, 2009.

Diner, Dan. *Beyond the Conceivable: Studies on Germany, Nazism, and the Holocaust*. Berkeley: California University Press, 2000.

Dinnerstein, Leonard. "Jews and the New Deal." *American Jewish History* 72, no. 4 (1983): 461–76.

———. *Anti-Semitism in America*. New York: Oxford University Press, 1994.

Dittes, James E. Review of *Christian Beliefs and Anti-Semitism*, by Charles Y. Glock and Rodney Stark. *Review of Religious Research* 8, no. 3 (1967): 183–87.

Doblin M. Ernest, and Claire Pohly. "The Social Composition of the Nazi Leadership." *American Journal of Sociology* 51, no. 1 (1945): 42–49. doi:10.1086/219712.

Douglas, Mary. *Risk Acceptability according to the Social Sciences*. New York: Russell Sage Foundation, 1985.

———. *Purity and Danger: An Analysis of the Concepts of Pollution and Taboo*. London: Routledge & Kegan Paul, 1966.

Draenger, Gusta D. *Justyna's Narrative*. Amherst: University of Massachusetts Press, 1996.

Drumont, Édouard. *La France juive*. Paris: Marpon et Flammarion, 1886.

Dubois, William E. B. *Black Reconstruction in America, 1860–1880*. New York: Free Press, 1935.
Dunning, Eric, and Stephen Mennell. "Elias on Germany, Nazism and the Holocaust: On the Balance between "Civilizing" and "Decivilizing" Trends in the Social Development of Western Europe." *The British Journal of Sociology* 49, no. 3 (1998): 339–57.
Durkheim, Émile. *De la division du travail social*. Paris: F. Alcan, 1893.
———. *Les règles de la méthode sociologique*. Paris: F. Alcan, 1895.
———. *Éducation et sociologie*. Paris: Les Presses universitaires de France, 1922.
Duverger, Maurice. *I Metodi delle Scienze Sociali*. Milan: Etas Kompass, 1967.
Dwork, Debóra, and Robert Jan van Pelt. *Holocaust: A History*. New York: W. W. Norton, 2003.
Eaton, Jonathan. *Political Economy*. London: Lawrence & Wishart, 1949.
Edelheit, Abraham J., and Hershel Edelheit. *History of the Holocaust: A Handbook and Dictionary*. Boulder, CO: Westview, 1994.
Edelman, Marek. *Getto walczy: Udzial Bundu w obronie getta warszawskiego*. Warsaw: Nakladem C. K. "Bundu," 1945.
Einstein, Albert. *Ideas and Opinions*. New York: Random House, 1954.
Einwohner, Rachel L. "Gender, Class, and Social Movement Outcomes: Identity and Effectiveness in Two Animal Rights Campaigns." *Gender and Society* 13, no. 1 (1999): 56–76. http://www.jstor.org/stable/190240.
———. "Opportunity, Honor, and Action in the Warsaw Ghetto Uprising of 1943." *American Journal of Sociology* 109, no. 3 (2003): 650–75.
———. "Leadership, Authority, and Collective Action: Jewish Resistance in the Ghettos of Warsaw and Vilna." *American Behavioral Scientist* 50, no. 10 (2007): 1306–26. doi:10.1177/0002764207300160.
———. "Availability, Proximity, and Identity in the Warsaw Ghetto Uprising: Adding a Sociological Lens to Studies of Jewish Resistance." In *Sociology confronts the Holocaust*, edited by Judith M. Gerson, and Diane. L. Wolf, 277–90. Durham, NC: Duke University Press, 2007.
———. "The Need to Know: Cultured Ignorance and Jewish Resistance in the Ghettos of Warsaw, Vilna, and Łódż." *The Sociological Quarterly* 50, no. 3 (2009): 407–30.
Eisenstadt, Shmuel N. *Paradoxes of Democracy: Fragility, Continuity, and Change*. Washington, DC: Woodrow Wilson Center Press, 1999.

Elias, Norbert. *Über den Prozess der Zivilisation*. Basel: Verlag Haus zum Falken, 1939.

———. *Humana conditio*. Bologna: il Mulino, 1987 [1985].

———. *The Germans: Power Struggles and the Development of Habitus in the Nineteenth and Twentieth Centuries*. Oxford: Polity, 1996 [1989].

Engelking, Barbara. "Reflections on the Subject of Polish-Jewish Relations during World War II." *Polish Sociological Review* 137 (2002): 103–7.

Epstein, Simcha. "From Anti-Semitism of 19th Century to Nazi Anti-Semitism." Paper presented at Yad Vashem, Jerusalem, August 22, 2011.

Epstein, Simon. *Histoire du peuple juif au XXè siècle: De 1914 à nos jours*. Paris: Hachette littératures, 1998.

Etzioni, Amitai. *The Monochrome Society*. Princeton, NJ: Princeton University Press, 2003.

Evans, Richard J. *Rethinking German History: Nineteenth-Century Germany and the Origins of the Third Reich*. London: Allen & Unwin, 1987.

———. *The Coming of the Third Reich*. London: Allen Lane, 2003.

———. *The Third Reich at War*. New York: Penguin, 2009.

———. Review of *The Night of Broken Glass: Eyewitness Accounts of Kristallnacht*, by Uta Gerhardt and Thomas Karlauf, *The Guardian*, April 11, 2012. Accessed May 8, 2012. http://www.guardian.co.uk/books/2012/apr/11/night-broken-glass-kristallnacht-review.

Ezra, Michael. "The Eichmann Polemics: Hannah Arendt and Her Critics." *Democratiya* 9 (2007): 141–65.

Fabbrini, Sergio, and Francesco Morata, eds. *L'Unione Europea: Le politiche pubbliche*. Rome-Bari: Laterza, 2002.

Fackenheim, Emil L. "Jewish Values in the Post-Holocaust Future: A Symposium." *Judaism* 16, no. 3 (1967): 266–99.

———. "Jewish Faith and the Holocaust: A Fragment." *Commentary*, August 1, (1968): 30–36.

———. *Quest for Past and Future*. Boston: Beacon, 1968.

———. *God's Presence in History: Jewish Affirmations and Philosophical Reflections*. New York: New York University Press, London: University of London Press, 1970.

———. *The Jewish Return into History: Reflections in the Age of Auschwitz and a New Jerusalem*. New York: Schocken, 1978.

———. *To Mend the World: Foundations of Post-Holocaust Jewish Thought*. Bloomington: Indiana University Press, 1982.

Faris, Robert E. L., and William Form, "Sociology." *Encyclopædia Britannica Online*, 1–11. Accessed September 1, 2015. http://www.britannica.com/topic/sociology.

Featherstone, Mike. *Global Culture: Nationalism, Globalization and Modernity*. London: Sage, 1990.

Fehér, Ferenc, Ágnes Heller, and György Márkus. *Dictatorship over Needs*. Oxford: Blackwell, 1983.

Fein, Helen. *Accounting for Genocide: National Response and Jewish Victimization during the Holocaust*. New York: Free Press, 1979.

———. "The Holocaust and Auschwitz: Revising Stereotypes of Their Victims." *Contemporary Sociology* 9, no. 4 (1980): 495–98.

———. "Reduction by Review." *Contemporary Sociology* 10, no. 2 (1981): 168–70.

———. Review of *The Holocaust and the Crisis of Human Behavior*, by George M. Kren, and Leon Rappoport, *Contemporary Sociology* 11, no. 1 (1982): 69–70.

———. *Genocide Watch*. New Haven, CT: Yale University Press, 1992.

———. *Genocide: a Sociological Perspective*. Newbury Park, CA: Sage, 1993.

———. *Human Rights and Wrongs: Slavery, Terror, Genocide*. Boulder, CO: Paradigm, 2007.

Feinstein, Stephen C. "Art of the Holocaust and Genocide: Some Points of Convergence." *Journal of Genocide Research* 1, no. 2 (1999): 233–55. doi:10.1080/14623529908413953.

Fine, Robert, and Charles Turner, eds. *Social Theory after the Holocaust*. Liverpool: Liverpool University Press, 2000.

Fleck, Christian. "Per un profilo prosopografico dei sociologi di lingua tedesca in esilio." In "L'Europa in esilio: La migrazione degli intellettuali verso le Americhe tra le due guerre", edited by Renato Camurri. *Memoria e Ricerca: Rivista di storia contemporanea* 16, no. 31 (2009): 81–101.

Fleck, Christian, and Albert Müller. "Bruno Bettelheim and the Concentration Camps." *Journal of the History of the Behavioral Sciences* 33, no. 1 (1997): 1–37. doi:10.1002/(SICI)1520-6696(199724)33:1<1::AID-JHBS1>3.0.CO;2-Y.

Fleming, Donald, and Bernard Bailyn, eds. *The Intellectual Migration: Europe and America, 1930–1960*. Cambridge, MA: Harvard University Press, 1969.

Fleming, Gerald. *Hitler und die Endlösung*. Wiesbaden: Limes, 1982.

Flores, Marcello. "Autoritarismo, totalitarismo, comunismi." *I Viaggi di Erodoto* 22 (1994): 236–45.
Fogelman, Eva. *Conscience and Courage: Rescuers of Jews during the Holocaust.* New York: Anchor Doubleday, 1994.
Foucault, Michel. *Surveiller et punir: Naissance de la prison.* Paris: Gallimard, 1975.
Fox, John P. Review of *Political Violence under the Swastika: 581 Early Nazis*, by Peter H. Merkl, *International Affairs* 53, no. 2 (1977): 304–5.
Frank, Andre G. *The Development of Underdevelopment.* New York: Monthly Review Press, 1966.
Frank, Anne. *I diari di Anna Frank: Edizione Critica.* Edited by David Barnouw and Gerrold Van der Stroom. Turin: Einaudi, 2002.
Freeman, Michael. "Genocide, Civilization and Modernity." *British Journal of Sociology* 46, no. 2 (1995): 207–23.
Frentzel-Zagórska, J. "Leading Politicians on Jedwabne." *Polish Sociological Review* 137, no. 11 (2002): 129–35.
Freud, Sigmund. *Das Unbehagen in der Kultur.* Vienna: Internationaler Psychoanalytischer Verlag, 1930.
Friedländer, Henry. *The Origins of Nazi Genocide: From Euthanasia to the Final Solution.* Chapel Hill: North Carolina University Press, 1995.
Friedman, Philip. *Their Brothers' Keepers: The Christian Heroes and Heroines Who Helped the Oppressed Escape the Nazi Terror.* New York: Crown, 1957.
———. *Roads to Extinction: Essays on the Holocaust.* Philadelphia: Jewish Publication Society of America, 1980.
Friedrich, Carl J., and Zbigniew Brzezinski. *Totalitarian Dictatorship and Autocracy.* Cambridge, MA: Harvard University Press, 1956.
Fromm, Erich. "Zul Gefühl der Ohnmacht." *ZfS* 6, no. 1 (1937): H. 1, S. 95–118.
———. *Escape from Freedom.* New York: Farrar and Rinehart, 1941.
Gallino, Luciano. *Globalizzazione e disuguaglianze.* Rome-Bari: Laterza, 2000.
Gamson, William A. *Talking Politics.* New York: Cambridge University Press, 1992.
Gamson, William A., and David S. Meyer. "Framing Political Opportunity". In *Comparative Perspectives on Social Movements*, edited by Doug McAdam, John D. McCarthy, and Mayer N. Zald, 275–90. Cambridge: Cambridge University Press, 1996.
Garfinkel, Harold. *Studies in Ethnomethodology.* Englewood Cliffs, NJ: Prentice-Hall, 1967.

Garliński, Józef. *Fighting Auschwitz: The Resistance Movement in the Concentration Camp.* London: J. Friedmann, 1975.

Garz, Detlef, Sandra Tiefel, and Fritz Schütze. "An alle, die Deutschland vor und während Hitler gut kennen: Autobiographische Beiträge deutscher Emigranten zum wissenschaftlichen Preisausschreiben der Harvard University aus dem Jahr 1939." *Zeitschrift für Qualitative Forschung* 8, no. 2 (2007): 179–88.

Gay, Peter. *Weimar Culture: The Outsider as Insider.* In *The Intellectual Migration: Europe and America, 1930–1960,* edited by Donald Fleming and Bernard Bailyn. Cambridge, MA: Harvard University Press, 1969.

———. "My German Question." *American Scholar* 67, no. 4 (1998): 25–49.

Gay, Ruth. *Unfinished People: East European Jews Encounter America.* New York: Norton, 1996.

Geldwert, Jake. *From Auschwitz to Ithaca: The Transnational Journey of Jake Geldwert,* Bethesda, MD: CDL Press, 2002.

Gellner, Ernest. *Causa e significato nelle scienze sociali.* Milan: Mursia, 1992.

Gerdmar, Anders. *Roots of Theological Anti-Semitism: German Biblical Interpretation and the Jews, from Herder and Semler to Kittel and Bultmann.* Leiden: Brill, 2008.

Gerhardt, Uta. *Talcott Parsons on National Socialism.* New York: Aldine de Gruyter, 1993.

———. "Scholarship, Not Scandal." *Sociological Forum* 11, no. 4 (1996): 623–30.

———. *Talcott Parsons: An Intellectual Biography.* Cambridge: Cambridge University Press, 2002.

Gerhardt, Uta, and Thomas Karlauf, eds. *The Night of Broken Glass: Eyewitness Accounts of Kristallnacht.* Malden, MA: Polity, 2012 [2009].

Gerlach, Christian. *Krieg, Ernährung, Völkermord: Forschungen zur deutschen Vernichtungspolitik im Zweiten Weltkrieg.* Hamburg: Hamburger Edition, 1998.

Gerson, Judith M., and Diane L. Wolf, eds. *Sociology Confronts the Holocaust: Memories and Identities in Jewish Diasporas.* Durham, NC: Duke University Press, 2007.

Gerth, Hans. "The Nazi Party: Its Leaders and Composition." *American Journal of Sociology* 45, no. 4 (1940): 517–41. http://www.jstor.org/stable/2770263.

Gerth, Nobuko. *Hans Gerth: "Between Two Worlds." Hans Gerth—eine Biographie 1908–1978.* Opladen/BRD: VS-Verlag, 2005.

Giaccardi, Carmen, and Mauro Magatti. *La globalizzazione non è un destino: Mutamenti strutturali ed esperienze soggettive nell'età contemporanea.* Rome-Bari: Laterza, 2001.

Giddens, Anthony. *The Nation-State and Violence.* London: Polity, 1985.

———. *The Consequences of Modernity.* Cambridge: Polity, 1990.

———. *Modernity and Self-Identity: Self and Society in the Late Modern Age.* Stanford, CA: Stanford University Press, 1991.

Gilroy, Paul. *The Black Atlantic: Modernity and Double Consciousness.* London: Verso, 1993.

Girard, Patrick. "Historical Foundations of Antisemitism." In *Survivors, Victims, and Perpetrators: Essays on the Nazi Holocaust,* edited by Joel E. Dinsdale, 55–77. Washington, DC: Emisphere, 1980.

Giuntella, Vittorio E. *Il nazismo e i Lager.* Roma: Studium, 1979.

Gläser, Elizabeth, and Hermann Wellenreuther. *Bridging the Atlantic: The Question of American Exceptionalism in Perspective.* Washington, DC: Cambridge University Press, 2002.

Gleanson, Abbott. *Totalitarianism: The Inner History of the Cold War.* Oxford: Oxford University Press, 1995.

Goffman, Erving. *Asylums: Essays on the Social Situation of Mental Patients and Other Inmates.* New York: Anchor, 1961.

Goldhagen, Daniel J. *Hitler's Willing Executioners: Ordinary Germans and The Holocaust.* New York: Alfred A. Knopf, 1996.

Goldman, Shalom. Review of *A Concise History of American Antisemitism,* by Robert Michael. *American Jewish History* 92, no. 3 (2004): 381–83.

Goldstein, Bernard. Review of *The Sociological Eye: Selected Papers,* by Everett C. Hughes, *The American Journal of Sociology* 92, no. 2 (1986): 459–60. doi:10.1086/ajs.92.2.2780158.

Goodwin, Jeff. *No Other Way Out: States and Revolutionary Movements, 1945–1991.* Cambridge: Cambridge University Press, 2001.

Goodwin, Jeff, and James M. Jasper. "Caught in a Winding, Snarling Vine: The Structural Bias of Political Process Theory." *Sociological Forum* 14 (1999): 27–54.

Goodwin, Jeff, James M. Jasper, and Francesca Polletta. *Passionate Politics: Emotions and Social Movements.* Chicago: University of Chicago Press, 2001.

Goodwin, Jeff, and Steven Pfaff. "Emotion Work in High-Risk Social Movements: Managing Fear in the U.S. and East German Civil Rights Movements."

In *Passionate Politics*, edited by Jeff Goodwin, James M. Jasper, and Francesca Polletta, 282–302. Chicago: University of Chicago Press, 2001.

Gottlieb, Roger S. "The Concept of Resistance: Jewish Resistance during the Holocaust." *Social Theory and Social Practice* 9, no. 1 (1983): 31–49.

Gouldner, Alvin W. *The Coming Crisis of Western Sociology*. New York: Basic Books, 1970.

———, ed. *Studies in Leadership: Leadership and Democratic Action*. New York: Garland, 1987.

Gozzini, Giovanni, and Giambattista Sciré. *Il mondo globale come problema storico*. Bologna: Archetipo, 2007.

Gradowski, Salmen. *Sonderkommando: Diario da un crematorio di Auschwitz, 1944*. Venice: Marsilio, 2002.

Graeber, Isacque, and Steuart Henderson Britt, eds. *Jews in a Gentile World: The Problem of Anti-Semitism*. New York: Macmillan, 1942.

Grant, Madison. *The Passing of the Great Race*. New York: C. Scribner, 1916.

Graziosi, Andrea. "Rivoluzione archivistica e storiografica sovietica." *Contemporanea* 8, no. 1 (2005): 57–85.

Greilsammer, IIlan. *Il sionismo*, Bologna: il Mulino, 2007 [2005].

Gross, Jan T. *Polish Society under German Occupation: The Generalgouvernement, 1939–1944*. Princeton, NJ: Princeton University Press, 1979.

———. *Revolution from Abroad: The Soviet Conquest of Poland's Western Ukraine and Western Belorussia*. Princeton, NJ: Princeton University Press, 1988.

———. *Neighbors: The Destruction of the Jews Community in Jedwabne, Poland*. Princeton, NJ: Princeton University Press, 2001.

Grossman, Chaika. *The Underground Army: Fighters of the Białystok Ghetto*. New York: Holocaust Library, 1987.

Gubert, Renzo, and Luigi Tomasi, eds. *Teoria Sociologica ed investigazione empirica: La tradizione della Scuola sociologica di Chicago e le prospettive della sociologia contemporanea*. Milan: FrancoAngeli, 1995.

Gurewitsch, Brana, ed. *Mothers, Sisters, Resisters: Horal Histories of Women Who Survived the Holocaust*. Tuscaloosa: University of Alabama Press, 1998. Accessed September 8, 2011. http://www1.yadvashem.org/yv/en/education/newsletter/18/couriers.asp.

Gurferin, Murray I., and Morris Janowitz. "Trends in Wehrmacht Morale." *The Public Opinion Quarterly* 10, no. 1 (1946): 78–84.

Gusfield, Joseph R. Review of *The Magic Background of Modern Anti-Semitism: An Analysis of the German-Jewish Relationship*, by Adolf Leschnitzer. *American Journal of Sociology* 62, no. 4 (1957): 429.

Gutman, Israel. *The Jews of Warsaw, 1939–1943: Ghetto Underground Revolt.* Bloomington: Indiana University Press, 1982.

———. *Resistance: The Warsaw Ghetto Uprising.* Boston: Houghton Mifflin Company, 1994.

———. "Goldhagen—His Critics and His Contribution." *Yad Vashem Studies* 26 (1998): 329–64.

Gutman, Israel, and Shmuel Krakowski. *Unequal Victims: Poles & Jews during World War II.* New York: The Holocaust Library, 1986.

Habermas, Jurgen. *Il discorso filosofico della modernità.* Rome-Bari: Laterza, 1987 [1985].

Halbwachs, Maurice. *La Mémoire collective.* Paris: Presses universitaires de France, 1950.

Halpert, Burton P. "Early American Sociology and the Holocaust: the Failure of a Discipline." *Humanity & Society* 31 (2007): 6–23.

Hamilton, Richard F. *Who Voted for Hitler?* Princeton, NJ: Princeton University Press, 1982.

Hartshorne, Edward Y., Jr. *The German Universities and National Socialism.* London: Allen and Unwin, 1937.

———. "The German Universities and the Government." *Annals of the American Academy of Political and Social Science* 200 (1938): 210–34.

Harvey, David. *The Condition of Postmodernity: An Enquiry into the Origins of Cultural Change.* Oxford: Blackwell, 1989.

Heberle, Rudolf. *From Democracy to Nazism: A Regional Case Study on Political Parties in Germany.* Baton Rouge: Louisiana State University Press, 1945; reprinted New York: H. Fertig, 1970.

———. Review of *The German Dictatorship: The Origins, Structure and Effects of National Socialism*, by Karl D. Bracher. *American Journal of Sociology* 78, no. 6 (1973): 1545–50.

Heermance, Edgar L. Review of *The Growth of an Institution: The Chicago Real Estate Board*, by Everett C. Hughes. *American Journal of Sociology* 37, no. 5 (1932): 817–18.

Heidenrich, John G. *How to Prevent Genocide: A Guide for Policymakers, Scholars, and the Concerned Citizen.* Westport, CT: Praeger, 2001.

Heinsohn, Gunnar. "What Makes the Holocaust a Uniquely Unique Genocide?" *Journal of Genocide Research* 2, no. 3 (2000): 411–30.

Heller, Celia S. *Mexican American Youth: Forgotten Youth at the Crossroads.* New York: Random House, 1966.

———. *On the Edge of Destruction: Jews of Poland between the Two World Wars.* New York: Columbia University Press, 1977.

———. Review of *When Light Pierced the Darkness: Christian Rescue of Jews in Nazi-Occupied Poland,* by Nechama Tec, *American Journal of Sociology* 93, no. 1 (1987): 221–22. http://www.jstor.org/stable/2779692.

Helmes-Hayes, Richard C. "Studying 'Going Concerns': Everett C. Hughes on Method." *Sociologica* 2 (2010): 1–27. Accessed February 23, 2016. doi:10.2383/32714.

Helmes-Hayes, Richard C., and Marco Santoro, "Introduction" *Sociologica* 2 (2010): 1–10.

Helmreich, William B. *Against All Odds: Holocaust Survivors and the Successful Lives They Made in America.* New York: Simon & Schuster, 1992.

Henderson, Charles R. "Rise of the German Inner Mission." *American Journal of Sociology* 1, no. 5 (1896): 583–95.

Herbert, Ulrich, hrsg. *Nationalsozialistische Vernichtungspolitik, 1939–1945: Neue Forschungen und Kontroversen.* Frankfurt: Fischer, 1998.

Herf, Jeffrey. *Reactionary Modernism: Technology, Culture, and Politics in Weimar and the Third Reich.* New York: Cambridge University Press, 1984.

Herman, Edward S., and Noam Chomsky, *Manufacturing Consent: The Political Economy of the Mass Media.* New York City: Pantheon, 1988.

Hilberg, Raul. *The Destruction of the European Jews.* Chicago: Quadrangle, 1961; New York and London: Holmes & Meier, 1985.

———. *Perpetrators, Victims, Bystanders: The Jewish Catastrophe, 1933–1945.* New York: HarperCollins, 1992.

Hillesum, Etty. *An Interrupted Life: The Diaries of Etty Hillesum, 1941–1943.* New York: Pantheon, 1983.

———. *Letters from Westerbork.* New York: Pantheon, 1986.

Hirsch, Walter. "The Autonomy of Science in Totalitarian Societies." *Social Forces* 40, no. 1 (1961): 15–22. doi:10.2307/2573466.

Hirshaut, Julian. "Paviak Memoirs." In *Anthology on Armed Jewish Resistance, 1939–1945*, edited by Isaac Kowalski, 493–506. Brooklyn: JCPH, 1991.

Hochfeld, Julian. "Poland and Britain: Two Concepts of Socialism." *International Affairs* 1 (1957): 2–11.
Hofer, Walther. *Il nazionalsocialismo: Documenti, 1933–1945.* Milan: Feltrinelli, 1964 [1957].
Hoffman, Martin L. *Empathy and Moral Development: Implications for Caring and Justice.* Cambridge: Cambridge University Press, 2000.
Holter, Øystein G. "A Theory of Gendercide." *Journal of Genocide Research* 4, no. 1 (2002): 11–38.
Homans, George C. *The Human Group.* New York: Harcourt, Brace, 1950.
Honigsheim, Paul. Review of *Racial State: The German Nationalities Policy in the Protectorate of Bohemia-Moravia,* by Gerhard Jacoby. *American Journal of Sociology* 51, no. 3 (1945): 259.
Hoover, Glenn E. "The Failure of the Social Sciences." *American Journal of Economics and Sociology* 3, no. 1 (1943): 89–96.
Horkheimer, Max. "Die Juden und Europa." *Zeitschrift für Sozialforschung* 8, no. 1/2 (1939):115–37.
———. *Eclipse of Reason.* New York: Oxford University Press, 1947.
Horkheimer, Max, and Samuel H. Flowerman. *Studies in Prejudice.* New York: Harper & Brothers, 1949–1950.
Horkheimer, Max, and Theodore L. W. Adorno. *Dialectic of Enlightenment.* Edited by Gunzelin Schmid Noerr. Translated by Edmund Jephcott. Stanford: Stanford University Press, 2002 [1947].
———. eds. *Lezioni di sociologia.* Turin: Einaudi, 2001 [1956].
Horkheimer, Max, Erich Fromm, and Herbert Marcuse. *Studien über Autorität und Familie: Forschungsberichte aus dem Institut für Sozialforschung.* Paris: Felix Alcan, 1936.
Horowitz, Irving L. *Genocide: State Power and Muss Murder.* New Brunswick, NJ: Transaction, 1976.
———. "Bodies and Souls." Review of *Accounting for Genocide: National Response and Jewish Victimization during the Holocaust,* by Helen Fein. *Contemporary Sociology* 9, no. 4 (1980): 489–492.
———. "Reply to Fein." *Contemporary Sociology* 10, no. 2 (1981): 170–71.
———. *Taking Lives: Genocide and State Power.* New Brunswick, NJ: Transaction, 1982.
———. "Counting Bodies: The Dismal Science of Authorized Terror." *Patterns of Prejudice* 23, no. 2 (1989): 4–15.

Horowitz, Ruth. *Honor and the American Dream: Culture and Identity in a Chicano Community.* New Brunswick, NJ: Rutgers University Press, 1983.

Howerth, Ira W. "What Are Principles of Sociology?" *American Journal of Sociology* 31, no. 4 (1926): 474–84.

Hughes, Everett C. Review of *Modern Industry*, by Ernest L. Bogart, and Charles E. Landon. *American Journal of Sociology* 33, no. 5 (1928): 849.

———. Review of *Race, Nation, Person: Social Aspects of the Race Problem: A Symposium*, by Joseph M. Corrigan and G. Barry O'Toole. *American Journal of Sociology* 50, no. 4 (1945): 320–21.

———. "The Knitting of Racial Groups in Industry." *American Sociological Review* 11, no. 5 (1946): 512–19.

———. "The Gleichshaltung of the German Statistical Yearbook." *The American Statistician* 9, no. 5 (1955): 8–11. Accessed March 2, 2016. http://www.jstor.org/stable/2685502.

———. Review of *Race and Nationality in American Life*, by Oscar Handlin. *American Journal of Sociology* 63, no. 1 (1957): 119.

———. "Good People and Dirty Work." *Social Problems* 10, no. 1 (1962): 3–11. http://www.jstor.org/stable/799402.

———. "Rejoinder to Rose." *Social Problems* 10, no. 4 (1963): 390.

———. "*Letter from Everett C. Hughes.*" *Social Problems* 11, no. 4 (1964): 433.

———. "A Letter to the Membership from the Outgoing President." *American Sociological Review* 29, no. 1 (1964): 116–17.

———. *The Sociological Eye: Selected Papers.* New Brunswick, NJ: Transaction, 1971.

———. "Comments: Everett C. Hughes." *American Sociologist* 13, no. 4 (1978): 248–49.

———. *On Work, Race, and the Sociological Imagination.* Chicago: University of Chicago Press, 1994.

———. "Innocents Abroad, 1948, or How to Behave in Occupied Germany." *Sociologica* 2 (2010): 1–8. Accessed March 28, 2012. doi:10.2383/32715.

———. "Memorandum on Total Institutions." *Sociologica* 2 (2010): 1–5. Accessed March 28, 2012. doi:10.2383/32719.

———. "Outline for the Sociological Study of an Occupation." *Sociologica* 2 (2010): 1–3. Accessed March 28, 2012. doi:10.2383/32716.

Hughes, Henry S. *The Sea Change. The Migration of Social Thought, 1930–1965.* New York: Harper & Row, 1975.

Husserl, Edmund. "Ideen zu einer reinen Phänomenologie und phänomenologischen Philosophie. Erstes Buch: Allgemeine Einführung in die reine Phänomenologie." In *Jahrbuch für Philosophie und phänomenologische Forschung*. Halle: Max Niemeyer Verlag, 1913. Accessed September 8, 2012. http://www.freidok.uni-freiburg.de/volltexte/5973/pdf/Husserl_Ideen_zu_einer_reinen_Phaenomenologie_1.pdf.

Inglehart, Ronald. *Modernization and Postmodernization: Cultural, Economic, and Political Change in 43 Societies*. Princeton, NJ: Princeton University Press, 1997.

Jäckel, Eberhard. *Hitler's Weltanschauung: A Blueprint for Power*. Middletown, CT: Wesleyan University Press, 1972.

Jacobs, Janet L. "Women, Genocide and Memory: The Ethics of Feminist Ethnography in Holocaust Research." *Gender and Society* 18 (2004): 233–38.

Jacobs, Steven L. "The Papers of Raphael Lemkin: A First Look." *Journal of Genocide Research* 1, no. 1 (1999): 105–14.

Jacobsen, Michael H., and Sophia Marshman, "The Four Faces of Human Suffering in the Sociology of Zygmunt Bauman—Continuity and Change." *Polish Sociological Review* 161, no. 1 (2008): 3–24.

Jacobson, Matthew F. *Special Sorrows: The Diasporic Imagination of Irish, Polish, and Jewish Immigrants in the United States*. Cambridge MA: Harvard University Press, 1995.

Janowitz, Morris. "German Reactions to Nazi Atrocities." *American Journal of Sociology* 52, 2 (1946): 141–46. doi:10.1086/219961.

Jasper, James M. *The Art of Moral Protest*. Chicago: University of Chicago Press, 1997.

Jaspers, Karl. *La questione della colpa: Sulla responsabilità politica della Germania*. Milan: Raffaello Cortina, 1996 [1946].

Jay, Martin. *The Dialectical Imagination: A History of the Frankfurt School and the Institute of Social Research, 1923–1950*. London: Heinemann, 1973.

Jedlowski, Paolo. M*emoria, esperienza e modernità: Memorie e società nel XX secolo*. Milan: Angeli, 2002.

———. *Il racconto come memoria: Heimat e le memorie d'Europa*. Turin: Bollati Boringhieri, 2009.

———. "Memoria collettiva." *Dizionario di Storiografia*. http://www.pbmstoria.it/dizionari/storiografia/lemmi/264.htm.

Johnson, Charles S. Review of *The American Race Problem*, by Edward B. Reuter. *American Journal of Sociology* 33, no. 4 (1928): 647–49.

Jonas, Hans. *Der Gottesbegriff nach Auschwitz: Eine judische Stimme.* Frankfurt: Suhrkamp, 1987.

Judaken, Jonathan. "So What's New? Rethinking the "New Antisemitism" in a Global Age." *Patterns of Prejudice* 42, no. 4/5 (2008): 531–60.

Judt, Tony. *Postwar: A History of Europe Since 1945.* New York: Penguin, 2005.

———. *Reappraisals: Reflections on the Forgotten Twentieth Century.* New York: Penguin, 2008.

Junker, Klaus. "Research under Dictatorship: The German Archaeological Institute, 1929–1945." *Antiquity* 72 (1998): 282–92.

Kalberg, Stephen. "The German Sonderweg De-Mystified: A Sociological Biography of a Nation." *Theory, Culture and Society* 9, no. 3 (1992): 111–24.

Kaldor, Mary. *Le nuove guerre: La violenza organizzata nell'età globale.* Rome: Carocci, 2003 [1999].

Kalekin-Fishman, Devorah, and Lauren Langman, "Introductory Background." *Current Sociology* 56, no. 4 (2008): 507–16.

Kaplan, Chaim A. *Scroll of Agony: The Warsaw Diary of Chaim A. Kaplan.* Bloomington: Indiana University Press, 1999.

Karády, Victor. *The Jews of Europe in the Modern Era.* Budapest: Central European University Press, 2004.

Karpf, Anne. *The War After: Living with the Holocaust.* London: Heinemann, 1996.

Karski, Jan. *Story of Secret State.* Boston: Houghton Mifflin, 1944.

Kater, Michael H. "Everyday Antisemitism in Pre-War Nazi Germany: The Popular Bases." *Yad Vashem Studies* 16 (1984): 129–59.

Katz, Elihu. Review of *Sociology Confronts the Holocaust: Memories and Identities in Jewish Diasporas*, by Judith M. Gerson, and Diane L. Wolf. *Social Forces* 87, no. 4 (2009): 2221–2222. Accessed October 2, 2009. doi:10.1353/sof.0.0198.

Katz, Elihu, and Ruth Katz, "Life and Death among the Binaries: Notes on Jeffrey Alexander's Constructionism," in *Remembering the Holocaust: A Debate*, edited by Alexander, Jeffrey, Martin Jay, Bernhard Giesen, Michael Rothberg, Robert Manne, Nathan Glazer, Elihu Katz, and Ruth Katz, 156–70. New York: Oxford University Press, 2009.

Katz, Fred E. "A Sociological Perspective to the Holocaust." *Modern Judaism* 2, no. 3 (1982): 273–96.

_____. *Ordinary People and Extraordinary Evil: A Report on the Beguilings of Evil.* Albany: SUNY Press, 1993.

Katz, Steven T. *The Holocaust in Historical Context.* Vol. 1, *The Holocaust and Mass Death Before the Modern Age.* New York: Oxford University Press, 1994.

Kaufman, Debra R. "Introduction: Gender, Scholarship and the Holocaust." *Contemporary Jewry* 17, no. 1 (1996): 3–18.

Kaufman, Walter C. "Status, Authoritarianism, and Anti-Semitism." *American Journal of Sociology* 62, no. 4 (1957): 379–82.

Kazmierska, Kaja. "Memory and Oblivion: Extermination in Poles' Collective Experience." *Polish Sociological Review* 137 (2002): 109–12.

Keen, Mike F. Review of *Talcott Parsons on National Socialism*, by Uta Gerhardt. *American Journal of Sociology* 99, no. 5 (1994): 1359–61.

Kellas, James G. *Nazionalismi ed etnie.* Bologna: il Mulino, 1993.

Kellner, Douglas. Review of *The Frankfurt School: Its History, Theories, and Political Significance*, by Rolf Wiggershaus. *American Journal of Sociology* 100, no. 5 (1995): 1369–71.

Kermish, Joseph. *To Live with Honor and Die with Honor!: Selected Documents from the Warsaw Ghetto Underground Archives "O.S." [Oneg Shabbath].* Jerusalem: Yad Vashem, 1986.

Kern, Stephen. *The Culture of Time and Space, 1880–1918: With a New Preface.* Cambridge, MA: Harvard University Press, 2003.

Kershaw, Ian. *Der Hitler-Mythos: Volksmeinung und Propaganda im Dritten Reich.* Stuttgart: Deutsche Verlagsanstalt, 1980.

_____. *The Nazi Dictatorship: Problems and Perspectives of Interpretation.* London: Edward Arnold, 1985.

Kimura, Akio. "Genocide and the Modern Mind: Intention and Structure." *Journal of Genocide Research* 5, no. 3 (2003): 405–20.

King, Ryan D., and William I. Brustein. "A Political Threat Model of Intergroup Violence: Jews in Pre–World War II Germany." *Criminology* 44, no. 4 (2006): 867–91. doi:10.1111/j.1745-9125.2006.00066.x.

Kirchheimer, Otto. "Criminal Law in National Socialist Germany." *Studies in Philosophy and Social Sciences* 8, no. 3 (1939), 444–63.

Kirkpatrick, Clifford. Review of *Why Hitler Came Into Power*, by Theodore Abel. *American Sociological Review* 4, no. 3 (1939): 410–11.

Kirshner, Sheldon. "Warsaw Ghetto Commander Forgives Tormentors (an interview with Marek Edelman)." *Canadian Jewish News*, November 9, 1989.

Klausner, Samuel Z. Review of *The Story of an Underground: The Resistance of the Jews of Kovno (Lithuania) in the Second World War*, by Zvie A. Brown and Dov Levin. *American Journal of Sociology* 69, no. 4 (1964): 421–22.

Klee, Ernst, Willi Dreßen, and Volker Rieß. *Bei tempi: Lo sterminio degli ebrei raccontato da chi l'ha eseguito e da chi stava aguardare*. Florence: La Giuntina, 1990.

Klemperer, Victor. *LTI: La lingua del terzo Reich*. Florence: La Giuntina, 1998 [1947].

———. *Testimoniare fino all'ultimo*. Milan: Mondadori, 2000.

Klibanski, Bronka. "In the Ghetto and in the Resistance: A Personal Narrative." In *Women in the Holocaust*, edited by Dalia Ofer and Lenore J. Weitzman, 175–86. New Haven, CT: Yale University Press, 1998.

Klug, Brian. "The Collective Jew: Israel and the New Antisemitism." *Patterns of Prejudice* 37, no. 2 (2003): 117–38.

Kogon, Eugen. *Der SS-Staat: Das System der deutschen Konzentrationslager*. Munich: Alber, 1946.

Kohn, Hans. "The Totalitarian Philosophy of War." *Proceedings of the American Philosophical Society* 82 (1940), 57–72.

Kolakowski, Leszek. "A Pleading for Revolution: A Rejoinder to Z. Bauman." *Archives Europeenes de Sociologie* 12, no. 1 (1971): 52–60.

Kolbi-Molinas, Alexa R. *The Secret of Redemption. Memory and Resistance: A Lesson for the 21st Century*. New York: The Elie Wiesel Foundation for Humanity, 2000.

Korbonski, Andrzej. "Civil-Military Relations in Poland between the Wars: 1918-1939." *Armed Forces and Society* 14 (1988): 169–89.

Korczak, Janusz. *Diario del ghetto*. Milan-Trent: Luni, 1997.

Korzec, Pawel. "Antisemitism in Poland as an Intellectual, Social, and Political Movement." In *Studies on Polish Jewry, 1919-1939* edited by Joshua A. Fishman, 12–104. New York: Yivo Institute for Social Research, 1974.

Kosík, Karel. *La nostra crisi attuale*. Rome: Editori Riuniti, 1969.

Krausnick, Helmut. "Judenverfolgung." In *Anatomie des SS-Staates*, Band 2, edited by Hans Buchheim, Martin Broszat, Hans-Adolf Jacobsen, and Helmut Krausnick, 338–55. Olten; Freiburg: Walter, 1965.

Krieken, Robert van. "The Barbarism of Civilization: Cultural Genocide and the 'Stolen Generations.'" *British Journal of Sociology* 50, no. 2 (1999): 297–315.

Kristel, Conny. "Survivor as Historians: Abel Herzberg, Jacques Presser and Loe de Jong on the Nazi Persecution of the Jews in the Netherlands." In *Holocaust Historiography in Context. Emergence, Challenges, Polemics and Achievements*, edited by David Bankier, and Dan Michman, 207–24. Jerusalem: Yad Vashem; New York: Berghahn, 2008.

Kron, Claus-Dieter. "L'esilio degli intellettuali tedeschi negli Stati Uniti dopo il 1933." In *L'Europa in esilio: La migrazione degli intellettuali verso le Americhe tra le due guerre*, edited by Renato Camurri. *Memoria e Ricerca: Rivista di storia contemporanea* 16, no. 31 (2009): 13–26.

Krzemiński, Ireneusz. "Polish-Jewish Relations, Anti-Semitism and National Identity." *Polish Sociological Review* 137 (2002): 25–51.

Kühl, Stefan. *The Nazi Connection: Eugenics, American Racism, and German National Socialism*. Oxford: Oxford University Press, 1994.

Kulka, Otto Dov. "Singularity and its Relativization: Changing Views in German Historiography on National Socialism and the 'Final Solution.'" *Yad Vashem Studies* 19 (1988): 151–86.

Kulka, Otto Dov, and Eberhard Jäckel, eds. *The Jews in the Secret Nazi Reports on Popular Opinion in Germany, 1933–1945*. New Haven, CT: Yale University Press, 2010.

Kuper, Adam, and Jessica Kuper, eds. *The Social Science Encyclopedia*. London: Routledge, 1985.

Kuper, Leo. *Passive Resistance in South Africa*. New Haven, CT: Yale University Press, 1957.

———. *An African Bourgeoisie: Race, Class, and Politics in South Africa*. New Haven, CT: Yale University Press, 1965.

———. *Race, Class and Power: Ideology and Revolutionary Change in Plural Societies*. London: Duckworth, 1974.

———. *The Pity of It All: Polarisation of Racial and Ethnic Relations*. London: Duckworth; Minneapolis: University of Minnesota Press, 1977.

———. Review of *Accounting for Genocide*, by Helen Fein. *Ethnic & Racial Studies* 3, no. 2 (1980): 238–40.

———. *Genocide: Its Political Use in the Twentieth Century*. New York: Penguin, 1981.

———. *The Prevention of Genocide*. New Haven, CT: Yale University Press, 1985.

Kuper, Leo, P. Sargant Florence, and C. Madge, eds. *Living in Towns: Selected Research Papers in Urban Sociology*. London: Cresset, 1953.

Kurkowska-Budzan, Marta. "Imaging Jedwabne the Symbolic and the Real." *Polish Sociological Review* 137 (2002): 113–16.

Kwiet, Konrad, and Jürgen Matthäus, eds. *Contemporary Responses to the Holocaust*. Westport, CT: Praeger, 2004.

LaCapra, Dominick. *History and Memory after Auschwitz*. Ithaca, NY: Cornell University Press, 1998.

——. *Writing History, Writing Trauma*. Baltimore: Johns Hopkins University Press, 2001.

Lammers, Cornelis J. Review of *The Order of Terror: The Concentration Camp*, by Wolfgang Sofsky. *Organization Studies* 16, no. 1 (1995): 139–56. doi:10.1177/017084069501600107.

Lanzmann, Claude. *Shoah*. Milan: Rizzoli, 1987.

Laqueur, Walter. *Il terribile segreto: La congiura del silenzio sulla "soluzione finale."* Florence: La Giuntina 1983.

——. *The Changing Face of Anti-Semitism: From Ancient Times to the Present Day*. New York: Oxford University Press, 2006.

Laska, Vera. *Women in the Resistance and in the Holocaust: The Voices of Eyewitnesses*. Westport, CT: Greenwood, 1983.

Laski, Harold. "Foundations, Universities, and Research." In *The Dangers of Obedience and Other Essays*, edited by Harold Laski, 150–77. New York: Harper, 1930.

Leites, Nathan C. Review of *Symposium on the Totalitarian State: Proceedings of the American Philosophical Society LXXXII*. *American Journal of Sociology* 47, no. 6 (1942): 1010.

Lemarchand, René. "Disconnecting the threads: Rwanda and the Holocaust reconsidered." *Journal of Genocide Research* 4, no. 4 (2002): 499–518. doi:10.1080/146235022000000436.

Lemkin, Raphael. *Axis Rule in Occupied Europe: Laws of Occupation, Analysis of Government, Proposals for Redress*. Washington, DC: Carnegie Endowment for International Peace, 1944.

Lentin, Ronit. *Israel and the Daughters of the Shoah: Reoccupying the Territories of Silence*. New York: Berghahn, 2000.

——, ed. *Re-presenting the Shoah for the Twenty-first Century*. New York: Berghahn, 2004.

_____. "Memories for the Future." *International Sociology* 24, no. 2 (2009): 173–84. doi:10.1177/0268580908101064.

Lévai, Eugene. *Black Book on the Martyrdom of Hungarian Jewry*. Zurich: Central European Times, 1948.

Levi, Primo. *Se questo è un uomo*. Turin: Einaudi, 1958.

Levinas, Emmanuel. *Trascendenza e intelligibilità*. Genoa: Marietti, 1990.

Levine, Peter. *Ellis Island to Ebbets Field: Sport and the American Jewish Experience*. New York: Oxford University Press, 1992.

Levis-Sullam, Simon. *L'archivio antiebraico: Il linguaggio dell'antisemitismo moderno*. Rome-Bari: Laterza 2008.

Levy, Daniel, and Natan Sznaider. *Erinnerung im globalen Zeitalter: Der Holocaust*. Frankfurt: Suhrkamp, 2001.

_____. "Memory Unbound: The Holocaust and the Formation of Cosmopolitan Memory." *European Journal of Social Theory* 5, no. 1 (2002): 87–106. doi:10.1177/1368431002005001002.

_____. "The Institutionalization of Cosmopolitan Morality: the Holocaust and Human Rights." *Journal of Human Rights* 3, no. 2 (2004): 143–57. doi:10.1080/1475483042000210685.

_____. "The Cosmopolitanization of Holocaust Memory: From Jewish to Human Experience." In *Sociology Confronts the Holocaust*, edited by Judith M. Gerson and Diane L. Wolf, 313–30. Durham, NC: Duke University Press, 2007.

Lewin, Kurt. *Field Theory in Social Science*. New York: Harper & Row, 1951.

Lewis, Bernard. *Semites and Anti-Semites: An Inquiry into Conflict and Prejudice*. New York: W. W. Norton, 1987.

Liao, Tim F., and Carolyn Hronis. "The Polish Peasant and the Sixth Life Course Principle." *Polish Sociological Review* 158 (2007): 173–85.

Lijphart, Arend. *The Trauma of Decolonization: The Dutch & West New Guinea*. New Haven, CT: Yale University Press, 1966.

Linden, Robin Ruth. *Making Stories, Making Selves: Feminist Reflections on the Holocaust*. Columbus: Ohio State University Press, 1993.

Lippman, Matthew. "A Road Map to the 1948 Convention on the Prevention and Punishment of the Crime Genocide." *Journal of Genocide Research* 4, no. 2 (2002): 177–95.

Lipset, Seymour M. *Political Man: The Social Bases of Politics.* Garden City, NY: Doubleday, 1960.

———. *Istituzioni, partiti, società civile.* Edited by L. Morlino. Bologna: il Mulino, 2009.

Lipstadt, Deborah. *The Eichmann Trial.* New York: Schocken, 2011.

Lisus, Nicola A., and Richard V. Ericson, "Misplacing Memory: The Effect of Television Format on Holocaust Remembrance." *British Journal of Sociology* 46, no. 1 (1995): 1–19.

Lochner, Louis P. *Tycoons and Tyrants: German Industry from Hitler to Adenauer.* Chicago: Henry Regnery, 1954.

Lowenthal, Leo. "Terror's Atomization of Man." *Commentary* 1, no. 3 (1946): 1–8.

Löwith, Karl. *Mein Leben in Deutschland vor und nach 1933: Ein Bericht.* Stuttgart: J. B. Metzler, 1986.

Löwy, Michael, and Eleni Varikas. "Racisme et eugénisme pendant l'entre-deux-guerres. Précurseurs et alliés du nazisme aux Etats-Unis." *Le Monde Diplomatique* (April 2007): 22–23.

Lozowick, Yaacov. *Hitler's Bureaucrats: The Nazi Security Police and the Banality of Evil.* London: Continuum, 2002.

Lubetkin, Tzivia. *In the Days of Destruction and Revolt.* Tel Aviv: Beit Lohamei Haghetaot, 1981.

Luhmann, Niklas. *Sociologia del rischio.* Milan: Mondadori, 1996 [1991].

Lukács, Georg. *Geschichte und Klassenbewusstsein: Studien über marxistische Dialektik.* Berlin: Malik-Verlag, 1923.

Lupovitch, Howard N. "Traversing the Rupture: Antisemitism and the Holocaust in Hungary." *Patterns of Prejudice* 37, no. 4 (2003): 429–36.

Lynd, Robert S., *Knowledge for What? The Place of the Social Sciences in American Culture.* Princeton, NJ: Princeton University Press, 1939.

Lynd, Robert S., and Helen M. Lynd, *Middletown: A Study in Contemporary American Culture.* New York: Harcourt, Brace, 1929.

———. *Middletown in Transition: A Study in Cultural Conflicts.* New York: Harcourt, Brace, 1937.

MacCoun, Robert J., Elizabeth Kier, and Aaron Belkin. "Does Social Cohesion Determine Motivation in Combat? An Old Question with an Old Answer." *Armed Forces & Society* 32, no. 4 (2006): 646–654. doi:10.1177/0095327X05279181.

Malmgreen, Gail. "Labor and the Holocaust: The Jewish Labor Committee and the Anti-Nazi Struggle." *Labor's Heritage* 3, no. 4 (1991): 20–35.

Mann, Michael. *The Sources of Social Power.* Cambridge: Cambridge University Press, 1986.

Mantelli, Brunello. "Campi di sterminio." In *Storia della Shoah: La crisi dell'Europa, lo sterminio degli ebrei e la memoria del XX secolo*, edited by Marina Cattaruzza, Marcello Flores, Simon Levis-Sullam, and Enzo Traverso, 2:536–59. Turin: Utet, 2005–2006.

March, James G., and Herbert A. Simon. *Organizations.* Cambridge, MA: Blackwell, 1993.

Marchetti, Valerio. "Resistenza ebraica, antisemitismo, totalitarismo." In *Nazismo, fascismo, comunismo: Totalitarismi a confronto*, edited by Marcello Flores, 259–87. Milan: Bruno Mondadori, 1998.

Marcuse, Herbert. *One-Dimensional Man: Studies in the Ideology of Advanced Industrial Society.* Boston: Beacon, 1964.

———. *Kultur und Gesellschaft.* Frankfurt: Suhrkamp, 1965.

Markle, Gerald E. *Meditations of Holocaust Traveler.* Albany: SUNY Press, 1995.

Marrus, Michael R. *The Holocaust in History.* Lebanon, NH: University Press of New England, 1987.

Marrus, Michael R., and Robert O. Paxton. *Vichy France and the Jews.* New York: Basic Books, 1981.

Martinelli, Alberto. *La modernizzazione.* Rome-Bari: Laterza, 2004.

Mason, Timothy W. *The Primacy of Politics: Politics and Economics in National Socialist Germany.* In *The Nature of Fascism*, edited by Stuart J. Woolf, 165–95. London: Weidenfeld and Nicolson, 1968.

Massing, Paul W. *Rehearsal for Destruction: A Study of Political Anti-Semitism in Imperial Germany.* New York: Fertig, 1967.

Mathews, Shailer. "The Christian Church and Social Unity." *American Journal of Sociology* 5, no. 4 (1900): 456–69.

Mayers, David A. Review of *Values and Violence in Auschwitz: A Sociological Analysis*, by Anna Pawełczyńska. *American Journal of Sociology* 85, no. 6 (1980): 1485–87.

Mazower, Mark. *Dark Continent: Europe's 20th Century.* New York: Knopf, 1998.

McLung Lee, Alfred. *Principles of Sociology.* New York: Barnes & Noble, 1951.

McWilliams, Carey. *A Mask for Privilege: Anti-Semitism in America.* Boston: Brown and Company, 1948.

Mead, Margaret. Review of *Race: Individual and Collective Behavior*, by Edgar T. Thompson and Everett C. Hughes. *American Journal of Sociology* 65, no.

1 (1959): 110–12.

Mechanicus, Philip. *Year of Fear*. New York: Hawthorn, 1969.

Meed, Vladka. *On Both Sides of the Wall: Memoirs from the Warsaw Ghetto*. New York: Holocaust Library, 1979.

Melchior, Malgorzata. "Threat of Extermination in Biographical Experience of the Holocaust Survivors." *Polish Sociological Review* 137 (2002): 53–70.

Melucci, Alberto, ed. *Fine della modernità?* Milan: Guerini Studio, 1998.

Memmi, Albert. *Portrait d'un Juif*. Paris: Gallimard, 1962.

Merkl, Peter H. *Political Violence under the Swastika: 581 Early Nazis*. Princeton, NJ: Princeton University Press, 1975.

Merton, Robert K. *Social Theory and Social Structure: Toward the Codification of Theory and Research*. Glencoe, IL: Free Press, 1949.

Messina, A. Valeria. "Nel campo di Auschwitz." *Free Ebrei: Rivista di identità ebraica contemporanea* 4, no. 2 (2015). http://www.freeebrei.com/anno-iv-numero-2-luglio-dicembre-2015/nel-campo-di-auschwitz-a-cura-di-adele-valeria-messina; *Deportate, Esuli e Profughe* 30 (2016): 202–26. http://www.unive.it/nqcontent.cfm?a_id=200057.

Michael, Robert. *A Concise History of American Antisemitism*. New York: Rowman and Littlefield, 2005.

Michel, Henri. *The Shadow War: European Resistance, 1939–1945*. New York: Harper & Row, 1972.

Michlic, Joanna. *Coming to Terms with the "Dark Past": The Polish Debate about the Jedwabne Massacre*. Jerusalem: SICSA, 2002.

Michman, Dan, ed. *Belgium and the Holocaust: Jews, Belgians, Germans*. Jerusalem: Yad Vashem, 1998.

———. *Pour une historiographie de la Shoah: Conceptualisations, terminologie, définitions et problèms fondamentaux*. Paris: In Press Éditions, 2001.

Milgram, Avraham, Carmit Sagui, and Shulamit Imbar, eds. *Every Day Life in the Warsaw Ghetto, 1941*. Jerusalem: Yad Vashem, 1993.

Milgram, Stanley. *Obedience to Authority: An Experimental View*. New York: Harper & Row, 1974.

Mill, John S. *Auguste Comte and Positivism*. Ann Arbor: University of Michigan Press, 1961.

Mills, Charles W. *The New Men of Power: America's Labor Leaders*. Urbana: University of Illinois Press, 1948.

———. *White Collar: The American Middle Classes.* Oxford: Oxford University Press, 1951.
———. *The Power Elite.* New York: Oxford University Press, 1956.
———. *The Sociological Imagination.* New York: Oxford University Press, 1959.
Momigliano, Arnaldo. *Sesto contributo alla storia degli studi classici e del mondo antico.* Vol. 1. Rome: Edizioni di storia e letteratura, 1980.
Mommsen, Hans. *Auschwitz, 17. Juli 1942: Der Weg zur europäischen "Endlösung der Judenfrage."* Munich: Deutscher Taschenbuch Verlag, 2002.
Moore, Barrington, Jr. *Soviet Politics—The Dilemma of Power: The Role of Ideas in Social Change.* Cambridge, MA: Harvard University Press, 1950.
———. *Social Origins of Dictatorship and Democracy: Lord and Peasant in the Making of the Modern World.* Boston: Beacon, 1966.
———. *Injustice: The Social Bases of Obedience and Revolt.* White Plains, NY.: Sharpe, 1978.
Moore, Deborah D. *To the Golden Cities: Pursuing the American Jewish Dream in Miami and Los Angeles.* New York: Free Press, 1994.
Morawska, Ewa. *Insecure Prosperity: Small-Town Jews in Industrial America, 1890–1940.* Princeton, NJ: Princeton University Press, 1996.
Morgan, J. Graham. Review of *On Work, Race, and the Sociological Imagination*, by Everett C. Hughes. *Canadian Journal of Sociology* 21, no. 4 (1996): 575–77.
Morlino, Luciano. *Democrazie e democratizzazioni.* Bologna: il Mulino, 2003.
Morris, Aldon D. *The Origins of the Civil Rights Movement: Black Communities Organizing for Change.* New York: Free Press, 1984.
Morris, Aldon D., and Carol McClurg Mueller, eds. *Frontiers in Social Movement Theory.* New Haven, CT: Yale University Press, 1992.
Morse, Arthur D. *While Six Million Died: A Chronicle of American Apathy.* New York: Random House, 1967.
Morton, Jeffrey S., and Neil V. Singh. "The International Legal Regime on Genocide." *Journal of Genocide Research* 5, no. 1 (2003): 47–69.
Mosca, Gaetano. *Elementi di scienza politica.* Turin: Bocca, 1923.
Mosse, George L. *Die Nationalisierung der Massen: Politische Symbolik und Massenbewegungen von den Befreiungskriegen bis zum Dritten Reich.* Frankfurt: Campus, 1993.
Moyn, Samuel. "Antisemitism, Philosemitism and the Rise of Holocaust Memory." *Patterns of Prejudice* 43, no. 1 (2009): 1–16. doi:10.1080/00313220802636023.

Mueller, John. "Changing Attitudes towards War: The Impact of the First World War." *British Journal of Political Science* 21 (1991): 1–28.
Musial, Bogdan. "Jewish Resistance in Poland's Eastern Borderlands during the Second World War, 1939–41." *Patterns of Prejudice* 38, no. 4 (2004): 371–82.
Musil, Robert. *L'uomo senza qualità*. Turin: Einaudi, 2005 [1930–1933].
Musolff, Andreas. "What Role do Metaphors Play in Racial Prejudice? The Function of Antisemitic Imagery in Hitler's *Mein Kampf*." *Patterns of Prejudice* 41, no. 1 (2007): 21–43.
Neumann, Franz. *Behemoth: The Structure and Practice of National Socialism, 1933–1944*. New York: Oxford University Press, 1942.
———. *The Democratic and the Authoritarian State: Essays in Political and Legal Theory*. Glencoe, IL: Free Press, 1957.
Neumann, Franz, Herbert Marcuse, and Otto Kirchheimer. *Il nemico tedesco: Scritti riservati sulla Germania nazista (1943–1945)*. Edited by Roberto Laudani. Bologna: il Mulino, 2012.
Neurath, Paul M. *The Society of Terror: Inside the Dachau and Buchenwald Concentration Camps*. Edited by Christian Fleck and Nico Stehr. Boulder, CO: Paradigm, 2005.
Nidam-Orvieto, Iael. "Fighting Oblivion: The CDEC and Its Impact on Italian Holocaust Historiography." In *Holocaust Historiography in Context: Emergence, Challenges, Polemics and Achievements*, edited by David Bankier and Dan Michman, 293–304. Jerusalem: Yad Vashem, and New York: Berghahn, 2008.
Nielsen, Jens K. "The Political Orientation of Talcott Parsons: The Second World War and Its Aftermath." In *Talcott Parsons: Theorist of Modernity*, edited by Roland Robertson and Bryan S. Turner. London: Sage, 1991.
Nirenstajn, Albert. *Ricorda cosa ti ha fatto Amalek*. Turin: Einaudi, 1958.
Noiriel, Gérard. *Immigration, antisémitisme et racisme en France (XIX–XX siècle): Discours publics, humiliations privées*. Paris: Fayard, 2007.
Nora, Pierre. "Mémoire collective." In *La nouvelle histoire*, edited by Jacques Le Goff, Roger Chartier, and Jacques Revel, 398–401. Paris: Retz, 1978.
Norwood, Stephen H., "Legitimating Nazism: Harvard University and the Hitler Regime, 1933–1937." *American Jewish History* 92, no. 2 (2004): 189–223.
Novick, Peter. *The Holocaust in American Life*. New York: Houghton Mifflin, 1999.
Nussbaum, Marta. *The Fragility of Goodness: Luck and Ethics in Greek Tragedy and Philosophy*. Cambridge: Cambridge University Press, 2001.

Oberschall, Anthony. *Social Movements: Ideologies, Interests, and Identities.* New Brunswick, NJ: Transaction, 1993.

O'Connell, Charles. "Social Structure and Science: Soviet Studies." PhD diss., UCLA, 1990.

Ofer, Dalia, and Lenore J. Weitzman, eds. *Women in the Holocaust.* New Haven, CT: Yale University Press, 1998.

Ogburn, William Fielding: "Introduction." *American Journal of Sociology* 38, no. 6 (1933): 823–24.

O'Lessker, Karl. "Who Voted for Hitler? A New Look at the Class Basis of Nazism." *American Journal of Sociology* 74, no. 1 (1968): 63–69.

Olick, Jeffrey K. "Genre Memories and Memory Genres: A Dialogical Analysis of May 8, 1945, Commemorations in the Federal Republic of Germany." *American Sociological Review* 64 (1999): 381–402.

———. Review of *Roots of Hate: Anti-Semitism in Europe before the Holocaust,* by William I. Brustein. *American Journal of Sociology* 109, no. 3 (2005): 945–48.

Olsak-Glass, Judith. Review of *Poland's Holocaust: Ethnic Strife, Collaboration with Occupying Forces and Genocide in the Second Republic, 1918–1947,* by Tomasz Piotrowski. *Sarmatian Review* 19, no. 1 (1999): 1–4. Last accessed March 28, 2011. http://www.ruf.rice.edu/~sarmatia/199/glass.html.

Oppenheimer, Martin. "Footnote to the Cold War: The Harvard Russian Research Center." *Monthly Review* 48 (1997): 7–17.

———. "Social Scientists and War Criminals." *New Politics* 6, no. 23 (1997). Accessed May 31, 2011. http://nova.wpunj.edu/newpolitics/issue23/oppenh23.htm.

———. "To the Editor." *Sociological Forum* 12, no. 2 (1997): 339–341.

———. "The Sociology of Knowledge and the Holocaust: A Critique." In *Sociology Confronts the Holocaust: Memories and Identities in Jewish Diasporas,* edited by Judith M. Gerson, and Diane L. Wolf, 331–36. Durham, NC: Duke University Press, 2007.

Ordover, Nancy. *American Eugenics: Race, Queer Anatomy, and the Science of Nationalism.* Minneapolis: University of Minnesota Press, 2003.

Ossowski, Stanisław. "Prawa 'historyczne' w socjologii." *Przegląd filozoficzny* 37 (1935): 3–32.

———. *Struktura kłasowa w społecznej świadomości.* Łódź, Wrocław: Zakład narodowy imienia Ossolińskich, 1957.

———. *O osobliwościach nauk społecznych.* Warsaw: PWN, 1962.

Ostow, Robin. *Jews in Contemporary East Germany: The Children of Moses in the Land of Marx.* New York: St. Martin's, 1989.

Outhwaite, William, Tom Bottomore, Ernest Gellner, Paolo Jedlowski, Robert Nisbet, and Alain Touraine, eds. "Modernità." In *Dizionario delle scienze sociali,* 440–441. Milan: il Saggiatore, 1997.

Overy, Richard J. *The Inter-War Crisis, 1919–1939.* London: Longman, 1994.

———. *Interrogations: The Nazi Elite in Allied Hands, 1945.* New York: Viking Penguin, 2001.

Pace, Fabio M. "L'impossibile ritorno: Gli ebrei in Polonia dalla fine della guerra al pogrom di Kielce." In *Il ritorno alla vita e il problema della testimonianza: Studi e riflessioni sulla Shoah,* edited by Alessandra Chiappano and Fabio Minazzi, 127–54. Florence: Giuntina, 2007.

Palmer, Alison. Review of *Genocide Watch,* by Helen Fein, and *Final Solutions: Biology, Prejudice, and Genocide,* by Richard M. Lerner. *Ethnic & Racial Studies* 18, no. 1 (1995): 148–50.

Paolucci, Gabriella, ed. *Cronofagia: La contrazione del tempo e dello spazio nell'era della globalizzazione.* Milan: Guerini, 2003.

Papcke, Sven, and Martin Oppenheimer. "Value-Free Sociology: Design for Disaster German Social Science from Reich to Federal Republic." *Humanity & Society* 8, no. 3 (1984): 272–82.

Parisella, Antonio. *Sopravvivere liberi: Riflessioni sulla storia della Resistenza a cinquant'anni dalla Liberazione.* Rome: Gangemi, 1997.

Parisi, Valentina. "Samizdat: Problemi di definizione." *eSamizdat* 8 (2010–2011): 19–29. Accessed March 28, 2012. http://www.esamizdat.it/rivista/2010-2011/index.

Park, Robert E. Review of *The Jews,* by Hilair Belloc, and *Patriotism of the American Jew,* by Samuel W. McCall. *American Journal of Sociology* 30, no. 4 (1925): 486–88.

———. Review of *Are the Jews a Race?* by Karl J. Kautsky. *American Journal of Sociology* 32, no. 4 (1927): 671.

———. Review of *I Am a Woman: And a Jew,* by Leah Morton, and *I, the Jew,* by Maurice Samuel. *American Journal of Sociology* 33, no. 5 (1928): 829–30.

———. Review of *Jews without Money,* by Michael Gold. *American Journal of Sociology* 37, no. 4 (1932): 669–70.

Park, Robert E., Ernest W. Burgess, and Roderick D. McKenzie. *The City*. Chicago: University of Chicago Press, 1925.
Parsons, Talcott. "Propaganda and Social Control." *Psychiatry* 5 (1942): 551–72.
———. "The Problem of Controlled Institutional Change: An Essay in Applied Social Science." *Psychiatry* 8 (1945): 79–101.
———. *The Social System*. Glencoe, IL: Free Press, 1951.
———. *Professioni e libertà*. Edited by Marco Santoro. Rome: Armando, 2011.
Parsons, Talcott, and Bernard Barber, "Sociology 1941–1946." *American Journal of Sociology* 53 no. 4 (1948): 245–57.
Parsons, Talcott, and Edward A. Shils. *Toward a General Theory of Action*. Cambridge, MA: Harvard University Press, 1951.
Pasquino, Gianfranco. "I partiti strutture del consenso: Ascesa e declino." *I Viaggi di Erodoto* 8 (1994): 259–70.
———. "Democrazia ed eccezionalismo." Review of *Istituzioni, partiti, società civile*, by Seymour M. Lipset. *New York Review of Books*, March 2010. Accessed May 2, 2010. http://www.larivistadeilibri.it/2010/03/pasquino.html.
Pawełczyńska, Anna. "Values and Violence Sociology of Auschwitz." *Polish Sociological Bulletin* 3 (1976): 5–17.
———. *Values and Violence in Auschwitz: A Sociological Analysis*. Translated by Catherine S. Leach. Berkeley: University of California Press, 1979. Polish edition: *Wartości A Przemoc: Zarys socjologicznej problematyki Oświęcimia*. Warsaw: Państwowe Wydawnictwo Naukowe, 1973.
Peace, Timothy. "Un antisemitisme nouveau? The Debate about a 'New Antisemitism' in France." *Patterns of Prejudice* 43, no. 2 (2009): 103–21.
Pei, Yu. "Global History and National Historical Memory." *History* 42, no. 3 (2009): 25–45.
Pellegrino, Giuseppina. "Introduction: Studying (Im)mobility through a Politics of Proximity." In *The Politics of Proximity: Mobility and Immobility in Practice*, edited by Giuseppina Pellegrino, 1–14. Aldershot: Ashgate, 2011.
Pells, Richard H. *Radical Visions & American Dreams: Culture and Social Thought in the Depression Years*. Middletown, CT: Wesleyan University Press, 1973.
Petrusewicz, Marta. "Fine della Polonia innocente: Analisi di un dibattito." *Passato e Presente* 20, no. 56 (2002): 153–66.

Pierre, Andrew J., and Lucy E. Despard. Review of *Genocide Watch*, by Helen Fein. *Foreign Affairs* 71, no. 3 (1992): 167.
Pinchuk, Ben-Cion. *Shtetl Jews under Soviet Rule: Eastern Poland on the Eve of the Holocaust*. Cambridge, MA: Basil Blackwell, 1991.
Pingel, Falk. *Häftlinge unter SS-Herrschaft: Widerstand, Selbstbehauptung und Vernichtung im Konzentrationslager*. Hamburg: Hoffmann & Campe, 1978.
Pinto, Vincenzo. *I sionisti*. Milan: M&B Publishing, 2001.
Piotrowski, Tadeusz. *Vengeance of the Swallows: Memoir of a Polish Family's Ordeal under Soviet Aggression, Ukrainian Ethnic Cleansing and Nazi Enslavement, and Their Emigration to America*. Jefferson, NC: McFarland, 1995.
_____. *Ukrainian Integral Nationalism: Chronological Assessment and Bibliography*. Toronto: Alliance of the Polish Eastern Provinces, with the Polish Educational Foundation in North America, 1997.
_____. *Poland's Holocaust: Ethnic Strife, Collaboration with Occupying Forces and Genocide in the Second Republic, 1918–1947*. Jefferson, NC: McFarland, 1998.
Pizzorno, Alessandro. *Le radici della politica assoluta e altri saggi*. Milan: Feltrinelli, 1993.
Platt, Jennifer. *A History of Sociological Research Methods in America, 1920–1960*. Cambridge: Cambridge University Press, 1996.
Poggi, Gianfranco. *La vicenda dello stato moderno: Profilo sociologico*. Bologna: il Mulino, 1978.
Pohl, Dieter. *Nationalsozialistische Judenverfolgung in Ostgalizien 1941–1944: Organisation und Durchführung eines staatlichen Massenverbrechens*. Munich: Oldenbourg, 1996.
Polanyi, Karl. *The Great Transformation*. New York: Farrar and Rinehart, 1944.
Poliakov, Léon. *Histoire de l'antisémitisme: L'Europe suicidaire (1870–1933)*. Vol. 4. Paris: Calmann-Lévy, 1977.
Pollock, Friedrich. "Is National Socialism a New Order?" *SPSS* 9, no. 3 (1941): 440–55.
Polonsky, Antony, and Joanna B. Michlic, eds. *The Neighbors Respond: The Controversy over the Jedwabne Massacre in Poland*. Princeton, NJ: Princeton University Press, 2004.
Pooley, Jefferson. "Edward Shils' Turn against Karl Mannheim: The Central European Connection." *The American Sociologist* 38, no. 4 (2007): 364–82.

Porat, Dina. *The Blue and the Yellow Star of David: The Zionist Leadership in Palestine and the Holocaust, 1939–1945*. Cambridge, MA: Harvard University Press, 1990.

Porter, Jack N. "The Holocaust as a Sociological Construct." *Contemporary Jewry* 14, no. 1 (1993): 184–87.

———. "Toward a Sociology of National Socialism." Review of *Talcott Parsons on National Socialism*, by Uta Gerhardt. *Sociological Forum* 9, no. 3 (1994): 505–11.

———. "Talcott Parsons and National Socialism: The Case of the 'Ten Mysterious Missing Letters.'" *Sociological Forum* 11, no. 4 (1996): 603–11.

———. "Toward a Sociology of the Holocaust." *Contemporary Jewry* 17 (1996): 145–48.

Porter, Jack N., and Steve Hoffman. *The Sociology of the Holocaust: A Teaching and Learning Guide*: Washington, DC: ASA, 1999.

Postone, Moishe. "AntiSemitism and National Socialism." In *Germans and Jews since the Holocaust*, edited by Anson Rabinbach and Jack D. Zipes, 302–14. New York: Holmes and Meier, 1986.

———. Review of *Modernity and Holocaust*, by Zygmunt Bauman. *American Journal of Sociology* 97, no. 5 (1992): 1521–23.

Pressac, Jean-Claude. *Le macchine dello sterminio: Auschwitz, 1941–1945*. Milan: Feltrinelli, 1994.

Presser, Jacob. *The Destruction of the Dutch Jews*. New York: Dutton, 1969.

Putnam, Robert D. *The Comparative Study of Political Elites*. Englewood Cliffs, NJ: Prentice-Hall, 1976.

Rapaport, Lynn. *Jews in Germany after the Holocaust: Memory, Identity, and Jewish-German Relations*. Cambridge: Cambridge University Press, 1997.

———. Review of *The Society of Terror: Inside the Dachau and Buchenwald Concentration Camps*, by Paul M. Neurath. *American Journal of Sociology* 112, no. 4 (2007): 1263–65. Accessed March 4, 2016. doi:10.1086/513546.

———. Review of *Sociology Confronts the Holocaust: Memories and Identities in Jewish Diasporas*, edited by Judith M. Gerson and Diane L. Wolf. *American Journal of Sociology* 113, no. 6 (2008): 1794–96.

Rauty, Raffaele. *Società e metropoli: La scuola sociologica di Chicago*. Rome: Donzelli, 1995.

Reike, Theodor. *Listening with the Third Ear: The Inner Experience of a Psychoanalyst*. New York: Farrar, Straus, 1948.

Reitlinger, Gerald. *The Final Solution: The Attempt to Exterminate the Jews of Europe, 1939–1945*. London: Vallentine Mitchell, 1953.

Reitz, Charles. "Marcuse in America—Exile as Educator: Deprovincializing One-Dimensional Culture in the U.S.A." *Fast Capitalism* 5, no. 2 (2009). Accessed June 30, 2016. https://www.uta.edu/huma/agger/fastcapitalism/5_2/Reitz5_2.html.

Rejak, Sebastian. "Judaism Facing the Shoah: American Debates and Interpretations." *Dialogue & Universalism* 13, no. 3/4 (2003): 81–102.

Rheingold, Howard. *The Virtual Community: Homesteading on the Electronic Frontier*. Boston: Addison-Wesley, 1993.

Rich, Norman. *Hitler's War Aims, II: The Establishment of the New Order*. New York: Norton, 1974.

Ricœur, Paul. *La memoria, la storia, l'oblio*. Milan: Cortina, 2003.

Ridolfi, Maurizio, ed. *La storia contemporanea attraverso le riviste*. Soveria Mannelli: Rubbettino, 2008.

Riezler, Kurt. Review of *Pouvoir: Les génies invisibles de la cite*, by Gugliemo Ferrero. *American Journal of Sociology* 48, no. 3 (1942): 424–25.

Ringelblum, Emmanuel. *Sepolti a Varsavia: Appunti dal Ghetto*. Milan: il Saggiatore, 1965.

Ringelheim, Joan M. "Women and the Holocaust: A Reconsideration of Research" *Signs* 10, no. 4 (1985): 741–61.

Rittner, Carol, Stephen D. Smith, and Irena Steinfeldt, eds. *The Holocaust and the Christian World: Reflections on the Past, Challenges for the Future*. New York: Continuum, 2000.

Roach, Jack L. "Reply." *American Journal of Sociology* 71, no. 1 (1965): 76–77.

Robbins, Richard. Review of *The Sociological Eye: Selected Papers*, by Everett C. Hughes. *British Journal of Sociology* 23, no. 3 (1972): 362.

Rock, Paul. Review of *The Order of Terror: The Concentration Camp*, by Wolfgang Sofsky. *British Journal of Sociology* 49, no. 1 (1998): 159–60.

Rock, Stella. "Introduction: Religion, Prejudice and Conflict in the Modern World." *Patterns of Prejudice* 38, no. 2 (2004): 101–8.

Rockaway, Robert. Review of *Henry Ford and the Jews: The Mass Production of Hate*, by Neil Baldwin. *American Jewish History* 89, no. 4 (2001): 467–69.

Rogin, Michael. Review of *Who Voted for Hitler?* by Richard F. Hamilton. *American Journal of Sociology* 89, no. 3 (1983): 754–57.

Rokkan, Stein. *Stato, nazione e democrazia in Europa*. Bologna: il Mulino, 2002.

Romanienko, Lisiunia A. Review of *Poland's Holocaust: Ethnic Strife, Collaboration with Occupying Forces and Genocide in the Second Republic, 1918-1947*, by Tomasz Piotrowski. *Humanity and Society* 24, no. 1 (2000): 99–100. doi:10.1177/016059760002400110.

Rose, Arnold M. "Comment on 'Good People and Dirty Work.'" *Social Problems* 10, no. 3 (1963): 285–86.

Rose, Gillian. *Judaism and Modernity: Philosophical Essays*. Cambridge, MA: Basil Blackwell, 1993.

Rosen, Donia. *Forest, My Friend*. Jerusalem: Yad Vashem, 1985.

Rosenberg, Morris. Review of *The Political Behavior of American Jews*, by Lawrence H. Fuchs. *American Journal of Sociology* 62, no. 4 (1957): 428–29.

Rosenthal, Erich. Review of *Children of the Gilded Ghetto: Conflict Resolutions of Three Generations of American Jews*, by Judith R. Kramer and Seymour Leventman. *American Journal of Sociology* 68, no. 6 (1963): 724–25.

Roth, Guenther. "Partisanship and Scholarship." In *Authors of Their Own Lives: Intellectual Autobiographies by Twenty American Sociologists*, edited by B. M. Berger, 383–409. Berkeley: University of California Press, 1990.

Rousset, David. *L'univers concentrationnaire*. Paris: Éditions de Minuit, 1946.

Rozett, Robert. "Jewish Resistance." In *The Historiography of the Holocaust*, edited by Dan Stone, 341-63. New York: Palgrave Macmillan, 2004.

Rubenstein, Richard L. *The Cunning of History: The Holocaust and the American Future*. New York: Harper Colophon, 1978.

———. "Was Dietrich Bonhoeffer a 'Righteous Gentile'?" *International Journal on World Peace* 17, no. 2 (2000): 33–46.

Rubenstein, Richard L., and John K. Roth. *Approaches to Auschwitz, Revised Edition: The Holocaust and Its Legacy*. Louisville, KY: Westminster John Knox, 2013.

Rudwick, Elliott M. *W. E. B. Du Bois: Propagandist of the Negro Protest*. New York: Atheneum, 1968.

Rummel, Rudolph J. *Democide: Nazi Genocide and Mass Murder*. New Brunswick, NJ: Transaction, 1992.

———. *Death by Government*. New Brunswick, NJ: Transaction, 1994.

———. "Genocide." In *Enciclopedia del Novecento*, III Supplement (2004). http://www.treccani.it/enciclopedia/genocidio_%28Enciclopedia-Novecento%29/.

Rupnow, Dirk. "Racializing Historiography: Anti-Jewish Scholarship in the Third Reich." *Patterns of Prejudice* 42, no. 1 (2008): 27–59.

Rürup, Reinhard. "A Success Story and Its Limits: European Jewish Social History in the Nineteenth and Early Twentieth Centuries." *Jewish Social Studies* 11, no. 1 (2004): 3–15.

Russel, James W. "Intellectual Partnerships and Grudges: Gerth's Relationship with Charles W. Mills." *Critical Sociology* 27, no. 3 (2001): 147–58.

———. Review of *Hans Gerth: "Between Two Worlds,"* by Nobuko Gerth. *Contemporary Sociology* 32, no. 5 (2003): 655–56.

Said, Edward W. *Reflections on the Exile and Other Essays*. Cambridge, MA: Harvard University Press, 2000.

Salomon, Kim. *Refugees in the Cold War: Towards a New International Regime in the Early Postwar Era*. Lund, Sweden: Lund University Press, 1991.

Salomoni, Antonella. *L'Unione Sovietica e la Shoah: Genocidio, resistenza, rimozione*. Bologna: il Mulino, 2007.

———. "L'Europa orientale: Transizioni, stabilizzazioni, nuove identità." In *La storia contemporanea attraverso le riviste*, edited by Maurizio Ridolfi, 149–64. Soveria Mannelli: Rubbettino, 2008.

———. "I libri sulla Shoah: Una guida storiografica suddivisa per periodi e per temi." *Storicamente* 5, no. 23 (2009). Accessed October 24, 2009. doi:10.1473/stor200.

———. "State-sponsored Anti-Semitism in Postwar USSR: Studies and Research Perspectives." *Quest: Issues in Contemporary Jewish History* 1 (2010). http://www.quest-cdecjournal.it/focus.php?id=212.

Salvati, Mariuccia. "Antifascismo e totalitarismo nelle scienze sociali tra le due guerre." *Contemporanea* 4 (2002): 623–50.

Samin, Amir. *Imperialism and Unequal Development*. New York: Monthly Review Press, 1977.

Sanbonmatsu, John. "The Holocaust Sublime: Singularity, Representation, and the Violence of Everyday Life." *American Journal of Economics and Sociology* 68, no. 1 (2009): 101–26.

Santoro, Marco. "Postscript: 'Hughesian Sociology' and the Centrality of Occupation." *Sociologica* 2 (2010): 1–13.

Sarapata, Adam, and Wlodzimierz Wesolowski. "The Evaluation of Occupations by Warsaw Inhabitants." *American Journal of Sociology* 66, no. 6 (1961): 581–91.
Sarfatti, Michele. *La Shoah in Italia: La persecuzione degli ebrei sotto il fascismo.* Turin: Einaudi, 2005.
Savitz, Leonard D., and Richard F. Tomasson. "The Identifiability of Jews." *American Journal of Sociology* 64, no. 5 (1959): 468–75.
Scarbrough, Elinor. Review of *Anti-Semitism in Germany: The Post-Nazi Epoch since 1945*, by Werner Bergmann and Rainer Erb. *American Journal of Sociology* 103, no. 5 (1998): 1441–42.
Schaffner, Bertram. *Fatherland: A Study of Authoritarianism in the German Family.* New York: Columbia University Press, 1948.
Schaller, Dominik J., and Jürgen Zimmerer, eds. *The Origins of Genocide: Raphael Lemkin as a Historian of Mass Violence.* New York: Routledge, 2009.
Schein, Edgar H. "A Social Psychologist Discovers Chicago Sociology." *Academy of Management Review* 14, no. 1 (1989): 103–4.
Scherrer, Christian P. "Towards a Theory of Modern Genocide. Comparative Genocide Research: Definitions, Criteria, Typologies, Cases, Key Elements, Patterns and Voids." *Journal of Genocide Research* 1, no. 1 (1999): 13–23. doi:10.1080/14623529908413932.
Schleunes, Karl A. *The Twisted Road to Auschwitz: Nazi Policy toward German Jews, 1933–1939.* Urbana–Champaign: University of Illinois Press, 1970.
Schneider, Dorothee. "Polish Peasants into Americans: U. S. Citizenship and Americanization among Polish Immigrants in the Inter-War Era." *Polish Sociological Review* 158, no. 2 (2007): 159–71.
Schneigert, Zbigniew. "Obozy NKWD jeńców polskich z lat 1939-1941 w Małopolsce Wschodniej." *Semper Fidelis* (Wrocław) 3, no. 4 (1992): 24–29.
Schorske, Carl E. *German Social Democracy, 1905–1917: The Development of the Great Schism.* Cambridge, MA: Harvard University Press, 1955.
Schütz, Alfred. *The Phenomenology of the Social World.* Evanston, IL: Northwestern University Press, 1967.
Schwartz, Michael. *Radical Protest and Social Structure: The Southern Farmers' Alliance and Cotton Tenancy, 1880-1890.* Chicago: University of Chicago Press, 1976.

Schweitzer, Albert. Review of *Political Violence under the Swastika: 581 Early Nazis,* by Peter H. Merkl. *Contemporary Sociology* 7, no. 4 (1978): 460–61.

Scott, W. Richard. *Le organizzazioni*. Bologna: il Mulino, 2005.

Segal, Sheila F. *Women of Valor: Stories of Great Jewish Women Who Helped Shaped the Twentieth Century*. West Orange, NJ: Behrman House, 1996.

Segev, Tom. *The Seventh Million: The Israelis and the Holocaust*. New York: Henry Holt, 2000.

Sémelin, Jacques. *Senz'armi di fronte ad Hitler: La Resistenza civile in Europa, 1939–1943*, Turin: Sonda, 1993.

——. "Resistenza civile nel 1943: Dalla sopravvivenza alla liberazione." In *La resistenza non armata*, edited by Giorgio Giannini, 39–46. Rome: Editrice Sinnos, 1995.

——. "Toward a Vocabulary of Massacre and Genocide." *Journal of Genocide Research* 5, no. 2 (2003): 193–210.

——. *Purificare e distruggere: Usi politici dei massacri e dei genocidi*. Turin: Einaudi, 2007.

Shabas, William A. *Genocide in International Law: The Crime of Crimes*. New York: Cambridge University Press, 2009.

Shaffer, Gavin. "Assets or "Aliens"? Race Science and the Analysis of Jewish Intelligence in Inter-War Britain." *Patterns of Prejudice* 42, no. 2 (2008): 191–207.

Shaul, Esh. "Words and Their Meanings: Twenty-Five Examples of Nazi-Idiom." *Yad Vashem Studies* 5 (1963): 133–67.

Sheehan, James J. "Barrington Moore on Obedience and Revolt." *Theory & Society* 9, no. 5 (1980): 723–34.

Sherman, Ari J. *Island Refugee*. London: Paul Elek, 1973.

Shils, Edward A. "Limitations on the Freedom of Research and Teaching in the Social Sciences." *Annals of the American Academy of Political and Social Science* 200 (1938): 144–64. http://www.jstor.org/stable/1022348.

——. *The Present State of American Sociology*. Glencoe, IL: Free Press, 1948.

——. *The Calling of Sociology and Other Essays on the Pursuit of Learning*. Chicago: University of Chicago Press, 1980.

Shils, Edward A., and Morris Janowitz. "Cohesion and Disintegration in the Wehrmacht in World War II." *Public Opinion Quarterly* 12 (1948): 280–315.

Shirer, William L. *The Rise and Fall of the Third Reich*. New York: Simon & Schuster, 1960.

Shokeid, Moshe. "Immigration and Factionalism: An Analysis of Factions in Rural Israeli Communities of Immigrants." *British Journal of Sociology* 19, no. 4 (1968): 385–406.
Siebert, Renate. *Il razzismo: Il riconoscimento negato.* Rome: Carocci, 2003.
Sierakowiak, Dawid. *Il diario di Dawid Sierakowiak: Cinque quaderni dal ghetto di Lodz.* Turin: Einaudi, 1997.
Silverman, Max. *Facing Postmodernity: Contemporary French Thought on Culture and Society.* London: Routledge, 1999.
Simmel, Ernst. *Anti-Semitism, a Social Disease.* New York: International Universities Press, 1946.
Simmel, Georg. *Über sociale Differenzierung.* Leipzig: Duncker & Humblot, 1890.
———. *Philosophie des Geldes.* Leipzig: Duncker & Humblot, 1900.
———. *Die Großstädte und das Geistesleben.* Dresden: Petermann, 1903.
———. *Soziologie: Untersuchungen über die Formen der Vergesellschaftung.* Leipzig: Duncker & Humblot, 1908.
Simon, Herbert A. "A Behavioral Model of Rational Choice." *Quarterly Journal of Economics* 69, no. 1 (1955): 99–188. doi:10.2307/1884852.
———. *Administrative Behavior: A Study of Decision-Making Processes in Administrative Organization.* New York: Free Press, 1976.
Simpson, Christopher. *Blowback: The First Full Account of America's Recruitment of Nazis, and Its Disastrous Effect on Our Domestic and Foreign Policy.* New York: Weidenfeld and Nicolson, 1988.
Simpson, Ida H. "Continuities in the Sociology of Everett C. Hughes." *Sociological Quarterly* 13, no. 4 (1972): 547–59.
Skocpol, Theda. *States and Social Revolutions: A Comparative Analysis of France, Russia, and China.* New York: Cambridge University Press, 1979.
Smelser, Neil J. "Psychological Trauma and Cultural Trauma." In *Cultural Trauma and Collective Identity*, edited by Jeffrey C. Alexander, Ron Eyerman, Bernhard Giesen, Neil J. Smelser, and Piotr Sztompka, 31–59. Berkeley: University of California Press, 2004.
Smelser, Neil J., and Paul B. Baltes, eds. *International Encyclopedia of the Social & Behavioral Sciences.* Amsterdam: Elsevier, 2001.
Smith, Anthony D. *Nations and Nationalism in a Global Era.* Cambridge, MA: Blackwell, 1995.
Smith, Bradley F. *The Shadow Warriors: OSS and the Origins of the CIA.* New York: Basic Books, 1983.

Smolar, Aleksander. "Jews as a Polish Problem." *Daedalus* 116, no. 2 (1987): 31–73.

Snow, David A., and Robert D. Benford. "Ideology, Frame, Resonance, and Participant Mobilization." In *From Structure to Action: Comparing Social Movements Research across Cultures*, edited by Bert Klandermans, Hanspeter Kriesi, and Sidney Tarrow, 197–218. Greenwich, CT: JAI Press, 1988.

Socco, Carlo. "Landscape, Collective Memory and Cultural Identity." Paper presented at the forum Italian Landscapes for the Government of Transformations, organized by Benetton Foundation, Castelfranco Veneto, May 26–29, 1999.

Sofsky, Wolfgang. *The Order of Terror: The Concentration Camp*. Chichester, West Sussex: Princeton University Press, 1997 [1993].

Sombart, Werner. *Die Juden und das Wirtschaftsleben*. Leipzig: Duncker & Humblot, 1911.

Sorokin, Pitirim A. *Fads and Foibles in Modern Sociology and Related Sciences*. Chicago: Henry Regnery, 1956.

Sorokin, Pitirim A., and Walter A. Lunden. *Power and Morality: Who Shall Guard the Guardians?* Boston: Porter Sargent, 1959.

Soyer, Daniel. *Jewish Immigrant Associations and American Identity in New York, 1880–1939*. Cambridge, MA: Harvard University Press, 1997.

Spargo, John. "Christian Socialism in America." *American Journal of Sociology* 15, no. 1 (1909): 16–20.

Spencer, Herbert. *The Principles of Sociology*. New York: D. Appleton, 1880–97.

Spicer, Kevin P. *Hitler's Priests: Catholic Clergy and National Socialism*. DeKalb: Northern Illinois University Press, 2008.

Spiro, Jonathan P. *Defending the Master Race: Conservation, Eugenics, and the Legacy of Madison Grant*. Lebanon, NH: University Press of New England, 2008.

Spurr, Michael A. "'Playing for Fascism': Sportsmanship, Antisemitism and the British Union of Fascists." *Patterns of Prejudice* 37, no. 4 (2003): 359–76.

Stangneth, Bettina. *Eichmann before Jerusalem: The Unexamined Life of a Mass Murderer*. New York: Alfred A. Knopf, 2014 [2011].

Stanton, Gregory H. "The 8 Stages of Genocide." Washington, DC, 1996. Accessed March 24, 2010. http://www.genocidewatch.org/aboutgenocide/8stagesofgenocide.html.

Starnawski, Marcin. "Nationalist and the Ultra-Conservative Press in Contemporary Poland: A Case Study of Nasz Dzennik." *Patterns of Prejudice* 37, no. 1 (2003): 65–81.
Stein, Maurice, and Arthur J. Vidich, eds. *Sociology on Trial*. Englewood Cliffs, NJ: Prentice-Hall, 1963.
Stein, Stuart D. "Conceptions and Terms: Templates for the Analysis of Holocausts and Genocides." *Journal of Genocide Research* 7, no. 2 (2005): 171–203.
Steinfeldt, Irena, Arieh B. Saposnik, Ephrat Balberg, and Stephen D. Smith. *How Was It Humanly Possible?* Jerusalem: Yad Vashem, 2002.
Steinmetz, George. Review of *German White-Collar Workers and the Rise of Hitler*, by Hans Speier. *American Journal of Sociology* 93, no. 5 (1988): 1262–64.
Stember, Charles H., Marshall Sklare, and George Salomon. *Jews in the Mind of America*. New York: Basic Books, 1966.
Stern, Alexandra M. *Eugenic Nation: Faults and Frontiers of Better Breeding in Modern America*. Berkeley: University of California Press, 2005.
Stiglitz, Joseph E. *Whither Socialism?* Cambridge, MA: MIT Press, 1996.
———. *Globalization and Its Discontents*. New York: W. W. Norton, 2002.
Stola, Dariusz. "Jedwabne: How Was It Possible." *Polish Sociological Review* 137, no. 6 (2002): 91–102.
Stone, Dan. "Modernity and Violence: Theoretical Reflections on the Einsatzgruppen." *Journal of Genocide Research* 1, no. 3 (1999): 367–78.
Strauss, Anselm. "Everett Hughes: Sociology's Mission." In *Classical Tradition in Sociology: The American Tradition*, edited by Jeffrey C. Alexander, Raymond Boudon, and Mohamed Cherkaoui, 2:92–106. London: Sage, 1997.
Strzembosz, Tomasz. *Odbijanie i uwalnianie więźniów w Warszawie 1939-1944*. Warsaw: PWN, 1972.
Stueber, Karsten R., and Hans H. Kögler, eds. *Empathy and Agency: The Problem of Understanding in the Human Sciences*. Boulder, CO: Westview, 2000.
Suhl, Yuri. *They Fought Back*. New York: Schocken, 1967.
Sułek, Antoni. A Sociologist Looks at "Neighbors." *Polish Sociological Review* 137, no. 5 (2002): 71–89.
Swett, Pamela E. Review of *Seeing Hitler's Germany: Tourism in the Third Reich*, by Kristin Semmens. *Reference & Research Book News*, November 1, 2005.

Świebocki Henryk, ed. *People of Good Will*. Oświęcim: Auschwitz-Birkenau State Museum, 2009.

Sznaider, Natan *Jewish Memory and the Cosmopolitan Order*. Cambridge: Polity, 2011.

Sztompka, Piotr. "The Renaissance of Historical Orientation in Sociology." *International Sociology* 1, no. 3 (1986): 321–37. doi:10.1177/026858098600100308.

Talmon, Jacob L. *The Origins of Totalitarian Democracy*. London: Seecker and Warburg, 1952.

Tarde, Gabriel. *La logique sociale*. Le Plessis-Robinson: Institut Synthélabo, 1999 [1895].

Tec, Nechama. *Dry Tears: The Story of a Lost Childhood*. New York: Oxford University Press, 1984.

———. *When Light Pierced the Darkness: Christian Rescue of Jews in Nazi-Occupied Poland*. New York: Oxford University Press, 1986.

———. *In the Lion's Den: The Life of Oswald Rufeisen*. New York: Oxford University Press, 1990.

———. *Defiance: The Bielski Partisans*. Oxford: Oxford University Press, 1993.

———. *Jewish Resistance: Facts, Omissions, and Distortions*. Washington, DC: Research Institute of the United States Holocaust Memorial Museum, 2001.

———. *Resilience and Courage: Women, Men and the Holocaust*. New Haven, CT: Yale University Press, 2003.

———. "La resistenza ebraica: Definizioni e interpretazioni storiche." In *Storia della Shoah: La crisi dell'Europa, lo sterminio degli ebrei e la memoria del XX secolo*, edited by Marina Cattaruzza, Marcello Flores, Simon Levis-Sullam, and Enzo Traverso, 2:684–715. Turin: Utet, 2005–2006.

Tenenbaum, Joseph. *Race and Reich: The Story of an Epoch*. New York: Twayne, 1956.

Tent, James F., ed. *Academic Proconsul: Harvard Sociologist Edward Y. Hartshorne and the Reopening of German Universities, 1945–1946. His Personal Account*. Trier: Wissenschaftlicher Verlag Trier, 1998.

Tester, Keith. *Il pensiero di Zygmunt Bauman*. Gardolo: Erickson, 2005 [2004].

Tester, Keith, and Michael H. Jacobsen. *Bauman before Postmodernity: Invitation, Conversations and Annotated Bibliography, 1953–1989*. Aalborg: Aalborg University Press, 2005.

———. "Bauman before Exile—A Conversation with Zygmunt Bauman." *Polish Sociological Review* 3, no. 155 (2006): 267–74.
Thomas, William Isaac. *The Unadjusted Girl: With Cases and Standpoint for Behavior Analysis.* Boston: Little, Brown, 1923.
Thompson, Edward P. *The Making of the English Working Class.* London: Gollancz, 1963.
Thyssen, Fritz. *I Paid Hitler.* New York: Farrar and Rinehart, 1941.
Tillich, Paul. "The Totalitarian State and the Claims of the Church." *Social Research* 1 (1934): 405–33.
Tilly, Charles. *From Mobilization to Revolution.* Reading, MA: Addison-Wesley, 1978.
Todorov, Cvetan. *Face à l'extrême.* Paris: Éditions du Seuil, 1991.
———. *Les abus de la mémoire.* Paris: Les Editions Arlèa, 1995.
Tollet, Daniel. Review of *The Holocaust and the German Elite: Genocide and National Suicide in Germany, 1871-1945,* by Ranier C. Baum. *Annales: Économies, Sociétés, Civilisations* 39, no. 4 (1984): 734–36.
Tönnies, Ferdinand. *Gemeinschaft und Gesellschaft.* Berlin: Karl Curtius, 1912.
Tooze, Adam. *The Wages of Destruction: The Making and Breaking of the Nazi Economy.* London: Allen Lane, 2006.
Torpey, John. Review of *The Order of Terror: The Concentration Camp,* by Wolfgang Sofsky. *Contemporary Sociology* 26, no. 6 (1997): 719–20.
Toscano, Mario A. *Spirito sociologico.* Milan: FrancoAngeli, 1998.
Totten, Samuel, Paul R. Bartrop, and Steven L. Jacobs. *Dictionary of Genocide.* New York: Greenwood, 2007.
Totten, Samuel, William S. Parsons, and Israel W. Charny, eds. *Century of Genocide: Eyewitness Accounts and Critical Views.* New York: Garland, 1997.
Touraine, Alaine. *Production de la société.* Paris: Éditions du Seuil, 1973.
Trapanese, Enzo V., ed. *Sociologia e Modernità: Problemi di storia del pensiero sociologico.* Rome: La Nuova Italia Scientifica, 1997.
Traverso, Enzo, ed. *Insegnare Auschwitz: Questioni etiche, storiografiche, educative della deportazione e dello sterminio.* Turin: Bollati Boringhieri, 1995.
———. *Il totalitarismo: Storia di un dibattito.* Milan: Bruno Mondadori, 2002.
———. *The Origins of Nazi Violence.* New York: The New Press, 2003.
———. *Auschwitz e gli intellettuali: La shoah nella cultura del dopoguerra.* Bologna: il Mulino, 2004 [1997].
———. *Cosmopoli: Figure dell'esilio ebraico-tedesco.* Verona: Ombre Corte, 2004.

———. "Immigrazione, antisemitismo e razzismo: Una sola storia?" *Contemporanea* 12, no. 1 (2009): 203–10.

———. *Fire and Blood: The European Civil War (1914–1945)*. London: Verso, 2016.

Trow, Martin A. *Right-wing Radicalism and Political Intolerance: A Study of Support for McCarthy in a New England Town*. New York: Arno, 1980.

Trunk, Isaiah. *Judenrat: The Jewish Councils in Eastern Europe under Nazi Occupation*. New York: Macmillan, 1972.

Turda, Marius, and Paul J. Weindling. *Blood and Homeland: Eugenics and Racial Nationalism in Central and Southeast Europe, 1900–1940*. Budapest: Central European University Press, 2007.

Turner, Friedrich J. *The Frontier in American History*. Tucson: University of Arizona Press, 1986.

Turri, Eugenio. *Il paesaggio come teatro: Dal territorio vissuto al territorio rappresentato*. Venice: Marsilio, 1998.

Tutu, Desmond. *No Future without Forgiveness*. New York: Doubleday, 1999.

———. *God Has a Dream: A Vision of Hope for Our Time*. New York: Doubleday, 2004.

Ulatowska, Hanna K., and Danuta Kadzielawa, "Legacy through Language and Photography of an Auschwitz Survivor." In *Survivors of Nazi Persecution in Europe after the Second World War*, edited by David Cesarani, 2:267–80. Middlesex, UK: Vallentine Mitchell, 2011.

Unger, Michael. *In Those Terrible Days*. Jerusalem: Yad Vashem, 2002.

Vago, Raphael. "The Traditions of Antisemitism in Romania." *Patterns of Prejudice* 27, no. 1 (1993): 107–19.

———. "Shoah and Genocide." Paper presented at the International School for Holocaust Studies for the ICHEIC Program for Holocaust Education in Europe, Yad Vashem, Jerusalem, August 28, 2011.

Varon, Benno W. *Professions of a Lucky Jew*. New York: Cornwall, 1992.

Vidich, Arthur J. The Department of Social Relations and 'Systems Theory' at Harvard: 1948–50. *International Journal of Politics, Culture and Society* 13, no. 4 (2000), 607–48.

Vidich, Arthur J., and Stanford M. Lyman. *American Sociology*. New Haven, CT: Yale University Press, 1985.

Vienne, Philippe. "The Enigma of the Total Institution: Rethinking the Hughes-Goffman Intellectual Relationship." *Sociologica* 2 (2010): 1–5. Accessed March 28, 2012. doi:10.2383/32720.

———. "Introduction to Everett C. Hughes' 'Memorandum on Total Institutions.'" *Sociologica* 2 (2010): 1–5. Accessed March 28, 2012. doi:10.2383/32718.

Vrba, Rudolf, and Alan Bestic. *I Cannot Forgive*. London: Sidgwick and Jackson, 1963.

Vromen, Suzanne. "Collective Memory and Cultural Politics: Narrating and Commemorating the Rescue of Jewish Children by Belgian Convents during the Holocaust." In *Sociology Confronts the Holocaust*, edited by Judith M. Gerson and Diane L. Wolf, 134–53. Durham, NC: Duke University Press, 2007.

———. *Hidden Children of the Holocaust: Belgian Nuns and Their Darling Rescue of Young Jews from the Nazis*. Oxford: Oxford University Press, 2008.

Walker, Bruce. "Ideological, Bedfellows: College Professors and the Media Tell Us That There Are Right-wing Totalitarians and There Are Left-wing Totalitarians, but Is This an Accurate Assessment?" *The New American* 25, no. 23 (November 9, 2009): 31–38.

Waller, James. *Becoming Evil: How Ordinary People Commit Genocide and Mass Killing*. Oxford: Oxford University Press, 2002.

Wallerstein, Immanuel. *The Modern World-System*. New York: Academic Press, 1974.

———. "Citizens All? Citizens Some! The Making of the Citizen." *Comparative Studies in Society and History* 45, no. 4 (2003): 650–79.

Wasserstein, Bernard. *Britain and the Jews of Europe, 1939-1945*. Oxford: Clarendon, 1979.

Wat, Aleksander. *My Century: The Odyssey of a Polish Intellectual*. Berkeley: University of California Press, 1988.

Weber, Max. *Die Börse*. 1894. Accessed February 15, 2012. http://www.zeno.org/Soziologie/M/Weber,+Max/Schriften+zur+Soziologie.

———. *Economy and Society: An Outline of Interpretive Sociology*. Berkeley: University of California Press, 1978.

Weil, Friedrich D. Review of *The Holocaust and the German Elite: Genocide and National Suicide in Germany, 1871-1945*, by Ranier C. Baum. *American Journal of Sociology* 89, no. 3 (1983): 751–54.

Weindling, Paul J. *Epidemics and Genocide in Eastern Europe, 1890–1945*. New York: Oxford University Press, 2000.

Weinreich, Max. *Hitler's Professors: The Part of Scholarship in Germany's Crimes against the Jewish People*. Yiddish Scientific Institute, 1946.

Weinstein, Allen, and Alexander Vassiliev. *The Haunted Wood: Soviet Espionage in America – the Stalin Era*. New York: Random House, 1999.
Welzer, Harald. "On the Rationality of Evil: An Interview with Zygmunt Bauman." *Thesis Eleven* 70 (2002): 100–12.
West, Nigel. *Venona: The Greatest Secret of the Cold War*. London: HarperCollins, 1999.
Whitaker, Leighton C. *Understanding and Preventing Violence: The Psychology of Human Destructiveness*. Boca Raton, FL: CRC Press, 2000.
Wiener, Jon. "Talcott Parsons' Role Bringing Nazi Sympathizers to the U.S." *The Nation*, March 6, 1989, 305–9.
Wiesel, Elie. *La Nuit*. Paris: Les Éditions de Minuit, 1958.
Wieviorka, Annette. *L'era del testimone*. Milan: Cortina, 1999.
Wiggershaus, Rolf. *The Frankfurt School: Its History, Theories, and Political Significance*. Cambridge, MA: MIT Press, 1994.
Wilkanowicz, Stefan, ed. *Gli straordinari abitanti di Oświęcim: Come aiutarono I prigionieri del KL Auschwitz*. Oświęcim: Museo Statale di Auschwitz-Birkenau, 2007.
Winch, Peter. *The Idea of a Social Science and Its Relation to Philosophy*. London: Routledge Classics, 2008.
Winkler, Allan M. *The Politics of Propaganda: The Office of War Information, 1942–1945*. New Haven, CT: Yale University Press, 1978.
Winks, Robin. *Cloak and Gown: Scholars in the Secret War, 1939–1961*. New York: Morrow, 1987.
Winter, J. Alan. Review of *The Death of American Antisemitism*, by Spencer Blakeslee. *Review of Religious Research* 44, no. 2 (2002): 204–5.
Wirth, Louis. "The Ghetto." *American Journal of Sociology* 33, no. 1 (1927): 57–71.
_____. *The Ghetto*. Chicago: University of Chicago Press, 1928.
_____. "Problems and Orientations of Research in Race Relations in the United States." *British Journal of Sociology* 1, no. 2 (1950): 117–25.
Wissmann, Friedrich, and Ursula Blömer, hrsg. *Es ist Mode geworden, die Kinder in die Lesslerschule zu schicken: Dokumente zur Privaten Waldschule von Toni Lessler in Berlin Grunewald*. Oldenburg: BIS-Verlag, 2010.
Wistrich, Robert S. *Socialism and the Jews: The Dilemmas of Assimilation in Germany and Austria-Hungary*. London: Associated University Presses, 1982.

———. *Hitler and the Holocaust: How and Why the Holocaust Happened*. London: Phoenix Press, 2001.
Wolf, Joan B. Review of *Women in the Holocaust*, by Dalia Ofer and Lenore J. Weitzman. *American Journal of Sociology* 105, no. 1 (1999): 296–98.
Wolin, Richard, and Seyla Benhabib. "Eichmann, Arendt, and 'The Banality of Evil.'" *Jewish Review of Books*. Accessed November 2, 2014. https://jewishreviewofbooks.com/articles/1317/eichmann-arendt-and-the-banality-of-evil/.
Wood, E. Thomas, and Stanisław M. Jankowski. *Karski: How One Man Tried to Stop the Holocaust*. New York: J. Wiley, 1994.
Woolf, Linda, and Michael Hulsizer. "Psychosocial Roots of Genocide: Risk, Prevention, and Intervention." *Journal of Genocide Research* 7, no. 1 (2005): 101–28.
Woolford, Andrew. "Making Genocide Unthinkable: Three Guidelines for a Critical Criminology of Genocide." *Critical Criminology* 14 (2006): 87–106. doi:10.1007/s10612-005-3197-7.
———. Review of *The Society of Terror: Inside the Dachau and Buchenwald Concentration Camps*, by Paul M. Neurath. *Canadian Journal of Sociology Online*, September–October (2006). Accessed March 4, 2016. http://www.cjsonline.ca/reviews/societyofterror.html.
Wormser-Migot, Olga. *Le système concentrationnaire nazi (1933–1945)*. Paris: PUF, 1968.
Worrell, Mark P. "*Es Kommt Die Nacht*: Paul Massing, the Frankfurt School, and the Question of Labor Authoritarianism during World War II." *Critical Sociology* 35, no. 5 (2009): 629–35.
Wrong, Dennis H. "Truth, Misinterpretation, or Left-Wing McCarthyism?" *Sociological Forum* 11, no. 4 (1996): 613–21. http://www.jstor.org/stable/684908.
Wuthnow, Robert. "On Suffering, Rebellion, and the Moral Order." *Contemporary Sociology* 8, no. 2 (1979): 212–15.
Wyman, David S. *Paper Walls: America and the Refugee Crisis, 1938–1941*. Amherst: University of Massachusetts Press, 1968.
Young, James E. *Writing and Rewriting the Holocaust: Narrative and the Consequences of Interpretation*. Bloomington: Indiana University Press, 1988.
Young-Bruehl, Elisabeth. *Hannah Arendt, 1906–1975: Per amore del mondo*. Turin: Bollati Boringhieri, 1990.

Zappalà, Salvatore. *La tutela internazionale dei diritti umani: Tra sovranità degli Stati e governo mondiale*. Bologna: il Mulino, 2011.

Zertal, Idith. *Israel's Holocaust and the Politics of Nationhood*. Translated by Chaya Galai. Cambridge: Cambridge University Press, 2005.

Zimmermann, Michael. *Rassenutopie und Genozid: Die nationalsozialistische "Lösung der Zigeunerfrage."* Hamburg: Christians, 1996.

Znaniecki, Florian. "The Object Matter of Sociology." *American Journal of Sociology* 32, no. 4 (1927): 529–84.

Znaniecki, Florian, and William I. Thomas. *The Polish Peasant in Europe and America. Monograph of an Immigrant Group*, vols. 1–4. Chicago: University of Chicago, 1918–1920.

Zuckerman, Yitzhak. *A Surplus of Memory: Chronicle of the Warsaw Ghetto Uprising*. Berkeley: University of California Press, 1993.

Index

A
Abel, Theodore, 41, 66, 69–70, 73, 79, 80n200
academic and cultural circumstances of Holocaust studies, xxxii
accountability, 23, 36, 53, 82, 85, 134, 262, 285, 305–306, 309, 316, 320–321, 339, 346
Accounting for Genocide (Helen Fein), xvi, xxxii, 3, 125, 201, 205, 208, 220–223, 225, 227–228, 230–232
   Ben-Baruch's criticism, 231–232
   case studies of the Netherlands, Hungary, and the Warsaw ghetto, 207, 210–211, 221, 225, 228–229
   concepts of socialism and Zionism, 225–226
   correlation between anti-Semitism and profession of Catholicism, 219
   debate on, 219, 222–234
   Horowitz's criticism, 222–233
   Jewish leadership, 228–230
   Jewish victims, 203, 206, 210–211, 221–222, 232
   model and method in comprehending the "Jewish victimization," 213–214, 220, 223–224
   national sovereignty, principle of, 216
   notion of solidarity, 214–216, 214n194, 215n198, 218, 220–221, 229, 232–234
   role of churches and their attitudes in genocidal practices, 207–208, 210, 212, 218–219, 232
   role of the allied governments, 221
   role of the Jewish Councils and other Jewish institutions, 219–221
   victimization, 207, 212–213, 220, 223–225, 229
   "victims' view," 221, 221n211, 227, 232
Adorno, Theodore L. W., 8n22, 12–15, 18, 20–21, 21n55, 22–23, 75, 290, 292, 316, 332
   conception of Nazism, 17, 23
   Dialectic of Enlightenment, 16, 20, 290, 292
   Minima Moralia, 15, 22–23
   Negative Dialectics, 22, 23
Agudat Israel, 163
Alberoni, Francesco, 150, 359
Alexander, Jeffrey, xxxvi, 312, 335–348
Alexandros, Joseph, 49
Allen, Michael T., 121, 251, 385, 388
Allport, Gordon, 41
Aly, Götz H., 4, 248
Amalgamated Clothing Workers of America (ACWA), 24
American authoritarianism, 23
American Jewish Committee (AJC), 24
American mass society, 23
American positivism, 109
American Sociological Association, xviv, 53–54
American Sociological Review (ASR), xxv, 106n236
American sociology, xv, xvi, xviii, 15, 20, 38, 106n236, 107, 109–110, 112–113
   chronological approach, xxx–xxxi
   literature review, xvii, xxi, xxiii–xxx, 334, 381, 385, 389
Anders, Günther, 21, 21n55
Anna, Zarzycka, 129
anti-Semitic intelligentsia, 5

anti-Semitism, xv–xvi, xxxi–xxxii, xxxiv–xxxvi, 4–6, 8–10, 12, 14, 16–18, 20–26, 29, 32–33, 36–37, 45, 86, 88, 97, 107–108, 114–115, 119, 121, 161–163, 165–166, 180, 203, 206–208, 211–212, 215–219, 226, 228–230, 232, 234, 257, 263, 269–271, 273–275, 273n81, 277–278, 288, 299, 302–308, 310, 314, 320, 320n28, 344–346, 354, 377–379, 384–385
  assimilation between Nazism and, 344–345
  authoritarianism and, 29
  Brustein's *Roots of Hate*, 377–379
  Frankfurt School reactions on anti-Semitism. *See* Frankfurt School reactions on anti-Semitism
  Hitler's racist, 20
  Horkheimer and Adorno's theory on, 17–18
  in American labor, 24
  in Poland, of 1960s, 166, 273–275, 273n81, 277–279, 288, 302, 304
  in religious circles, 354
  in *Roots of Hate*, 320
  of the Enlightenment, 17–18, 21
  of Roosevelt and Churchill, 346
  prejudice in German society, 16–17
  prewar, 54, 180, 206–207, 211, 217, 229–230, 232
  profession of Catholicism and, 219
  solidarity and, 214–215, 217–218. *See also Accounting for Genocide* (Helen Fein)
Arendt, Hannah, xxxiii, 12, 46, 81n201, 90, 107–108, 117–120, 208–209, 219–220, 257, 265, 274, 308, 330, 332, 346, 384–385, 389
  Eichmann in Jerusalem: A Report on the Banality of Evil, 385
Arendt controversy, 46, 118–120
Auschwitz, xxxiii–xxxiv, 21–23, 121–123, 125–126, 128–129, 128n14, 131–141, 137–138n33, 143, 143n46, 146–148, 150–152, 154–160, 222, 252, 261, 272, 284, 315, 329, 339, 346, 391
  as modern state, 159–160

community of prisoners and mechanisms of functioning, 131–135
  constitution of community of solidarity in, 134
  division of prisoners, 143n46
  marketplaces, 147–150
  Pawełczyńska's description of, 137–138n33, 139–140
  physical space of, 136–140
  role of conspiratorial organizations in, 152–153
  survival of Jewish community in, 140–154
  types of forces in, 133
Auschwitz e gli intellettuali (Enzo Traverso), xiv, 13, 27n70

B
Bacon, Gershon C., 164, 168
Balkan crisis, 118, 235, 301, 330–331, 335, 347
Banality of evil, xxxii–xxxiii, xxxv, 8, 10, 80, 81n201, 82, 84n207, 101, 107, 117–120, 257–258, 261, 350, 385, 389
  The Banality of Evil (Hannah Arendt), 46, 108, 118, 385
Bandera, Stepan, 177
Banton, Michael, 294–295
Bartoszewski, Władysław, 173
Baudelaire, Charles, 285
Baum, Rainer C., 236, 238, 248–250, 252, 255
  on Holocaust, 248–251
  process of naturalization of the Jews, 250
  The Holocaust and the German Elite, 115, 248
Bauman, Janina, 268, 272–273
Bauman, Zygmunt, xv–xx, xxii, xxiv, xxxv–xxxvi, 87, 90, 97, 118, 130n18, 168, 197, 223, 239, 258–260, 268–292, 274n86, 294–297, 299–309, 311, 322, 334, 384, 387, 389
  anti-Semitism in *Endlösung*, 307
  birth and education, 269–271
  cause of real socialism, 279

citizenship, concept of, 308
English exile life, xxxv, 271–272
glocalization, 334
Holocaust as a product of modernity, 281–288
Lager, 283
Legislators and Interpreters, 283
life at Poland, 269–271
Memories of Class, 271, 280, 282
Modernity and the Holocaust, xv–xvii, xix–xx, xxiv, xxxv, 97, 168, 268, 271–272, 275, 282, 286–288, 291, 294–295, 297, 300–303, 307, 311, 389
modernity thesis of the Holocaust, 304–309
power social forces, concept of, 276
samizdat strategy, 290–294
social suffering, concept of, 144, 272, 275–282, 300–301, 309, 388
socioeconomic relationship between capitalist class and labor force, 277–278
sociological lesson, 288–290
structural and procedural characteristics of modern society, 286
totalitarian ideology, 272, 279, 282–284, 290–292, 292n131, 297
Winter in the Morning, 272, 280, 282
Beck, Ulrich, 312, 320–321, 323–324, 327–330, 332, 334, 336
 definition of criminal state, 329
 distinction between national and international, 327
 globalization of Holocaust, 325, 327–335
 principle of cosmopolitanism, 323–324
 "risk society," 321, 336
Beilharz, Peter, 272, 286, 292, 294
Benahbib, Seyla, 117
Ben-Baruch, Benjamin M., 201, 203–204, 207, 210, 213, 231–234
Benjamin, Walter, 7n21, 8n22
Berger, Alan L., 352–353
Berlin Wall, collapse of, xvi, xix–xx, xxxiv, 107, 118, 204, 222, 257, 275, 291, 296, 310–311, 348–349
Bernard, Jessie, 106n237
Bettauer, Hugo, 226

Binder, Eliszewa/Elza, 351–352, 352n107
Black civil rights movement, 83, 162
Blau, Peter, 106n237
Bloxham, Donald, 247
Blumer, Herbert, 106n237, 363
Bogart, Ernest L., 114
Bosnian conflict (1992–95), 180, 331
Brandt, Willy, 124, 133
Bridenthal, Renate, 349
Brodzikowską-Pohorecka, Zofia, 129
Broszat, Martin, 307
Brustein, William I., 251, 310, 320, 320n28, 377–379, 377n183
Bulgarian Orthodox Church, 218
Burgess, Ernest W., 364
Burundian genocide, 236

C

Carnegie Corporation, 54
Cassese, Antonio, 237
Charny, Israel W., 233, 235
Chinoy, Ely, 99–100
Churchill, Winston, 47, 329, 346
Cieplinski, Feigue, 170
Clark, Ian, 359
Clinard, Marshall B., 106n237
Cohn, Norman, 250
 Warrant for Genocide, 250
collective action, xxxiv, 186–187, 268, 313, 357–359, 361, 363–364, 367, 371–372, 374–376
 conditions of, 363–366
 in Warsaw, Vilna, and Łódź, 366–377
 Warsaw Ghetto uprising of 1943, 356–362
collective memory studies of the Holocaust, 313–320
 category of globalization, xxxvi, 305, 312–313, 319, 321–322, 324–325, 327–335, 343, 379–380, 387
 Levy and Sznaider's work, 123, 312, 317, 319–328, 330–332, 330–331n58, 334–335, 347, 388
 modern, 318
 national, 317–318
Collomp, Catherine, 24

Congress of Industrial Organizations (CIO), 24
Cooley, Charles Horton, 113
cosmopolitan memory, 313, 320, 323–324, 328, 332–335, 354
cosmopolitan memory of the Holocaust, xxxvi, 235, 334, 347–348, 379
Cymet, David, 180
Czerniaków, Adam, 367–368

D

Dahrendorf, Ralf, 252
Daniels, Arlene K., 98
Dank, Barry, xvi, 168
Davies, Norman, 48
Davis, David S., 100–101
democide, 237–238
denazification program, 316
Dialektik der Aufklärung, 20
Die Grosstädte und das Geistesleben (Georg Simmel), 93
Donovan, William, 43
Drumont, Édouard, 87
Dunning, Eric, 294, 297–300
Durkheim, Émile, 29, 31, 61, 91, 99, 105, 133–134, 150, 203, 249, 280, 285, 302, 327, 334–336, 341, 358, 362
    Les règles de la méthode sociologique, 134, 335, 362
    unity of a society, 335–348
Duverger, Maurice, 2
Dworecki, Chaim, 267

E

Ebert, Friedrich, 189–190
EBSCO database, xxiv, xxvi–xvii, xxvin, 96n220, 107
Eichmann trial of 1962, xxxiii, 10, 19, 83, 108, 115, 117, 303, 329–330, 345, 385
Einwohner, Rachel L., xxxvi, 267, 355–377, 388
Elias, Norbert, 275n89, 295, 297–300, 378n186
    The Germans, 297
Ellwood, Charles A., 115

Enlightenment, 17–23, 225, 273n81, 292–293, 333
Entzauberung, 288
Euripides's tragedy, 339
European Jewry, 2, 257, 265, 314, 330
Evans, Richard J., 39
    German Universities and National Socialism, 38–39, 385

F

Fackenheim, Emil L., xxxiii, 6, 20, 84, 96, 123, 222, 231, 231n240, 386–387
Faris, Robert E. L., 15
Fay, Sidney, 41
Fein, Helen, xviii, xxii, xxxiv, xxxvii, 3, 90, 118, 124–125, 201–234, 210n187, 214n194, 215n198, 257, 269, 320n28
    Accounting for Genocide. See *Accounting for Genocide*
Feuerman, Juliusz, 351–352, 352n107
Fidelio, Gisella, xxv
Fleck, Christian, xxv, 19, 204
Form, William, 15
Frankfurt School reactions on anti-Semitism, xxxii, 8n22, 10, 14–26, 31, 40, 63, 72, 121, 124, 285, 290, 292, 302–303, 381–383, 385
    anti-Semitism in American labor, 24
    as an expression of Enlightenment mentality, 22
    as totalitarian principle of identity, 22
    Auschwitz concentration and death camp, 21–23
    between 1943 and 1947 the sociological theory of, 17
    chasm between theory and empirical research, 15–16
    dialectic of the Enlightenment, 17–18
    Dialektik der Aufklärung, 20
    grading of anti-Semitism, 26
    Nazi society, 23–24
    process and uses of rationalization, 17, 20, 23, 288
    totalitarian capitalism of the Third Reich, 20
    under Weimar Republic, 17
Franz, Günther, 76

Freeman, Michael, 295–297
Freikorps, 298
Fromm, Erich, 8n22, 12–13, 36
    Escape from Freedom, 12
Furnivall, J. S., 246

G

Gaulle, Charles de, 303
Geldwert, Jake, 350
genre studies of the Holocaust, 348–355
genocide, xv, xvii, xx–xxii, xxiv, xxxiv–xxxv, 2, 4–7, 9, 19, 21, 29, 35, 88, 118–119, 154–155, 158, 161, 167, 170, 181, 202–207, 209–210, 213–214, 216–217, 221, 223, 227, 231, 233–248, 241n12, 250–252, 254, 261, 282–284, 290, 294–297, 300–303, 307, 309, 312, 318, 324–333, 335, 341, 345, 347, 352, 361, 371, 376, 384, 390
    as an "anodious scourge," 245
    Balkans, ethnic cleansing in, 118, 235
    Burundian genocide, 236
    extermination of European Jews, 247, 319
    factors leading to, 246
    Kuper's contributions, 241–248, 254
    Maya Indians genocide (1981–83), 236
    in article 2 of the Convention, 241
    in "plural societies," 245
    international convention on, 239–240
    of Armenians, 202, 212, 223, 243, 246–247
    of Jews in Poland, xxxiv, 161–169, 179
    of the Jews as a cultural trauma, 341–348
    recognition of the Holocaust as, 345
    role of international organizations, 243–247
    significance of, 239–241
    Sikh genocide of 1984, 236
    state sponsored, xxxv, 241–251
Gerhardt, Uta, 27–29, 32–33, 37, 41–42, 45–47, 46n121, 49n131, 53–54, 204
Gerlach, Christian, 5
German working class, 183, 186
Gerson, Judith M., xviii, xxi–xxiii, 18, 313, 379

Giddins, Franklin H., 113
globalization of memory, 327–335
God's Presence in History (Emil Fackenheim), 84
Goldstein, Bernard, 101
"Good People and Dirty Work," xxxiii, 1, 80–84, 84n207, 86, 90, 92, 95–96, 99–104, 106–108, 106n237, 115–116, 384
    categories of "dirty work" and "good people," 10, 81–83, 85–94, 98–104, 108, 116, 119, 121, 155
    central aspects in "Good People," 86
    criticism of, 95–102
    The Ghetto (Louis Wirth), 115–116
    theory and evidence related to concept of "good people and dirty work," 90–93
Gouldner, Alvin W., 152
Gross, Irina, 172
Gross, Jan T., xxxiv, 166n97, 167, 172, 180, 304, 311
Grossman, Atina, 349
Gurland, A.R.L., 25
Gutman, Israel, 266, 367

H

Habermas, Jürgen, 43, 290n123, 321, 347
Halbwachs, Maurice, 313, 317–318, 320, 342, 344
Halpert, Burton P., xv–xvi, 112–114
Hartshorne, Jr., Edward Y., 34, 37–45, 47, 121, 155, 163, 204, 385, 389–390
    collapse of German universities under Nazism, 40
    Nazi Madness, 41–42
Harvard Russian Research Center (HRRC), 46, 48–49, 51, 53–54, 56
Heberle, Rudolf, 66–71, 73, 77, 192, 387
    extreme Right movement, 69
    From Democracy to Nazism, 66–67, 69
    NSDAP's growing consensus, 67
    residents of Schleswig-Holstein, study of, 67–68, 71, 74, 76
    socio-geography (*Soziografie*) research of, 67

Heller, Celia S., xxxii, 124, 161–170, 180, 234. *See also On the Edge of Destruction* (Celia S. Heller)
Helmes–Hayes, Richard C./Rick, xxviii, 91n218, 95, 95n219, 107, 120, 120n255
Herbert, Ulrich, 5, 119
Herf, Jeffrey, 36, 299
Hilberg, Raul, xv, xxxvii–xxxviii, 3, 7–9, 26n66, 208nn181–182, 210n186, 211, 226, 246, 248, 260, 265, 314, 353, 367, 369–370, 385, 389
Hitler, Adolf, xxiii–xxiv, 4, 6–7, 13, 20, 40, 43, 59, 65–66, 69–70, 73, 75, 80, 89, 96–97, 104, 113–114, 123, 174–175, 179, 185, 192, 195–196, 202, 205, 209, 226, 248–250, 298, 377, 384, 387, 390, 390n6
Hofer, Walther, 191
Holocaust as trauma, idea of, 319–320
Holocaust in Poland, 164, 170, 180
  Gross's work, 180
  Heller's work, 161–170, 180
  Piotrowski's work, 169–176, 179–182
"Holstein Switzerland" (*Holsteinische Schweiz*), 67
Hoover, Glenn E., 106, 110
Horkheimer, Max, 8, 8n22, 15, 18, 20–21, 23, 36, 288, 290, 292
  conception of Nazism, 23
  Eclipse of Reason, 16, 288
Horowitz, Irving L., xxxv, 221–233, 226n225, 233n242, 236, 238, 248, 250, 252, 255, 257, 359
  Genocide, 243–244, 250
  social and political context of genocidal states, 250–251
  Taking Lives, 250
Hughes, Everett C., xxviii, xxx, xxxiii, 1–2, 10, 25, 62, 80–108, 81n201, 91n208, 95n219, 106n237, 110–112, 114–121, 163, 192, 257–258, 314n11, 381–382, 384–385, 389
  American sociology, 107, 109–110, 112–120
  anti-Semitism, 86, 88, 97, 107–108, 114–115, 119, 121, 384
  concept of division of labor, 91–95
  consequences of racial prejudice, 84–85, 87, 89
  criticism of "Good People," 95–102
  extermination in Nazi society, 83, 85–89
  extermination of the Jews, 81–83, 85, 116–117, 121
  ghettoization of the Jews, 115–116
  "Good People and Dirty Work." *See* "Good People and Dirty Work"
  instance of self-alignment ("*self-coördination*"), 107–112
  moral–spatial competition, 92
  nature of National Socialist state, 92
  Nazi modern society, 94–95
  research on banality of evil, xxxii–xxxiii, 80, 82, 101, 107, 117–120. *See also* Banality of evil
  society of good people, 87
  "sociological eye," 91, 95
  sociology of, 86–95, 120n255
  solidarity, 90–92, 94, 98–100, 115
  "The Gleichshaltung of the German Statistical Yearbook," 2, 80–81, 100, 102–107, 192
Husserl, Edmund, 343
Huxley, Aldous, 12–13

I

Injustice, 182, 184–185, 190, 193, 198, 200. *See* Moore, Barrington, Jr.
Institute for Social Research, 8, 21–22
Institute on the Holocaust and Genocide, 235
International Center for Transitional Justice, 244
International Ladies Garment Workers' Union (ILGWU), 24
Israel's representation of the Holocaust, 347, 350
Italian Society for the Study of Contemporary History (Sissco), xxv

J

Jacobs, Janet L., 352
Jacobsen, Michael H., 276
Janowitz, Morris, 8, 57–66, 387

on *Wehrmacht*, 31, 57–65. See *Wehrmacht*
organic solidarity within German army, 57–58
Wilhelmine military ethics, 58
Jaspers, Karl, 85, 89
Jewish children, studies of, 352–355
Jewish Labor Committee (JLC), 24–25
"Jewish problem" of sociology, xiv, xix, xxi
Jewish Scientific Institute (JIVO), 168
Jews in a Gentile World (Isacque Graeber and Steuart H. Britt), 32
Jews in Poland, xxxiv, 161–182
  anti-Semitism and, xxxiv–xxxvi, 161–166, 180, 263, 269–271, 273–275, 273n81, 277–278, 304
  assimilation and acculturation, 162–165
  forms of resistance, 164, 264, 367
  killing by Soviet partisan units, 177–182
  social, political, and cultural aspects of, 162–163
Jews of Jedwabne, 166–167, 180, 311
Judenräte, 220

K

Kaiserreich society, 297, 299
Kaiser Wilhelm Institute, 40
Kaplan, Marion, 349
Karlauf, Thomas, 42, 204
Karpf, Anne, 319
  The War After: Living with the Holocaust, 319
Katz, Fred E., xvi, xxxv, 256–261, 350
  case of Rudolf Höss, 261
  causes for extermination, xxxv, 257–260
  death camps functioned as factories, 258–259
  factors leading to destruction of European Jewry, 257–258
  modernity of extermination, 258
  notions of bureaucratization and routinization, 258
  Ordinary People and Extraordinary Evil, 350
Kaufman, Debra, xx

Keen, Mike F., 236
Kennan, George F., 49
Kershaw, Ian, xxxv, 5
Khrushchev Thaw, 38, 49, 69, 103, 108, 128n14, 291, 385
Kirchheimer, Otto, 8, 41, 389
Klajman, Jack, 365, 365n152
Kluckhohn, Clyde, 44, 48, 50–51, 53
Kłodziński, Stanislaw, 128
Kosovocaust, 331, 347
Kossak-Szczucka, Zofia, 178, 264
Krieken, Robert van, 300–301
Kristallnacht, 41, 54, 344
Krohn, Claus-Dieter, 14
Kulka, Otto Dov, xxxvii, 5
Kuper, Hilda, 242
Kuper, Leo, xxxv, 221–223, 233, 235–236, 238, 241–248, 252, 254–255
  An African Bourgeoisie, 243
  education, 242
  genocide, 235, 238, 241–247, 250, 252, 254
  interpretation of the Holocaust, 235, 242
  Passive Resistance in South Africa, 243
  The Prevention of Genocide, 243, 247

L

Landon, Charles E., 114
Langer, William, 43
Lee, Alfred McClung, 106
Lee, Elizabeth Briant, 106
Lemkin, Raphael, 223, 223n216, 239–242, 241n12, 245, 295–296, 329. See Genocide
  Axis Rule in Occupied Europe, 240
Levine, Louis, 111
Levy, Daniel, xxxiv, 123, 310–312, 317, 319–323, 325–328, 330–332, 330–331n58, 334–335, 347, 388
Linden, Robin, 349–350
Linenthal, Edward, 346–347
Lipset, Seymour M., xxxiii, 2, 10, 66, 68–80, 73n187, 192, 387
  analysis of Hitler's electoral constituency, 1928–33, 66–80
  apartheid case, 72, 242, 242n14

distinction between "left" and "right" political tendencies, 70–71
examination of voting behavior of Germans, 71
extremist movements, 68
Heberle's study and, 66–71, 73, 77, 192, 387
man living in the *polis*, 73n187
National Socialism, 67, 72–73, 78
on authoritarianism, 71–72, 72n187, 75, 79
on Protestant reformism, 75
Political Man, 66, 68–70, 75, 80
sociological notion of mass, 71–72
view of Nazism, 69, 73, 79
Lithuania, 5, 168, 172, 174, 216, 216n201, 369
Lowenthal, Leo, 8n22, 15, 18, 25
Lynd, Robert, 15, 170, 385

M

MacIver, Robert, 15, 18n46, 385
Madge, Charles, 242
Making the Fascist State (Herbert W. Schneider), 115
Mandela, Nelson, 242
Marcuse, Herbert, 8n22, 43, 292, 292n131
  One-Dimensional Man, 292, 292n131
Markle, Gerald E., xx
Marshman, Sophia, 276
Marxism, neo-Marxism, 20, 74, 126n11, 130, 195, 276, 279
Mason, Edward, 49
mass ideology, xxxii, 10
Massing, Paul, 25
Maya Indians genocide (1981–83), 236
Mazurkiewicz, Maria, 129
McKenzie, Roderick D., 364
Melson, Robert, 233
Melucci, Alberto, 150, 358, 358n129
Mennell, Stephen, 294, 297–300
Merkl, Peter, 5, 194, 196, 234, 385
Mikhnovskyi, Mykola, 175
modernity, Holocaust as a product of, 281–288
Mommsen, Hans, 4
Moore, Barrington, Jr., xxxiv, 124, 182–188, 186n145, 190–200, 192n154, 234, 387

attitudinal acceptance of oppression by prisoners and power of concentration camps, 197–200
bases of society, 184
Bettelheim's experience, 197, 199–200, 265
census of employment and the *Parteistatistik*, 191–194
forms of nationalism, 185–186
German working class, study of, 186–191
Injustice, 182
National Socialist German Workers Party, 190
social composition of the NSDAP, 190–196
Social Origins of Dictatorship and Democracy, 183
Soviet Politics, 183
Mossad, 19
Müller, Ludwig, 104, 308

N

national collective memory, 317–319
National Response and Jewish Victimization, 223
National Socialism, 8, 13, 26–30, 32–34, 36–39, 45, 53, 57, 62n165, 67, 72–73, 78, 88, 100, 113, 161, 190, 204, 232, 292, 299–300, 302, 377, 384, 388
National Socialistische Fuhrungsoffiziere (NSFO), 64
National Socialist society, 61, 82, 93–95, 98, 101
National Socialist state, 2, 82, 90, 92–93, 103, 197, 232, 293
Nationalsozialistische Deutsche Arbeiterpartei (NSDAP), xxxiii, 5–6, 29, 66–71, 74, 76, 78–79, 93, 104, 188, 190–193, 195–196, 251
  analysis of support, 74, 76, 80
  electoral consensus, 74
Nazi militants, autobiographical accounts of, 194–197
Neurath, Paul M., 18–19, 18n46, 19n49, 121, 204, 314n11, 381, 384, 389
  Society of Terror, 19

Nielsen, Jens K., 52–53
Night (Elie Wiesel), 83
Nissebaum, Yitzhak, 140
Noiriel, Gérard, 308
Nuremberg Laws, 8, 104, 154, 308
Nuremberg trials, 236, 254, 315, 321, 328
Nussbaum, Martha, 340

O

O'Connell, Thomas Charles, 47–48, 47n126, 50–53
Ofer, Dalia, 310, 350
Ogburn, William, 108
Olick, Jeffrey K., 319, 377
On the Edge of Destruction (Celia S. Heller), 161
    distinction between periods welcomed and persecuted by Poles, 164–166
    forms of resistance, 164
    memorial of Jews, 166–167
    Piłsudski regime (1926–35), 163
    social, political, and cultural aspects of Jews, 163–164
    term "edge," 161
Oppenheimer, Martin, xx, xxii, xxviii–xxix, xxxn, 45–47, 46n121, 49–50, 49n131, 53
Ossowska, Maria, 130
Ossowski, Stanisław, 126–128, 126n11, 130, 130nn18,21, 270, 274, 289

P

Papcke, Sven, xxix
Park, Robert E., 90, 102, 364
Parsons, Talcott, xxvii, xxxii, 10, 16, 26–57, 72, 109, 121, 204, 236, 381–384, 386, 388–390
    about totalitarianism, 38–39
    authoritarian structure of the German family, 31
    background, 28
    establishment of Harvard Russian Research Center, 46, 48, 51, 53
    examination of National Socialism and its consequences, 29–34, 38–39, 45, 53–54
    genocide of Jews, 35
    German society, 35–36
    Harvard Research Center in Creative Altruism, 38
    historical role of liberal scholars in the early Cold War, 50–51
    Holocaust, xxx, 27, 35–37, 39, 44–45, 53–56
    letters to Kluckhohn, 48, 51, 56
    real problem for America, 32–33
    role in bringing Nazi collaborators to the United States, 44–57
    role played by institutions in maintenance of social order, 29–30
    sociological aspects of the Fascist Movements, 29
    sociology of Nazism, 27, 34–35, 47
    Uta Gerhardt's 1993 work about, 27–29, 32–33, 37, 41–42, 45–47, 46n121, 49n131, 53–54, 204
Pasquino, Gianfranco, 75
Paton, Alan, 243
Pawełczyńska, Anna, xxviii, xxxiv, 122, 124–129, 126n11, 131–134, 136–141, 137–138n33, 141n42, 143–144, 147, 150–152, 154–156, 158–160, 234, 254, 256, 386, 388
    analysis of the Nazi concentration camp system, 130
    as a political prisoner, 129
    as a scholar of resistance, 127
    community of prisoners and mechanisms of functioning of the Auschwitz system, 131–135
    "degeneration of authoritarian power," 158
    description of Auschwitz, 137–138n33, 139–140
    discourse of resistance, 140–154
    followers of the Nazis as a social "gang," 156
    industrialized mass murder, 158–159
    Nazi organizations as criminals, 154–159
    Nazi totalitarian politics, 129, 133, 135
    organized resistance movement, 131, 139, 145–146, 149–150, 152
    political objectives, 129

stages of Nazi criminal
institutionalization,
156–157
theme of the *Amidah*, 140
themes of law or constitutional rights,
154–159
understanding of concepts of sociology,
criminology, and history,
128, 128n14
Values and Violence in Auschwitz, 126,
128, 130, 214n194
Piotrowski, Tadeusz, 169–175, 178–182
Pizzorno, Alessandro, 150
Platt, Jennifer, 111
Pohl, Dieter, 5
Poland, xxviii, xxxiv–xxxv, 88, 127–128,
133–134, 136, 141, 141n42, 142, 152,
161–173, 169n104, 175–176, 178–180,
203, 206, 216, 216n201, 239,
263–264, 268–273, 273n81, 274,
277, 279–280, 290–291, 298, 304,
306, 369, 373, 386
arrival of Russians in, 172–173
aspects of Polish collaboration, 177–182
constitution of 1921, 172
ethnic minorities, 169, 171–172, 180
Polish nationalism, xxxiv–xxxv, 161,
171–177, 234, 304
relationships between Poles and
Ukrainians, 174–177
social problems of Polish society, 171
Poliakov, Léon, 3
Pollock, Friedrich, 8n22, 25
Poppe, Nicholas, 48–51, 49n132, 50n135, 56
Porter, Jack N., xx, xxvii, 7, 27, 37, 44–47,
46n121, 49n131, 50–53
Posmysz-Piasecka, Zofia, xxviii, 339
post-Holocaust sociological studies,
3, 311
anti-Semitism, 4–5, 14–26
*Anti-Semitism among American
Labor: Report on a
Research Project
Conducted by the Institute
of Social Research of
Columbia University*, 16
categories of "totalitarian order"
and "anti-Semitic
discrimination," 9–14

Chicago School, xxviii, xxxiii, 25, 57, 62,
65, 77, 82, 86n210, 89, 102,
104–108, 114–115, 119, 121,
132, 139, 156, 170, 363,
364n149
comparison of Holocaust and other
genocidal types, 6
Dialectic of Enlightenment. *See Dialectic
of Enlightenment*
Eclipse of Reason. *See Eclipse of Reason*
Frankfurt School reactions on
anti-Semitism. *See*
Frankfurt School reactions
on anti-Semitism
Freiburg School of thought, xxxvii, 4–5
functionalists/structuralists views,
3–4, 118
genocide. *See* genocide
"Good People and Dirty Work." *See*
"Good People and Dirty
Work"
intentionalists views, xxxvii–xxxviii, 4,
118, 201, 294
issues in dealing with genocide of the
Jews, 19
link between fascism and anti-
Semitism, 8
Nazi anti-Jewish policy, 4
Nazi criminal law, 8
Neurath's work concentration camps,
19. *See* Neurath, Paul M.
of Talcott Parsons, 26–57
relevance of sociology or of
sociological tools, 7
Rubenstein's and Hilberg's studies, 7
Studies in Prejudice, 16
post-Holocaust sociology of 1950s–60s,
2, 291
post-Holocaust sociology of 1970s,
122–234
Fein's work. *See* Fein, Helen
Heller's work. *See On the Edge of
Destruction* (Celia S.
Heller)
microsociological issues, 125
Moore's work. *See* Moore,
Barrington, Jr.
Pawełczyńska's work. *See*
Pawełczyńska, Anna

Piotrowski's work. *See* Piotrowski, Tadeusz
post-Holocaust sociology of 1980s, 235. *See also* genocide
    Baum's contribution.
        See Baum, Rainer C.
    Bauman's contribution.
        See Bauman, Zygmunt
    Horowitz's contribution. *See* Horowitz, Irving L.
    Katz's contribution. *See* Katz, Fred E.
    Kuper's contribution. *See* Kuper, Leo
    Sofsky's contribution. *See* Sofsky, Wolfgang
    Tec's contribution. *See* Tec, Nechama
Postone, Moishe, 289, 294, 301–302
    Anti-Semitism and National Socialism, 302

R

racism, 4, 22, 37, 72, 85–87, 96–98, 110, 114, 161, 217, 231, 327, 377
Rapaport, Lynn, xxii
Reagan, Ronald, 279
Reitlinger, Gerald, 3, 246
resistance, xxxiv–xxxvi, 7, 19, 65, 100, 115, 122, 127, 129–133, 131n23, 136–137, 139–141, 143–154, 164–165, 199, 207–208, 214–215, 220, 225–227, 229, 234, 239, 242–243, 261, 264–267, 288, 303, 309, 348, 350, 352–353, 355–356, 356n122, 358–363, 362n141, 364, 366–369, 371–377, 380, 386, 388
    as communication, 144–147
    as movement and organization, 150–154
    elements of love and compassion in, 141
    inner, 130, 143. *See also* theme of the Amidah
    in the *Lager*, 141–143
    in Warsaw, Vilna, and Łódź, 366–377
    marketplaces and, 147–150
    places to practice, 143–144
responsibility, 2, 7–8, 43, 56, 60, 82, 89, 98, 119, 167, 182, 190, 214n194, 221, 236, 250, 255, 259–260, 287, 306, 309, 315, 320–321, 324, 327, 329, 339, 346, 376

Rethinking the Holocaust (Yehuda Bauer), 3, 6
Ridolfi, Maurizio, xxv
Ringelblum, Emmanuel, 179, 228, 265
Robbins, Richard, 98n226, 99
Rockefeller Foundation, 67, 108
Roman Catholic Church, 219
Romanienko, Lisiunia A., 180–181
Roots of Hate (William Brustein), 320, 377
Rose, Arnold M., 97, 107
Ross, Edward A., 113
Rubinstein, Richard L., 6
Rufeisen, Oswald, 178
Ruhr, 186–190, 259
Rummel, Rudolph J., 237–238
    distinction between genocide, political murder, and mass murder, 238
Russell-Einstein Manifesto, 10
Russel Sage Foundation, 109

S

Salomoni, Antonella, 218, 312
Samchuk, Ulas, 176
samizdat phenomenon, 290–294
sanctification of life, 140. *See* theme of the *Amidah*
Santoro, Marco, 109, 120n255
Satter, David, 120
Schleunes, Karl A., 4
Schorske, Carl E., 183
Schulman, Faye, 177
Schütz, Alfred, 254, 343, 359, 376
Segev, Tom, 390–391
    The Seventh Million, 390
Shawcross, Sir Hartley, 245
Shils, Edward A., xxxiii, 10, 57–66, 109–110, 387
    connection between Nazi Party and the army, 58
    organic solidarity within German army, 57–58
    on *Wehrmacht*. *See Wehrmacht*
    Wilhelmine military ethics, 58–59
Sikh genocide of 1984, 236
Simmel, Georg, 38, 93, 148, 208, 214, 249, 253, 285, 384
Simpson, Christopher, 47–49, 53
Simpson, Ida H., 99–101

Six-Day War, 1967, xxxii–xxxiii, 2, 19, 83, 96, 122–123, 385–386
Smelser, Neil J., 362
Smith, Roger, 233
Smolar, Aleksander, 172
Social Forces, 29, 124
social justice, 182
social memory, 317, 342
social movements, post-Holocaust sociology of, 1, 355–377, 384
   Warsaw Ghetto uprising of 1943, 356–362
   Zionist youth movement, 360
Social Problems, 81, 83, 97, 106–107, 106n237, 115, 124
social sciences, xxxii, 1–2, 53, 59, 109–110, 112, 201, 234, 270, 295, 304, 309, 311, 349
sociological delay, xxxvii, 19, 51, 83, 95, 121, 132, 381
sociological orientation, xxxiv
"Sociological Perspectives on the Holocaust and Post-Holocaust Jewish Life," October 2001 Conference, xviii–xxiv
   general scholarly consensus, xvii–xviii
Sociology Confronts the Holocaust, xxi–xxii, 313
Sofsky, Wolfgang, xxxv, 237, 251–256, 258–259
   categories of absolute power, 253
   concentration camp system, 252–253, 255–256
   Lager, 253–255
   The Order of Terror, 237, 251–252, 254, 256
   social relationships, 253
Sophocles's tragedy, 339, 344
Sorokin, Pitirim A., 38, 382–387
Spagnolo, Carlo, xxv
Stangneth, Bettina, 117, 119–120
state-sponsored genocide. *See* genocide
Status, Authoritarianism, and Anti-Semitism (Walter C. Kaufman), 115
Strzelecki, Jan, 130
Studies in Philosophy and Social Science (SPSS), 17, 24
Sullam, Simon Levis, 217
Sussman, Marvin B., 106n237
systems theory, 44
Sznaider, Natan, xxxvi, 123, 294n139, 310–312, 317, 319–323, 325–328, 330–332, 330–331n58, 334–335, 347, 388

T

Taylor, Fraser, 42
Tec, Nechama, xxxiii, 239, 261–268, 351
   Bielski otriad, 262, 265–268
   conceptions of resistance, 264–268
   Defiance, xxxv, 239, 261, 264
   division of labor, concept of, 268, 351
   Dry Tears, xxxv, 261
   issue of anti-Semitism, 263–264
   The Lion's Den, 261
   persecution of minorities, 263
   Resilience and Courage, 351
   sociological categories of genocide, 261–268
   When Light Pierced the Darkness, 261–263
Thatcher, Margaret, 279
Third Arab-Israeli War, 1967, 122
Thomas, William I., 61
Thompson, Edward P., 183
Tolischus, Otto D., 161–162
Tollik, Janina, 129
totalitarian power, xxxiii, 11, 70, 98, 102, 133, 138, 157, 183, 198, 290, 297, 363, 370, 373
Touraine, Alain, 150–151, 357, 358n129, 360
tragic/tragedy, idea of, 337–341
transnational memory, 322, 324
Trapanese, Enzo, 110
trauma, representation of, 317–320, 336–348
Traverso, Enzo, xvi, 13–14, 16–17, 23, 27n70, 82, 121, 314–316, 335, 389
Treaty for the Protection of Minorities, 171
Treaty of Versailles, 76, 249, 341
Trow, Martin, 73
Turner, Frederick J., 77
Tutu, Desmond, 242, 242n14

U

Ulatowska, Hanna K., xxviii

UN Convention on Genocide,
    242, 246, 248, 295, 328
unity of a society, 335–348
Universal Declaration of Human
    Rights (UDHR), 328
UN Universal Declaration of Human
    Rights, 23

V
Vago, Raphael, 325
Verlag, S. F., 20
Vietnam War (1954–75), xxx, 15, 56, 96,
    108, 124, 202, 345–347, 349,
    383–386
Vromen, Suzanne, 352–354

W
Waller, James, 385
Ward, Lester F., 113
Warsaw Ghetto uprising of 1943, 356–362,
    356n124
Wasserstein, Bernard, 120
Wat, Aleksander, 181
Weber, Max, 7, 20, 28–29, 36, 86, 110,
    136, 148, 155, 158, 255, 260, 276,
    285–288, 348n97, 361, 366–367

Wehrmacht, xxxiii, 57–63, 65
    as a primary social group, 59, 61–63
    ideological nature, 58
    "passionate aggressiveness" of, 57
    role in Third Reich policies of
        extermination, 60–61
    social cohesion of, 59, 61–62, 64
    social control exercised among
        members, 63
    soldiers of, 58, 61–62
    support of Hitler and his policies, 59
Weitzman, Lenore J., 310, 350
Wiener, Jon, 45, 47–50, 52–53
Wolf, Diane L., xix, xxi–xxiii, 18, 313, 350,
    379
Wolin, Richard, 117
Wrong, Dennis H., 47, 53

Y
Yom Kippur War, xxxiii, 125, 130, 234,
    303, 386
Young, Michael, 244

Z
Zimmermann, Michael, 5
Zuckerman, Yitzhak, 265

www.ingramcontent.com/pod-product-compliance
Lightning Source LLC
Chambersburg PA
CBHW052009290426
44112CB00014B/2173